# Environmental Economics and Development

# Environmental Analysis and Economic Policy

*Series Editors:* Kenneth Button
*Professor of Public Policy*
*The Institute of Public Policy, George Mason University, USA*

Peter Nijkamp
*Professor in Regional, Urban and Environmental Economics*
*Free University, Amsterdam, The Netherlands*

1. Global Aspects of the Environment (Volumes I and II)
   *Robert U. Ayres, Kenneth Button and Peter Nijkamp*
2. Environment, Land Use and Urban Policy
   *David Banister, Kenneth Button and Peter Nijkamp*
3. Environmental Valuation (Volumes I and II)
   *Kenneth G. Willis, Kenneth Button and Peter Nijkamp*
4. Environment and Transport
   *Yoshitsugu Hayashi, Kenneth Button and Peter Nijkamp*
5. Environmental Economics and Development
   *J(Hans). B. Opschoor, Kenneth Button and Peter Nijkamp*
6. Environmental Instruments and Institutions
   *Thomas Tietenberg, Kenneth Button and Peter Nijkamp*
7. Ecosystems and Nature
   *R. Kerry Turner, Kenneth Button and Peter Nijkamp*

Wherever possible, the articles in these volumes have been reproduced as originally published using facsimile reproduction, inclusive of footnotes and pagination to facilitate ease of reference.

For a list of all Edward Elgar published titles visit our site on the World Wide Web at
http://www.e-elgar.co.uk

# Environmental Economics and Development



*Edited by*

## J(Hans). B. Opschoor

*Rector of the Institute of Social Studies, The Hague, The Netherlands and Professor of Environmental Economics, Free University of Amsterdam, The Netherlands*

## Kenneth Button

*Professor of Public Policy, The Institute of Public Policy, George Mason University, USA*

*and*

## Peter Nijkamp

*Professor in Regional, Urban and Environmental Economics, Free University, Amsterdam, The Netherlands*

ENVIRONMENTAL ANALYSIS AND ECONOMIC POLICY

**An Elgar Reference Collection**
Cheltenham, UK • Northampton, MA, USA

Published by
Edward Elgar Publishing Limited
Glensanda House
Montpellier Parade
Cheltenham
Glos GL50 1UA
UK

Edward Elgar Publishing, Inc.
136 West Street
Suite 202
Northampton
Massachusetts 01060
USA

A catalogue record for this book is available from the British Library.

**Library of Congress Cataloguing in Publication Data**

Environmental economics and development / edited by J(Hans). B. Opschoor,
Kenneth Button and Peter Nijkamp.
(Environmental analysis and economic policy: 5)
A collection of 28 journal articles and book chapters previously
published between 1984–1997.
Includes index.
1. Environmental economics. 2. Economic development.
3. Sustainable development. 4. Environmental policy.
I. Opschoor, Johannes B. (Johannes Baptist), 1944– . II. Button, Kenneth.
III. Nijkamp, Peter. IV. Series V. Series: An Elgar reference collection.
MK
HD75.6.E562 1999
333.7—dc21 99–14856
CIP

ISBN 1 85898 740 7

Printed and bound in Great Britain by Biddles Ltd, Guildford and King's Lynn

# Contents

# Acknowledgements

The editors and publishers wish to thank the authors and the following publishers who have kindly given permission for the use of copyright material.

Academic Press, Inc. for article: Sverre Grepperud (1996), 'Population Pressure and Land Degradation: The Case of Ethiopia', *Journal of Environmental Economics and Management*, **30** (1), January, 18–33.

*Ambio* for article: Partha Dasgupta (1992), 'Population, Resources, and Poverty', *Ambio*, **21** (1), February, 95–101.

Blackwell Publishers Ltd for article: Ernst Mohr (1996), 'Sustainable Development and International Distribution: Theory and Application to Rainforests', *Review of International Economics*, **4** (2), June, 152–71.

Cambridge University Press for articles: Sujata Gupta and Stephen G. Hall (1996), 'Carbon Abatement Costs: An Integrated Approach for India', *Environment and Development Economics*, **1** (1), February, 41–63; Karl-Göran Mäler and Mohan Munasinghe (1996), 'Macroeconomic Policies, Second-Best Theory and the Environment', *Environment and Development Economics*, **1** (2), May, 149–63; J.B. Opschoor and S.M. Jongma (1996), 'Bretton Woods Intervention Programmes and Sustainable Development', *Environment and Development Economics*, **1** (2), May, 183–202.

Earthscan Publications Ltd/Kogan Page Ltd for excerpt: John A. Dixon, David E. James and Paul B. Sherman (1989), 'Risk and Uncertainty in Dryland Development and Management', in John A. Dixon, David E. James and Paul B. Sherman (eds), *The Economics of Dryland Management*, Chapter 8, 163–92.

Earthscan Publications Ltd/Kogan Page Ltd and St Martin's Press, Inc. for excerpt: Robert Repetto, William Magrath, Michael Wells, Christine Beer and Fabrizio Rossini (1992), 'Wasting Assets: Natural Resources in the National Income Accounts', in Anil Markandya and Julie Richardson (eds), *Environmental Economics*, Chapter 25, 364–88.

Elsevier Science BV for articles: Edward B. Barbier (1990), 'Alternative Approaches to Economic–Environmental Interactions', *Ecological Economics*, **2** (1), April, 7–26; Amitrajeet A. Batabyal (1994), 'An Open Economy Model of the Effects of Unilateral Environmental Policy by a Large Developing Country', *Ecological Economics*, **10** (1), May, 221–32.

Elsevier Science Ltd for article: Mohan Munasinghe (1993), 'Environmental Issues and Economic Decisions in Developing Countries', *World Development*, **21** (11), 1729–48.

Island Press for excerpt: Herman E. Daly (1992), 'Developing Economies and the Steady State', in *Steady-State Economics*, Chapter 7, 148–67.

Johns Hopkins University Press for excerpt: Salah El Serafy and Ernst Lutz (1989), 'Environmental and Natural Resource Accounting', in Gunter Schramm and Jeremy J. Warford (eds), *Environmental Management and Economic Development*, Chapter 3, 23–38.

Kluwer Academic Publishers BV for articles: Ernst Lutz and Herman Daly (1991), 'Incentives, Regulations, and Sustainable Land Use in Costa Rica', *Environmental and Resource Economics*, **1**, 179–94; Theodore Panayotou (1994), 'Conservation of Biodiversity and Economic Development: The Concept of Transferable Development Rights', *Environmental and Resource Economics*, **4**, 91–110; Mohammad Ferdous Alam, Ishak Haji Omar and Dale Squires (1996), 'Sustainable Resource Use, Economic Development, and Public Regulation: The Multiproduct Gill Net Fishery of Peninsular Malaysia', *Environmental and Resource Economics*, **7** (2), March, 117–32; Haynes C. Goddard (1997), 'Using Tradeable Permits to Achieve Sustainability in the World's Large Cities: Policy Design Issues and Efficiency Conditions for Controlling Vehicle Emissions, Congestion and Urban Decentralization with an Application to Mexico City', *Environmental and Resource Economics*, **10** (1), July, 63–99; Kanchan Chopra and S.C. Gulati (1997), 'Environmental Degradation and Population Movements: The Role of Property Rights', *Environmental and Resource Economics*, **9** (4), June, 383–408.

Macmillan Press Ltd for excerpts: Iwan J. Azis (1997), 'Linking Pollution and Macroeconomic Variables: An Indonesian Example', in Manas Chatterji and Yang Kaizhong (eds), *Regional Science in Developing Countries*, Chapter 17, 243–56, 360–63; Peter Nijkamp and Hans Opschoor (1997), 'Urban Environmental Sustainability: Critical Issues and Policy Measures in a Third-World Context', in Manas Chatterji and Yang Kaizhong (eds), *Regional Science in Developing Countries*, Chapter 5, 52–73.

Oxford University Press, Inc. for excerpt: David W. Pearce and Jeremy J. Warford (1993), 'Evaluating Environmental Damage and Benefits', in *World without End: Economics, Environment, and Sustainable Development*, Chapter 5, 97–144, references.

David W. Pearce and R. Kerry Turner for their own excerpt: (1990), 'Environment and the Developing Countries', in *Economics of Natural Resources and the Environment*, Chapter 22, 342–59.

Plenum Publishing Corporation for article: David Feeny, Fikret Berkes, Bonnie J. McCay and James M. Acheson (1990), 'The Tragedy of the Commons: Twenty-Two Years Later', *Human Ecology*, **18** (1), March, 1–19.

University of Chicago Press for article: John M. Antle and Gregg Heidebrink (1995), 'Environment and Development: Theory and International Evidence', *Economic Development and Cultural Change*, **43** (3), April, 603–25.

University of Wisconsin Press for article: Richard B. Norgaard (1984), 'Coevolutionary Development Potential', *Land Economics*, **60** (2), May, 160–73.

John Wiley & Sons Ltd for excerpt: Hamish Main and Stephen Wyn Williams (1994), 'Marginal Urban Environments as Havens for Low-Income Housing: Third World Regional Comparisons', in Hamish Main and Stephen Wyn Williams (eds), *Environment and Housing in Third World Cities*, Chapter 9, 151–70.

World Bank for article and excerpt: Gunnar S. Eskeland and Emmanuel Jimenez (1992), 'Policy Instruments for Pollution Control in Developing Countries', *World Bank Research Observer*, **7** (2), July, 145–69; Ramon Lopez (1992), 'The Environment as a Factor of Production: The Economic Growth and Trade Policy Linkages', in Patrick Low (ed.), *International Trade and the Environment: An Overview*, Chapter 9, Discussion Paper 159, 137–55, references.

Every effort has been made to trace all the copyright holders but if any have been inadvertently overlooked the publishers will be pleased to make the necessary arrangement at the first opportunity.

In addition the publishers wish to thank the Library of the London School of Economics and Political Science and the Marshall Library of Economics, Cambridge University for their assistance in obtaining these articles.

# Series Preface

*Kenneth Button and Peter Nijkamp*

The environment has been a dominant theme for research and public policy during the latter part of the twentieth century and there is no sign that this will change as we move to the new millennium. The global interest in environmental matters in part stems from the increased pressures that a mounting population and increased production puts on the planet's natural resource base. Additionally, as personal incomes rise and leisure time becomes more freely available in the developed world, concern with more immediate human needs give way to an interest in preservation and conservation for future generations and for others. Science has also contributed by both highlighting emerging environmental problems and discovering the importance of many components of the natural environment for medical and other uses.

Historically, the interest in the environment can be traced through several phases, each with its own particular emphasis. The interest is also far from new and in antiquity there were often laws governing such things as the removal of night soil and the use of noisy wagons into towns. Traditionally, also the natural environment was seen as a source of the necessities of life and was controlled through farming techniques to ensure that food was adequate to maintain the population. Land use was controlled and water resources were often regulated at the local and regional levels.

With the Industrial Revolution came population growth, urbanization and the accelerated exploitation of natural resources. Malthus advanced ideas of over population while others, such as Jevons, became concerned about the finite nature of such resources as coal. The new technologies contaminated water courses and the widespread use of carbon fuels led to atmospheric pollution. In cities, dirt, noise and urban decay led to new ideas of town planning and ideal cities.

Much of the interest in the latter part of the last century centred around public health. As knowledge of how disease was spread – urban authorities in particular sought to improve the local environment by such measures as sewage control and clean water supply to reduce the spread of germs and infection. This trend, much later, spread to policies embodied in various pieces of clean air legislation to reduce local atmospheric pollution that causes smog and other harmful effects.

Wealthy societies, and the better off within poorer societies, with the time and resources to expand, became concerned with the built environment and in shaping nature in ways they found aesthetically pleasing. Over the centuries this has led to landscaping of the countryside and the provision of parks and gardens in urban areas.

The twentieth century has seen many of these trends continue although some of the problems, such as depletion of natural resources, initially appeared less severe as new sources were found in Africa, South America and Asia. Difficulties in feeding and otherwise sustaining the burgeoning populations of these regions, however, resurrected Malthusian concerns over whether the planet could sustain itself. Increasing reliance on fossil fuels for energy and the geographical concentration of the main reserves of oil in politically unstable areas resurrected concern over natural resource reserves in the post Second World War period.

More fundamental to modern debates has been the global orientation of recent concerns. This has been accompanied by a much more popular interest in the state of the natural environment. Kenneth Boulding's development of the idea of 'spaceship earth' attracted much attention, as did the rather doom ladened prophesies of the Club of Rome, but this was subsequently overshadowed by the publication of the Brundtland Report, *Our Common Future*, with its emphasis on the need to maintain resources for future generations. With the report came the much touted, but universally ambiguous, concept of sustainable development.

Just as the academic interest in the environment has evolved so has the institutional setting in which the topic is debated and researched. In a very general way as our understanding of the environment has progressed and as technology has developed so there has been a movement out from micro-policy making in the hands of city councils, lords of the manor and the like to macro-policy making, involving global agencies such as the United Nations and World Bank. Indeed, one of the pressing issues of contemporary environmental debate is the appropriate jurisdiction for different levels of government.

For those interested in researching environmental topics, either from the standpoint of the beginner or of that of an expert wishing to expand an established basis of knowledge, there are practical problems. Environmental analysis extends across virtually all academic disciplines although many such as economics and engineering have specific sub-areas of interest specifically devoted to environmental issues. The multidisciplinary and transdisciplinary nature of environmental research makes it difficult to keep track of the key literature. To those new to the field there is the added problem of tracing back to find classic papers or research results. There are now a large number of specialist journals that deal with environmental topics but this is often adding to the problem of collecting information rather than reducing it. While these journals and periodicals provide explicitly environmental research findings, other general journals in economics, sociology, geography, engineering, medicine, biology and so on still continue to publish important findings.

The aim of this series of edited books is to provide both a set of reference volumes for those already in the field and to facilitate newcomers with accessible core material. The aim is not to offer readings on the purely scientific issues but rather to limit the papers to those concerned with social science aspects of the environment. This does not mean that we have excluded papers with a natural science orientation but rather the focus is on the softer debates and research. There are seven volumes in the series. The papers have all been previously published but do not constitute a set of traditional classics. While many of the articles have an established pedigree, equally there are less often referenced pieces. The aim of each volume is to paint a picture of how a topic area has developed, provide an indication as to some of the key contributions to this development but also look at some of the more recent literature that covers policy considerations.

The books cover a wide range of topic areas. At one extreme there are the macro-oriented volumes edited with Bob Ayres looking at the *Global Aspects of the Environment* while, in conjunction with Kerry Turner, there is a collection concerned with *Ecosystems and Nature*. Also at the aggregate level, edited with Hans Opschoor, there is a volume which focuses on *Environmental Economics and Development*. At the other extreme there are volumes concerned with micro-issues such as that along with Ken Willis that deals with *Environmental*

*Valuation* and with David Banister on *The Environment, Land Use and Urban Policy*. Transport's impact on the environment is multifaceted and can be severe hence there is a volume edited with Yoshi Hayashi, *The Environment and Transport* dealing exclusively with that subject. Finally, edited with Tom Tietenberg there is a collection that looks more generally at *Environmental Instruments and Institutions*.

We accept that there are many omissions from the collections and that others may have made different selections or have structured the material differently. Space limits what can be included and there is much more that could have been justified in a larger exercise (although this would add further to deforestation). We have also had to omit work by many eminent and important scholars for the same reason. As for structuring the material, a number of possible cuts are possible, the ones selected here just seem logical to us and would seem to fit with the needs of both researchers and, possibly, teachers.

# Economics, Environment and Development: Introduction

*J(Hans). B. Opschoor, Kenneth Button and Peter Nijkamp*

Development is a form of change in social processes and institutions broadening the set of options that people have to improve their livelihoods and determine their futures (United Nations Development Programme, 1995). As part of this, economic development is the process of change of economic activities and institutions aimed at the removal, or at least the suppression, of scarcity by expanding the availability of goods and services and enhancing the access to these resources that enables the continued production of these goods and services.

These definitions allude to the issues that are put centrally in this volume: the links between economic activity, on the one hand, and environmental quality and the availability of natural resources, on the other. In general, the natural environment is economically significant as: (1) a source of raw materials; (2) a set of sinks for absorbing wastes and recycling; and (3) a provider of essential life supports. Economic activity, as a basis for development and human welfare, has to be possible over time; this means that its sustainability is an issue. Sustainability has several dimensions, one of which is environmental: sustainable development has been defined as a process of change in which the exploitation of resources, the direction of investment and the orientation of technological development and institutional change are all compatible and satisfy current human needs and aspirations without jeopardizing the future potential for satisfying these needs (after World Commission on Environment and Development (WCED), 1987).

In this volume we will attempt to survey the territory of environment–development linkages and some of the tensions that are implicit in the notion of sustainable development. As Gunnar Myrdal (1970) said: there is no view without a viewpoint. We will approach the field from a wide, economic angle that will allow for a systematic coverage of a variety of development issues.

## Environment and Development

### *The Economic Process and Its Environmental Base*

Analytically, economists have looked at the economic process as one of a circulation of goods and services between various agents (producers, traders, consumers, investors, etc.), in which labour, capital and primary commodities are turned into intermediate products and consumer products to finally be consumed; simultaneously, economists saw a flow of money in the opposite direction. The origins of labour and primary commodities, as well as the destination of these final products beyond the act of consumption, remained very much a mystery in traditional economic models – except that some pre-classical economists (the 'Physiocrats') attributed it all to 'land'. More recently, environmental economics (especially in its more ecologically inspired branches) has come to regard this process of circulation as being embedded in natural processes within ecosystems characterized by flows (such as biogeochemical cycles of nutrients, ecological succession and regeneration) and stocks of non-renewable and renewable resources: 'All economic development takes place within natural ecosystems ... Development brings about very varying degrees of modification, but always remains subject to the ecological limitations which operate within natural systems' (Dasmann, Milton and Freeman, 1973).

For an adequate elaboration of environmental issues from a developmental perspective, this ecological approach to economic cycles must be given some more spatial resolution (James, Nijkamp and Opschoor, 1989). A minimum of that is achieved by regarding this process of circulation as taking place within and between two countries or regions, say A and B, exchanging (through trade or otherwise) goods and services, means of exchange and technologies. Each of these countries draws on a set of natural assets or resources within its own territory, but may also tap shared or common resources. Each of these countries releases the residuals of its productive and consumptive activities in its own environmental compartments (air, water, soils), but some might directly enter the 'national' compartments of the other country. And, more importantly, environmental degradation may indirectly spill over into the other country's environment or affect the productivity of natural resource systems there (or that of the common resources), through ecological processes of transportation of materials and the modification of systems, as referred to above. Finally, for this to be interesting in the context of global development, one may assume some asymmetries between these two regions or countries (now to be labelled 'North' and 'South') in terms of, for example, demands for natural resources relative to their own resource endowments, their levels of environmental pollution and waste generation per unit of land, their levels of income or consumption per capita, their roles in the development of technology, and their influence on political processes and institutions (e.g. those regulating international trade and the transfer of intellectual properties and technology). This allegedly rather simple analytical framework already points at the following list to which attention should be devoted in a reader on the subject at hand:

1. Differences in environment–economy relationships within developed versus less developed regions.
2. Different patterns of development in each of these, related to the politico-economic dynamics between the regions.
3. International or transboundary environmental problems related to national or regional economic activity and development (on a bilateral up to a global scale).

Of course, there are other ways to give more spatial resolution to the analysis, such as distinguishing different spatial scales (e.g. urban, regional). These will be given less systematic attention, with the exception of urban issues.

*The International Debate on Environment and Development*

In political terms, environment, or 'ecology', and the process of economic development were described by some early researchers as being linked as early as the 1950s (e.g. De Vries, 1951). This link became more manifest from the late 1960s. The first official document to contain fundamental principles of environmental management was *Development and Environment*, the Founex Report of 1971, one of the main inputs into the 1972 Stockholm Conference on Environment and Development – the first international conference on the subject.

The accelerated concern with environmental issues around 1970 emerged mainly out of the problems experienced by the industrially advanced countries in consequence of the process of economic growth. These concerns were not predominant in developing countries, which were, and are, interested first and foremost in environmental problems related to 'poverty and (the) very lack of development' of their societies: problems to be overcome by development and growth (Founex Report 1971). Yet it was recognized that economic growth in developing countries would give rise to further environmental pressures, which had to be taken into account by those countries. Moreover, the Founex Report expressed concern over adverse impacts in the fields of trade, aid and technology transfer due to environmental concerns in the industrialized world, but some more hopeful perspectives were discerned as well: environmental concerns might reawaken attention to poverty elimination and strengthen support for social policies; commodity prices might rise and industries might relocate.

The debate about environment–development issues in 1971 and since has discerned two direct, and two indirect, categories of environment–development interactions:

1a. Environmental pressure or degradation of (national) environmental assets directly related to socio-economic activity levels in developing countries (e.g. emissions of water pollutants, stock impacts of harvesting activities).
2a. Environmental pressure reductions due to changes in the types of economic activity or the technologies deployed in them, due to improved livelihoods.
3a. Socio-economic spillovers in the form of changed economic conditions for developing countries as a result of policies of, or dominated by, developed countries.
4a. Environmental spillovers in the form of transboundary disseminations of environmental degradation from one country to another, or through global environmental change.

In fact, (1a) and (2a) are elaborations on issue (1), whereas (3a) and (4a) are identical to (2) and (3).

*Environmental Policy*

Developing countries generally, but especially as their income levels are lower, have a higher dependency on primary economic activities (mining, fishing, forestry, agriculture) and hence on natural resources. These resources include forests (livelihoods, wood, etc.), land/soils (degradation aspect) and water systems (habitats of fish, water for irrigation and drinking). Moreover, the quality of the various environmental compartments (air, water, soils) is increasingly threatened by pollution, with impacts on living conditions beyond levels that are considered tolerable by developing countries' populations and administrations, especially in urban settings. Hence both the resource aspect and the environmental quality concern now enter into decision making and politics.

Nowadays not only the industrialized developed countries but also those outside the

Organization for Economic Cooperation and Development (OECD) recognize that natural resource degradation as well as pollution have become impediments to economic development and to poverty alleviation, and are on a track towards sustainable development.

If we take the results of the Rio de Janeiro Conference on Environment and Development of 1992 as indicative of where the policy debate stands, the following points are relevant to the subject matter of this volume because they relate to environment and development issues in an economically significant way:

1. The need to address environmental issues from a developmental perspective (cf. the Founex Report of 1971 and that of the WCED 1987) is firmly established: sustainability and poverty eradication are dealt with in the main documents coming out of Rio as intricately related topics, and principles addressing these include:

- the right to development (Declaration of Rio, Principle 3);
- national sovereignty over national natural resources (Principle 2);
- the need for integrated development with priority given to the poor (Principles 4–6);
- common concerns for all nations but differentiated with respect to effective responsibilities, according to level of development (Principle 7);
- the desirability of prices expressing social and environmental costs, and the use of economic incentives to merge economics and environment in the decisions of economic agents and make polluters and resource consumers pay (Principle 16).

2. In these notions one hears echos of the Founex and WCED Reports. By now – that is, more than five years after the Conference in Rio, and more than ten years since the publication of the Brundtland Report (WCED, 1987) – concerns over the sustainability of development are well established, and some principles of sustainable development, as listed above, are in the process of being codified in national legislation (Directorate-General Environmental Management, 1996) and international agreements (see, for example, the International Treaty on Climate Change).

3. A crucial consideration in the statements and principles referred to above is the need to merge environment and economics at all levels of decision making. In fact, one could argue that the main gain of the 1992 UN Conference over that of 1972 is the recognition of the role of economic approaches in the issues of environment and development, as argued for forcefully by the 1987 Report of the WCED. In 1990 Pearce and Turner observed that 'that part of environmental economics which deals with developing country problems is in its infancy' (see Chapter 1 of this volume). It still is, as is reflected by the dates of publication of the contributions to this volume. But it is growing rapidly.

## Economics, Environment and Development: The Literature

### *Viewpoints and Expectations*

How might economic analysis help in improving the management of natural resources and environmental quality in developing countries? How could economic analysis help in merging environmental and economic considerations in the decision making of economic and political agents? We address these issues by asking questions related to the reasons for economic approaches ('why') and to their focus ('how').

Why would decision makers or academics be interested in an economic approach of environment–development interactions?

One first contribution would be to show the potential economic benefits of resource and environmental management (Pearce and Turner, Chapter 1). This would entail showing the economic values of different levels of natural capital stocks and environmental quality and hence implies the availability of adequate and appropriate tools for carrying out such valuations in the absence of institutional arrangements, making such valuations endogenous in decision making by economic agents. Generalizing this, there is a need for quantifying or measuring the demand for environmental quality and its supply (Antle and Heidebrink, Chapter 3).

Second, sustainability considerations may imply that current levels of costs are higher than when environmental and social long-term considerations are not to be captured by relevant current cost and prices. In the longer run, the net value of that may still be positive as future levels of welfare would be enhanced, and the design of appropriate institutions (e.g. property rights and regimes of access) and policy instruments achieving such cost internalization would be a significant contribution to making development processes more sustainable in an efficient way (Pearce and Turner, Chapter 1). Obviously, this would have to be based on a profound analysis of what institutional failures currently drive the economic process in less sustainable directions, or render them inefficient or inequitable (Opschoor, 1996).

Thirdly, in reality it may not yet be possible to attach economic values to various states of the environment, and short-term considerations or high levels of time preference may pose impediments to achieving optimal institutional arrangements. In such situations policy makers may opt for second-best solutions such as setting environmental standards or objectives. Even then economic analysis may be of use, as reaching environmental objectives in cost-effective ways would be more socially desirable than reaching those objectives in less efficient ways. Furthermore, as has often been demonstrated (e.g. Munasinghe, Chapter 2), economic analysis might help in identifying or designing alternative, more efficient projects or programmes to achieve a set of societal objectives. Thus economic analysis of projects, programmes and strategies of development would enable decision makers to find and implement more cost-effective approaches. The other side of this coin would be the analysis of negative environmental spin-offs of macroeconomic and economy-wide developmental policies designed without explicit consideration of environmental and resource issues. At any rate, in the absence of adequate possibilities for valuing all relevant states of the environment and changes therein, a third role for economic analysis is to elucidate and study trade-offs between environmental and economic considerations relevant to different developmental options.

Fourth, there is a need for understanding, more fundamentally, the nature as well as the dynamics of the relationship of the interactions between economic processes (e.g. growth paths) and their environmental contexts. This can be done from an historical or evolutionary perspective (e.g. Wilkinson, 1973; Norgaard, Chapter 6) and by taking a system approach (e.g. Barbier and Daly, Chapters 4 and 5, respectively). In the latter, the interactions between economic activity levels, resources, population and so on are modelled and analysed so as to arrive at a better understanding of the longer-term repercussions (in terms of sustainability and sometimes also distribution or equity) of the endogenous dynamics of these systems.

We now turn to the 'how' question. As should already be clear from our answer to the 'why' question, the two types of interaction (resource extraction and pollution) can and should be studied both from an analytical perspective (i.e. attempting to understand the relationships between economic and environmental systems) and from a developmental or normative position (i.e. attempting to design more desirable institutions and policy instruments, especially taking into account the asymmetrical position of so-called developing countries in terms of their access to environmental sources and sinks). Both perspectives will be covered by the contributions to this volume.

This distinction between analytical and normative approaches is only one of the aspects of paradigm and methodology that need to be addressed here. Another is the distinction between an historical, or contextual, approach, and a more systems-oriented approach; this volume is biased towards the latter. One could also distinguish between qualitative and quantitative approaches, the latter being further differentiated between empirically based and the mere numerical; we have attempted to base this volume as much as possible on empirical ground. One could also distinguish between various levels: micro, meso, macro – all are represented in this reader.

This rather pluralistic approach has to do with a pragmatic recognition that different types of question may require different types of approach and that one should not be too dogmatic about such issues (see also Opschoor and Klaassen, 1991).

*Outline of Reader*

This reader presents twenty-eight contributions, mostly by academics from environmental and ecological economics, very often based in developing countries or in institutions dealing with development and environment issues. We have organized the volume in six parts: (1) general aspects, (2) resource utilization and management, (3) valuation and accounting of environmental change, (4) environmental policy instruments, (5) adjustment, trade and the environment, and (6) distributional issues.

Above we learned to distinguish resource-related issues from pollution-related issues, and below we shall label these R-issues and P-issues. R-issues are explicitly focused on in Part II on resource utilization and management, and in most of Part III on valuation; R-issues are implicitly addressed also in Part V on adjustment and trade and Part VI on distributional issues. P-issues are central to Part IV on policy instruments and Part VI on distribution, and occasionally appear in Parts III and IV as well. Specific types of resource investigated include land, forests, fisheries and biodiversity.

We have also come across four different features of environment–development linkages; these are addressed by contributions in the various Parts of this volume as follows:

- environmental pressure related to socio-economic activity levels in developing countries: Parts I, II and IV;
- environmental pressure and poverty: Part VI;

- environment, development and changing international economic conditions: Part V;
- international environmental problems and policies: Part VI.

Part III is mainly methodological in nature, and as such has a rather different position.

Finally, in terms of contributions expected from economics, we refer to the answers to the 'why' question to derive a list of objectives: valuation, institutional analysis and reform, trade-off and policy evaluation, and analysis of fundamental aspects of environment–development interactions. The latter are central to Part I (and to some degree also Part II); valuation issues are the core of Part III; institutional aspects crop up in Part II but are the key issue of Part IV; and trade-offs and policy analysis are addressed in Parts V and VI.

We shall proceed by reviewing the individual contributions in more detail, following essentially the order in which they appear.

In Part I some general features of the environment–development interface are presented. The contribution by Pearce and Turner (Chapter 1) sets the scene by picturing the environmental issues and their relevance to development, as well as their inter-relatedness. Understandably, the focus is on R-issues. They also indicate how an economic approach might help in drawing attention to, and addressing, these issues. They show how price as well as non-price incentives can be built into decision making so as to enable economic agents to incorporate considerations of sustainability. The function of economic analysis of both R- and P-issues is elaborated by Munasinghe (Chapter 2), who discusses environmental analysis and several more or less innovative techniques of environmental economics, in project analysis, resource accounting, multiobjective decision support systems, and so on; this more or less sets the scene for Part III of this reader. Munasinghe remains close to the mainstream approach and to World Bank practices, and this enables a comparison with other paradigms and perspectives presented subsequently in Part I.

Antle and Heidebrink (Chapter 3) explicitly abstain from attempting to put values on environmental assets, and opt for a trade-off-oriented approach where income per capita and some aggregate measure of environmental services are traced in their co-development over time. In doing so they develop the hypothesis of an 'environmental transition', which they at least partially validate with some empirical data. This subject or hypothesis is so important that we shall come back to it towards the end of this Introduction. In Chapter 4, Barbier develops an approach in essentially the same vein: by modelling these interactions with environmental and economic performance indicators in separate dimensions, or by addressing the trade-off between environmental quality and income or welfare. His qualitative, analytical approach arrives at a different outcome than the previous chapter: there may not be a smooth environmental transition; the future might lead economies into states of widespread and unsustainable ecological disruption. The model results also indicate ways out of such futures: resource-saving innovations in production and consumption, changes in organizational and managerial capabilities, changes in patterns of consumption.

Daly (Chapter 5) takes these issues further by developing a radically different, normative approach where economic performance is to be judged by its allocative efficiency (the utility it generates), its fairness or equitability, and its adherence to the ecologically determined maximum scale of the economy as determined by the level of economic activity per capita and the population size. Drawing on the experiences of Brazil, and assuming that sustainable welfare of the majority of the population is the objective, he points at 'solutions' such as population control and redistribution to get away from unsustainable paths of economic growth. Norgaard's evolutionary analysis in Chapter 6 actually provides the reader with some hope that such explicit shifts in developmental approach as called for by Barbier, and especially by Daly, might arise in a less confrontational manner than one might expect *ex ante*, if one is justified in assuming that the interactions between societies and their physical environments show a co-evolutionary pattern over time and in the very long run. That is, economies have adapted, and will adapt, to changes in their environments (and vice versa) much along the lines suggested by historical analyses such as Wilkinson's (1973). Rather than extrapolations of behaviour in linear modes, one should look for adaptive, recursive options and their adoption by society, and for mechanisms to enhance and accelerate these processes of adaptation.

In Chapter 7, which concludes this Part, Iwan Azis puts the reader back on the ground of less speculative analysis of economy–environment interactions under different institutional regimes, by using an input–output-based general equilibrium model and applying it to the Indonesian economy and possibilities to endogenise environmental pricing through a tax on pollution. Thus this Chapter not only takes up some of the issues addressed in Chapters 1 and 5, but it adds the value of introducing another type of modelling of environment–economy interactions and of setting the scene for Part III.

Part II deals with issues related to the use and management of natural resources. Earlier in this Introduction we emphasized the significance of resource issues when addressing environment–economy interactions with special reference to developing countries.

Writing on environmental issues in a global context, Hardin as long ago as 1968 developed the metaphor of the 'tragedy of the commons' to indicate the degradation of free-access resources used by self-interested agents in the absence of mechanisms for collective decision making: such agents would run down these resources even if this were against their collective interest. This metaphor has been regarded as particularly relevant to the resource use regimes in many developing countries. In Chapter 8, Feeny *et al.* review the empirical evidence of resource use to find that in a surprising number of cases users have actually developed mechanisms to restrict access and to enforce rules in the collective interest. Resource-based environmental collapse is avoidable, and it thus makes sense to explore how.

Before doing this we must look into one relevant dynamic aspect of resource use in developing countries: its link with population growth. In Chapter 9 Grepperud explores the relevance of the 'Population Pressure Hypothesis' (PPH), according to which resource degradation is directly related to population pressure, more or less along Malthusian lines. An alternative hypothesis would be Boserup's, which suggests that, as pressure mounts, resource users will change their technologies and thus develop away from resource scarcities. Grepperud investigates the links between population pressure and land degradation on the Ethiopian Highlands using a cumulative logit model, and finds in favour of the PPH (thus rejecting Boserupian adaptations). Interventions explicitly aiming at reducing erosion risks by introducing new farming methods and new inputs are called for. On the same subject Chopra and Gulati come out very differently, based on their analysis of developments in western India (Chapter 10). To begin with, in that context people respond by migrating out of regions with mounting pressure on resources, thus alleviating the pressure on the resource base. Second, the analysis suggests that the creation of appropriate common property rights on hitherto open access land resources would lead to improvements in environmental resource management and resource quality, thus effectively taking away the need for outmigration and allowing higher levels of population to be supported by the same resource base.

In Chapter 11 Alam, Omar and Squires combine the two aspects of production technologies and institutional reforms by investigating through an optimization model how regulations on fishing gear and multi-species fishery management would, in the case of Malaysian sea fisheries, produce a sustainable use of the resource. Lutz and Daly add another feature to this bouquet of types of measure to improve resource use by economies, by reviewing qualitatively a mix of prevailing and plausible incentives and regulations, from a broad perspective cutting across all relevant economic activities, in order to arrive at suggestions for sustainable forest management in Costa Rica (Chapter 12). This paper has been included in order to show that in choosing between different types of methodology one may easily opt for the elegance of modelling approaches but this elegance may be at the expense of relevance.

More on resource management can be found in the chapters in Part III on resource accounting, in Chapter 13 on a specific economic policy instrument for managing land use in conservation areas, and in Chapter 24 where the connection is made with the issue of poverty.

Part III is a methodological Part, dealing with valuation and accounting in the contexts of R-issues and P-issues.

The normative economic approach to sustainability assumes rising genuine income per capita; to be disposed of in whatever preferred mix, via consumption or investment. This presupposes that the income-generating potential embedded in the per capita stocks of assets, or capital, available to society is, at the very least, left intact. Assets include produced assets, human capital and natural assets. Reductions in the stocks of these assets would have to be accounted for and the value of these assets would have to be depreciated accordingly, so as to reduce gross income and to yield genuine net income; hence the wish to value these stocks, or at least the changes in them.

Valuation of stock is notoriously difficult, and even more so in the case of natural assets. One complication is the assumptions to be made on the nature of the underlying production function: should one assume the possibility of substitution of produced assets and human capital for dwindling natural assets? Or should one assume that at least some assets are 'essential', that is, cannot be substituted but are to remain available according to some fixed coefficient, Leontief-type production function (see Opschoor, 1997)? Second, how should possibilities for technological innovation be incorporated? Third, how to deal with time preference and the interests of future generations, especially when natural resources may be essential and their exhaustion may be irreversible? Finally, what operational methods should be or could be applied? On the first of these issues, the notions of 'weak' and 'strong' sustainability have been proposed: leaving overall per capita capital intact is referred to as weak sustainability, whereas leaving essential natural assets intact is called strong sustainability. Going for strong sustainability would ensure the availability of essential resources over time, thus bypassing most of the questions related to valuation, but at the expense of the risk of over-precaution at present. The latter risk is substantial and hence many agents in the development process (especially those with a background in economics) prefer the weak version of sustainability (e.g. the World Bank).

In Part III the focus is on operational valuation and accounting methods. Pearce and Warford (Chapter 14) provide a theoretical background for, and an overview of, methods to value environmental change. They introduce the notions of non-use value and total economic value and give numerous examples of applying these concepts as well as a range of practical tools for measuring them in developing countries. These methods are potentially useful in project evaluation, policy analysis, and in environmental and resource accounting. Repetto *et al.* (Chapter 15) and El Serafy and Lutz (Chapter 16) provide two alternative methods for treating natural resources and changes in the levels of their stocks in national accounting systems; Repetto's methodology has been applied, for example, to oil resources and soil erosion valuation in Indonesia. Finally, in Chapter 17, Dixon, James and Sherman provide a framework for dealing with risk and uncertainty in dryland management and development. Many of the methods they discuss imply the need to apply some type of valuation in order to arrive at estimates of distributions of net benefits of management strategies. A key feature here is uncertainty about processes in the natural environment (e.g. rainfall patterns in time and space), as opposed to types of uncertainty rooted in the socio-economic aspects of environment–development relationships.

Part IV is devoted to economic approaches to environmental policy instruments in developing countries. The use of economic instruments such as charges and tradeable permits has often been advocated in the context of OECD economies (see Opschoor and Turner, 1994), especially because of their efficiency-related features. However, often it is doubted whether these instruments can be used in the setting of developing economies. Surveys (e.g. Panayotou, 1994) have made clear that one should not underestimate these possibilities and that, in fact, a very wide range of applications can be found in developing countries. Eskeland and Jimenez introduce the subject by presenting, in qualitative terms, the range of options for policy instruments for pollution control (Chapter 18). It is important to follow the authors in paying attention not only to the efficiency side of instruments but also to distributional aspects.

Gupta and Hall develop an interesting modelling approach combining micro and macro modelling, to test the impacts of several policy instruments, including an emissions tax, on carbon emissions in India (Chapter 19). Reinvesting the revenues from a carbon tax in new carbon-abating technologies would accelerate the adoption of cleaner technology. In Chapter 20 Goddard shows how in one particular megapolis, tradeable vehicle use permits might lead to drastic and efficient reductions in emissions of traffic-originated air pollutants, at least in theory and taking into account some institutional features typical of the Mexican context (especially the aversion to fuel taxes). In Chapter 13 Panayotou develops the notion of tradeable or Transferable Development Rights from an instrument used in the conservation of urban sites to one applicable in the field of biodiversity conservation, and attempts to reconcile concerns over biodiversity with those over economic development.

Part V puts environment and development concerns in the wider, international context. In this Part the impacts of changes in international trade regimes and structural adjustment policies as advocated by the World Bank and International Monetary Fund are explored.

Lopez (Chapter 21) presents a theoretical approach of the economic and environmental impacts of unilateral trade liberalization in a small developing economy, using general equilibrium analysis. Mäler and Munasinghe develop an analytical framework to trace the impacts of second-best policies (such as purely macroeconomic policies in disregard of environmental externalities) on the environment (Chapter 22). From their general equilibrium analysis it follows that, if environmental externalities are substantial, then the root causes (i.e. the market failures or property rights problems) should be addressed explicitly and/or macroeconomic policies should be modified in order to reduce or compensate the effects of ignoring these realities. Opschoor and Jongma (Chapter 23) trace in some detail how the various types of intervention usually advocated in the context of stabilization and structural adjustment of economies may impact on the environment via such externalities. They advocate short-run ('retrofitting') and long-run ('integrative') approaches for effectively modifying macroeconomic policies.

The final Part, Part VI, is devoted to several types of distributional features: intragenerational distributional inequality within economies, international distributional aspects related to policies on global environmental issues, and urban–rural distributional issues.

In Chapter 24 we step back to the scene set in Part I to look at household behaviour, including reproductive behaviour, from a resource allocative perspective; Dasgupta finds that for poor households environmental degradation is both a cause and an effect of increased family size. Appropriate policies would have to take into account the value of children in different settings, as producer and insurance goods, and would include measures for the alleviation of poverty and for the expansion of the range of financial and economic options open to poor households.

The next two chapters discuss the international distributional impacts of dealing with international environmental issues. Mohr (Chapter 25) shows how an uneven sharing between North and South of costs and benefits of a subset of such policies (aimed at enhancing sustainability in one region; for example, to protect tropical rain forests) stands in the way of progress in reaching and implementing international agreements. Batabyal (Chapter 26) extends this to show that, in general, there are plausible reasons for especially larger developing countries to abstain from implementing environmental policies unilaterally. The policy relevance of such analyses is clear, especially now that the role of the larger developing economies (such as Indonesia, Brazil, India and China) in dealing with global environmental issues is becoming increasingly prominent at the same time that their willingness to go along with extending international agreements is becoming less clear (cf. the developments up until the end of 1997 in relation to the International Convention on Climate Change).

Our last two chapters deal with issues related to urban development. Main and Wyn Williams (Chapter 27) discuss on empirical grounds how urbanization, and especially migration to urban settings by the rural poor, is leading to a situation of increasing exposure to environmental risks of an increasing share of the rapidly growing urban populations in developing countries. In theory, the use of government controls to curb this may be less appropriate than working via property rights and market mechanisms, but in practice – and especially for the poorest segments – substantial direct public actions will remain necessary. In Chapter 28 Nijkamp and Opschoor attempt to develop an approach towards urban sustainability. Again, efficiency alone is insufficient, and equity and environmental considerations are brought in explicitly. Attention is drawn to the relevance of financial constraints on any policy towards sustainable cities, and the need for public–private partnerships is emphasized.

### *The Environmental Kuznets Curve*

In this final section we wish to address one specific issue that arose in Section I, namely the plausibility of an 'environmental transition'. In preparing for the UN Conference on Environment and Development of 1992, the question has been raised whether the relationship between economic development and environmental impact could not be represented by an inverted U: starting from low levels of development (as measured by per capita income) environmental pressure would rise with income growth, but decreasingly so, eventually to level off and even drop (increasingly so) at high income levels. This relationship is referred to as the 'Environmental Kuznets Curve' (because of its resemblance to the relationship between per capita income and inequality suggested by Kuznets in 1955) or the 'Environmental Transition Hypothesis' (Antle and Heidebrink, Chapter 3 of this volume).

Antle and Heidebrink have analysed empirically the relationships between the development of per capita income and two proxies for natural assets: (1) the total area of parks and protected areas in a country, and (2) a measure of afforestation. Their analysis supports the Environmental Transition Hypothesis (see also Panayotou, 1993). Findings such as these have triggered a vast amount of empirical work, the upshot of which may be summarized as follows (after Arrow *et al.*, 1995; De Bruyn and Opschoor, 1997; Grossman and Krueger, 1996; Opschoor, 1997; Shafik and Bandyopadhyay, 1992; World Resources Institute, 1991, and others).

Environmental Kuznets Curves, even if they have been found for individual pollutants and materials in individual countries, may be less apparent, or may even vanish to be inverted Us, when considered at a more aggregate level of environmental throughput and/or in a supranational context. At the moment the OECD countries may be entering a phase of re-linking of income growth and degradation – and this at least for the time being puts a halt to the optimistic belief in Environmental Kuznets Curves as a general 'law'.

Moreover, insofar as Environmental Kuznets Curves do show the desired shape, they say very little about the system-wide consequences of environmental utilization. For example, this type of analysis appears to ignore the long-run risks to ecological processes in cases of accumulative and irreversible environmental changes. But even if we could ignore these system-wide and dynamic effects, and even if Environmental Kuznets Curves as found reflected a general phenomenon, they often imply a reduction of metabolism only beyond fairly high average incomes which, given the current levels and distribution of income and people, would entail that globally environmental utilization will keep on growing for at least a number of decades, with subsequent unsustainability. Thus the environmental transition might be forestalled by irreversible ecological damage. This calls for work and interventions aimed at the adoption of more sustainable technologies and patterns of production and consumption, and the institutions to boost these. Development will entail that at the global level incomes will rise; investments, technology and management, as well as institutional reform, will have to help in making this growth become environmentally sustainable before serious irreversibility problems arise.

## References


Arrow, K., Bolin, B., Costanza, R., Dasgupta, P., Folke, C., Holling, C.S., Jansson, B.-O., Levin, S., Maler, K.-G., Perrings, C. and Pimental, D. (1995), 'Economic Growth, Carrying Capacity and the Environment', *Science*, **268**, 520–21. Reprinted in *Ecological Economics*, **15** (2), 91–5.

Dasmann, R.F., Milton, J.P. and Freeman, P.H. (1973), *Ecological Principles for Economic Development*, London and New York: John Wiley & Sons.

De Bruyn, S.M. and Opschoor, J.B. (1997), 'Developments in the Throughput–Income Relationship: Theoretical and Empirical Observations', *Ecological Economics*, **20** (3), 255–69.

De Vries, E. (1951), *The Earth is Paying: The Wealth of the Earth and its Significance for the World Economy and Politics* (in Dutch), The Hague: Alabani.

Directorate-General Environmental Management (1996), *Report on the International Conference on Codifying Rio Principles in National Legislation*, Den Haag (Netherlands): Ministry of Housing, Spatial Planning and Environment, Nr 1996/4.

Founex Report (1971), *Development and Environment*. Published in UNEP (1981).

Grossman, G.M. and Krueger, A.B. (1996), 'The Inverted U: What Does It Mean?', *Environment and Development Economics*, **1** (1), 119–22.

James, D.E., Nijkamp, P. and Opschoor, J.B. (1989), 'Ecological Sustainability and Economic Development', in F. Archibugi and P. Nijkamp (eds), *Economy and Ecology: Towards Sustainable Development*, Dordrecht: Kluwer Academic Publishers.

Kuznets, S. (1955), 'Economic Growth and Income Inequality', *American Economic Review*, **XLV**, 1, 1–24.

Myrdal, G. (1970), *The Challenge of World Poverty*, New York: Random House.

Opschoor, J.B. (1996), 'Institutional Change and Development Towards Sustainability', in R. Costanza, O. Segura and J. Martinez-Alier (eds), *Getting Down to Earth: Practical Applications of Ecological Economics*, Washington, DC: Island Press.

Opschoor, J.B. (1997), 'The Hope, Faith and Love of Neoclassical Environmental Economics', *Ecological Economics*, **22**, 281–3.

Opschoor, J.B. and Klaassen, G.A.J. (1991), 'Economics of Sustainability or the Sustainability of Economics: Diffrent Paradigms', *Ecological Economics*, **4**, 93–115.

Opschoor, J.B. and Turner, R.K. (eds) (1994), *Economic Incentives and Environmental Policies: Principles and Practice*, Dordrecht and New York: Kluwer Academic Press.

Panayotou, Th. (1993), 'Empirical Tests and Policy Analysis of Environmental Degradation at Different Stages of Economic Development', Technology and Employment Programme, WP 238, ILO, Geneva.

Panayotou, Th. (1994), *Economic Instruments for Environmental Management and Sustainable Development*, Environmental Economics Series, Paper No 16, UNEP, Nairobi.

Reed, D. (ed.) (1996), *Structural Adjustment, the Environment, and Sustainable Development*, London: WWF/Earthscan.

Shafik, N. and Bandyopadhyay, S. (1992), 'Economic Growth and Environmental Quality: Time-Series and Cross-Country Evidence', *World Bank Working Papers*, WPS 904, Washington, 52 pp.

United Nations Development Programme (1995), *Human Development Report 1995*, Oxford: Oxford Economic Press.

United Nations Environment Programme (1981), *In Defence of the Earth: Basic Texts on Environment: Founex, Stockholm, Cocoyoc*, Nairobi: UNEP.

Wilkinson, R.G. (1973), *Poverty and Progress: An Ecological Model of Economic Development*, Utrecht and Antwerp: Aula/Het Spectrum (Dutch translation).

World Commission on Environment and Development (WCED) (1987), *Our Common Future*, Oxford: Oxford University Press.

World Resources Institute, UN Environmental Programme, UN Development Programme, World Bank (1997), *World Resources 1996–97*, Oxford and New York: Oxford University Press.

# Part I
# General Aspects

# [1]

# ENVIRONMENT AND THE DEVELOPING COUNTRIES

## 22.1 THE PROBLEM

Natural and man-modified resources in developing countries exhibit extensive interdependence. The extent of tree cover has a direct influence on soil fertility and water run-off rates: the trees serve both a protective and moisture-retaining function. As tree cover is reduced through clearance for agriculture, timber production and fuelwood demand, so the carrying capacity of the recovered and surrounding soils may be reduced, depending on the land management regime that succeeds deforestation. Agricultural productivity declines and livestock may be moved to more marginal grazing land. As soils dry out, the risks of flood and wind erosion increase. In the limit, desertification occurs. The water run-off takes soil from the land to produce sediment in rivers, irrigation channels, reservoirs and natural lakes, reducing the water resource input to agriculture, polluting drinking-water supplies, reducing the capacity of hydropower reservoirs, raising water levels and increasing the size of flood plains, and damaging fishery resources. As the demand for woodfuels grows and tree cover is reduced, so the stock of trees diminishes as the resource is 'mined' instead of being managed on a sustainable basis. With fuelwood scarcity comes the diversion of animal dung from its traditional role as soil nutrient to direct burning for fuel. Reduced dunging of the land further impairs soil fertility.

Soil fertility, water as irrigation and trees as a protective input to fertility and the source of fodder inputs to livestock are thus closely interrelated resources. In the absence of imported food or large supplies of fertiliser, the impact of any mismanagement of this resource base shows up in reduced output of food and reduced quality, and perhaps quantity, of water for human consumption. Of equal importance, resource mismanagement is recursive: damage to the resource base now makes the ability to recover from that damage, or from exogenous events such as reduced rainfall, less in the future. Thus as soils reduce in humus so hitherto manageable variations in rainfall become catastrophic events, and previous catastrophes increase in size. The adaptability and renewability of the resource system is impaired, with consequent costs to be borne in the near- and long-term future by existing and future generations.

Developing countries, especially poor ones, have a more immediate dependence on their renewable resources than have developed countries. In the latter case, dependency is still present, but the role of technology and the application of capital makes the linkage more 'roundabout'. The sophistication of water treatment plants, for example, makes the issue of water pollution less immediately damaging, important though it is. Since rural communities in developing countries drink water directly from its source, the reliance on the self-cleansing properties of natural rivers and lakes is more direct. The pollution of those supplies thus has immediate health effects. The same contrast between developing and developed countries holds for forests and woodland. The transition to fossil fuels in developed countries is largely complete, but woodfuels and crop residues are a basic and extensive source of fuel in developing countries. As trees are depleted so the rural household (and many urban ones too) has less capability to cook food and provide a source of heat. That reduced capability is not offset, other than at the margin, by substitution of fossil fuels, due to income constraints.

While there is a complex of reasons at work, it is primarily the pressure of increased population that has led to a situation in many developing countries where the rate at which land and water renewable resources are being used is in excess of the regenerative capacity of those resources. In short, renewable resources are being 'mined' in much the same way as exhaustible resources: their stock is being reduced. But the rate of depletion of renewable resources causes greater concern for the reasons given above: the depletion of any one of them impacts on the availability of the others; the rates of depletion feed back on the ability of the resources to renew themselves; and the resources are directly consumed as water and fuel, and both directly and indirectly as food. It is these three features:

- directness of impact
- resource interconnectedness
- damage to regenerative capacity

that provide the fundamental rationale for concern about natural resource mismanagement in developing countries. The rest of this chapter is devoted to an expansion of this theme.

## 22.2 THE DEPENDENCE ON NATURAL RESOURCES

### Fuel

Many developing countries have a substantial reliance upon woodfuels (fuelwood and charcoal) and, to a lesser extent, crop wastes as their source of energy. Table 22.1 shows the percentage degree of reliance on these 'traditional' fuels. Countries with the highest reliance on traditional fuels also tend to be the poorest. Indeed, in many ways, the extent to which traditional fuels are used

**Table 22.1** Developing country dependence on traditional fuels (traditional fuels as a percentage of total primary energy)[a].

| | | | |
|---|---|---|---|
| Nepal | 93 | Senegal | 60 |
| Malawi | 92 | Yemen AR | 58 |
| Tanzania | 91 | Fiji | 55 |
| Guinea-Bissau | 89 | Indonesia | 49 |
| Ethiopia | 89 | Sri Lanka | 45 |
| Sudan | 83 | Botswana | 45 |
| Paraguay | 83 | St Vincent | 44 |
| Niger | 80 | St Lucia | 39 |
| Uganda | 71 | Costa Rica | 38 |
| Kenya | 71[b] | Bolivia | 35 |
| Gambia | 70 | Morocco | 35 |
| Haiti | 70 | Zambia | 35 |
| Bangladesh | 70[c] | Zimbabwe | 30 |
| Solomon Islands | 66 | Turkey | 24 |
| Liberia | 64 | | |

[a]Defined as woodfuels = fuelwood and charcoal. In some cases bagasse and other crop residues are included.
[b]Authors' estimate.
[c]A range of 69–76 per cent is implied in the Bangladesh Energy Assessment.
*Source*: Computed from World Bank / UNDP *Energy Assessments* for each country, except Kenya. Estimates are for 1980–83 except for Indonesia (1978), Haiti (1979) and Kenya (1984).

can be regarded as an (inverse) indicator of the stage of economic development. Table 22.1 reveals two fundamental facts. First, if the sources of woodfuels are not sustained, there will be a major direct impact on the population. Second, that problem will be greatest in the poorest countries who can least afford to import petroleum product substitutes for direct household use of woodfuels, such as kerosene and liquid petroleum gas (LPG). (Note that electricity is also a very limited substitute since it is not used for cooking.)

There is in these statistics alone a cause for concern. The extent to which existing wood stocks are being depleted is more difficult to gauge, but Table 22.2 assembles some of the data and indicates that depletion of potentially renewable stocks is already a serious problem in a number of developing economies. For example, Nepal's annual consumption of wood appears to be more than 130 per cent greater than the mean annual increment in wood stocks (the 'sustainable yield'). Self-evidently, such situations must, unless

**Table 22.2** Illustrative examples of excess harvesting of wood over sustained yields[a].

| | | | |
|---|---|---|---|
| Uganda | +21 | Ethiopia | +150 |
| Malawi | +31 | Tanzania | +151 |
| Sahel[b] | +30 | Niger | +193 |
| Sudan | +71 | Haiti | +220 |
| N. Nigeria[b] | +73 | Yemen | +300 |
| Nepal | +132 | Mauritania | +893 |

[a]That is, harvest minus mean annual yield from existing stock. All estimates relate to a year in the period 1979–81.
[b]From D. Anderson and R. Fishwick, *Fuelwood Consumption and Deforestation in African Countries*, World Bank Staff Paper, No. 704, World Bank Washington DC, 1984.
*Source*: Apart from Note b, taken from data in World Bank/UNDP *Energy Assessments* for these countries.

corrected, lead to the eventual loss of the resource. If initial stocks are very high then excess consumption at levels shown in Table 22.2 could be argued to be tolerable for the near future. But the gravity of the situation can be revealed with two examples.

In Haiti, the United Nations Development Programme has estimated a reduction in the forest area of 59 per cent between 1956 and 1977. The World Bank conservatively estimates the annual current rate of decline at 5 per cent. Yet over 70 per cent of Haiti's energy demands are met from domestic wood supplies and 98 per cent of household energy demand is met from fuelwood and charcoal. With only some 200,000 hectares of forest left, Haiti illustrates the seriousness of the problem of direct consumption of a renewable fuel resource. In Nepal, forest area has shrunk from 6.4 million hectares in 1963–1964 to about 4.0 million in 1980 and the forests are disappearing at the rate of 100,000 hectares per annum. Fuelwood demand in Nepal could be met by an additional 1.2 million hectares of high-yield plantations, a planting rate of 50,000 hectares per annum by 1990 and 100,000 hectares per annum in the 1990s to get into reasonable balance by 2000.

## Water

Water serves several functions. In terms of direct use it is required for human consumption and livestock, comprising some 5 per cent and 3 per cent of world water use, respectively. Irrigation accounts for 70 per cent of world use of water, and industry and mining for 22 per cent. Table 22.3 shows water use for selected developing countries, and reveals that irrigation use generally accounts for even higher proportions of total water use in developing countries. Estimates of per capita drinking water suggest ranges of 65–290 litres per day per capita for Africa for urban households with connections, 20–45 litres per day for urban households with public standposts, and 15–35 litres per day for rural households. The corresponding ranges for Southeast Asia are 75–165, 25–50 and 30–70. Table 22.4 shows estimates of the percentage of the population with access to safe drinking water in countries where access is less than 20 per cent.

**Table 22.3** Percentage water use in selected developing countries.

| Country | Energy production | Irrigation | Industrial | Domestic consumption | Total water use ($10^9$ $m^3$) |
|---|---|---|---|---|---|
| Egypt | 1 | 91 | 3 | 5 | 30 |
| India | negative | 92 | 1 | 7 | 386 |
| Indonesia | negative | 86 | 2 | 12 | 42 |
| Pakistan | 0.4 | 97 | 0.3 | 2 | 118 |
| Phillipines | 10 | 72 | 4 | 14 | 14 |
| Thailand | 4 | 90 | 1 | 5 | 20 |
| Brazil | 5 | 20 | 30 | 50 | 10 |

*Source*: Computed from *The Global 2000 Report to the President*, Penguin Books, London, 1982, p. 147. Note that 'use' is not the same as 'consumption' since industrial water use is recycled to a considerable extent. Irrigation and drinking water are examples of consumptive uses.

The overall picture is clear. Developing countries have a marked direct dependence on natural resources – on wood for fuel and on untreated water for human consumption and cooking, for livestock,

**Table 22.4** Ranking of developing countries according to access to drinking water 1975–1980 (expressed as a percentage of population).

| | | | |
|---|---|---|---|
| Ethiopia | 4 | Lesotho | 14 |
| Mali | 6 | Central African Republic | 16 |
| Bhutan | 7 | Mauritania | 16 |
| Afghanistan | 10 | Papua New Guinea | 16 |
| Guinea-Bissau | 10 | Uganda | 16 |
| Nepal | 11 | Paraguay | 18 |
| Mozambique | 13 | Sri Lanka | 19 |
| Sierra Leone | 14 | | |

*Source*: UNICEF, *The State of the World's Children 1985*, UNICEF, Paris, 1985.

and for irrigation. Other resources play a similar role: fodder for livestock comes from trees, shrubs and pastures; crops depend on organic manures from animals and from crop residues; a considerable amount of food comes from the wild; medicines are frequently based on plants; the forests supply building materials, and so on. On this count alone, managing natural resources in a sustainable fashion is vital to the well-being and development prospects of the people of the developing world.

## 22.3 RESOURCE INTERCONNECTIONS

Land and water resources are interconnected in developing economies in ways which are more fragile than in the developed countries. While the same ecological cycles are at work, the capacity to distance people from the effects of interrupting those cycles is greater the richer the country is. The main linkages in resource systems are shown in Figure 22.1. The interconnectedness is shown by considering what happens if a single 'shock' to the system occurs, in this case removal of tree cover in excess of the sustainable yield. It is important to note that the links are not *necessary* ones, i.e. the consequences shown are not inevitable. In the first place, the negative impacts may be ameliorated by deliberate policy designed to reduce damage, e.g. by pollution clean-up, dredging of water channels, relocation of populations at risk from flood, and so on. Second, much will depend on what activity takes place when the removal of

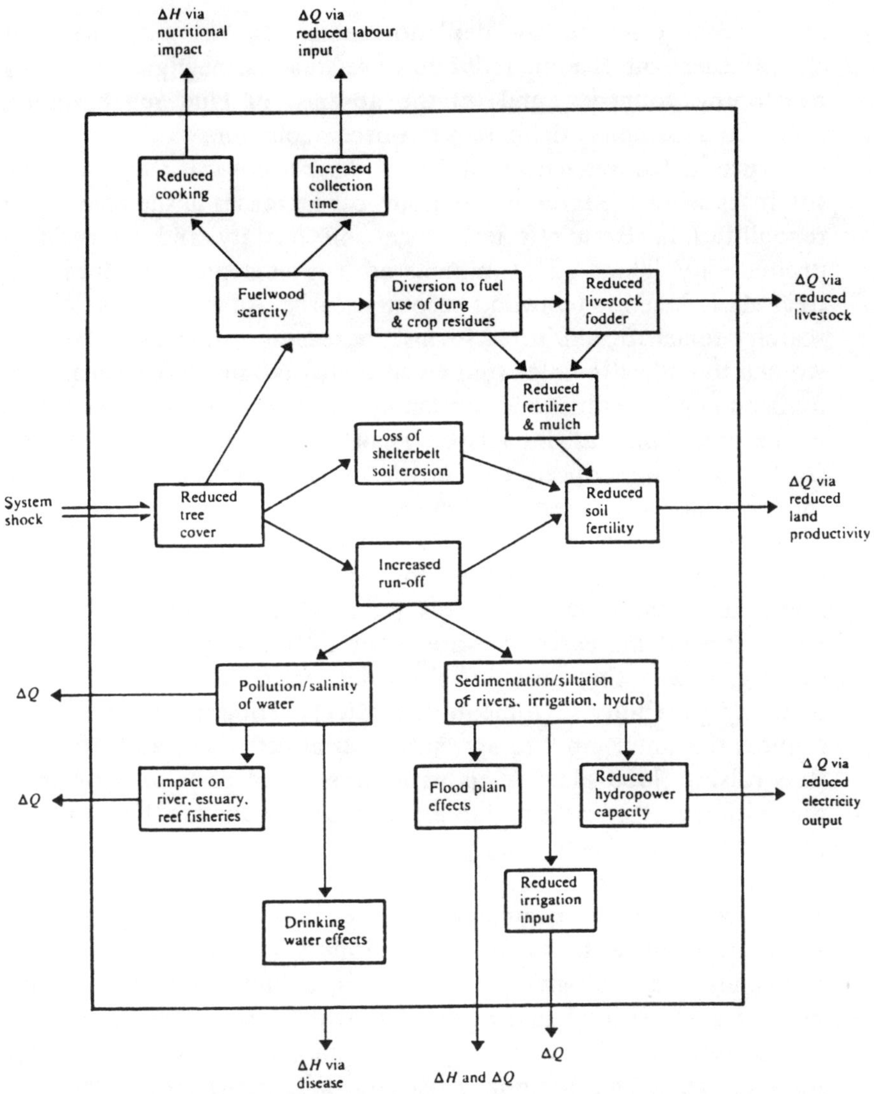


**Figure 22.1** Resource interconnections in developing countries.

tree cover takes place. Left alone, soil erosion may well occur, as it will if indiscriminate grazing is allowed. But if the land is terraced and farmed on a sustainable basis, soil run-off need not increase and many of the negative consequences of tree cover removal will not occur. The reasons for thinking that the 'negative consequence' model of resource interconnection is still appropriate arise from (*a*) the factual evidence on depletion episodes, (*b*) the fact that expenditures on damage reduction are small or negligible in many developing countries, and (*c*) the absence of land rehabilitation policy to accompany deliberate resource depletion.

Figure 22.1 shows various linkages. As tree cover is reduced so the soil loses wind shelter and water run-off increases in the absence of rehabilitation. Both effects reduce soil fertility and hence land productivity. These direct impacts are supplemented by others. As trees are reduced so fuelwood becomes scarce. Adaptive behaviour to scarcity tends to take three forms: increasing distances walked by women to collect remoter sources of fuelwood, increased burning of dung and crop residues and, utimately, abandoning one cooked meal in the day. This has impacts on health ($\Delta H$) and on food output ($\Delta Q$). In turn, reduced tree cover directly impacts on livestock fodder, especially in semi-arid environments and upland watersheds (this link is not shown in Figure 22.1). Increased burning of dung and crop residues deprives the soil of chemical, physical and microbiological inputs and thus reduces soil fertility further. As water run-off increases so water sources are subject to increased salinity, so affecting agricultural output via irrigation channels and affecting potability. Sedimentation affects irrigation channels and reduces the water input to agriculture. It affects rivers and estuaries, thus raising flood plain levels with consequent costs to agriculture and with increased risks of damage to property and life. Hydropower reservoirs become silted and generation capacity is reduced.

Obviously, these linkages will be affected by other causal factors. Irrigation alone, for example, will be the major contributing factor to salinisation of water, and salinisation is additionally a natural outcome of hydrologic cycles. That is, salinity and waterlogging problems are exacerbated by the removal of tree cover but are not primarily caused by it. Inadequate drainage is widely cited as the main cause, so that the policy issue at stake is the proper design of new systems and rehabilitation of defective sysstems.

## 22.4 THE ECONOMIC COST OF RESOURCE DAMAGE

The combination of the close dependence on natural resources and the fragility of the interconnections between them does much to explain why natural resource management is important in the developing world. The fragility issue should not be exaggerated. Anyone who has worked in arid zones, for example, will know that even these areas, which look like traditional picture images of the desert in the dry season, can be transformed into lush greenness in the wet season. But the opposite is also possible. Lush forests can be quickly converted into infertile land after clearance and used for intensive livestock farming; whole mountain-sides can be stripped of vegetation as erosion removes top soil. This environmental damage has an economic cost. Some examples follow.

**Fuelwood**

As fuelwood becomes scarce due to deforestation, so the time taken to collect the wood increases due to the longer distances that have to be travelled. Increased collection times have a clear opportunity cost in terms of foregone farm output or other activity. There were an estimated 2.25 million rural households in Kenya in 1980. In that year, it is estimated that 1.1 million of these were in regions where tree stocks were beginning to be 'mined'. Taking the daily unskilled labour rate at that time to be US $2.6 per day, then even an extra one hour per day per household in collection time could be valued at 26 cents per household, or $290,000 per annum. Such procedures raise issues about the economic valuation of time but offer some guideline to the orders of magnitude involved. If anything, the procedure will exaggerate costs since foregone farm output will not be valued at the unskilled labour rate and because there are other adjustments to fuelwood scarcity such as choosing more 'efficient' woods, brewing less beer, and so on.

The primary use for woodfuels is cooking. As wood becomes scarce, so cooking habits may change, sometimes to the detriment of nutrition. Fuel scarcity also inhibits the introduction of new nutritious foods such as soya beans, due to the extra cooking time required. The cost of such dietary changes, and the foregone benefits from the inability to introduce new foods, is obviously complex to estimate and no empirical work appears to be available. But it is a positive cost which must be debited to resource mismanagement.

Apart from collection time and nutrition effects, fuelwood scarcity has a third impact. As the wood becomes scarce, so animal dung and crop residues are burned rather than being applied to the soil as fertiliser and soil conditioners. A study by Newcombe (1984)

**estimates that up to 90 per cent of cattle dung produced in Eritrea, and 60 per cent in Tigrai and Gondar, Ethiopia, is used as fuel. By estimating the crop-response functions, it is possible to calculate the incremental grain production that would result if the dung was applied to the land. Multiplying this incremental yield by the market price of the grain gives an implicit price for the dung. A second approach to valuation is to estimate the nutrient value of the dung and value this at the price of imported fertiliser (this is a minimum value since there are non-chemical benefits to soil from using dung). A third approach is to observe what prices are actually paid for dung – in Ethiopia dung is sold to urban markets. The resulting estimates produced by Newcombe were, per tonne of dung:**

| | Ethiopian Birr | US$ (1983) |
|---|---|---|
| Market price | 99–238 | 47–114 |
| Fertiliser substitute | 45 | 22 |
| Grain response | 128–189 | 61– 91 |

As an illustration we can take Newcombe's estimate of dung burned in Ethiopian households at 7.9 million tonnes per annum. It follows that the foregone agricultural output by diverting dung to fuel uses is some US$600 million (an average grain-response value of $76 multiplied by 7.9 million tonnes) in a year.

### Sedimentation of hydro-reservoir capacity

A major cause of sedimentation of rivers, irrigation channels and dams is deforestation. Sediment loads carried in major rivers can be very large indeed. The Lo and Ching rivers in the People's Republic of China carry sediment that corresponds to an erosion rate for the drainage area of some 1,500 tonnes per hectare per year. Rates in the five major river basins of the world vary from 2.8 to 302 tonnes/hectare/year, compared with so-called 'tolerable rates' of 10 tonnes. One recipient of sedimentation is dams. Sfeir-Younis (1985) has simulated the effects of sedimentation on 200 major dams built from 1940 onwards. At a 1 per cent constant sedimentation rate per annum, the 'live' storage capacity of the dams will be reduced by *one-third* by the year 2000. At increasing sedimentation rates (1 per cent to 4 per cent per annum), some two-thirds of capacity would be lost.

Again, as a purely illustrative calculation, we can estimate the direct cost of foregone electricity production through sedimentation. Hydropower capacity in 100 developing countries contributed 445,000 gigawatt hours (GWh) out of a total electricity demand of 1,090,000 GWh in 1980, i.e. 41 per cent. Taking the *lower* of Sfeir-Younis' scenarios the losses to these dams in the year 2000 would be 148,000 GWh. The amount of oil needed to produce this amount of electricity is approximately 37 million tonnes. At a 1988 world price of US$15 per barrel, this would amount to a direct cost due to sedimentation of over US $4,000 million. This is for a *single* year (2000).

## 22.5 ECONOMIC INCENTIVES AND NATURAL RESOURCE MANAGEMENT POLICY

Given that natural resource management is important in the developing world, how might economic analysis help in improving it? The first way in which it can help is to demonstrate the economic value of good resource management. In large part, decision-making in developing economies is very much focused in ministries of finance and economic planning. Indeed, this bias is fairly familiar in the developed world where treasury departments often seem to wield more power than the government departments that have spending programmes. Environmental policy is not likely to be seen to be important unless its economic dimensions can be indicated. As we have seen, this is largely an exercise in the valuation of environmental functions.

The second way in which economics can help is to indicate the effects of devising incentives to manage resource sustainably. Some of the relevant considerations are outlined below.

Because environmental economics is rooted in the foundations of neoclassical economics, it tends to emphasise the role that incentives can play in securing a more rational management of natural resources. Its presupposition is that 'rational economic man' is as helpful an abstraction for rural Africa as it is for a Western consumer. Rational economic man is assumed to respond to economic signals in a continuous fashion so as to maximise his (or her) own welfare. One way of testing the reasonableness of this construct is to see in practice how resource management responds to changes in incentives. In reality this is difficult because of the evidence which suggests that changes in *individual* incentives may do little to encourage wise resource management. It seems more likely that what has to be manipulated is a *package* of incentives. This is very likely to consist first of enabling incentives aimed at the resource user, such as more secure land tenure, clarification of resource rights, access to credit (which frequently follows on from security of tenure), and information (extension) projects. Once the user is 'enabled' to respond, the issue becomes one of altering the economic signals to the resource user, e.g. producer prices. The implication is that 'wrong' signals induce environmental degradation and that the resource user may well perceive and understand that the degradation process is coming about because of his own actions. But those actions have to be seen as responses to external incentives. Given that set of signals, resource degradation may, perversely, be a rational economic response.

**The producer price argument**

It is widely argued that the most efficient and administratively simple alteration to incentives is the raising of producer prices. Most developing countries have some form of price control in official markets, although the existence of widespread black markets reduces the impact of the controls. The result is that farmgate prices are often markedly below the 'border' price for internationally traded goods, the price received (f.o.b.) for exports or the price paid (c.i.f.) for imports. Table 22.5 shows illustrative ratios for selected widely traded commodities in Kenya, Malawi and Tanzania. It will be observed that Kenya maintains producer prices very close to world prices for coffee and tea, but Malawi tobacco growers receive less than one-third of the world price and Tanzanian tobacco growers receive 50–70 per cent of the world price. A similar picture arises for Tanzanian cotton and coffee, with procurer prices being around 50 per cent of world prices (the exception being cotton in 1985 due to world price changes).

The argument might be that raising producer prices close to world prices will increase the incomes of farmers, enabling them to secure surpluses which can be re-invested in resource conservation, and to expand supply. But reality is likely to be far more complex and the current state of research is simply not adequate to pronounce on the

**Table 22.5** Ratios of producer prices to international prices.

| | Kenya | | Malawi | Tanzania | | |
|---|---|---|---|---|---|---|
| | Coffee | Tea | Tobacco | Tobacco | Cotton | Coffee |
| 1970 | 0.91 | | 0.30 | 0.78 | 0.73 | |
| 1971 | 0.90 | 0.79 | 0.33 | 0.84 | 0.61 | |
| 1972 | 0.98 | 0.77 | 0.29 | 0.84 | 0.57 | 0.57 |
| 1973 | 0.96 | 0.77 | 0.27 | 0.84 | 0.35 | 0.43 |
| 1974 | 0.97 | 0.67 | 0.20 | 0.68 | 0.33 | 0.43 |
| 1975 | 1.01 | 0.75 | 0.20 | 0.70 | 0.52 | 0.36 |
| 1976 | 0.96 | 0.74 | 0.23 | 0.65 | 0.42 | 0.30 |
| 1977 | 0.93 | 0.89 | 0.22 | 0.63 | 0.46 | 0.35 |
| 1978 | 1.02 | 0.85 | 0.30 | 0.70 | 0.56 | 0.39 |
| 1979 | 0.99 | 0.75 | 0.24 | 0.51 | 0.51 | 0.29 |
| 1980 | 1.04 | 0.83 | 0.23 | 0.47 | 0.53 | 0.41 |
| 1981 | 0.89 | 0.89 | 0.20 | 0.50 | 0.62 | 0.53 |
| 1982 | 0.82 | 0.86 | 0.18 | 0.50 | 0.73 | 0.52 |
| 1983 | 0.90 | 0.68 | 0.31 | 0.70 | 0.67 | 0.47 |
| 1984 | 0.83 | 0.98 | 0.28 | 0.55 | 0.65 | 0.47 |
| 1985 | | | 0.29 | 0.72 | 1.03 | 0.50 |

*Source*: U. Lele, 'Agricultural growth, domestic policy and extension assistance to Africa: Lessons of a quarter century', Paper presented at the 8th Agricultural Sector Symposium, Washington DC, January 1988.

nature of the linkage from producer price to agricultural supply response to natural resource effects. Some authorities argue that price increases encourage switches between crops, but have no effect on aggregate output. Others suggest that the aggregate response is also positive.

The natural resource dimension adds further complexity. Positive supply response is likely to be through an extension of agricultural margins rather than an intensification through application of technology, fertilisers, etc. This will be more obviously the case where there is limited access to technology or limited capability to adopt it. But extended margins may involve clearance of hitherto forested land or movements into previously marginal arid areas. In both cases there are environmental costs in terms of increased desertification risks which affect medium- to long-run agricultural yields. Even with intensive responses there are issues of the type of crop which is encouraged. The presumption is that bush and tree crops provide extensive root structures and canopy cover and are therefore less erosive than many root crops such as cassava, maize, millet and sorghum. If so, policy has to consider the social costs of encouraging expansion of erosive crops.

### The portfolio argument

Economic theory suggests a link between undeveloped capital markets and natural resource degradation. Given the essentially unequal distribution of incomes in developing countries, there are always institutions and individuals seeking outlets for money surpluses. With the widespread presence of exchange control and the absence of well-developed property and capital markets, such surpluses tend to gravitate to a few legitimate outlets and, of course, to some illegitimate ones. Livestock ownership is an example of legitimate investment, as is land purchase by absentee landlords. As long as this encouragement exists there is a tendency to over-stock on common land, and hence an incentive to degrade pasture. If land titlement also depends on clearance of vegetation, as it does in many cases, the same incentive exists to deforest and devegetate.

It is difficult to assess how important this portfolio argument is in the current state of knowledge. It would appear to be significant in some Latin American countries.

### Exchange rates

Exchange rates are simply prices of one currency in terms of another, but the rate set for this price can have effects on natural resources. A typical situation in developing countries is the over-valuation of exchange rates, i.e. holding them above what the market rate would be if market forces were allowed to operate. Over-valuation tends to come about because of expansionary monetary and fiscal policies which push up domestic prices relative to those of principal trading partners, and through policies of protecting indigenous industrial sectors with import quotas and tariffs which keep domestic industrial prices high.

If the exchange rate is over-valued, agricultural exports are discouraged because the exporter receives less in local currency for any exports than would be the case with a lower exchange rate. Effectively, then, an over-valued exchange rate will have the same effect as maintaining low producer prices. Over-valuation thus produces an implicit tax on domestic production. Moreover, over-valuation makes imported commodities artificially cheap, so that domestic farmers find themselves competing with effectively subsidised imported foodstuffs. What evidence there is suggests that over-valuation – measured by real rates of currency appreciation – does result in lower rates of growth of agricultural output. Although the 'automatic' response to over-valued exchange rates is to suggest a devaluation, this may have little impact on farmers' incentives due to the presence of middle men, district traders, processors and trading monopolies. This network of intermediaries may soak up the benefits to exports of any devaluation, leaving producer margins little changed. In effect, the devaluation creates a 'rent' which is dissipated by those with economic power, leaving the farmer unaffected.

What does this mean for natural resource management? As with domestic prices, the issue is one of how to increase agricultural output without generating environmental degradation which then feeds back as lower yields in the medium and long term. The exchange rate evidence suggests that over-valued rates do harm agricultural output, but the impact on natural resources will depend on the types of crops encouraged (so that relative prices matter as well as absolute prices) and on the type of farmer-response. These have not yet been systematically studied.

### Non-price incentives

Many other incentives are likely to be important in a package of measures designed to stimulate sustainable increases in agricultural production. Measures are also likely to be location-specific. But one type of incentive is very widely recommended in many studies – a change in the form of land tenure.

The basic argument is that tenure insecurity reduces the farmer's incentive to invest in land improvement. The sequence of relationships is shown in Figure 22.2. But there is a debate over the effect of tenurial change on natural resources and there is a great deal more to be learned before any significant conclusions can be reached. The basic contrast is made between common property systems and sets of individual land rights. In the former, land is managed by the community as a whole. In the latter, land is effectively 'privatised' by individuals. It is widely mooted that 'the tragedy of the commons' ensues in common property regimes since each individual has an incentive to increase personal gains, e.g. by adding more personal

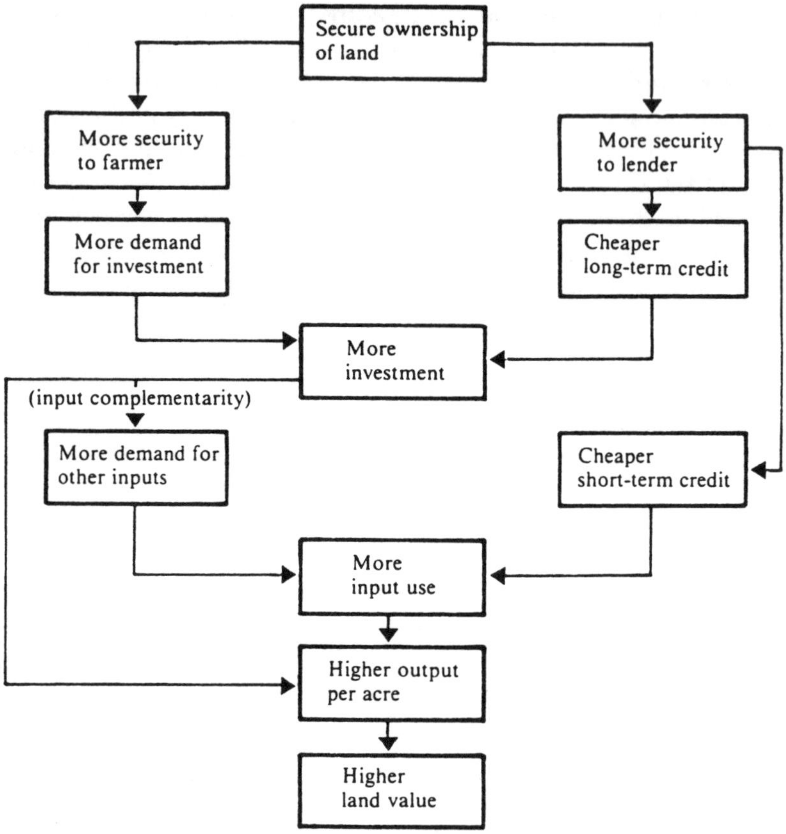


**Figure 22.2** Land tenure and agricultural output.

livestock to common grazing land, knowing that the costs of environmental degradation will be shared with others. That is, a personal cost–benefit calculation is inconsistent with the common good (see Chapter 16).

Much of the literature based on this idea is overly simplistic, but the main germ of the idea has validity. Several observations are in order:

1. Common property regimes are not static or homogeneous. There are many examples of them working well and, in particular, working well in terms of sustaining the stock of natural environmental capital on common land. What matters is the set of

communal rules applied to each person and the sanctions for breaking those rules. In many African contexts there are close, effective rules of social cohesion which guarantee proper resource management.

2. The 'tragedy of the commons' is more aptly applied to *open-access* resources, i.e. those for which there are no communal rights at all. Such an arrangement is distinct from a common property arrangement, and while economic theory would predict that some open-access resources can achieve an equilibrium short of extinction, it is clear that these resources are at grave risk of destruction.
3. Privatisation often occurs 'naturally' as land starvation sets in and the opportunity cost of over-grazing and resource over-use becomes clear. Privatised ownership is more widespread than might appear. Moreover, common-property systems frequently contain significant household and farm rights on an individual basis.
4. Many changes in pastoral societies are nonetheless altering some common property resources *back* to open-access resources. Factors of relevance here are improvements in transport for people and animals, government declarations making grazing land public property, competition between ethnic groups, loss of social cohesion in rural areas and rapid population growth.

Blanket recommendations that common-property regimes be replaced by privatised ones are simplistic. Too little is known about the costs and benefits of changing tenurial regimes and there is little option but to approach the issue on a case-by-case basis. There must, however, be a presumption, on the evidence available, that a more efficient agriculture would ensue from clearer titling, leasing and registration of land.

## 22.6 CONCLUDING NOTE

That part of environmental economics which deals with developing country problems is in its infancy. This chapter has attempted to give no more than the flavour of the kinds of issues that need to be tackled. There are a great many others. The significant point, however, is that the interconnections between environment and economy are far more direct and, arguably, more important in the developing world than they are in the developed world. This may show up in the importance of the concept of sustainable development (see Chapter 3) for the developing world, although we regard it as important also in the developed countries where economies and environments may only superficially appear to be 'decoupled'.

# [2]

*World Development*, Vol. 21, No. 11, pp. 1729–1748, 1993.
Printed in Great Britain.

0305–750X/93 $6.00 + 0.00
Pergamon Press Ltd

# Environmental Issues and Economic Decisions in Developing Countries



MOHAN MUNASINGHE*
*The World Bank, Washington, DC*

**Summary.** — This paper explains the key role of environmental economics in incorporating environmental concerns into decision making and in facilitating the more efficient management of natural resources as a step toward sustainable development. It reviews concepts and techniques for valuation of environmental impacts for use in conventional cost-benefit analysis, as well as key related aspects including environmental impacts of economywide policies, multicriteria analysis, risk and uncertainty, and discount rate issues. Several developing country case studies are summarized which cover a range of practical valuation methods. The evidence presented suggests that the valuation techniques for determining "use values" may be applied successfully in appropriate cases, but examples involving "nonuse values" are rare. The use of multiobjective decision methods also needs to be explored, where economic valuation is not feasible.

## 1. INTRODUCTION

In recent times, the environment has emerged as a major area of concern worldwide. Pollution is the perceived threat in most industrialized countries. Meanwhile, the developing world recognizes that both pollution and natural resource degradation have become an impediment to economic development and the alleviation of poverty. The world is currently exploring the concept of sustainable development — an approach that will permit continuing improvements in the quality of life with a lower intensity of resource use, thereby leaving for future generations an undiminished or even enhanced stock of natural resources and other assets (WCED, 1987; Pezzey, 1993).

Environmental assets provide three main types of essential services to humanity. First, the environment is a basic source of raw materials and inputs that support economic activities. Second, the environment is the sink which absorbs and recycles (normally at little or no cost to society) the waste products of human society. Finally, the environment provides essential life support functions (such as the blocking of harmful ultraviolet rays by the stratospheric ozone layer), without which many living organisms would cease to exist.

The diversity of short-term needs, as well as long-term goals, suggests that there is no universally "correct" approach to sustainable development. The concept of sustainable development has evolved to encompass three major points of view: economic, social, and ecological. All three concepts must be reconciled and effectively operationalized, to successfully achieve sustainable development (Munasinghe, 1993).

The economic approach to sustainability is based on the Hicks-Lindahl concept of the maximum flow of income that could be generated while at least maintaining the stock of assets (or capital) which yield these benefits (Solow, 1986; Maler, 1990). Problems of interpretation arise in identifying the kinds of capital to be maintained and their substitutability, as well as in valuing these assets, particularly ecological resources. The issues of uncertainty, irreversibility and catastrophic collapse pose additional difficulties (Pearce and Turner, 1990).

The ecological view of sustainable development focuses on the stability of biophysical systems. Of particular importance is the viability of subsystems that are critical to the global stability of the overall ecosystem (Perrings, 1991). Protection of biological diversity is a key aspect. Furthermore, "natural" sys-

*The author is particularly grateful to Noreen Beg. Special thanks are owed also to Ernst Lutz. In addition, assistance is acknowledged from Edward Barbier, Robin Bates, Jan Bojo, Wilfrido Cruz, John Dixon, John English, Gunnar Kohlin, Karl-Goran Maler, David Pearce, Adelaida Schwab, Jeremy Warford and Dale Whittington. Final Revision accepted: May 14, 1993.

tems may be interpreted to include all aspects of the biosphere, including man-made environments such as cities. The emphasis is on preserving the resilience and dynamic ability of natural systems to resist shocks and adapt to change, rather than conservation of some "ideal" static state.

The sociocultural concept of sustainability seeks to maintain the stability of social and cultural systems, including the reduction of destructive conflicts (UNEP, IUCN and WWF, 1991). Both intragenerational equity (especially elimination of poverty), and intergenerational equity (involving the rights of future generations) are important aspects of this approach. Preservation of cultural diversity across the globe, and the better use of knowledge concerning sustainable practices embedded in less dominant cultures, should be pursued. Modern society would need to harness pluralism and grassroots participation into a more effective decision making framework for socially sustainable development.

This paper reviews how environmental economics facilitates the efficient use of natural resources, as well as man-made capital and human resources — an objective which is a vital prerequisite for sustainable development. Attention is focused on the key role of environmental economics in helping value environmental resources more precisely, and in internalizing the costs and benefits of using such resources into the conventional calculus of economic decision making.

## 2. LINKING ECONOMICS AND THE ENVIRONMENT

### (a) *The role of environmental economics*

Environmental economics helps in identifying efficient natural resource management options that facilitate sustainable development. It is an essential bridge between the traditional techniques of decision making and modern environmental analysis. Environmental economics helps us incorporate ecological concerns into the framework of human society, as shown in Figure 1.

The right-hand side of the diagram indicates the hierarchical nature of modern society. The global and transnational level consists of sovereign nation states. In the next level are individual countries, each having a multisectored macroeconomy. Various economic sectors (such as industry and agriculture) exist in each country. Finally, each sector consists of different subsectors and projects.

Unfortunately, the environmental analysis cannot be carried out readily using the above socioeconomic structuring. The left side of Figure 1 shows one convenient environmental breakdown in which the

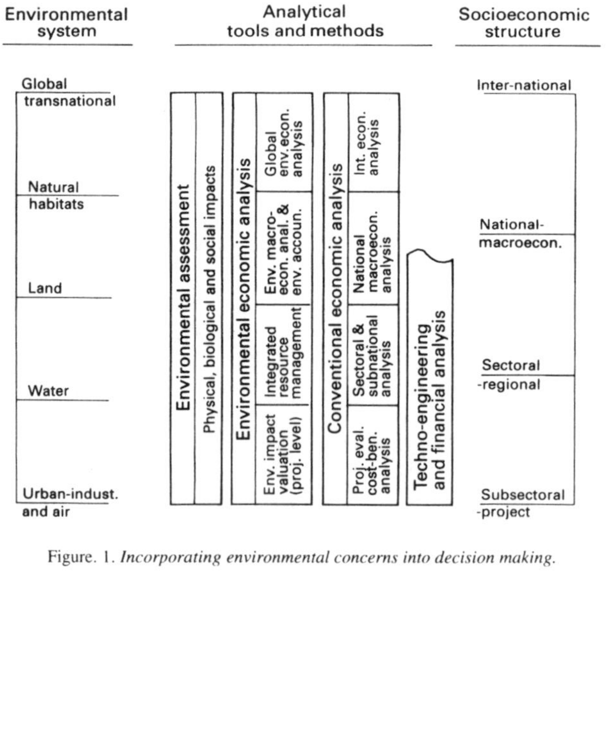


Figure. 1. *Incorporating environmental concerns into decision making.*

issues are related to: (i) global and transnational (e.g., climate change, ozone layer depletion); (ii) natural habitat (e.g., forests and other ecosystems); (iii) land (e.g., agricultural zone); (iv) water resource (e.g., river basin, aquifer, watershed); and (v) urban-industrial (e.g., metropolitan area, airshed). In each case, a holistic environmental analysis would seek to study a physical or ecological system in its entirety. Complications arise when such natural systems cut across the structure of human society. For example, a forest ecosystem (such as the Amazon) could span several countries, and also interact with many economic sectors within each country.

The causes of environmental degradation arise from human activity (ignoring natural disasters and other events of nonhuman origin), and therefore, we begin on the right side of Figure 1. The physical effects of socioeconomic decisions on the environment must then be traced through to the left side. The techniques of environmental assessment (EA) have been developed to facilitate this difficult analysis. For example, destruction of a primary moist tropical forest may be caused by hydroelectric dams (energy sector policy), roads (transport sector policy), slash and burn farming (agriculture sector policy), mining of minerals (industrial sector policy), land clearing encouraged by land-tax incentives (fiscal policy), and so on. Disentangling and prioritizing these multiple causes (right side) and their impacts (left side) will involve a complex analysis.

Meanwhile, the usual decision making process on the right side of Figure 1 relies on technoengineering, financial and economic analyses of projects and policies. In particular, conventional economic analysis has been well developed in the past, and uses techniques such as project evaluation/cost-benefit analysis (CBA), sectoral/regional studies, multisectoral macroeconomic analysis, and international economic analysis (finance, trade, etc.) at the various hierarchic levels.

Figure 1 also shows how environmental economics plays its bridging role, by mapping the EA results onto the framework of conventional economic analysis. A variety of environmental economic techniques including valuation of environmental impacts (at the local/project level), integrated resource management (at the sector/regional level), environmental macroeconomic analysis and environmental accounting (at the economywide level), and global/transnational environmental economic analysis (at the international level), facilitate this process of incorporating environmental issues into traditional decision making. Since there is considerable overlap among the analytical techniques described above, this conceptual categorization should not be interpreted too rigidly.

Once the foregoing steps are completed, projects and policies must be redesigned to reduce their environmental impacts and shift the development process toward a more sustainable path. Clearly, the formulation and implementation of such policies is itself a difficult task. In the deforestation example described earlier, protecting this single ecosystem is likely to raise problems of coordinating policies in a large number of disparate and (usually) noncooperating ministries and line institutions (i.e., energy, transport, agriculture, industry, finance, forestry, etc.).

### (b) *Recent developments*

While the environmental economic theory developed and its application spread throughout the developed world in the 1970s, the incorporation of environmental issues into development planning is a relatively recent phenomenon (Dasgupta and Maler, 1990). Much of the literature on applications of environmental economics in developing countries has emerged since the mid-1980s (see, for example, Dixon and Hufschmidt, 1986). The Brundtland Report recognized the role of economics in sustainable development — both in assessing costs of environmental degradation in developing countries, and in designing relevant incentives to limit such degradation (WCED, 1987).

Decision makers in most developing countries now accept that poor management of the environment has become a significant barrier to development. Since sustainable development includes other long-standing, high priority objectives such as economic growth and poverty eradication, scarce resources (both natural and man-made) must be used as efficiently as possible. The conventional approach relied on the systematic analyses of economic decisions (in particular, investment and pricing policies) that influenced the production of goods and services. As discussed earlier, however, this focus on economic efficiency, is a necessary but not sufficient condition for sustainable development.

In 1989, the World Bank issued its guidelines for environmental impact assessment of projects, as the natural culmination of many years of increasing concern about the environmental dimension of development (World Bank, 1989). Thus environmental analysis has been elevated to the same level of importance as the three existing aspects of project evaluation: financial, economic and technical analyses. In particular, valuation of environmental impacts permits environmental concerns to be incorporated effectively into project decisions.

### (c) *Conventional project evaluation*

The approach used by the World Bank in a typical project cycle includes several well-defined steps: identification, preparation, appraisal, negotiations and financing, implementation and supervision, and evaluation. Cost-benefit analysis (CBA), which seeks to assess project costs and benefits, is the key element in the appraisal stage. Benefits are defined by how a project enhances human welfare. Project costs are measured in terms of opportunity costs — the benefits foregone by not using scarce resources in the best alternative application.

Beyond this economic test, it was mentioned that a number of other aspects (including technical, environmental, and financial criteria), also need to be considered in project appraisal. In particular, the financial and economic analyses of projects are different. The former focuses on the money profits accruing to the project enterprise or firm, based on market or financial costs. The economic analysis of a project measures economic effects on the whole economy, using shadow prices that reflect opportunity costs. Externalities are valued, wherever practical. Well-known criteria such as net present value, internal rate of return and benefit-cost ratio are routinely used in the cost-benefit test of a project.

In the idealized world of perfect competition, the interaction of many profit-maximizing producers and utility-maximizing consumers gives rise to a situation that is called Pareto-optimal, where prices reflect the marginal economic costs, scarce resources are efficiently allocated and, for a given income distribution, no one person can be made better off without making someone else worse off (Bator, 1957). In the real world, however, distortions due to monopoly practices, external economies and diseconomies (such as environmental impacts which are not internalized in the private market), interventions in the market process through taxes, import duties and subsidies, all result in market (or financial) prices for goods and services which may diverge substantially from their shadow prices or true economic values. Furthermore, the reliance on strict efficiency criteria for determining economic welfare implies the passive acceptance of the existing (skewed) income distribution — this may be socially and politically unacceptable, especially if there are large income disparities. Such considerations necessitate the use of appropriate shadow prices (instead of market prices), to determine the optimal investment decisions and policies, especially in the developing countries where market distortions are more prevalent than in the industrialized countries (Dasgupta, Marglin and Sen, 1972; Little and Mirrlees, 1974; Munasinghe, 1990a; Ray, 1984; Squire and van der Tak, 1975).

Two basic types of shadow prices exist, either efficiency or socially oriented. In brief, efficiency shadow prices try to establish the actual economic values of inputs and outputs, while socially oriented shadow prices take account of the fact that the income distribution among different societal groups may not be consistent with overall national objectives. This may call for special adjustments, for example, by giving greater weight to benefits and costs accruing to the poor relative to the rich. In practice, such formal weighting schemes are seldom used in project evaluation — instead, income distributional and other social issues are addressed through direct targeting of beneficiaries and similar ad hoc approaches. In our analysis, we will place primary emphasis on efficiency shadow pricing.

Nonpriced inputs and outputs must be shadow-priced to reflect their economic opportunity costs. Major categories of such nonpriced inputs and outputs are public goods and externalities (especially environmental impacts). Public goods are basically those goods and services that are accessible to all without payment once they have been made available, such as transportation facilities, and police protection. Externalities are defined as beneficial or adverse effects imposed on others, for which the orginator of these effects cannot charge or be charged (as the case may be). Unfortunately, many externalities are not only difficult to measure in physical terms, but even more difficult to convert into monetary equivalents. Often therefore, the approach taken is to impose regulations and standards, expressed in physical measurements only, that try to limit the perceived external damages. This approach, however, could be improved by comparing the costs of compliance with the damages avoided.

To derive a consistent set of economic shadow prices for goods and services, a common yardstick or numeraire to measure value is necessary. The choice of the numeraire, like the choice of a currency unit, should not change the results of economic decision making, provided the same consistent framework and assumptions are used in the analysis. One convenient numeraire is a unit of uncommitted public income at border shadow prices (Little and Mirrlees, 1974). Essentially, this unit is the same as freely disposable foreign exchange available to the government, but expressed in terms of local currency units converted at the official exchange rate. The border-priced numeraire is particularly relevant for foreign exchange-scarce developing countries. It represents the set of opportunities available to a country to purchase goods and services on the international market.

### (d) *National accounts and macroeconomic performance*

To adequately include environmental concerns in economic analyses, standard income-accounting techniques must be reexamined. Gross domestic product (GDP) is the commonly used growth measure, based on transactions in markets. GDP is the basis on which many aspects of macroeconomic policy are determined. Its shortcomings, however, include neglect of income distributional concerns, nonmarket activities, and even more crucial, environmental degradation. In terms of the environment, there are three weaknesses in the current national accounting framework: (i) national accounts may not represent welfare accurately, because the balance sheets do not fully include environmental and natural resources, and therefore, important changes in the status of such resources are neglected; (ii) the depreciation of natural capital essential for human life — such as a nation's stock of air, soil, water, minerals and wilderness areas — are not included usually in national accounts; and (iii) cleanup costs (e.g., expenditures incurred to restore the environment) often serve to inflate national income, while offsetting environmental damages are not included (Lutz and Munasinghe, 1991). The resulting GDP estimates are incorrect because harmful outputs such as pollution are overlooked, while beneficial inputs related to environmental needs are implicitly undervalued.

To overcome these deficiencies, it is necessary to develop a system of national accounts (SNA) which will yield an Environmentally-adjusted Net Domestic Product (EDP) and an Environmentally-adjusted Net Income (EDI). National level decision makers rely on the conventional SNA to formulate economic policies. Thus, a supplementary environmentally adjusted SNA and corresponding performance indicators would encourage them to reassess the macroeconomic situation in light of environmental concerns, and trace the links between economywide policies and natural resource management (Muzondo, Miranda and Borenberg, 1990).

The World Bank has worked closely with the United Nations for the past decade, to better incorporate environmental concerns into the present round of revisions of the SNA framework. The interim system for environmentally adjusted economic accounts (SEAA) was proposed (Bartelmus, Stahmer and van Tongeren, 1989). The SEAA seeks to maintain the essential integrity of the existing SNA; but at the same time, encourages the collection and compilation of relevant data on environmental and natural resources — through a new set of satellite accounts. These satellite accounts constitute an important step toward the eventual goal of computing the EDP and EDI (Repetto et al., 1989; Peskin with Lutz, 1990). Recently, the World Bank and UN Statistical Office have completed two joint case studies for Mexico and Papua New Guinea, to determine how such accounts could be prepared (van Tongeren *et al.*, 1991, Bartelmus, Stahmer and von Tongeren, 1989).

### (e) *Economywide policies and the environment*

Fiscal and monetary policies, structural adjustment programs, and stabilization measures all have an effect on the natural resource base, but these complicated interactions are not well understood. The ideal approach is a "general equilibrium" analysis that traces both the economic and environmental effects of economywide policy reforms. Such comprehensive methods, however, are not possible in developing countries where data and skills are scarcer. "Partial" approaches that help to identify the most important impacts of economywide policies, may be more practical.

No simple generalizations are possible, but many instances of environmental damage are due to market failures and policy distortions, exacerbated by unemployment, landlessness and poverty (Munasinghe, Cruz and Warford, 1993). Therefore, broad policy reforms which usually promote efficiency or reduce poverty, also should be generally beneficial for the environment. Some of these reforms, however, may have negative environmental effects, depending on the preexisting (and often localized) constraints — such as inadequately defined property or resource rights. The challenge is to trace the complicated paths by which such policy changes ultimately affect incentives for efficient resource use at the firm or household level. The objective is not necessarily to modify the original broader policies (which have conventional economic or poverty related goals), but rather to design more specific or localised complementary measures. The latter would help mitigate negative effects or enhance positive impacts of the original policies on the environment. Such complementary actions would include both market-based approaches (such as Pigouvian taxes on environmental externalities or allocation of limited pollution rights coupled with marketable permits), as well as nonmarket methods (such as command-and-control techniques). This process of articulating a range of policies becomes more difficult when economywide reform programs address very broad macroeconomic issues.

#### (i) *General economywide policies*

In the 1980s, debtor countries adopted emergency stabilization programs which necessitated currency devaluations, controls on capital, and interest rate increases. When income levels dropped, tax revenues decreased accordingly. As unemployment increased, governments fell back upon expansionary financing policies, which led to increases in consumer prices. Such policies often drove the poorest groups onto marginal lands, resulting in soil erosion and desertification. Fuel price increases and lowered incomes caused deforestation and soil degradation, as the poor were forced to use fuelwood and animal dung for heating and cooking.

Real currency devaluations increase international competitiveness, and raise production of internationally tradable goods (e.g., forestry and agricultural products). If the agricultural response occurs through crop substitution, environmental impact would depend on whether the substitute crop had environmental benefits (e.g., tea, cocoa, rubber) or was environmentally damaging (e.g., tobacco, sugarcane, corn). Environmental impacts would also depend on whether increased production led to farming on new land (which could result in increased deforestation) or resulted in more efficient use of existing farmland. Increasing the competitiveness of exports increases the opportunity cost of keeping timber unharvested which could lead to forest depletion (Capistrano and Kiker, 1990).

Exchange rate overvaluation results in negative terms of trade, and decreased competitiveness of products and lower farmgate prices, which could push small cultivators onto marginal lands in an attempt to offset the effects of poor prices. Furthermore, skewed prices for agricultural outputs (arising from an incorrect exchange rate) sometimes encourages shifts into production of crops that may be more environmentally harmful. Since an overvalued exchange rate is often associated with poor export performance and foreign exchange shortages, devaluation may provide a double saving in foreign exchange — more export earnings from forestry products, as well as foreign exchange saved through import substitution from agricultural crops planted on deforested land.

In a recent review of the links between growth, trade policy and the environment, Lopez (1991) argues that the output from a natural resource such as a forest or fishery (where the production depends critically on the stock) also will be affected by other factors like property rights. Thus, if trade policy increased the value of output (e.g., timber or fish exports), then the degree of ownership would influence how production and resource stocks were managed — reactions might range from more investment in and maintenance of assets (if environmental costs were internalized by owner-users), to rapid depletion (when the users had no stake in the resource stock).

(ii) *Structural adjustment*

The conditionalities in the World Bank's structural adjustment loans (SALs) cover many of the elements discussed above: increases in agricultural prices, currency devaluations, and removal of agricultural subsidies (Sebastian and Alicbusan, 1989). Export taxes are often recommended as a means of generating public revenues, but they result in lower agricultural prices. Again, environmental impacts depend on the nature of the crops. SALs also call for reductions in energy subsidies, to decrease pollution and encourage energy efficiency, but this may force poor consumers to use more fuelwood and animal dung, thereby increasing deforestation and decreasing soil fertility.

SALs usually entail the adoption of policies designed to: promote trade liberalization — by removing barriers to external trade, and encouraging exports; and implement institutional reform — through privatization, encouraging foreign investment, better training and marketing, and reform of land ownership. The benefits and costs of such measures are highly country-specific. There is some concern that encouraging foreign investment and privatization might lead to the growth of "pollution havens", given the weakness of environmental regulations in most developing countries. Trade liberalization also could encourage the growth of energy-intensive and/or highly polluting industry. Pollution caused by industrialization, however, could be offset by afforestation (although this does not necessarily compensate residents of polluted areas), and limited by appropriate taxation policies that encouraged the use of pollution abatement technologies. In a recent review of the Latin American experience, Birdsall and Wheeler (1991) conclude that open economies are not necessarily more prone to pollution. They argue that the inflow of foreign technology and capital would tend to bring in better pollution standards. At the same time, it is the pollution-intensive heavy industries sector that has generally benefited from protective industrial and trade policies.

(iii) *Sectorial policies*

Several recent studies examine the effects of sectoral policies on the environment (Repetto, 1988; Sebastian and Alicbusan, 1989). Some countries subsidize urban consumers by placing price ceilings on food. In such cases, the environmental consequences will be the same as for currency overvaluation, as both result in lowered incentives to increase production of internationally tradable crops. Two classic studies by Mahar (1989) and Binswanger (1991) highlighted how distorted public policies have exacerbated environmental problems in the Brazilian Amazon region over several decades. Mahar showed that poor and landless peasants have contributed to deforestation, basically responding to incentives such as highways that opened up jungle areas, government land grants, access to public infrastructure, and cash subsidies. Some of the blame is attributable directly to government settlement projects. Large-scale livestock as well as iron ore smelting (in the Carajas area) have contributed to land degradation. Binswanger, focusing on the agricultural sector, argued that tax and land distribution policies, and the provision of credit to farmers, not only encouraged deforestation but also worsened income distribution (by favoring larger landowners). More recently, Lutz and Young (1992) have stressed that rational agricultural policies that eliminated subsidies for farm inputs (such as fertilizers and pesticides) could provide both economic and environmental gains.

Schneider *et al.* (1993) argue that unsustainable destruction of the Amazon is the result of farmers, ranchers and loggers responding predictably and rationally to distorted incentives arising from poor government policies and political instability.

## 3. INCORPORATING ENVIRONMENTAL IMPACTS ON DECISION MAKING

### (a) *Valuation of environmental costs and benefits*

Determine the environmental impacts of a project or policy, is the first step toward incorporating environmental concerns into conventional economic decision making. These biological, physical and social impacts are determined by comparing the "with" and the "without" project scenarios. To determine such impacts, the economist will have to rely on the expertise of engineers, ecologists, agronomists, social scientists, and other experts. An important issue, outside the scope of this paper, is that such physical impacts are complex and often poorly understood. Economically valuing the environmental impacts is the second step in taking the environment into account. A number of concepts of value, and practical valuation techniques have been developed to trace the welfare impacts of these changes.

#### (i) *Basic concepts of economic value and classification of valuation techniques*

Conceptually, the total economic value (TEV) of a resource consists of its use value (UV) and nonuse value (NUV). Use values may be broken down further into the direct use value (DUV), the indirect use value (IUV) and the option value (OV) (potential use value). One needs to be careful not to double count both the value of indirect supporting functions and the value of the resulting direct use (Aylward and Barbier, 1992). One major category of non-use value is existence value (EV). We may write: TEV = UV + NUV or TEV = [DUV + IUV + OV] + [NUV]

Figure 2 shows this disaggregation of TEV in schematic form. Below each valuation concept, a short description of its meaning and a few typical examples of the environmental resources underlying the perceived value, are provided. Thus, direct use value is determined by the contribution an environmental asset makes to current production or consumption. Indirect use value includes the benefits derived basically from functional services that the environment provides to support current production and consumption. Option value is the willingness to pay today based on the future benefit to be derived

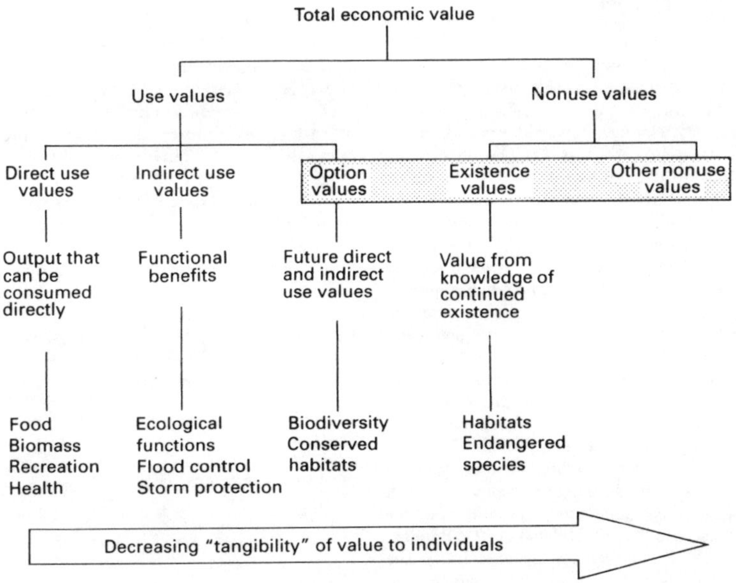


Source: Adapted from Pearce (1991)

Figure 2. *Categories of economic values attributed to environmental assets.*

from an unutilized asset when the option to use it will be exercised (for a more detailed explanation, see Bishop, 1982). Existence value arises from the satisfaction of merely knowing that the asset exists, although the valuer has no intention of using it.

Option values and nonuse values are shaded in the figure, to caution the analyst concerning some of the ambiguities associated with defining these concepts — as shown in the examples, they can spring from similar or identical resources. Economic theory clearly defines TUV (see next section), but there tends to be considerable overlap and ambiguity in the breakdown categories, especially with regard to nonuse values. Therefore, these categories are useful mainly as an indicative guide, but the distinctions often become irrelevant in practical estimation since the objective is to measure TUV rather than its components (Randall, 1991). Use values tend to be conceptually clearer, whereas nonuse values are linked to more altruistic motives (Schechter and Freeman, 1992).

Option value, as defined technically by Smith (1987a) is the algebraic difference between *ex-ante* option price (a sum paid to preserve the environmental option regardless of the future state of the environment) and *ex-post* expected consumer surplus (consumer surplus from use value, weighted by the probabilities of the respective states of nature. Randall (1991) notes the discrepancies that may arise from combining *ex-post* measures of option value with *ex-ante* measures of other values. Quasi-option value (QOV), which focuses on the intertemporal aspects of development, is perhaps most relevant to environmental economists in deciding whether to delay a project, given the possibility of irreversible environmental losses. QOV arises from new information that might emerge in the future regarding the value of a natural resource which would be irreversibly lost if the project was undertaken today (Arrow and Fisher, 1974). Fisher and Hanemann (1987) conclude that "[quasi-]option value can be calculated empirically given appropriate biological, engineering, and economic data and that it may be substantial relative to conventionally estimated benefits."

Nevertheless, whatever the conceptual basis of economic value, there are several practical techniques that permit us to estimate a monetary value for many environmental assets and impacts. The basic concept of economic valuation underlying all these techniques is the willingness to pay (WTP) of individuals for an environmental service or resource (for details, see Braden and Kolstad, 1991; Randall, 1991). This WTP is based on the area under the compensated or Hicksian demand curve which indicates how demand varies with price while keeping the user's utility level constant. Equivalently, the WTP for an environmental asset could be defined in terms of the difference between the values of two expenditure functions. The latter are the minimum amounts required to achieve a given level of utility (or welfare) before and after varying the price of, access to, and/or quality of the environmental resource in question, while keeping all other aspects constant. Problems of measurement arise because the commonly estimated demand curve is the Marshallian one — which indicates how demand varies with the price of the environmental good, while keeping the user's income level constant. In practice, it has been shown that the Marshallian and Hicksian estimates of WTP are in good agreement for a variety of conditions, and in a few cases the Hicksian function may be derived, once the Marshallian demand function has been estimated (Willig, 1976; Braden and Kolstad, 1991). An economic measure related to WTP is what people are willing to accept (WTA) as compensation for environmental damage. WTP and WTA could diverge (Cropper and Oates, 1992). In practice either or both measures are used for valuation, and therefore references to WTP below may be broadly interpreted to include WTA also.

Table 1 categorizes valuation methods, according to which type of market they rely on, and by considering how they make use of actual or potential behavior.

(ii) *Direct effects valued on conventional markets*

Methods considered in this section are based on how a change in environmental quality directly affects actual market-related production.

*Effect on production*: An investment decision often has environmental impacts, which in turn affect the quantity, quality or production costs of a range of productive outputs that may be valued readily in economic terms. In the case study on soil conservation in Lesotho, increased production from conserved land is estimated. In the valuation of a Peruvian rainforest, the values of different produc-

Table 1. *Taxonomy of relevant valuation techniques*

| | Conventional market | Implicit market | Constructed market |
|---|---|---|---|
| Based on actual behavior | — Effect on production<br>— Effect on health<br>— Defensive or preventive Cost | — Travel cost<br>— Wage differences<br>— Property values<br>— Surrogate goods | — Artificial market |
| Based on potential behavior | — Replacement cost<br>— Shadow project | | — Contingent valuation |

tion schemes are compared. Other examples include impacts on tropical wetlands (Barbier, Adams and Kimmage, 1991) and the effects of sedimentation on coral diversity and fish production (Hodgson and Dixon, 1988).

*Effect on health*: Approach is based on health impacts caused by pollution and environmental degradation. One practical measure that is relevant is the value of human output lost due to ill health or premature death. The loss of potential net earnings (called the human capital technique) is one proxy for foregone output, to which the costs of health care or prevention may be added (as a form of replacement/preventive expenditure). The above measure assumes that earnings reflect the value of marginal product and that medical treatment costs are well defined. The method also encounters difficulties when the cause-effect link between environmental quality and ill-health is unclear, or the sickness is chronic (i.e., of long duration).

This technique seeks to avoid ethical controversies associated with valuing a single life, attempting instead to place a value on the statistical probability of ill-health or death (akin to the actuarial values used by life insurance companies). Moreover, governments and public health authorities routinely set priorities and allocate health expenditures which affect human well-being. This in turn provides a baseline for determining implicit values placed by society on various health risks.

*Defensive or preventive costs*: Often, costs may have been voluntarily incurred by communities or individuals to mitigate or undo the damage caused by an adverse environmental impact. For example, if the drinking water is polluted, extra filtration and/or purifying chemicals may need to be used. Then, such additional defensive or preventive expenditures (*ex-post*) could be taken as a minimum estimate of the benefits of mitigation. The assumption is that the benefits of avoided environmental degradation at least exceed the costs of avoidance. The advantage of the technique is that defensive or preventive outlays (already made) are easier to determine than the value of the original environmental damage. One weakness is the defensive actions are sometimes decided upon quite arbitrarily with little reliance on market forces, so that the costs bear little relation to the potential environmental benefit. Recently, Harrington, Krupnick and Spofford (1989) evaluated the economic damages of a waterborne disease outbreak, emphasizing that the valuation of averting behavior requires the establishment of a relationship between observable defensive expenditure, and nonobservable willingness to pay.

(iii) *Potential expenditure valued on conventional markets*

This section summarizes techniques in which potential or future actions could be valued in conventional markets to provide a measure of environmental degradation, provided there is a high degree of certainty that such actions will be undertaken.

*Replacement cost and shadow project*: If an environmental resource that has been impaired is likely to be replaced in the future by another asset that provides equivalent services, then the costs of replacement may be used as a proxy for the environmental damage. This is an *ex-ante* measure similar to the (*ex-post*) defensive costs approach. It may be argued that the benefits from the environmental resource should be at least as valuable as the replacement expenses. The replacement cost approach has been applied to protecting groundwater resources in the Philippines, by determining the cost of developing alternative water sources (Munasinghe, 1990c). The same technique of estimating potential *ex-post* mitigation expenditures due to the increased costs of health care, is used in the Manicaland case study.

A shadow project is usually designed specifically to offset the environmental damage caused by another project. The cost of the shadow project reflects an institutional judgement on the value of environmental assets that are thereby restored. The approach has been discussed in the context of project-level sustainability. The original project and shadow project together form a sustainable package which helps to maintain undiminished, some vital stock of environmental resources. For example, if the original project was a dam that inundated some forest land, then the shadow project might involve the replanting of an equivalent area of forest, elsewhere. Often, the equivalency criterion is hard to satisfy exactly — in the above example, the two tracts of forest may have the same volume of biomass, but could differ widely in terms of biodiversity.

(iv) *Valuation using implicit (or surrogate) markets*

Often, relevant market data are not available in directly usable form, to value environmental resources. In many such cases, analysis of indirect market data (e.g., using statistical and econometric methods) permits the valuation to be carried out implicitly. A variety of such surrogate market-based methods — including travel cost, the "hedonic" methods (property value and wage differential), and proxy goods — as well as their applicability under different circumstances, are described below.

*Travel cost*: This method seeks to determine the demand for a recreational site (e.g., number of visits per year to a park), as a function of variables like consumer income, price, and various socioeconomic characteristics. The price is usually the sum of observed cost elements such as entry price to the site; costs of travelling to the site; and foregone earnings or opportunity cost of time spent. The consumer surplus associated with the demand curve provides an estimate of the value of the recreational site in question. More sophisticated versions include comparisons (using regression analysis) across sites, where environmental quality is also included as a variable that affects demand (for a detailed survey, see Mendelsohn, 1987 and Bockstael, McConnell and Strand, 1991). Until a few years ago, most applications of this technique were to be found in the market economies, but quite recently, several examples have emerged involving developing world applications. The travel cost for domestic trips to a forest is estimated in the Costa Rica case study. In the other study on the value of elephants in Kenya, the travel cost of tourists from Europe and North America is used to estimate consumer surplus.

*Property value*: In areas where relatively competitive markets exist for land, it is possible to decompose real estate prices into components attributable to different characteristics such as house and lot size, proximity to schools, shops and parks, etc. (Cropper and Oates, 1992). To value an environmental variable like air or water quality, the method seeks to determine that component of the property value attributable to the relevant environmental variable. Thus, the marginal WTP for improved local environmental quality is reflected in the increased price of housing in cleaner neighborhoods. This method has limited applicability in developing countries, because it requires a well-functioning housing market, as well as sophisticated information and tools of statistical analysis. Jimenez (1983) used this technique to explain changes in housing prices in a Manila slum area, upgraded partly due to water and sanitation service improvements.

*Wage differences*: As in the case of property values, the wage differential method attempts to relate changes in an economic price variable (i.e., the wage rate), to environmental conditions. The underlying assumption is that there is some component of the wage that is determined by the environmental pollution or hazard associated with the job or work site. The technique is relevant when competitive labor markets exist, where wages (that reflect the marginal product of labor) equilibrate the supply and demand for labor (see earlier discussion on shadow pricing). One concern is that the approach relies on private valuations of health risks, rather than social ones. In this context, the level of information on occupational hazards must be high, for private individuals to make meaningful tradeoffs between health-risk and remuneration. Finally, the effects of all factors other than environment (e.g., age, skill level, job responsibility, etc.) that might influence wages must be accounted for, to eliminate bias and isolate the impacts of environment.

*Proxy marketed goods*: This method is useful when an environmental good or service has no readily determined market value, but a close substitute exists which does have a competitively determined price. In such a case, the market price of the substitute may be used as a proxy for the value of the environmental resource. Barbier, Adams and Kimmage (1991) provide an example involving marketed and nonmarketed fish substitutes.

(v) *Valuation using constructed markets*

In cases, where market information cannot be used directly or indirectly, market-like behavior needs to be deduced through construction or simulation. The methods summarized below depend on direct questions, surveys or marketing experiments.

*Artificial market*: Such markets are constructed for experimental purposes, to determine consumer WTP for a good or service. For example, a home water purification kit might be marketed at various price levels, or access to a game reserve may be offered on the basis of different admission fees, thereby facilitating the respective estimation of values placed by individuals on water purity or on the use of a recreational facility.

*Contingent valuation*: When relevant market behavior is not observable, the contingent valuation method (CVM) puts direct questions to individuals to determine how much they might be willing-to-pay (WTP) for an environmental resource, or how much compensation they would be willing-to-accept (WTA) if they were deprived of the same resource. The contingent valuation method is more effective when the respondents are familiar with the environmental good or service (e.g., water quality) and have adequate information on which to base their preferences. CVM is likely to be far less reliable when the object of the valuation exercise is a more abstract aspect like existence value.

Generally, declared WTA tends to be significantly greater than the corresponding WTP. This may be partly attributable to "strategic bias" where respondents feel they would be better off inflating the amounts they would receive rather than the sums to be paid out, if the hypothetical questions posed were somehow to become a reality in the future. In the case of poorer individuals, WTP may be limited by the ability-to-pay, whereas WTA is not. The questionnaires have to be carefully designed, implemented and interpreted to overcome the above mentioned difficulties, as well as other types of bias. (For details, see *The Energy Journal*, 1988.) Munasinghe (1990a) provides several early examples of the application of CVM to value the quality of electricity services in developing countries.

A recent review by Pearce and Markandya (1989) compared valuation estimates obtained from market-based techniques and CVM, using results from seven studies carried out in industrial nations. They found that the corresponding estimates overlapped within an accuracy range of plus or minus 60%. The conclusion is that CVM, cautiously and rigorously applied, could provide rough estimates of value that would be helpful in economic decision making especially when other valuation methods were unavailable. The case study using the CVM for estimating the value of elephants in Kenya (see below) shows that it is possible to achieve an understanding of the order of magnitude of the benefits through modest methods. The other study, on WTP for water services in southern Haiti, tests the CVM for different biases, indicating the limits of its reliability.

### (b) *Multiobjective decision making*

The methods described above seek to estimate costs and benefits of a given project in monetary terms. When environmental impacts cannot be easily valued in monetary terms, multiobjective decision making is an alternative approach which may facilitate better choices among projects or policies available.

Desirable objectives need to be specified. These often exhibit a hierarchical structure. The highest level represents the broad overall objectives often vaguely stated and, hence, not very practical (e.g., improving the quality of life). Some of these, however, can be broken down into more operational lower level attributes (e.g., income), so that the extent to which the latter are met may be practically assessed. Sometimes only proxies are available (e.g., if the objective is "to enhance recreation opportunities," the attribute "number of recreation days" can be used). Value judgements may be required to choose the proper attribute (especially if proxies are involved), but measurements do not have to be in monetary terms (the single criterion used in economic cost-benefit analysis). More explicit recognition is given to the variety of nonmonetary concerns associated with planning decisions.

An intuitive understanding of the fundamental of multiobjective decision making can be provided by a two-dimensional graphical exposition such as in Figure 3. Assume that a scheme has two noncommensurable and conflicting objectives, $Z_1$ and $Z_2$. For example, $Z_1$ could be the additional project cost required to protect biodiversity, and $Z_2$, some index indicating the loss of biodiversity. Assume further that alternative projects or solutions to the problem (*A*, *B* and *C*) have been identified. Clearly, point *B* is superior (or dominates) to A in terms of both $Z_1$ and $Z_2$ because *B* exhibits lower costs as well as less biodiversity loss relative to *A*. Thus, alternative *A* may be discarded. We cannot, *A* however, make such a simple choice between solutions *B* and *C* since the former is better than the latter with respect to objectived $Z_1$ but worse with respect to $Z_2$. In general, more points (or solutions) such as *B* and *C* may be identified to define the set of all nondominated feasible solution points that form an optimal tradeoff curve or curve of best options.

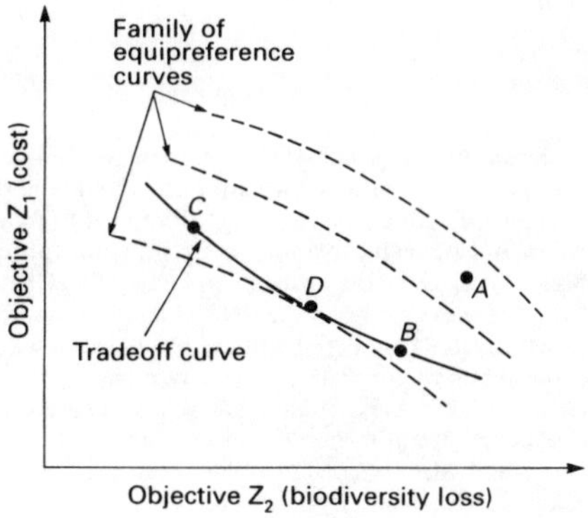


Figure 3. *Multicriteria tradeoffs.*

For an unconstrained problem, further ranking of alternatives cannot be conducted without the introduction of value judgements. Specific information has to be elicited from the decision maker to determine the most preferred solution. In its most complete form such information may be summarized by a family of equipreference curves that indicate the way in which the decision maker or society trades off one objective against the other — typical equipreference curves are illustrated in Figure 3. The preferred alternative is that which results in the greatest utility — which occurs (for continuous decision variables as shown here) at the point of tangency *D* of the best equipreference curve, with the tradeoff curve.

Several multicriteria methods have been developed (Romero and Rehman, 1987; Petry, 1990; Munasinghe, 1992). Which practical method in particular is suitable to determine the "best" alternative available, depends upon the nature of the decision situation. The advantage of multiobjective decision models is that they allow for more accurate representation of decision problems, since several objectives can be accounted for. A key question, however, concerns whose preferences are to be considered. Various interested groups will often assign different priorities to the respective objectives. Nevertheless, in constructing the model the analyst communicates information about the nature of the problem, and clarifies why factors are important and how they interact. While developing country applications are scarce, a recent study by Meier and Munasinghe (1992) seeks to incorporate (nonvalued) environmental considerations into energy decision making in Sri Lanka.

(c) *The discount rate*

Economists typically use a forward-looking approach in which past (or sunk) costs and benefits are ignored, while a discount rate is applied to future costs and benefits to yield their present values. Standard criteria for cost-benefit analysis (CBA), such as the net present value (NPV) and internal rate of return (IRR) are derived in this way. The issue of choosing an appropriate discount rate has been discussed in the context of general CBA for many years (Dasgupta, Marglin and Sen, 1972; Harberger, 1976; Little and Mirrlees, 1974). Two concepts help to shape the discount (or interest) rate in a market economy. First, there is the rate of time preference of individuals which determines how they compare present-day with future consumption. Second, there is the rate of return on capital, which determines how an investment (made by foregoing today's consumption) would yield a stream of future consumption (net of replacement). In an ideally functioning market, the interest rate which equilibrates savings and investment, also equals both the marginal rates of time preference and return on capital. In practice, government policy distortions and market failures lead to divergences between the rates of time preference and return on capital. Furthermore, the social rate of time preference may be less than the individual time preference rate, because long-lasting societies are likely to have a bigger stake in the more distant future than relatively short-lived individuals.

The long-term perspective required for sustainable development suggests that the discount rate might play a critical role in intertemporal decisions concerning the use of environmental resources (Lind and Arrow, 1982). The rate of capital productivity is very high in many developing countries, because of capital scarcity, and the rate of time preference also is elevated because of the urgency of satisfying immediate food needs rather than ensuring long term food security (Pearce and Turner, 1990). Projects with social costs occurring in the long term and net social benefits occurring in the near term will be favored by higher discount rates. Conversely, projects with benefits accruing in the long run will be less likely to be undertaken under high discount rates. Thus, some environmentalists have argued that discount rates should be lowered to facilitate environmentally sound projects meeting the CBA criteria. This would lead, however, to more investment projects of all types, thereby possibly threatening fragile environmental resource bases. Norgaard (1991) argues that lowering discount rates can in fact worsen environmental degradation — by lowering the cost of capital and thereby lowering the cost of production, more is consumed in the near-term relative to the case where discount rates were higher. Further, using a very low discount rate to protect future generations is inequitable, since it would penalize the present generation and increase inequalities across time periods — especially when the present contained widespread poverty (Pearce, 1991).

In order to facilitate such intergenerational transfers, one option is to impose a sustainability constraint, whereby current well-being is maximized without reducing the welfare of future generations below that of the current generation. In practice, this would entail monitoring and measurement of capital stocks (man-made, human and natural), and a broad investment policy which sought to ensure that compensating investments offset depreciation of existing assets (Pearce, 1991). Theoretically, the aim would be to ensure that the overall stock of assets is preserved or enhanced for future generations, but practical application of this principle would be difficult.

In summary, the following conclusions may be reached, within the context of environmental cost-benefit analysis: the normal range of opportunity cost of capital (e.g. 6–12%) may be used as the discount rate; efforts should be made to ensure that compensating investments offset capital stock degradation arising from policy and project decisions; and in the case of projects leading to irreversible damage, CBA should be adapted to the extent possible, to include the foregone benefits of preservation in the computation of costs.

(d) *Risk and uncertainty*

Risk and uncertainty are an inherent part of economic decisions. Risk represents the likelihood of occurrence of an undesirable event like an oil spill. In the case of uncertainty, the future outcome is basically unknown. Therefore, the risk of an event may be estimated by its probability of occurrence, whereas no such quantification is possible for uncertainty since the future is undefined. The risk probability and severity of damage could be used to determine an expected value of potential costs, which would be used in the CBA. The use of a single number (or expected value of risk), however, does not indicate the degree of variability or the range of probability values that might be expected. Additionally, it does not allow for individual perceptions of risk. The risk probability may be used to devise an insurance scheme to protect against the risk.

In the case of uncertainty, it is not possible to estimate the expected value of costs or insure against an unknown eventuality. The increasing scale of human activity, the complex of environmental and ecological systems, and the lack of knowledge of how these systems might be affected, all emphasize the need to deal with uncertainty more explicitly. A cautious approach is the key to dealing with uncertainty. Global warming is an illustrative example. In the past, the greenhouse effect of CO2 emissions was not known or recognized as a risk. At the present time, there is still considerable uncertainty about the future impacts of global warming, but given the large magnitude of potential consequences, caution is warranted.

The traditional and simple way of incorporating risk and uncertainty considerations in project level CBA has been through sensitivity analysis. Using optimistic and pessimistic values for different variables can indicate which variables will have the most pronounced effects on benefits and costs. We note that while sensitivity analysis need not reflect the probability of occurrence of the upper or lower values, it is useful for determining which variables are most important to the success or failure of a project (Dixon *et al.*, 1988). More sophisticated approaches to analyze risk and uncertainty are available (Braden and Kolstad, 1991).

The issue of uncertainty plays an important role in environmental valuation and policy formulation. Option values and quasi-option values are based on the existence of uncertainty. Option value (OV) is essentially the "premium" that consumers are willing to pay to avoid the risk of not having something available in the future (see the study on the valuation of elephants in Kenya). The sign of option value depends upon the presence of supply and/or demand uncertainty, and on whether the consumer is risk averse or risk loving. Quasi-option value (QOV) is the value of preserving options for future use in the expectation that knowledge will grow over time. If a development takes place that causes irreversible environmental damage, the opportunity to gain knowledge through study of flora and fauna is lost. Increased benefits to be derived through future knowledge expansion (which is independent of exploitation) leads to a positive QOV. This suggests that the resource exploitation should be postponed until increased knowledge facilitates a more informed decision. If information growth depends on the use taking place, which is unlikely in an environmental context, then QOV is positive (negative) when the uncertainty applies to the benefits of preservation (exploitation) (Pearce and Turner, 1990; Fisher and Hanemann, 1987).

Bromley (1989) suggests that the way in which policy makers address uncertainties depends on their perception of the existing entitlement structure. The interests of the future are only protected by an entitlement structure that imposes a duty on current generations to consider the rights of future generations (or, as he terms them, "missing markets" because "future generations are unable to enter bids to protect their interests"). Without such a structure, decision makers may tend to ignore costs to future generations, and minimize costs to current generations at the expense of the future. If the entitlement structure is adjusted, the policymaker can then examine three policies to protect the interests of future generations: mandated pollution abatement; full compensation for future damages (e.g., by taxation); and an annuity to compensate the future for costs imposed in the present. In the face of uncertainty, the first option might be the most efficient.

Other important sources of uncertainty linked with environmental issues include uncertainty over land tenure (which leads to deforestation and unsustainable agricultural practices), and uncertainty of resource rights (which can accelerate the rate of depletion of a nonrenewable resource). Policy makers can address these issues by instituting land reforms, and by designing appropriate taxation policies that return rents to public sources rather than to private agents.

## 4. CASE STUDIES OF VALUATION OF ENVIRONMENTAL IMPACTS

Few good developing country case studies of environmental impact valuation are available. Some selected examples are outlined briefly, to illustrate the implementation of the techniques discussed earlier, and explore their strengths and limitations in situations where the practitioner is likely to be more constrained than in the industrialized world (for details, see Munasinghe, 1993). These illustrations apply primarily to the direct and indirect use value categories shown in Figure 2.

### (a) *Effect on production method*

#### (i) *Cost-benefit analysis of land improvement in Lesotho (Bojö, 1991)*

The Farm Improvement with Soil Conservation (FISC) project was initiated in Southern Lesotho in 1985, with the overriding aim of raising agricultural production among smallholder farming households through soil conservation measures, subsidized inputs, and afforestation. In pursuit of this goal the project has rehabilitated old terrace structures, constructed new ones and added other structures for conservation. It has promoted the use of hybrid maize and sorghum, the planting of fodder grasses, and tree planting. It has also promoted rotational grazing on communal rangeland. "Conservation," in this study, is defined as "the promotion of optimum use of land in accordance with its capability so as to assure its maintenance and improvement."

A financial analysis compares a "high input" alternative implying the use of commercial fertilizer and hybrid seed, with the "traditional" alternative implying no use of fertilizer and locally saved seeds (as opposed to hybrids). The calculation (valid for one year only), does not take into consideration the impacts on soil conservation. Calculations for maize and sorghum show a negative real marginal IRR of 21–30%, respectively. An economic analysis distinguishes between productivity impacts due to increased use of commercial inputs, and impacts due to increased soil conservation. Costs are primarily labor and material input costs. Primary benefits include increased production of sorghum and maize (in terms of the incremental yield due to conservation, relative to future decline in yield due to erosion), fruit, fuelwood, and fodder. Given the assumptions regarding the rate of growth of project implementation factors, the results of the base case are an NPV of –M 7.0 million at a discount rate of 10% and -M 5.6 million at 1%. Conservation crop benefits are more significant at a lower discount rate, as they are slow to materialize.

Qualitatively, the project makes a significant loss in comparison to the resources invested. In terms of the main goal of the project — to raise agricultural production among smallholder farming households — the project cannot be termed successful. The benefits of soil conservation, however, may have been underestimated in the desire to improve crop yields (FISC has a "production," as opposed to a "preservation" orientation). There is demand uncertainty arising from lack of information on future population, food habits, agricultural technology, and capacity to import food; and supply uncertainty about the possibility of droughts leading to soil losses. Thus, soil conservation efforts could have a positive option value, to be incorporated into the stream of costs and benefits. Again, if long-term protection of the land has a higher priority than immediate productivity increases, this would justify subsidization of cover crops such as fodder grasses at the expense of traditional cropping. Aside from the debatable benefits of its "production" as opposed to "conservation" oriented approach, FISC serves as an important model in terms of its emphasis on consultation and community participation, and its reliance on low-cost, labor-intensive field techniques.

(ii) *Valuation of an Amazonian rainforest (Peters, Gentry and Mendelsohn, 1989)*

Most financial appraisals of tropical forests have focused exclusively on timber resources and have ignored the market benefits of nonwood products, thereby encouraging destructive logging and widespread forest clearing. To illustrate the values of nonwood forest products, the authors present data concerning inventory, production and current market value for all commercial tree species occurring in one hectare of Amazonian forest. They arrive at a combined NPV of $6820 for a fruit and latex production and selective cutting project, with logging contributing just 7% of the total. This greatly exceeds an estimated NPV of $3184 for timber and pulpwood obtained from a one hectare plantation, and an NPV of $2960 for fully stocked cattle pastures.

In extrapolating the value of the project (which is based on the value of one hectare), attempts could have been made to incorporate elasticities of demand for the products. Another concern is the use of returns per hectare as the unit of comparison between different uses. A recent study (World Bank, 1992) concludes that an appropriate analysis would compare returns per productive unit, including land, labor and capital valued at their opportunity cost. Since land in the Amazon is generally abundant relative to labor, returns to labor would better predict the market outcome than returns to land. This deduction is confirmed by behavior in the market, where forest extractivism has tended to vanish wherever reasonable alternative employment was available.

(b) *Valuing health: Economic costs and benefits of tobacco projects (Barnum, 1991)*

This study analyzes the net worldwide impact, of existing World Bank tobacco-related projects appraised during 1974–91. The aim is to determine net benefits as an indicative guide in formulating a Bank policy on lending for tobacco. First, the incremental effects on world output and price are calculated. It is estimated that the added global supply lowers the price by $20.5 per metric ton. Global benefits and costs are then estimated.

Benefits and costs identified are: the benefit from added consumer's surplus, the benefit from added producer's surplus; the value of life lost from premature death; the indirect cost of added morbidity; and the direct cost of added morbidity. Summing across the net benefits and costs above gives an annual net benefit in 1991 of –$612,000,000. It is estimated that an additional ton of tobacco produced by a new project in 1991 will have net annual global benefits of –$7,500.

Several key assumptions in the analysis, however, must be questioned. 0.65 deaths are estimated from all tobacco related causes per metric ton of tobacco consumed, and based on an average ratio of 4.0 for total smoking mortality to tobacco caused lung cancer mortality in the United States during 1965–85. Such a statement requires further analysis. In addition, on a global level, US figures do not necessarily apply, as there is little documentation of tobacco caused lung cancer (as opposed to, say, industrial pollution caused lung cancer) in developing countries. Another questionable assumption is that only 10% of tobacco starts are made by well informed consumers. The author's claim is not necessarily true, that the information gap for tobacco is the same as for alcohol. Finally, the study does not consider the costs of passive smoking, which may be as great or even greater than the costs of direct tobacco consumption (Markandya and Pearce, 1989).

(c) *Travel cost and contingent valuation methods*

(i) *Consumer surplus from visits to a rainforest in Costa Rica (Tobias and Mendelsohn, 1991)*

This study measures the value of ecotourism at a tropical rainforest site in Costa Rica using the travel cost method. Travel behavior reveals that Costa Rican visitors are willing to pay $35 per household to visit the site. The study finds that visitation is highly correlated with education (and therefore probably income), and that households in areas with high population densities make more trips. The paper only considers domestic visits, although foreign visitors to the site outnumbered domestic visitors by four to one in 1988. Foreign visitation is likely to be worth far more than domestic, as foreign visitors have higher travel costs, and a greater value of travel time because of higher earnings. Additionally, they provide foreign exchange. Nevertheless, if we use the same value of $35 per visit for all visitors, this would result in an NPV of $1250 per hectare. This figure is one to two times the purchase price currently paid by the reserve for the acquisition of new lands.

A linear demand function is utilized, rather than the more popular semi-log functional form, since visitation rates from many zones were zero. In a similar study, Willis and Garrod (1991) argued that the semi-log functional form was superior to the linear one — for the Clawson-Knetsch Zonal Travel Cost Method. They also found that the zonal travel cost method probably overestimated consumer surplus in the travel cost studies they reviewed. The individual travel cost method (utilized in this study) comes closer to contingent valuation results. It is unclear whether the Costa Rican case study assesses the cost (in foregone earnings) of time spent at site. It does mention the "cost of travel time." It would have been useful to have a clearer definition of this element.

As in this Costa Rican example, most travel cost studies look at single-purpose, single-destination trips. A more general methodological problem is how to deal with multiple destination trips. In most cases of international tourism to developing countries the travel cost would need to be attributed to many activities at a number of sites. The problem then becomes to elicit the specific value given to a certain site. An ongoing World Bank study on environmental valuation of a forestry development and conservation project in Madagascar is attempting to do this (Kramer *et al.*, 1992). Their model utilizes a household production framework in which the household examines cost functions for specific activities within the potential destination countries to compare the expected satisfaction and cost of trips of various bundles of activities. This demands much however, from the empirical data. A survey of tourists was used to collect travel cost and itinerary data that includes the distribution of time between activities for each individual, the costs of pursuing the activities, and the features of the various activities that lead to differences across individuals in their ability to undertake them.

(ii) *The value of viewing elephants on safaris in Kenya (Brown and Henry, 1989)*

The travel cost method was utilized to estimate a demand function of safaris in Kenya. The analysis is based on the 80% of tourists who come to Kenya from Europe and North America. Surveys of tour operators and visitors provided data for the estimation of land costs, air fare and travel time costs. Travel time costs were weighted at 30% to reflect the fact that vacation time is valued at lower than the gross wage rate. A weighted average consumers surplus of $725 per visitor is estimated, giving a total consumer surplus in the range of $182–218 million annually, depending on the assumed level of visitation. To identify the contribution elephants make to the value of a safari, tourists were asked to allocate the enjoyment of their trip over various categories of experience. Elephants represented 12.6% of total enjoyment. Therefore, the estimated economic value of a safari yields a viewing value for elephants of $23–27 million per year.

In order to assess consumer WTP to maintain the elephant population at current levels through increased enforcement activity, a survey was designed, utilizing the contingent valuation approach. Attempts were made to adjust for biases. The average value was $89 while the median was $100. This example of option value yields an annual viewing value of $22–27 million, and $25–30 million respectively, based on 250,000–300,000 adult safaris per year.

To conclude, both methods produced annual viewing values for elephants of around $25 million dollars. Although rough, such estimates are a useful guide.

(iii) *The willingness to pay for water services in Haiti (Whittington et al., 1990)*

The contingent valuation method was used in this study to estimate consumers' willingness to pay for an improved water system in a village in southern Haiti. The project was executed by CARE. The research team devised tests in an attempt to correct biases that could threaten the validity of the survey results, such as strategic bias, starting point bias, and hypothetical bias. An ordered probit model applied to the survey results demonstrated that WTP for a new water system (whether for a public standpost or a private connection) was positively correlated to income, the cost of obtaining water from existing sources, and the education of household members. It was negatively correlated with the individual's perception of water quality at the traditional source used before the construction of the improved water supply system. The sex of the respondent was statistically significant in the model for public standposts, but not in the model for private connections. The mean of WTP bids for public standposts represented 1.7% of household income, while the mean WTP bid for private connections was 2.1% of household incomes. These bids are significantly lower than the 5% rule-of-thumb often used in rural water-supply planning for maximum "ability to pay" for private connections. The bids are based, however, on the assumption that the public standposts are already in place.

The results of this study show that it is possible to do a contingent valuation survey among a very poor, illiterate population and obtain reasonable, consistent answers. Contingent valuation has the potential to become a viable method in developing countries: both for collecting information on individuals' willingness to pay for a wide range of public infrastructure projects, and for environmental protection services (such as the treatment of industrial wastewater flowing through residential areas).

### (d) *Contingent valuation method applied to estimate option and nonuse values*

An ongoing World Bank study seeks to determine nonuse values of tropical forests in Madagascar (Kramer *et al.*, 1992). Since hardly any developing country examples are available in this category, four US examples are cited below. They all used the contingent valuation approach to obtain actual measures for option, existence, and/or bequest values. A survey by Schulze *et al.* (1983) attempted to measure annual household willingness to pay (WTP) to preserve visibility in the Grand Canyon — both user and existence values are estimated separately. A study by Brookshire, Eubanks and Randall (1983) measured the option price (option value plus expected consumer surplus) and existence value of grizzly bears and bighorn sheep in Wyoming — both of these species being endangered by human activity in the area. Walsh, Loomis and Gillman (1984) sought to determine the use, option, bequest and existence values of wilderness areas to be protected in Colorado. Finally, Samples, Dixon and Gowen (1986) determined that existence value based on an individual's WTP to preserve a particular animal is significantly influenced by information provided about the animal's characteristics and endangered status.

## 5. CONCLUSIONS

One essential step toward economically efficient management of natural resources and formulating a practical strategy for sustainable development, is the effective incorporation of environmental concerns into decision making. Traditionally, the economic analysis of projects and policies (including the techniques of shadow pricing), has helped countries make more efficient use of scarce resources. "External effects," especially those arising from adverse environmental consequences, often have been neglected in the past.

This paper has described the critical role of environmental economics in bridging the gap between conventional development decision making and the new more environmentally sensitive approach. The paper has focused on concepts and techniques for valuation of environmental impacts of projects and policies that enable such environmental considerations to be explicitly considered in the conventional cost-benefit calculus used in economic decision making. The process of internalizing these environmental externalities may be facilitated by extending the techniques of neoclassical economic theory, with particular reliance on willingness-to-pay as a measure of value. Problems caused by discounting, risk and uncertainty were discussed. When economic valuation of environmental impacts is difficult, reliance may have to be placed on multiobjective methods.

There are an increasing number of attempts to both improve and make use of economic techniques to value environmental assets in developing countries. While the academic literature focuses mainly on the development of techniques, for practitioners, the important concern is to make use of the advances most relevant to their own areas of application (see reference list).

Certain specific shortcomings and difficulties associated with the case studies were discussed earlier. More generally, we may conclude that greater application to practical problems in a developing country is required (rather than further theoretical development), of the environmental valuation concepts and techniques presented in this paper. Such work can indicate orders of magnitude of impacts, eliminate gross environmental errors, and help identify the critical environmental indicators to which decisions should be sensitive.

Valuation techniques for determining use values may be applied successfully in appropriate cases.

Examples involving the estimation of nonuse values however, are virtually nonexistent in the developing world, and still scarce but becoming more common in the industrialized nations. The use of multiobjective decision methods also needs to be explored more systematically.

REFERENCES

Anderson, D., The Economics of Afforestation — A Case Study in Africa, The World Bank Occasional Paper No. 1/New Series (Baltimore, MD: The Johns Hopkins University Press, 1987).

Arrow, K. J., and A. C. Fisher, "Environmental preservation, uncertainty, and irreversibility," Quarterly Journal of Economics, Vol. 88 (1974), pp. 313–319.

Attaviroj, P., "Soil erosion and land degradation in the Northern Thai Uplands," in J. A. Dixon, D. E. James and P. B. Sherman (Eds.), Dryland Management: Economic Case Studies (London: Earthscan Publications, 1990).

Aylward, B., "The economic value of ecosystems: 3 — biological diversity," LEEC Gatekeeper Series No. GK91-03 (London: IIED/UCL London Environmental Economics Centre, June 1991).

Aylward, B., and E. B. Barbier, "Valuing environmental functions in developing countries," Biodiversity and Conservation, Vol. 1 (1992), pp. 34–50.

Barbier, E. B., "The economic value of ecosystems: 2 — tropical forests," LEEC Gatekeeper Series No. GK91–01 (London: IIED/UCL London Environ-mental Economics Centre, January 1991).

Barbier, E. B., "The economics of controlling degradation: Rehabilitating gum arabic systems in Sudan," LEEC Discussion Paper No. DP90–03 (London: IIED/UCL London Environmental Economics Centre, June 1990).

Barbier, E. B., "The economic value of ecosystems: 1 — tropical wetlands," LEEC Gatekeeper Series No. GK89–02 (London: IIED/UCL London Environmental Economics Centre, August 1989).

Barbier, E. B., W. M. Adams and K. Kimmage, "Economic valuation of wetland benefits: The Hadejia-Jama'are Floodplain, Nigeria," LEEC Discussion Paper No. DP91–02 (London: IIED/UCL London Environmental Economics Centre, April 1991).

Barde, J. P., and D. W. Pearce (Eds.), Valuing the Environment: Six Case Studies (London: Earthscan Publications, June 1991).

Barnum, H. N., "A note on the economic costs and benefits of bank tobacco projects," Mimeo (Washington, DC: The World Bank, 1991).

Barnum, H. N., "Evaluating healthy days of life gained from health projects," Social Science & Medicine, Vol. 24, No. 10 (1987), pp. 833–841.

Bartelmus, P., C. Stahmer, and J. van Tongeren, "Integrated environmental and economic account — Framework for an SNA satellite system," Review of Income and Wealth (1989).

Bator, F. J., "General equilibrium, welfare and allocation," American Economic Review (March 1957), pp. 22–59.

Binswanger, H. P., "Brazilian policies that encourage deforestation in the Amazon," World Development, Vol. 19 (July 1991), pp. 821–829.

Birdsall, N., and D. Wheeler, "Openness reduces industrial pollution in Latin America: The missing pollution haven effect," Paper presented at the Symposium on International Trade and the Environment (Washington, DC: The World Bank, November 1991).

Bishop, R. C., "Option value: An exposition and extension," Land Economics, Vol. 58, No. 1 (February 1982), pp. 1–15.

Bockstael, N. E., K. E. McConnell and I. Strand, "Recreation," in J. B. Braden, and C. D. Kolstad (Eds.), Measuring the Demand for Environmental Quality (New York: Elsevier, 1991), pp. 227–270.

Bojö, J., "The Economics of Land Degradation: Theory and Applications to Lesotho", Dissertation for the Doctor's Degree in Economics (Stockholm: Stockholm School of Economics, 1991).

Bojö, J., "Benefit-Cost Analysis of the Farm Improvement with Soil Conservation Project in Maphutseng, Mohale's Hoek District, Lesotho", in J. A. Dixon, D. E. James and P. B. Sherman (Eds.), 1990, op. cit.

Bojö, J., "Economic analysis of agricultural development projects: A case study from Lesotho," EFI Research Report (Stockholm: Stockholm School of Economics, 1990).

Braat, L. C., and J. B. Opschoor, "Risks in the Botswana Range-Cattle System," in J. A. Dixon, D. E. James and P. B. Sherman (Eds.), Economics of Protected Areas (Washington, DC: Island Press, 1990).

Braden, J. B., and C. D. Kolstad (Eds.), Measuring the Demand for Environmental Quality (New York: Elsevier, 1991).

Bromley, D. W., "Entitlements, missing markets, and environmental uncertainty," Journal of Environmental Economics and Management, Vol. 17 (1989), pp. 1181–1194.

Brookshire, D. S., L. S. Eubanks and A. Randall, "Estimating option prices and existence values for wildlife resources," Land Economics, Vol. 59, No. 1 (February 1983).

Brown Jr., G., and W. Henry, "The economic value of elephants," Discussion Paper 89–12 (London: London Environmental Economics Centre, 1989).

Capistrano, D., and C. F. Kiker, "Global economic influences on tropical closed broadleaved forest depletion, 1967–1985," Paper presented at the International Society for Ecological Economics Conference (Washington, DC: World Bank, May 1990).

Cocklin, C., "Mathematical programming and resources planning I: The limitations of traditional optimization," *Journal of Environmental Management*, Vol. 28 (1989), pp. 127–141.

Cropper, M. L., and W. E. Oates, "Environmental economics: A survey," *Journal of Economic Literature*, Vol. XXX (June 1992), 675–740.

Dasgupta, P., and K. G. Maler, "The environment and emerging development issues," Paper presented to the Annual Conference on Development Economics (Washington, DC: World Bank, 1990).

Dasgupta, P. S., Marglin and A. K. Sen, *Guidelines for Project Evaluation* (New York: UNIDO, 1972).

Dixon, J. A., De James, and P. B. Sherman (Eds.), *Economics of Protected Areas* (Washington, DC: Island Press, 1990).

Dixon, J. A., R. Carpenter, L. Fallon, P. Sherman, and S. Manipomoke, *Economic Analysis of the Environmental Impacts of Development Projects* (London: Earthscan in association with the Asian Development Bank, 1988).

Dixon, J. A., and M. M. Hufschmidt (Eds.), *Economic Valuation Techniques for the Environment: A Case Study Workbook* (Baltimore, MD: Johns Hopkins University Press, 1986).

Durojaiye, B. O., and A. E. Ikpi, "The monetary value of recreational facilities in a developing economy: A case study of three centers in Nigeria," *Natural Resources Journal*, Vol. 28, No. 2 (1988), pp. 315–328.

Energy Journal, Special Issue on Electricity Reliability, Vol. 9 (December 1988).

Finney, C. E., and S. Western, "An economic analysis of environment protection and management: An example from the Philippines," *The Environmentalist*, Vol. 6, No. 1 (1986).

Fisher, A. C., and M. Hanemann, "Quasi option value: Some misconceptions dispelled," *Journal of Environmental Economics and Management*, Vol. 14 (1987), pp. 183–190.

Fleming, W. M., "Phewa Tal catchment management programme: Benefits and costs of forestry and soil conservation in Nepal," in L. S. Hamilton (Ed.), *Forest and Watershed Development and Conservation in Asia and the Pacific* (Boulder, CO.: Westview Press, 1983).

Gigengack, A. R. *et al.*, "Global modelling of dryland degradation," in J. A. Dixon, D. E. James and P. B. Sherman (Eds.), *Economics of Protected Areas* (Washington, DC: Island Press, 1990).

Gilbert, A., "Natural resource accounting: A case study of Botswana", in J. A. Dixon, D. E. James and P. B. Sherman (Eds.), *Economics of Protected Areas* (Washington, DC: Island Press, 1990).

Grandstaff, S., and J. A. Dixon, "Evaluation of Lumpinee Park in Bangkok, Thailand," in J. A. Dixon and M. M. Hufschmidt (Eds.), *Economic Valuation Techniques for the Environment: A Case Study Workbook* (Baltimore: Johns Hopkins University Press, 1986).

Hanley, N. D., "Valuing rural recreation benefits: An empirical comparison of two approaches," *Journal of Agricultural Economics*, Vol. 40, No. 3 (1989), pp. 361–374.

Harberger, A. C., *Project Evaluation: Collected Papers* (Chicago: University of Chicago Press, 1976).

Harrington, W., A. J. Krupnick, and W. O. Spofford, Jr., "The economic losses of a waterborne disease outbreak," *Journal of Urban Economics*, Vol. 25, No. 1 (1989), pp. 116–137.

Hartunian, N. S., C. N. Smart, and M. S. Thompson, *The Incidence and Economic Costs of Major Health Impairments* (Lexington, MA D. C. Heath, 1981).

Hodgson, G., and J. A. Dixon, "Logging versus fisheries and tourism in Palawan," Paper No. 7 (Honolulu, HI: East West Center, 1988).

Holmberg, G., "An economic evaluation of soil conservation in Kitui District, Kenya," in J. A. Dixon, D. E. James and P. B. Sherman, *Economics of Protected Areas* (Washington, DC: Island Press, 1990).

Hufschmidt, M. M., D. E. James, A. D. Meister, B. T. Bower, and J. A. Dixon, *Environment, Natural Systems, and Development: An Economic Valuation Guide* (Baltimore, MD: Johns Hopkins University Press, 1983).

Jimenez, E., "The magnitude and determinants on home improvement in self-help housing: Manila's Tondo Project," *Land Economics*, Vol. 59, No. 1 (1983), pp. 70–83.

Kim, S., and J. A. Dixon, "Economic valuation of environmental quality aspects of upland agricultural projects in Korea," in J. A. Dixon and M. M. Hufschmidt (Eds.,) *Economic Valuation Techniques for the Environment* (Baltimore: Johns Hopkins University Press, 1986).

Kramer, R. A., M. Munasinghe, N. Sharma, E. Mercer, and P. Shyamsundar, "Valuing and protecting tropical forests: A case study of Madagascar," Paper presented at the IUCN World Parks Congress (Caracas: February 1992).

Liebman, J., "Some simple-minded observations on the role of optimization in public systems decisionmaking," Interfaces, Vol. 6 (1976), pp. 102–108.

Little, I. M. D., and J. A. Mirrlees, *Project Appraisal and Planning for Developing Countries* (New York: Basic Books, 1974).

Little, I. M. D., and J. A. Mirrlees, "Project appraisal and planning twenty years on," Paper presented at the Annual Conference on Development Economics (Washington, DC: World Bank, April 26–27, 1990).

Lind, R. C., and K. J. Arrow (Eds.), *Discounting for Time and Risk in Energy Policy*, (Baltimore, MD: Johns Hopkins University Press, 1982).

Lopez, R., "The environment as a factor of production: The economic growth and trade policy linkage," Mimeo (College Park: University of Maryland, College Park, December 1991).

Luenberger, D., *Introduction to Linear and Non-linear Programming* (Reading, MA: Addinson-Wesley, 1973).

Lutz, E., and M. Munasinghe, "Accounting for the environment," *Finance and Development*, Vol. 28 (March 1991), pp. 19–21.

Lutz, E., and M. Young, "Integration of environmental concerns into agricultural policies of industrial and developing countries," World Development, Vol. 20, No. 2 (1992), pp. 241–253.

MacRae, D., Jr., and D. Whittington, "Assessing preferences in cost-benefit analysis: Reflections on rural water supply evaluation in Haiti," *Journal of Policy Analysis and Management*, Vol. 7, No. 2 (1988), pp. 246–263.

Mahar, D., *Government Policies and Deforestation in Brazil's Amazon Region* (Washington, DC: World Bank, 1989).

Maler, K. G., "Economic theory and environmental degradation: A survey of some problems," *Revista de Analisis Economico*, Vol. 5, No. 2 (November 1990), pp. 7–17.

Markandya, A., and D. W. Pearce, "Environmental considerations and the choice of the discount rate in developing countries," ENV Department Working Paper No. 3 (Washington, DC: World Bank, May 1988).

Markandya, A., and D. W. Pearce, "Social costs of tobacco smoking," *British Journal of Addiction*, Vol. 84, No. 10 (1989), pp. 1139–1150.

McConnell, K. E., and J. H. Ducci, "Valuing environmental quality in developing countries: Two case studies,"

Paper prepared for session on "Contingent Valuation Surveys in Developing Countries," AEA/AERE Annual Meetings (Atlanta, GA: 1989).

Meier, P., and M. Munasinghe, "Incorporating environmental concerns into energy sector decisionmaking," ENV Department (Washington, DC: World Bank, January 1992).

Mendelsohn, M., "Modelling the demand for outdoor recreation," *Water Resources Research*, Vol. 23, No. 5 (1987), pp. 961–967.

Mitchell, R. C., and R. T. Carson, *Using Surveys to Value Public Goods: The Contingent Valuation Method* (Washington, DC: Resources for the Future, 1989).

Munasinghe, M., *Environmental Economics and Sustainable Development*, World Bank Environmental Paper No. 3 (Washington, DC: World Bank, 1993).

Munasinghe, M., *Water Supply and Environmental Management* (Boulder, CO: Westview Press, 1992).

Munasinghe, M., *Electric Power Economics* (London: Butterworths Press, 1990a).

Munasinghe, M., *Energy Analysis and Policy* (London: Butterworths Press, 1990b).

Munasinghe, M., "Managing water resources to avoid environmental degradation," ENV Working Paper No. 41 (Washington, DC: World Bank, 1990c).

Munasinghe, M., "Operationalizing Sustainable Development — An Economic Viewpoint", *Finance and Development* (December 1993).

Munasinghe, M., W. Cruz, and J. Warford, "Do economy-wide policies hurt the environment," *Finance and Development* (September 1993).

Muzondo, T. R., K. M. Miranda, and A. L. Borenberg, "Public policy and the environment," IMF Working Paper (Washington, DC: International Monetary Fund, June 1990).

Norgaard, R. B., "Sustainability as intergenerational equity: The challenge to economic thought and practice," Internal Discussion Paper, Asia Regional Series, Report No. IDP 97 (Washington, DC: World Bank, June 1991).

Pearce, D. W., "Economic valuation and the natural world," Report prepared for *World Development Report 1992: Development and the Natural World* (Washington, DC: World Bank, August, 1991).

Pearce, D. W., "An economic approach to saving the tropical forest," LEEC Paper 90–96 (London: London Environmental Economics Centre, 1990).

Pearce, D. W., E. B. Barbier, A. Markandya, S. Barrett, R. K. Turner and T. Swanson, *Blueprint 2: Greening the World Economy* (London: Earthscan Publications Ltd., 1991).

Pearce, D. W., and A. Markandya, *Environmental Policy Benefits: Monetary Valuation* (Paris: OECD, 1989).

Pearce, D. W., and K. Turner, *Economics of Natural Resources and the Environment* (London: Harvester Wheatsheaf, 1990).

Perrings, C., "Ecological sustainability and environmental control" (Australia: Centre for Resource and Environmental Studies, Australian National University, 1991).

Peskin, H. M., and E. Lutz, "A survey of resource and environmental accounting in industrialized countries," Environment Working Paper No. 37 (Washington, DC: World Bank, 1990).

Peters, C. M., A. H. Gentry, and R. O. Mendelsohn, "Valuation of an Amazonian Rainforest," *Nature*, Vol. 339 (June 29 1989), pp. 655–656.

Petry, F., "Who is afraid of choices? A proposal for multi-criteria analysis as a tool for decisionmaking support in development planning," *Journal of International Development*, Vol. 2 (1990), pp. 209–231.

Pezzey, J., "Economic Analysis of Sustainable Growth and Sustainable Development," World Bank Environment Paper No. 2 (Washington, DC: World Bank, 1993).

Phantumvanit, D., "A case study of water quality management in Thailand," in Y. J. Ahmad (Ed.), *Analysing the Options*, UNEP Studies, 5 (Oxford: Pergamon Press Ltd., 1982).

Phelps, C. E., "Death and taxes: An opportunity for substitution," *Journal of Health Economics*, Vol. 7 (1988), pp. 1–24.

Randall, A., "Total and non-use values," in J. B. Braden and C. D. Kolstad (Eds.), *Measuring Demand for Environmental Quality* (New York: Elsevier, 1991).

Randall, A., and J. R. Stoll, "Existence value in a total valuation framework," in *Managing Air Quality and Scenic Resources at National Parks and Wilderness Areas* (Boulder, CO: Westview Press, 1983).

Ray, A., *Cost Benefit Analysis* (Baltimore MD: Johns Hopkins University Press, 1984).

Repetto, R., "Economic policy reform for natural resource conservation," ENV Department Working Paper No. 4 (Washington, DC: World Bank, May 1988).

Repetto, R., W. Magrath, M. Wells, C. Beer, and F. Rossini, *Wasting Assets: Natural Resources in the National Income Accounts* (Washington, DC: World Resources Institute, 1989).

Romero, C., and T. Rehman, "Natural resource management and the use of multiple criteria decision making techniques: A review", *European Journal of Agricultural Economics*, Vol. 14 (1987), pp. 61–89.

Samples, K. C., J. A. Dixon, and M. M. Gowen, "Information disclosure and endangered species valuation," *Land Economics*, Vol. 62, No. 3 (August 1986).

Schechter, M., and S. Freeman, "Some reflections on the definition and measurement of nonuse value," Mimeo (Haifa: Natural Resources and Environmental Research Center and Department of Economics, University of Haifa, June 1992).

Schneider, R., G. Platais, D. Rosenblatt and M. Webb, "Sustainability, yield loss and 'imediatismo'," Laten Dissemination Note 1 (Washington, DC: World Bank, April 1993).

Schulze, W. D., D. S. Brookshire, E. G. Walther, K. Kelley MacFarland, M. A. Thayer, R. L. Whitworth, S. Ben-David, W. Malm and J. Molenar, "The economic benefits of preserving visibility in the National Parklands of the Southwest," *Natural Resources Journal*, Vol. 23 (January 1983).

Sebastian, I., and Alicbusan, A., "Sustainable development: Issues in adjustment lending policies," ENVPR Working Paper No. 1989–6 (Washington, DC: World Bank, October 1989).

Smith, V. K., "Non-use value in benefit cost analysis, and the treatment of option value," *Southern Economic Journal*, Vol. 54, No. 1 (1987a), pp. 19–26.

Smith, V. K., "Uncertainty, benefit-cost analysis, and the

treatment of option value," *Journal of Environmental Economics and Management*, Vol. 14, No. 3 (1987b), pp. 283–292.

Society for Promotion of Wastelands Development, "Economic and social change in a small rural community in the degraded lower Shivalik Hill Range in North India," in J. A. Dixon, D. E. James and P. B. Sherman (Eds), *Economics of Protected Areas* (Washington, DC: Island Press, 1990).

Society for Promotion of Wastelands Development, "Dryland management options in wastelands development: Jawaja Block, Rajasthan (India)," in J. A. Dixon, D. E. James and P. B. Sherman (Eds.), *Economics of Protected Areas* (Washington, DC: Island Press, 1990).

Solow, R., "On the integenerational allocation of natural resources," *Scandinavian Journal of Economics*, Vol. 88, No. 1 (1986), pp. 141–149.

Squire, L., and H. van der Tak, *Economic Analysis of Projects* (Baltimore: Johns Hopkins University Press, 1975).

Statistical Office of the United Nations (UNSO), *SNA Handbook on Integrated Environmental and Economic Accounting Draft*, (New York: UNSO, October 1990).

Thomas, V., "Evaluating pollution control: The case of Sao Paulo," in G. S. Tolley and V. Thomas (Eds.), *The Economics of Urbanization and Urban Policies in Developing Countries* (Washington, DC: The World Bank, 1987).

Tobias, D., and R. Mendelsohn, "Valuing ecotourism in a tropical rain-forest reserve," *Ambio*, Vol. 20, No. 2 (April 1991).

Turner, R. K., "Wetland conservation: Economics and ethics," in D. Collard, D. W. Pearce and D. Ulph (Eds.), Economics, Growth and Sustainable Environments: Essays in Memory of Richard Lecomber (London: Macmillan, 1988), pp. 121–159.

United Nations Environment Programme, International Union for the Conservation of Nature, and the World Wildlife Fund, *Caring for the Earth* (New York, United Nations, 1991).

van Tongeren, J., S. Schweinfest, E. Lutz, M. Gomez Luna, and F. Guillen Martin, "Integrated environmental and economic accounting: A case study for Mexico," Environment Working Paper No. 50 (Washington, DC: World Bank, December 1991).

Walsh, R. G., J. B. Loomis, and R. A. Gillman, "Valuing option, existence and bequest demands for wilderness," *Land Economics*, Vol. 60, No. 1 (February 1984).

Wang, G., W. Wu and F. Li, "Economic evaluation of land levelling in Weibei Dry Upland, Shaanxi, China," in J. A. Dixon, D. E. James and P. B. Sherman *Economics of Protected Areas* (Washington, DC: Island Press, 1990).

Wang, G., and L. Han, "Economic evaluation of dryland peanut growing with perforated plastic mulch," in J. A. Dixon, D. E. James and P. B. Sherman, *Economics of Protected Areas* (Washington, DC: Island Press, 1990).

Whittington, D., J. Briscoe, X. Mu, and W. Barron, "Estimating the willingness to pay for water services in developing countries: A case study of the use of contingent valuation surveys in Southern Haiti," *Economic Development and Cultural Change*, Vol. 38, No. 2 (January 1990).

Whittington, D., A. Okorafor, A. Okore, and A. McPhail, "Strategy for cost recovery in the rural water sector: A case study of Nsukka District, Anambra State, Nigeria," Draft, Infrastructure and Urban Development Dept. (Washington, DC: The World Bank, 1989).

Willig, Robert, D., "Consumer's surplus without apology," *American Economic Review*, Vol. 66, No. 4 (September 1976), pp. 589–597.

WIllis, K. G., and G. D. Garrod, "An individual travel-cost method of evaluating forest recreation," *Journal of Agricultural Economics*, Vol. 42, No. 1 (January 1991), pp. 33–42.

World Commission on Environment and Development (WCED), *Our Common Future* (Oxford: Oxford University Press, 1987).

World Bank, "Brazil: An analysis of environmental problems in the Amazon," Report No. 9104-DR, Vol. 2, Annex 5 (Washington, DC: The World Bank, 1992).

World Bank, *Operational Manual* (Washington, DC: World Bank, 1989).

41-63
(95)

# [3]

## Environment and Development: Theory and International Evidence*

O10

Q20

selected Countries

Q28

John M. Antle
*Montana State University*

Gregg Heidebrink
*Southern Methodist University*

The environmental effects of economic development have significant implications for a wide array of policy questions facing both low- and high-income countries today. Internationally, agricultural research centers are considering how to incorporate sustainability issues into their research agendas, while international lending institutions are taking a close look at the environmental consequences of industrial projects. Domestically, the North American Free Trade Agreement has brought the relationship between economic development and environmental quality to the forefront of U.S. public policy debate.[1]

It is surprising that despite the postwar growth of development economics, the genesis of environmental economics, and the fusion of ideas from both fields into the theme of sustainable development, economists have not made much progress in describing the impacts of long-term economic growth on environmental quality. Yet a vigorous public debate has arisen between individuals who maintain that environmental degradation is a necessary outcome of economic growth and those who believe that economic growth and environmental quality go hand in hand. This debate was highlighted at the 1992 United Nations Conference on Environment and Development in Rio de Janeiro.

In part this debate hinges on the properties of the aggregate demand for and supply of environmental quality. If the income elasticity of demand for environmental quality or amenities is high, then the increased prosperity engendered by economic growth could lead to significantly higher demand for environmental quality. Proponents of economic growth believe this demand will translate into a higher realized level of quality, as both public and private institutions and organi-


0013-0079/95/4303-0039$01.00

zations respond to political and market forces. This line of reasoning raises numerous questions about the structure of both the demand for and supply of environmental quality.

In his 1971 presidential address to the American Agricultural Economics Association, Vernon Ruttan hypothesized that "in relatively high-income economies the income elasticity of demand for commodities and services related to sustenance is low and declines as income continues to rise, while the income elasticity of demand for more effective disposal of residuals and for environmental amenities is high and continues to rise. This is in sharp contrast to the situation in poor countries where the income elasticity of demand is high for sustenance and low for environmental amenities." However, Ruttan qualified this hypothesis by noting that "quantitative evidence with respect to the demand for environmental services is inadequate at this time."[2]

One of the major themes of environmental economics research in high-income countries has been the measurement of the demand for environmental quality.[3] Yet Ruttan's observation concerning the lack of quantitative evidence about the aggregate income elasticity of demand for environmental quality—in either low- or high-income countries—remains nearly as true today as it was in 1971. There likewise has been little quantification of the supply of environmental amenities, the supply side of the environment-development equation.

One reason for this gap in knowledge has been the lack of data with which to estimate the relevant income elasticities. Until recently, there were no systematic attempts to document quantitatively the state of the environment in both developing and developed countries. National accounts data generally lack sufficient detail to ascertain the level of public spending on environmental protection. Private and international organizations have only recently begun to attempt to fill the data void.[4] As these data have become available, a number of studies have focused on quantitative assessment of the environment-development question, principally using data on industrial emissions and indexes of urban air quality. Several of these studies have estimated a quantitative relationship between certain environmental indicators and per capita incomes across countries and over time.[5]

A related problem is that environmental quality is a concept without a universally agreed upon definition. Is environmental quality best measured by the availability of clean drinking water, by an urban air-quality index, by the amount of land in national parks, or by the number of endangered species? Each of these measures falls along a continuum. At one end of this continuum are measures related to human standards of living. At the other end are measures that relate to ecological conditions such as viability and stability of the ecosystem. Each of these dimensions is likely to be relevant to people, but possibly at different income levels. At low per capita incomes, people may be willing to pay for the health benefits of clean drinking water but may not be willing to pay for species preservation; yet at higher income levels individuals are indeed willing to pay taxes to support preservation of wilderness areas and to preserve species. Therefore, the relationship between income and the demand for environmental quality is likely to depend on the type of measure used to represent environmental quality.

In this article we develop a stylized model of the environment-development trade-offs faced by countries during the process of economic growth. This model provides a conceptual framework for understanding the public debate over growth and environmental quality. The analysis shows that, even in a world in which environmental quality is not valued in markets, economic growth does not necessarily lead to environmental degradation. Indeed, the analysis shows that market economies generally will maintain their environmental capital stocks at positive, and possibly increasing, levels. It is simply not economically rational for a market economy to exhaust the environmental capital stock. This analysis also provides a theoretical foundation for empirically examining Ruttan's hypothesis and testing the hypothesis of the "environmental transition."

The environmental transition hypothesis is generated by combining Ruttan's hypothesis about the demand for environmental quality with likely patterns of economic growth. The environmental transition hypothesis states that economic growth is likely to be accompanied by environmental degradation at low income levels. However, as income grows, the accompanying increase in the demand for environmental protection is hypothesized to bring about a development path characterized by both economic growth and environmental quality improvements. Subsequent sections of the article use recently available data from low- and high-income countries to estimate the relationship between income and two classes of environmental amenities, parklands and forests. These two indicators can be interpreted as related to a broad set of environmental amenities associated with environmental quality, ranging from those affecting human living standards to those related to general ecosystem health, and thus are appropriate for testing the environmental transition hypothesis. The empirical results provide support for the environmental transition hypothesis; the two variables representing environmental quality are negatively related to income in countries with less than \$1,200–\$2,000 income per capita, while in higher-income countries, these environmental amenities are positively related to income with an elasticity that typically exceeds unity. The article concludes with a discussion of the implications of these findings for the environment-development debate.

**The Environment-Development Trade-off**

The conventional production possibilities frontier shows the supply-side trade-offs an economy faces in the production of market goods, given its resource endowment and technology. In this section a transformation frontier is defined between market goods and environmental services. To model this frontier, consider an economy where the production of market goods is $x = x(L, K, Z)$, where $L$ is labor and other variable inputs devoted to production of market goods, $K$ is the environmental capital stock devoted to market goods production (land, timber, water resources, etc.), and $Z$ is the conventional capital stock (structures, machinery, etc.).[6] This function is assumed to exhibit the usual concavity properties, and it is assumed that $x_K < 0$ is possible for high levels of $K$ utilization just as a negative marginal product is possible for conventional capital in the production process. We focus on this point here because environmental resources may be unpriced and thus there will be a tendency to use these resources up to the point of zero marginal product. Environmental services are produced according to the function $e = e(E)$, where $E$ is the environmental capital stock (parks, forests, rivers, etc.). This function is also assumed to be concave, but the marginal product of environmental capital is assumed to be positive, $e_E > 0$, because there does not appear to be a reason why there would be diminishing marginal returns to the environmental capital stock. Otherwise, both production functions are assumed to exhibit neoclassical properties.

A transformation surface between market goods and environmental services is defined as the combinations of $x$ and $e$ that are produced as resources are transferred from one production activity to the other. For this stylized analysis, it is further assumed that environmental capital ($E$) can be transformed into $K$ on a one-for-one basis. Let $R$ denote a unit of capital that is transferred from $E$ to $K$. It follows that $-dE/dR = dK/dR = 1$. Now suppose labor and conventional market capital are optimally allocated in each sector, given prices and the quantities of $E$ and $K$. Under these assumptions, proof of the concavity of the production possibilities frontier is straightforward. Applying the envelope theorem, it follows that

$$\frac{de}{dR} = e_E \frac{dE}{dR} = -e_E$$

and

$$\frac{dx}{dR} = x_K \frac{dK}{dR} = x_K,$$

and therefore the marginal rate of transformation from $e$ to $x$ is

$$\mathrm{MRT}_{e,x} = \frac{de}{dx} = -\frac{e_E}{x_K}.$$

Differentiating this last expression with respect to $R$, and using $dE/dR = -1$, yields

$$\frac{d\mathrm{MRT}_{e,x}}{dR} = \frac{e_{EE}}{x_K} + \frac{e_E x_{KK}}{x_K^2}.$$

Thus, the transformation frontier is negatively sloped and concave unless $x_K$ is negative, in which case a positively sloped, convex segment is possible. The transformation function's shape is illustrated in figure 1. The negatively sloped, concave segment between points $A$ and $B$ follows from the assumption that $e_E > 0$ and $x_K > 0$ until zero marginal returns to $K$ are achieved at point $B$. Below this point, $x_K < 0$ and the frontier is convex with a positive slope.[7]

The shape of the transformation frontier has important implications for the properties of general equilibrium in the economy. For simplicity, assume that the environmental services are public goods for which there are no markets or market prices. The equilibrium of the supply side of the economy is achieved where the marginal rate of technical substitution equals the relative prices of the two goods. Since the price of a pure public good is zero in a market economy, the market equilibrium occurs at point $B$, where the slope of the frontier approaches infinity. The shape of the transformation frontier thus ex-

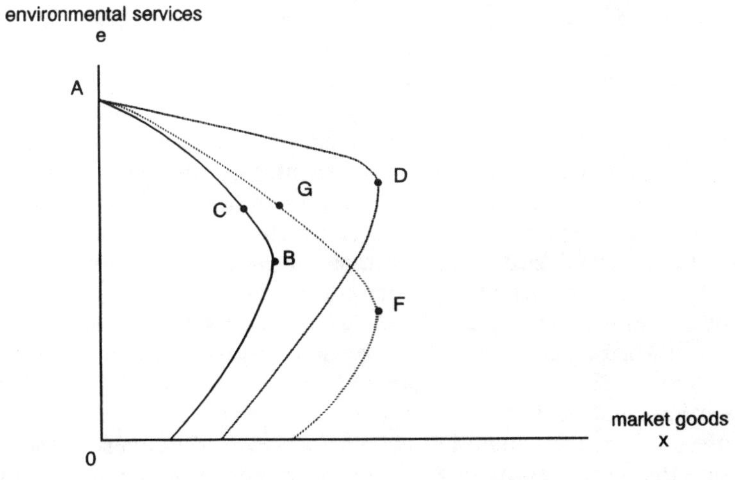


FIG. 1.—Production possibilities between market goods and environmental services.

plains why, even in a world in which environmental quality is not valued in markets, a positive level of environmental quality is obtained. Even though environmental capital is unpriced, the private sector will not use it beyond the point of zero marginal productivity in a given production period. Thus, it simply is not economically rational for the market economy to exhaust the environmental capital stock at any point in time.

But over time, as an increasing amount of environmental capital, *E*, is converted to production of market goods, *E* must decline unless it is renewable at a higher rate than that at which it is being consumed. As *E* (and thus *K*) becomes scarce, its shadow value increases. In response to this increase in the value of environmental capital, in the following section we argue that either through resource markets or through the political process, actions are likely to be taken to reverse the process of environmental decline.

**Economic Growth and the Demand for Environmental Quality: The Environmental Transition**

Two opposing themes have dominated the debate over environment and economic growth: the antigrowth view, that growth and development are inherently damaging to the environment;[8] and the progrowth view, that economic growth and a concomitant increase in per capita incomes are the key factors in protecting the environment.[9]

The notion that economic growth is inherently damaging to the environment appears to be a logical deduction given the production possibilities frontier just derived. In figure 1, as long as society is at a point above *B* on the solid curve (as it must be in a market economy, unless it is forced to a point below *B* by government action), a movement along the production possibilities frontier (PPF) toward point *B* necessarily entails a reduction in environmental services. However, this conclusion is valid only in a static world where an economy is constrained to a fixed transformation curve. In such a world, economic growth can only be achieved via a more intensive use of environmental capital. Of course, modern economic growth has been driven by more than resource exploitation; technological change has also played a major role. Figure 1 illustrates that technological change shifts the PPF *ACB* so that a higher level of market goods production could correspond to either more (point *D*) or fewer (point *F*) environmental services in a market economy. Thus, even for market economies in which environmental quality is a pure public good, economic growth and environmental quality improvement are not necessarily incompatible if growth is accompanied by technical change. Moreover, in the case where the frontier shifts to *AGF*, which would lead to a market equilibrium with lower environmental quality and fewer environmental services being produced, it is possible for public policies (e.g., environmental regulations) to move the economy to a point such as *G*, where more market goods and more environmental services are produced. Conversely, government policies that subsidize the exploitation of the environment, such as public-sector water projects, could move the economy to a point along the PPF below *D* or *F* where the marginal product of environmental capital is negative.

It is important to emphasize that the vertical axis of figure 1 measures environmental services, not environmental capital. Assuming that there is no technological progress in natural processes that yield environmental services, then the point at which the production possibilities frontier intercepts the vertical axis in figure 1 is fixed at point *A*. This means that to increase flows of environmental services, the environmental capital stock must be rebuilt or renewed. This rebuilding can be accomplished in many cases by reducing the use of the environmental capital in the production of market goods, as when technological progress in the production of market goods results in increased efficiency in the use of environmental capital. However, it is important to note that some components of the environmental capital stock are not renewable. The use of an aggregate representation of environmental capital masks these differences among types of environmental capital. In cases where a nonrenewable resource approaches exhaustion and there is no possibility for substitution with other resources or technology, then the phenomenon of irreversibility becomes a consideration.

The point along the PPF at which a society chooses to produce and consume is an empirical question. It depends on supply factors—how the economy's PPF is shifting and how public policy evolves—and demand factors—how preferences are expressed as economic growth occurs. Conceptually, the demand side can be introduced by specifying an aggregate preference function that depends on quantities of environmental services and market goods, along with other exogenous demand factors such as population. This preference function defines an income-expansion path in the $(x, e)$ space for each set of relative prices (note that when $e$ is a nonmarket good, the price for $e$ is a shadow price, not a market price). Figure 2 illustrates an income expansion path consistent with Ruttan's hypothesis, horizontal up to some threshold level of income, but sloping upward beyond that point.

If growth were neutral with respect to environment in the sense that the PPF shifted in a horizontal fashion, then the growth path of a laissez-faire market economy would follow a horizontal line through point *B* in figure 3. Because $e$ has no price, equilibrium production and consumption are determined solely by the supply side. However, economic growth in many developing economies appears to be associated with environmental degradation. Thus, it is hypothesized that the shift in the PPF typically resembles the movement from points *B* to *C*

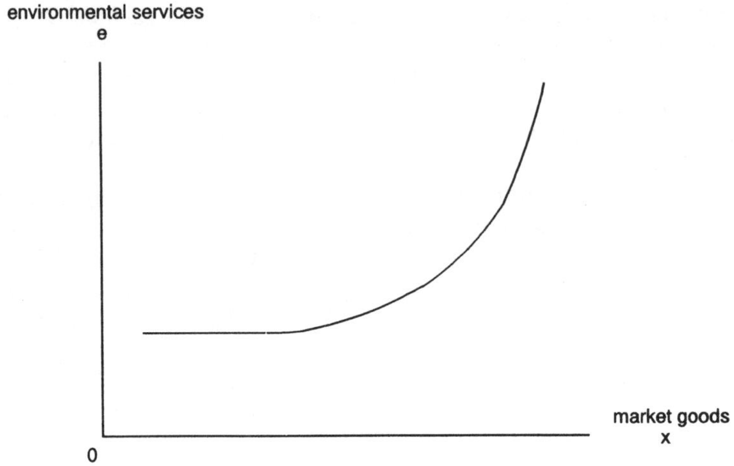


FIG. 2.—Income expansion path hypothesized by Ruttan

in figure 3. If the income elasticity of demand for environmental quality is low or zero in LDCs, the equilibrium growth path in low-income countries will typically correspond to this path.

As income grows, it is hypothesized that the demand for environmental goods rises rapidly beyond some point, as illustrated in figure 2. If environmental services are pure public goods, the demand for environmental quality must be expressed through the public sector. Theories of government behavior suggest that government policies respond to the pressures exerted by organized interests, and this should

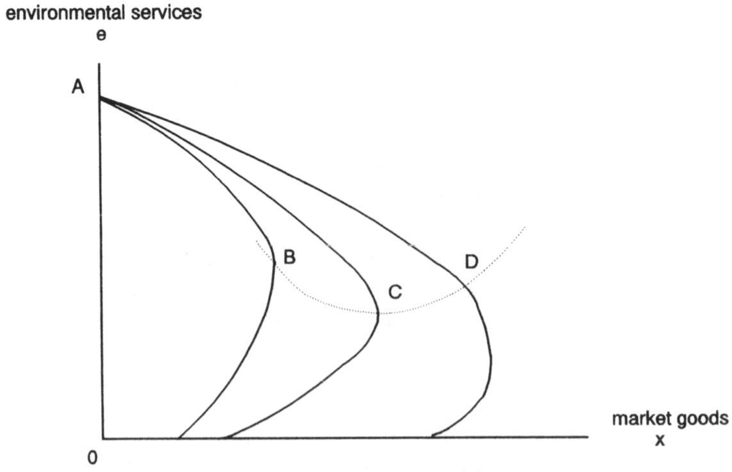


FIG. 3.—Economic growth and the environmental transition

be true in the case of environmental interests. To the degree that market interests in agriculture and other sectors are better organized than environmental interests in developing countries, governments will be slow to respond to environmental demands in early stages of development. Eventually, though, environmental voices should be heard as incomes rise and environmental interests become better organized.

When the demand for environmental services begins to be expressed, the economy's growth path is hypothesized to turn from a southeasterly path to a northeasterly one. Figure 3 is drawn to represent a growth path that reflects this environmental transition. Under this scenario, equilibria during early stages of development (points *B* to *C*) correspond to increases in market goods but reductions in environmental services. Beyond some point, however, income growth raises the demand for environmental services and an equilibrium growth path is achieved (points *C* to *D*) along which both market goods and environmental services are increasing.[10] The remainder of the article is devoted to estimating the relationship between environmental quality and income to test the hypothesis of the environmental transition.

**Empirical Specification, Data, and Results**

To investigate Ruttan's hypothesis about the income elasticity of demand for environmental services, a system of demand and supply functions should be identified and estimated. This is possible in principle but difficult in practice because the data are inadequate. On the demand side, not only are price data for nonmarket goods lacking, even data measuring aggregate prices for market goods are incomplete in many developing countries. Furthermore, it is not clear what other variables should be included in such a demand equation. Demographic, cultural, and other preference effects may be important, but these factors are difficult to measure and data are not available for many countries. Additionally, since many preference factors are likely to be highly correlated with income, it would be difficult to disentangle their effects with a single cross section of data.

On the supply side, relevant price data are also lacking. Factors affecting the behavior of the public sector could be measured and included in the supply equation, such as type of political system.[11] As with the demand side, however, many of these factors are highly correlated with income and it is difficult to differentiate their effects in a cross-sectional study.

Because only a single cross section of data is available for analysis, the above considerations suggest that a simple model specification is appropriate. Thus, in the following analysis the quantity of an environmental amenity (parklands and rate of afforestation, as described below) is specified as a function of the country's resource endowment, population, and per capita income. An individual's demand for a public good can be specified as $q = d(p, y)$, where $p$ is price and $y$ is per capita income. Following T. E. Borcherding and R. T. Deacon, the degree to which the good is public or private can be represented by a function $\psi(N)$, where $N$ is population.[12] This function takes on the value $N$ if the good is purely private, and the value 1 if the good is purely public. Thus, letting $e$ be the total quantity of the environmental service, $q = e/\psi(N)$, it follows that $e = \psi(N)d(p, y)$. Letting the inverse supply function of the environmental service be $p = s(e, E)$, substitution of this function into the demand function and solving for $e$ yields the reduced-form equation $e = r(E, y, N)$. The quantity variables on the right-hand side of this reduced form (land area, forest area, population) may not identify either a supply function or a demand function. The income parameter is likely to be measuring the effects of income and other variables correlated with income. Considering that the data sample consists of both low- and high-income countries (listed in the Appendix), the estimated equations are interpreted as measuring the long-run equilibrium growth path that is the product of both supply and demand factors. One drawback to this reduced-form approach is that it does not allow a satisfactory test of Ruttan's elasticity-of-demand hypothesis because the estimated equation is not necessarily a demand equation. However, these reduced-form equations are suitable for testing the environmental transition hypothesis of a U-shaped long-run equilibrium growth path.

*Data and Variable Definitions*

Environmental quality is a concept without a universally agreed upon definition. Is environmental quality best measured by an air-quality index, the amount of land in national parks, or the number of endangered species? Each of these measures falls along a continuum. At one end of this continuum are measures related to human standards of living. At the other end are measures that relate to ecological conditions such as viability and stability of the ecosystem. Measurement of environmental quality is further complicated by its multidimensional nature. Compounding these conceptual problems is a scarcity of either time-series or cross-sectional data on measures of environmental quality. Therefore, one major factor in selecting measures of environmental quality is the availability of a variable for a large number of low- and high-income countries.

The total area of parks and protected areas (PARKS) in a country has several factors to recommend it as an indicator of the demand for environmental quality. The PARKS variable exists for a wide range of countries, both more and less developed, and captures aspects of both the human and ecological concepts of environmental quality. Finally, PARKS is also a measure that should reflect both the public's demand for environmental amenities and the government's actions to satisfy that demand.

As a measure of environmental services to be used to test the environmental transition hypothesis, however, the PARKS variable may be misleading. Recall that the theoretical model discussed above assumes that in early stages of development the environmental capital stock is large because there has been relatively little economic development. At this stage the demand for environmental services should be low and governments should have little political incentive to devote public lands to parks and protected areas, even though the environmental capital stock is relatively large. Only with income growth should there arise a demand for the environmental services derived from parks. Thus, the association of PARKS with income across low- and high-income countries may reflect primarily the demand-side phenomenon illustrated in figure 2, in which case only a positive relationship between PARKS and income would be found.[13] A better variable might include both official parks and other undeveloped lands, but such a variable is unavailable. It is also possible that at low income levels land is very abundant and governments will establish parks even though the public demand is not great. At a later time, population growth may increase land scarcity and parklands may be returned to agricultural or other uses. In this case, a negative relationship between PARKS and income could exist. Finally, PARKS does not capture environmental degradation due to illegal encroachment, nor does it adjust to changes in quality due to wear and tear or overuse.

Another potential drawback to PARKS is that the model outlined in the previous section specifies environmental services as a flow variable, yet PARKS is a measure of a stock. Using PARKS as a proxy for services implicitly assumes that the flow of environmental services is proportional to the quantity of PARKS. Fortunately, this assumption is consistent with the assumption made above that the production of environmental services is monotonically increasing in the quantity of environmental capital.

The average annual deforestation rate during the 1980s (listed as DEFOR in the Appendix) was also available for a wide range of countries. In the regression analysis that follows, a measure of afforestation, AFFOR, is used as a dependent variable (afforestation is defined as the negative of the deforestation variable presented in the Appendix). The AFFOR variable captures a different aspect of environmental quality than PARKS, because afforestation rates are a product of the interplay of market forces, government action, and the values placed on resources by the public.

The AFFOR variable may be better than the PARKS variable to test the environmental transition hypothesis in that it may capture the impact of development on the environmental capital stock better than

PARKS. However, AFFOR is also not a measure of environmental services but, rather, a measure of the rate of investment (if positive) or disinvestment (if negative) in the environmental capital stock. Thus, AFFOR could also be a misleading measure for a test of the environmental transition. For example, forests in an environmentally sensitive area could be in the process of being protected and reforested while other private lands were being cut, and the AFFOR variable could indicate that deforestation was taking place. Yet the environmental services derived from forests, such as recreation and biodiversity, could actually be increasing.

The most obvious choice of a measure of relative resource abundance to associate with PARKS is the total area of the country (AREA). Similarly, the total forested area (FOR) was chosen to represent the environmental capital stock associated with AFFOR. The AREA variable was also used to represent the environmental capital stock in the AFFOR equation, because deforestation often occurs where arable land is scarce. Per capita gross national product (GNPPC) was chosen as a measure of aggregate income for both regressions. Population (POP) is included in the model, as indicated in the above derivation of the reduced form.

When estimating aggregate demand for private market goods, the quantity demanded is measured on a per capita basis. In this model, however, environmental quality is assumed to be a public good. Therefore, as noted in the preceding discussion of the reduced-form equation for the demand and supply of a public good, the total aggregate quantity of PARKS and AFFOR is specified as the dependent variable. The data sources and a listing of the data are provided in the Appendix.[14]

*Empirical Results*

Figures 4–6 present the data graphically. Figure 4 suggests a U-shaped pattern between PARKS per square kilometer of land area and GNP per capita. The graph shows that the low-income countries are very heterogeneous with regard to parkland; there are a few countries with very large percentages of their areas in parks, whereas there is also a substantial number with less than 2% of their area in parks. Most of the middle- and high-income countries have more than 2% of their area in parks, and about half of them have more than 5%.

Figures 5 and 6 show the relationship between average annual afforestation per 1,000 square kilometers of forest land and GNP per capita. Figure 5 presents the data for 35 countries for which AFFOR is less than −500, that is, for those countries with more than 500 square kilometers average annual deforestation. These countries are all low-income, with an average per capita income of $1,204 (see table 1).[15] This graph shows a pronounced U-shape pattern in the low-income countries. Clearly, deforestation tends to increase with income

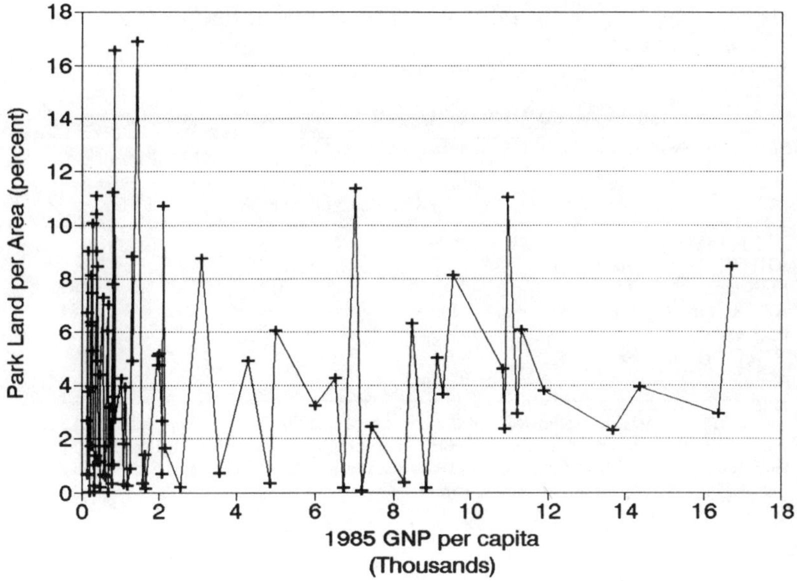


FIG. 4.—Parkland and GNP per capita

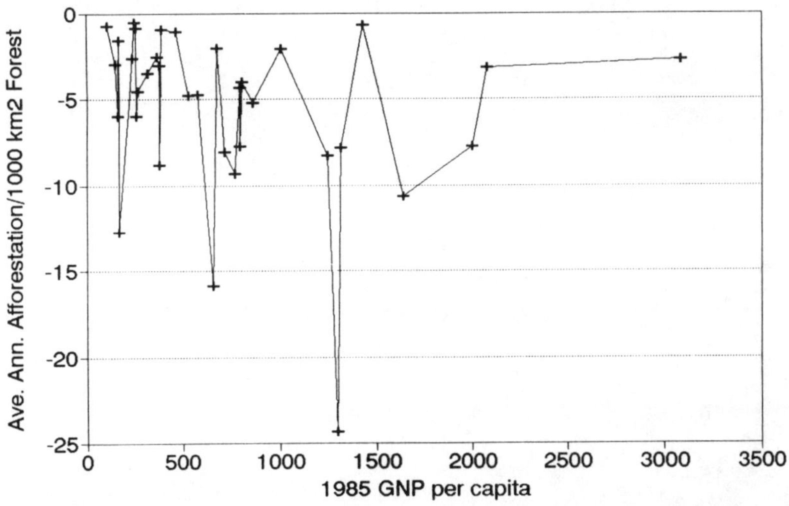


FIG. 5.—Afforestation and GNP per capita with AFFOR < −500

TABLE 1

MEANS OF VARIABLES USED IN REGRESSIONS PRESENTED IN TABLES 2 AND 3

| | | AFFOR | |
|---|---|---|---|
| | PARKS | Full Sample | AFFOR < −500 |
| PARKS (km$^2$ × $10^{-3}$) | 36.8 | | |
| AFFOR (km$^2$ × $10^{-3}$) | | −2.1 | −5.0 |
| FOR (km$^2$ × $10^{-6}$) | | .331 | .487 |
| AREA (km$^2$ × $10^{-6}$) | 1.009 | 1.046 | 1.181 |
| POP ($10^{-6}$) | 43.6 | 47.3 | 53.1 |
| GNPPC (1985 US$ × $10^{-3}$) | 3.2 | 3.2 | 1.2 |
| *N* | 93 | 82 | 36 |

NOTE.—Variable definitions and sources presented in the Appendix: PARKS = parklands and protected areas; AFFOR = average annual afforestation rate; FOR = forested area; AREA = land area; POP = population; GNPPC = gross national product per capita; *N* = number of observations.

up to a point and then diminish in this group of countries. The pattern is influenced by several countries with high rates of deforestation. Brazil has the highest level of deforestation (almost 70 kilometers per 1,000 square kilometers of forest). Figure 6 shows the AFFOR data for the middle- and high-income countries. All of these countries—with the exception of the large negative value that corresponds to Trinidad and Tobago, a small country with a very high deforestation

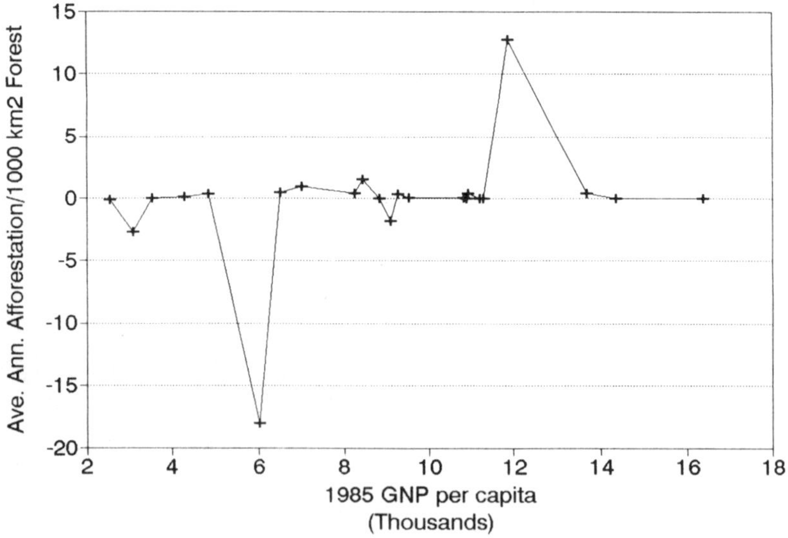


FIG. 6.—Afforestation and GNP per capita in middle- and high-income countries.

rate—have small rates of deforestation or positive rates of afforestation. Combining the two figures shows there is a positive trend in afforestation as income increases.

To quantify these relationships more precisely, the two equations, one for PARKS and one for AFFOR, were estimated using ordinary least squares. To capture the nonlinearity hypothesized to exist between the dependent variables and income, the equations were specified as quadratic in income. Possible nonlinearities in the other variables were also tested by specifying equations linear in AREA, FOR, and POP, and quadratic models in all variables. Testing for heteroscedasticity failed to reject the null hypothesis of spherical disturbances. Estimates of equations with regional dummy variables did not differ substantially from those presented below without regional dummies.[16]

Table 2 presents OLS estimates of the PARKS equation for a full quadratic specification and with all quadratic terms except $GNPPC^2$ suppressed. The results in table 2 provide support for the environmental transition hypothesis: PARKS is found to be a convex function of GNP per capita, although the coefficient on $GNPPC^2$ is not highly statistically significant in the full quadratic model. However, other quadratic terms are highly significant and show positive interactions between GNPPC and AREA and GNPPC and POP, and diminishing marginal effects of AREA. As shown in table 4, these parameter estimates imply that the income elasticity of demand for environmental

TABLE 2

OLS Estimates of the PARKS Equation, 93 Countries

| | Model 1 | Model 2 |
|---|---|---|
| Intercept | 8.044 | 15.736 |
| AREA | 32.196 | 31.461 |
| $AREA^2$ | −3.622 | |
| AREA × POP | .022 | |
| GNPPC | −6.834 | −15.303 |
| $GNPPC^2$ | .325 | 1.492 |
| GNPPC × AREA | 2.613 | |
| GNPPC × POP | .078 | |
| | (3.392) | |
| POP | .093 | −.082 |
| | (.511) | (−1.512) |
| $POP^2$ | −.000 | |
| | (−.672) | |
| $R^2$ | .884 | .643 |
| $F$ | 73.806 | 39.533 |
| $N$ | 93 | 93 |

Note.—*t*-statistics in parentheses. The data are scaled as indicated in table 1.

services is near zero in countries with per capita incomes less than about $1,200. The income elasticity for higher income countries is found to be positive and generally greater than one. As noted above, it is to be expected that the PARKS equation would identify demand behavior at higher income levels. Thus, these estimates are consistent with Ruttan's hypothesis that the income elasticity is low in low-income countries and positive in the higher income countries.

Table 3 presents the OLS estimates of the AFFOR equation. The AFFOR model was estimated for the full sample and for the group for which there was a significant level of deforestation. This latter group was identified on the basis of the properties of the data illustrated in figures 5 and 6. Because the high-income countries generally have low negative or positive afforestation, it was suspected that the relationship

TABLE 3

OLS Estimates of the AFFOR Equation

| | Full Sample | | AFFOR < 500 | |
|---|---|---|---|---|
| Intercept | −.301 | .282 | −.513 | 3.969 |
| | (−.854) | (.246) | (−.986) | (2.674) |
| FOR | 1.039 | −15.516 | 16.556 | −7.271 |
| | (.848) | (−8.391) | (2.636) | (−1.659) |
| $FOR^2$ | 8.025 | | −4.716 | |
| | (3.218) | | (.533) | |
| FOR × POP | .021 | | −.051 | |
| | (.376) | | (−4.583) | |
| AREA | −1.576 | 3.323 | −7.989 | −5.368 |
| | (−2.458) | (3.923) | (−2.028) | (−1.862) |
| $AREA^2$ | .525 | | 5.838 | |
| | (2.183) | | (1.976) | |
| AREA × FOR | −7.468 | | −6.278 | |
| | (−4.013) | | (−.750) | |
| AREA × POP | −.055 | | .011 | |
| | (.890) | | (4.570) | |
| GNPPC | −.153 | −.979 | −1.473 | −2.038 |
| | (−.928) | (−1.608) | (−1.831) | (−1.260) |
| $GNPPC^2$ | .007 | .110 | 1.210 | .355 |
| | (.566) | (2.432) | (2.700) | (3.668) |
| GNPPC × FOR | 2.064 | | −13.756 | |
| | (5.475) | | (−2.847) | |
| GNPPC × AREA | .118 | | 2.810 | |
| | (1.070) | | (1.404) | |
| GNPPC × POP | −.063 | | −.002 | |
| | (−1.128) | | (−1.250) | |
| POP | .052 | .006 | −.001 | −.017 |
| | (1.103) | (.512) | (−.069) | (2.477) |
| $POP^2$ | 0 | | −0 | |
| | (.491) | | (−.854) | |
| $R^2$ | .981 | .603 | .996 | .901 |
| $F$ | 245.719 | 23.047 | 349.018 | 54.391 |
| $N$ | 82 | 82 | 36 | 36 |

Note.—$t$-statistics in parentheses. The data are scaled as indicated in table 1.

between AFFOR and income might be different between the two groups. The results in table 3 show this is indeed the case. The linear and quadratic specifications were estimated for the full sample and for the group defined by AFFOR < −500. For both samples, the full quadratic model explains a very high percentage of the variation in the data; this is particularly striking when one considers that these are cross-sectional data. The full-sample estimates indicate a significant positive relationship between AFFOR and GNP per capita in the restricted model, but the convex, U-shaped relationship is not supported by the data in the full quadratic model. However, the convex relationship is found in the AFFOR < −500 group, and this result is robust to alternative specifications (e.g., linear vs. quadratic in the FOR and AREA variables). Thus, the estimates from the AFFOR < −500 sample are also consistent with the environmental transition hypothesis.

Table 4 summarizes the relationships between AFFOR and per capita income. The income elasticity is found to be less than zero at less than $2,049 GNP per capita and positive above that level. An income elasticity calculated at the sample mean for countries with income greater than $2,049 is very large and positive because many of those countries have values of AFFOR near zero. At a more representative level of deforestation for a middle-income country, for example, a country with GNP per capita equal to $3,000 and AFFOR equal to −2000, the parameter estimates imply an income elasticity of 3.45. At a per capita income of $500, the income elasticity is found to be −0.37.

To summarize, if these relationships are interpreted as demand functions, then the data presented in table 4 show that the income elasticity of demand for environmental services is low or negative in

TABLE 4

INCOME ELASTICITIES FOR PARKS AND AFFORESTATION

| | Income at Zero Elasticity (US$) | Low Income | | High Income | |
|---|---|---|---|---|---|
| | | Income (US$) | Elasticity | Income (US$) | Elasticity |
| PARKS | 1,224 | 500 | −.01* | 14,000 | 1.94† |
| AFFOR | 2,049 | 500 | −.37‡ | 3,000 | 3.45§ |

* Based on parameters of the full quadratic equation in table 2, with PARKS = 20,000.

† Based on parameters of the full quadratic equation in table 2, with PARKS = 60,000.

‡ Based on parameters of the AFFOR < −500 sample equation, calculated at the AFFOR < −500 group sample means.

§ Based on parameters of the AFFOR < −500 sample equation, calculated at AFFOR = −2,000.

low-income countries, and greater than unity in higher-income countries, as hypothesized by Ruttan. As noted above, however, these equations should be interpreted as reduced forms instead of structural equations. Therefore, these income elasticities are more appropriately interpreted as indicating the growth path of the environmental transition illustrated in figure 3.

**Conclusion**

This article develops a stylized model of the environment-development trade-offs faced by countries during the process of economic growth. Ruttan's hypothesis about the income elasticity of demand for environmental quality is combined with a model of the supply of market and nonmarket goods to obtain the hypothesis of the environmental transition. The environmental transition hypothesis states that economic growth is likely to be accompanied by environmental degradation at low income levels, but as income grows the demand for environmental protection also tends to increase, leading to a development path characterized by both economic growth and environmental quality improvements. The empirical section of the article used recently available data from low- and high-income countries to estimate the relationship between income and two classes of environmental amenities, parks and forests. The empirical results support the environmental transition hypothesis—environmental amenities are negatively related to income in countries with less than about $1,200–$2,000 income per capita, and in higher-income countries the environmental amenities are positively related to income with an income elasticity that is greater than unity.

The tendency for market economies to follow the growth path described here as the environmental transition should not be taken as a justification for complacency about environmental problems in developing countries. As the experience in high-income countries has shown, it cannot be assumed that market economies automatically solve their environmental problems. Costly, time-consuming technological and institutional innovations may be required. Moreover, the relationships captured in the cross-sectional data paint a long-run picture; it may take a country with a $500 per capita income many decades to raise its income enough to have a discernible impact on the demand for environmental services. However, note that the estimates of the environmental transition presented here were obtained using data representing components of the environmental capital stock—forests and parklands—that are associated with services such as recreation or species diversity that are often assumed to be demanded by relatively high-income individuals. These findings therefore suggest that the demand for all environmental services, including those related to basic needs such as drinking water and sanitation, as well as those associated with forests and parks, are positively related to income at relatively low income levels.

There remains the troubling possibility that the environmental transition could be forestalled by irreversible environmental damage, which could in turn lead to lower incomes and yet more environmental degradation. Indeed, it is this possibility that seems to underlie much of the concern about sustainable development, particularly in the context of tropical deforestation and soil erosion. One way to restate the sustainable development problem is to ask whether a country is following a growth path that leads to the environmental transition, and how long it will take the country to achieve the transitional phase of development.

The findings reported in this article are preliminary and need to be buttressed by further research. The finding of a U-shaped growth path consistent with the environmental transition hypothesis raises many as-yet-unanswered questions about which we can only speculate without better data. There are several possible explanations for the environment-income relationship switching signs. This relationship may be affected by political and other socioeconomic factors not explored in this study. At the present time, it is not possible to verify whether Ruttan's hypothesis about the income elasticity is the primary factor, or whether the supply-side shifts in the production possibilities frontier are the major factor. The finding of the environmental transition threshold in the range $1,200–$2,000 per capita, well above the income level of some developing countries, raises the question of whether or not institutional or technological innovations can significantly lower this threshold. Moreover, some countries, such as Costa Rica, appear to have successfully achieved the environmental transition at relatively low income levels, whereas other countries with higher income levels have not. It is important to understand why there are large differences across countries with respect to their environmental conditions.

Two important shortcomings of the available data limit our ability to differentiate the demand- and supply-side effects. First, reliable data are available for only a few environmental indicators. In addition to the parklands and forest data used in this article, meaningful indexes of water and air quality, species diversity, and other indicators are needed. At the present time, such data are available for only a few localities in a small number of countries. Time-series data for each country are also needed. Without time-series data, it will be difficult to sort out the effects of income from all of the other possible supply-side and demand-side effects that are correlated with large differences in income.

## Appendix

TABLE A1

| Country | PARKS (km$^2$) | DFOR (km$^2$) | FOR (km$^2$) | AREA (km$^2$) | GNPPC (US$) |
|---|---|---|---|---|---|
| Brazil | 120,312 | 90,500 | 5,144,800 | 8,512,000 | 1,640 |
| Burkina Faso | 7,389 | 800 | 47,350 | 274,000 | 150 |
| Burma | 30.56 | 677,000 | 190 | ... | ... |
| Cameroon | 17,022 | 1,900 | 233,000 | 475,000 | 810 |
| Canada | 229,618.6 | −3,833 | 4,364,000 | 9,976,000 | 13,680 |
| Central African Republic | 39,040 | 550 | 358,900 | 623,000 | 260 |
| Chile | 127,811.1 | 500 | 75,500 | 757,000 | 1,430 |
| China | 98,138.44 | 0 | 1,150,470 | 9,561,000 | 310 |
| Columbia | 56,129.65 | 8,900 | 517,000 | 1,139,000 | 1,320 |
| Congo | 13,531 | 220 | 213,400 | 342,000 | 1,110 |
| Costa Rica | 4,514 | 1,240 | 17,980 | 51,000 | 1,300 |
| Côte d'Ivoire | 19,580 | 5,100 | 98,340 | 322,000 | 660 |
| Denmark | 1,253.29 | 0 | 4,840 | 43,000 | 11,200 |
| Dominican Republic | 5,504.34 | 40 | 6,290 | 49,000 | 790 |
| Egypt, Arab Republic | 6,173 | 1,001,000 | 610 | ... | ... |
| El Salvador | 221.51 | 50 | 1,410 | 21,000 | 820 |
| Ethiopia | 24,243 | 880 | 271,500 | 1,222,000 | 110 |
| Finland | 8,034 | 0 | 232,250 | 337,000 | 10,890 |
| France | 44,496.32 | −52.5 | 150,750 | 547,000 | 9,540 |
| Germany, Federal Republic | 27,535.48 | −100 | 72,070 | 249,000 | 10,940 |
| Ghana | 11,750.75 | 720 | 86,930 | 239,000 | 380 |
| Greece | 985.63 | −2.5 | 57,540 | 132,000 | 3,550 |
| Guatemala | 970.83 | 900 | 45,420 | 109,000 | 1,250 |
| Guinea | 130 | 860 | 106,500 | 246,000 | 320 |
| Haiti | 77 | 20 | 480 | 28,000 | 310 |
| Honduras | 3,575 | 900 | 39,970 | 112,000 | 720 |
| Hungary | 4,771.63 | 93,000 | 1,950 | ... | ... |
| India | 129,988.9 | 15,000 | 642,000 | 3,288,000 | 270 |
| Indonesia | 140,451 | 9,200 | 1,168,950 | 1,919,000 | 530 |
| Ireland | 245.92 | −25 | 3,800 | 70,000 | 4,850 |
| Israel | 1,272.03 | 21,000 | 4,990 | ... | ... |
| Italy | 12,861.95 | −137 | 80,630 | 301,000 | 6,520 |
| Japan | 22,728.02 | 0 | 252,800 | 372,000 | 11,300 |
| Jordan | 343 | 0 | 500 | 98,000 | 1,560 |
| Kenya | 30,954.02 | 390 | 23,600 | 583,000 | 290 |
| Lesotho | 68.05 | 30,000 | 470 | ... | ... |
| Liberia | 1,307 | 490 | 20,400 | 111,000 | 470 |
| Libya | 1,550 | 1,760,000 | 7,170 | ... | ... |
| Madagascar | 10,313.12 | 1,560 | 132,000 | 587,000 | 240 |
| Malawi | 10,669 | 1,500 | 42,710 | 118,000 | 170 |
| Malaysia | 17,137.21 | 2,550 | 209,960 | 330,000 | 2,000 |
| Mali | 8,761 | 360 | 72,500 | 1,240,000 | 150 |
| Mauritania | 11,730 | 130 | 5,540 | 1,031,000 | 420 |
| Mauritius | 36.11 | 0 | 30 | 2,000 | 1,090 |
| Mexico | 14,133.52 | 6,150 | 483,500 | 1,973,000 | 2,080 |
| Morocco | 2,983.59 | 130 | 32,360 | 447,000 | 560 |
| Nepal | 9,541 | 840 | 21,210 | 141,000 | 160 |
| Netherlands | 1,509.14 | −15 | 3,550 | 41,000 | 9,290 |
| New Zealand | 30,583.7 | −250 | 95,000 | 269,000 | 7,010 |
| Nicaragua | 433 | 1,210 | 44,960 | 130,000 | 770 |
| Niger | 81,097.4 | 670 | 25,500 | 1,267,000 | 250 |
| Nigeria | 9,600.82 | 4,000 | 147,500 | 924,000 | 800 |

TABLE A1 (*Continued*)

| Country | PARKS (km²) | DFOR (km²) | FOR (km²) | AREA (km²) | GNPPC (US$) |
|---|---|---|---|---|---|
| Norway | 12,748.38 | 0 | 87,010 | 324,000 | 14,370 |
| Oman | 530 | 300,000 | 6,730 | . . . | . . . |
| Pakistan | 72,732.59 | 90 | 24,800 | 804,000 | 380 |
| Panama | 8,259.79 | 360 | 41,650 | 77,000 | 2,100 |
| Papua New Guinea | 31.43 | 230 | 381,750 | 462,000 | 680 |
| Paraguay | 11,185.38 | 2,120 | 197,100 | 407,000 | 860 |
| Peru | 54,829.35 | 2,700 | 706,400 | 1,285,000 | 1,010 |
| Philippines | 5,224 | 1,430 | 95,100 | 300,000 | 580 |
| Portugal | 4,386.33 | −166 | 29,760 | 92,000 | 1,970 |
| Rwanda | 2,620 | 50 | 2,300 | 26,000 | 280 |
| Saudi Arabia | 4,150 | 0 | 2,000 | 2,150,000 | 8,850 |
| Senegal | 21,772.59 | 500 | 110,450 | 196,000 | 370 |
| Sierra Leone | 1,007 | 60 | 20,550 | 72,000 | 350 |
| Singapore | 24.34 | 1,000 | 7,420 | . . . | . . . |
| South Africa | 58,017.51 | 1,221,000 | 2,010 | . . . | . . . |
| Spain | 24,860.79 | −67.5 | 108,110 | 505,000 | 4,290 |
| Sri Lanka | 6,870.28 | 580 | 16,590 | 66,000 | 380 |
| Sweden | 17,129.27 | −5,720 | 278,420 | 450,000 | 11,890 |
| Switzerland | 1,199.89 | 0 | 11,240 | 41,000 | 16,370 |
| Thailand | 40,159.12 | 3,970 | 156,750 | 514,000 | 800 |
| Togo | 4,630 | 120 | 16,840 | 57,000 | 230 |
| Trinidad and Tobago | 160.88 | 90 | 2,080 | 5,000 | 6,020 |
| Tunisia | 444.55 | 50 | 2,970 | 164,000 | 1,190 |
| Turkey | 2,460.26 | 0 | 201,990 | 781,000 | 1,080 |
| United Kingdom | 15,530.84 | −385 | 21,780 | 245,000 | 8,460 |
| United States | 791,460.5 | 1,590 | 2,959,890 | 9,363,000 | 16,690 |
| Uruguay | 282.78 | 176,000 | 1,650 | . . . | . . . |
| Venezuela | 79,732.8 | 2,450 | 338,700 | 912,000 | 3,080 |
| Yugoslavia | 6,869.97 | −110 | 104,900 | 256,000 | 2,070 |
| Zaire | 88,270 | 3,700 | 1,775,900 | 2,345,000 | 170 |
| Zambia | 63,590 | 700 | 295,100 | 753,000 | 390 |
| Zimbabwe | 27,592.67 | 800 | 198,200 | 391,000 | 68 |

NOTE.—These data are used in the empirical analysis. Values for AREA and for 1985 GNP per capita (GNPPC) are from the *World Development Report 1987* (Washington, D.C.: World Bank, 1987). PARKS measures the total area of designated parks and protected areas within a country as of 1988 and is from the 1989/90 *Environmental Data Report* published by the United Nations Environment Program. Values for FOR and DEFOR are from *World Resources 1990–91* published by the World Resources Institute (WRI) and from the *OECD Environmental Data Compendium 1987* and *The State of the Environment,* both published by the Organization for Economic Cooperation and Development (OECD). FOR measures the extent of forest and woodland and refers to "natural stands of woody vegetation in which trees predominate." DFOR measures "the permanent clearing of forest lands for use in shifting cultivation, permanent agriculture, or settlements" and is the negative of the variable AFFOR used in the empirical analysis. DFOR observations for most countries are taken from the WRI report and measure average annual deforestation during the 1980s. Values for the OECD members are from the two OECD publications and represent average annual deforestation from 1980 to 1984. Ellipses indicate data were not available.

## Notes

* John M. Antle acknowledges support from Resources for the Future, where he is a University Fellow. The research reported here was conducted in 1991 when Gregg Heidebrink was a Carthage Fellow at the Political Economy Research Center, Bozeman, Montana.

1. Technical Advisory Committee, *Sustainable Agricultural Production: Implications for International Agricultural Research* (Rome: Food and Agriculture Organization of the United Nations, 1989); Inter-American Development Bank (IADB), *Annual Report 1990* (Washington, D.C.: IADB, 1990); D. G. Abler and D. Pick, "NAFTA, Agriculture, and the Environment in Mexico," *American Journal of Agricultural Economics* 75 (August 1993): 794–98; J. M. Antle, "Environment, Development, and Trade between Low and High Income Countries," *American Journal of Agricultural Economics* 75 (August 1993): 784–88; U.S. Department of Agriculture, "Agriculture in a North American Free Trade Agreement: Analysis of Liberalizing Trade between the United States and Mexico," Foreign Agriculture Economic Report no. 246 (USDA Economic Research Service, Washington, D.C., September 1992).

2. V. W. Ruttan, "Technology and the Environment," *American Journal of Agricultural Economics* 53 (1971): 707–17, quotes on 707–8.

3. J. B. Braden and C. D. Kolstad, eds., *Measuring Demand for Environmental Quality* (New York: North-Holland, 1991).

4. World Resources Institute, *World Resources 1990–91* (Oxford: Oxford University Press, 1990); World Resources Institute, *World Resources 1992–93* (Oxford: Oxford University Press, 1992); United Nations Environment Programme, *Environmental Data Report* (Oxford: Alden, 1987); Organization for Economic Cooperation and Development (OECD), *OECD Environmental Compendium 1987* (Paris: OECD, 1987), and *The State of the Environment* (Paris: Alden, 1991); World Bank, *World Development Report 1992: Development and the Environment* (Oxford: Oxford University Press, 1992).

5. World Bank, chap. 1; R. E. B. Lucas, D. Wheeler, and H. Hettige, "Economic Development, Environmental Regulation and the International Migration of Toxic Industrial Pollution," in *International Trade and the Environment,* ed. P. Low, World Bank Discussion Papers 159 (Washington, D.C.: World Bank, 1992); M. Radetzki, "Economic Growth and the Environment," in Low, ed.; M. S. Bernstram, *The Wealth of Nations and the Environment* (London: Institute of Economic Affairs, 1991).

6. For a discussion of the environment as a capital stock, see S. El Serafy, "The Environment as Capital," in *Ecological Economics,* ed. R. Constanza (New York: Columbia University Press, 1991).

7. Observe that this curvature property of the production possibilities frontier does not arise from the existence of externalities. With externalities, nonconvexities of the technology could occur with the usual implications for existence of equilibria (W. J. Baumol and W. E. Oates, *The Theory of Environmental Policy,* 2d ed. [Cambridge: Cambridge University Press, 1988], chap. 8).

8. H. E. Daly and J. B. Cobb, Jr., *For the Common Good: Redirecting the Economy toward Community, the Environment, and a Sustainable Future* (Boston: Beacon, 1989).

9. Bernstram.

10. This northeasterly growth path may occur because the demand for *e* is expressed through environmental policies that move the economy along the frontier, but they may also occur because the shifting of the frontier is endogenous to policy and shifts more in a northeasterly direction, as in R. A. McCain, "Endogenous Bias in Technical Progress and Environmental Policy," *Ameri-*

*can Economic Review* 68 (1978): 538–46. And it is also possible, as noted above, that technological innovation in the private sector will result in a growth path like *C* to *D* in fig. 3.

11. R. D. Gastil, *Freedom in the World* (Westport, Conn.: Greenwood, 1987).

12. T. E. Borcherding and R. T. Deacon, "The Demand for the Services of Non-Federal Governments," *American Economic Review* 62 (1972): 891–901.

13. Another problem is that in countries where tourism is an important industry, the existence of parks may reflect the demand for recreation associated with the incomes of tourists, not the domestic population. Cause and effect are difficult to determine in this example, however. Tourism could be a consequence of local demand for parks rather than a cause of it.

14. Other studies have investigated pollution intensity (e.g., Lucas, Wheeler, and Hettige; and Radetzki), pollution per capita (e.g., World Bank [n. 4 above], fig. 4), and air-pollution concentrations (e.g., World Bank, chap. 1; and Bernstram). The reduced-form equation $e = r(E, y, N)$, however, shows that a model derived from a system of demand and supply equations for a public good can be specified with total quantity on the left-hand side, and with environmental capital, population, per capita income, and possibly other demand and supply shift variables on the right-hand side.

15. The United States is the only high-income country in the AFFOR $< -500$ group. It is not included in fig. 5 to maintain the income scale for the other countries, which have much lower incomes.

16. The model was also estimated for the low-income sample excluding "outliers" such as Brazil. The results were also robust with respect to the treatment of these outliers. The AFFOR equation was also estimated using the least absolute error method of estimation (G. G. Judge, R. C. Hill, W. E. Griffiths, H. Lutkepohl, and T. C. Lee, *The Theory and Practice of Econometrics* [New York: Wiley, 1985]) to investigate robustness of results, and the parameter estimates were found to be quite stable. The World Bank's data on deforestation (World Bank, table 33) show a smaller value for Brazil. Similar results to those in table 3 were obtained using the World Bank data.

64-83
[90]

# [4]

*Ecological Economics*, 2 (1990) 7–26
Elsevier Science Publishers B.V., Amsterdam – Printed in The Netherlands

## ALTERNATIVE APPROACHES TO ECONOMIC–ENVIRONMENTAL INTERACTIONS

Q20
Q24

EDWARD B. BARBIER

*London Environmental Economics Centre, International Institute for Environment and Development, 3 Endsleigh Street, London WC1H 0DD (Great Britain)*

(Accepted 8 September 1989)

ABSTRACT

Barbier, E.B., 1990. Alternative approaches to economic–environmental interactions. *Ecol. Econ.*, 2: 7–26.

The key questions raised by recent developments in resource and environmental economics have been what useful economic functions does the environment provide and how are these functions affected by the process of economic–environmental interaction? This paper distinguishes between two different formal approaches to answering these questions: the more conventional approach which is concerned with the optimal allocation of economically valuable exhaustible resources and an alternative analysis that considers the trade-off between, on the one hand, environmental quality, and on the other, resource depletion and waste generation by the economic process. To illustrate and extend the latter approach, a model is constructed to show how this trade-off might lead to continuously declining environmental quality and a future ecological constraint. Society must therefore optimally allocate output between consumption and services to improve the environment and choose between increased capital accumulation and environmental degradation. Although strict application of such a model may be limited, it has wider implications for the role of technological change and the value of the environment in any system experiencing deteriorating environmental quality

INTRODUCTION

Economic analysis of resource and environmental problems has been extensively developed in recent years. To distinguish its general approach from those of other scientific disciplines, this analysis has relied on one guiding principle, i.e. "that the satisfaction of any value requires the use of scarce productive services of some type, and we must necessarily have some way to allocate them" (Herfindahl, 1974a, p. 5). The crucial questions that

Based on a paper presented at the 13th Annual Convention of the Eastern Economic Association, Washington, DC, March 5–7, 1987.

environmental and resource economists have been asking, therefore, are what useful economic functions does the environment provide and how are these functions affected by the process of economic–environmental interaction?

This paper distinguishes between two different formal approaches to answering these questions: the more conventional approach which is concerned with the optimal allocation of economically valuable exhaustible resources [1] and an alternative analysis that considers the trade-off between, on the one hand, environmental quality and, on the other, resource depletion and waste generation by the economic process. To illustrate and extend the latter approach, a model of economic–environmental interaction is constructed to show how this trade-off might lead to continuously declining environmental quality and a future ecological constraint.

Although strict application of such a model may be limited, it has wider implications for the role of technological innovations and the value of the environment in any system experiencing deteriorating environmental quality. The concerns, and indeed some of the propositions suggested in this model, are not new. It builds on earlier attempts to integrate environmental dimensions into growth models, and the experiences learned from incorporating ideas from thermodynamics and ecology into economics. The model of this paper therefore demonstrates the physical dependency of economic activity on the sustainability of crucial natural resource systems and ecological functions, and indicates the economic costs, or trade-offs, resulting from the failure to preserve sustainability and environmental quality. The objective is 'sustainable' growth and development, and it mirrors the increasing concern over new – possibly irreversible – environmental dangers, such as the greenhouse effect, ozone-layer depletion, land degradation, deforestation, and so forth, rather than reiterating the previous concern with material and energy shortages per se. In short, the alternative approach is more applicable to the emerging problems of *environmental degradation*, which require a different method of analysis than the conventional problem of *depletion of a specific resource stock.*

## CONVENTIONAL APPROACHES

Following the classic work by Hotelling (1931), the conventional economic approach is to treat natural resources as comparable to other assets of wealth in the economy worth 'holding' in the present. Consequently, the conventional definition of natural resources is usually limited to those environmental resources providing economically valuable productive services

---

Notes on p. 17.

in the economic system, meaning that only one function of the natural environment – as supplier of the raw material and energy inputs to the economic process – is considered relevant to the phenomenon of natural-resource scarcity. Since they are valuable commodities traded in markets, as these resources become increasingly scarce, their prices will rise relative to those of other goods.

What makes certain material and energy-yielding natural resources worth holding compared to other assets, therefore, is the expected threat of future scarcity from over-exploitation and depletion. Hence the conventional economic approach is to ask what is the optimal rate of extraction or depletion of these economically valuable resources. Ideally, for any particular resource, this will depend on its relative scarcity, and thus (shadow) price, over time compared to other assets (both 'natural' and economic), which in turn should depend on the availability of substitutes, technological innovation, economies of scale, market imperfections, the pattern of property rights and whether the resource is 'renewable'.

The general convention is to "call extractive resources renewable or non-renewable depending on whether they exhibit economically significant rates of regeneration" (Fisher and Peterson, 1977, p. 681). In the case of strictly 'non-renewable' resources, it may be optimal to deplete the resource completely if the availability of future technologies and perfect substitutes mean that exploitation of the resource is no longer 'essential' for future production (Dasgupta and Heal, 1974, 1979; Solow, 1974b; Stiglitz, 1974; Kamien and Schwartz, 1978; Dasgupta and Stiglitz, 1981). That is, because the future scarcity of the resource has been mitigated, the resource is not worth holding compared to other income-earning assets, and the optimal choice may be to exhaust the resource quickly and invest in these other assets. Even in the case of renewable resources, such as a forest valued for its timber, exhaustion may be optimal if the resource is growing at a slow rate, harvesting costs are low and its value appreciates more slowly than the market rate of interest (Clark, 1976; V.L. Smith, 1977).

Thus the conventional approach to natural resource scarcity usually engenders optimism, i.e., "there seems to be little reason to worry about the exhaustion of resources which the market already treats as economic goods" (Nordhaus and Tobin, 1977, p. 402; see also Barnett and Morse, 1963; Beckerman, 1974; Solow, 1974a). For those resources of the environment used as basic material and energy inputs, market forces should dictate the optimal rate of exploitation automatically and effectively. [2]

Notes on p. 17.

ALTERNATIVE APPROACHES

An alternative approach to resource and environmental problems is to recognize that there is not just one but three important functions performed by scarce environmental resources: first, as emphasized by conventional approaches, the environment provides useful material and energy inputs for the economic process; second, the environment assimilates the waste by-products generated by this process; and third, the natural environment provides certain utility-yielding services, or ecological functions, that are essential for supporting the economic system and human welfare. [3] The latter range from recreational, health, cultural, educational, scientific and aesthetic services to the maintenance of essential climatic and ecological cycles and functions (Freeman, 1979; Pearsall, 1984; Barbier, 1989a).

Together, these three economic functions of the environment underline the physical dependency of the economic process and human welfare on ecological stability and the sufficiency of potentially scarce environmental resources. The fundamental scarcity problem, therefore, is that as the environment is increasingly being exploited for one set or uses, say, to provide new sources of raw material and energy inputs and to assimilate additional waste, the quality of the environment may deteriorate over time. The consequence is an increasing 'relative' scarcity of essential environmental services and ecological functions (Barbier, 1989a). In other words, if "the environment is regarded as a scarce resource", then the "deterioration of the environment is also an economic problem" (Hueting, 1980, pp. 1, 3).

Such an approach may lead to applying different criteria for the economic exploitation of environmental resources. For example, where conventional criteria might justify the cutting down of a forest, alternative criteria might justify preservation if the expected loss of value resulting from the decline in genetic diversity, soil quality, ecological stability, natural beauty, etc. were considered too high (Krutilla and Fisher, 1985). In other words, only by looking at the *total economic value* provided by *all* the functions of an environmental asset, is it possible to weigh the environmental benefits of preservation foregone against the net benefits of development (Pearce, Barbier and Markandya, 1990).

There are a growing number of studies emphasizing the environmental costs of economic activity, such as "the transformation and loss of whole environments as would result, for example, from clear cutting a redwood forest, or developing a hydroelectric project in the Grand Canyon" (Fisher, Krutilla and Cicchetti, 1972, p. 605; see also Arrow and Fisher, 1974;

Notes on p. 17.

Krutilla and Fisher, 1985; Miller and Menz, 1979; Turner, 1988; Southgate, 1989). Thus Krutilla and Fisher (1985) demonstrate that irreversible conversion of natural areas in fixed supply may have a high opportunity cost by foreclosing the future option of deriving environmental services from these areas. Other studies have stressed the essential utility-yielding role of natural ecosystems and their environmental functions (Freeman, 1979; Hueting, 1980; Farnworth et al., 1981; Pearsall, 1984; Farber and Costanza, 1987; Turner, 1988; Barbier, 1989a; Barbier and Markandya, 1989). The conventional approach to optimal resource depletion has also been broadened to incorporate the conditions that allow the preservation of natural environments containing resources used as productive inputs (Krautkraemer, 1985; Southgate, 1989), or to embrace an integrated approach to a variety of resource allocation problems (Dasgupta, 1982; V.K. Smith and Krutilla, 1977). In addition, analysis of optimal choice over time among consumption, accumulation and environmental quality has been the focus of a number of studies (Vousden, 1973; Maler, 1974; Becker, 1982; Barbier, 1989a; Barbier and Markandya, 1989). On still a broader front, Norgaard (1984, 1985) discusses the "coevolutionary development" of ongoing feedback and interaction between social and ecological systems, whereby the feedback mechanisms previously maintaining the ecosystem are assumed by or shifted to the social system.

The model of this paper follows, and hopefully clarifies, these approaches by addressing a situation where economic-environmental interaction not only leads to increasing 'relative' scarcity of utility-yielding environmental services, but as environmental quality declines, there is also the possibility of widespread ecological disruption and disturbances. That is, in the long run, an absolute ecological constraint may arise because the increasing environmental degradation inflicted by the economic process irrevocably disrupts natural ecosystems. Permanently impairing essential environmental functions on which economic activity and human welfare depend (Daly, 1979; Barbier, 1989a).

Such a model may be appropriate in cases where cumulative resource depletion and waste generation by the economic process lead to severe ecological disruption and the collapse of human livelihoods. For example, with continuous tropical deforestation, there may be adverse local and interregional ecological disturbances that radically alter rainfall patterns, climate and species diversity. The result may be a catastrophic decline in the ability of the forest area and neighboring regions to support dependent economic systems and human populations (Myers, 1984; Sioli, 1985; Southgate, 1989). Similarly, climatic changes resulting from excess emission of greenhouse gases from industrial activity may significantly affect agricultural productivity and thus the ability of some regions of the world to feed their populations (Oram, 1985; Barbier, 1989b). Intensive agricultural production on marginal lands can lead to accelerating problems of soil erosion, watershed degradation and even desertification (American Farmlands Trust, 1984; Barbier, 1988; Nelson, 1988; Southgate, 1988). Long-term combustion of fossil fuels emitting $SO_x$ and $NO_x$ pollution may increase 'acid rain' to levels intolerable for forest and freshwater ecosystems, thus destabilizing livelihoods dependent on fishing and forestry activities (WRI/IIED, 1986, chapter 10).

## A MODEL OF ECONOMIC–ENVIRONMENTAL INTERACTION

The following model analyzes the prospect of irreversible damage to the natural environment arising from resource depletion and waste generation; the outcome is a steady decline in environmental quality leading to potential long-run disruptions to important ecological systems and functions. In order to capture these 'relative' and 'absolute' scarcity impacts of increasing environmental degradation over time, several assumptions are adopted.

First, to indicate the dependency of human welfare on essential environmental services and ecological functions, a stock variable representing environmental quality, $X_t$, [4] is included along with consumption, $C_t$, as arguments in the social welfare function, $U$:

$$U = U(C_t, X_t) \tag{1}$$

with $U_c(C_t) > 0$, $U_{cc}(C_t) < 0$, $U_x(X_t) > 0$, $U_{xx}(X_t) < 0$. Equation (1) indicates that at any time $t$ social welfare is a concave, increasing function of consumption and environmental quality. To simplify analysis, the welfare function is additively separable, i.e.

$$U_{cx} = U_{xc} = 0$$

Second, it is assumed that at any time $t$ any output, $Q_t$, produced by the economic system that is not used for consumption, for providing environmental improvement services, $V_t$, or for replacing depreciated capital, $wK_t$, leads to a net accumulation in the capital stock, $K_t - K_{t-1}$:

$$K_t - K_{t-1} = Q_t - (C_t + V_t) - wK_t \tag{2}$$

Capital depreciates at the constant rate $w$. Environmental improvement services can be divided between those that directly improve environmental quality through, say, conservation practices, resource management, pollution clean-ups etc., and those that indirectly improve $X_t$ by increase recycling and abatement of waste residual otherwise emitted into the environment.

Notes on p. 17, 18.

Third, following the 'relative' scarcity argument of the 'alternative' approach, it is assumed that at any time $t$ as the economic process extracts resources, $R_t$, from the environment and generates (net) waste, $N_t$, increasing environmental degradation, $S_t - S_{t-1}$, occurs and, as a result, environmental quality declines:

$$S_t - S_{t-1} = f(R_t, N_t) \tag{3}$$

$$X_t = X(S_t, V_t) \tag{4}$$

$$X_t < X_{t-1} \tag{5}$$

with $f_r(R_t) > 0$, $f_n(N_t) > 0$, $X_s(S_t) < 0$ and $X_v(V_t) > 0$. Equation (4) shows that environmental quality is a decreasing function of environmental degradation, $S_t$, and an increasing function of environmental improvement services, $V_t$. A crucial assumption is that, since $S_t - S_{t-1} > 0$ throughout any time period $t$, then $X_t$ must also be declining (conditions 3 and 5). That is, environmental degradation occurs each period because the economic process must require some resource inputs, $R_t$, for production and generate some net waste, $N_t$. However, to suggest that the result is lower environmental quality each period implies that: (a) the level of environmental improvement services, $V_t$, is insufficient to counteract the increased environmental degradation, and (b) ecosystems are unable to 'repair' the resulting damage to crucial functions, cycles and resources through converting the energy flow from the sun or utilizing any inputs of material and energy from neighboring ecosystems. These are clearly strong assumptions that may not hold for all economic–environmental systems. [5]

Fourth, in order to incorporate the 'absolute' ecological constraint discussed above, the life of the economic–environmental system is assumed to be finite, where terminal time $T$ is that period at the end of which environmental degradation reaches some maximum level, $\bar{S}$, driving environmental quality to some minimum level, $\underline{X}$, and thus irrevocably destabilizing the entire economic-environmental system. This constraint on the system can be summarized as:

$$t_0 \le t < T, \qquad \underline{X} < X_t \quad \text{and} \quad U = U(C_t, X_t) \tag{6}$$

$$\lim_{t \to T} t, \qquad \lim_{S_t \to \bar{S}} X(S_t), \qquad \underline{X} \quad \text{and} \quad \lim U \to 0$$

The size of the population and its growth often impact on the environment. However, in this approach this affect has been left our of consideration.

Notes on p. 18.

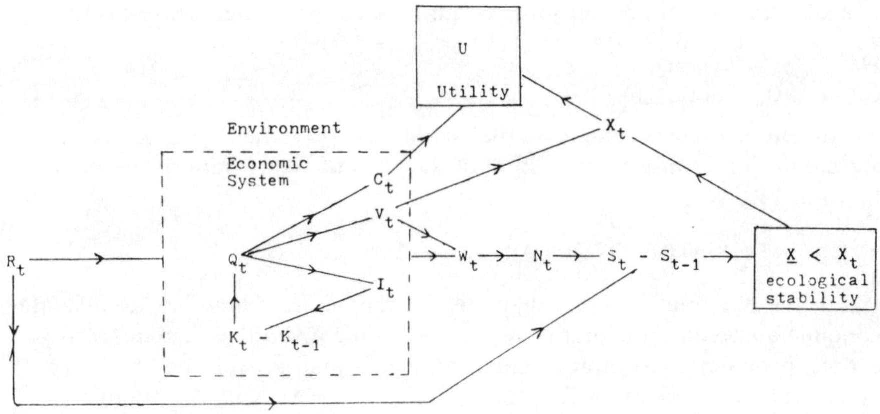


Fig. 1. Flow diagram of economic-environmental interaction.

Assuming population growth is constant, the remaining functional relationships of the model can be simplified to:

$$Q_t = Q(K_t) \quad \text{with} \quad Q_k(K_t) > 0 \text{ and } Q_{kk}(K_t) < 0 \tag{7}$$[6]

$$R_t = R(Q_t) \quad \text{with } R_q(Q_t) > 0 \tag{8}$$

$$N_t = W(Q_t) - B(V_t) \tag{9}$$

with $B_v(V_t) > 0$, $B_{vv}(V_t) < 0$ and $W_q(Q_t) > 0$. That is, production is a function of the capital stock; resource use and waste generation, $W_t$, are functions of total output; and net waste generation is $W_t$ less any recycling, $B_t$.

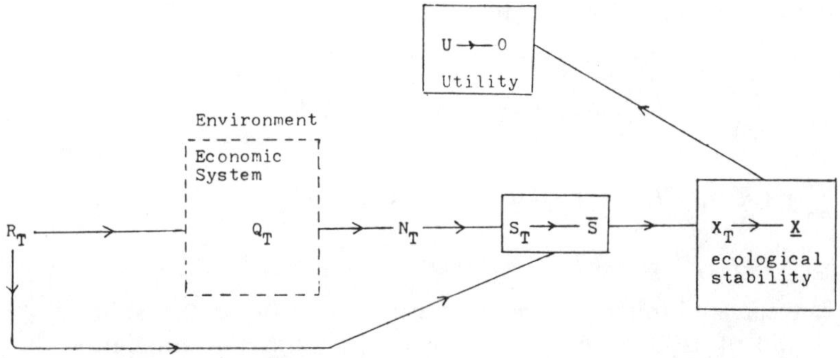


Fig. 2. Long-run ecological constraint.

Notes on p. 18.

Finally, the initial and terminal conditions of the model are respectively:

$$K_0 = \underline{K}, \qquad S_0 = \underline{S} \tag{10}$$

$$K_T \geq \overline{K} \geq 0, \qquad S_T \geq \overline{S} \tag{11}$$

The functional relationships of the model for period $t_0 \leq t \leq T$ are summarized in Fig. 1, and the operation of the absolute constraint in period $T$ is shown in Fig. 2.

OPTIMAL ALLOCATION OVER TIME

Thus the planning problem suggested by the model is how best to allocate economic and environmental resources over time given the current 'relative' scarcity problem of declining environmental quality and the threat of a future ecological constraint on the entire system. A dynamic discrete time optimization problem can be constructed from the model with the aid of a few substitutions.

Substituting (7)–(9) into (3) yields:

$$S_t - S_{t-1} = f(R(Q(K_t)), W(Q(K_t)) - B(V_t)) = g(K_t, V_t) \tag{12}$$

with $g_k(K_t) > 0$ and $g_v(V_t) < 0$. That is, as capital accumulation leads to production growth and – in the absence of technological change – more resource throughput, whereas environmental improvement services reduce waste through recycling, then environmental degradation is essentially an increasing function of $K_t$ and a decreasing function of $V_t$ at time $t$.

Expressions (12) and (4) can be substituted for $X_t$ in the social welfare function (1), which is now summed over the finite planning period $[t, T]$ and discounted at the rate $0 < r < 1$:

$$U = \sum_{t=1}^{T} \frac{1}{(1+r)^{t-1}} U(C_t, X(S_{t-1} + g(K_t, V_t), V_t)) \tag{13}$$

A Lagrangean function, $L^*$, can now be formed from (13), (2), (10) and (11):

$$\begin{aligned} L^* = & \sum_{t=1}^{T} \frac{1}{(1+r)^{t-1}} U(C_t, X(S_{t-1} + g(K_t, V_t), V_t)) \\ & + \sum_{t=1}^{T} p_t(K_{t-1} + Q_t(K_t) - (C_t + V_t) - wK_t - K_t) \\ & + p_0(\underline{K} - K_0) + p_{T+1}(K_T - \overline{K}) + u(\underline{S} - S_0) + a(S_T - \overline{S}) \end{aligned} \tag{14}$$

The Lagrangean multiplier $p_t$ can be interpreted as the utility value of an additional unit of capital, i.e. the social value of capital accumulation that becomes available in period $t$. Similarly, the multiplier $u$ represents the social value of an increase in the initial level of environmental degradation,

$S_0$, whereas $a$ indicates the social value of a 'relaxation' in the binding terminal constraint, as represented by an increase in $\bar{S}$.

Thus the dynamic optimization problem is to maximize (14) by optimal choice of $C_t$, $V_t$ and $K_t$. Assuming $C_t$, $V_t$, $K_t$ and $S_t > 0$, the first-order conditions are:

$$\frac{dL^*}{dC_t} = \frac{1}{(1+r)^{t-1}} U_c(C_t) - p_t = 0 \qquad t = 1, \ldots, T \quad (15)$$

$$\frac{dL^*}{dV_t} = \frac{1}{(1+r)^{t-1}} U_x(X_t)(X_s(S_t)\, g_v(V_t) + X_v(V_t)) = 0 \qquad t = 1, \ldots, T \quad (16)$$

$$\frac{dL^*}{dK_t} = \frac{1}{(1+r)^{t-1}} U_x(X_t)\, X_s(S_t)\, g_k(K_t) + p_{t+1} - p_t + p_t(Q_k(K_t) - w) = 0 \qquad t = 1, \ldots, T \quad (17)$$

$$\frac{dL^*}{dK_0} = p_1 - p_0 = 0 \quad (18)$$

$$\frac{dL^*}{dS_0} = U_x(X_1)\, X_s(S_1)(1 + g(K_1, V_1)) - u = 0 \quad (19)$$

$$\frac{dL^*}{dS_T} = \frac{1}{(1+r)^{T-1}} U_x(X_T)\, X_s(S_T) + a = 0 \quad (20)$$

As specified, the complexity of the model prevents characterization of a final solution to these equations. Interpretation of these conditions, however, does provide some useful insights into society's allocative choices when faced with the unique 'relative' and 'absolute' scarcity constraints of the model. For example, condition (15) can be substituted into condition (16) to yield:

$$\frac{U_c(C_t)}{U_x(X_t)} = X_s(S_t)\, g_v(V_t) + X_v(V_t) \qquad t = 1, \ldots, T \quad (21)$$

This suggests that the marginal rate of substitution of $X_t$ for $C_t$ is equated in each period with the impacts on the environment of a marginal increase in environmental improvement services. These services either protect the environment directly, $X_v(V_t)$, or indirectly by recycling waste and thus reducing some of the negative impact of the economic process on the environment, $X_x(S_t)\, g_v(V_t)$. Thus condition (21) defines the optimal trade-off between increased consumption and provision of services to improve the environment. That is, at any time $t = 1, \ldots, T$ any allocation of output between $C_t$ and $V_t$ must obey this rule.

Condition (17) can be rearranged as:

$$p_{t+1} - p_t = p_t(Q_k(K_t) - w) + \frac{1}{(1+r)^{t-1}} U_x(X_t)\, X_s(S_t)\, g_k(K_t)$$

$$t = 1, \ldots, T \quad (22)$$

which indicates that the social value of capital is changing in each period according to the benefits of marginal capital productivity net of depreciation, $p_t(Q_k(K_t) - w)$, less the discounted marginal damage of the environmental degradation accompanying this increased productivity, $U_x(X_t)\, X_s(S_t)\, g_k(K_t)$. Capital accumulation that is not replacing depreciated stock leads to increased output and thus socially valuable consumption and environmental improvement services. At the same time, however, the increased output requires a greater use of resources by the economic system, which in turn increases environmental degradation. The former can be considered the benefits of capital accumulation and the latter the costs. If in any period the costs exceed the benefits of capital accumulation, then its social value will decline. If the costs equal the benefits, the value remains constant, i.e.

$$\text{if} \quad p_t(Q_k(K_t) - w) = \frac{1}{(1+r)^{t-1}} U_x(X_t)\, X_s(S_t)\, g_k(K_t)$$

$$\text{then} \quad p_{t+1} - p_t = 0 \qquad t = 1, \ldots, T \quad (23)$$

Expressions (22) and (23), therefore, are the rule governing the optimal rate of capital accumulation, and thus growth, in the economy.

Condition (18) states that the social value of additional capital in the first planning period and the period before are equal; i.e., the social value of capital is unchanged up to the first period. Condition (19) shows that the negative social value of a decline in the initial state of the environment must be equal to the marginal damage of an increase in environmental degradation in the first period. Any such increase in $S_0$ must be a social cost, for it both lowers initial environmental quality, $X_1$, and it brings the system that much closer to the level of environmental degradation that causes its 'collapse', $\bar{S}$. In contrast, an increase in $\bar{S}$ would prolong the life of the economic–environmental system and is therefore beneficial to society. From condition (20), this benefit is equivalent to the marginal utility of a decrease in environmental degradation in the last period.

To summarize, this model has derived the optimal conditions for allocating economic and environmental resources in an interdependent economic–environmental system where any resource depletion and waste generation by the economic process leads to deteriorating environmental quality and an eventual ecological collapse. As the model has stressed that the state, or quality, of the environment is an essential determinant of social welfare, environmennetal improvement services are recognized as a socially valuable component of economic output, and in every period, society must optimally allocate output between consumption and services to improve the environment. Although the key to expanding output is capital accumulation, the cost of capital accumulation and production growth is increased environmental degradation. If this cost exceeds the benefits of economic expansion, then the social value of capital accumulation and thus growth declines. Under certain conditions determining the social welfare function, e.g., individuals' giving more weight to environmental quality than consumption in their utility considerations, society may opt for slower or for even no production growth and to allocate an increasing share of output to environmental improvement services. Such allocative choices are clearly consistent with a preference for ecological preservation over increased aggregate consumption, a preference that is perhaps spurred by apprehension over the type of future 'absolute' ecological constraint included in this model.

Thus the quantitative results of the model clearly depend on: (a) the relative preferences of individuals, (b) the development of technology, and (c) the resilience and regenerative capacity of ecosystems and life-support functions. It is to these wider issues that the paper now turns.

## WIDER IMPLICATIONS: TECHNOLOGY, TASTES AND TIME

As noted in section one, conventional approaches to natural resource scarcity often indicate that technological innovation, substitution and improvements in resource management can be mitigating factors in overcoming increasing relative scarcity. The crucial question is whether the type of scarcity effects envisioned by the above model can also be mitigated by technological innovations and proper environmental management. The answer must be yes, albeit with some qualifications. One key is, of course, slowing down the rate of environmental degradation to a level low enough that there is little appreciable or significant deterioration in vital ecological functions or natural resource systems. As suggested by equation (3) of the model, this invariable calls for innovations that can slow down the rate of resource throughput in the economy by reducing the inflows of material and energy required from the environment and the outflows of waste. There are essentially two broad types of resource-saving innovations that can be applied to economic activity:

(1) Resource-saving innovations in the process of production:

(a) *factor-substitution*, e.g. labor-power for energy, resource-saving capital for energy and materials;

(b) *reuse of scrap and waste materials*, i.e. improvements in recovery and recycling producer and consumer waste;

(c) *increased efficiency of resource conversion and utilization*, i.e. obtaining the maximum amount of end-use energy and material for production of final goods and services from the primary inflows of resources into the economic system.

(2) Other resource-saving innovations:

(a) *improved organizational techniques*, i.e. better organization of production, distribution and consumption activities to reduce resource inefficiencies and resource use;

(b) *changes in the composition of output*, e.g. from non-durables to durables, from resource-using goods to services, etc.;

(c) *changes in product quality and / or design*, e.g. reducing sizes and weights of vehicles, eliminating 'built-in-obsolescence', re-designing throwaway packages and containers, improving energy-efficiency in appliances, etc.

The technology necessary to achieve these resource-saving innovations may already exist, or is easily achievable, in the advanced industrialized countries. As a recent report from the U.S. Office for Technical Assessment (OTA, 1988) has indicated, thanks to the revolution in information technology, resource savings of 40–60% of current use could be *feasible* in the near future for the United States *without* any sacrifice in economic growth. However, as Page (1977) has emphasized, what is technologically feasible in terms of resource saving may not actually be realized unless some conservation criterion, such as keeping the resource base intact for future generations, is accepted as a valid macro-economic policy goal. Perhaps the recent policy debate over the use of a 'carbon tax' to reduce emissions, encourage resource-saving innovations and thus mitigate any possible $CO_2$-induced 'global warming' is one indication that policy makers are increasingly taking into account long-term considerations of future economic security and welfare.

As implied by equation (4), better techniques of environmental improvement and management could also mitigate any decline in envrionmental quality. The quality of the environment will generally be improved by a variety of innovations ranging from improvements in resource, land and water management to developments in ecologically appropriate planning of tourist facilities, conservation areas and environmental policies to the dissemination of new conservation skills and training. Particularly in the case of agricultural systems, where "ecosystems are transformed into hybrid agroecosystems for the purpose of food or fibre production" (Conway, 1985, p. 34), the result may also be a direct increase in production. For example, in the Sahel small farmers struggle to produce a predominantly millet-based cropping system under conditions of drought, high temperature and marginal soil fertility. Through the introduction of improved multi-cropping techniques, new drought and pest-resistant varieties of cowpeas and no-tillage mulching, water run-off and soil erosion were reduced and yields increased (IITA, 1985, pp. 22–26). Similar examples from around the world show how improved land-management techniques and cropping systems – accompanied by appropriate economic policies, incentives and investment strategies – can overcome land and watershed degradation (American Farmlands Trust, 1984; Barbier, 1988; Nelson, 1988; Southgate, 1988).

Despite optimism that the combination of resource-saving and environmental management techniques could indefinitely postpone the type of binding ecological constraint suggested by condition (6), there a number of reasons why such innovations may not be 'automatically' or 'effectively' implemented in response to declining environmental quality.

First, in the conventional case of increasing scarcity of raw materials, the existence of identifiable markets for these resources means that the price system can automatically respond to this increasing scarcity and thus induce the appropriate innovative responses. However, many environmental resources exist outside the economic system as integral components of complex resource and ecological systems, and are thus nonmarketed common property resources. Although "markets indirectly and other institutions directly influence the allocation of these resources" for use as resource inputs and waste assimilation as opposed to preservation, "unfortunately none of these can be relied upon to provide the information on the marginal valuations of the resources involved in these allocations" (Smith and Krutilla, 1979, p. 281). As Pearce (1985, p. 21) has argued, even if external environmental costs imposed by resource depletion are estimated, "there is nothing in the conventional concept of an external costs to account for the decay of ecological processes themselves", and as a result, "in the absence of perfect information and both perfect and instantaneous response to ecological disequilibrium, the system can be unsustainable." Without a mechanism for conveying this information, the appropriate technological response to environmental degradation is not assured.

Furthermore, the appropriateness and effectiveness of technological innovation in halting environmental deterioration depend on a clear understanding of the ecological impacts of pollution and resource depletion. However, changes in the state of the environment and its resources usually involve substantial qualitative changes and interactions. The aggregate effects on ecological functions and systems may in some cases by an unusual capacity for resilience and regenerative capacity, whereas in others, a tendency towards rapidly reinforcing disturbance and disruption (Conway, 1985). Because such changes are rarely stable, frequently irreversible and often cumulative and discontinuous, environmental systems almost never 'settle' to an equilibrium state in response to perturbations and disturbances. Even in the relatively simple case of a constant input of pollution into a stream ecosystem, the environmental system may or may not reach an equilibrium condition for years, as the pollutant may differentially affect the survival rate and perhaps even the course of evolution of species in the stream. In the case of multiple pollutants, the combined changes rarely equal the sum of the separate effects (Norgaard, 1985, p. 384).

In addition, there may be physical limits on the extent to which resource-saving innovations can reduce resource throughput in the economic process. It may be possible, as noted above, to reduce current U.S. resource use by 40–60% and still have reasonable economic growth, but any further reductions may not be feasible under even the most optimistic technological assumptions. As argued by Daly (1977, 1979) and Georgescu-Roegen (1971, 1979), the source of these restrictions stem from the first and second laws of thermodynamics as analogously applied to the economic process:

(1) from the first law, as material and energy can neither be created nor destroyed, production and consumption must require some inputs of material and energy from the environment and generate some waste.
(2) from the second law, as material and energy used in transformation must irrevocably dissipate or decay, some degradation of material and energy from a useful to a useless state by the economic process is inevitable and irreversible.

In other words, resource-saving innovations may minimize, but they cannot eliminate, resource throughput in the economic process. Given uncertainty over ecological processes and environmental change, even the minimum resource-throughput level required to sustain an economic process may continue to damage the environment, particularly if it has been subject to stress from past resource-using technologies for a significant period of time, or if the regenerative capacity/resilience of affected ecosystems is low. Many current environmental problems, such as the global greenhouse effect, land degradation in resource-poor areas, deforestation and so forth, contain elements of this problem.

Finally, just as conditions (21)–(23) indicate that optimal allocation of output between consumption, environmental improvement services and investment is influenced by the relative preferences of consumption to environmental quality and changes in the social value of capital, choices of resource-saving and environmental management innovations over other possible technological 'mixes' will be dictated by individuals' tastes and preferences. The classic problem here, of course, is that choice of innovations today will affect both future consumption and environmental quality, yet there is no method available to measure the intensity of future preferences and the preferences of future generations. For example, very little of the yield-enhancing technical progress in U.S. agriculture over the postwar period was induced by concern about the cumulative effects of soil erosion, and has thus contributed to the current problems of soil degradation on erodible croplands, which is now an urgent and pressing concern (Crosson and Stout, 1983). In assessing both future and present reactions to environmental degradation, the crucial problem remains that "the level of the shadow price of environmental functions is largely indeterminate because insufficient information is available on the preferences for environmental functions" (Hueting, 1980, p. 141).

In sum, resource-saving technological and environmental management innovations should in principle be capable of overcoming the type of scarcity effects depicted by the model of this paper. However, because the main indicator of these scarcity effects – the relative decline in the quality of the environment and ecological functions – occurs largely outside the institutional mechanisms of the economic system, and at best, is only indirectly and partially captured by the market through impacts on productivity, human health, resource management costs, etc., the appropriate innovative responses may not be automatically forthcoming. Moreover, given the complexity of ecological relationships, their often unstable responses to stresses and shocks, the uncertainty over future and even current preferences for environmental functions and resources, and the physical limits to resource-saving techniques, the effectiveness of innovations in ameliorating environmental deterioration may be constrained. If this is the case, then the trade-off between consumption and environmental improvement services, and between more production growth and increased environmental preservation, suggested by conditions (21)–(23) may be unavoidable.

## SUMMARY AND CONCLUSION

The model of this paper has confirmed the general conclusion of many alternative approaches to natural resource scarcity that if individuals express preferences for essential environmental resources and functions which are perceived to be deteriorating over time, then it may be optimal to consider trade-offs between consumption and services to improve the environment and between more rersource-using growth and environmental preservation. With its strong assumption of increasing environmental degradation leading to ecological collapse, the model may be strictly applicable to only a limited number of economic–environmental systems. Its general insights, however, are more widely applicable to any situation where economic activity leads to declining environmental quality and loss of ecological functions. To borrow Hueting's (1980) phrase, this is the "new scarcity" that is affecting all global systems, including the advanced industrialized economies. Given the uncertainties surrounding appropriate and effective innovative responses, there must be concern that "we could get into serious difficulty simply because of inability to cope in time with... deterioration in the quality of the environment" (Herfindahl, 1974b, pp. 272–273). As "no one model provides the means for understanding how the ends of both economic growth and ecological sustainability might be achieved" (Norgaard, 1985, p. 388), further developments in both the conventional and alternative approaches described in this paper are necessary for improving our understanding of the complex interaction between economic and environmental systems.

ACKNOWLEDGEMENTS

I am indebted to my fellow participants at the 13th Annual Convention (5–7 March 1987, Washington, DC) for comments. I would also like to thank Robert Costanza, Partha Dasgupta, Roefie Hueting, David Pearce, Henry Peskin, Somnath Sen, Ron Smith and Dennis Snower for their suggestions and comments. Any errors in thinking or exposition are, of course, my own.

NOTES

[1] According to Dasgupta and Heal (1979, p. 3), "a resource is exhaustible if it is possible to find a pattern of use which makes its supply dwindle to zero.

[2] As Dasgupta and Heal (1979, pp. 5–7) point out, however, although in theory "capital-resource substitution may be sufficient to overcome the 'drag' imposed by an essential and exhaustible resource", in practice this requires "a complete set of forward markets", a condition which "is certainly not met" in actual market systems, and "as a consequence resource markets may be unstable, and will almost certainly display 'market bias', in the sense of depleting the resource at a rate different from an optimal rate". Quite clearly, the problem is "uncertainty about future resource stocks and about future technology."

[3] d'Arge (1972) provides an alternative classification of these functions into four categories: "(a) source of raw materials; (b) space for waste accumulation and storage; (c) assimilation-regenerative capability for chemically or biologically active wastes; and (d) determinant of health and life style, and of aesthetic satisfactions."

[4] Following Becker (1982) and Maler (1974), it is assumed that environmental quality is measured by a stock of environmental goods that yield a flow of services proportional to that stock in each time period. However, Becker (1982) defines this stock variable as "the differences between the level of pollution for which life ceases and the current level of pollution." Similarly, Maler (1974) in his intertemporal models considers that only the quality and flow of waste residuals and recycling have an impact on environmental quality. Here, it is assumed that environmental quality may be effected not only by (net) waste generation but also by resource depletion and services to improve the environment, such as conservation and resource management. For a given type of ecosystem with its associated energy flow, a measure of environmental quality may include, in addition to Becker's definition, the ecosystem's biomass (i.e., the volume or weight of total living material found above or below ground) plus some measure of the distribution of nutrients and other materials between the biotic (living) and abiotic (nonliving) components of the ecosystem. Such a measure is discussed in more detail in (Barbier, 1986, chapter 8), and is more consistent with this model's

broader concept of deteriorating environmennetal quality, or environmental degradation, which "comprises not just the loss of environmental quality that impinges on the senses, but also the damage to the damage to the natural purification and regenerative processes of the environment itself" (Pearce, 1985, p. 21).

[5] In fact, it may be possible to make this condition explicit by constructing an index of environmental degradation that is proportional to some measure of $R_t$ and $N_t$ (Barbier, 1986, chapter 8).

[6] Note that, as discussed above and indicated in Fig. 1, some beneficial services of the environment, such as maintenance of soil, air and water quality or of climatic stability, directly aid economic production. This would suggest that environmental quality, $X_t$, should also be included in the production function for economic output, $Q_t$. Recent discussions of the 'sustainability' of production in the Third World imply this relationship (Conway, 1985; Pearce, Barbier and Markandya, 1989). However, to simplify analysis in this model, the more traditional production function for the economy is employed. Instead, the stream of benefits provided by environmental quality to production activities are included as part of the overall contribution of $X_t$ to welfare. Hence, $X_t$ in equation (1) can be interpreted as representing both the direct utility-yielding impacts of environmental quality on individuals and the indirect impacts on overall social welfare through assisting production and other intermediate economic activities. This in any case may be a more appropriate way of accounting for these latter services, as their benefits are often 'externalities' to private production and consumption allocation decisions.

## REFERENCES

American Farmland Trust, 1984. Soil conservation in America: What do we have to lose? Washington, DC, 193 pp.

Arrow, K.J. and Fisher, A.C., 1974. Environmental preservation, uncertainty, and irreversibility. Q. J. Econ., 88: 312–319.

Barbier, E.B., 1986. Alternative economic approaches to natural resource scarcity. Ph.D. thesis, Economics Department, Birkbeck College, Univ. London, 416 pp.

Barbier, E.B., 1988. The economics of farm-level adoption of soil conservation measures in the uplands of Java. Environ. Dep. Work. Pap. 11, World Bank, Washington, DC, 31 pp.

Barbier, E.B., 1989a. Economics, natural resource scarcity and development: Conventional and alternative views. Earthscan Publ., London, 223 pp.

Barbier, E.B., 1989b, the global greenhouse effect: economic impacts and policy considerations. Nat. Resour. Forum, 1: 20–32.

Barbier, E.B. and Markandya, A., 1989. The conditions for achieving environmentally sustainable development. LEEC Pap 89-01, IIED/UCL London Environmental Economics Centre, 25 pp.

Barnett, H.J. and Morse, C., 1963. Scarcity and Economic Growth: The Economics of Natural Resource Availability. Johns Hopkins University Press, Baltimore, MD, 288 pp.

Becker, R.A., 1982. Intergenerational equity: the capital–environment trade-off. J. Environ. Econ. Manage., 9: 165–185.

Beckerman, W., 1974. In Defense of Economic Growth. Cape, London, 187 pp.

Clark, C.W., 1976. Mathematical Bioeconomics: The Optimal Management of Renewable Resources. Wiley, New York, 352 pp.

Conway, G.R., 1985. Agroecosystem analysis. Agric. Adm., 20: 31–55.

Crosson, P.R. and Stout, A.T., 1983, Productivity Effects of Cropland Erosion in the United States. Johns Hopkins University Press, Baltimore, MD, 203 pp.

Daly, H.E., 1977. Steady-state Economics. Freeman, San Francisco, CA, 185 pp.

Daly, H.E., 1979. Entropy, growth and the political economy of scarcity. In: V.K. Smith (Editor) Scarcity and Growth Reconsidered. Johns Hopkins University Press, Baltimore, MD, pp. 67–85.

d'Arge, R.C., 1972. Economic growth and the natural environment. In: A.K.Kneese and B.T. Bower (Editors), Environmental Quality Analysis: Theory and Method in the Social Sciences. Johns Hopkins University Press, Baltimore, MD, pp. 1–25.

Dasgupta, P.S., 1982. The Control of Resources. Basil Blackwell, Oxford, 223 pp.

Dasgupta, P.S. and Heal, G., 1974. The optimal depletion of exhaustible resources. In: Rev. Econ. Stud. Symp. Economics of Exhaustible Resources, pp. 3–28.

Dasgupta, P.S. and Heal, G., 1979. Economic Theory and Exhaustible Resources. Cambridge University Press, Cambridge, 501 pp.

Dasgupta, P.S. and Stiglitz, J.E., 1981. Resource depletion under technical uncertainty. Econometrica, 49: 85–104.

Farber, S. and Costanza, R., 1987. The economic value of wetland systems. J. Environ. Manage., 24: 41–51.

Farnworth, E.G., Tidrick, T.H., Jordan, C.F. and Smathers, W.M., Jr., 1981. The value of natural ecosystems; an economic and ecological framework. Environ. Conserv., 8: 275–282.

Fisher, A.C. and Peterson, F.M., 1977. The exploitation of extractive resources, a survey. Econ., J., 87: 681–721.

Fisher, A.C., Krutilla, J.V. and Cicchetti, C.J., 1972. The economics of environmental preservation, a theoretical and empirical analysis. Am. Econ. Rev., 62: 605–619.

Freeman, A.M., III, 1979. The Benefits of Environmental Improvement. Johns Hopkins University Press, Baltimore, MD, 272 pp.

Georgescu-Roegen, N., 1971. The Entropy Law and the Economic Process, Harvard University Press, Cambridge, MA, 457 pp.

Georgescu-Roegen, N., 1979. Energy analysis and economic valuation. South. Econ. J., 45: 1023–1058.

Herfindahl, O.C., 1974a. Is resource economics unorthodox? In: D.B. Brooks (Editor), Resource Economics: The Selected Works of Orris C. Herfindahl. Johns Hopkins University Press, Baltimore, MD, pp. 3–6.

Herfindahl, O.C., 1974b. Effects of resource depletion and economic growth on the quality of life. In. D.B. Brooks (Editor), Resource Economics: The Selected Works of Orris C. Herfindahl. Johns Hopkins University Press, Baltimore, MD, pp. 255–273.

Hotelling, H., 1931. The economics of exhaustible resources. J. Polit. Econ., 39: 137–175.

Hueting, R., 1980. New Scarcity and Economic Growth: More Welfare Through Less Production? North-Holland, Amsterdam, 269 pp.

IITA, 1985. Research Highlights for 1984. International Institute of Tropical Agriculture, Ibadan, Nigeria, 114 pp.

Kamien, M.I. and Schwartz, N.L., 1978. Optimal exhaustible resource depletion with endogenous technical change. Rev. Econ. Stud., 45: 179–196.

Krautkraemer, J.A., 1985. Optimal growth, resource amenities and the preservation of natural environments. Rev. Econ. Stud., 52: 153–170.

Krutilla, J.V. and Fisher, A.C., 1985. The Economics of Natural Environments: Studies in the Valuation of Commodity and Amenity Resources (2nd Edition). Johns Hopkins University Press, Baltimore, MD, 300 pp.

Maler, K.G., 1974. Environmental Economics: A Theoretical Inquiry. Johns Hopkins University Press, Baltimore, MD, 267 pp.

Miller, J.R. and Menz, F.C., 1979. Some economic considerations for wildlife preservation. South. Econ. J., 45: 718–729.

Myers, N., 1984. The Primary Source: Tropical Rain Forests and Our Future. Norton, New York, 337 pp.
Nelson, R., 1988. Dryland management: the 'desertification' problem. Environ. Dep. Work. Pap. 8, World Bank, Washington, DC, 42 pp.
Nordhaus, W.D. and Tobin, J., 1977. Growth and natural resources. In: R. Dorfman and N.S. Dorfman (Editors). Economics of the Environment (2nd Edition), Norton, New York, pp. 479–488.
Norgaard, R., 1984. Coevolutionary development potential. Land Econ., 60: 1601–173.
Norgaard, R., 1985. Environmental economics: an evolutionary critique and a plea for pluralism. J. Environ. Econ. Manage., 12: 382–394.
Oram, P.A., 1985. Sensitivity of agricultural production to climatic change. Clim. Change, 7: 129–152.
OTA, 1988. Technology and the American Economic Transition. Office for Technical Assessment, Washington, DC, 131 pp.
Page, T., 1977. Conservation and Economic Efficiency: An Approach to Materials Policy. Johns Hopkins University Press, Baltimore, MD, 266 pp.
Pearce, D.W., 1985. Sustainable futures: economics and the environment. Inaugural lecture, Univ. College London, 30 pp.
Pearce, D.W., Barbier, E.B. and Markandya, A.M., 1990. Sustainable Development: Economics and Environment in the Third World. Edward Elgar, London, 217 pp.
Pearsall, S.H., III, 1984. In absentia benefits of nature preserves: a review. Environ. Conserv., 11: 3–10.
Sioli, H., 1985. The effects of deforestation in Amazonia. Geogr. J., 151: 197–203.
Smith, V.K. and Krutilla, J.V., 1979. Summary and research issues. In: V.K. Smith (Editor), Scarcity and Growth Reconsidered. Johns Hopkins University Press, Baltimore, MD, pp. 276–290.
Smith, V.L., 1977. Control theory applied to natural and environmental resources: an exposition. J. Environ. Econ. Manage., 4: 1–24.
Solow, R.M., 1974a. The economics of resources or the resources of economics. Pap. Proc. Am. Econ. Rev., 64: 1–14.
Solow, R.M., 1974b. Intergenerational equity and exhaustible resources. Rev. Econ. Stud. Symp. Economics of Exhaustible Resources, pp. 123–137.
Southgate, D., 1988. The economics of land degradation in the third world. Environ. Dep. Work. Pap. 2, World Bank, Washington, DC, 17 pp.
Southgate, D., 1989. Efficient management of biologically diverse tropical forests. LEEC Pap. 89-03, IIED/UCL London Environmental Economics Centre, 19 pp.
Stiglitz, J.E., 1974. Growth with exhaustible natural resources; efficient and optimal growth paths. Rev. Econ. Stud. Symp. Economics of Exhaustible Resources, pp. 123–137.
Turner, R.K., 1988. Wetland conservation: economics and ethics. In: D. Collard, D.W. Pearce and D. Ulph (Editors), Economics, Growth and Sustainable Environments: Essays in Memory of Richard Lecomber. Macmillan, London, pp. 121–159.
Vousden, N., 1973. Basic theoretical issues of resource depletion. J. Econ. Theory, 6: 126–143.
WRI and IIED (World Resources Institute and International Institute for Environment and Development), 1986. World Resources 1986. Basic Books, New York, 353 pp.

# [5]
# DEVELOPING ECONOMIES AND THE STEADY STATE

Herman E. Daly

> An increase in the rate of growth tends to aggravate both external dependence and internal exploitation. Thus higher rates of growth, far from reducing underdevelopment, tend to worsen it, in the sense of tending to increase social inequalities.
>
> Celso Furtado (1974)

It is absolutely a waste of time as well as morally backward to preach steady-state doctrines to underdeveloped countries before the overdeveloped countries have taken any measure to reduce either their own population growth or the growth of their per-capita resource consumption. Therefore, the steady-state paradigm must first of all be adopted and applied in the overdeveloped countries. That does not mean, however, that the underdeveloped countries can be left out of consideration. For one thing, the underdeveloped countries are not ever going to develop (recall the "impossibility theorem" of Chapter 1) unless the overdeveloped countries moderate their demands on world resources and absorption capacities. One of the major forces necessary to push the overdeveloped countries toward a SSE will be Third World outrage at their overconsumption. In addition, underdeveloped countries will have to revise their expectations downward regarding their own growth. Although per-capita consumption levels are too low and must still grow, population size need not grow and must, in fact, be significantly slowed down as a precondition for increasing the growth rate of per-capita consumption. Investment can be used either to increase the standards of a given population or to increase the population at given standards. Underdeveloped countries must, regardless of the actions of overdeveloped countries, reduce their population growth.

The starting point in development economics should be the "impossibility theorem" mentioned in Chapter 1: that a U.S.-style high mass consumption economy for a world of 4 billion people is impossible, and even if by some miracle it could be achieved, it would certainly be short lived. Even less realistic is the prospect of an ever growing standard of consumption for an ever growing population. The raw materials concentrated in the earth's crust and the capacity of ecosystems to absorb either large quantities or exotic qualities of waste materials and heat set a limit to the number of person-years that can be lived in the "developed state," as that term is understood today in the United States and in the Third World.

This impossibility theorem is arrived at by common sense reasoning and does not depend on opaque computer models with their "counterintuitive" results. Models such as those sponsored by the Club of Rome are useful and informative, but the steady-state position is not dependent on them. Just as in the Middle Ages all Holy Thought had to be expressed in Latin, so in the Age of Analysis all Correct Thought must, it would seem, be expressed in the binary language of computer codes. There is a real danger of the computer model becoming a large black box containing a giant syllogism that carries us with the speed of light from dialectically fuzzy premises to analytically precise conclusions. While I have great admiration for the work sponsored by the Club of Rome (Meadows et al., 1972; Mesarovic and Pestel, 1974), I nevertheless think that we are wise to resist assurances of truth unless we can grasp the entirety of argument in intellectual intuition and see it illuminated as a whole by the natural light of reason. Complex computer models are aids to, but not substitutes for, this kind of more intimate understanding.

As a simple intuitive demonstration of the impossibility theorem, consider the following. If it requires roughly one third of the world's annual production of nonrenewable resources to support that 6 percent of the world's population residing in the United States in that developed condition to which the rest of the world is thought to aspire, then it follows that present resource flows would allow the extention of the U.S. standard to a maximum of 18 percent of the world's current population, with nothing left over for the other 82 percent. And without the services rendered by the other 82 percent, the rich 18 percent would have so much work to do that they could not possibly do it and, even if they could, they would have no time or energy left over to enjoy their riches. It is clear that a middle-class U.S. standard is possible for much less than 18 percent because it depends on having many poorer people available to do the dirty work; a significant share of resources must be devoted to sustaining them, even at their lower level, and hence would not be available to support the high consumption levels of the hypothetical 18 percent.

It will be objected by some that the solution is simply to increase world resource flows by some factor such that world resource use per capita will equal U.S. resource use per capita. That factor turns out to be about six.* In order to increase world resource flows sixfold, the rest of the world would have to attain the U.S. level of capitalization and technical extracting and processing capacity. This enormous increase in capital would require a long period of accumulation; moreover, even if it could be done overnight, it would require an immense increase in resource flows during that short accumulation period. To supply the rest of the world with the average per-capita "standing crop" of industrial metals already embodied in existing artifacts in the ten richest nations would require more than sixty years' production of these metals at 1970 rates (Brown, 1970).

But neglecting the enormous resource requirements of increasing the capital stock, for how long could the biosphere sustain the depletion and pollution generated by even the sixfold increase in the throughput of materials and energy required to maintain the miraculously accumulated capital? There is much evidence that present rates of usage are irreversibly damaging ecological life-support systems. Furthermore, a sixfold increase in *net, usable* throughput implies a much greater than sixfold increase in gross throughput and environmental impact, due to the law of diminishing returns. To mine poorer grade and less accessible minerals and to dispose safely of large quantities of wastes will require enormous increases in energy and capital devoted to mining, refining, transportation, and pollution control. To get our sixfold increase in net energy and materials throughput, the gross throughput must increase by much more than sixfold. There is a limit to the process of throwing ever larger quantities of capital into the exploitation of ever poorer, more remote, and more dangerous sources of energy and materials.

Nothing illustrates the amazing shallowness of orthodox development economics more convincingly than the realization that it has been for the last twenty years attempting an impossible goal. Yet the establishment worldwide of the Western, middle-class material lifestyle has been the explicit goal of most of our aid and development programs. As a means

---

*Let $M$ be the factor, $R$ be annual world resource production; 4 billion is the world population, and 210 million is the U.S. population; then:

$$\frac{M \cdot R}{4 \times 10^9} = \frac{0.33R}{2.1 \times 10^8} \rightarrow M = 6.35$$

to that end, as well as an end in itself, rich countries are urged to continue growing. According to former chairman of the Council of Economic Advisers, Dr. Paul W. McCracken, "The action most urgently needed in the world economy is for the strong economies to be willing to accept higher levels of living. Their reluctance to do so seems to be of Calvinistic proportions" (1975). In other words, the rich must consume more for the sake of the poor! How could such a respected economist make such an apparently absurd statement? Or, more instructively, what premises must be accepted for McCracken's statement to be reasonable? If resources were unlimited in supply, and the only limiting factor in economic growth were aggregate demand, and if the distribution of income did not matter as long as the absolute incomes of all were increasing, and if we look only at the short run—then the statement would be reasonable. Keynesian pump-priming is evidently the paradigm within which McCracken views world development.

But these assumptions are grossly unrealistic. Resource supplies are, in fact, increasingly limited; distribution is as important as absolute levels; we cannot ignore the long run, and the rich can remain at their more than sufficient material standard without necessarily being Calvinists. The rich should not be urged to devote their leisure to senseless consumption. Better that they should consume less, freeing resources for the poor, who can create their own markets by selling necessities to each other, instead of having to sell ever more extravagant luxuries to the jaded and harried rich.

From the impossibility theorem it follows that the important development questions for the remainder of the century will be:

(1) How will the limited number of person-years of "developed living" be apportioned among nations and among social classes within nations?

(2) How will the total be divided between the present generation and all future generations?

(3) Could not the total number of person-years lived from now until extinction be increased by having a smaller number of people simultaneously alive in each generation, thereby avoiding some of the permanent destruction of renewable resources and life support systems that results when their short-run carrying capacity is overstressed?

(4) Could not our standards of per-capita consumption be lowered in exchange for an increase in person-years lived?

(5) Should the burden of scarcity fall mainly on the present or the future? On the standard of per-capita consumption, or the numbers of people? On the rich or on the poor?

Lest we think that these questions are unanswerable, it should be noted that varying answers have been given in recent United Nations conferences in Stockholm (Environment), Bucharest (Population), and Rome (Food). The leaders of the overdeveloped countries seemed to say that the increasing world burden of scarcity should fall on numbers of people in Third World countries. Let the poor limit their populations. The leaders of the underdeveloped countries seemed to be saying that the burden should fall on the high per-capita consumption of the overdeveloped. Let the rich limit their consumption. Both seemed willing to pass as much of the burden as possible on to the future.

If we heroically assume goodwill on both parts, the solution is simple; without goodwill there is no solution at all. The overdeveloped should limit consumption growth (and population growth), and the underdeveloped should limit population growth, while increasing per-capita consumption only up to equality with the stabilized or reduced levels of the overdeveloped countries. Both groups should move to a steady state at a common level of capital stocks per person and stabilized or reduced populations. Welfare or service can still increase with improvements in efficiency as discussed in Chapter 4.

In principle, the solution is so simple. Why then does it strike us as so hopelessly utopian and unrealistic? Partly because of lack of goodwill internationally—it is hard to be optimistic about nations limiting goods when they cannot even agree to limit the production of "bads," to end the arms race. It could easily happen that increasing scarcity will lead nations to devote more rather than less resources to weapons, in order to appropriate by force the remaining resources from other countries. With proliferation of nuclear weapons to underdeveloped countries, however, this may become an expensive conquest.

In addition to lack of goodwill internationally, the existence of class conflicts within each group of nations makes our simple solution "unrealistic." The overdeveloped countries will not want to limit consumption, because growing consumption is what buys off social conflict and keeps attention diverted from the divisive issue of distribution of wealth and income. In the United States growth is a substitute for redistribution. The leaders of underdeveloped countries are often not anxious to limit the populations of their own lower-class majorities, because cheap and abundant labor is a benefit to the owners of land and capital, the ruling class, which of course limits its own progeny. Cheap labor means higher profits that can be reinvested for faster growth and thus more rapid attainment of international power and prestige for the elite (Daly, 1970). If we were just a little cynical we might suspect that the reluctance of some Third World elites to support population control, or even family planning, bore some analogy to the reluctance of foxes to advocate birth control for rabbits.

Thus internal class conflicts, as well as international enmity, will make agreement difficult and will predispose both parties to accept the wishful thinking of technological optimists who advocate that we have faith in the Great Breakthrough that will invalidate the impossibility theorem. All that is needed, they say, are larger research and development budgets, greater offerings to the Technological Priesthood who gave us the Green Revolution, Nuclear Power, and Space Travel. That these technological saviors have created more problems than they have solved is conveniently overlooked. The mythology of technological omnipotence is by itself very strong, but when backed by class interests in avoiding the radical policies required by the steady state, it becomes a full-fledged idolatry.

As long as we remain trapped by the ideology of competitive growth, there is no solution. We are reminded of the South Indian monkey trap, in which a hollowed-out coconut is fastened to a stake by a chain and filled with rice. There is a hole in the coconut just large enough for the monkey to put his extended hand through but not large enough to withdraw his fist full of rice. The monkey is trapped only by his inability to reorder his values, to recognize that freedom is worth more than the handful of rice. We seem to be in a similar position. The value of growth is rigidly held in first place, and we are trapped into a system of increasing environmental disruption and gross injustices by our inability to reorder values, to open our fist and let go of the growth paradigm. Although it is hard on rational grounds to be optimistic about our getting out of the growth trap, we must, nevertheless, adopt an existential attitude of hope, without which no efforts at all would be made. Hope and despair are existential attitudes that we bring to the world from within our being. Optimism and pessimism are rational expectations about the probable course of events. Therefore, it is possible to be a hopeful pessimist without contradiction.

The split in point of view between the overdeveloped and underdeveloped is in some ways new but has its roots in the old division between Marx and Malthus. The Marxian and Malthusian traditions represent the major competing explanations of poverty in Western thought (Daly, 1971). The difference between them is reflected in the two meanings of the word "proletariat," and the differing theories of poverty implicit therein. The literal Latin meaning of proletariat is "those with many offspring," and the full ancient Roman sense of the word is "the lowest class of a people, whose members, poor and exempt from taxes, were useful to the republic only for the procreation of children." The correlation between proletarian and prolific is implicit in our very language and is given explicit theoretical development in the Malthusian tradition. The second meaning of proletariat is the Marxian definition as "nonowners of the means of production, who must sell their labor power to the capitalist in order to live." By Marx's time the literal meaning of the word had been lost, and it was used as a synonym for "the laboring class, the poor, the common people." Marx's definition completed the alienation of the word from all connection with its literal meaning. Implicit in the Marxian definition, and explicitly developed in Marxian thought, is the theory that poverty results from the social relations of production not from the proliferation of the proletariat.

But are these two views really mutually exclusive or logically incompatible? If we consider that poverty means "low per-capita income of a class" and that per-capita income is the ratio of total income *(Y)* to total population *(P)* for the class, then we can say, as a first approximation, that the Malthusian tradition explains low *Y/P* by pointing to a large or rapidly growing denominator and its causes. In contrast, Marxians explain the poverty of a class by showing why the numerator is low or growing very slowly, or even declining. To the extent that *Y* and *P* are independent, the two explanations are complementary. Certainly there are limits to the independence of *Y* and *P*. Given *Y*, there is a maximum *P* which can subsist and a minimum *P* technically necessary for the production of the given *Y*. But within the limits set by subsistence and technology (which grow wider with time), the two terms of the fraction can vary in relative independence, and instead of Marx *versus* Malthus we have Marx *and* Malthus. Even when *Y* and *P* cannot be treated independently, there still exist complementarities between the Marxian and Malthusian views, since there is no reason that we cannot recognize two-way causation, with both *Y* and *P* capable of autonomous change.

The big conflict between Marx and Malthus does not lie in any *logical* incompatibility between their theories of poverty, but in an *ideological* incompatibility between their pet remedies. Marx's remedy calls upon worker solidarity and overthrow of the capitalist system. Since the proletarians are the grave diggers of capitalism, it will not do to restrict their numbers, at least not until after the revolution. Malthus, by contrast, took capitalism as given and urged individual prudence, restraint, and responsibility in marriage and reproduction as the way to combat poverty. The neo-Malthusians urged contraception, while Malthus favored abstinence. For Marx, overpopulation was relative to capitalist institutions. For Malthus, overpopulation was absolute, defined by the limits imposed by nature independent of human social arrangements. Once again there is no *logical* conflict between the views. We can easily recognize the existence of both absolute and relative overpopulation. To deny either in defense of the other is nonsensical, though frequently done in ideological debate. To explain poverty, which is low per-capita income, *Y/P*, for a class, the Marxian tradition explains class differences in the numerator (income) as resulting mainly from a class monopoly on ownership of the means of production. The Malthusian tradition explains class differences in the denominator as resulting from the practice or nonpractice of birth limitation, or ownership versus nonownership of the means of limiting reproduction. The "means of limiting reproduction" includes not only contraceptive knowledge and devices but also the minimum cultural level of education and self-discipline necessary for their effective use—just as "means of production" means not only machines, but also the technical and managerial will and ability to use them. Could not this simple union of the two historically dominant theories of poverty be made to yield a more useful and informative set of categories than we presently have?

We have defined poverty as a low $Y/P$ for a class; but as yet we have not defined a "class." Our definition of class is not in terms of numerical size of per-capita income, so that all members of the class would be homogeneous with respect to size, but rather in terms of underlying *social* characteristics (differential property ownership and differential fertility), which largely determine the size of $Y/P$. Our resulting categories, homogeneous with respect to fertility and property ownership, will contain varying levels of per-capita income, but these differing per-capita income levels are not the result of differential property or fertility (except at a narrow within-category level) and are determined by chance differences in intelligence, opportunity, preference, and so on.* Hence within categories, we would expect families to be distributed much more normally about a mean per-capita income representative of that class, since the factors mainly responsible for skewness, differential property and fertility, have been held constant. By following the implications of the previous section and moving from a monistic to a dualistic conception of both $Y$ and $P$, we can make a large gain in within-category homogeneity at a relatively small cost in terms of multiplying categories.

The Marxian tradition insists on distinguishing two kinds of $Y$—that which goes to laborers largely as wages, $Y_w$, and that which goes to capitalists largely as returns to property, $Y_p$. Hence $Y = Y_w + Y_p$. These two categories of income follow different laws of growth and embody the fundamental Marxian criterion for class division. Income to laborers and income to property owners are both functionally and ethically different and should not be indiscriminately lumped together.

The neo-Malthusian tradition distinguishes two kinds of $P$—those who control reproduction, $P_c$, and those who do not, $P_n$. Hence $P = P_c + P_n$. These two populations follow different laws of growth and embody the fundamental neo-Malthusian criterion for class division. That they really form two statistically distinct populations, at least at an international level, has been shown by a United Nations study (1963). A frequency distribution of countries by gross reproduction rate (GRR) is strikingly bimodal. Developed countries have a GRR of less than 2.0, while underdeveloped countries have a GRR greater than 2.0, with almost no countries falling in the dividing range around 2.0. For high-fertility countries the unweighted mean GRR was 2.94, while for the

*From a welfare viewpoint, the existence of effective choice is more important than the numerical level of a family's per-capita income (the family may choose high leisure or many children in preference to a high per-capita income). Possession and control of the means of production and the means of limiting reproduction are necessary to make these choices effective.

low-fertility countries it was 1.41, or less than half as large. The difference between the two means (1.53) is over twenty-one times the standard error (0.07), clearly showing that we are dealing with two distinct populations and that the line of distinction is controlled versus uncontrolled fertility.

Furthermore, the fact that, at the international level, the division of countries by fertility criteria and the division by wealth or level of development criteria tend to coincide, is highly significant. The study found a remarkably high inverse relation between income and fertility on an international level when the world was divided into two fertility blocs. Almost all countries with GRR $> 2.0$ are in Asia, Africa, and Latin America. Almost all countries with GRR $< 2.0$ are in the developed parts of the world, and practically no countries have GRRs in the neighborhood of the 2.0 dividing point. The exceptions (high-fertility Albania and low-fertility Israel, Japan, Argentina, and Uruguay) only tend to prove the rule, since for their regions they are not only demographic exceptions but also economic exceptions and still conform to the rule of inverse association of fertility and economic development. However, *within* each bloc there appears to be no association at all between fertility and level of development.

With two kinds of income, $Y_w$ and $Y_p$, and two kinds of population $P_c$ and $P_n$, we have four possible types of per-capita income: $Y_p/P_c$, $Y_p/P_n$, $Y_w/P_c$, $Y_w/P_n$. To each of these types corresponds a social class with its own per-capita income distribution. If we knew the size and the rates of growth, and the percentage of the population contained in each of these four per-capita income classes, we would have a vastly better picture than that obtained by lumping everything together. The first category, $Y_p/P_c$, combines control of production and reproduction and is characteristic of an upper class or stable bourgeoisie—stable because, with both population control and property, they are unlikely to fall into the proletariat. The last category, $Y_w/P_n$, is characteristic of a stable proletariat. With no property income and uncontrolled fertility, there is little chance of rising out of the proletariat. The intermediate categories represent transitional, unstable phases. The proletarians who control fertility may accumulate a small capital and rise out of the lower class. The bourgeois family that fails to control fertility may dissipate its capital and fall into the lower class.

Most growth models in the contemporary literature trace the path of aggregate $Y/P$ (or just aggregate $Y$) according to various assumptions and are quite incapable of distinguishing among the infinitely many combinations of the four components that could correspond to any given aggregate per-capita GNP. The tacit assumption, if these models are to be included in the economist's tool kit rather than in his toy box, is that the average per-capita incomes of the four classes increase more or less proportionately. If not, then an important element of change is being omitted. A case in point is northeast Brazil, the largest poor area in the Western Hemisphere, which has had an annual growth rate in per-capita income of around 3.4 percent in the 1960s (Daly, 1970). But almost all of this growth has taken place in the upper-class per-capita income ($Y_p/P_c$) with that of the lower-class category ($Y_w/P_n$) remaining constant at best, perhaps even decreasing. At the same time, the percentage of the total population in the latter category has been increasing while that in former was decreasing! Conventional growth models thus leave out the most important feature of economic change in this region. The fourfold typology easily encompasses both even and uneven growth and is sensitive to the differences between them.

If we reject this fourfold disaggregation of per-capita income, we must do it on one of two grounds: 1. Disaggregation is not necessary, in which case it must be argued that equal growth of the four per-capita incomes is a realistic description of the process of economic growth for all countries. This, as just indicated, can be refuted. 2. Disaggregation is desirable, but the particular Marxian-Malthusian disaggregation here advocated is not a good one. Then, of course, we would be obliged to offer a better one. There may well be a better disaggregation, but it is argued below that the Marxian-Malthusian criteria have a very high degree of universality and deep-rootedness.

"The first principle of all human history is, of course, the existence of living human individuals," we are informed by Marx. The continued existence of living human individuals is the result of the two life-sustaining processes of production (to maintain human organisms) and reproduction (to replace human organisms). These two processes, then, are the most basic in society, and differential control over them gives us the first principles of division into social classes. The two processes are the basic force functions that generate class differences. Production provides the means for the short-term maintenance (and enjoyment) of life; reproduction provides for the long-term continuation (and enjoyment) of life. The basic social unit in the productive process is the firm and in the reproductive process, the family. In neither case is it the individual, who is a middle-run disequilibrium process; that is, he dies. But the firm and the family do not necessarily die and may be viewed as long-term equilibrium processes capable of indefinite, though not eternal, self-replacement.

Given the two fundamental life processes, let us note some ways in which they are analogous. Production is essentially reproduction of commodities by commodities. Reproduction is the production of people by people. We have two self-renewing sets, people and commodities, which are dependent on each other for their self-renewal. Both processes require specialization and division of labor, both are time consuming.

The biological term "gestation period" is widely used in economics. The first political economist, William Petty, could not resist calling land the mother and labor the father of wealth, and since earliest times the fertility of soil and the fertility of woman have been associated. The aggregate stocks of people and commodities both have birth (production) rates and death (consumption) rates, age structures, and life expectancies (durabilities). From a strictly physical point of view, the maintenance of these two stocks is accomplished by the same process: the importation of low-entropy matter-energy from the environment and the exportation of the same quantity of high-entropy matter-energy (waste) back to the environment. Both people and commodities are entropy converters, capable of mutually dependent self-renewal as long as the supply of low entropy holds out. This much is familiar from the discussion of Chapter 2, in which the SSE was defined in terms of the same stocks of people and artifacts.

The important question from a social viewpoint is: Who controls these two processes and to what purpose? Our social classes are defined on the basis of differing participation in and *control over* the two processes of production and reproduction. Control over production is, under capitalism, vested in capital, in the broad sense of property. He who owns the means of production by and large controls the process of production and directs it to his own purposes. Property hires, organizes, and directs labor. Our two classes are laborers and property owners—the fundamental Marxian division of classes. To what end do capitalists control the process? To the maximization of their private profit, according to the classical economists, to Marx, and to the neoclassical economists.

Control over the reproductive process has likewise been vested in the owners of the means of reproduction, that is, under capitalism in men and women, who own their own bodies. Under slavery the control over reproduction was still vested in the owner, who was, of course, the master not the slave. But the control of reproduction has, for the majority of mankind throughout history, been left to the natural consequences of the sex urge as unconsciously conditioned by social custom. Only since the middle of the nineteenth century has there been, and only for a minority, an effective rational barrier between the sex act and its natural outcome in proliferation. That the *desire* for (but not possession of) such a rational barrier, effective contraception, is a cultural and historical universal has been admirably demonstrated by Norman E. Himes in his classic *Medical History of Contraception* (1936). The attainment of this desire is relatively recent and still limited to a minority of the world's people. The incompleteness of what Himes termed the "democratization of contraception" means that the owners of the means of reproduction really do not *control* the process in any rational sense, because they do not possess effective means of limiting reproduction.

On the frontispiece of his classic study, Himes has the following quotation from Lippert: "The farther a notion reaches back into primitive times for its origin, the more universal must be its extent, and its power in history is rooted in this universality." It is to Himes' great credit to have shown that, contrary to popular opinion, the desire to control conception is a cultural and historical universal—not a recent product of birth-control propaganda. The control of *numbers* (effected by abortion and infanticide as well as by contraception) is even more universal, extending in all probability back to our prehuman ancestors. It is hardly necessary to argue the universality of property. Both individual and collective property holding have been traced back through human history and into the animal kingdom in the instinct of territoriality.

In sum, the deep-rootedness and universality of the two criteria is apparent. Can we imagine more basic lines of division for defining social classes than differential control over the two basic life processes? Is it at all surprising that in the history of economic thought, each of the two great traditions of explaining poverty should have seized upon one of these criteria as providing the key to understanding and combating poverty? That the two traditions should have been seen as mutually exclusive substitutes rather than as complements is an unfortunate historical circumstance that economists must now strive to put right.

To show how, in spite of severe data limitations, these categories might be usefully applied, let us consider the case of northeast Brazil in the 1960s, which in terms of conventional development criteria has been a great success (Daly, 1970). Total GNP for the region has grown at between 6 and 7 percent (say, 6.5) annually, with population growing at around 3.1 percent annually and per-capita income thus growing at around 3.4 percent—well above the hemispheric goal of 2.5 percent expressed at the Punta del Este conference. Add the fact of sparse density and there appears to be no population problem at all.

But let us apply the concepts just considered in order to go behind the misleading average and ask what is happening to each type of per-capita income and the corresponding social class. As a first approximation, let us take $Y_w/P_c$ and $Y_p/P_n$ to be empty categories; that is, there is a high inverse correlation between wealth and fertility. In other words, by our definition there is no middle class—only a stable bourgeoisie *($Y_p/P_c$)* and a stable proletariat *($Y_w/P_n$)*. If we consider that a typical completed bourgeois family has four surviving children, while a typical completed proletarian family has eight surviving children, then over one generation (say 25 years) the bourgeois family doubles (4 children ÷ 2 parents) and the proletarian family quadruples (8 children ÷ 2 parents). If over the same 25-year period the total income of each class grows at the same 6.5-percent rate at which the total income of both classes taken together has been growing, then the total income of each class will have increased by a factor of $(1.065)^{25} = 4.8$. Therefore, the per-capita income of the bourgeois family will have increased, over one generation, by a factor of $4.8/2 = 2.4$; that of the proletarian family will have increased by a factor of only $4.8/4 = 1.2$.

Even this meager increase of 20 percent over 25 years for the proletarians disappears when we recall our very optimistic assumption of equal growth rates for the total incomes of the two classes. Total income of the proletariat surely grows at less than the average 6.5 percent, while total income of the bourgeoisie surely grows more rapidly. This is because the proletariat lacks bargaining power due to nonownership of property, lack of labor unions, and lack of education; and because inflation tends to benefit property income at the expense of labor income and to benefit those who have access to credit. Thus it appears extremely likely that the per-capita income of the proletariat has not increased at all, while that of the bourgeoisie has increased very rapidly indeed. The bourgeoisie becomes richer and relatively less numerous; the proletariat remains equally poor and becomes both absolutely and relatively more numerous. Looking at aggregate per-capita GNP, we can see only "economic growth." Looking at the fourfold disaggregation forces us to distinguish between growth in the sense of "improvement" and growth in the sense of "swelling." And we are led to recognize the key role played by differential fertility in the dynamics of swelling. The rather more important role of differential property ownership has been more generally recognized intellectually, even if avoided politically.

Finally, in a world increasingly polarized into right and left, might not the inclusion of the true insights of both the Marxian and neo-Malthusian traditions in our informational categories go at least some distance toward uniting these factions to a common development effort? The underlying moral viewpoint capable of embracing the best in both traditions is that stated in Mark 2:28: "The Sabbath was made for man, not man for the Sabbath." If this rule applies to sacred institutions, then it must apply with even greater force to secular institutions. The institutions, laws, and conventions governing the dual life-sustaining processes of production and reproduction are to serve man, not vice versa. Man was not made to serve Mammon—nor the goddess of fertility.

Let us take a further look at the specific case of Brazil as representative of the conflict between development and the environment. At international conferences Brazil has been noted for hard-line stands against any environmental constraints on economic development. Brazil also has achieved one of the highest growth rates in the world. This accomplishment can be viewed from at least three very different perspectives—the neoclassical, the neo-Marxian, and the neo-Malthusian. Old economic doctrines never die, they just add the prefix "neo" and continue their subversive or apologetic existences.

Keynes warned us that economists are more powerful than commonly realized: "Practical men who believe themselves to be quite exempt from any intellectual influences, are usually the slaves of some defunct economist. Madmen in authority, who hear voices in the air, are distilling their frenzy from some academic scribbler of a few years back" (1936, p. 383). Prior to 1964 in Brazil, both neoclassical and neo-Marxian "voices in the air" spoke to those in authority. Since the revolution of 1964 the neo-Marxians have been placed beyond the pale. Neo-Malthusians have never been a dominant force anywhere, especially not in Brazil. Their inclusion here is based not on their past importance but on my estimate of their future importance. The neoclassical paradigm thus has, for now, a virtual monopoly on official Brazilian economic thinking. Neoclassical economics has been applied with originality and imagination and, within its own terms, has been highly successful. Let us examine the nature of the Brazilian neoclassical development strategy first in a sympathetic way and then give it a more critical look from the neo-Marxian and neo-Malthusian perspectives, especially the latter.

The current technocratic military regime in Brazil has based its development strategy overwhelmingly on its ability to maintain a very high rate of growth in real GNP, arguing that this would make unnecessary any direct confrontation with the politically divisive issues of redistribution (exit neo-Marxians) and population control (exit neo-Malthusians, if any). If GNP continues to grow at 10 percent per year, it will double every seven years, quadruple every fourteen years, and so forth. Surely, it is argued, the poor will benefit more from this rapid doubling than from any "premature" or "emotional" redistribution, which would kill incentives and lead to economic stagnation. It is considered natural that income distribution should become more unequal in the early stages of rapid growth—after all, universal poverty is highly egalitarian and any movement away from that position is bound to have nonuniform effects and therefore increase the inequality of income distribution. As for the nearly 3-percent rate of demographic growth that the "demophobes" fear, that too is "solved" by economic growth. If the 10-percent rate of GNP growth is maintained, then a 3-percent rate of demographic growth means that per-capita GNP will grow at about 7 percent and double every ten years. If, by heroic and expensive effort, the population growth rate were cut to 1 percent per year, then per-capita income would grow at 9 percent and double every eight years instead of every ten years—not a significant difference and certainly not worth the enormous effort. Besides, people are needed to colonize the Amazon, which is viewed as a great potential source of agricultural and mineral wealth and as a temptation to greedy foreigners. Furthermore, the "demographic transition thesis" holds that as incomes increase, the birth rate automatically tends to fall, so that rapid economic growth is itself the best birth-control policy.

In sum, rapid growth in aggregate GNP is the turnpike to development, and redistribution and fertility reduction are bumpy, dirt-road detours that will at best slow the journey down and at worst rattle the car to pieces. The best strategy is to stay on the turnpike and pay the relatively cheap toll.

Reality is always more complex than our descriptions of it, and I would not claim that this brief sketch does total justice to Brazilian development policy, but I believe it captures the essential strategy. There are, however, countercurrents. Everyone recognizes that income distribution became more concentrated during the intercensal period 1960–1970, and the regime has expressed concern. The literacy program (MOBRAL) and some educational and social welfare expenditures have no doubt benefitted the poor. Some influential Brazilians (Mario Simonsen and Rubens Costa, for example) have long argued for a voluntary family-planning program. Moreover, Brazil ratified the Bucharest World Plan of Action on Population. It remains to be seen whether that is an index more of the vacuity of the action plan than of Brazil's intention to worry about population growth (*"Brasil admite,"* 1974).

The successful policies undertaken to promote growth include: tax incentives for exports and for investment, especially investment in poor regions; reduction of inflation and monetary correction, or "indexing" to correct the worst distortions of the remaining inflation; adjustable exchange rates and frequent minidevaluations to discourage foreign exchange speculation; welcoming foreign capital from a diverse mix of countries; administrative enforcement of tax laws; and other measures. I will not describe these policies in detail, since it is clear enough that the goal of growth was being achieved (at least until the oil crisis of 1974). Rather, let us take a closer look at that goal itself and judge its adequacy from our other two perspectives.

We need not be Marxian to appreciate the importance of the main points of what I have called the neo-Marxian tradition. The major emphasis of that tradition is on social justice and on breaking the monopoly of economic and political power of the elite class. Brazil is governed by a military dictatorship. In recent elections most Brazilians, in spite of the benefits of economic growth, cast their somewhat meaningless ballots for the opposition party. Social justice has not been served by the worsening distribution of income. In 1960 the poorest 80 percent of the population received 46 percent of total national income, while in 1970 they received only 37 percent. Correspondingly, over the same period the share of the richest 20 percent increased from 54 percent to 63 percent, while the richest 1 percent increased its share from about 12 percent to about 18 percent (Simonsen, 1972, p. 51). To put it bluntly, the great majority of the population has, since the revolution, gotten both a reduced share of the national product and a reduced voice in national affairs. Hence the popular saying, "Brazil is doing well, but the Brazilian is doing badly."

But is the Brazilian majority getting worse off absolutely as well as relatively? Between 1960 and 1970 the *absolute* income of the lower 80 percent taken as a whole increased by 8.4 percent, while that of the richest 20 percent increased by 55.4 percent. For the richest 1 percent the increase was 103.2 percent (Simonsen, 1972, p. 53). Within the large category of the poorest 80 percent, there were no doubt many people (especially in poor areas like the northeast) whose absolute real incomes did not rise at all, or actually declined. But the data are too global to permit more than a guess at the actual numbers. However, the falling purchasing power of the real minimum wage (actual inflation has been greater than the anticipated inflation used in calculating the minimum wage adjustments) suggests that many of the poor are getting worse off absolutely.

It is sometimes argued that the pursuit of growth will eventually require a more even distribution of income in order to have a mass market in which to sell the growing output. This is not very convincing, for two reasons: First, there are export markets available. Second, the upper 20 percent of Brazil's 110 million people consists of 22 million consumers (almost equal to the entire population of Argentina), who can provide adequate markets for each other, with little need to sell much beyond rice and beans to the lower 88 million. As growth continues, the product mix shifts more to luxuries and consumer durables and away from basic necessities. The increase in luxury consumption of a minority at the expense of the basic needs of the majority is, of course, the real meaning of income inequality and the real cost of a "trickle-down" development policy.

The one thing that the poor definitely get more of than the rich is children. Completed family size differs probably by a factor of about 2 between the richest 20 percent and the poorest 80 percent. That is a crude estimate, but it is unmistakably clear, as we have already seen, that differential fertility is an important determinant of per-capita income distribution, a point generally ignored by neo-Marxians and neoclassicals alike. It seems that differential population growth in Brazil has promoted aggregate economic growth at the expense of the lower class. The high fertility of the lower class serves to perpetuate an unlimited supply of labor at a constant low wage. This helps to keep profits high, and, since most investment comes from profit earners, the result is more investment and faster growth than would be the case if labor were scarce and wages were being bid up. The cheap service of abundant labor is a key part of the Brazilian growth pattern and is of enormous benefit to the upper and middle classes, who have not only cheap labor for their factories and *fazendas* but also cheap domestic servants for their households. Jonathan Swift observed a similar condition in his time. Explaining how his rational Houyhnhnms limited their reproduction to one of each sex, Swift wrote, "But the race of inferior Houyhnhnms bred up to be servants, is not so strictly limited upon this article; these are allowed to produce three of each sex to be domestics in the noble families" (Swift, 1952, p. 166).

But what of the demographic transition thesis that fertility falls as income increases? For one thing, the real income of the masses hardly seems to be rising at all, and for another the thesis itself may be just wishful thinking. Rising per-capita income may be as much the result of lowered fertility as the cause, and the expectation that a process that took place over centuries in Europe will be repeated in the Third World in a matter of decades inspires skepticism. Death control did spread in a matter of decades, but procreating is a much more popular activity than dying, and social values that evolved during a history in which mortality was high, must, for survival, favor high fertility. A lowering of fertility will take a long time at best and may never take place if governments sit back and wait for some automatic transition to occur as a by-product of economic growth (Teitelbaum, 1975). It is a fact that illiteracy has declined with economic growth, but on the basis of that commonplace no one invents a "literacy transition thesis" and counsels Brazil not to waste money on MOBRAL because economic growth will automatically induce literacy!

The neo-Malthusian view has recently been generalized from a demographic focus to a concern for total ecological balance among population, resources, and environment. Since the Brazilian strategy is so heavily committed to rapid growth, it is a question of great interest whether and for how long a growth rate of 10 percent can be sustained by the natural ecosystem of which the Brazilian economy is a subsystem. What is politically and economically expedient may turn out to be biophysically unacceptable. Very little study has been devoted to this question, because it is considered a nonproblem. The official view is that, "in relation to the special human carrying capacity of the earth, it is obvious that it is infinitely greater than present levels" (Osorio de Alameda, 1973). Since the growth-based strategy would be rendered untenable by any imminent limits to growth in the form of steeply rising costs resulting from minerals depletion, environmental pollution, or ecological disruption, the regime simply declares by fiat that any such limits are infinitely remote. Any research that might cast doubt on this "obvious" fact is not likely to be welcomed, just as economic and demographic research on fertility is limited by a kind of taboo (Lyra Madeira, 1971, p. 42). This denial of the problem is hardly surprising, since most politicians in the United States take the same attitude and dismiss any argument that growth must be limited as "doomsaying."

Admittedly, Brazil is a large country with abundant resources and plenty of space in which to spread the inevitable pollution resulting from production and consumption. But the resource and waste-disposal demands of other countries also impinge upon Brazil and provide an important reason for the large inflow of foreign investment that has been a major factor in rapid growth. Such investments offer foreign countries an alternative to importing raw materials and further polluting home environments—a prospect that is doubly attractive to polluted and resource-poor countries, such as Japan. Ironically, Brazil already is experiencing the environmental problems of overdevelopment before it has solved the traditional problems of underdevelopment. With the help of West Germany, the most intractable of all problems of overdevelopment, managing fission power, will soon increase Brazil's prestige while decreasing its national well-being. The enormous ecological destruction being wrought on the Amazon jungle in the name of development has been admirably documented by Goodland and Irwin (1975). Therefore, it is simplistic to argue that pollution replaces hunger and that rapid growth has substituted lesser for greater evils. The problems of underdevelopment and overdevelopment do not cancel out; instead, they add together or perhaps even multiply.

A famous formerly exiled Brazilian, Celso Furtado, is one of the few economists to have recognized the increasingly apparent contradiction of our present concept of development: that an upper-middle-class standard of per-capita resource consumption for the current world population of 4 billion is simply impossible (Furtado, 1974).

The Brazilian elite suspects that "environmentalism" is part of a plot to stifle their growth and thwart the destiny by which Brazil is "condemned to greatness." Certainly it is unreasonable to expect the poor to limit their resource consumption until after the rich have limited theirs. This applies not only between rich and poor nations but also between social classes within nations.

Perhaps the real goal of "development" in Brazil has nothing to do with individual welfare of the majority and everything to do with national power. The mercantilists proclaimed this goal openly, and perhaps the regime is really more neomercantilist than neoclassical. If the goal is to maximize the economic and military power of the "nation" (meaning the current elite), then nothing more need be said. We can assume that we know other peoples' real goals and then interpret contradictory behavior as an aberration or a mistake. Or we can assume that behavior is always rational and consistent and that the real goal, which may be secret or even unconscious, is exactly what the behavior implies. According to which view we adopt, the regime will appear either neoclassical or neomercantilist. But if the goal is to increase the welfare of the majority of Brazilians in the present and future generations, then it seems clear that Brazil will have to get off the rapid-growth turnpike and follow the slower, bumpy road of redistribution and population control. At least those two elements of the steady-state program are already relevant to Brazil, and probably to a number of other Third World countries as well.

While not referring specifically to Brazil, Raul Prebisch, head of ECLA, recently expressed to a U.S. audience a certain disenchantment with growth in Latin America:

> Reference has been made to the so-called high rates of growth that are possible in Latin America. I do not share the rejoicing over this prospect. Indeed the high rates of growth that have been attained by some countries are accompanied by a growing disparity in income distribution and by the lack of ability of the economic system to absorb with satisfactory productivity the continuous increment in the labor force.
>
> The introduction of the consumption society means that we are "benefitting" from all the "delights" of your patterns of consumption such as pollution, irresponsible use of nonrenewable resources, growing congestion in the cities, and erosion of some human values that we would like to preserve [Prebisch, 1974, p. 40].

The growth ethic will have to end sometime, and the neo-Malthusians will have their day, perhaps sooner than anyone thinks. But in the meantime it seems inevitable that the rhythmic crescendo of the GNP samba will drown out the somber Greek chorus of rational foresight. Now that the Brazilians have learned to beat us at our own game of industrial growthmanship, it seems rather ungracious to declare that game obsolete. We can sympathize with Brazilian disbelief and suspicion regarding the motives of the neo-Malthusians. But the dialectic of change has no rule against irony.

The purpose of this chapter has been not to offer a treatise on the Third World but merely to show that while the SSE has, quite appropriately, been discussed mainly in the context of overdeveloped countries, it is not at all irrelevant to underdeveloped countries. As Richard Wilkinson has noted:

> Predictions of when the resources which modern industrial technology depends on will run out are usually within the same time scale as the predictions of when many underdeveloped countries may reach industrial maturity. The industrial nations cannot avoid having to change their whole resource-base and technology for a second time, but some of the pre-industrial nations might manage to avoid making more than one change [Wilkinson, 1973, p. 216].

Hopefully, the underdeveloped are not condemned to repeat the mistakes of the overdeveloped.

## REFERENCES

*"Brasil Admite o Livre Planejanento Familiar," O Globo,* August 5, 1974, p. 4.

Brown, Harrison. "Human Materials Production as a Process in the Biosphere," *Scientific American,* September 1970.

Daly, Herman E. "The Population Question in Northeast Brazil: Its Economic and Ideological Dimensions," *Economic Development and Cultural Change*, July 1970, 536–574.

Daly, Herman E. "A Marxian-Malthusian View of Poverty and Development," *Population Studies*, March 1971, 25–37.

Furtado, Celso. *O Mito do Desenvolvimento Economico*. Rio de Janeiro: *Editora Paz e Terra S. A.*, 1974.

Goodland, Robert J. A., and Howard S. Irwin, *Amazon Jungle: Green Hell to Red Desert*. New York: Elsevier Scientific Publishing Co., 1975.

Himes, Norman E. *A Medical History of Contraception*. Baltimore: Williams & Wilkins, 1936.

Keynes, J. M. *The General Theory of Employment, Interest, and Money*. New York: Harcourt Brace Jovanovich, 1936.

Lyra Madeira, João. "*Migraçoẽs Internas no Planejamento Econômico*," in Manoel Costa, ed., *Migraçoẽs Internas no Brasil*. Rio de Janeiro: *Instituto de Planejamento Economico e Social*, 1971.

McCracken, Paul W. "A Way Out of the World's Slump," *Wall Street Journal*, September 17, 1975, p. 16.

Meadows, D. H. et al. *The Limits to Growth*. New York: Universe Books, 1972.

Mesarovic, Mihajlo, and Edward Pestel. *Mankind at the Turning Point*. New York: Dutton, 1974.

Osorio de Almeida. Statement of the Brazilian Representative to the 17th Session of the U.N. Population Commission, Geneva, October 3, 1973.

Prebisch, Raul. "Third World Viewpoint," in George M. Dalen and Clyde R. Tipton, Jr., eds., *The Dilemma Facing Humanity*. Columbus, Ohio: Battelle Memorial Institute, 1974.

Simonsen, Mario Henrique. *Brasil 2002*. Rio de Janeiro: *APEC Editora, S.A.*, 1972.

Swift, Jonathan. *Gulliver's Travels*. Chicago: University of Chicago Great Books Edition, 1952. Originally published in 1726.

Teitelbaum, M. S. "Relevance of the Demographic Transition Thesis to Developing Countries," *Science*, May 2, 1975, 420–425.

United Nations. *Population Bulletin of the United Nations, No. 7*. New York: United Nations, 1963.

Wilkinson, Richard. *Poverty and Progress: An Ecological Perspective on Economic Development*. New York: Praeger, 1973.

104-17
[84]

# [6]

## Coevolutionary Development Potential

*Richard B. Norgaard*

1120
7210
7220

Q20
011

If economic development is real—not simply one group exploiting others or this generation living better at the expense of the next—then economic systems must have an inherent potential for development. Existing economic thought on the potential for sustainable development is neither explicit nor consistent with knowledge accumulated in the natural sciences. Neoclassical economists assume that the potential resides in our ability to devise technologies which augment the quality of labor and capital and which allow for the continued exploitation of lower quality stock resources. This assumption has been the focus of intermittent debate over the nature and limits of technological change and natural resources development since the beginnings of economics. The debate has influenced the development of biology and affected resource management policies. While the debate has raised disturbing issues within economics, it has resulted neither in resolutions nor in new directions in economic thought.

The sustainability debate has not been productive because it has been set within an inadequate framework. The neoclassical model assumes that factors of production and the products of economic activity come in discrete units related only in the process of economic production or through markets. This simplification has proven very powerful for explaining market phenomena. But neither natural resources and environmental services as factors of production nor environmental impacts as products of economic activity come in discrete units. The assumptions of the model are incongruent with the nature of the real world. It is ironic that environmental problems in economics are thought of as problems of market failure rather than as evidence of the applicable limits of the market model.

Alternative economic models are no better. Marxist models assume that capitalists exploit workers. Resource use and environmental problems can only be explored as aspects of this exploitation. Structuralist models similarly restrict issues regarding resources and the environment to a presumed underlying structural problem. The key ideas of institutional economics are general; they do not constrain institutionalists to a particular model structure. Within the general consensus that institutions are important and evolve on their own, a few institutional economists have considered the nature of environmental systems (Kapp 1950; Ciriacy-Wantrup 1963). Overall, however, institutionalists have emphasized institutions apart from nature. Some have reached pessimistic conclusions about the long run (Heilbroner 1980) while others have waxed optimistic (Brinkman 1980). Like the neoclassical model, none of the alternative models focuses on resources and environ-

Associate Professor, Department of Agricultural and Resource Economics, University of California, Berkeley.

*Giannini Foundation, Working Paper No. 245. The following people provided much needed suggestions, encouragement, and guidance into unfamiliar literatures: Sam Barakat, Martin Cohen, Paul Craig, Luis Crouch, Jr., Herman Daly, Paul Ehrlich, Ernst Haas, John Harte, Alan Larson, Kari Norgaard, Laurel Prevetti, Jeff Romm, Ben Shaine, Lee Travers, and Alan Trefeissen. I regret that I have not been able to produce a final draft upon which all the various experts whom I have been dependent upon can completely agree. Ruth E. Oscar provided research assistance and substantive as well as editorial comments. Catherine Taylor, editor, helped me completely transform the third draft into an article. I am also grateful for the comments of Dan Bromley and two anonymous reviewers.

*Land Economics*, Vol. 60, No. 2, May 1984
0023-7639/84/002-0160 $1.50/0

mental systems and incorporates assumptions that are appropriate for the investigation of the sustainability of economic development.

The coevolutionary development paradigm (Norgaard 1981, 1983, and 1984) is designed to address whether economic development can be maintained over the long run. In turn, the paradigm reframes what real development can mean. This paper describes the coevolutionary development process, documents that it stems from a real potential, and raises doubts about the desirability of growth based on stock-resource exploitation.

## I. THE COEVOLUTIONARY DEVELOPMENT PROCESS

In biology, coevolution refers to an evolutionary process based on reciprocal responses between two closely interacting species (Ehrlich and Raven 1964; Baker and Hurd 1968). Coevolutionary explanations have been given for the shape of both the beaks of hummingbirds and the flowers they feed on, the behavior of bees and the distribution of flowering plants, the biochemical defenses of plants and the immunity of their insect prey. The concept can be broadened to encompass any ongoing feedback process between two evolving systems, including social and ecological systems.

Dunn (1971) and Boulding (1978) describe economic development in evolutionary terms by identifying isomorphisms in social and ecological systems along the lines suggested by Bertalanffy (1968). Both Dunn and Boulding draw analogies between ecological and social systems, between genetic mutation and technological and social innovation, between survival of the fittest and economical and institutional competition, and between efficiently tapping the sun's energy and maximizing profits. Coevolution, however, is an interactive rather than a parallel or analogous process. For this reason, the coevolutionary model was developed from the work of cultural ecologists where social and ecological interaction is the distinguishing concept (Steward 1955; Rappaport 1968; and Harris 1979). The cultural ecology perspective, however, has largely evolved from studies of primitive societies in homeostatic equilibrium with their environment. Except for Harris, few cultural ecologists have addressed the global issues of economic development of interest to economists.

One way to look at the interaction of ecological and social systems is through energy flows.[1] Coevolutionary development can be envisioned as a sequential process involving a surplus of energy beyond that necessary to maintain the social and ecological systems in their present states. A surplus of energy would be defined as more than the ecological system needs to maintain its present mix of biomass and more than the social system needs to maintain the size and welfare of its population. The surplus energy may be either directed to, or fortuitously result in, a new interaction between the social and ecological systems. If this new interaction is favorable to society, results in a continuing energy surplus, and if this surplus is invested in further beneficial change, coevolutionary development is taking place.[2]

Sociosystems and ecosystems are maintained through numerous feedback mechanisms. Coevolution occurs when at least one feedback is changed, which then initiates a reciprocal process of change. An important feature of this process is that feedbacks that previously maintained an equilibrium in the ecosystem may be assumed by or shifted to the social system. Eugene Odum (1969) characterizes agricultural development as a transformation of the ecosystem to reduced numbers of species and usually lower combined

[1] "To coevolve" and "coevolution" refer to any positive (in the cybernetic sense) feedback. Social and ecological systems are always responding to each other, or coevolving. This process may correct for an initial setback or could be destructive itself from a human perspective (Norgaard 1981). Coevolutionary development is a coevolutionary process that benefits man. "Benefit" and "development" are left as undefined as they generally are in the development literature. The coevolutionary model refines our understanding of the possible but does not define what is good.

[2] The classic energy analysis in ecology is edited by Howard Odum and R. F. Pigeon (1970). Howard Odum's (1971) attempt to apply an energy analysis to environmental and social systems is interesting but intellectually much less satisfying.

efficiency of nutrient recycling, higher but less stable rates of production, and low biomass stocks relative to natural conditions. As people push ecosystems in this direction to suit their own needs, they intervene in nutrient cycles and disturb some equilibrating mechanisms that evolved within the ecosystem. Coevolutionary development occurs faster, or is perhaps only possible, if the sociosystem compensates for these natural system losses. New sociosystem functions may entail, for example, managing legumes to replace portions of lost nutrient cycles, weeding to offset natural succession, and combating herbiverous insects to compensate for lost natural pest control mechanisms. These new sociosystem functions are costs because they involve managerial effort, the acquisition of knowledge, the use of natural resources, and the establishment and maintenance of institutions. Ecosystem modification need not entail more sociosystem involvement. But when it does, the costs of these new activities must be deducted from the gross benefits of the new interaction.

Coevolutionary development has been taking place for thousands of years. The rise of paddy rice culture in Southeast Asia is an instructive example. The land-extensive practice of slash-and-burn agriculture was gradually abandoned over many centuries as investments were made in dikes, terraces, and water delivery systems for increasingly intensive paddy agriculture. The benefits from this ecological transformation came in the form of superior weed control and greater nutrient retention. The environmental system modification process, however, was not unilateral. In order to maintain the ecological system in its modified form and to acquire the benefits of modification, individuals changed their behavior and the social system adapted to assist and reinforce appropriate individual behavior. In the case of paddy rice, the benefits from ecological transformation could only be acquired through complex social changes that facilitated property ownership, water management, and labor exchanges (Boserup 1965; Geertz 1963).

Economic views of Western history typically emphasize the dramatic increase in the productivity of the few individuals still working in agriculture. This increase is generally attributed to a continual decrease in environmental constraints on farmers. The coevolutionary perspective emphasizes the increase in individual task specialization and the increase in the cultural or institutional complexity of maintaining feedback mechanisms between specialized actors within the social system and between the social system and the ecosystem. The coevolutionary view emphasizes an increasingly important, and frequently more complex, interaction between man and his environment.

Western agriculture was once a small-scale, labor-intensive, polycultural, and near-subsistence interaction between the social and ecological systems. The systems coevolved to a large-scale, mechanized and energy-intensive, monocultural, commercial farming interaction. This new agricultural interaction is maintained by a highly complex system of farm-implement and agrochemical industries, a highly developed marketing system, and government institutions to generate and disseminate knowledge, develop new inputs, regulate markets, absorb risk, subsidize capital, limit the distributional effects of adjustments, and control environmental and health impacts. The various sociosystem elements in part evolved in reaction to the ecosystem's responses to human activities. While monocultural systems brought increasing returns to scale with mechanization, their instability and the increased risk borne by a farmer with a single crop encouraged the use of agrochemicals and risk-spreading institutions. Similarly, ecosystem responses to agrochemicals led to new institutions to regulate pesticides and water pollution as well as to new research programs in agricultural experiment stations. Equally important, the institutional responses typically encouraged further changes in similar directions. Crop insurance and regulated markets, for example, reduce the risks of monocultural production and make it more attractive. Today's agricultural systems have soil features, weed dynamics, and insect-crop interactions that reflect coevolution with the sociosystem, while today's agricultural institutions reflect the vulnerability of disturbed soil to wind and water erosion, the adaptations of insect populations to chemical control, and the susceptibility of monocultural systems to variations in weather.

Western agriculture was transformed by factor augmentation, by increasing the rate of use of separate factors of production. The most significant change was in the use of purchased inputs produced from stock resources. The ecological system responded to this change, initiating a coevolutionary response with the social system that continues today. Coevolutionary development, however, was not being realized. Coevolutionary processes have unveiled the negative aspects of stock-exploitive technologies or, at best, offset the negative effects. To improve upon the past, we need a better understanding of the nature of coevolutionary potential.

## II. THE NATURE OF COEVOLUTIONARY POTENTIAL

> . . . life is a member of the class of phenomena which are open or continuous systems able to decrease their internal entropy at the expense of substances or free energy taken in from the environment and subsequently rejected in a degraded form. (J. E. Lovelock 1979, p. 4)

Since the beginnings of agriculture until the significant use of stock resources a little more than a century ago, the human population has doubled more than eight times. This growth can most easily be explained as the result of a process of capturing coevolutionary potential. During the past century, increases in population and economic well-being primarily came from the augmentation of factors of production—physical capital accumulated, the quality of the labor force improved, and stock resources were exploited at much higher rates. While social and ecological systems coevolved, growth came through an increased flow of imputs. In this increased flow, stock resources played a new and proportionately larger role. Though the rate of population doubling increased dramatically with the significant exploitation of stock resources, it has doubled less than twice.[3] Seven millenia of coevolutionary agricultural development and a longer, earlier history of progress in hunting and gathering, provides empirical testimony that outweighs the record of factor-augmented growth by at least seventy centuries to only somewhat more than one.

Coevolutionary potential stems from two phenomena which form the major premises of the coevolutionary development argument. First, evolution has been a negentropic process. Planet Earth, at least with respect to human needs, has acquired a better order through evolution. Second, knowledge and the ability to learn have been incorporated in the perceptual systems of individuals and the cultural systems of societies through evolutionary processes including natural selection. Since these phenomena are described in parts of the natural science literature rarely cited in the economics literature, they will be developed in some detail. A third premise, that additional coevolutionary potential still exists, is also key to the argument.

From a perspective limited to people and Planet Earth, evolution has been a negentropic process.[4] Four and a half billion years ago, Earth did not have the order that allows us to exist today. Whether by chance or by design, life somehow started. Gradually life transformed its own environment. The nitrogen molecules in the atmosphere are a product of the early anaerobic life forms while oxygen molecules are largely a product of later net plant growth. By evolutionary and coevolutionary processes, various species evolved to

[3] This characterization and temporal division of our past economic development is simplistic both for emphasis and due to space limitations. The calculations are based on a world population of about 5 million when agriculture began some 5,000 to 10,000 years ago, a population of about 1.6 billion in 1880, and a population of some 4.5 billion now (Grigg 1974). Other estimates still confirm that there have been many more doublings through coevolutionary development than through stock-exploitive development.

[4] The second law of thermodynamics can be stated in a variety of interrelated ways. One is that all physical processes (or work) reduce the availability of energy for further work. Another is that concentrations (of anything) tend to disperse, structure tends to disappear, order becomes disorder. These and other definitions are presented in lay terms in Ehrlich, Ehrlich, and Holdren (1977, p. 33–35).

form the highly diverse and complex ecosystems of today. The oxygen we breathe, the plants and animals we eat, and the hydrocarbons we tap to fuel our industries are products of biological processes. Even the ordering of minerals improved for us over eons by various physical processes stemming from solar energy and the gradual cooling of the earth. From a human perspective, entropy on Planet Earth has decreased.[5]

Evolution has not defied the second law of thermodynamics. The increase in order and in the availability of energy is only a local phenomenon. Plants have captured some of the sun's energy and, with the assistance of other organisms, used it to create certain forms of order that happen to be beneficial to people. But energy in the solar system overall is dissipating, proceeding from potential to kinetic, still becoming less and less available. The sun will die in perhaps another 4 and a half billion years, but for now and the forseeable future, life is capturing more of the sun's energy in a form that is more beneficial for us than it was in the beginning.[6]

Though it is obvious that Earth has a superior order now, misinterpretations of the second law of thermodynamics have masked this reality.[7] Life maintains order, not in spite of the laws of entropy, but because of DNA and the energy that plant life captures from the sun. From simple amoebae to complex vertabrates, life is a process of maintaining order, of maintaining the processes of life and the characteristics of particular species. This order is encoded as information in the arrangement of the bases of DNA molecules.[8] Single-celled organisms and tissue cells in higher organisms replicate by a process whereby paired chains in the DNA molecule split, reform they paired parts, and provide the information necessary for reconstructing the characteristics of new cells. Individual cells form and die, but the cell's order lives on and the orderly life processes provided by each cell type continue. Similarly, individuals die but species can live on through sexual reproduction.

Order, however, is not simply maintained. The diverse gene pools of each species are constantly subjected to the selective pressures of changing physical and biological factors. In addition, mutations occur through imperfect DNA replication and DNA damage. A small proportion of mutations facilitate the functioning of the organism in its environment

---

[5] The idea that the earth was unusually well-suited for life to evolve and that evolution further favored humar life was first explored by Henderson (1913). We have here the tautest of tautologies. Detail after detail can be listed and described as to how the environment is uniquely suited to people. Humans as we know ourselves, of course, would not be here if the environment were not the way it is, for we evolved with the environment. Lovelock (1979) and Jantsch (1980) have recently developed the argument that, while chance has played an important role, evolution has largely occurred within a global system with numerous, intricate, self-regulating mechanisms which have buffered change and kept evolution from "spinning out" on a destructive course. Dyson (1979, pp. 245–53) also acknowledges this possibility. Kamshilov (1976) presents a distinctly Soviet view on the orderliness of evolution, society's current disruptive role, and the challenge of living with and ultimately directing the evolution of the biosphere. The idea that evolution favors human survival was well-developed by Thomas Huxley and Herbert Spencer and to some extent by Darwin himself (Greene 1981). The idea is sustained in the writings of Julian Huxley (Greene 1981) and Teilhard de Chardin (1959). Recently, Peter Corning (1983) has given a new impetus to this tradition. Most evolutionists today follow what they claim to be the true Darwinian tradition and are content with the combination of deterministic, endogenous biological responses to exogenous environmental changes as an explanation for the course of evolution (Gould 1980 and 1982).

[6] Blum (1968) presents a thorough discussion of evolution and entropy. See also: Boulding (1981, ch. 5) or Schrodinger (1944, ch. 6).

[7] Georgescu-Roegen (1971), for example, acknowledges the incredible energy and long life of our sun and its importance to economic well-being over the long run. His references to biological processes and evolution (ch. 8), however, are limited to the directionality of life for the individual of a species and the irreversibility of biological processes. He associates these phenomena with the directionality and irreversibility of the second law rather than seeing them as characteristics of biological processes. Rifkin's (1980) popularization of the importance of entropy makes similar errors by analogy.

[8] Gatlin (1972) has written on the nature of the encoding, the amount of information that can be encoded, and how different forms of encoding can enhance replication or allow the development of more information (complexity). Social scientists might better initiate their introduction to this material with the summaries by Boulding (1978, ch. 5), Dunn (1970, ch. 2), or Schrodinger (1944, ch. 2 and 3) and then take up a text such as Ayala and Valentine (1979).

and, in turn, change the biotic selective pressures on other species. Evolution necessarily went from the simple to the more complex, but how ecosystems developed such a multitude of different and diversely interdependent species remains a mystery.

Animals, even amoebae, learn.[9] The sensory systems of even the most simple animals enable them to recognize different stimuli. Similarly, the brains of even the less developed species deduce cause and effect and extrapolate experience to new situations. Western thought has emphasized formal learning and neglected the innate. This has led to the view of past evolution as a chance process. Quite the contrary, learning, knowledge, and evolution have been intertwined from somewhere near the beginning. This means that the fitness of animal species, especially the vertebrates, is partly related to the correctness of their perceptions as to the nature of reality and to their ability to learn. To some extent, reality has coevolved with perceptions of reality.[10]

Animals not only learn but learn together. Ants, wolves, and humans have learned—in very different ways—to live in social groups. The survival of individuals and of the species now depends on their social behavior. In some cases social roles have become genetically encoded, while in others culture is the sole repository. Cultures evolve through random change, deliberate trial, error, and learning, and through natural selection. Cultural adaptations survive if they make the culture more fit. Information with considerable survival value becomes incorporated in culture in ways which individuals do not understand or even perceive. The new sociobiology literature uses a coevolutionary framework to describe how cultural adaptations have influenced genetic selection while genetic factors have, in turn, influenced cultural selection. Looking at the world this way, it is futile to distinguish between natural and cultural factors for over time they have become hopelessly intertwined.

Agriculture has long relied on cultural knowledge for ecosystem management through shifting the mix of species. Deliberate planting and watering, hand weeding, plowing, flooding, and burning are direct means of favoring productive species, reducing the competition for nutrients by "weeds," and nurturing species that complement each other. Plants complement one another by providing shade, by having associated soil microorganisms that fix nitrogen or help other plants absorb mineral nutrients, and by hosting predators of other plant's pests. The optimal management of interacting species in an ecosystem can be compared with the optimal

---

[9] With this paragraph we enter into the controversial realm of sociobiology. The initial forays into the intersection of social and biological science by Lorenz (1966) and Wilson (1975) were repelled by arguments from both social and biological scientists (see the readings edited by Caplan 1978). Neither Lorenz's nor Wilson's initial genetic explanations of social behavior formally acknowledged the roles of perception, learning, conscious decision-making, and culture in the evolution of behavior. Both authors quickly remedied these deficiencies. Lorenz (1973) produced an informal synthesis of genetic and cultural evolution that emphasized perception and learning and the broader philosophical significance of the synthesis itself. Lumsden and Wilson (1981) developed vastly superior formal models that integrate genetic and cultural evolution and the roles of perception systems and the mind. Numerous others also saw the explanatory potential of integrating genetic and cultural evolution and attempted models of various forms and degrees of mathematical formality (Cavalli-Sforza and Feldman 1981; Durham 1976 and 1978; Jantsch 1980; Pulliam and Dunford 1980, and many others that I have not read). Given the level of generality of the presentation in this paper, the differences between the various syntheses are relatively unimportant. A key outcome of all of the integrations is that genetic (both individual and group) and cultural selection are inseparable, for each is constantly influencing the other. Both types of selection are "natural." Durham and later Lumsden and Wilson use the term "coevolution" to emphasize the inseparability of the process.

[10] This characterization of knowledge contrasts with the conventional wisdom stemming from centuries of Western philosophy and science that the mind can be thought of as a computer microchip, that the sensory systems provide means of entering data, and that science is the software that gives thinking its starting point, logical pattern, and direction. The characterization presented here cuts through the "mind-body problem," eliminates issues of subjective vs. objective, and accepts the limitations and effects of the instruments of perception (Lorenz 1973). Each of these have puzzled Western philosophers heretofore because they lack an evolutionary epistemology. This characterization also accounts for the isomorphisms between biological and social systems noted by Boulding and Dunn.

control of nonmarket effects in an economic system (Tullock 1971).

People have been affecting, and been affected by, their environment for some time, up to three and a half million years. Agroecosystem management has indirectly influenced the course of evolution for organisms with rapid regeneration times, from microorganisms to insects. Simultaneously, people have directly selected individuals within populations of species—from corn to cows—for reproduction based on preferred characteristics. Both agroecosystem management and deliberate selective pressure have been culturally learned and reinforced. Individuals learn selection and management techniques from others. Society maintains and allocates shared resources including fields and water. Appropriate behavior is enforced. Cultural ecologists have shown for traditional societies how values, kinship, customs, rituals, and taboos are related to the maintenance of an interaction with an ecosystem.[11] To a large extent culture also guides modern agricultural societies, but modernization has entailed a continual substitution of formal institutions and objective knowledge for culture and cultural knowledge as we commonly think of them.

Modernization of agriculture in Third World countries has emphasized factor augmentation through new inputs and training for farmers. The cultural knowledge and traditional agroecosystems that evolved over centuries have not only been ignored but destroyed. Lacking a philosophy and science of development that incorporates coevolutionary processes, we have given insufficient respect to the importance of building on or learning from how ecological and social systems have interacted and affected each other in the past. Agroecology has emerged recently as a new field through the work of plant and insect ecologists interested in agricultural development. Agroecologists think of agriculture as a process of ecosystem management. They learn about ecological systems by studying how traditional farming systems have coevolved. Traditional farming systems represent a resource of coevolutionary knowledge which can be augmented with scientific knowledge and which, to some extent, can be used to improve the sustainability, productivity, and stability of modern agricultural systems.[12]

Coevolutionary development potential is far from exhausted. The existing favorable ecological order is sustained through the photosynthesis of only 0.25% of the sun's energy that strikes the land surface. Even modern cornfields only capture 2% while up to 13% could be captured through photosynthesis.[13] The long-run potential for DNA to provide more order is enormous.[14] Neither ecological nor social systems are static, and cultural learning is still taking place.

The existence of coevolutionary potential is certain. There is the historical record itself—seven millenia of coevolutionary agricultural development and a longer, earlier history of progress in hunting and gathering. How this potential might be captured and what kind of future coevolutionary development might hold is unclear. Coevolutionary development may be limited to food, clothing, shelter, and health. Skyscrapers, high-speed, long-distance travel, and similar products might only be possible through the use of

[11] One reason I have avoided defining the objectives of development and the sorts of development that "benefit" people (see footnote 1) is that values are endogenously determined. Shifts in values have been critical in the past to the coevolution of social and ecological systems. Harris (1979), Netting (1977), and Rappaport (1968) are good examples of the cultural ecology literature. A review of how values have affected and have been affected by recent development experiences in Asia can be found in Lasswell, Lerner, and Montgomery (1976).

[12] See for example, Gliessman, Garcia, and Amador (1981), Chacon and Gliessman (1982), and Altierri, Letourneau, and Davis (1982).

[13] The 0.25% and 2% figures come from Eugene Odum (1971, ch. 3). The 13% figure comes from Anderson (1979, ch. 6).

[14] Gatlin (1972, p. 4) notes that the DNA chains of the higher plants and animals can encode about ten to the power of 54 pieces of information. Ayala and Valentine (1979, p. 81–82) note that man, who is heterozygous at but about 6.7% of 100,000 gene loci, can potentially produce 10 to the power of 2017 genetically different offspring, not counting the potential for change through mutation. Geneticist Alan Larson has pointed out that these estimates are based on electrophoretically detected protein variation which results in a gross underestimate of the total variation (personal communication). The number of atoms in the known universe is thought to be but 10 to the power of 70.

stock resources. On the other hand, inner-city ghettos, the destruction of indigenous cultures, and nuclear holocaust might also be avoided along a coevolutionary development path. Needless to say, the future along either path is uncertain.

Due to the fragmentation of knowledge in science today, scientists and laypeople alike can neither significantly question our current development path nor conceive of a significantly different path. Our society's emphasis on atomistic and mechanistic thinking makes it difficult to comprehend, let alone capture, coevolutionary development potential. Even if systems and evolutionary thinking were much better developed, coevolutionary potential can only be captured slowly. Society will make the transition to this slower rate of growth only through a better understanding of the costs and limits of stock-exploitive growth.

## III. STOCK-RESOURCE EXPLOITATION IN A COEVOLUTIONARY WORLD

During the last century, increases in population and in economic well-being have primarily come from stock-resource exploitation. The potential for this growth was inherent in our ability to discover and adopt new technologies. But Georgescu-Roegen has shown that most technological change simply allows us to exploit low-entropy resources faster and thereby transform the favorable order of the natural world into a homogeneous garbage dump sooner. He correctly critiques increases in well-being that come strictly through augmenting factors of production. Current stock-exploitive growth necessarily comes at the expense of future generations.[15]

Increasing entropy seems first and most noticeably to be taking an institutional toll. Resources do not simply run out or even necessarily become "physically," in an on-site production sense, more difficult to extract. Ever more sophisticated technology to exploit increasingly intractable stock resources, however, requires continuous improvements in human skills and organization. In 1870 about 0.25% of the population of the United States between 18 and 65 years of age was enrolled in higher education. Some were there learning to develop and utilize new technologies. In 1920 almost 1% of the working-age population was investing in higher education rather than working. This proportion rose to 6.2% by 1970 and 9.7% by 1980. In addition, a larger proportion of the students were acquiring knowledge for the development and maintenance of technologies and institutions. This dramatic increase is representative of other changes in our society. Research and development have become substantial sectors in the economy. Private and public bureaucracies have arisen to capture the economic gains and minimize the social and environmental side effects of new technologies.

The social transformations necessary for the advance and use of stock-exploitive technologies have limits. The costs of education, the productivity of our research and development efforts, and the size and effectiveness of our bureaucracies are frequently identified as the major factors limiting economic advance today. A simple extrapolation of higher education attendance documents these limits. At current rates of increase, 100% of the working-age population will be attending school all the time by the year 2063 (Norgaard 1983). These transformations have one thing in common. The rapid increases in the demand for education, research and development, and bureaucratic organization and operation are all based on Western science. In this sense, we are experiencing the limits of objective knowledge.

These limits can be expressed in coevolutionary terms. In the neoclassical view, the costs of exploiting a stock resource are the discounted net gains of exploiting the resource later. From the coevolutionary vantage, this is an underestimate of the costs for at least two reasons.

[15] Georgescu-Roegen bridged the gap, albeit imperfectly, as indicated in footnote 7, between economics and thermodynamics but was unable to convince economists of the significance of the second law. Indeed, more controversy than enlightenment ensued and the bridge is rarely traversed. Georgescu-Roegen (1975) and Herman Daly (1983) document numerous instances where economic arguments defy the second law. The best resolutions of the controversies—or improvements in the bridge—have been made by Burness, Cummings, Morris, and Paik (1980).

First, stock resources can be used to initiate or assist coevolutionary development. This option may prove especially valuable within a social and ecological interaction that is not generating a surplus at the time but none the less has further coevolutionary potential. From the neoclassical perspective, this can be thought of as an opportunity cost of using a stock resource for exploitive development now rather than waiting to use it to initiate or guide coevolutionary development later. This cost might be expressed as a probability-weighted sum of the discounted higher costs using other resources for reaching alternative social and ecological system interactions and the discounted value of any interactions foregone. From the coevolutionary vantage, it is not clear what interest rates are or how to predict the nature, let alone the probabilities, of future interactions.

The second user cost is probably more significant but is no easier to quantify. Both the social and the ecological systems evolve during stock exploitation. But this evolution is not coevolutionary. Each system evolves not strictly in response to the other system but in response to the exploitation of stock resources. The two systems become "wedged" apart relative to a coevolutionary interaction.[16] After stocks are exhausted, it is unlikely that the ecological and social systems would be in a position for subsequent coevolutionary interaction. Ecologists warn us of the potential consequences of species extinction and irreversible ecosystem transformations (Dasmann et al. 1973; Ehrlich and Ehrlich 1981; Farvar and Milton 1972; Myers 1979). Social systems suffer from similar transformations. Nearly a decade after the OPEC embargo, institutions in both the developed and developing countries are still changing, at great cost, to complement the new relative prices for energy-related goods and services. In the United States the tendency to switch to other stock resources such as coal and oil shale rather than to flow resources used in the past such as solar and wind power is probably better explained by the extinction of appropriate institutions and the compatibility of current institutions than by relative costs in a narrower technological sense. In Alaska, the Middle East, and other areas with oil, social institutions, fed by oil revenues, are evolving largely independently of whether they assist in the development of a sustainable social and ecological interaction.

Both coevolutionary and stock-exploitive development paths take social and ecological systems to states from which other development paths may be difficult or impossible to reach and follow. Some paths presumably retain more options and flexibility; they eliminate fewer options and allow changes at lower cost. Coevolutionary development paths may retain more options in addition to the fact that they retain stock-resource exploitation options. Certainly, given the limits imposed by the second law of thermodynamics on factor-augmenting growth, staying on a coevolutionary path avoids the transition costs of finding and converting to such a path after stock resources have been depleted.

Economic thought typically stems from and reinforces real-world institutions. There is good reason to believe that stock resources are overexploited because current economic thought and social institutions ignore coevolutionary potential and coevolutionary user costs. These additional user costs include (1) the losses associated with not being able to use stock resources for later investment in coevolution, and (2) the losses associated with returning to and/or accepting a less advantageous coevolutionary path after the stock resource is depleted. Ignoring coevolutionary user costs results in an overuse of stock resources.

Looking at resource allocation in a broader economic context, ignoring coevolutionary user costs distorts the relative costs of factors and prices of products. Skills associated with stock-resource exploitation are overvalued relative to skills associated with environmental management. Stock-resource-

[16] Ellul (1954) and Winner (1977) coincidentally describe the rise of a technological-based social organization and the autonomy of technology in the same time frame as the rise of stock-resource exploitive development. Their analyses likewise emphasize the simultaneous decline of natural philosophy and cultural systems based on relations to the land.

intensive products are underpriced relative to labor and other flow-resource-intensive products. Research effort is overallocated to exploitation technologies relative to environmental management technologies. If a coevolutionary view of development had been adopted along with other views, our economy would probably be significantly different and less precarious.

## V. TEN CONCLUDING COMMENTS

A broad array of ideas new to economics have been related in this paper. Though a major objective of the paper has been to stress interactive relationships, I will conclude with an itemized list of important points.

First, the neoclassical view of economic development as a process of augmenting factors of production stems from the basic assumption that factors are separable. Atomism has a long history in philosophy and the physical sciences. The benefits of modern technology stem from the scientific advances based on the atomistic assumption, but the social and environmental costs of modern technology can also be attributed to this view of the world. A different and historically antecedent view contends that human welfare and tenure on earth depends on the maintenance of a harmonious relationship with the natural world. This perspective is grounded morally in many religions and has been developed further by philosopher-naturalists. Formal knowledge about ecology and evolution during the past century has provided an increasingly strong scientific foundation for this perspective. Far more than the atomistic-mechanistic world view, the harmony-with-nature world view has provided much of the philosophical and scientific bases for the conservation and environmental movements and for the resulting resource and environmental policies.

Second, the coevolutionary, or harmony-with-nature, development process has an underlying scientific basis. Plants that capture more of the energy from the sun have an advantage. Plants and animals that establish viable relationships with each other also have an advantage. The DNA encoding of these roles is not replicated perfectly. Nature keeps rolling the dice and some new adaptations survive while, in turn, new adaptations put new biotic pressures on other species. New adaptations for animals include the ability to perceive, interpret, and learn. Fitting well has become a conscious process. And for many species—but especially for humans—perceiving, interpreting, and learning is a social as well as an individual process that influences and is influenced by the nature of the collective consciousness.

And this is the third important conclusion. As one of the social species, our survival depends on the appropriateness of our social consciousness of our relationship to the environment. Value systems, institutions, and specific technologies evolve in the context of the overall consciousness, in the context of how we predict ecosystem responses and interpret our ecological options.

Fourth, we are not experiencing coevolutionary development through the realization of coevolutionary potential. Knowledge, institutions, and even tastes have evolved during the past century around atomistic and mechanistic paradigms rather than evolutionary paradigms. The transformation and management of ecosystems based on prescriptions from atomistic and mechanistic paradigms leads to immediate quantifiable gains to identifiable factors of production. These initial gains, however, have repeatedly been followed by costly consequences for social and ecological systems. These consequences have necessitated additional corrective social changes and bureaucratic developments that would not have been necessary if the initial changes had been designed with a coevolutionary paradigm in mind.

Fifth, the coevolutionary perspective gives a better picture of the nature of the social and ecological problems that accompany the factor-augmentation approach to development. From this vantage, stock-resource exploitive development appears to be driving a wedge between the social and ecological systems such that they no longer respond directly to each other. Each system responds first to phenomena of stock-resource exploitation. The social system responds to the ecological system only because of the detrimental ecological response to stock exploitation. Similarly, the ecological system responds to changes in the social system from stock-resource exploitation. The coevolutionary feedback system has been blocked and rerouted; the prospects for coevolutionary development in the future have diminished.

Sixth, the coevolutionary vantage highlights the uncertainty of the future. Possible courses of coevolution are unknown. Not only do new components and interactions evolve over time, but the rules of evolution themselves evolve. The ability to predict consequences, supposedly the true test of a science, is not a strength of evolutionary paradigms. The real uncertainty of the future does not increase as we shift from an atomistic-mechanistic world view to a coevolutionary view. Indeed, to the extent that the coevolutionary perspective leads to more realistic reactions to new conditions, uncertainty should decrease.

Seventh, it is difficult to imagine how we will continue to work with ecological and economic thought from here and return to a coevolutionary path, optimally combine the two perspectives on development, or use the coevolutionary perspective to foresee and plan for the coevolutionary ramifications of the neoclassical approach to development. Specifically, it is difficult to imagine institutional changes that would ensure that coevolutionary user costs be reflected in economic decisions. It seems unlikely that these costs can be neatly accounted for in property rights, liability rules, procedural rules, or new bureaucratic structures. Current institutions presume a certain amount of certainty and separability. Property rights, as well as other institutions, are established and maintained on the premise that actions have limited effect on definable components and that these effects do not change over time. The gains from taking a coevolutionary world view probably will be more easily captured through the development of ecological and evolutionary philosophies, land ethics, and social pressure than through legislation; through a clear move away from formal analysis and prediction toward the use of cultural knowledge; and through a move away from large, formal, centralized, inertia-bound bureaucracies toward smaller, regional institutions. These thoughts, however, are the beginnings of yet another paper.

Eighth, the paper provides a link between economic and ecological paradigms. A grand synthesis is not the intention but rather an appeal for theoretical pluralism. Receptivity to alternative vantages on reality facilitates new insights and exposes old myths, enriching both economics and ecology.

Ninth, the coevolutionary development paradigm provides a new perspective on environmental and cultural transformation. New arguments for change and preservation cut across the existing divisions and promise to redefine environmentalists and developers, stock-resource optimists and pessimists, and cultural libertarians, protectionists, and reformers. Over the past decade, these factions have entered into a costly stalemate and have established permanent fronts. A redrawing of the lines and redefinition of the interests could prove very productive in the future.

Tenth, all models evolve in response to particular questions. In turn, the questions one chooses to pursue, especially in the social sciences, are linked to premises about the nature and state of the world. The classical economic model evolved more than one and a half centuries ago to explore markets and the relation of individual economic actors and the state at a time when feudalism was giving way to capitalism. With the virtual acceptance of capitalism, the neoclassical model began to focus nearly a century ago on justifying the efficiency per se of market transactions. The assumptions of the neoclassical model are adequate for such a narrow focus. Few people today doubt the efficiency of the market except with respect to environmental management and intertemporal natural resource allocation. One of the major issues of the latter half of this century is whether and how development might be sustained. The assumptions of the neoclassical model are inappropriate for these questions. The coevolutionary model incorporates relationships between people and their environments based on recent advances in natural science and experience with modern social systems. The model is thereby more appropriate for exploring relationships between resources, environmental systems, and social systems over the long run.

### References

Altieri, Miquel A.; Letourneau, Deborah K.; and Davis, James R. 1982. "Developing Sustainable Agroecosystems." *Bio-Science.*

Anderson, Russell E. 1979. *Biological Paths to Energy Self-Reliance.* New York: Van Nostrand Reinhold Company.

Ayala, Francisco, and Valentine, James. 1979. *Evolving: The Theory and Process of Organic Evolution.* Menlo Park, Calif.: Benjamin/ Cummings Publishing.

Baker, Herbert G., and Hurd, Paul D. 1968. "Intrafloral Ecology." *Annual Review of Entomology* 13:385–414.

Bertalanffy, Ludwig von. 1968. *General System Theory.* New York: George Braziller.

Blum, Harold F. 1968. *Time's Arrow and Evolution.* Princeton: Princeton University Press.

Boserup, Ester. 1965. *The Conditions of Agricultural Growth: The Economics of Agrarian Change under Population Pressure.* Chicago: Aldine.

———. 1981. *Population and Technological Change: A Study of Long Term Trends.* Chicago: University of Chicago Press.

Boulding, Kenneth E. 1978. *Ecodynamics: A New Theory of Societal Evolution.* Beverly Hills, Calif.: Sage Publications.

———. 1981. *Evolutionary Economics.* Beverly Hills, Calif.: Sage Publications.

Brinkman, Richard L. 1980. "Mankind at the Starting Point." *Journal of Economic Issues* XIV (June):567–82.

Burness, Stuart; Cummings, Ronald; Morris, Glenn; and Paik, Inja. 1980. "Thermodynamic and Economic Concepts as Related to Resource Use Policies." *Land Economics* 55 (Feb.):1–9.

Caplan, Arthur L. ed. 1978. *The Sociobiology Debate.* New York: Harper and Row.

Cavalli-Sforza, L. L., and Feldman, M. W. 1981. *Cultural Transmission and Evolution.* Princeton: Princeton University Press.

Chacon, J. C., and Gliessman, S. R. 1982. "Use of the 'Non-Weed' Concept in Traditional Tropical Agroecosystems of South-Eastern Mexico." *Agro-Ecosystems* 8.

Corning, Peter A. 1983. *The Synergism Hypothesis: A Theory of Progressive Evolution.* New York: McGraw-Hill.

Daly, Herman. 1983. "The Circular Flow of Exchange Value and the Linear Throughput of Matter-Energy: A Case of Misplaced Concreteness." Manuscript in draft.

———, ed. 1974. *Toward A Steady-State Economy.* San Francisco: W. H. Freeman.

———, ed. 1980. *Economics, Ecology, and Ethics.* San Francisco: W. H. Freeman.

Dasmann, Raymond F.; Milton, John P.; and Freeman, Peter H. 1973. *Ecological Principles for Economic Development.* New York: John Wiley and Sons.

Dunn, Edgar S., Jr. 1971. *Economic and Social Development: A Process of Social Learning.* Baltimore: The Johns Hopkins University Press.

Durham, William H. 1976. "The Adaptive Significance of Cultural Behavior." *Human Ecology* 4 (2):89–121.

———. 1978. "Toward a Coevolutionary Theory of Human Biology and Culture." In *The Sociobiology Debate,* Arthur L. Caplan ed. New York: Harper and Row.

Dyson, Freeman. 1979. *Disturbing the Universe.* New York: Harper and Row.

Ehrlich, Paul R., and Ehrlich, Anne. 1981. *Extinction: The Causes and Consequences of the Disappearance of Species.* New York: Random House.

———; ———; and Holdren, John P. 1977. *Ecoscience: Population, Resources, Environment.* San Francisco: W. H. Freeman.

———, and Raven, Peter H. 1964. "Butterflies and Plants: A Study of Coevolution." *Evolution* 18:586–608.

Ellul, Jacques. 1954. *La Technique.* Paris: Armand Colin. (Translated by John Wilkinson and published as *The Technological Society.* New York: Random House, 1964.)

Farvar, M. T., and Milton, John P. eds. 1972. *The Careless Technology: Ecology and International Development.* New York: Natural History Press.

Gatlin, Lila L. 1972. *Information Theory and the Living System.* New York: Columbia University Press.

Geertz, Clifford. 1963. *Agricultural Involution: The Processes of Ecological Change in Indonesia.* Berkeley: University of California Press.

Georgescu-Roegen, Nicholas. 1971. *The Entropy Law and the Economic Process.* Cambridge, Mass.: Harvard University Press.

———. 1975. "Energy and Economic Myths." *Southern Economic Journal* 41(3):347–381.

Gliessman, S. R., and Amador, A. M. 1980. "Ecological Aspects of Production in Traditional Agroecosystems in the Humid Lowland Tropics of Mexico." *Tropical Ecology and Development.*

———; Garcia, R.; and Amador, A. M. 1981. "The Ecological Basis for the Application of Traditional Agricultural Technology in the Management of Tropical Agro-Ecosystems." *Agro-Ecosystems* 7:173–85.

Gould, Stephen J. 1982. "Darwinism and the Expansion of Evolutionary Theory." *Science* 216 (Apr. 23):380–7.

———. 1980. "Is a New General Theory of Evolution Emerging?" *Paleobiology* 6(1):119–30.

Goulet, Denis. 1971. *The Cruel Choice: A New Concept in the Theory of Economic Development.* New York: Athenem.

———. 1977. *The Uncertain Promise: Value Conflicts in Technology Transfer.* New York: IDOC/North America.

Greene, John C. *Science, Ideology, and World View.* Berkeley: University of California Press.

Grigg, D. B. 1974. *The Agricultural Systems of the World: An Evolutionary Approach.* Cambridge: Cambridge University Press.

Harris, Marvin. 1979. *Cultural Mate ialism: The Struggle for a Science of Culture.* New York: Random House.

Heilbroner, Robert L. 1980. *An Inquiry into the Human Prospect.* New York: W. W. Norton and Company.

Henderson, Lawrence J. 1913. *The Fitness of the Environment.* New York: Macmillan and Company.

Jantsch, Erich. 1980. *The Self-Organizing Universe: Scientific and Human Implications of the Emerging Paradigm of Evolution.* Oxford: Pergamon Press.

Kamishlov, M. M. 1974. *Evolution of the Biosphere.* Moscow: MIR Publishers. (Translated by Minna Brodskaya and published in English in 1976.)

Kapp, K. William. 1950. *The Social Costs of Private Enterprise.* Cambridge, Mass.: Harvard University Press.

Lasswell, Harold; Lerner, Daniel; and Montgomery, John D. 1976. *Values and Development: Appraising Asian Experience.* Cambridge, Mass.: The MIT Press.

Lorenz, Konrad. 1966. *On Aggression.* New York: Harcourt Brace Jovanovich.

———. 1977. *Behind The Mirror: A Search for a Natural History of Knowledge.* New York: Harcourt Brace Jovanovich. (Originally published in German in 1973 by R. Piper and Company Verlag.)

Lovelock, J. E. 1979. *Gaia: A New Look at Life on Earth.* Oxford: Oxford University Press.

Lumsden, Charles J., and Wilson, Edward O. 1981. *Genes, Mind, and Culture: Coevolutionary Process.* Cambridge, Mass.: Harvard University Press.

Myers, Norman. 1979. *The Sinking Ark.* New York: Pergamon Press.

Netting, Robert McC. 1977. *Cultural Ecology.* Menlo Park, Calif.: Cummings Publishing Co.

Norgaard, Richard B. 1984. "Coevolutionary Agricultural Development." Forthcoming in *Journal of Economic Development and Cultural Change.* (Jan.). (Also available as Giannini Foundation. University of California. Working Paper No. 163.)

———. 1983. "Resource Scarcity and the Sociology of Economics." Draft manuscript available from author.

———. 1982. "Resource Economics and Development Economics: Synthesis or Reformulation?" Center for Resource Policy Studies. University of Wisconsin. Working Paper 19. (Also available as Giannini Foundation, University of California. Working Paper No. 203.)

———. 1981. "Sociosystem and Ecosystem Coevolution in the Amazon." *Journal of Environmental and Economic Management* 8 (Sept.):238–54.

Odum, Eugene P. 1969. "The Strategy of Ecosystem Development." *Science* 164 (Apr. 18):262–70.

———. 1971. *Fundamentals of Ecology,* 3rd Edition. Philadelphia: W. B. Saunders.

Odum, Howard T. 1971. *Environment, Power, and Society.* New York: Wiley.

———, and Pigeon, R. F., eds. 1970. "A Tropical Rainforest. A Study of Irradiation and Ecology at El Verde, Puerto Rico." Washington, D. C. National Technical Information Service.

Pulliam, H. Ronald, and Dunford, Christopher 1980. *Programmed to Learn: An Essay on the Evolution of Culture.* New York: Columbia University Press.

Rappaport, Roy A. 1968. *Pigs for the Ancestors: Ritual in the Ecology of a New Guinea People.* New Haven, Conn.: Yale University Press.

Rifkin, Jeremy. 1980. *Entropy: A New World View.* New York: Viking Press.

Schrodinger, Erwin. 1944. *What is Life?* Cambridge: Cambridge University Press.

Steward, Julian H. 1968. "Cultural Ecology." In *International Encyclopedia of the Social Sciences,* David L. Sills (ed). 4:337–44. New

York: Macmillan.

———. 1977. *Evolution and Ecology: Essays on Social Transformation,* eds. Jane C. Steward and Robert F. Murphy. Urbana: University of Illinois Press.

Teilhard de Chardin, Pierre. 1959. *The Future of Man.* (Translated by Norman Denny. New York: Harper and Row, 1964.)

Tullock, Gordon. 1971. "Biological Externalities." *Journal of Theoretical Biology* 33:565–76.

von Ciriacy-Wantrup, S. 1963. *Resource Conservation: Economics and Policies.* Berkeley: University of California, Division of Agricultural Sciences.

Wilson, Edward O. 1975. *Sociobiology: The New Synthesis.* Cambridge, Mass.: Harvard University Press.

Winner, Langdon. 1977. *Autonomous Technology: Technics-Out-Of-Control As a Theme in Political Thought.* Cambridge, Mass.: The MIT Press.

118-35

[97]

(5)

# [7]

# Linking Pollution and Macroeconomic Variables: An Indonesian Example

Iwan J. Azis

Q25

O13

O11

Increasingly, environmental issues have become an integral part of economic planning and decision-making in many countries. The consensus seems to suggest that the solution approach would be to internalize the externalities, since many of the environment-cum-economic issues involve problems of externalities. There seems to be little disputes about the need to apply monetary prices for environmental resources, for example, air, river water and so on, which, as often practised, have always been exploited without real monetary costs (market imperfection). Another case often found is the failure to assign some prices or costs on pollution, which is frequently considered a 'bad' outputs. Even if costs are incurred, more often than not these are far below the optimal level, creating a divergence between private and social returns.

Incorporating a pollution charge will imply, on the other hand, higher costs, which may also mean greater inefficiency for the economy. This applies to cases in which incorporating pollution into economic calculation is done either through a preventive act (for example, operating pollution-reducing equipment), or by incurring a special tax that corresponds to the pollution emitted. While some complications related to technological constraints may be involved in the first case, likely to increase the costs even further, the tax solution is often considered to be more practical and less costly. Even in a typical developing country with a considerable scale of (inefficient) administrative bureaucracy, taxing the polluters would still seem to be more feasible and has higher degree of effectiveness than imposing a certain standard on producing sectors across the board.

There remain, however, questions regarding the level of pollution that society can tolerate, based upon which the size of cleaning-up activities can be determined which may be financed at least partially by pollution taxes. There is then a question of who would be in charge of the pollution clean-up, private or public sectors? Policy-makers are also bound to determine the appropriate (optimal) pollution tax rate, based upon which the internal mechanism of the economy will generate maximum social welfare measured by some utility functions. But perhaps most important of all, along with increased awareness about environmental problems, policy-makers in many developing countries are often still in need of a more concrete understanding of the intricate mechanism connecting environmental factors with other standard macroeconomic indicators. This is often considered necessary before any policy can be implemented effectively.

The model presented in this chapter deals with some of these questions by capturing macroeconomic variables, but with the explicit topic of pollution tax. The country case study is Indonesia. The model is in the category of computable general equilibrium (CGE) and it is a modification from S. Robinson's stylist model (Robinson, 1990). Following the description of the model, a set of simulation results based on Indonesian data is exposed.

## THE MODEL

In an economy-wide model with a pollution factor, it is quite natural to expect some modifications to be made in the standard utility function. There are various forms of utility function one could apply. Following Robinson (1990), we shall adopt a standard Stone–Geary function where the minima or subsistence parameters, $g_i$, are constant:

$$U = \prod_i (C_i - g_i)^{\beta i} = (TNP - NP)^{\beta m} \prod_k (C_k - g_k)^{\beta k} \quad (17.1)$$

There are two categories of sector in the economy: market goods (consisting of $h = 1, 2, \ldots, m - 1$) and non-market goods, that is, the pollution-cleaning activity ($m$). The consumption for cleaning is related to the minima $g_m$; in this case, it is defined as the difference between the amount of dirt and the level of emission society can tolerate. Thus, the cleaning activity is treated as goods which have prices or an economic value. If the consumption for cleaning ($C_m$) is assumed to be zero, that is, its market is missing, the left side of the utility expression, $(NP - TNP)^{\beta m}$, reflects the actual dirt after cleaning beyond the tolerable level of pollution, where $\beta$ is the marginal expenditure coefficient. From this specification, any reduction in the pollution will tend to pull the utility level downwards. The net effect, however, depends on the interplay of pollution reduction and the increased consumption of 'market goods', $C_t$.

The net pollution is simply the total emission minus whatever level of cleaning activity:

$$NP = \sum_i pc_i Q_i - G_m \tag{17.2}$$

From the utility maximization, a linear expenditure system (LES) is generated, which, in the tradition of standard CGE model becomes the equation representing the demand for the commodity market:

$$P_k C_k = P_k g_k + mc_k YPS \tag{17.3}$$

The income expression, *YPS*, is defined as incomes that are not committed to purchasing the minima. By convention, it is called the 'supernumerary income', the algebraic definition of which will be exposed later.

Viewed from the production side, the optimal solution in terms of pollution tax, the size of cleaning activity and the corresponding utility level, will all depend on the nature of the production function being adopted. In particular, variable elasticity of substitution (VES) between factor inputs is likely to generate different results in each sector, since the response of factor proportions to factor–price changes will not be the same inter-sectorally. The specific form of the VES function being used in the model is:

$$Q_i = A_i K_i^{(1-\delta\rho)}[L_i + (\rho - 1)K_i]^{\delta\rho} \tag{17.4}$$

where $\sigma(k) = 1 + [(\rho - 1)/(1 - \delta\rho)] \cdot k$; $k$ being the capital–labour ratio, and $1/k > [(1 - \rho)/(1 - \delta\rho)]$; $0 < \delta < 1$; and $0 <= \delta\rho <= 1$[1]

The output price is specified in a straightforward manner:

$$\bar{P} = \prod_i P_i^{\beta_i} \quad \text{set as numeraire} \tag{17.5}$$

where only the market sectors are counted in the cost of living index:

$$CPI = \prod_k P_k^{\beta_k} \tag{17.6}$$

To generate the income equation we first need to have the value-added price:

$$PV_i = P_t - tn_i P_i - \sum_j A_{ji} P_j - t_i \qquad (17.7)$$

Notice that in the above equation the pollution tax, $t_i$, is further subtracted from the net price.

The commodity market will be cleared on the basis of total demand being equal to total supply:

$$C_i + G_i + \sum_j A_{ij} Q_j = Q_i \qquad (17.8)$$

In the factor market side, factor returns are simply derived from the first-order condition:

$$W_K = A_i(1 - \delta\rho)[(\rho - 1) + (L_i/K_i)]^{\delta\rho}$$
$$+ A_i \delta\rho(\rho - 1)[(\rho - 1) + (L_i/K_i)]^{\delta\rho - 1} \qquad (17.9)$$

$$W_L = A_i \delta\rho[(\rho - 1) + (L_i/K_i)]^{(\delta\rho - 1)} \qquad (17.10)$$

and the market is cleared via the equalization of factor demand and factor supply, where the latter is assumed to be constant:

$$\sum_i L_i = \bar{L} \qquad (17.11)$$

$$\sum_i K_i = \bar{K} \qquad (17.12)$$

Given the value-added prices stated earlier, the private incomes are composed of two elements: incomes from production activities accrued to private sectors, and government transfers which, for simplicity, are assumed to be entirely channelled back to the consumers. There is no reason why we have to impose such a simplified assumption; but since it implies no loss of generalization, at this stage we shall maintain this assumption, for simplicity:

$$YP = \sum_i PV_i Q_i + GR - \sum_i P_i G_i \qquad (17.13)$$

The algebraic definition of 'supernumerary income' is:

$$YPS = YP - \sum_k P_k g_k \qquad (17.14)$$

which, as stated earlier, is the income not committed to purchasing the minima.

For the purpose of simulating various scenarios under which different levels of cleaning activity are proposed, government expenditure for this activity are set as the policy instrument (exogenously determined):

$$G_m = \overline{G_m} \tag{17.15}$$

One can easily modify the model by connecting this item with revenues from pollution tax or other forms of 'prices' attached to pollution externalities. It should be clear that, the more cleaning that is done, the greater the reduction in pollution will be, and consequently utility will increase.

On the revenue side, all proceeds from pollution tax are accrued to the government. Again, for simplicity, let us assume that no condition is imposed on the specific use of those revenues:

$$GR = \sum_i [t_i Q_i + tn_i P_i] \tag{17.16}$$

where

$$t_i = t_P \cdot pc_i \tag{17.17}$$

Below is a description of all the variables contained in the above model:

$m$ = cleaning activity (non-market sector)
$i$ = 1, 2, . . . , $m$
$h$ = 1, 2, . . . , $m - 1$ (market sector)

$NP$ = net pollution emission
$pc$ = pollution coefficient per unit of output
$Q$ = output level
$G_m$ = cleaning activity
$PV$ = net or value-added price
$CPI$ = consumers' price (cost of living) index
$P$ = producers' price
$tn$ = indirect tax rate
$t$ = sectoral tax on pollution
$A$ = input–output coefficient
$t_p$ = pollution tax per unit of emission
$W_L$ = wages
$W_k$ = capital return

$U$ = utility
$TNP$ = tolerable level of emission
$C$ = final demand
$g$ = minimum consumption (the minima)
$GR$ = government revenues
$YP$ = private incomes
$YPS$ = private supernumerary incomes[2]
$mc$ = private marginal cost (outside cleaning activity)
$L$ = labour
$K$ = capital
$\beta$ = marginal expenditure share
$\rho$ = coefficient of substitution
$\delta$ = distributive parameter.

The set of equations presented above only represents the basic model, but it is already capable of serving the main purpose of the analysis. Naturally, further refinements can and must be made if the model is to be applied in a real situation.

With the above specification, we simulate the model in two steps: first, no pollution tax is imposed, so that only government cleaning activity will determine the quality of the environment, and hence the utility level; second, pollution tax is imposed in addition to the cleaning activity. The hypothesis related to these two steps alludes to the superiority of imposing pollution tax as one form of internalizing the externalities, which often is the consensus on how to deal with environment-cum-economic issues. Furthermore, it is also expected that the model simulation will yield an optimal pollution tax that will be consistent with the utility maximization framework. Finally, to make use of the VES produc-tion function, we shall also attempt to compare results from several scenarios under different parameters of substitution implied in such a function.

## DATA REQUIREMENT

A close connection between pollution emission as a by-product, the cleaning activity as one of the goods sectors, and the overall economic activities, ought to be represented in the data set that will be used in the model. It is precisely for this reason that an input–output (IO) table becomes the logical candidate for the data set. The incorporation of intermediate inputs in matrix A also justifies the use of an IO framework. However, unlike in most IO applications, physical units are required in this model. One certainly cannot integrate the pollution emission into the IO table if the table contains only numbers in monetary units. Pollution, like the cleaning activity, is in the category of non-market sector, where no price is currently attached to it. In many countries we find this situation occurs relatively frequently; Indonesia is by no means an exception. It is, in fact, only through the model simulation we are led to argue that a certain price has to be imposed on environmental goods.

On the basis of data availability for pollution emission by sectors, the original sixty-six sectors of the 1985 Indonesian IO table are grouped into twelve sectors, plus one cleaning activity (sector number 13). The following is the list of those twelve sectors: 1. Paddy; 2. Other food crops; 3. Other agriculture; 4. Animal husbandry; 5. Forestry; 6. Fisheries; 7. Mining and quarrying; 8. Food industry; 9. Other industries; 10. Oil and gas refining; 11. Electricity, gas and water; 12. Other.

The next step was to obtain the average price level for each sector. Since no price data for aggregate sectors are available, we had to work with disaggregate data. For this purpose, a concordance of sectoral codes or classifications needed to be constructed. In the case of the non-manufacturing sector, we used the weighted average of a three-digit-based IO classification to yield an average price for a one-digit sector. For the manufacturing sector, a concordance of a three-digit IO with a five-digit ISIC was first carried out before a weighted average of unit price was generated. Unfortunately, not all industries can be treated in this way, either because of non-uniformity in the unit of production being recorded, for example, carpets (sectoral code 080) and cosmetics (098), or simply because no price data are available, for example, medicines (097), traditional medicines (100), coal-related manufacture (103); and aircraft industry (131). Consequently, these industries have to be grouped into the two-digit IO classification.

At this stage, the type of pollution being examined is confined to the $CO_2$ emission, the data being obtained from sources available at the Ministry of Environment and Population. Whenever data on sectoral pollution were suspected of being unreliable, a method known as the 'analytic hierarchy process' (AHP) was adopted to reveal the experts' perception. This approach was also applied to inspecting the reliability of data on the production of the cleaning activity. It is important to note that, eventually, the required information on sectoral pollution was measured in terms of per-unit output emission ('dirt-coefficient'), suggesting that obtaining data on absolute amounts of pollution is necessary.

## RESULTS OF MODEL SIMULATION

One of the policy questions often posed concerns the issue of the trade-off between economic development and environmental considerations. Conventional macroeconomists would tend to confirm the presence of the trade-off, especially when economic growth is to be contrasted with policies to protect the environment. However, there are more and more people who now believe that the two should not be in conflict. Indeed, the message of the UN Rio Conference in 1992 was, among other things, to suggest a development path in which efforts to protect the environment would not be in conflict with economic development. The proposed concept, 'sustainable development', recommends basically that economic development and the environment should go hand-in-hand, rather than to operating separately.

While it is certainly an attractive conjecture, the difficulties involved in its application are enormous. In the context of the model presented here, we shall examine various scenarios with respect to the size of cleaning activity and the imposition of pollution tax, through which the nature of trade-off can be analyzed. Given the fact that GDP is perhaps the most often used indicator to measure economic growth, it will first be defined in the model:

$$GDP = \sum_i (C_i + G_i) \qquad (17.18)$$

Another indicator worth comparing is the extent of government net revenues when environmental considerations are taken into account in the undertaking of macroeconomic policies, that is, imposing a pollution tax and conducting cleaning activities. This can be retrieved from the difference between revenues accrued from pollution tax and the monetary costs of cleaning (recall that in this version we assume that all cleaning is done by the government):

$$NPREV = t_i Q_i - P_m G_m \qquad (17.19)$$

where NPREV is the net pollution revenue.

Given the model specification, several types of simulation can be generated, the choice of which will depend on the questions at hand. Two types of simulation presented here will take government cleaning, $G_m$, as the policy variable.[3] The size of this government demand for cleaning will have ramifications for various macroeconomic variables, including the endogenously determined pollution tax appearing in the model, and at the same time it will directly determine environmental quality (net emission, *NP*). In this respect, the connection between development path and environmental quality can be captured. Hence, the non-linear optimization problems involves two decision variables: government cleaning, $G_m$ and pollution tax ($t_i$ and $t_p$). The solution to such a problem is a market equilibrium which maximizes social welfare.

The first experiment assumes that no pollution tax is imposed. In other words, the ultimate level of environmental quality will depend only upon how much pollution is emitted by production sectors and how much cleaning has been done by the government. Table A.1 displays the results of simulation at various levels of government cleaning, ranging from 980 to 1100 units. With this setting, it is clear that 1055 unit of cleaning gives the highest utility level, and hence this is considered the optimal level (see Appendix, pp. 359–63, for Tables A.1–4.)

Notice that the rejoinder to the issue of trade-off will depend on the range of $G_m$ as well as the choice of variable being used. More specifically, when we use *GDP* as the indicator of economic growth, at any $G_m$ below the optimal level, no sign of trade-off is observed; the improved environmental quality measured by declining net dirt gives a persistent increase, not only in utility but also in the values of real GDP. This pattern remains even when the level of real consumption steadily declines. Obviously, this is explained by the fact that the increased output of cleaning has more than offset the decline in consumption of market goods. At the same time, consumption patterns have also changed. As some sectors suffer from a decreasing price, the demand for these goods have increased, for example, in 'Other' (sector number 12), or, vice versa, when the price increases, consumption tends to decline, for example, 'Other food crops' (number 2) and 'Oil and gas refining' (number 10).

The presence of trade-off is detected beyond the optimum level of cleaning. While the environmental condition improves as the government spends more on cleaning activities (from 1055 to 1100 units); the GDP and consumption levels decline steadily.

The second experiment imposes pollution tax on the problem, such that the obtained solution will be the first-best welfare maximum, that is, at $G_m$ = 995 and $t_p$ = 35086.9 as observed from Table A.2 with the same level of cleaning as in the preceding experiment, a higher utility level is achieved if pollution tax is imposed. At the benchmark value of cleaning ($G_m$ = 1055), the utility is 1.6 per cent higher than in the previous case. Intuitively, this is supported by a quite straightforward interpretation: the amount of pollution is reduced by two forces, government cleaning and increased costs of pollution via a pollution tax imposed on polluters. Eventually, this will lead to a more pronounced change in the structure of production and consumption.

Take, for example, the 'Forestry' sector (number 5). In the series of nine experiments, the pollution tax per unit of forestry output is steadily increasing along with the increased cleaning activity. As shown in Table A.2, this induced a persistent increase in the product price of the respective sector from 17371.8 in Experiment 1 to 17373.7 in Experiment 9. This could be the case where producers transfer the burden of pollution tax to consumers, a practice often adopted by producers in order to maintain their profit level. Consequently, the consumption share of this sector declines, although only slightly, from 0.0913 to 0.0912 per cent. A similar case, with a sharper decline, occurs in the 'Mining and quarrying' sector (number 7), that is, from 1.2832 to 1.2826 per cent.

At any rate, one can see immediately the power of pollution tax to affect environmental condition as well as other economic variables in the economy. At the bench-mark value of cleaning, for example, the net dirt shown in Table A.2 is less than half of the level in the case of no pollution tax seen in Table A.1 (52.5 compared to 117.1). Furthermore, at lower levels of cleaning, the pollution tax tends to have a higher net impact on pollution generation. From Experiment 1 to Experiment 2 the marginal net dirt of pollution tax is 6.3951, whereas from Experiment 8 to Experiment 9 the marginal net dirt is 6.3766. If further experiments with greater levels of cleaning are conducted, the gap will probably widen.

At the market equilibrium and welfare maximizing point ($G_m$ = 995 and utility = 679.6115) the optimal pollution tax per unit of emission is 35086.9. Beyond that level, even if the government intends to increase cleaning activities that will lead to a further decline in net dirt, the utility level will steadily *decrease*. This indicates that within such a range the results are second-best welfare maxima, with pollution tax being optimal, given non-optimal values of $G_m$. Such a pattern is prompted by the level of pollution tax that is considered too burdensome. Indeed, pollution tax steadily increased up to Experiment 7, although in the last two experiments a different pattern was detected.

From the model mechanism, the implicit price elasticities of demand induced optimal pollution tax per unit of output at the maximum welfare solution that varies widely from a low 70.2 for 'Animal husbandry' (sector number 4) to a high 10526.1 for 'Oil and gas refining' (number 10). Obviously, such results are also affected by the pollution coefficients specified in the baseline table.

As indicated earlier, the specification of variable elasticity of substitution (VES) in the production function allows us to set different degrees of input substitution in each sector. Results of running the model at a same level of optimal $G_m$, 995 unit, but with different substitution parameters in each sector (see Table A.3) are listed in Table A.4.

Notice that Scenario A is basically adopting a Cobb–Douglas function, whereas Scenarios B and F use CES function. The other scenarios presumably reflect more realistic situations and specify the variable elasticity of the substitution function inter-sectorally. As shown in Table A.4, the optimal utility level is different in each scenerio, but the optimal level of $G_m$ remains the same, that is, 995 units.

Let us take the comparison between Scenario A and Scenario E. In Scenario E, there are six sectors (including the cleaning sector) assumed to have a greater ease of substitution between the two inputs. These sectors are, in general, labour-intensive categories. On the other hand, there are seven sectors that have elasticity of substitution lower than unity, implying less flexibility in adapting their technology (these are mostly capital-intensive sectors).

It is observed from Table A.4 that at the optimal level, Scenario E generates a higher utility level but a slightly lower GDP and consumption level than in Scenario A. Such results can be traced from changes in sectoral prices. As the rate of pollution tax per unit of emission ($t_p$) becomes higher, raising the sectoral pollution tax per unit of output ($t_i$), the output price of many sectors will increase. In fact, in this particular case, the price increased in seven sectors, and it is expected that this will transform into a reduction in the consumption level. Since the consumption share of these sectors already covered as much as 86 per cent of total consumption, we can expect there will be a decline in total consumption. This is indeed the case.

How do we explain the lower utility in Scenario E? Notice that the net emission (*NP*) is higher in this scenario. Therefore, given the specification of utility function in Equation 17.1, one can observe that despite the lower consumption of 'market goods', $C_h$, the higher *NP* have more than offset such a reduction, bringing about a higher utility level. Obviously, we cannot generalize from this situation. The net effect of pull and push forces coming from these two components will vary case by case.

In the government sector, total revenues accrued from pollution tax amount to Rp 38.9 billion, which is slightly higher than the pollution tax revenues under Scenario A. Furthermore, the obtained price of the cleaning activity is found to be lower. Therefore the net pollution revenue (*NPREV*) is higher in Scenario E.

Some generalization, however, can still be addressed, for example, when we compare the case of the Cobb–Douglas function and the lower-than-unity elasticity of substitution (CES) function (comparing Scenarios A and B). Similar to the previous case, output level in Scenario B is higher. With constant $pc_i$, this implies a greater emission (*NP*). Furthermore, pollution tax is also lower, inducing a price decline and consumption increase in many sectors. It turns out that those sectors experiencing a price decline (numbers 1, 2, 3, 8, 9, 10 and 11) represent more than 84 per cent of total consumption. Therefore, eventually, overall consumption will increase, and so will GDP (see again Table A.4).

The greater magnitude of *NP* has pulled the utility level downwards significantly. Consequently, although consumption of 'market goods' has increased, this appears to be insufficient to avert the utility reduction. Unlike in the previous case, the price unit of the cleaning activity is now lower than the level under Scenario A. Unfortunately, however, the reduction in pollution tax revenues is even greater. In effect, as we observe from Table A.4, the net pollution revenue (*NPREV*) is lower than in Scenario A. Results from Scenario F, when compared with Scenario A, imply the opposite of those found in the previous comparison between Scenario A and Scenario B. Scenarios C and D are basically variations of the other scenarios.

Therefore, it is clear that the adoption of the VES function provides more flexibility during analysis. When more accurate and reliable data on elasticity of substitution ($\sigma$) for each sector are available, the necessary adjustment can be made directly; $\sigma = 1$ and $\sigma =$ constant across sectors are obviously special cases of the VES function.

## CONCLUSIONS

The CGE framework presented in this chapter is a modification of Robinson's model on the interconnection between environmental and economic variables. More specifically, the model is designed to demonstrate the nexus between pollution, market failure and optimal policy in an economy-wide framework. The optimality in this case alludes to the maximum utility that is jointly determined by the consumption of conventional 'market' goods and that of pollution-related environmental quality. Unlike Robinson's model, the one presented here assumes neither equal factor returns nor identical elasticity of substitution between sectors. In this respect, more flexibility is gained.

From the application to the Indonesian case, it is demonstrated that, under different levels of cleaning, the standard macro aggregates and pollution variables can be determined simultaneously through endogenous price setting. The superiority of a pollution tax in affecting the condition of the environment and other economic variables is shown by comparing the simulation results from the scenario *with* and *without* imposing this tax. The use of this model is also capable of unravelling the nature of trade-off between growth and environment that is often addressed.

Obviously, numerous refinements should be made before the model can be applied in real cases. Extension of the model to conceal income and other forms of transfer payments between different income groups will enrich the analysis, since in reality different income groups are likely to perceive differently the importance of environmental quality *vis-à-vis* consumption of conventional goods. In this respect, the utilization of a social accounting matrix (SAM), rather than a standard input–output framework along with a more elaborate utility function is certainly desirable. The explicit treatment of different types of pollution will also make the analysis more complete. Nothwithstanding these points, however, as it stands now the model is already capable of serving the main purpose of the analysis.

## Notes

1. The derivation of the functions is shown in Iwan J. Azis (1985) *Elements of Interregional Interaction* (Jakarta: PT Pembimbing Masa) pp. 79–82.
2. Not all incomes are spent on minimum consumption; the unspent part is called supernumerary income.
3. Obviously, cleaning is only one of many activities on which the government will spend its budget. However, to concentrate on the issue of controlling pollution emission, without a loss of generality, at this stage we shall temporarily restrict the analysis of government expenditure to only the cleaning activities.

## References

Azis, I. J. (1994) 'Internalization of Externalities: An Environment CGE Model for Indonesia', in A. Anwar, T. K. Wie and I. J. Azis (eds), *The Thought, Implementation and Pioneering Work of Economic Development* (Jakarta: Gramedia) (in Indonesian).

Azis, I. J. (1981) *Elements of Interregional Interaction* (Jakarta: PT Pembimbing Masa).

Robinson, S. (1991) *Pollution Failure and Optimal Policy in an Economywide Framework*, Working Paper No. 559, Department of Agricultural and Resource Economics, University of California at Berkeley.

Saaty, T. L. (1991) *Multicriteria Decision Making, The Analytic Hierarchy Process: Planning, Priority Setting, Resource Allocation* (2nd edn) (Pittsburgh, Penn.: RWS Publications).

Table A.1 Alternative scenarios without pollution tax

| | | | | | | | | | |
|---|---|---|---|---|---|---|---|---|---|
| Clean | 980 | 995 | 1010 | 1025 | 1040 | 1055 | 1070 | 1085 | 1100 |
| Utility | 668.75 | 668.75 | 668.76 | 668.76 | 668.76 | 668.76 | 668.76 | 668.76 | 668.76 |
| Real GDP | 32851.89 | 32861.58 | 32871.26 | 32880.95 | 32890.64 | 32900.32 | 32910.01 | 32919.70 | 32929.38 |
| Net dirt | 192.98 | 177.81 | 162.64 | 147.48 | 132.31 | 117.14 | 101.98 | 86.81 | 71.64 |
| Prices: | | | | | | | | | |
| Sector 1 | 183.00 | 183.00 | 183.00 | 183.00 | 183.01 | 183.01 | 183.01 | 183.01 | 183.01 |
| Sector 2 | 279.38 | 279.39 | 279.40 | 279.40 | 279.41 | 279.42 | 279.42 | 279.43 | 279.43 |
| Sector 3 | 398.74 | 398.74 | 398.74 | 398.74 | 398.74 | 398.74 | 398.74 | 398.74 | 398.74 |
| Sector 4 | 2612.18 | 2612.19 | 2612.20 | 2612.21 | 2612.22 | 2612.23 | 2612.24 | 2612.26 | 2612.27 |
| Sector 5 | 17976.63 | 17976.94 | 17977.25 | 17977.55 | 17977.86 | 17978.17 | 17978.48 | 17978.79 | 17979.10 |
| Sector 6 | 819.98 | 820.00 | 820.01 | 820.02 | 820.04 | 820.05 | 820.07 | 820.08 | 820.10 |
| Sector 7 | 30588.79 | 30589.87 | 30590.96 | 30592.04 | 30593.12 | 30594.21 | 30595.29 | 30596.37 | 30597.46 |
| Sector 8 | 37261.13 | 37261.38 | 37261.64 | 37261.89 | 37262.14 | 37262.40 | 37262.65 | 37262.90 | 37263.16 |
| Sector 9 | 13097.62 | 13097.64 | 13097.66 | 13097.68 | 13097.70 | 13097.72 | 13097.73 | 13097.75 | 13097.77 |
| Sector 10 | 35552.37 | 35553.59 | 35554.81 | 35556.03 | 35557.25 | 35558.47 | 35559.69 | 35560.91 | 35562.13 |
| Sector 11 | 94645.56 | 94646.64 | 94647.72 | 94648.80 | 94649.88 | 94650.96 | 94652.04 | 94653.12 | 94654.20 |
| Sector 12 | 75001.64 | 75000.41 | 74999.18 | 74997.95 | 74996.72 | 74995.49 | 74994.26 | 74993.03 | 74991.80 |
| Clean | 999.95 | 999.99 | 1000.03 | 1000.07 | 1000.11 | 1000.15 | 1000.19 | 1000.23 | 1000.27 |
| Private income | 97590.30 | 97575.74 | 97561.18 | 97546.63 | 97532.07 | 97517.51 | 97502.95 | 97488.39 | 97473.83 |
| Total output | 88489.48 | 88490.78 | 88492.09 | 88493.39 | 88494.69 | 88495.99 | 88497.28 | 88498.58 | 88499.88 |
| Net pollution revenue | −979.95 | −994.99 | −1010.03 | −1025.07 | −1040.11 | −1055.16 | −1070.20 | −1085.25 | −1100.30 |

*Table* A.2 Alternative scenarios without pollution tax

| | | | | | | | | | |
|---|---|---|---|---|---|---|---|---|---|
| Clean | 980 | 995 | 1010 | 1025 | 1040 | 1055 | 1070 | 1085 | 1100 |
| Utility | 679.61 | 679.61 | 679.61 | 679.61 | 679.61 | 679.60 | 679.60 | 679.59 | 679.58 |
| Real GDP | 27222.78 | 27233.33 | 27243.89 | 27254.44 | 27264.99 | 27275.55 | 27286.10 | 27305.03 | 27315.58 |
| Net dirt | 128.32 | 113.16 | 98.00 | 82.85 | 67.69 | 52.53 | 37.37 | 22.30 | 7.14 |
| Prices: | | | | | | | | | |
| Sector 1 | 306.92 | 306.93 | 306.94 | 306.95 | 306.96 | 306.97 | 306.98 | 306.76 | 306.77 |
| Sector 2 | 373.77 | 373.78 | 373.79 | 373.81 | 373.82 | 373.83 | 373.84 | 373.67 | 373.68 |
| Sector 3 | 482.55 | 482.56 | 482.57 | 482.57 | 482.58 | 482.58 | 482.59 | 482.43 | 482.44 |
| Sector 4 | 2070.51 | 2070.48 | 2070.45 | 2070.43 | 2070.40 | 2070.38 | 2070.35 | 2071.23 | 2071.20 |
| Sector 5 | 17371.77 | 17371.93 | 17372.10 | 17372.26 | 17372.43 | 17372.59 | 17372.75 | 17373.56 | 17373.72 |
| Sector 6 | 760.19 | 760.20 | 760.20 | 760.21 | 760.21 | 760.22 | 760.22 | 760.32 | 760.32 |
| Sector 7 | 27066.98 | 27067.42 | 27067.85 | 27068.29 | 27068.73 | 27069.17 | 27069.61 | 27075.90 | 27076.34 |
| Sector 8 | 48321.21 | 48322.16 | 48323.11 | 48324.07 | 48325.02 | 48325.97 | 48326.92 | 48306.65 | 48307.60 |
| Sector 9 | 24494.29 | 24495.09 | 24495.89 | 24496.69 | 24497.50 | 24498.30 | 24499.10 | 24478.76 | 24479.57 |
| Sector 10 | 38332.38 | 38333.34 | 38334.29 | 38335.24 | 38336.19 | 38337.14 | 38338.09 | 38333.33 | 38334.28 |
| Sector 11 | 100882.07 | 100883.27 | 100884.48 | 100885.68 | 100886.89 | 100888.10 | 100889.31 | 100876.52 | 100877.74 |
| Sector 12 | 67415.71 | 67414.62 | 67413.54 | 67412.46 | 67411.38 | 67410.29 | 67409.21 | 67418.97 | 67417.89 |
| Clean | 628.91 | 628.91 | 628.91 | 628.91 | 628.91 | 628.91 | 628.91 | 629.57 | 629.57 |
| Private income | 99759.50 | 99744.64 | 99729.78 | 99714.92 | 99700.06 | 99685.19 | 99670.33 | 99654.13 | 99639.27 |
| Total output | 74505.26 | 74508.35 | 74511.44 | 74514.53 | 74517.62 | 74520.71 | 74523.80 | 74548.24 | 74551.33 |
| Net pollution revenue | 38268.54 | 38256.20 | 38243.86 | 38231.52 | 38219.18 | 38206.83 | 38194.49 | 38113.74 | 38101.40 |

*Table* A.3 Alternative scenarios of sectoral RHO

| | *Scenario A* | *Scenario B* | *Scenario C* | *Scenario D* | *Scenario E* | *Scenario F* |
|---|---|---|---|---|---|---|
| 1. Paddy | 1 | 0.99 | 1.05 | 1.05 | 1.07 | 1.05 |
| 2. Other food crops | 1 | 0.99 | 1.05 | 1.05 | 1.07 | 1.05 |
| 3. Other agriculture | 1 | 0.99 | 1 | 0.995 | 0.989 | 1.05 |
| 4. Animal husbandry | 1 | 0.99 | 1 | 1.05 | 1.07 | 1.05 |
| 5. Forestry | 1 | 0.99 | 1 | 0.99 | 0.989 | 1.05 |
| 6. Fishery | 1 | 0.99 | 1.05 | 1.05 | 1.07 | 1.05 |
| 7. Mining & quarrying | 1 | 0.99 | 1 | 0.99 | 0.985 | 1.05 |
| 8. Food industry | 1 | 0.99 | 1 | 0.995 | 0.989 | 1.05 |
| 9. Other industries | 1 | 0.99 | 0.995 | 0.995 | 0.989 | 1.05 |
| 10. Oil & gas refinery | 1 | 0.99 | 0.99 | 0.99 | 0.985 | 1.05 |
| 11. Electricity, gas & water | 1 | 0.99 | 0.99 | 0.99 | 0.985 | 1.05 |
| 12. Others | 1 | 0.99 | 1 | 1.1 | 1.105 | 1.05 |
| 13. Cleaning | 1 | 0.99 | 1.05 | 1.05 | 0.85 | 1.05 |

*Table* A.4 Alternative scenarios using different RHO

| | *Scenario A* | *Scenario B* | *Scenario C* | *Scenario D* | *Scenario E* | *Scenario F* |
|---|---|---|---|---|---|---|
| Clean | 995 | 995 | 995 | 995 | 995 | 995 |
| Utility | 679.61 | 679.45 | 679.50 | 679.69 | 679.61 | 680.50 |
| Real GDP | 27233.33 | 27265.08 | 27254.75 | 27219.88 | 27234.87 | 27065.72 |
| Net dirt | 113.16 | 113.28 | 113.23 | 113.11 | 113.16 | 112.61 |
| Prices: | | | | | | |
| Sector 1 | 306.93 | 305.87 | 306.23 | 307.44 | 306.94 | 312.67 |
| Sector 2 | 373.78 | 372.98 | 373.24 | 374.15 | 373.76 | 378.16 |
| Sector 3 | 482.56 | 481.79 | 482.05 | 482.94 | 482.58 | 486.71 |
| Sector 4 | 2070.48 | 2074.69 | 2073.24 | 2068.33 | 2070.28 | 2047.88 |
| Sector 5 | 17371.93 | 17375.66 | 17373.80 | 17368.45 | 17369.90 | 17352.54 |
| Sector 6 | 760.20 | 760.64 | 760.46 | 759.90 | 760.09 | 757.85 |
| Sector 7 | 27067.42 | 27097.50 | 27085.05 | 27046.83 | 27060.03 | 26906.41 |
| Sector 8 | 48322.16 | 48224.52 | 48256.97 | 48368.90 | 48322.80 | 48850.67 |
| Sector 9 | 24495.09 | 24397.34 | 24430.31 | 24543.23 | 24497.32 | 25023.24 |
| Sector 10 | 38333.34 | 38311.21 | 38316.59 | 38339.06 | 38327.61 | 38453.63 |
| Sector 11 | 100883.27 | 100822.91 | 100841.52 | 100909.33 | 100879.91 | 101212.20 |
| Sector 12 | 67414.62 | 67461.82 | 67448.13 | 67397.34 | 67420.15 | 67162.64 |
| Clean | 628.91 | 632.06 | 630.89 | 627.10 | 628.64 | 611.95 |
| Pollution tax | 35086.92 | 34791.80 | 34891.44 | 35232.40 | 35093.91 | 36679.98 |
| Net pollution revenue | 38256.20 | 37930.27 | 38040.04 | 38417.41 | 38264.23 | 40018.40 |

# Part II
# Resource Utilization and Management

# [8]

*Human Ecology, Vol. 18, No. 1, 1990*



# The Tragedy of the Commons: Twenty-Two Years Later

**David Feeny,[1] Fikret Berkes,[2] Bonnie J. McCay,[3] and James M. Acheson[4]**

*Hardin's Tragedy of the Commons model predicts the eventual overexploitation or degradation of all resources used in common. Given this unambiguous prediction, a surprising number of cases exist in which users have been able to restrict access to the resource and establish rules among themselves for its sustainable use. To assess the evidence, we first define common-property resources and present a taxonomy of property-rights regimes in which such resources may be held. Evidence accumulated over the last twenty-two years indicates that private, state,* and *communal property are all potentially viable resource management options. A more complete theory than Hardin's should incorporate institutional arrangements and cultural factors to provide for better analysis and prediction.*

**KEY WORDS:** co-management; common property; fisheries; forests; grazing lands; sustainable development; water resources; wildlife.

> It was twenty years ago today; Sgt. Pepper taught the band to play
> (John Lennon and Paul McCartney (1967). *Sgt. Pepper's Lonely Hearts Club Band.* Northern Songs Ltd.).

## INTRODUCTION

Garrett Hardin's *The Tragedy of the Commons* was published 22 years ago (Hardin, 1968). Although it focused attention on overpopulation, the

[1]Departments of Economics and Clinical Epidemiology and Biostatistics, McMaster University, Hamilton, Ontario L8S 4M4 Canada.
[2]Institute of Urban and Environmental Studies, Brock University, St. Catharines, Ontario L2S 3A1 Canada.
[3]Departments of Human Ecology and Anthropology, Rutgers University, P.O. Box 231, New Brunswick, New Jersey 08903.
[4]Department of Anthropology, University of Maine, Orono, Maine 04460-0158.



0300-7839/90/0300-0001$06.00/0 

dominant legacy of the paper has been its metaphor of common-property resource management. In the intervening years, the ideas that Hardin popularized have become the most widely accepted explanation for overexploitation of resources that are commonly held. The essential idea was that resources held in common, such as oceans, rivers, air, and parklands, are subject to massive degradation. Hardin was neither alone nor novel in making the argument. He noted that Lloyd had made the same point in a series of lectures in the 1830's (Lloyd, 1968). Two modern resource economists, Gordon (1954) and Scott (1955), are usually credited with the first statement of the conventional theory of the commons, although Hardin does not mention them. In this paper, we examine the accumulated evidence pertaining to common-property resource management and provide a critique of the conventional theory expounded by Hardin.

Although Hardin was referring to global concepts such as carrying capacity, his observations about resources held in common are considered by many as the definitive insight. To make his points about the need for major social change to deal with problems such as overpopulation, resource depletion, and air and water poullution, Hardin (1968) relied upon a thought experiment. He asked the reader to imagine what would happen to a metaphorical village commons if each herder were to add a few animals to his herd. His metaphor highlighted the divergence between individual and collective rationality. If each herdsman found it more profitable to graze more animals than the pasture could support, because each took all the profit from an extra animal but bore only a fraction of the cost of overgrazing, the result would be a tragic loss of the resource for the entire community of herders. Thus Hardin concluded that "freedom in the commons brings ruin to all" (Hardin, 1968, p. 1244).

This conclusion has been accorded by some the status of scientific law. The tragedy of the commons has become part of the conventional wisdom in environmental studies, resource science and policy, economics, ecology, and political science (McEvoy, 1988, p. 214) and is featured in textbooks (Nebel, 1987, pp. 484-485; Lineberry, 1983, pp. 579-580). J. A. Moore, author of a major environmental education project for the American Society of Zoologists, states: "Hardin's Tragedy of the Commons should be required reading for all students ... and if I had my way, for all human beings" (Moore, 1985, p. 602). It has also been used in formulating resource-management policy, as recently shown for Atlantic Canada fisheries (Matthews, 1988).

To avoid the tragedy, Hardin (1968; Hardin and Baden, 1977) concluded that the commons could be privatized or kept as public property to which rights to entry and use could be allocated. Hardin has been widely cited as having said that resource degradation was inevitable unless common property was converted to private property, or government regulation of uses and users was instituted. In a later paper, Hardin (1978) specifically recognized two general solutions, and presumably no others: private enterprise and socialism (control by government). Hardin argued that if we do not act in one of these two ways, we "acquiesce in the destruction of the commons" (Hardin, 1968, p. 1245).

We examine the evidence on factors associated with successful vs. unsuccessful exploitation of common-property resources, focusing in particular on communally-held resources. Surprisingly little careful empirical work on common property followed Hardin's seminal publication. However, several recent volumes summarize a growing and rich body of evidence relevant to common-property resource management (National Research Council, 1986; McEvoy, 1986, 1988; Marchak *et al.,* 1987; McCay and Acheson, 1987; Wade, 1987; Fortmann and Bruce, 1988; Pinkerton, 1989; Berkes, 1989; Cordell, 1989; Ostrom, forthcoming). A few definitions will be presented before examining this new evidence in the light of the predictions of Hardin's model.

## DEFINITIONS AND CONCEPTS

Common-property resources include fisheries, wildlife, surface and groundwater, range, and forests. It is important to delineate the characteristics shared by these resources, and to distinguish between the resource and the property-rights regime in which the resource is held (National Research Council, 1986).

Common-property resources share two important characteristics. The first is excludability (or control of access). That is, the physical nature of the resource is such that controlling access by potential users may be costly and, in the extreme, virtually impossible. Migratory resources such as fish, wildlife, and groundwater pose obvious problems for regulating access. Similarly, range and forest lands typically pose problems of exclusion. For large bodies of water, the global atmosphere, and radio frequency bands, exclusion is even more problematic.

The second basic characteristic of common-property resources is subtractability, that is, each user is capable of subtracting from the welfare of other users. Even if users cooperate to enhance the productivity of their resource, for instance by replanting trees, the nature of the resource is such that the level of exploitation by one user adversely affects the ability of another user to exploit the resource. Subtractability (or rivalry) is the source of the potential divergence between individual and collective rationality. If one user pumps more water from an aquifer, other users will experience an increase in pumping costs as aggregate use approaches or exceeds recharge capacity. If one user harvests fish, the catch per unit of fishing effort of other fishermen declines. Hence, we define common-property resources as *a class of resources for which exclusion is difficult and joint use involves subtractability* (Berkes *et al.,* 1989, p. 91).

The definition here resembles one given by Elinor Ostrom (1986, p. 604; see also Fortmann and Bruce, 1988, p. 2). Ostrom underscores the importance of the distinction between the intrinsic nature of the resource and the property-rights regime under which it is held, by defining the class of resources as "common-pool resources." Because of the widespread use of the term common property for certain kinds of resources, we have chosen to use this term to refer to the *resource* and the term communal property to refer to one of the four basic property-rights *regimes.*

In order to facilitate analysis, we define four categories of property rights within which common-property resources are held: open access, private property, communal property, and state property. These are ideal, analytic types. In practice, many resources are held in overlapping, and sometimes conflicting combinations of these regimes, and there is variation within each. It is nevertheless important to distinguish these four basic property-rights regimes (Ciriacy-Wantrup and Bishop, 1975; for similar distinctions see also Berkes *et al.,* 1989, p. 91; Bromley, 1986, 1989b, pp. 872-875; Bromley and Cernea, 1989, pp. 3-5; Demsetz, 1967, p. 354; Gibbs and Bromley, 1989, pp. 24-27; Godwin and Shepard, 1979, p. 267; Jacobs and Munro, 1987, p. 442; Libecap, 1986, p. 33; Marchak, 1987, pp. 4-5; Ostrom, 1986).

*Open access* is the absence of well-defined property rights. Access to the resource is unregulated and is free and open to everyone. Many offshore ocean fisheries before the twentieth century, or the global atmosphere provide examples.

Under *private property,* the rights to exclude others from using the resource and to regulate the use of the resource are vested in an individual (or group of individuals such as a corporation). Private-property rights are generally recognized and enforced by the state. Unlike rights under open access, private-property rights usually are exclusive and transferable (Regier and Grima, 1985). Examples include forests and rangelands that are held privately.

Under *communal property,* the resource is held by an identifiable community of interdependent users. These users exclude outsiders while regulating use by members of the local community. Within the community, rights to the resource are unlikely to be either exclusive or transferable; they are often rights of equal access and use. Some inshore fisheries, shellfish beds, range lands, and forests have been managed as communal property; similarly, water-users associations for many groundwater and irrigation systems can be included in this category. The rights of the group may be legally recognized. In other cases the rights are *de facto,* depending on the benign neglect of the state. Some scholars use the term common property, or simply a common, to refer exclusively to the regime we classify as communal property (Ostrom, 1986; Bromley, 1986, 1989a,b; Marchak, 1988-1989; Blaikie and Brookfield, 1987, pp. 186-187).

Finally, under *state property,* or state governance, rights to the resource are vested exclusively in government which in turn makes decisions concerning access to the resource and the level and nature of exploitation. Examples include forests and rangelands held by the government or crown-owned, and resources such as fish and wildlife that may be held in public trust for the citizenry. The category of state property may refer to property to which the general public has equal access and use rights such as highways and public parks. The nature of the state property regime also differs from the other regimes in that, in general, the state, unlike private parties, has coercive powers of enforcement.

Although the nature of the property-rights regime under which the resource is held is important, that information is not sufficient to draw valid conclusions concerning behavior and outcomes. One theme of the paper is that one must understand a whole host of institutional arrangements governing access to and use of the resource. Knowledge of the property rights is necessary but not sufficient. Many of the misunderstandings found in the literature may be traced to the assumption that common property is the same as open access. Hardin's prediction of the inevitability of over-exploitation follows from this assumption. Yet the assumption is inaccurate and it has led to a great deal of confusion. Based on our definition of common property, an approach to testing Hardin's hypothesis is to examine two broad challenges in the management of common-property resources: (1) the exclusion of other potential users, and (2) the regulation of use and users to ameliorate the problems associated with subtractability. Evidence on each will be examined for each of the property-rights regimes listed above.

In evaluating evidence to test Hardin's hypothesis, a criterion with which to classify the outcome as a success or failure is needed. The choice of any particular standard is arbitrary, but we will use *ecological sustainability* as the working criterion of success, that is, whether the resource in question has been used "without compromising the ability of future generations to meet their own needs" (World Commission on Environment and Development, 1987, p. 8). Sustainability is a rough index of management success; it does not necessarily imply that resource utilization is optimal from either ecological or economic points of view (see World Conservation Strategy, 1980). Note that the criterion of sustainability is both human, and resource-centric regarding the source of valuation, not exclusively one or the other.

## EVIDENCE ON EXCLUSION

*Open Access.* The evidence supports Hardin's argument concerning degradation due to the inability to regulate access to resources held as open access. Examples are many, and include the classic case of the historical depletion of various whale stocks in the open ocean. Several examples, however, reveal a point not mentioned by Hardin. In many cases, the tragedy occurred only after open-access conditions were created, often as a consequence of the destruction of existing communal land-tenure and marine-tenure systems. A number of these cases involved the imposition of colonial rule, as in sub-Saharan Africa (Johnson and Anderson, 1988), the Pacific Islands (Johannes, 1978), and northwest North American salmon rivers (Berkes, 1985, and references therein).

*Private Property.* The establishment and enforcement of private property rights have frequently provided the institutional arrangements for successful exclusion. Private-property rights may not, however, be sufficiently precise for solving the exclusion problem. A classic example is the exploitation of oil pools in much of the United States. In an 1889 Pennsylvania Supreme Court decision, the doctrine of law of capture was applied to oil. Private property rights in oil were assigned only upon extraction. In practice, this means that each owner of surface rights has the incentive to accelerate their pumping of oil to the surface. The result is a duplication of drilling and other capital costs, substantial reduction in the overall rate of recovery, and dissipation of economic rents. A remedy to the problem has long been recognized—to define property rights in the underground pool as a unit (unitization) before extraction rather than after. In jurisdictions (such as Wyoming) in which unitization is required before drilling on land leased for oil exploration, greater efficiency has been achieved. In spite of the potential gains for all users through unitization, this form of contract is uncommon in other jurisdictions (such as Texas and Oklahoma) because the high cost of private contracting inhibits its adoption. Private property rights and the incentives they afford are not always sufficient to achieve efficient exploitation (Libecap and Wiggins, 1985; Wiggins and Libecap, 1985).

There is an enforcement problem with all types of property rights, including private property. For common-property resources, which by definition pose exclusion problems, such enforcement can be costly. Well recognized *de jure* rights of the medieval lord, and even contemporary landlords, to fish and game have been routinely violated by poachers (McCay, 1987; Thompson, 1975). The extent to which the community regards private-property rights as legitimate affects the cost of enforcement. The difficulty of enforcing private claims to common-property resources is exacerbated by competing claims to communal rights in those resources. This is evident in the United States oyster industry, where a private property regime, including leasehold, is not politically acceptable in many areas (McCay, 1987) regardless of the fact that it is logical, feasible, and demonstrably more efficient (Agnello and Donnelley, 1984).

*Communal Property*. Hardin did not consider the possibility of exclusion under communal-property regimes. By exclusion we mean the power to exclude people other than members of a defined community. Evidence suggests that successful exclusion under communal property is the rule rather than the exception. Well-documented contemporary cases include Amerindian community hunting and fishing lands in James Bay, eastern subarctic Canada (Berkes, 1977, 1987; Feit, 1987). Here, the communal-property regime collapsed as a result of incursions by outsiders and recovered with the re-establishment of exclusion at least twice since the nineteenth century (Feit, 1986). Other examples come from the Pacific islands where communal-property regimes have collapsed in some areas but continue to be viable in many others (Johannes, 1978, 1982; Ruddle and Akimichi, 1984; Ruddle and Johannes, 1985).

Communal property is not confined to remote and sparsely populated areas. Cooperative-based coastal fisheries in Japan provide many successful examples of communal-property systems. These fishing communities hold legally guaranteed exclusive fishing rights in coastal areas (Ruddle, 1987, 1989). One of the major conclusions of the National Research Council conference (1986, p. 621) was that legal recognition of communal rights, as in Japanese coastal fisheries, was crucial for the success of communal-property regimes. Many of the island nation states in the Pacific are creating formal legal guarantees of traditional communal-property rights (Ruddle and Johannes, 1985; Baines, 1989). Even when there is no legal recognition of communal property, the exclusion of outsiders by local users through such means as threats and surreptitious violence is not uncommon (Acheson, 1975; McEvoy, 1988). The persistence of community-based lobster fishing territories in Maine is merely one example, but an important one because it occurs in a country and culture in which the belief in right of free access is deeply held (Acheson, 1987, 1988).

The examples given thus far are for fish and wildlife for which exclusion is particularly difficult because of the migratory nature of the resource. Successful exclusion can also be found for other resource types, including grazing lands, forests, and water resources (National Research Council, 1986; Fortmann and Bruce, 1988; Dani, *et al.*, 1987; Maass and Anderson, 1978).

Pressure on the resource because of human population growth, technological change, or economic change, including new market opportunities, may contribute to the breakdown of communal-property mechanisms for exclusion. The role of population growth is especially controversial. For example, some argue that in the case of East Africa, the carrying capacity of rangelands under any management regime has been exceeded (Talbot, 1986). Other cases indicate that population is merely one of many interrelated social and economic problems (Jodha, 1985; Johnson and Anderson, 1988; Peters, 1987; Fortmann and Roe, 1986).

Communal-property regimes fail to provide for exclusion for other reasons as well. Many of these failures are associated with the appropriation of the resource by politically or militarily powerful groups, or by other factors such as land reform that disrupt existing communal management systems (Jodha, 1987). Others are associated with problems of scale and internal organization. The social and political characteristics of the users of the resource and how they relate to the larger political system affect the ability of local groups to organize and manage communal property (Ostrom, 1987, 1988, forthcoming).

*State Property.* Exclusive state governance of the resource has in many cases been sufficient to provide for adequate exclusion. However, difficulties in exclusion are not necessarily overcome by declaring the resource to be state property. A vivid example comes from Nepal. Alarmed by deforestation, the government nationalized forests in 1957, converting what were often communal forests into *de jure* state property. But the result more closely approximated the creation of *de facto* open access. Villagers whose control of nearby forests had been removed often succumbed to the incentives of law of capture. Deforestation accelerated instead of decelerated. In the face of worsening conditions the government began to experiment in 1976 with the re-creation of communal-property rights (Arnold and Campbell, 1986; Bromley and Chapagain, 1984).

Similar evidence on exclusion is found in the management of state forests in Niger and Thailand. In both countries state property has often been treated as open access. In response to the growing crisis of degradation in Niger, some farmers began in the 1980's to extend their private property rights in arable land to include the trees, which are *de jure* state property (Thomson *et al.*, 1986, 1989; Feeny, 1988a).

Another problem with state governance is that imperfections in the political process will often be mirrored in resource management (McEvoy, 1988). In some cultures, free access to certain resources for citizens at large is viewed as a right. In other cases, the state is especially responsive to the interests of the elite (Feeny, 1982, 1988b; Jodha, 1985). Some instances of apparent tragedies of the commons are more accurately construed as examples of government failure (Anderson, 1987; Marchak, 1988-1989).

The logic of the argument of *The Tragedy of the Commons* is that we should not observe sustainable management of common-property resources and the exclusion of some uses or users, under regimes other than private or state property. But as we have illustrated, exclusion is feasible, if not always successful, under private, state, *and* communal-property regimes. Furthermore, private or state ownership is not always sufficient to provide for exclusion.

## EVIDENCE ON REGULATIONS OF USE AND USERS

*Open Access.* Hardin's predictions that incentives for successful resource management are absent from or weak in open access regimes are in general consistent with the evidence. In such regimes, under conditions in which demand exceeds the capacity of the resource to sustain itself, and where the technology is available to exploit the resource at a high level, many species, including the North American passenger pigeon and the bison, have become extinct, or virtually extinct. In the context of the day, free and unregulated use of resources such as the bison initially made sense. To illustrate the individual rationality that lay behind ecological tragedy, Hardin (1978) invokes the image of Kit Carson shooting bison on the plains, taking only the tongue and leaving the rest. This is not economically irrational if one considers that the game was then abundant but the hunter's time was scarce. Depletion occurred rapidly, before countervailing institutional arrangements or changing cultural values could prevent it.

*Private Property.* Privatization usually provides incentives for rational exploitation of the resource. If the owner has property rights in the resource and those rights are tradeable, both the costs and benefits will accrue to the same owner and will be reflected in the market price of the resource, giving the owner the pecuniary incentive to refrain from destructive use. These incentives, however, are not necessarily consistent with sustainable use. Suppose a redwood planted for $1 is worth $14,000 at maturity—which may take 2000 years. The implied rate of return would be less than 0.5%, well below the rates of return generally available to investors. Although planting a redwood may make ecological sense, it does not make economic sense under a private-property regime (Hardin, 1979).

More realistically, Clark (1973) has shown that for relatively slow-growing and late-maturing species such as whales, it may be economically optimal to deplete the resource rather than to use it sustainably. For the Antarctic blue whale with a maximum sustainable yield level of probably no more than 5% a human-rate of time preference (discount rate) of greater than this 5% would be sufficient to lead to its extinction, even under exclusive and enforceable private-property rights. These rights permit the owner to maximize the present value of the resource, yet the resource is not protected from extinction.

*Communal Property*. There is abundant evidence, contrary to Hardin, on the ability of social groups to design, utilize, and adapt often ingenious mechanisms to allocate use rights among members. The medieval English commons featured in Hardin's paper, like many other historic and contemporary commons, were often subject to comprehensive systems of regulation. For example, stinting was often practiced, that is, limiting the number of head that each owner could graze. Not only was access exclusive to certain members of the village, but their rights were often closely regulated (McCloskey, 1976; Cox, 1985; Campbell and Godoy, 1986; Dahlman, 1980; Fenoaltea, 1988). A plethora of scholars have noted in passing that the commons operated successfully for several hundred years in medieval England, and have questioned if a tragedy of the sort described by Hardin (1968) ever occurred widely (Schumacher, 1979, p. 139; Repetto, 1985, p. 145; Potter, 1974, p. 813; Dasgupta, 1983, p. 13; Marchak, 1988-89, p. 9).

Forest and meadow commons in Japanese villages were also the subject of elaborate regulations. Village leaders set opening and closing dates for the harvest of certain products. In some villages, thatch was harvested collectively; bundles were then randomly assigned to each household. This device permitted the aggregate level of utilization to be controlled while giving each household an incentive to be reasonably conscientious in its harvesting effort. Guards patrolled the common lands to prevent poaching both by villagers and outsiders. Written rules provided a graduated schedule of fines for violators. Harvesting tools were also regulated. Regulations legislated by villagers ensured sustainable use of common lands for generations (McKean, 1982, 1986).

In the Japanese case, forest and meadow lands and irrigation works were held as communal property while crop lands were held privately. This is not an isolated example of the co-existence of two property-rights regimes. There are other cases indicating the ability of users to match appropriately the resource with the regime (Netting, 1976). In some societies, the same resource may alternate back and forth between communal and private control seasonally or over the long term (Bauer, 1987; Vondal, 1987; Acheson, 1989b; Wade, 1986, 1987).

Not all examples of successful regulation are historic or based on longstanding tradition. In a study of Turkish coastal fisheries, successful regulation was found to have evolved within 15 years in two cases (Alanya, Tasucu), and 9 years in one case (Berkes, 1986a). Alarmed by the increasing numbers of users and escalating conflicts, fishermen in Alanya developed a system to regulate use: fishing sites were spaced sufficiently apart to avoid interference, and fisherman agreed among themselves to fish in rotation to ensure equitable access to best sites, with their starting position determined by drawing lots. Although only half of the licensed fishermen belonged to the local marketing cooperative, the authority under which the system was operated, all participated in the process for creating and maintaining it (Berkes, 1986b).

Self-regulation of resource use to improve livelihood was also achieved by a local marketing cooperative of New Jersey fishermen. Because large catches depressed prices on the New York fresh fish market, a cooperative was formed to enhance producers' bargaining power. This cooperative decided on total catch levels for the fleet, and provided for the sharing of revenues regardless of the catch levels of individual boats. The pooling of revenues reduced the incentives to over-fish. Although the system was devised to raise prices, a spillover benefit may have been conservation (McCay, 1980).

A case from South India provides another example. In a village in Andhra Pradesh, villagers at the tail end of a large government-run irrigation scheme found that they were particularly vulnerable to fluctuations in water supply after the end of the rainy season. Although the traditional practice, in which households attempted to have plots at various locations throughout the village, reduced the variability in household agricultural production, villagers realized that careful management of village water resources could further increase and stabilize yields. A village water-user's association was formed and rules were developed. Irrigators were hired to manage the allocation of water; salaries were paid through taxes levied on landowners, based on the area irrigated. Along any particular irrigation ditch, fields closest to the source of the water could only be watered after downstream fields had been adequately wetted. The fact that prominent village landowners owned plots throughout the village helped to ensure their assistance in organizing a village-wide system of irrigation (Wade, 1986, 1987).

These case studies illustrate that people are not helpless but are able to organize, to monitor resource use by members, to allocate use rights among members, and to adjust aggregate utilization levels to maintain sustainable use of the resource (McEvoy, 1988). These cases, and those detailed elsewhere, indicate that under the appropriate circumstances, voluntary collective action is feasible and effective (McCay, 1978; National Research Council, 1986; McCay and Acheson, 1987; Ostrom, forthcoming; Wade, 1986, 1987).

*State Property.* Government ownership (state governance) permits the formulation of appropriate regulations for resource use. It also provides for the expression of public interest and for accountability. But state governance does not necessarily ensure sustainable use. Given that the officials who make decisions do not have the same time horizon or interests as private owners, the general public, or the government itself, this is not surprising.

One of the oft-mentioned problems of state ownership is the proliferation of such regulations. Smith points out, for example, that in a New England regional fishery, the combination of quotas, allocations, and trip limitations generated more than 100 different limits, with the result that there was widespread violation of the law (Smith, 1988). Noncompliance of users and *de facto* open access has led to an assertion by some that better protection can be achieved under private- rather than state-property regimes.

State ownership is seldom associated with successful management in less-developed countries. The professional resource-management infrastructure of the state is usually poorly developed and enforcement of regulations problematic. In India, for example, communally-held forests were nationalized before the state had developed the capacity for management. Local communities are, however, starting to re-assert their cultural traditions of conservation (Gadgil, 1985, 1987; Gadgil and Iyer, 1989). In much of South Asia, Africa, and elsewhere, poorly-defended state property, in conjunction with population pressure, has led to widespread poaching of government forest and other resources. Repetto argues that "villagers who ruthlessly cut trees for firewood and fodder in government forests will zealously nurture and protect groves that belong to them or—if their community is sufficiently strong—to their village" (Repetto, 1986, pp. 30-31).

The logic of the argument of "The Tragedy of the Commons" is that private owners or state managers can and often do manage resources successfully. That is, these two property-rights regimes would provide the incentives to regulate use in a fashion consistent with sustainability. Implicitly Hardin argues that these incentives would be absent or weak for other regimes. However, the evidence indicates that complex interactions among the characteristics of the resource, the property-rights regime and other institutional arrangements, and the socio-economic environment contribute to the degree of management success. Success in the regulation of uses and users is not universally associated with any particular type of property-rights regime. Communal property, private property, and government property have all been associated both with success and failure.

## CONCLUSIONS

Hardin's model is insightful but incomplete. His conclusion of unavoidable tragedy follows from his assumptions of open access, lack of constraints on individual behavior, conditions in which demand exceeds supply, and resource users who are incapable of altering the rules. Actual common-property situations often do not conform to all four of these assumptions. This leads us to amend Hardin's heuristic fable. The "tragedy" may start as in Hardin (1968). But after several years of declining yields, the herdsmen are likely to get together to seek ways to (1) control access to the pasture, and (2) agree upon a set of rules of conduct, perhaps including stinting, that effectively limits exploitation. Whether or not the intended self-regulation works depends on a number of factors. Here the simple model breaks down – no single metaphor can tell the full story. The medieval English commons usually were regulated by the community, sometimes effectively, sometimes not. The outcome was never so clear and deterministically predictable as in Hardin's model.

Thus, a major conclusion of the paper is the rejection of the simple one-to-one relationship between property-rights regime and outcome postulated by Hardin. The Hardin argument overlooks the important role of institutional arrangements that provide for exclusion and regulation of use. It also overlooks cultural factors (Feeny, 1988b; Charles, 1988). In order to understand the outcome, one needs to know the nature of the resource, the whole array of decision-making arrangements, including the property-rights regime, and the nature of the interactions among users and regulators (Oakerson, 1986; Godwin and Shepard, 1979, p. 266; McEvoy, 1988, p. 229). Complex interactions are an important characteristic of commons situations, and models of the commons must take these interactions into account (for a review of the mathematics of describing complex interactive systems, see West and Shlesinger, 1990). Success may be found under three, not just two property-rights regimes.

The original Hardin paper did, however, allude to the potential viability of communal property. Hardin's (1968, p. 1247) phrase, "mutual coercion, mutually agreed upon" is consistent with communal-property arrangements, although he appears to have meant state institutions under representative government. Societies have the capacity to construct and enforce rules and norms that constrain the behavior of individuals. In many societies and in many situations, the capacity for concerted social action overcomes the divergence between individual and collective rationality. The cases discussed in this paper provide ample evidence of the ability of groups of users and local communities to organize and to manage local resources effectively. Contrary to assumptions by many common-property analysts, these communal-property arrangements have persisted. A diversity of societies in the past and present have independently devised, maintained, or adapted communal arrangements to manage common-property resources. Their persistence is not an historical accident; these arrangements build on knowledge of the resource and cultural norms that have evolved and been tested over time.

The new interest in communal property arrangements is perhaps related to the resurgence of interest in grass-roots democracy, public participation, and local-level planning. State property regimes in which officials exercise exclusive decision-making powers have been falling into disfavor. Given that there are many situations in which users have the capacity for self-management, it makes administrative and economic sense to involve them in resource management. Communities of resource users are, however, no longer relatively isolated and resources often have multiple uses. Therefore, complete devolution may not be appropriate; it makes sense for the state to continue to play a role in resource conservation and allocation among communities of users. Shared governance or state regulation jointly with user self-management is thus a viable option. Such co-management can capitalize on the local knowledge and long-term self-interest of users, while providing for coordination with relevant uses and users over a wide geographic scope at potentially lower transaction (rule-enforcement) cost (McCay, 1988; Acheson, 1989a; Pinkerton, 1989).

Further, the logic of communal property can also be applied to resources that are global (rather than local) in scope. Here, tragedies are more difficult to prevent. This is perhaps why the World Conservation Strategy (1980) and the World Commission on Environment and Development (1987) both emphasized the global commons. Problems such as ozone depletion and carbon dioxide accumulation in the atmosphere are clearly global tragedies of the commons in the making. The solution of such problems will necessarily involve co-management on a large scale. The 1987 Montreal Protocol to protect the ozone layer is an example of international co-management. The case of oil pollution on the high seas, with various international conventions going back to 1954 (Cuyvers, 1984), and leading to reductions in accidental oil spills in the 1980's, the Alaska spill notwithstanding, demonstrates that international cooperation can be effective (World Resources Institute, 1988, p. 330).

The problem posed by Hardin over 20 years ago captured the attention of a multi-disciplinary collection of scholars and practitioners, including anthropologists, development planners, ecologists, economists, geographers, political scientists, resource scientists, and sociologists. *The Common Property Resource Digest,* published since December 1986, is distributed to more than 3500 individuals and institutions. Hardin's model provided insights and focused attention on important analytical issues. However, as with many seminal but simple models, Hardin's analysis has been shown by subsequent studies to be overly simplified and deterministic. As is the usual process in science, theory will have to be revised to take into account the new evidence (Feeny, 1989).

A new and more comprehensive theory for common-property resources must be able to account for sustainable resource management under communal-property regimes. The theory should be capable of accommodating user self-organization or the lack of it. Such a model can better explain whether and under what conditions sustainable resource management will occur, rather than simply predicting the demise of all resources held in common.

## ACKNOWLEDGMENTS

The authors acknowledge the helpful comments of Mina Kislalioglu, Donald McCloskey, Stuart Mestelman, Elinor Ostrom, Henry Regier, Darrell Tomkins, and two anonymous referees. The usual disclaimer applies. The Common Property Resource Digest is available from 332E Classroom Office Building, 1994 Buford Avenue, University of Minnesota, St. Paul, Minnesota 55108.

## REFERENCES

Acheson, J. M. (1975). The lobster fiefs: Economic and ecological effects of territoriality in the Maine lobster industry. *Human Ecology* 3: 183-207.

Acheson, J. M. (1987). The lobster fiefs, revisited: Economic and ecological effects of territoriality in the Maine lobster industry. In McCay, B. J., and Acheson, J. M. (eds.), *The Question of the Commons.* University of Arizona Press, Tucson, pp. 37-65.

Acheson, J. M. (1988). *The Lobster Gangs of Maine.* University Press of New England, Hanover, and London.

Acheson, J. M. (1989a). Where have all the exploitings gone? Co-management of the Maine lobster industry. In Berkes, F. (ed.), *Common Property Resources.* Belhaven, London, pp. 199-217.

Acheson, J. M. (1989b). Economic anthropology and the management of common property resources. In Plattner, S. (ed.), *Economic Anthropology.* Stanford University Press, Stanford, pp. 351-378.

Agnello, R. J., and Donnelley, L. P. (1984). Regulation and the structure of property rights: The case of the U.S. oyster industry. *Research in Law and Economics* 6: 165-172.

Anderson, E. N., Jr. (1987). A Malaysian tragedy of the commons. In McCay, B. J., and Acheson, J. M. (eds.), *The Question of the Commons.* University of Arizona Press, Tucson, pp. 327-343.

Arnold, J. E. M., and Campbell, J. G. (1986). Collective management of hill forests in Nepal: The community forestry development project. National Research Council, Proceedings of the Conference on Common Property Resource Management, National Academy Press, Washington, D.C., pp. 425-454.

Baines, G. B. K. (1989). Traditional resource management in the Melanesian South Pacific: A development dilemma. In Berkes, F. (ed.), *Common Property Resources.* Belhaven, London, pp. 273-295.

Bauer, D. (1987). The dynamics of communal and hereditary land tenure among the Tigray of Ethiopia. In McCay, B. J., and Acheson, J. M. (eds.), *The Question of the Commons.* University of Arizona Press, Tucson, pp. 217-230.

Berkes, F. (1977). Fishery resource use in a subarctic Indian community. *Human Ecology* 5: 289-307.

Berkes, F. (1985). Fishermen and the "tragedy of the commons." *Environmental Conservation* 12: 199-206.

Berkes, F. (1986a). Marine inshore fishery management in Turkey. National Research Council, Proceedings of the Conference on Common Property Resource Management, National Academy Press, Washington, D.C., pp. 63-83.

Berkes, F. (1986b). Local-level management and the commons problem: A comparative study of Turkish coastal fisheries. *Marine Policy* 10: 215-229.

Berkes, F. (1987). Common-property resource management and Cree Indian fisheries in subartic Canada. In McCay, B. J., and Acheson, J. M. (eds.), *The Question of the Commons.* University of Arizona Press, Tucson, pp. 66-91.

Berkes, F. (ed.) (1989). *Common Property Resources: Ecology and Community-Based Sustainable Development*. Belhaven, London.

Berkes, F., Feeny, D., McCay, B., and Acheson, J. M. (1989). The benefits of the commons. *Nature* 340: 91-93.

Blaikie, P., and Brookfield, H. (1987). Common property resources and degradation worldwide. In Blaikie, P., and Brookfield, H. (eds.), *Land Degradation and Society*. Methuen, London, pp. 186-196.

Bromley, D. W. (1986). Closing comments. National Research Council, Proceedings of the Conference on Common Property Resource Management, National Academy Press, Washington, D.C., pp. 593-598.

Bromley, D. W. (1989a). *Economic Interests and Institutions*. Blackwell, Oxford.

Bromley, D. W. (1989b). Property relations and economic development: The other land reform. *World Development* 17: 867-877.

Bromley, D. W., and Cernea, M. M. (1989). The management of common property natural resources. Washington, D.C.: World Bank Discussion Paper No. 57.

Bromley, D. W., and Chapagain, D. P. (1984). The village against the center: Resource depletion in South Asia. *American Journal of Agricultural Economics* 66: 868-873.

Campbell, B., and Godoy, R. A. (1986). Commonfield agriculture: The Andes and medieval England compared. National Research Council, Proceedings of the Conference on Common Property Resource Management. National Academy Press, Washington, D.C., pp. 323-358.

Charles, A. (1988). Fishery socioeconomics: A survey. *Land Economics* 64: 276-295.

Ciriacy-Wantrup, S. V., and Bishop, R. C. (1975). "Common property" as a concept in natural resource policy. *Natural Resources Journal* 15: 713-727.

Clark, C. W. (1973). The economics of overexploitation. *Science* 181: 630-634.

Cordell, J. (ed.) (1989). *A Sea of Small Boats*. Cultural Survival, Inc., Cambridge.

Cox, S. J. B. (1985). No tragedy on the commons. *Environmental Ethics* 7: 49-61.

Cuyvers, L. (1984). *Ocean Uses and Their Regulation*. Wiley, New York.

Dahlman, C. (1980). *The Open Field System and Beyond: A Property Rights Analysis of an Economic Institution*. Cambridge University Press, Cambridge.

Dani, A. A., Gibbs, C. J. N., and Bromley, D. W. (1987). *Institutional Development for Local Management of Rural Resources*. East-West Center, Honolulu.

Dasgupta, P. S. (1983). *The Control of Resources*. Harvard University Press, Cambridge.

Demsetz, H. (1967). Toward a theory of property rights. *American Economic Review* 57: 347-359.

Feeny, D. H. (1982). *The Political Economy of Productivity: Thai Agricultural Development, 1880-1975*. University of British Columbia Press, Vancouver.

Feeny, D. H. (1988a). Agricultural expansion and forest depletion in Thailand, 1900–1975. In Richards, J. F. and Tucker, R. (eds.), *World Forests in the Twentieth Century*. Duke University Press, Durham, pp. 112-143, 281-287.

Feeny, D. H. (1988b). The demand for and supply of institutional arrangements. In Ostrom, V., Feeny, D., and Picht, H. (eds.), *Rethinking Institutional Analysis and Development: Issues, Alternatives and Choices*. Institute for Contemporary Studies Press, San Francisco, pp. 159-209.

Feeny, D. H. (1989). Where do we go from here?: Implications for the research agenda. McMaster University Department of Economics Working Paper 89-18.

Feit, H. A. (1986). James Bay Cree Indian management and moral considerations of fur bearers. In *Native People and Renewable Resource Management*. Alberta Society of Professional Biologists, Edmonton, pp. 49-65.

Feit, H. A. (1987). North American native hunting and management of moose populations. *Swedish Wildlife Research Viltervy* (Suppl. 1): 25-42.

Fenoaltea, S. (1988). Transaction costs, Whig history, and the common fields. *Politics and Society* 16: 171-240.

Fortmann, L., and Bruce, J. W. (eds.). (1988). *Whose Trees? Proprietary Dimensions of Forestry*. Westview, Boulder.

Fortmann, L., and Roe, E. M. (1986). Common property management of water in Botswana. National Research Coucnil, Proceedings of the Conference on Common Property Resource Management. National Academy Press, Washington, D.C., pp. 161-180.

Gadgil, M. (1985). Cultural evolution of ecological prudence. *Landscape Planning* 12: 285-299.
Gadgil, M. (1987). Diversity: Cultural and ecological. *Trends in Ecology and Evolution* 2(12): 369-373.
Gadgil, M., and Iyer, P. (1989). On the diversification of common property resource use by the Indian society. in Berkes, F. (ed.), *Common Property Resources*. Belhaven, London, pp. 240-255.
Gibbs, C. J. N., and Bromley, D. W. (1989). Institutional arrangements for management of rural resources: Common-property regimes. In Berkes, F. (ed.), *Common Property Resources*. Belhaven, London, pp. 22-32.
Godwin, R. K., and Shepard, W. B. (1979). Forcing squares, triangles and ellipses into a circular paradigm: The use of the commons dilemma in examining the allocation of common resources. *Western Political Quarterly* 32: 265-277.
Gordon, J. S. (1954). The economic theory of a common-property resource: The fishery. *Journal of Political Economy* 62: 124-142.
Hardin, G. (1968). The tragedy of the commons. *Science* 162: 1243-1248.
Hardin, G. (1978). Political requirements for preserving our common heritage. In Brokaw, H. P. (ed.), *Wildlife and America*. Council on Environmental Quality, Washington, D.C., pp. 310-317.
Hardin, G. (1979). Why plant a redwood tree? In Miller, G. T. (ed.), *Living in the Environment* (2nd Ed.). Wadsworth, Belmont, pp. 206-207.
Hardin, G., and Baden, J. (eds.) (1977). *Managing the Commons*. Freemen, San Francisco.
Jacobs, P., and Munro, D. A. (eds.) (1987). *Conservation with Equity. Strategies for Sustainable Development*. International Union for the Conservation of Nature and Natural Resources (IUCN), Cambridge.
Jodha, N. S. (1985). Population growth and the decline of common property resources in Rajasthan India. *Population and Development Review* 11: 247-264.
Jodha, N. S. (1987). A case study of degradation of common property resources in India. In Blaikie, P., and Brookfield, H. (eds.), *Land Degradation and Society*. Methuen, London, pp. 196-207.
Johannes, R. E. (1978). Traditional marine conservation methods in Oceania and their demise. *Annual Review of Ecology and Systematics* 9: 349-364.
Johannes, R. E. (1982). Traditional conservation methods and protected marine areas in Oceania. *Ambio* 11: 258-261.
Johnson, D., and Anderson, D. (eds.) (1988). *The Ecology of Survival: Case Studies from Northeast African History*. Crook, London.
Libecap, G. D. (1986). Government policies on property rights to land: U.S. implications for agricultural development in Mexico. *Agricultural History* 60: 32-49.
Libecap, G. D., and Wiggins, S. N. (1985). The influence of private contractual failure on regulations: The case of oil field unitization. *Journal of Political Economy* 93: 690-714.
Lineberry, R. (1983). *Government in America* (2nd Ed.). Little Brown, Boston.
Lloyd, W. F. (1968). *Lectures on Population, Value, Poor-laws, and Rent. Delivered in the University of Oxford during the Years 1832, 1833, 1834, 1835, and 1836*. Reprints of Economic Classics, Kelley, New York.
Maass, A., and Anderson, R. L. (1978). *And the Desert Shall Rejoice. Conflict, Growth and Justice in Arid Environments*. MIT Press, Cambridge.
Marchak, M. P. (1987). Uncommon property. In Marchak, P., Guppy, N., and McMullan, J. (eds.), *Uncommon Property: The Fishing and Fish Processing Industries in British Columbia*. Methuen, Toronto, pp. 3-31.
Marchak, M. P. (1988-1989). What happens when common property becomes uncommon? *BC Studies* 80: 3-23.
Marchak, M. P., Guppy, N., and McMullan, J. (eds.) (1987). *Uncommon Property: The Fishing and Fish-Processing Industry in British Columbia*. Methuen, Toronto.
Matthews, R. (1988). Federal licensing policies for the Atlantic inshore fishery and their implementation in Newfoundland, 1973–1981. *Acadiensis* 17: 83-108.
McCay, B. J. (1978). Systems ecology, people, ecology and the anthropology of fishing communities. *Human Ecology* 6: 397-422.
McCay, B. J. (1980). A fishermen's cooperative, limited: Indigenous resource management in a complex society. *Anthropological Quarterly* 53: 29-38.

McCay, B. J. (1987). The culture of the commoners. Historical observations on Old and New World fisheries. In McCay, B. J., and Acheson, J. M. (eds.), *The Question of the Commons.* University of Arizona Press, Tucson, pp. 195-216.

McCay, B. J. (1988). Muddling through the clam beds: Cooperative management of New Jersey's hard clam spawner sanctuaries. *Journal of Shellfish Research* 7: 327-340.

McCay, B. J., and Acheson, J. M. (eds.) (1987). *The Question of the Commons. The culture and Ecology of Communal Resources.* University of Arizona Press, Tucson.

McCloskey, D. N. (1976). English open fields as behavior toward risk. *Research in Economic History* 1: 124-170.

McEvoy, A. F. (1986). *The Fisherman's Problem: Ecology and Law in the California Fisheries, 1850*–1980. Cambridge University Press, Cambridge.

McEvoy, A. F. (1988). Toward an interactive theory of nature and culture: Ecology, production, and cognition in the California fishing industry. In Worster, D. (ed.), *The Ends of the Earth: Perspective on Modern Environmental History.* Cambridge University Press, Cambridge, pp. 211-229.

McKean, M. A. (1982). The Japanese experience with scarcity: Management of traditional commons lands. *Environmental Review* 6: 63-88.

McKean, M. A. (1986). Management of traditional common lands (iriaichi) in Japan. National Research Council, Proceedings of the Conference on Common Property Resource Management, National Academy Press, Washington, D.C., pp. 533-589.

Moore, J. A. (1985). Science as a way of knowing—human ecology. *American Zoologist* 25: 483-637.

National Research Council (1986). *Proceedings of the Conference on Common Property Resource Management.* National Academy Press, Washington, D.C.

Nebel, B. J. (1987). *Environmental Science* (2nd Ed.). Prentice-Hall, Englewood Cliffs, New Jersey.

Netting, R., McC. (1976). What Alpine peasants have in common: Observations in communal tenure in a Swiss village. *Human Ecology* 4: 135-146.

Oakerson, R. J. (1986). A model for the analysis of common property problems. National Research Council, Proceedings of the Conference on Common Property Resource Management. National Academy Press, Washington, D.C., pp. 13-30.

Ostrom, E. (1986). Issues of definition and theory: Some conclusions and hypotheses. National Research Council, Proceedings of the Conference on Common Property Resource Management. National Academy Press, Washington, D.C., pp. 599-615.

Ostrom, E. (1987). Institutional arrangements for resolving the commons dilemma: Some contending approaches. In McCay, B. J., and Acheson, J. M. (eds.), *The Question of the Commons.* University of Arizona Press, Tucson, pp. 250-265.

Ostrom, E. (1988). Institutional arrangements and the commons dilemma. In Ostrom, V., Feeny, D., and Picht, H. (eds.), *Rethinking Institutional Analysis and Development.* Institute for Contemporary Studies Press, San Francisco, pp. 101-139.

Ostrom, E. *Governing the Commons.* Cambridge University Press, Cambridge (forthcoming).

Peters, P. E. (1987). Embedded systems and rooted models: The grazing lands of Botswana and the commons debate. In McCay, B. J., and Acheson, J. M. (eds.), *The Question of the Commons.* University of Arizona Press, Tucson, pp. 171-194.

Pinkerton, E. (ed.) (1989). *Co-operative Management of Local Fisheries.* University of British Columbia Press, Vancouver.

Potter, V. R. (1974). The tragedy of the Sahel commons. *Science* 185: 813.

Regier, H. A., and Grima, A. P. (1985). Fishery reserve allocation: An explanatory essay. *Canadian Journal of Fisheries and Aquatic Sciences* 42: 845-859.

Repetto, R. (ed.) (1985). *The Global Possible.* Yale University Press, New Haven.

Repetto, R. (1986). *World Enough and Time.* Yale University Press, New Haven.

Ruddle, K. (1987). Administration and conflict management in Japanese coastal fisheries. FAO Fisheries Technical Paper 273.

Ruddle, K. (1989). Solving the common property dilemma. Village fisheries rights in Japanese coastal waters. In Berkes, F. (ed.), *Common Property Resources.* Belhaven, London, pp. 168-184.

Ruddle, K., and Akimichi, T. (eds.) (1984). *Maritime Institutions in the Western Pacific.* National Museum of Ethnology, Osaka.

Ruddle, K., and Johannes, R. E. (eds ) (1985). *The Traditional Knowledge and Management of Coastal Systems in Asia and the Pacific.* Unesco, Jakarta.

Schumacher, E. F. (1979). *Good Work.* Harper and Row, New York.

Scott, A. D. (1955). The fishery: The objectives of sole ownership. *Journal of Political Economy* 63: 116-124.

Smith, M. E. (1988). Fisheries risk in modern contest. *Maritime Anthropological Studies* 1: 29-48.

Talbot, L. M. (1986). Rangeland destruction in East Africa. *Population and Development Review* 12: 441-452.

Thompson, F. P. (1975). *Whigs and Hunters.* Lane, London.

Thomson, J. R., Feeny, D. H., and Oakerson, R. J. (1986). Institutional dynamics: The evolution and dissolution of common property resource management. National Research Council, Proceedings of the Conference on Common Property Resource Management, National Academy Press, Washington, D.C., pp. 392-424.

Thomson, J. R., Feeny, D. H., and Oakerson, R. J. (1989). Institutional dynamics: The evolution and dissolution of common property resource management. McMaster University Department of Economics Working Paper 89-17.

Vondal, P. J. (1987). The common swamplands of Southeastern Borneo: Multiple use, management, and conflict. In McCay, B. J., and Acheson, J. M. (eds.), *The Question of the Commons.* University of Arizona Press, Tucson, pp. 231-249.

Wade, R. (1986). Common property reserve arrangement in South Indian villages. National Research Council, Proceedings of the Conference on Common Property Resource Management, National Academy Press, Washington, D.C., pp. 231-257.

Wade, R. (1987). *Village Republics: Economic Conditions for Collective Action in South India.* Cambridge University Press, Cambridge.

West, B. J., and Shlesinger, M. (1990). The noise in natural phenomena. *American Scientist* 78: 40-45.

Wiggins, S. N., and Libecap, G. D. (1985). Oil field unitization: Contractual failure in the presence of imperfect information. *American Economic Review* 75: 368-385.

World Commission on Environment and Development (1987). *Our Common Future.* Oxford University Press, Oxford.

World Conservation Strategy (1980). *World Conservation Strategy: Living Resource Conservation for Sustainable Development.* IUCN/UNEP/WWF, International Union for the Conservation of Nature and Natural Resources, Gland.

World Resources Institute (1988). *World Resources 1988-1989.* Basic Books, New York.

[9]

JOURNAL OF ENVIRONMENTAL ECONOMICS AND MANAGEMENT **30**, 18–33 (1996)
ARTICLE NO. 0002

# Population Pressure and Land Degradation: The Case of Ethiopia

SVERRE GREPPERUD[1]

*University of Oslo, Department of Economics, P.O. Box 1095, Blindern, N-0317, Oslo, Norway*

Received July 27, 1993; revised June 27, 1994

This paper tests the population pressure hypothesis (PPH) for the Ethiopian Highlands using quantitative methods. The hypothesis posits that under comparable physical conditions heavily eroded areas occur in highly populated regions. A severity of soil erosion index (SESI), a proxy for some types of water erosion, was chosen as the dependent variable. Because the dependent variable is categorical and ordinal, an ordinal cumulative logit model was chosen for the analysis. The findings imply that as pressure from people and livestock exceeds some threshold, a rapid degradation of land take place. 

## 1. INTRODUCTION

The literature of the 1970s generated a number of important hypotheses concerning possible harmful consequences of rapid population growth (Meadows *et al.* [25], NAoS [29]), but there has been remarkably little work examining their empirical relevance. This is particularly the case for issues concerning population and the environment. The intention of this paper is to test the Population Pressure Hypothesis (PPH)[2] which relates land degradation directly to population pressure. The hypothesis is frequently addressed, directly or indirectly, in papers on environmental degradation for developing countries (Kelley [23] and Srinivasan [31]).

Most empirical studies on land degradation analyze the impact of physical factors and farming practices on soil erosion, for selected test plots, creating constraints on analyzing factors such as land tenure and population pressure. Two studies of large-scale data on land degradation are Whitlow [33] and Kuru [24]. Both studies try to identify factors responsible for distinctive erosion patterns. Neither is convincing due to their partial character and inefficient statistical methods.[3] In this paper we perform a multivariate analysis to identify factors

[1] A previous and longer draft of this paper appeared in the World Bank's Environment Department Divisional Working Paper Series [18]. The author is indebted to J. English, S. Hansen, and T. Schweder for comments at various stages in the preparation of this paper. I also thank O. Burt and three anonymous referees for very constructive suggestions. The work related to this paper is sponsored by the World Bank, and the findings, interpretations, and conclusions expressed are entirely those of the author and should not in any matter be attributed to the World Bank or its affiliated organizations, or to members of its Board of executive directors or the countries they represent.

[2] The term PPH is to my knowledge first applied by Baikie and Brookfield [7].

[3] Whitlow [33] compares erosion and land tenure patterns for Zimbabwe in order to reveal any systematic tendencies. Kuru [24] includes several explanatory factors in his study on Ethiopia, among them population density. Most of his analysis, however, is done by scatter plots, providing information only on bivariate relationships.



0095-0696/96 $12.00

responsible for the observed spatial distribution of soil erosion for Ethiopia. Even though the data applied are not fully satisfactory, the analysis suggests interesting causal relationships that shed light on the impact of population on resource degradation. The key finding is that the probability of an area being classified above any given level of soil erosion rapidly increases as population exceeds the population-supporting capacity of its region.

The next section presents two opposing groups of theories concerning the role of population in relation to resource management; the Population Pressure Hypothesis and Boserupian theories. The subsequent sections outline the model, describe data, and present the results that follow from the testing of the PPH for the Ethiopian Highlands. In Section 3, the framework is introduced together with the selection of variables. Furthermore, data and their sources are described together with a discussion of their reliability. Following this, in Section 4, the estimation technique is described, while the results are presented in Section 5. The last section summarizes the findings and discusses their interpretation with reference to the historical circumstances of Ethiopia.

## 2. POPULATION PRESSURE AND AGRICULTURAL DEVELOPMENT

The FAO methodology [17] classifies the causes of soil erosion into physical factors like topography, climate and soils, and human factors. The physical factors may be considered as exogenous for land managers, with rain and wind being the agents that physically cause the removal of soil. Human factors are analyzed in some of the economic literature on development. High discount rates and low agricultural output prices have been blamed for depressing farmer incentives for soil conservation (see, e.g., Griffin and Stoll [19] and Barrett [5]). Another aspect is tenurial regimes which may discourage the adoption of soil conservation measures and encourage resource depletion. The role of agrarian institutions and effort incentives for maintaining and improving the quality of land are discussed in Bardhan [4] and Bose [8].

In the last few decades a neo-Malthusian set of hypotheses has emphasized the role of population on environmental degradation in developing countries. The theories stress population as a major cause of economic and social problems, neglect the role of development, and view resources as finite. The population pressure hypothesis is mentioned in several works on land degradation and population (Ruddle and Manshard [30], Eckholm [16], and World Bank [34]). When the population–land ratio increases, the processes of extensification and intensification take place.

In the process of extensification, as population increases, demand for fuel, building materials, and land for crops and livestock also increases, forcing people onto new land. More of the original vegetative cover of the land is removed, and new, less fertile land is brought into agricultural production. New, marginal land is less suitable for production and more erosion-prone as a result of poor soil properties, shallow soil, and unfavorable topographic and climatic conditions. People forced onto marginal land bring with them their old cultivation practices, which may not be suited to the new environment.

In the process of intensification, over time, demographic pressure forces people to intensify cultivation. This can occur parallel or subsequent to the process of extensification.[4] Eventually very limited opportunities remain to bring new land into use. To support their households, farmers intensify their agricultural activities on land already in use. In shifting cultivation, farmers may increasingly employ shorter intervals of fallowing, giving the land insufficient recovery time. New cultivation practices introduced to deal with increasing needs for food may not be well adapted to the local environment and may have harmful long-term consequences on the resource base. Livestock production may intensify as well, increasing the risks of overgrazing and making land more susceptible to soil erosion.

Attention must also be given to the interlinkages between cultivators and pastoralists, and to farms practicing simultaneous crop cultivation and livestock rearing (mixed farms) under increased demographic pressure. Under extensification, cultivators may push out pastoralists and turn former grassland into cropland, leaving pastoralists on a diminished land area or forcing them to more erosion-prone grassland. On mixed farms with no options for expanding onto new land, increasing household size results in competition between crops and livestock for the same land. Farmers are forced to rear the livestock on cropland between harvest and sowing, exposing the fragile land to compaction and removal of crop residues.

In general, the PPH ignores the possibility that farmers can adapt to a changing environment (demographic pressure) and stresses the harmful consequences of adopting new cultivation practices. This theory does not consider the possibilities farmers have to change or reverse a malign development. Several authors challenge this direct link between population density and land degradation, emphasizing the role of development in increasing the productivity of land and mitigating the process of soil mining.

Boserup [9] regards population as an independent variable in explaining agricultural development, and as a precondition for it to take place. As land becomes increasingly scarce, farmers adapt by changing cultivation practices and their use of inputs in order to preserve and improve their land. Boserup's central point is that changes in tools and farming techniques would not have come about without demographic pressure. She does not give explicit attention to preservation and improvement of land, but there are indications in her work that population growth does not involve negative effects on soil quality. She argues, "there can be no temptation to regard soil fertility exclusively as a gift of nature bestowed upon certain lands once and for all" (Boserup [9], p. 15). In a later work, however, she gives explicit attention to land degradation but in a way as to suggest that in some cases soil erosion actually induces desirable agricultural innovations [10].

Other theories stress the importance of the market mechanism. Over time prices respond to factor scarcity (of land, for example), promoting factor substitution and the introduction of new inputs. "As resources are depleted, rising prices reduce consumption and speed the search for substitutes, stimulating technological change" (World Bank [34], p. 80). In their theory of induced innovation, Hayami and Ruttan [20] stressed that factor use changes over time, leading to improved conservation of scarce resources and increased use of more abundant resources. Increasing labor–land ratios determine the path of technical change, leading to the mix of technology and new inputs associated with improved land management.

[4] There are circumstances in which intensification may precede extensification, e.g., where there are physical or political barriers to expansion.

Land degradation is widespread in Ethiopia and many country studies discuss population–environment links. Dejene [15] states that population growth has been an important cause of erosion in the Wollo province, in expanding land clearing onto marginal lands. In the conclusions from the Ethiopian Highland Reclamation Study (EHRS), population pressure is considered an important contributor to degradation in some areas of the northern Highlands. For these areas there are indications that both extensification and intensification are occurring. Both cultivation and grazing has spread to newer and more marginal areas and a persistent tendency to shorten the length of fallow periods between annual crops has been observed [11]. The rapid decline in land surface under forest that has occurred during the last four decades is mentioned as a primary cause of soil erosion [35]. Housing and increased demand for fuelwood and cultivable land due to population growth are often blamed for the rapid deforestation that has occurred in Ethiopia.

Other studies on Ethiopia attribute land degradation to ineffective government. See, for example, Bekele and Chole [6] and Kuru [24]. Over the last four decades, governmental institutions have failed to recognize the problem of land degradation. It is not so much a problem of getting the prices right, but in making available the organizations, infrastructure, and innovations required for conservation, research, advisory services, and education.

## 3. FRAMEWORK, DATA, AND LIMITATIONS

This study focuses on the Ethiopian Highlands. As defined by the Ethiopian Highland Reclamation Study, the area broadly comprises land 1,500 m above sea level and associated valleys. The study covers 44% of the national area and contains 88% of the population, 95% of the cropped area, and two-thirds of the livestock. It is dominated by subsistence farmers practicing mixed farming. Because of data limitations, *awrajas* are chosen as the observation unit.[5]

Below we select variables to test the hypothesis of a causal relationship between population pressure and land degradation. Other potential explanatory factors derived from both theory and Ethiopian evidence are also introduced.

The importance of livestock rearing and mixed farming in Highland agriculture justify the inclusion of a variable reflecting pressure from livestock. The same matters for physical factors (rain intensity, slope, and soils) and land use factors (cropping patterns and forest cover) which play a decisive part in theory. Ethiopian data indicate that 50 to 80% of annual soil loss occurs during the most intensive rainstorms [12]. Furthermore, Ethiopia contains many types of soils and the uneven topography of much of the Highlands leaves the central part of Ethiopia especially vulnerable to erosion. Finally, there are differences across the Highlands both in cropping practices and land tenure history. It was not possible to identify variation over time across observation units as concerning governmental policies, and the general impression is that soil conservation practices have not been a central part of traditional agriculture [12].[6] For this reason these factors were not considered.

[5] Highland *awrajas* range in size from 3,400 to 16,000 sq.km, but are seldom larger than 10,000 sq.km. The administrative boundaries of Ethiopia to some extent differ over sources. The boundaries this study is building upon are taken from the Master Land Use Plan [26] and the National Atlas of Ethiopia [28].

[6] One exception is the Konso area (a small area in the southwest of Ethiopia), where farmers have adapted to the environment by terracing, constructing drainage channels, rotating crops, and fallowing [32].

The framework for the Ethiopian Highlands,

$$Y = F(\mathbf{X}, \mathbf{H}) \tag{1}$$

is chosen, where **X** is a vector of all physical variables (rain intensity, slope, and soils) and **H** is a vector of all human variables and includes land use and farming system variables (cropland, forest cover, crops, tillage methods, and land tenure history) as well as pressure variables (people and livestock).

All data are from secondary sources and refer to 1983–1984. The study contains 47 observation units (*awrajas*).[7] No complete study of the erodability of different soils in Ethiopia has been done. However, from soil and geomorphology maps of Ethiopia [3] information on soil parent materials was available. A classification was undertaken based on three parent materials categories suggested by Wright [36].[8] The derived index representing the erodability of soils (SO) did not display substantial variation across the observation units. All *awrajas* were dominated by basic parent material, while calcareous and siliceous parent material composed smaller fractions of the total area. A variable for croplands (CPL) was also constructed measuring the ratio of area under crops to total area (MLUP [26]). Both variables were applied in the subsequent analysis, but they were both irrelevant (the estimates became approximately zero and were insignificant). For this reason both variables were not included in the tables presented below.

*Dependent Variable (Y)*

As dependent variable the soil erosion severity index (SESI) is chosen, which was assessed by Kuru [24] to act as a proxy for water erosion (except tunnel and bank erosion). Differences in the relative degree of soil erosion severity were obtained by assigning a composite-score distribution of 1 to 5, such that 1 denotes the least affected and 5 the most.[9] Kuru measured the area in each severity class for a given *awraja*; in this way his work provided proportional measures summing over the five categories for each *awraja*. In general, each *awraja* extends over two (in some cases three) adjacent classes but is often dominated by one. In order to provide a single estimate for the degree of soil erosion prevailing in a given unit, each *awraja* was assigned the value of its dominant class, in this way ending up with an ordered categorical dependent variable. The explanatory variables are listed below.

[7] Only 47 out of 102 *awrajas* could be defined as pure highland. The remaining *awrajas* are either pure lowland or have great discrepancies in their shares of Highland and Lowland areas.

[8] The categories were defined on the basis of information on genesis of landforms and parent materials. The basic category included volcanic and structural genesis of landforms. The calcareous category included evaporite, structural, and residual genesis of landforms. The siliceous category included alluvial, aeolian, structural, and residual genesis of landforms. According to Wright [36], basic and calcareous parent materials are much more resistant to erosion than siliceous parent materials, while basic is somewhat more resistant to erosion than calcareous parent materials. For this reason the basic, calcareous, and siliceous categories were assigned the values 4, 3, and 1, respectively. The estimate on each category's share of total area was then multiplied with the number representing its erodability.

[9] In order to produce a map depicting the extent of areas affected by different degrees of soil erosion severity, data were transferred from black and white multispectral scanning (MSS) imagery detail (178*178) onto available maps. This was carried out by using NASA's false color infrared composites of LANDSAT imagery. Originally the classifications, were done over six groups, but one category (wind erosion) is removed for this study, since it is experienced mainly by the Lowlands. More information on the definition of the categories and problems associated with their assessment; is available from the author on request.

*Physical Variables (X)*

*R*, *average wind speed*, is a proxy for rain intensity (erosivity). On the basis of data from 138 climatic stations across Ethiopia, figures on the average wind speed (m/s) were obtained (AtLUP [3]). In those *awrajas* without a station, data were compiled from *awrajas* located in similar climatic zones. This variable seems to be strongly correlated with the erratic influence from wind and rain, in that *awrajas* experiencing high wind speed are more frequently exposed to heavy rainstorms. Average wind speed decreases with lower altitude and when moving from the northern to the southern part of the highlands, which from the literature seems to be those areas where erosivity in general is lowest.

*S*, *slope dummy*, represents inter-*awraja* variation in topography. From MLUP [27] information on the percentage of each *awraja* above 30° slope was available. The observations for *S* proved to be almost entirely confined to two categories. Half of the *awrajas* showed no slopes above 30°, while the other half showed 20 to 40% of total area in this category. Consequently, a dummy variable *S* was designed that assigned one to *awrajas* with substantial areas above 30° slopes and zero to *awrajas* with almost no slopes above this gradient.

*Human Variables (H)*

*LG*, *language group dummy*, represents differences in tillage methods and land ownership prior to the 1975 agrarian reform. The dummy variable distinguishes between *awrajas* dominated by the Ethiosemitic language group (the value 1) and the Cushtic language group (the value 0). Variation in both farming systems and land tenure history seem to coincide with the two language groups. The plow farming culture of the northern highlands depends primarily on annual crops while the hoe culture of the south depends more on perennials [11]. Furthermore, the EHRS reports differences in land ownership before the 1975 agrarian reform where the north had various systems of communal or kinship land tenure while a private freehold system prevailed in the south, with most of the land owned by absentee landlords who allowed local people to cultivate it [12].[10]

*C*, *crop index*, represents crops' susceptibility to erosion. This variable was designed using data on the distribution of the 10 most important crops for each *awraja* (MLUP [26]). Each crop's share of total cropland is multiplied by its own *c* (crop) factor (Hurni [22]). A *c* factor measures and compares the ability of crops to protect the soil against erosion. A high *c* factor indicates less ability to protect the soil. This way an index is obtained where higher values means increased susceptibility to soil erosion.

*FC*, *forest cover*, is the ratio of remaining forest to total area (MLUP [27]).

*PP*, *population pressure*, is the ratio of population-supporting capacity (PSC) to rural population (MLUP [27]). This variable intends to reflect inter-*awraja* variation in pressure from people. PSCs are designed for each *awraja* by calculations on the minimum land area on which a family can subsist, taking into account among other things a household's basic nutrition needs, fuel needs, and food production.

[10] Since the Ethiopian maps on landownership prior to the 1975 agrarian reform (Constable [11]) and language groups (Westphal [32]) to a large extent coincided, it was decided not to treat them separately.

These data were used to estimate a variable showing how many people each *awraja* can support. PSCs were computed under varying assumptions about technological level. The analysis here assumes a low-input use technology, the base model, where land and labor are assumed to be the only inputs.

*LP, livestock pressure*, is the proxy for overstocking (MLUP [27]), the ratio of available dry matter (ADM) to demand for fodder (DFF). In calculating the demand for forage, livestock numbers were converted to total livestock units (TLU). The demand for forage was then calculated on the basis of 2% of the live weight of the average TLU required for maintenance. Available dry matter was calculated on the basis of data on land use and land cover, including estimates of crop residues and aftermath grazing on cropland. This variable acts as a proxy for the ratio between potential supply of fodder to actual demand for fodder. *LP* reflects higher pressure for lower values.

The PPH posits, ceteris paribus, that soil erosion is most serious in densely populated regions. For this study, the observed level of soil erosion is expected to increase for lower values of PP and LP. Low values of *PP* and *LP* reflect heavy pressure from people and livestock and a longer history in excess of a region's supporting capacity. If the statistical analysis does not identify such a relationship, the results support explanations challenging the PPH, such as that of Boserup, in that heavy pressure from people and livestock induce agricultural development and an improved management of land.

*Limitations and Assumptions*

The size of the observation units, combined with their enormous diversity of topography and climate, constitutes a hindrance for constructing variables suitable for this analysis. Even for small *awrajas* the variation within may be huge, thus reducing each observation's ability to reflect typical characteristics.

The reliability of the land degradation data is crucial for this analysis. It is of vital importance that the SESI applied give a good impression of the spatial distribution of the eroded condition for the soils. However, it is not of importance that the intervals between the categories can be meaningfully compared, only that the scale associated with certain values preserves an adequate ranking of the units.

The estimate of PSC is purely a technical measure and acts as a benchmark value comparing units with respect to land capability and a region's potential for agricultural production, for a given technological level. For this analysis the base model (low input level) is chosen. However, the level chosen should not alter the results, since only their assigned values, not the ranking of the observations units, would experience changes. The method applied to estimate PSCs builds on data on land degradation, as well as on soils, climate, and land evaluation (Higgins *et al.* [21]). Estimated rates of soil loss were translated into anticipated decreases in productivity. Since the rate of soil loss was related to the level of inputs and not regional differences, using carrying capacity as the dependent variable in the analysis does not risk having soil erosion as both the response and the explanatory variable in the analysis.

The choice of the dependent variable has strong implications for this analysis because of its cumulative nature. The eroded condition of soil at a given time is the result of both land use and climatic history. Hence, all explanatory variables included in the analysis need to reflect past relative relations among *awrajas*. The physical factors, being more or less constant over time, do possess this attribute. For some of the human factors the situation is more complex. This is especially the case for figures on population. Over time there is reason to believe in relative changes in population over regions, due to famines, different birth and mortality rates, migration, and resettlement schemes. The most severe shocks, though, postdate the census data used in this study, for example the severe famine of 1984 and large-scale resettlement programs (CSA [13]).[11]

## 4. STATISTICAL ESTIMATION PROCEDURES

### *Cumulative Logit Models*

When choosing an adequate statistical procedure, careful attention had to be paid to the principle of measuring the dependent variable. In our analysis this variable is an ordinal categorical variable. Hence, an ordinal logit analysis as outlined by Agresti [1] and Amemiya [2] can be used to estimate the soil degradation model for the Ethiopian Highlands. This method utilizes only the information available through the ranking of *awrajas* according to their eroded condition. Assuming linearity, Eq. 1 becomes (subscripts for observation units are omitted)

$$Y = \mathbf{X}\beta + \mathbf{H}\gamma + u, \tag{2}$$

where $Y$ is the unobservable continuous dependent variable, $u$ is a random disturbance, and the vectors of coefficients $\beta$ and $\gamma$ express the relationship between the degree of soil erosion and the vectors of explanatory variables **X** and **H**.

$Y$ is assumed to be observed ordinally ($Y^*$) over five ordered categories, where

$$Y_j^* = \begin{pmatrix} 1 & \text{if } \alpha_{j-1} < Y \leq \alpha_j \\ 0 & \text{otherwise} \end{pmatrix} \quad j = 1, \ldots, 5. \tag{3}$$

The cutpoint parameters ($\alpha$) are unobservable and $\alpha_0 = 0 < \alpha_1 < \alpha_2 < \alpha_3 < \alpha_4 < \alpha_5 = \infty$. The response probabilities, $P_j$, are determined by

$$\begin{aligned} P_1 + P_2 + \cdots + P_j &= P(Y \leq \alpha_j) \\ &= P(u \leq \alpha_j - \mathbf{X}\beta - \mathbf{H}\gamma) \\ &= F(\alpha_j - \mathbf{X}\beta - \mathbf{H}\gamma), \end{aligned} \tag{4}$$

where $F$ is the cumulative distribution function of the unobservable $u$. The logit function is nonlinear in the response probabilities $P_1, \ldots, P_5$.

[11] In this century Ethiopia has been exposed to four major famines, the most severe one was in 1984 when more than one million people died [15]. Until 1984, only 120,000 people had been resettled under an official program, about 30% of these were moved from Wollo to Wollega.

The choice of $F$ determines the model. It has been popular (Agresti [1]) to choose $F$ as the logistic distribution function. This works well in our case. This choice implies the linear cumulative logit model

$$\begin{aligned} L_j &= \operatorname{logit}\left[P(Y > \alpha_j)\right] \\ &= \log\left[\frac{\left[P(Y > \alpha_j)\right]}{\left[P(Y \leq \alpha_j)\right]}\right] \\ &= \alpha_j - \mathbf{X}\beta - \mathbf{H}\gamma \qquad j = 1, \ldots, 5. \end{aligned} \tag{5}$$

The logit model as formulated here is proportional, meaning that the effect from the explanatory variables is the same over all categories. Furthermore, the model provides a meaningful interpretation of the parameters as cumulative odds ratios. This is seen by subtracting the logits for different values of the explanatory variables,

$$\begin{aligned} & L_j(\mathbf{X} = \mathbf{X}_1, \mathbf{H}^*) - L_j(\mathbf{X} = \mathbf{X}_2, \mathbf{H}^*) \\ &= \beta(\mathbf{X}_1 - \mathbf{X}_2) \\ &= \log\left[\frac{P(Y > j|\mathbf{X} = \mathbf{X}_1, \mathbf{H}^*)}{P(Y \leq j|\mathbf{X} = \mathbf{X}_1, \mathbf{H}^*)}\right] - \log\left[\frac{P(Y > j|\mathbf{X} = \mathbf{X}_2, \mathbf{H}^*)}{P(Y \leq j|\mathbf{X} = \mathbf{X}_2, \mathbf{H}^*)}\right] \\ & \qquad j = 1, \ldots, 5. \end{aligned} \tag{6}$$

If $\beta = 0$, then $Y$ and $\mathbf{X}$ are independent. If $\beta > 0$, $Y$ tends to be larger at higher values of $\mathbf{X}$. The odds of making response $> j$ are $\exp[\beta(\mathbf{X}_1 - \mathbf{X}_2)]$ times higher at $\mathbf{X} = \mathbf{X}_1$ than $\mathbf{X} = \mathbf{X}_2$ (Agresti [1]).

## 5. RESULTS

The results obtained are presented in Table I, which contains two different specifications of the model. In the first two equations (columns (1) and (2)) the logit model is linear both in parameters and variables, as presented in Eq. (2). For the three other equations (columns (3)–(5)), negative reciprocal transformations for both pressure variables are undertaken, yielding a model that is still linear in parameters but nonlinear in pressure variables.

For columns (1) and (2) the only variable which entered with significant estimates was forest cover (FC), while both pressure variables suggest a weak and insignificant relationship in explaining soil erosion. The equations where negative reciprocal transformations of both $PP$ and $LP$ are undertaken seem to explain the data better than is the case for columns (1) and (2). The measures of fit, the likelihood ratio chi-square ($c$), and the percent of correct predictions (pcp), experience an improvement.[12] Additional variables have become significant (at the 5% level) and an increase in magnitude is observed for $S$, $LG$, $LP$, and $PP$, while

[12] A random sample of numbers from 1 to 5 would generate a $pcp$ at 20%.

TABLE I
Linear Model: Ordinal Logit Analysis

| Explanatory variables | Logit estimates (1) | (2) | (3) | (4) | (5) |
|---|---|---|---|---|---|
| Physical variables | | | | | |
| *S* | 0.331 | 0.395 | 0.835 | 0.798 | 0.768 |
| | (0.33) | (0.41) | (0.61) | (0.71) | (0.70) |
| *R* | 0.414 | 0.404 | 0.290 | 0.290 | 0.287 |
| | (1.80) | (1.88) | (1.01) | (1.03) | (1.01) |
| Land use | | | | | |
| *FC* | −0.102 | −0.099 | −0.089 | −0.089 | −0.085 |
| | (2.84) | (2.73) | (1.91) | (2.01) | (1.99) |
| Farming system | | | | | |
| *LG* | 0.772 | 0.741 | 1.901 | 1.918 | 2.020 |
| | (0.95) | (0.94) | (2.07) | (2.08) | (2.18) |
| *C* | −0.038 | | −0.021 | | |
| | (0.21) | | (0.13) | | |
| Population pressure | | | | | |
| *PP* | −0.277 | −0.276 | | | |
| | (0.58) | (0.60) | | | |
| $-1/(PP)^3$ | | | −0.327 | −0.336 | −0.363 |
| | | | (2.01) | (2.08) | (2.16) |
| Livestock pressure | | | | | |
| *LP* | −0.034 | −0.035 | | | |
| | (0.67) | (0.68) | | | |
| $-1/LP$ | | | −1.823 | −1.77 | |
| | | | (2.20) | (2.26) | |
| $-1/(LP)^2$ | | | | | −0.733 |
| | | | | | (2.08) |
| *c* | 45(7 d.f.) | 45(6 d.f.) | 51(7 d.f.) | 51(6 d.f.) | 49(6 d.f.) |
| | p = 0.000 | p = 0.000 | p = 0.000 | p = 0.000 | p = 0.000 |
| *pcp* | 44.68 | 44.68 | 59.57 | 59.57 | 55.31 |

*Notes.* *T*-statistics are in parenthesis. The variable *c* is the likelihood ratio Chi-square, assessing the overall fit of the model (all alternatives are equally likely). The variable *pcp* is the percentage of correct predictions.

*R* has declined. The variable for crops (*C*) seems unimportant since the logit estimate is close to zero and insignificant.

In the following, column (4) is commented upon in more detail. The signs of all estimators were as expected. Regions are more likely classified as heavily eroded at large values of *S* (slope), *R* (rain intensity), and *LG* (language group), and less likely at large values of *FC* (forest cover), *LP*, and *PP*. Of these, the coefficients for *R* and *S* are not significant (at the 5% level).

When interpreting the logit estimates in terms of cumulative odds ratios, the results become more intuitive and yield a sufficient basis for judging them. The odds of soil erosion being above any level *j*, is estimated to be 2.20 times higher for *S* (dummy) and 1.33 higher for *R* (increments of 1 m/s). While the odds for being in a higher erosion class are 6.82 for *LG* (dummy) and 2.22 for *FC* (10 percentage point decrease in forest cover).

Since the odds ratios for the pressure variables depend on the level at which the changes are occurring, larger changes for both variables are investigated and presented in Table II to give a clearer impression of the magnitude of the parameters generated at different levels. For both pressure variables, 0.1-unit changes in scale are considered for five different levels, as well as two 0.5-unit changes of scale. The odds ratios decrease as the level increases for the same absolute change in scale. For *PP*, the odds ratio more than doubles for a 0.1-unit change in scale at level 0.6 compared with the same change at level 0.7. For a 0.5-unit decrease, a move *PP* from a unit where population equals the supporting capacity (a level of 1.0) to a unit where population is twice the supporting capacity boosts the odds for being at a higher level of soil erosion by 9.67 times. For a similar decrease in supply of fodder compared with demand, the odds ratio is 5.52 times higher. A 0.5-unit decrease in *PP* and *LP* at the level of 0.9 causes a dramatic increase in the odds ratios for both variables, but especially for *PP* (99.8).

Figure 1 depicts the development in odds ratios for *PP* and *LP* for a 0.01-unit decrease in level (for marginal increases in population and livestock pressure) and confirms the conclusions from Table II; the probability of greater erosion in the region accelerates rapidly.

To conclude, the pressure variables did not seem important in explaining the distribution of soil erosion over regions for the equations presented in columns (1) and (2). Substantial increases in both variables are required to raise the odds ratios. Reciprocal transformations of both pressure variables substantially improves the analysis. Both variables become significant, and as they approach critical levels, their impact on the dependent variable is strong and increases rapidly. This matters especially for *PP* but for *LP* as well.

As for forest cover (*FC*), the odds for the soil erosion severity index to exceed any given erosion level *j* (more seriously eroded) increases with reduction in cover. The result seem to support views stressing the importance of forests in protecting the soils they actually occupy from erosion. However, the explanation may also be due to remaining forests being located in areas which are unproductive for cultivation, hence not exposed to human activities. The effect from forests may also be more indirect, by being a potential energy source, and thus may help to prevent the diversion of dung and cropland residues to use as fuel. If deforestation is a consequence of a growing population, the parameter value of *FC* should be taken into account when considering the effects of population on land degradation.

TABLE II

Logit Estimates and Odds Ratios for Decreases in *PP* and *LP*, Column 4

| Change level | *PP* log est. | | *PP* odds ratios | | *LP* log est. | | *LP* odds ratios | |
|---|---|---|---|---|---|---|---|---|
| | 0.1 | 0.5 | 0.1 | 0.5 | 0.1 | 0.5 | 0.1 | 0.5 |
| 0.5 | 2.45 | | 11.65 | | 0.86 | | 2.36 | |
| 0.6 | 1.09 | | 3.56 | | 0.57 | | 1.76 | |
| 0.7 | 0.55 | | 1.73 | | 0.41 | | 1.50 | |
| 0.8 | 0.31 | | 1.36 | | 0.30 | | 1.35 | |
| 0.9 | 0.18 | | 1.20 | | 0.23 | | 1.25 | |
| 0.9 | | 4.60 | | 99.80 | | 2.39 | | 10.91 |
| 1.0 | | 2.27 | | 9.67 | | 1.71 | | 5.52 |

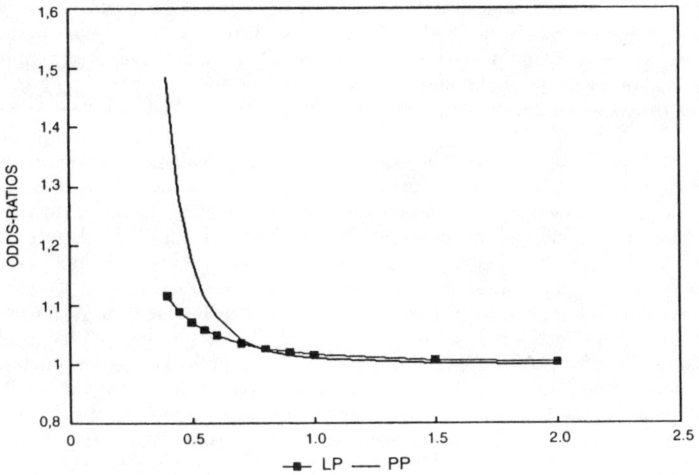


FIG. 1. Odds ratios for marginal changes in *PP* and *LP*, for the equation in column 4 of Table I.

The parameter value of the dummy variable for the two major language groups (*LG*) is both significant and strong. It is unlikely that this surprisingly strong effect merely reflects differences in tillage systems and land tenure history. As with forest cover, the strength of this effect may partly reflect differences in settlement history. In addition, northern Ethiopia seems to have suffered more external shocks, such as famine and war, than the south. Whatever the reasons, this north–south dimension in Ethiopian agriculture appears significant in explaining soil erosion.

In addition to the soil (*SO*) and cropland (*CPL*) variables, crops (*C*), slope (*S*), and rain intensity (*R*) turned out to be insignificant in explaining soil erosion, even though the proxy on rain intensity (*R*) is fairly strong. The results concerning crops (*C*) and croplands (*CPL*) do not necessarily conflict with the conclusions of the EHRS [11]. That study claimed that 80% of all erosion occurred on croplands. Though variation in croplands across *awrajas* (as a percentage of total area) do not explain the distribution of soil erosion severity, erosion may still occur on croplands.

However, caution must be applied when interpreting the results. The causes of soil erosion have continuous and cumulative effects on the resource base, hence the observed values of soil erosion represent outcomes of many actions by local people in the past. For this reason some of the identified partial impacts may be due to a longer history of settlement and exploitive land use. Such effects are most likely to be reflected in the parameters of the pressure variables, forest cover, and language group. It is, however, doubtful that the identified impacts are due to a longer land use history alone.

The single equation estimation assumes a one-way causal relationship between the variables, overlooking the possible influence of land degradation on farming systems and land cover. In the literature on Ethiopia there are, however, no indications of such changes on a larger scale. A more acute problem is whether land degradation has influenced the population distribution over time by forcing people to move from heavily eroded areas. That means there is a potential econometric problem of simultaneity. This problem does not necessarily threaten the conclusions of the analysis. Outmigration is most likely for heavily eroded areas, but there is a question as to what extent people migrate to areas outside each *awraja*. If outmigration has occurred, this will negatively bias the estimates.

The estimates of the pressure variables could also be positively biased because of the omittance of factors which are important in determining the spatial distribution of soil erosion. One obvious candidate is soils. Other studies on Africa conclude that soils differ with respect to their ability to resist erosion and Ethiopia exhibits broad landform differentiation. However, the index for erodability ($SO$) that was constructed and applied in this analysis turned out to be irrelevant. This was not surprising, considering that all observation units (with one exception) are dominated by the same parent material category. Since no alternative soil variables were introduced, this study builds upon an assumption of homogeneous landscape erodability for the Ethiopian highlands across *awrajas*. The validity of this assumption is important for the interpretations of the results. More information on Ethiopian soils and their erodability is needed both to evaluate the above assumption and to arrive at more conclusive statements about geomorphological conditions in Ethiopia. Soils are also important in determining settlement patterns, land use, and agricultural practices, and hence they affect erosion. Such effects, however, do not challenge the results derived from this analysis.

## 6. SUMMARY AND CONCLUSIONS

This study addresses the ongoing debate on population–environment links. The econometric analysis yields the statistically most satisfactory results when a negative reciprocal transformation of the pressure variables is performed. The results indicate that erosion is not so much due to the specific natural variables evaluated in this analysis but primarily to human activities. Statistically insignificant correlations were obtained from all physical variables, rain intensity, slope, and soil. Of the human factors evaluated, forest cover, language group, and the pressure variables were significant and displayed strong impacts on the observed level of soil erosion. The SESIs are shown to be significantly greater in regions mainly occupied by the language group which practices agriculture based on the production of grains/annual crops and makes extensive use of animal traction for plowing. Furthermore, the same area has a land tenure history dominated by various communal tenure systems. A negative correlation between forest cover as a percentage of total land and the level of soil erosion was estimated. The greater the share of forest, the lower the value of SESI. This was as expected and may be due to a range of factors such as more benign climatic conditions. However, large-scale reforestation programs may not be an optimal strategy for arresting erosion, since the pressure may increase on remaining pastures and croplands.

It is important that the assumptions this study builds upon are acknowledged when interpreting the results. The analysis is carried out by applying outcome variables on land degradation, focusing upon Malthusian processes which emphasize relatively few causal factors. However, it could be possible to have Malthusian outcomes from more complex non-Malthusian processes which may have acted over time in Ethiopia. The weak contribution identified from the physical factors evaluated questions the adequacy of some of the data to discern actual variations in these factors. One possible explanation is the level of aggregation; the size of the observation units inherently means huge physical diversities within each unit. The primary effect of this measurement problem is to inflate the disturbance variance in the statistical model and the standard errors on all parameter estimates. On the other hand, the potential problem of simultaneity would cause an underestimation of the point estimates of the parameters.

In spite of the limitations, the key finding of the study concerns the nature of the relationship between both pressure variables and land degradation. An exponential increase in the probability of having a high SESI is expected with greater pressure from people and livestock. The nature of these impacts does not uniquely support the PPH. As long as population and livestock are far below the supporting capacity of the region, a growing population and increasing population–land ratios are not expected to cause a rise in the SESIs. In fact, population growth could for such a situation act as a stimulus to improved resource management. Only when population is greater than the carrying capacity of land is a more rapid degradation of land identified. In statistical terms, this analysis supports the PPH (and rejects Boserupian theories) for regions exceeding some threshold or critical level. The results do not provide evidence for claiming that population growth inevitably causes land degradation, however, a growing population will, other things being equal, bring a region faster to the point where human activities have harmful consequences on the resource base. The accelerating impact may also be attributed to the fact that observed pressure on land from people most probably mirrors a longer history with population in excess of the population-supporting capacity of land.

The statistical reciprocal relationship between erosion and the pressure variables would probably not have been identified if substantial innovation had occurred in Ethiopia. The introduction of new inputs, implying different and more sustainable resource management, causing a divergence from the assumptions of the base model, could offset the identified link between erosion and pressure. This interpretation is confirmed by other studies on Ethiopia. Bekele and Chole [6] find that agricultural production systems have been practiced in Ethiopia since Biblical times without any substantial improvement. EHRS [12] reports reductions in the fallow periods of annual cropping and an increased use of marginal land in agricultural production.

Agriculture is the mainstay of the Ethiopian economy, dominated by subsistence production and widespread rural poverty [61]. Furthermore, transportation and communication is poorly developed and the country has been exposed to war, droughts, and political instability. At the time the data were collected, the mid-1980s, the country had been under Mengistu rule for about a decade. Both before and during this period little effort was given to foster technological change and there was great uncertainty in land rights after the 1975 land reform. These circumstances suggest limited possibilities for providing input and extension, creating substantial disincentives for the rural population and limiting the extent of peasant participation in the market economy. The Boserupian theories depend on a reservoir of technical knowledge and on the role of governments the application of this new knowledge when and where it is needed. Based on this analysis and our knowledge of the stock of technical knowledge available for the last decades, it seems that society, government, and world institutions in general have not succeeded.

## REFERENCES


1. A. Agresti, "Categorial Data Analysis," Wiley, New York (1990).
2. T. Amemiya, Qualitative response models: A survey, *J. Econom. Lit.* **19**(4), 1483–1536 (1981).
3. AtLUP (Assistance to Land Use Planning), Ethiopia, Technical Report 2, Vol. 1, maps, MoA/UNDP/FOA (1984).
4. P. K. Bardhan, Ed., "The Economic Theory of Agrarian Institutions," Clarendon Press, Oxford (1989).
5. S. Barrett, Optimal soil conservation and the reform of agricultural pricing policies, *J. Develop. Econom.* **36**, 167–187 (1991).
6. A. Bekele and E. Chole, "A Profile of the Ethiopian Economy," Oxford Univ. Press, London/Nairobi (1969).
7. P. Blaikie and H. Brookfield, Land Degradation and Society," Methuen, London (1987).
8. G. Bose, Interlinked contracts and moral hazard in investment, *J. Develop. Econom.* **41**, 247–273 (1993).
9. E. Boserup, "The Conditions of Agricultural Growth," Allen & Unwin, London (1965).
10. E. Boserup, "Population and Technology," Blackwell Sci., Oxford (1981).
11. M. Constable, "Resources for Rural Development in Ethiopia," EHRS Working Paper 17, FAO/MoA (1984).
12. M. Constable, "The Degradation of Resources and an Evaluation of Options to Combat It," Working Paper 19, FAO (1984).
13. CSA (Central Statistics Authority), "Population and Housing Census, Preliminary Report," Vol. 1, Addis Ababa, Ethiopia (1984).
14. CSA, Report on the results of the 1981 demographic survey, *Statist. Bull.* **46** (1985). [Addis Ababa, Ethiopia]
15. A. Dejene, "Environment, Famine and Politics in Ethiopia: A View from the Village," NORAD, Oslo (1987).
16. E. P. Eckholm, "Losing Ground," Norton, New York (1976).
17. FAO, "A Provisional Methodology for Soil Degradation Assessment," Rome (1979).
18. S. Grepperud, "Population–Environment Links: Testing a Soil Degradation Model for Ethiopia," Environment Department Divisional Working Paper 1994-46, World Bank (1994).
19. G. S. Griffin and J. R. Stoll, Evolutionary processes in soil conservation policy, *Land Econom.* **60**(1), 30–39 (1984).
20. Y. Hayami and V. Ruttan, Factor prices and technical change in agricultural development, *J. Polit. Econom.* **78**, 1115–1141 (1971).
21. G. M. Higgins *et al.*, "Potential Population Supporting Capacities of Lands in the Developing World," technical report, FAO/UNFPA, Rome (1982).
22. H. Hurni, "Erosion, Productivity, Conservation Systems in Ethiopia," Paper presented for the Fourth International Conference on Soil Conservation, Maracay, Venezuela (1985).
23. A. Kelley, The population debate: A status report and revisionist interpretation, mimeo, Centre for Demographic Studies, Duke University (1984).
24. A. Kuru, "Soil Erosion and Strategic Policy: The Case of Ethiopia," Publications of the Department of Environmental Conservation at the University of Helsinki No. 7 (1986).
25. D. H. Meadows *et al.*, "The Limits to Growth," Earth Island, London (1972).
26. MLUP (Master Land Use Plan), main report, UNDP/FAO, Rome (1988).
27. MLUP, Technical Report 1, Annexes 1–3, UNDP/FAO, Rome (1988).
28. NAoE (National Atlas of Ethiopia), Addis Ababa, Ethiopia (1984).
29. NAoS (National Academy of Sciences), "Rapid Population Growth," John Hopkins Univ. Press, Baltimore/London (1971).
30. K. Ruddle and W. Manshard, Renewable natural resources and the environment: pressing problems in the developing world, Tycooly International Publishing, Dublin (1981).

31. T. N. Srinivasan, "Population, Food and Rural Development," background paper prepared for the Working Group on Population Growth and Economic Development, Committee on Population, National Research Council, Washington, DC (1985).
32. E. Westphal, "Agricultural Systems in Ethiopia," Agricultural Research Report 826, Center for Agricultural Publishing and Documentation, Wageningen (1975).
33. R. Whitlow, A national soil erosion survey for Zimbabwe, *J. Soil Water Conserv.* **62** (1987).
34. World Bank, "The World Development Report," World Bank, Washington, DC (1984).
35. World Bank, "Ethiopia—Issues and Options in the Energy Sector, report of the UNDP/World Bank Energy Sector Assessment Program, World Bank, Washington, DC (1984).
36. C. Wright, "An Assessment of the Causes, Severity, Extent and Probable Consequences of Degradation in the Ethiopian Highlands," EHRS Working Paper 3, FAO/MoA (1986).

*Environmental and Resource Economics* **9:** 383–408, 1997.


# Environmental Degradation and Population Movements: The Role of Property Rights *

KANCHAN CHOPRA and S.C. GULATI
*Institute of Economic Growth, Delhi-110007, India*

Accepted 15 August 1996

**Abstract.** This study examines the linkages between environmental degradation (viewed primarily as deforestation and land degradation) and the movement of population from one region to another within a developing country. The hypothesis postulated is that the link between population and environmental degradation is mediated by the nature of property rights in land. This hypothesis is examined with the help of two alternative methodologies. Firstly, a simultaneous equations model using data for the arid and semi-arid region of Western India illustrates that outmigration from the region is largely the consequence of push factors such as environmental degradation and decrease in common land. Alternatively, micro experiments in environmental protection and the creation of common property rights on open access land in the same region indicate that the association between migrational change, creation of common property rights and participation indices is high. It can be concluded that once property rights are well defined with the help of appropriate institutional arrangements, labour moves towards the creation of common assets and an improvement in the environment takes place. Out migration is prevented and higher levels of population are supported by the same resources.

**Key words:** common property regimes, population movements, outmigration

## 1. Introduction

The last two decades have seen the emergence of environment-related issues as areas of immediate concern. Two major categories of threats to the environment can be distinguished between: (i) those associated with high levels of industrialization and the associated emissions and (ii) those arising out of rapid rates of natural capital depletion exemplified by forest degradation and soil erosion. In India, as in most other developing countries, it is the second that have been the focus of concern.[1] The gradual depletion of forest cover and the continued existence of large areas of wasteland which produce less than their potential capacity concomitant with higher rates of population growth continue to cause serious concern.

It is often postulated that poverty results in environmental degradation of the second kind indicated above and higher rates of population growth compound the adverse environmental impact. Such a contestation derives support from two kinds of arguments: an analytical and an empirical. The analytical argument is based on a modified type of 'tragedy of commons' stand. It seems plausible to argue

* The authors wish to thank Ms. Seema Bathla and Dr. Suresh Sharma for assistance in documentation, data collection and analysis.

that high levels of poverty and population growth constitute increased pressure on natural resources. Since such resources can often not be excluded from use by all groups, increased pressure of demand results in progressive deterioration. Rates of discount of the future are higher at low levels of income as satisfaction of present demand becomes the first priority. The consequent high levels of present demand which far exceed the rate of regeneration result in depletion of the environment.

The above manner of viewing the scenario is, however, over simplified. There now exists a large and growing literature which counters the above argument from an empirical perspective.[2] A number of other factors, in particular institutional structures, both of government and of market origin, are found to be significant contributors to degradation.On a more positive note, some kinds of changes in institutional structure are seen to be playing a useful role. Small communities, often with non-government and/or government support, are seen to come together with the express intention of preserving environmental resources linked with consumption patterns and livelihoods.[3] Such changes in the institutional framework are, in effect, a change in the nature of property rights. One of the outcomes of this change is an increase in the capacity of the environment to support larger populations. This paper aims at examining what effect this change has on the nature and magnitude of rural urban population movements. It is postulated that there exists a close association between this kind of internal migration and the clear specification of property rights on common land. Better specification of the latter leads to a reduction in the former. In other words, the link between population levels and environmental degradation is not simply arithmetic, but is mediated by the institutional framework within which it takes place.

## 2. Alternative Property Rights Structures and Environmental Degradation: An Overview

It is postulated in this paper that the nature of rights in property constitutes a significant determinant of the carrying capacity of natural resources, and hence the link between population movements and environmental degradation. A continuum of property rights can be distinguished between in any economy as the dominant control of ownership and user rights over these resource changes from one agency to another within it. Four important kinds of property rights arrangements which can be conceived to exist in a 'continuum' are: private, state, common and open access.[4] While private and state property are easily understood, it is important to define 'common property'. This consists in the setting up of a structure of rights and obligations with reference to the members of a specific group. Only members of that group are eligible to obtain access to the resource in question. This access carries with it certain obligations on the part of each member. Examples of such regimes can easily be located in village common lands or common sources of water. It is not an 'open access' regime in the sense that 'outsiders' do not have access.

Each of these forms of property rights defines in effect the bounds of control of the major right holder. However, no right in property can ever be absolute and undeterred. Even the most rigid private property institution is restricted by the dictates of what constitutes legal use. The state may impose additional limits. For instance, limits to he exercise of private property rights are often set by the state in view of the emerging significance of environmental or amenity values in adjacent property. In a similar manner, an extension of the frontier of private property has resulted in a reduction in the realm of common property. Alternatively, the inefficacy of state control as the dominant form of property ownership has led to the emergence of community forms of control. In general, if the players outside the bounds of any form of property right structure find that a change is to their advantage and if they are in a position to alter the structure of control, they shall attempt to do so. Whether or not thev are successful in their attempt shall depend, among other things, on their capability to meet the transaction cost of the change.

Common property institutions come about as the consequence of such shifts in the rights frontier. In such situations, they represent a more efficient form of social organisation. This is due to a number of factors, some related to the existence of environmental resources as commonly consumed commodities. It is found for instance that the management of ground water as a private property resource has often been the first step in a shift towards common property rights in water, as in the semi-arid region around Los Angeles.[5] The agreements to curtail water withdrawals, which were arrived at voluntarily, constituted an institutional change leading to a transformation from private towards common property rights.

The existence of a minimum economic scale factor may sometimes mean the superiority of a common property scheme of management. Small fragments of submarginal land often remain uncultivated under private property regimes. A pooling together of land with the creation of common infrastructural assets, once suggested and implemented as a possible option, results in an increase in land productivity.[6]

A rich diversity of property rights structures is therefore feasible and changes in the frontiers take place constantly. In this paper, it is postulated that institutional changes such as those defined above have an impact on productivity and hence on the links between population and environmental degradation. An analysis of this role is significant in particular in the context of migration.

## DETERMINANTS OF RURAL–URBAN MIGRATION AND A HYPOTHESIS

The literature on internal, in particular rural–urban migration in developing countries, has viewed the problem from a number of different angles.[7] In the early literature, rural urban migration was considered desirable as it provided an input into the growth of the industrial sector. Over time, it was found that, in most countries, migration far exceeded the rate of employment creation in most countries. It was, in part, this that led to a focus on the micro-economic foundations of the behaviour of individuals in the process of deciding to migrate. The Todaro hypothesis, which postulated that migration occurred in response to (a) rural–urban differences in expected rather than actual earnings and (b) the probability of getting work, comprised a major watershed in the work on migration. Simultaneously, social and cultural factors entering the migration decision did receive some attention. However, the overwhelming conclusion of most empirical studies is that people migrate for economic reasons. In the case of India, for instance, Greenwood's study found that migration was related positively and significantly to destination wage and negatively, and again significantly, to origin wage.[8]

In the above context, some studies examined the genesis of the expected income differentials between rural and urban areas. The existence of trade unions and other institutional factors that increased this wage differential was recognized. The effect of migration on the differences between source and destination areas also attracted attention. Considering the impact of an increasing population on the urban environment, it was recognized that rural–urban migration was not necessarily desirable. It was found in some studies, for instance, that internal migration may affect adversely the welfare of the source areas[9] while contributing little to expanded social welfare in urban areas.

Some factors affecting micro-economic behaviour of migrants have however received little attention. One of these is changing institutions in the rural sector which influence migrant behaviour primarily through their effect on the rural–urban income differential. Incomes in the rural economy are typically the sum of those obtained from private property resources and those received from common property resources. A strengthening of common property rights institutions is expected to increase the probability of obtaining a sustained level of income from them, thereby tending to reduce the rural–urban income differential and affecting adversely the propensity to migrate. In other words, the increased capacity of the resources to sustain populations becomes a disincentive to migrate. It is postulated in this paper that this is true in particular in arid and semiarid regions where common property resources constitute a large part of the consumption base of the poor[10] and where stress migration resulting from environmental degradation comprises a significant part of total migration.

## Testing the Hypothesis: Alternative Methodologies

This hypothesis can be tested either with a large data set referring to a uniform agro-climatic zone or with the help of an in-depth study of experiments in property right changes in smaller areas. Each approach has its usefulness. A cross-sectional analysis of a large data set can throw up interesting pointers, because it is amenable to econometric analysis. Secondary data based studies, on the other hand, are expected to capture the quantitative aspects of the relationship between outmigration, environmental degradation and the existence of common resources, including land.

However, common land can be identified only in a somewhat limited manner from secondary data sources. The exact nature of group duties and privileges of members of the group comprising the community cannot be specified at that level of aggregation. Land or resources that fall within the domain of a well-defined common property regime can, on the other hand, be identified far more correctly from a closer in depth study of micro-communities and the manner in which they relate to the resources available to them. Such studies of particular instances of the creation of common property rights help in giving substance to quantitative relationships obtained from empirical studies by focussing on qualitative aspects.

Both approaches have been attempted in this paper. In the first part of the paper the links between migration and environmental degradation are studied in a simultaneous equations framework using secondary data for the 89 districts (a district is an administrative division) comprising the arid and semi-arid part of India. The second part of the study consists of an in-depth examination of the hypothesis in the context of specific areas where efforts at the creation of common property regimes have taken place in the 1980s and the early 1990s. Some documentation of these exists (Agarwal and Narain 1989, Burra 1991, Development Alternatives 1988 and Gera undated among others). It is expected that possible changes in the nature of the relationship between internal migration and efficacy of common property regimes shall be thrown up.

## 3. The Study Region

The arid and semi-arid regions in the western and central parts of India are defined to include three zones from the Indian Planning Commission's agro-climatic classification of India. Important characteristics of these zones are given in Table I. From the viewpoint of administrative units, 89 districts falling in the central and western part of India constitute the study area. The selection of an ecological basis for analysis is a consequence of the contention that it leads to a better understanding of livelihood strategies and environmental situations. Livelihood systems tend to be built around ecological reality in the absence of outside interventions. Links with the outside economy must take this reality into account.

The Central Plateau and Hill region (Zone 8) consists of 46 districts from three states. The zone is interspersed with plateau and hill areas, the physiography being characterized by

(a) low hill ranges, mounds, narrow valleys with acute soil erosion and excessive run-off,
(b) undulating topography,
(c) vast areas of barren and uncultivated land.

This zone has a geographical area of 37,592.6 thousand ha, i.e. it accounts for 11.6% of the land mass of India, but it accommodates only 8% of its population with a density of 136 persons/km$^2$. The annual rainfall ranges from 490 mm to

Table I. Characteristics of zones

| | Units | Zone 8 | Zone 9 | Zone 14 |
|---|---|---|---|---|
| Geographical area | Thousand hectares | 37592.6 | 33221.9 | 17580 |
| Rainfall (annual average) | mm | 1030 | 904 | 17580 |
| Density of population | Persons/km$^2$ | 136.77 | 169.28 | 58.16 |
| Net sown area per captia | Hectares | 0.33 | 0.385 | 0.75 |
| Forest area | % of total area | 20.17 | 11.4 | 7.28 |
| Irrigated area | % of net sown area | 21.2 | 11.5 | 6.3 |
| Livestock density | Animals per hectare of GCA | 2.64 | 1.77 | 2.32 |
| Sheep and goats | % of livestock livestock | 36.41 | 29.78 | 72 |

Note: GCA is gross sown area, i.e. net sown area corrected for cropping intensity.

1570 mm. The 16 districts which fall in the state of Rajasthan have an annual rainfall of 500 mm or less. However, the sub-region of western Madhya Pradesh has a rainfall of about 1570 mm.

Per capita availability of forest area is 0.14 ha, net sown area is about 0.33 ha per capita with irrigated area being 0.07 ha per capita. The major source of irrigation is wells and tubewells which irrigate 55% of the area. Canals and tanks come second with 36%. Forests cover 20.17% of the reported area with variations between 4.2% and 38.86% across districts. Livestock–man ratio is 1.04 with cattle population comprising a large component and with variations between sub-regions. While the northern hills support only 1.9% of the total livestock population, the southern plains and the semi-arid eastern plains support 27% of the total population.

The Western Plateau and Hill Region (Agroclimatic Zone 9) comprises 34 districts from the three states of Rajasthan, Madhya-Pradesh and Maharashtra with a geographical area of 33,221.97 thousand ha. It has a population of 56.13 million with a density of 169 per km$^2$. The river basins are hilly and narrow in the west and broad and flat in the east. The rainfall varies between 580 and 1176 mm with an average of 904 mm. More than 70% of the area is either medium or deep black soil with high clay content and poor drainage. The net sown area is 65% of geographic area with little variation. Per capita net sown area is 0.385 ha, with 11.5% on an average being irrigated. Wells account for 71.3%, canals 25% and tanks 3.7% of this irrigated area. Forests occupy 11.3% of the geographical area with lands not available for cultivation constituting about 8.77%. Livestock population per hectare of gross sown area is 1.7, with cattle contributing 54%, buffaloes 13% and sheep and goats 29.78% of total livestock population.

The Western Dry Region (Agroclimatic Zone 14) consists of nine districts of Rajasthan, with a geographical area of 17580 thousand ha. the average rainfall is 395 mm with a very high year-to-year fluctuation. The population is 13.3 million and density is 58.16 persons/km$^2$. The zone has all the characteristics of hot deserts, namely scanty and erratic rainfall, high evaporation, non-existence of perennial rivers and sparse vegetation. The ground water table is often deep and very brackish. The soils are desertic with excessive permeability and low moisture holding capacity. The average land–man ratio is high with net sown area per person of 0.750 ha. However, only 6.3% of net sown area is irrigated.

Ground water is the major source of irrigation accounting for 92% of the net irrigated area. The forest cover is very poor at 7.28% of the geographical area and land designated as waste is 23.1%. Livestock density is 2.32 animals per hectare of gross sown area and 1.87 animals per person. Sheep and goats constitute 72% of livestock population and cattle and buffaloes share just one-fourth.

## A Simultaneous Equation System

As stated earlier, the nature and strength of linkages between population movement, changing property rights and the environmental degradation process in the region can be studied with the help of a simultaneous equations system. This paper examines the interactions by formulating a simultaneous structural system, with rural outmigration, environmental degradation, and property rights over land being treated as endogenous variables in the system, and selected demographic and developmental indicators being treated as exogenous to the system. A priori, the following kinds of interrelationships between levels, changes and inter spatial movements of population can be identified:

(a) increases in population result in pressures on land and water in rural environments;
(b) environmental degradation of the above kind results in so-called 'stress' outmigration from rural tracts;
(c) changing property rights in land and in common property resources can limit or even end stress outmigration from the rural tracts;
(d) a parallel stream of 'developmental' migration occurs as a consequence of employment opportunities in the urban non-agricultural sectors of the economy;
(e) both kinds of migration have their own impact on urban environments as well.

The 'stress' migration referred to in (b) and the 'developmental' migration referred to in (d) are both the consequence of differences in income between the origin and destination regions. As stated earlier, this difference can be affected in a substantial manner by the magnitude of income or consumption derived from common property resources and the certainty with which it is available. Further, the present model, while focusing attention on the hitherto neglected area of links between (b) and (c), does not ignore income and wage differentials as an influence on the level of migration. These factors are taken care of by the exogenous variables included in the simultaneous equations framework.

The simultaneous structural system designed to capture the combined impact of the above mentioned movements has four endogenous variables and eleven exogenous variables. The endogenous variables are:

(1) Environmental degradation index measured by change in structural composition of livestock. An increase in the percentage of sheep and goats in the total livestock is taken to imply a degradation in the environment as these animals survive better in degraded areas (CHSHGOTTLS). This indirect measure of environmental degradation is preferred to more direct measures such as forest degradation and fall in level of ground water because of availability of cross-section and time series data.
(2) Change in private property rights on agricultural land characterized by change in net sown area to total geographical area over the period 1974 to 1984 (CHNSATGA).
(3) Change in common land area over the same period (CHCOMLAND). To arrive at a proxy variable for this, an approximation for usable common access land is obtained for each district by excluding privately-owned, state-owned land and barren and un-cultivable land from geographical area.[11]
(4) Distress out-migration from rural tracts to towns, urban agglomerations and metropolitan centres because of push factors is approximated by change in sex composition in rural areas in favour of females (CHRSRTTSR). This is because distress migration is usually male dominated with the females staying behind and thus changing sex-composition would reflect the extent of outmigration from rural areas.

The system also includes 11 exogenous socioeconomic and developmental variables. Rainfall, irrigation and land-productivity are the weather and agriculture related variables. Employment opportunities provided by industrial development of the intended destination are represented by the extent of non-farm employment activities in factories and in mining and quarrying sectors and by the non-agricultural development index. Areas with a higher degree of non-farm related employment are also likely to have a higher level of urban incomes. Another exogenous variable, percent of literate to total population in a given district, also reflects the probability of urban employment, since the more literate presumably possess a higher probability of being absorbed in the urban labour force.

The district level non-agricultural development index is derived from 14 selected developmental variables encompassing sectoral aspects of the economic development process at the district level. The index is elicited through multi-variate factor analysis technique facilitating weights to be assigned to different developmental variables. The weights are based on factor loadings in the varimax-rotated factor structure of the interrelated developmental variables and the elicited Eigen values (Gulati 1992). Interestingly, the factor loadings of the elicited factor (NADI) turned out to be relatively much higher on the constituting non-agricultural developmental variables, viz. average daily employment in factories, in household industrial

Table II. List of selected variables

| No. | Var. abbreviation | Description of the variable |
|---|---|---|
| 1. | CHRSRTSR | Change in rural sex ratio to total sex ratio (females per 1000 males) |
| 2. | CHSHGOTTLS | Change in sheep and goats as percent of total live stock population |
| 3. | CHNSATGA | Change in net sown area per 1000 $km^2$ of geographical area |
| 4. | CHOMMLAND | Change in common land area as percent of geographical area |
| 5. | PGRE | Population growth rate in the 1980s |
| 6. | NADI | Non-agricultural development index |
| 7. | ANR | Average normal rainfall |
| 8. | CHFCA | Change in forest covered area as percent of geographical area |
| 9. | CHPCFGP | Change in per capita food-grain production |
| 10. | CHADEFPLP | Change in average daily employment per Lakh population |
| 11. | CHWEMQPLP | Change in workers employed in mining and quarrying per LAKH population |
| 12. | CHDEN | Change in density of population per $km^2$ |
| 13. | CHGIAGCA | Change in gross irrigated area to gross cropped area |
| 14. | LITEIG | Percent population literate in 1981 |
| 15. | PCFGP | Per capita food grain production in 1980 |

units, extent of urbanization, extent of electrification, bank advances for industrial activity, etc. Thus, the elicited indices for all the 89 districts reflect the extent of non-agricultural employment potentials in the districts which in turn are hypothesized to affect rural–urban population movements.

It is therefore correct to presume that income differentials and probabilities of urban employment as causal factors for migration are being included in the model. Higher demographic pressure on land is represented by population growth and increase in population densities. It can be concluded, therefore, that while our model focuses on the hitherto relatively ignored area of the linkages between migration and common property rights, it does contain exogenous variables that take into account the impact of more traditional influences on migration.

The notation for the variables selected is given in Table II.

The data used in the study are derived from secondary sources. Most of it is published data obtained from government sources.[12] For district wise forest area, satellite data obtained from the Forest Survey of India (Ministry of Environment and Forests, India 1991) are used. It is also important to note that a large number of variables are defined as changes between two points of time in the early and the late 1980s. The exercise is carried out using these and not panel data, primarily due to non availability of panel data for all variables used.

The simultaneous structural system depicts hypothesized relationships among variables comprising the four structural relations. The first structural relation depicts the extent of distress rural outmigration as measured by change in rural sex composition in favour of females in the district's sex ratio (CHRSRTTSR), as a function of:

(a) the environmental degradation variable represented by changes in proportion of sheep and goats to total livestock (CHSHGOTTLS);
(b) change in net sown area to total geographical area (CHNSATGA); and
(c) change in proportion of common land to total geographical area (CHCOMLAND).

The following equation defines the above relationship:

CHRSRTTSR = f(CHSHGOTTLS, CHNSATGA, CHCOMLAND, CHPCFGP, CHADEFPLP, CHWEMQPLP, LITEIG) (1)

The four exogenous variables included in this equation are, e.g., the land productivity variable, viz. change in per capita food production (CHPCGP); two non-agricultural employment variables, viz. change in average daily employment in factories per lakh population (CHADEFPLP) and change in employment in mining and quarrying sector (CHWEMQPLP); and a social development variable depicting extent of literacy in the district (LITEIG).

The independent variables in this equation represent the different factors that impact the outmigration from rural areas, outmigration that is of the 'stress' outmigration variety. Both the push and pull factors are included in this. Changes in land productivity and in net sown area are expected to have a negative effect on outmigration. Similarly environmental degradation process is contended to have a strong positive impact on rural–urban migrational patterns. Among the 'pull' factors, availability of employment opportunities in urban and industrial centres is most significant. The non-agricultural employment variables depicting extent of employment opportunities that have been included in the set of exogenous variables are the extent of employment in factories (CHADEFPLP) and employment in mining and quarrying sector (CHWEMQPLP). Furthermore, a social development related variable, the extent of literacy in the population (LITEIG), is also presumed to have a strong bearing on the migrational flows. It is generally contended that rural outmigrational streams are dominated by younger age groups and relatively more educated adult members to begin with. Subsequently, the adult outmigrants may be followed by other family members such as spouses and dependents.

The second structural relation postulates environmental degradation (as reflected in change in favour of sheep and goats in the livestock population (CHSHGOTTLS)) as a function of two endogenous variables, viz. change in common land area depicting community ownership rights on land (CHCOMLAND), stress migration from the rural tracts depicted by excessive change in rural sex composition to overall sex composition (CHRSRTTSR), and an exogenous variable, viz. change in forest covered area (CHFCA) as given below:

CHSHGOTTLS = f(CHCOMLAND, CHRSRTTSR, CHFCA) (2)

The exogenous variable has been included as several empirical studies have demonstrated that deforestation in several tracts has gone together with the changing composition of the livestock in favour of sheep and goats. These can be sustained easily by grazing on degraded tracts unlike other milch animals like cows and buffaloes which require more fodder.

In the third structural relation, change in private ownership of land is measured by change in net sown area to total geographical area (CHNSAPTGA). It is stated to be a function of one endogenous variable, viz. change in common land to total geographical area (CHCOMLAND) to capture the tendency towards privatisation.

CHNSATGA = f(CHCOMLAND, ANR, CHGIATGCA, PCFGP, NADI, CHDEN) (3)

The five exogenous variables that are postulated as affecting changes in net sown area are: (a) three agricultural variables, viz. annual normal rainfall (ANR), change in irrigational intensity (CHGIATGCA), and agricultural land productivity measured by per capita food production (PCFGP); and (b) two non-agricultural variables, i.e. non-agricultural development index (NADI) and population pressure on land variable as measured by change in density of population per square kilometre (CHDEN).

Change in net sown area is taken to stand for increase in private land ownership. The magnitude of change in privately owned croplands could have a strong inverse relationship with changes in common land areas. On the other hand, improvements in irrigation facilities (themselves sometimes a consequence of protection of common land) and greater availability of rain water are expected to have a strong bearing on land productivity and thus encourage extension of private property in land by increasing private returns form it. Similarly higher land productivity or better quality of land also encourages private ownership.

Non-agricultural development in the district may also influence migration outflows and thus land use patterns in the rural tracts. The non-agricultural development related outmigrational flows form the areas may influence changing property rights in two ways. By decreasing the pressure of population on land, they lower the need for increased privatization of land. Simultaneously, this outflow decreases the availability of labour for use on agricultural land and is expected to make it more difficult to manage increased land.

The fourth structural relation depicts the extent of change in common land area (CHCOMLAND) as determined by changes in net sown area (CHNSATGA), changes in forest covered area (CHFCA), improvements in land productivity (CHPCFGP), population growth (PGRSEV), and pressure of population on land (CHDEN).

CHCOMLAND = f(CHNSATGA, CHPCFGP, PGRSEV, CHDEN, CHFCA) (4)

This equation together with the earlier one captures the mutual dependence of common and private property resources in the specific context of land. Such interdependence was found to be a crucial variable in the analysis of the motivation for the protection of common land in a number of regions including, for example, the lower Sivaliks (Chopra and Kadekodi 1991). The realization that common land provides inputs of water (through increased ground water levels, for instance) and fodder to improve the productivity of privately owned fields often results in its protection. Such a linkage is often assumed to be reflected in the quality of the common land. Here, the assumption is that area changes with respect to common land shall also result as a consequence of this linkage.

Furthermore, the economies of scale factor may bring around private individuals with small land holdings to become a part of a common property scheme of management (WRI 1995). Small fragments of submarginal land holdings may be uneconomic under private property regimes and may come to be cared for better if institutional change to pool them were made possible. This equation helps us to see whether such tendencies get reflected in the macro-level data.

Land productivity can also be an important determinant of property rights structures over land. A higher level of productivity may result in privatization of common land. It is because of this that the land productivity variable (CHPCFGP) has been included as one of the determinants of land under common property rights regimes. In a similar vein, demographic pressures on land characterized by extent of population growth (PGRSEV) and its pressure on land as represented by change in density (CHDEN) have also been included as predictors of landownership patterns.

### PARAMETRIC ESTIMATES OF THE MODEL

The functional form of all the four structural relations is assumed to be intrinsically linear, i.e. linear in parameters. A perusal of the system reveals that all the structural relations are over identified and thus the three-state least squares system estimational procedure (3SLS) is used for eliciting consistent estimates of the structural coefficients. The estimated structural coefficients are presented in Table III. Theoretically, the ordinary least squares (OLS) estimates of the structured parameters are not only biased but also inconsistent (Intriligator 1980). It may be of interest to mention that the OLS procedure yielded estimates (not reported here) depicting directions of influence quite contradictory to the general expectations. However, the system method employed here seems to have eliminated the simultaneity bias and provided consistent estimates. The 3SLS estimates are asymptotically efficient under correct specification conditions. The estimates are discussed below.

A perusal of the parametric estimates in the first column of Table III reveals that the process of environmental degradation in the arid and semiarid zones of India has a significant and positive impact on distress rural outmigration. The degradation process accelerates rural outmigration.

Another factor depicting significant and negative impact on distress rural outmigration turns out to be changes in common property resources. A decrease in land under common property regimes accelerates the process of distress out-migration from rural areas.

Table III. 3SLS estimates of the model

| Explanatory variables | Dependent variables | | | |
|---|---|---|---|---|
| | CHRSRTTSR | CHSHGOTTLS | CHNSATGA | CHCOMLAND |
| Endogenous | | | | |
| CHRSRTTSR | – | 0.037* | – | – |
| | (11.77) | | | |
| CHSHGOTTLS | 26.639* | – | – | – |
| | (13.93) | | | |
| CHNSATGA | 2.055 | – | – | −3.554* |
| | (0.75) | | | (3.77) |
| CHCOMLAND | −4.072* | −0.174* | −0.075* | – |
| | (1.98) | (2.24) | (2.42) | |
| Exogenous | | | | |
| Intercept | −2504.5 | 83.211 | 109.00 | 594.64 |
| | (7.61) | (8.15) | (7.09) | (6.07) |
| ANR | – | – | 0.011* | – |
| | | | (3.06) | |
| CHGIAGCA | – | – | 0.032 | – |
| | | | (1.36) | |
| PCFGP | – | – | 0.010 | – |
| | | | (0.80) | |
| CHPCFGP | 0.241 | – | – | −0.276* |
| | (1.13) | | | (2.47) |
| CHFCA | – | 0.003 | – | −0.115* |
| | | (0.77) | | (2.82) |
| CHPDEPLP | −0.033 | – | – | – |
| | (0.68) | | | |
| CHNEMOPLP | −0.004 | – | – | – |
| | (0.34) | | | |
| NADI | – | – | −1.957* | – |
| | | | (1.93) | |
| PGRSEV | – | – | – | −0.015 |
| | | | | (0.02) |
| CHDEN | – | – | −0.035 | −0.587* |
| | | | (0.56) | (2.11) |
| LITEIG | −0.314 | – | – | – |
| | (0.33) | | | |
| $R^2$ | 0.92 | 0.91 | 0.49 | 0.50 |
| $\bar{R}^2$ | 0.91 | 0.91 | 0.45 | 0.47 |

The estimates of the equation for compositonal change in livestock (CHSHGOTTLS), a proxy variable for environmental degradation, are presented in the second column of Table III. A perusal of the estimates reveals that decrease in area of common land has a significant and negative impact on environmental degradation process. Alternatively, districts with similar levels of distress outmigration and changes in forest covered area but with larger land areas under common property rights depict lower environmental degradation. Furthermore, higher outmigration from rural tracts also depicts significant and positive relationship with environmental degradation process. Thus, higher extent of outmigration from rural tracts, ceteris paribus, depicts higher environmental degradation in arid and semi-arid zones over western parts of India.

A perusal of the estimates provided in the third column of Tanle III reveals that privatization of land has been at the expense of commonly owned land. Alternatively, districts with similar levels of agricultural resources such as annual rainfall, land productivity, outmigration potentials, etc., but with larger common ownership rights have depicted positive changes in private ownership rights over agricultural land. Possibly, the explanation could be in terms of larger encroachments on commonly owned land over the period.

Interestingly, higher normal rainfall districts within arid and semi-arid western zones of India have depicted significantly positive changes in private ownership rights over agricultural tracts. Among the demographic variables, we find that districts with lower nonagricultural development related migrational potential depict significantly higher changes in privately owned croplands. Alternatively, areas with a higher non-agricultural development potential depict much lower changes in privately owned croplands. When people have fewer alternate source of livelihood to look forward to in urban areas, they tend to think in terms of expansion of privately owned land.

The parametric estimates in the fourth column of Table III reveal that changes in common land areas and net sown areas are significantly and negatively associated. Possibly, expansion of privately owned cultivated lands is at the expense of shrinkage of common land areas. In other words, increases in net sown areas, largely privately owned, have a significant and negative impact on changes in common land areas.

It seems that common property resources such as land under governmental and community ownership rights have often been encroached upon by private individuals. Such encroachment of common land areas for cultivation is a significant source of their shrinkage. However, there seems to exist complementarity between privately and commonly owned agricultural land areas.

Looked at from another viewpoint, it is seen that districts with lower land productivity have experienced significantly higher improvements in common land areas or common ownership rights over agricultural land. Alternatively, regions with higher improvements in land productivity have depicted significant declines in common land areas.

The structural coefficients provide estimates of the direct effects of different predictors on the response variables in the system. In other words, solving the simultaneous structural system of four equations for the four endogenous variables in terms of the exogenous variables provides the reduced form coefficients of the model. The reduced form coefficient includes interaction effects also and can, therefore, be interpreted as the total effect of the exogenous variable on the endogenous one. In a static model the reduced form coefficients are the same as impact multipliers.

The estimated impact multipliers are presented in Appendix 2. The impact multiplier of an exogenous variable upon any endogenous variable is shown in the corresponding cell. For instance, 1% increase in gross irrigated area to gross cropped area (GIAGCA) will bring about 16% decline in distress outmigration from the rural tracts (RSRTTSR). Also, it will bring about 3% decline in proportion of sheep and goats to livestock composition (SHGOTTLS), implying an improvement in the environment to that extent. Furthermore, it brings about 4% increase in net sown area to total geographical area (NSATGA), and 15% decline in common land area (COMLAND). Interestingly, we find that total effects of all the agricultural variables on distress rural outmigration is consistent with general expectations. Higher irrigation intensity (GIAGCA), higher land productivity and changes therein (CHPCFGP), and regeneration of forests (CHFCA) leads to a reduction in the distress rural outmigration (CHRSRTSR) from districts over arid and semi-arid zones of India. Furthermore, improvements in non-agricultural employment opportunities, viz. employment in factories (ADEFPLP), employment in mining and quarrying sector (WEMQPLP), and overall non-agricultural development (NADI) encourage rural outmigration. In terms of factors operating in the source and destination areas, the results are quite consistent with the factors stated to be affecting rural outmigrational flows as discussed in the literature.

Similarly, we find that all the agricultural variables, viz. annual normal rainfall (ANR), irrigational intensity (GIAGCA), per capita foodgrain production (PCFGP) and improvements therein (CHPCFGP), forest covered area (FCA) depict significant effects on environmental conditions, cropland areas, and common land areas in expected directions. Improvements in irrigation intensity and improvements in per capita foodgrain production and forest covered area result in improvements in environmental conditions (characterized by reduction in sheep and goats as percent of total livestock population). Furthermore, the improvements depict increase in cropland areas or net sown area and reduction in common land areas.

The strong interconnections between the four crucial endogenous variables standing for distress rural outmigration (CHRSRTR), the environmental degradation process as measured by changing livestock composition in terms of proportion of sheep and goats to total livestock population (CHSGGOTTLS), and changes in land use patterns characterized by net sown area (CHNSTGA) and common land area (CHCOMLAND) are revealed through significant structural coefficients estimates of the simultaneous equations system. The multiple influences among the four endogenous variables become revealed by the structured formulations and estimated parameters of the system. The 3SLS system method of estimation provides consistent and efficient estimates of the structural coefficients. Thereby, the reduced form estimates of the system reveals that total effects of the significant exogenous variables are far more intense than their direct effects characterized by the estimated structural coefficients.

In brief, the distress rural outmigration in arid and semiarid zones over the Central and the Western parts of India seems to be largely because of push factors operative at place of origin such as environmental degradation process (CHSHGOTTLS) and shrinkage of common property resources (CHCOMLAND). Interestingly, we find that pull factors such as employment opportunities in non-agricultural sectors such as industrial units or mining and quarrying sectors do not have a significant impact on rural outmigration in the regions. Thus, in a sense, the outmigration flows from rural tracts in these regions have rightly been classified as distressed outmigration.

The system clearly reveals that distress outmigration from rural tracts in the arid and semiarid regions can be contained by regeneration of forests and pastureland, improving irrigational potential, and bringing more land under common property regime.

## 4. An Alternative Approach: Analysis of Micro Experiments

The econometric analysis undertaken above suggests directions that many of the hypothesized relationships are likely to take. By its very nature, however, it is not able to undertake an indepth study of the processes of creation of common property regimes. As stated in earlier sections, approximate measures of migration, environmental degradation and property rights changes have to be set up in order to use the array of available cross-section data. As an alternative approach, the following section undertakes an indepth analysis of selected experiments in the arid and semi-arid region. These micro-level experiments have been directed at poverty alleviation and environmental preservation in the last decade or so and have concentrated on change in the structure of property rights through participatory methods as the major policy intervention. This provides an alternative methodology for examination of the hypothesis regarding the linkage between outmigration and environmental degradation.

Whereas it is possible to pick up more authentic indices of property rights, environment and migration by following this approach, the nature of the information makes it imperative to adopt less sophisticated statistical techniques. The objective of the exercise is to compare the results obtained from the two alternative methods of analysis.

### Description of Projects, Subunits and Methodology

The projects selected are all located within the study area described in Section 4. Initiated and undertaken in the 1980s, they can be viewed as different kinds of experiments in combining changes in technology with those in property rights in order to achieve a degree of environmental protection, more specifically to arrest the ongoing process of degradation. The projects studied can be divided into three categories:

- pure technical interventions based on watershed technology;
- interventions aimed at improving the nature of property rights on forest land which in India is government owned but tends to become open access;
- technical interventions on land with ill-defined property rights.

The Tejpura watershed is located in district Jhansi which is a part of the Central Plateau and Hills Zone. This project undertaken in 1983 had six components (Maheshwari et al. 1990), which were integrated to increase productivity without attempting to take a view on and alter the social organization or the form that property rights took in the area. It was one of the earliest projects in which the watershed was treated as the unit of analysis and constituted an example of technical intervention in the form of soil and water conservation measures, afforestation, dry land horticulture and farm forestry measures. The project resulted in increased productivity on private lands and a higher level of cropping intensity which, in turn, led to higher farm incomes.

In contrast with the above project, the following projects included both property rights and technical interventions within their purview, while being confined to work on non-forest land:

(i) Jawaja project in Ajmer district,
(ii) Ubeshwar Vikas Mandal,
(iii) Ralegaon Siddhi in Ahmednagar.

The Harda project, the last of those being considered, was focused on changing property rights on forest land, ostensibly under the control of the Forest Department (Bahuguna 1992). However, keeping in mind the degradation of forests and the ground reality with regard to them, it is difficult to treat land to which the forest department has legal claim as exclusive to it. User rights of people do exist within the legal framework. Further, as well documented now, increase in biotic pressure has resulted in forest areas being treated more as open access property. Accepting this, an initiative which was taken in India in the form of Joint Forest Management aimed at creating a form of common property on it. The rights of the people and the Forest Department were both institutionalized. Harda in Hoshangabad district [Central Plateau and Hill Zone], is selected for an indepth study as an example of the implementation of joint forest management.

Table IV gives some characteristics of projects selected an indepth study. In each case, the location, period of work, nature of work and the migrational status of the district in which the project is located are given. The unit of work in some cases spreads over a number of villages and/or watersheds. The Harda project, for instance, is spread over six forest ranges; 150 forest protection committees were set up in 15 villages. The Jawaja project had an area of operation of 30 villages in Ajmer and Bhilwara districts but seven were selected by the project authorities for

Table IV. Some micro-experiments: interventions in technology and institutions

| | Location and zone | Period | Nature of intervention | Migrational status in initial year | Number of subunits studied |
|---|---|---|---|---|---|
| Tejpur | Jhansi: 8 | 1983–85 | Technical: on watershed | Immigration | 4 |
| Harda | Hoshangabad: 8 | 1991 onwards | Changing property rights forest land | Outmigration | 12 |
| Jawaja | Ajmer and Bhilwara: 8 | 1982 onwards | Technical cum institutional change | Both trends | 6 |
| R. Sidhi | Ahmednagar: 9 | 1976 onwards | Creation of common property rights | Outmigration | 4 |
| U.V.M. | Udaipur: 8 | 1986 onwards | Common property rights creation | Outmigration | 1 |

more indepth work from 1987 onwards. In this study 12 villages from the Harda project and six villages from the Jawaja project have been selected. The work in Ralegaon Sidhi was spread over four watersheds. UVM (Ubeshwar Vikas Mandal) also spreads its work over two blocks and a number of villages but one tribal hamlet for which detailed data were available has been selected for this study (Saint 1993).

The detailed strategy employed by the individual projects to create common property rights institutions varied from one project to the other. It is not possible to go into the details of these here. In general, the broad outline of the steps involved in the setting up of a common property regime can be laid down as follows:

- Identifying the land to be worked on and the group to whom rights accrue.
- Laying down the 'rules of the game' in the form of obligations of members of the group and rights accruing to them: this may include adoption of 'rotational grazing' or 'stall feeding'.
- Evolving a mechanism for ensuring that rules are followed.

In order to examine the nature and magnitude of linkage between different variables, data from sub-units (villages watersheds or forest ranges) for the different projects was merged to construct indices of environmental improvement, migrational resource base, creation of property rights and emergence of participation. This was made possible by the detailed information available at project level.[13] The association between these indices is highlighted through a chi-square test of association.

Four indicators of environmental improvement are identified. These are:

- a rise in ground water table,
- an increase in survival rate of trees planted,
- a decrease in illicit felling of fuelwood and cutting of fodder and
- a decrease in the population of sheep and goats.

Table V. Nature of association: results from micro experiments

| | Creation of property rights | Decrease in outmigration | Environmental improvement | Index of participation | Level of resource endowment |
|---|---|---|---|---|---|
| 1. Creation of property rights | – | – | – | – | – |
| 2. Decrease in outmigration | Highly significant | – | – | – | – |
| 3. Environmental improvement | Significant | Highly significant | – | – | – |
| 4. Index of participation | Significant | Highly significant | Highly significant | – | – |
| 5. Level of resource endowment | Insignificant | Insignificant | Insignificant | – | – |

Notes: Chi-square test of association between different attributes was performed to highlight the extent of association. The significance level of association is characterized as follows: (i) Highly significant: significance at 5% level; (ii) Significant: significance at 10% level. Number of observations: 27 (total number of sub-units in the projects studied).

A village or a watershed having one of these indicators as positive is given an index 1 for environmental improvement; if it has shown improvement in two factors, then the index is given a value of 2; if in more than two factors the index is placed at 3.

The resource base in measured in terms of land owned per capita, the land unit being defined as the one relevant form the viewpoint of the nature of work on the project. The categories considered vary from project to project and represent the total resource base available for carrying out the experiment of institutional or technical change. They may extend to private, common and forest land, as the case may require.

The level of participation of the people is difficult to quantify as documented in many studies which have dealt in depth with the issue (Chopra, Kadekodi and Murty 1990 and Wade 1987 among others). Here we have taken the percentage contribution by village people to the cost of asset building as the appropriate indicator. This contribution is, in most cases, the imputed value of labour contributed.

## Results from Micro-Experiments

Table V lists the nature of association between the attributes discussed above. The association between migrational change, creation of property rights and index of participation is found to be highly significant. Indices of environmental improvement are also associated with the above mentioned indices in a highly significant manner. It can therefore be concluded that the creation of property rights through assurance of access to returns decreases outmigration. Environmental improvement and higher rates of participation also seem to deter outmigration. Once property rights are clearly defined on non-private land, labour moves towards the creation of community assets and there is an improvement in the environmental situation. This implies an increase in the carrying capacity of hitherto degraded land.

It may be noted that environmental improvement and creation of institutions for control of resource use are marginally associated. This is perhaps because some kinds of environmental improvement such as increase in ground water levels can be the consequence of technical interventions on private land over which property rights are, by definition, well defined.

The level of resource endowment of the unit of operation does not seem to be associated significantly with the creation of property rights, migrational change or environmental improvement. This implies that the scale factor is not important in setting the process in operation. Even villages or watersheds with limited resources by way of per capita land at their disposal can initiate the process of institutional change. A lower relative resource endowment would probably mean that the income levels possible to be attained as a consequence of the change are not as high as in the case of better endowed villages/watersheds.

## Conclusions

The two alternative methodologies used to examine the hypothesis provide pointers in the same direction. The simultaneous equations framework based on secondary data indicates that in the arid and semi-arid regions of India a large part of outmigration is because of push factors such as environmental degradation and shrinkage of common property resources. The collation of evidence from micro experiments also suggests that the outmigration process becomes decelerated once property rights are well defined, either in the form of ownership rights or user rights. Simultaneously, inputs of labour for environmental protection start coming in. A similar process sis expected to emerge with respect to forest land once joint forest management takes roots. Institutional change which ensures that people get a return from the new focus adopted is a necessary ingredient for success.

Once property rights are carefully specified, the nature of the area of origin and the income it is able to provide changes. A higher level of consumption is possible with a greater degree of certainty. This changes the relative attractiveness of the areas of origin and destination for the migrant and affects the decision to migrate. Such a development is of crucial significance in the context of rising levels of population and pressures on the urban environment as well. These pressures decrease once higher levels of population can be supported within rural areas as indicated by the findings of this study. It can be concluded that the creation of institutions aimed at enforcing property rights on common property resources corrects the imbalance between the rural and urban environment. The development is simultaneously the consequence of a more realistic manner of understanding the manner in which people relate to natural resources.

**Appendix 1. Summary statistics for the selected variables**

| No. | Variable | Mean | S.D. | C.V.*100 | Skewness | Min. | Max. |
|---|---|---|---|---|---|---|---|
| 1. | CHRSRTSR | 98.07 | 9.23 | 9.41 | −8.80 | 13.30 | 105.70 |
| 2. | CHSHGOTTLS | 118.19 | 94.45 | 79.91 | 8.08 | 53.59 | 960.30 |
| 3. | CHNSATGA | 99.43 | 9.95 | 10.00 | −2.26 | 52.00 | 120.90 |
| 4. | COMLAND | 120.83 | 6.31 | 49.91 | 1.92 | 29.13 | 412.80 |
| 5. | PGRESEV | 26.89 | 5.93 | 22.05 | 1.24 | 15.00 | 50.92 |
| 6. | NADI | −0.36 | 0.74 | 211.42 | 1.36 | −1.50 | 2.24 |
| 7. | ANR | 881.66 | 310.22 | 35.18 | 0.30 | 164.00 | 1932.00 |
| 8. | CHFCA | 88.36 | 104.70 | 118.49 | 6.51 | 6.25 | 955.70 |
| 9. | CHPCFGP | 119.62 | 49.23 | 41.15 | 2.60 | 9.50 | 364.70 |
| 10. | CHADEFPLP | 190.11 | 177.79 | 93.47 | 3.40 | 21.77 | 1079.00 |
| 11. | CHWEMQPLP | 194.89 | 616.05 | 316.24 | 8.79 | 1.44 | 5850.00 |
| 12. | CHDEN | 130.39 | 20.59 | 15.79 | 3.78 | 84.29 | 247.00 |
| 13. | CHGIAGCA | 129.12 | 32.50 | 25.17 | 1.33 | 59.38 | 240.20 |
| 14. | LIT81 | 30.06 | 10.79 | 35.89 | 0.61 | 11.00 | 57.00 |
| 15. | PCFGP | 187.16 | 63.89 | 34.13 | 0.53 | 47.00 | 379.00 |

**Appendix 2. Reduced form coefficients of the system**

| Item | | Endogenous variables | | | |
|---|---|---|---|---|---|
| | | CHRSRTSR | CHSHGOTTLS | CHNSATGA | CHCMLAND |
| Intercept | | 289.9390 | 141.3205 | 87.80693 | 282.5741 |
| Exogenous variables | ANR | −0.05588 | −0.01140 | 0.014997 | −0.05330 |
| CHGIAGCA | | −0.16256 | −0.03317 | 0.04363 | −0.15506 |
| PCFGP | | −0.05080 | −0.01036 | 0.01363 | −0.04845 |
| CHPCFGP | | −0.40372 | −0.08390 | 0.02822 | −0.37630 |
| CHFCA | | −0.16590 | −0.03110 | 0.01176 | −0.15679 |
| CHADEFPLP | | 0.00373 | 0.00138 | 0 | 0 |
| CHWEMQPLP | | 0.00045 | 0.00017 | 0 | 0 |
| NADI | | 9.94214 | 2.02858 | −2.66821 | 9.48282 |
| PGRSEV | | −0.02046 | −0.00401 | 0.001533 | −0.02045 |
| CHDEN | | −0.62295 | −0.12074 | 0.012304 | −0.63073 |
| LITEIG | | 0.03545 | 0.01312 | 0 | 0 |

**Appendix 3. Characteristics of selected projects**

| Projects | Units | Tejpura | Harda |
|---|---|---|---|
| 1. Location | District state agroclimatic zone | Jhansi U.P. 8 | Hoshangabad M.P. 8 |
| 2. Period undertaken | | 1983–1985 | 1991– |
| 3. Unit of work | | Watershed | Forest ranges 6 village forest protection committee (150 in 15 villages) |
| 4. Nature of work | | Soil conservation Water resource development, Management of crop husbandry, Grass and farm forestry Afforestation | Grazing control Distribution of fuelstocks Physical irrigation works Mechanism for control created, Dissemination of information |
| 5. Ownership of land affected (ha) | Common: 30.19 | Private: 525.6 Govt. forest land: | Private: 1426 10060 |
| 6. Impact on property rights | | Marginal | Creation of rights on government owned forest land |
| 7. Population (no.) | | 1400 | 5158.00 |
| 8. Migrational status of district | Nature | Immigration | Outmigration |
| | Index | 0.41 | −0.27 |
| | Rank | 97 | 179 |
| 9. Natural growth index of district | Index | 0.49 | 0.88 |
| | Rank | 134 | 85 |
| 10. Primary impact | | Increase in productivity of private land of 226%: increase in cultivated area of 23.9%: annual farm income increased 8.5 times | Rotational grazing accepted: 36.9% closed to grazing; distribution of fuel stocks increased from 623 to 2489: 300% increase in two years in productivity of agricultural crops |
| 11. Externalities (secondary) | | Accumulation of ground water water table increased by 3–7 m at different seasons. | Area increased = 31.64% soyabean introduced |
| 12. Indications of success | | Increased incomes of people | Control over distribution and grazing accepted, fines imposed: 15 cases in 2 |

Ranges women members: 274 in 2 ranges

Appendix 3. Continued

| Projects | Units | Jawaja | | Ralegaon Siddhi |
|---|---|---|---|---|
| 1. Location | District state agroclimatic zone | Ajmer and Bhilwara Rajasthan 8 | | Ahmednagar Maharashtra 9 |
| 2. Period undertaken | | 1982 onwards | | 1976 onwards |
| 3. Unit of work | | Village – 30 | | Village – 1 (4 watersheds) |
| 4. Nature of work | | Plantation on private and common land Appropriate technology for development of common lands, contour channels, trenches, checkdams | | Plantation on watershed: soil and water conservation economy of fuel use: recycle of product |
| 5. Ownership of land affected (ha) | | Common – 1774 area worked – 289 or 16.3% of total common land | | Wasteland: 122.71 Govt. pastures: 50.78 Govt. forests: 136.8 Cultivable village panchayat: 3.95 |
| 6. Impact on property rights | | Creation of rights on common lands | | Creation of rights on common lands |
| 7. Population (no.) | | 9235 (in 7 villages) | | 1508.00 |
| | | Ajmer | Bhilwara | |
| 8. Migrational status of district | Nature | Immigration | Outmigration | Outmigration |
| | Index | 0.50 | –0.90 | –0.28 |
| | Rank | 93 | 304 | 181 |
| 9. Natural growth index of district | Index | 0.42 | 1.22 | –0.86 |
| | Rank | 140 | 48 | 301 |
| 10. Primary impact | | Average rate of survival of plantation on private and common land increased, technical interventions by way of checkdams, contour channels and trenches | | Increase in productivity of private land 20–50%. Increase in area cultivated, 233 ha or 37.2% water conservation: 40 new wells, rise in water table saving in fuel conservation of 16.2%, due to smokeless recycling of manure, biogas plant |
| 11. Externalities (secondary) | | Increase in productivity of crops | | Augmentation of ground water tree and grass covers |
| 12. Indication of success | | | | Migration reduced to zero from 200–250 people; 13.3–16.6% of the population. Self sufficiency in foodgrain. Import of foodgrains decreased from 60% to zero stock of 150 qtls. |

Appendix 3. Continued

| Projects | Units | UVM |
|---|---|---|
| 1. Location | District state<br>agroclimatic zone | Udaipur<br>Rajasthan 8 |
| 2. Period undertaken | | 1986– |
| 3. Unit of work | | Hamlet (part of multi-caste village)<br>selected for study |
| 4. Nature of work | | Development of community<br>pastures, rules for sharing<br>responsibilities determined,<br>development of private lift irrigation<br>and community well. |
| 5. Ownership of land<br>affected (ha) | | Common lands: 119<br>Revenue lands: 133<br>Private lands: 605<br>Miscellaneous: 15 |
| 6. Impact on property rights | | Common land put under community pasture<br>Rotational grazing<br>Existing rights<br>Abbreviated conflict but<br>creation of property rights |
| 7. Population (no.) | | 468–5000<br>(part of larger village) |
| 8. Migrational<br>status of<br>district | Nature<br><br>Index<br>Rank | outmigration<br><br>–0.82<br>288 |
| 9. Natural<br>growth<br>index of<br>district | Index<br><br>Rank | 0.97<br><br>76 |
| 10. Primary impact | | Vegetation cover increased from<br>5% in 1986 to 80% in 1993<br>(30% trees, 50% grass),<br>fodder productivity of<br>Rs. 90000 from pasture of<br>170 ha. |
| 11. Externalities<br>(secondary) | | Community well lift irrigation scheme<br>initiated, reduced soil erosion,<br>enhanced ground water recharge,<br>well distributed perennial stream flow<br>well distributed perennial stream flow |
| 12. Indication of success | | Initiative from villagers<br>for expansion to newer areas. |

Sources: Bahuguna (1992), Maheshwari R. C. et al. (1990) Society for Promotion of Wasteland Development (1989), Pangare and Pangare (1992) and Saint (1993).

## Notes

1. It is true that some emissions from agricultural activity and livestock also result in pollution of the environment. By and large, however, the qualitative and quantitative effects of these are not as damaging as those of the erosion of the natural capital base.
2. The World Resources institute Report (1995) accepts this repudiation of an oversimplified approach when it states that the manner in which w relate to our resources is also partly responsible for the environmental problems of the world. Bromley (1991) has put together evidence from a number of countries across the developing world to illustrate how intentional policies of governments in need of foreign exchange, well intended but misspecified policies and broad agricultural sector policies cause problems for land use and natural resources. See also Repetto and Holmes (1983) and Repetto and Gillis et al. (1988). For the impact of the market on natural resource use, see Gadgil (1992).
3. See, for instance, the listing of environmental organizations in India in World Wide Fund for Nature (1992).
4. The definitions and specifications of this continuum are discussed among others by Bromley (1991, 1992) and Ciriacy-Wantrup and Bishop (1975).
5. See Ostrom (1990) for an indepth analysis of institutional change with accompanying changes in property rights as it occurred in this region.
6. See Kadekodi and Chopra (1990) for a description and analysis of such a change in the structure of property rights which constituted the basis of an experiment in Bihar.
7. See Todaro (1980) for a survey of the earlier literature on internal migration in developing countries.
8. See Greenwood (1971a,b).
9. See, for example, Lipton (1976) and Connell et al. (1975).
10. For an empirical study of the contribution of common property resources to the consumption base of the poor in arid and semi-arid regions of India, see Jodha (1986).
11. It is to be noted that this is an independently defined variable and not a residual.
12. Centre for Monitoring the Indian Economy (1982 and later), which is listed as the source, collates data from different government sources and publishes it on a regular basis.
13. See Bahuguna (1992), Maheshwari et al. (1990), Pangare and Pangare (1992), Saint (1993), Society for Promotion of Wasteland Development (1989). Data were also collected from unpublished documents of the respective projects.

## References

Agarwal, A. and S. Narain (1989), *Towards Green Villages, a Strategy for Environmentally Sound and Participatory Rural Development*, New Delhi: Centre for Science and Environment.

Bahuguna, V. K. (1992), *Collective Resource Management: An Experience in Harda Forest Division*, IIFM Bhopal: Regional Centre for Wasteland Development (RCWD).

Bromley, D. W. (1991), *Environment and Economy: Property Rights and Public Policy*, Cambridge, MA, U.S.A.: Basil Blackwell.

Bromley, D. W. (1992), 'The Commons, Common Property and Environmental Policy', *Environmental and Resource Economics* **2**(1), 1–17.

Burra, N. (1991), *Women and Wasteland Development: A Review of N.G.O. Experience*, International Labour Organisation: Programme On Rural Employment And Development Department.

Center for Monitoring Indian Economy (CMIE) (1982), *District Level Data for Key Economic Indicators*, Bombay: The Centre for Monitoring Indian Economy.

Chopra, K., G. K. Kadekodi, and M. N. Murty (1990), *Participatory Development, People and Common Property Resources*, New Delhi and London: Sage Publications.

Chopra, K. and G. K. Kadekodi (1991), 'Participatory Institutions: The Context of Common and Private Property Resources', *Environmental and Resource Economics* (1), 353–372.

Ciriacy-Wanthrop, S. V. and R. C. Bishop (1975), 'Common Property as a Concept in Natural Resource Policy', *Natural Resources Journal* **15**, 713–727.

Connell, J. B. Dasgupta, R. Laishley, and M. Lipton (1975), *Migration from Rural Areas: the Evidence from Village Studies*. University of Sussex, Institute of Development Studies, Discussion Paper No. 39.

Development Alternatives, New Delhi (1988), *Common Property Resources Management*. Study in Ajmer and Jodhpur districts, Rajasthan.

Gadgil, M. (1992), 'State Subsidies and Resource Use in a Dual Society', in Agarwal, ed., *The Price of Forests*, New Delhi: Centre For Science and Environment.

Gera, P. (undated), *Farmers Participation in Externally Catalysed Irrigation System – The Case of the Johads*, New Delhi: Development Alternatives.

Greenwood, M. (1971a), 'An Analysis of the Determinants of Internal Labour Mobility in India', *Annals of Regional Science* **5**(1), 137–151.

Greenwood, M. (1971b), 'A Regression Analysis of Migration to Urban Areas of a Less Developed Country: The Case of India', *Journal of Regional Science* **11**(2), 253–262.

Gulati, S. C. (1992), 'Developmental Determinants of Demographic Variables in India: A District Level Analysis', *Journal of Quantitative Economics* **8**(1), 157–172.

Intriligator, M. D. (1980), *Econometric Models, Techniques, and Applications*, New Delhi: Princeton Hall of India Pvt. Ltd.

Jodha, N. S. (1986), 'Common Property Resources and the Rural Poor in Dry Regions of India', *Economic and Political Weekly* **XXX**(27), July 5, 1169–1181.

Kadekodi, G. K. and K. Chopra (1990), 'Cyclical Re-investment Strategy: An Alternative Approach to Rural Development', *Social Action* (40), 382–398.

Larson, B. A. and D. W. Bromley (1990), 'Property Rights, Externalities and Resource Degradation, Locating the Tragedy', *Journal of Development Economics* **33**, 235–262.

Lipton, M. (1976), 'Migration from Rural Areas of Poor Countries: The Impact on Rural Productivity and Income Distribution', Paper presented at *Research Workshop on rural Labour Market Interactions*, Washington, D.C.: International Bank for Reconstruction and Development.

Maheshwari, R. C., D. P. Singh, and V. M. Ambekar (1990), *A Case Study of Irrigated Watershed Management Tejpura, Jhansi*, Third IWRS National Symposium on Water Shed Development and Management, Kanpur.

Ministry of Environment and Forests, India (MOE) (1991), *The State of Forest Report*, Dehradun: Ministry of Environment and Forests, p. 7.

Ostrom, E., (1990), *Governing the Commons: The Evolution of Institutions for Collective Action*, U.S.A.: Cambridge University Press.

Pangare, G. and V. Pangare (1992), *From Poverty to Plenty, the Story of Ralegaon Siddhi*, Indian National Trust for Art and Cultural Heritage.

Repetto, R. and T. Holmes (1983), 'The Role of Population in Resource Depletion in Developing Countries', *Population and Development Review* **9**(4), 609–632.

Repetto, R. and M. Gillis, et al. (1988), *Public Policies and the Misuse of Forest Resources* (R. Repetto and I. Gills, eds.), Washington D.C.: World Resources Institute.

Saint, K. (1993), *Social Dynamics of Natural Resources Management – A Case Study in South Rajasthan Aravallis*. Ubeshwar Vikas Mandal, Udaipur.

Society For Promotion Of Wasteland Development (1989), *A Study of Jawaja Project*, New Delhi.

Todaro, M. P. (1980), 'Internal Migration in Developing Countries: A Survey', in A. Easterlin, ed., *Population and Economic Change in Developing Countries*, Chicago: University of Chicago Press.

World Resources Institute (WRI) (1995), *World Resources; A Guide to the Global Environment*, Delhi: Oxford University Press, pp. 83–106.

World Wide Fund for Nature (India) (1992), *Environmental N.G.O.s in India: A Directory*, New Delhi.

Wade, R. (1987), *Village Republics, Economic Conditions for Collective Action in South India*, Cambridge: Cambridge University Press.

200-215
[96]

# [11]

Q22
Ō13
Ō17
Q28
Malaysia

## Sustainable Resource Use, Economic Development, and Public Regulation
### *The Multiproduct Gill Net Fishery of Peninsular Malaysia*

MOHAMMAD FERDOUS ALAM[1], ISHAK HAJI OMAR[2] and DALE SQUIRES[3,*]
[1] *Department of Agricultural Finance, Bangladesh Agricultural University, Bangladesh*
[2] *Faculty of Economics and Management, University Pertanian Malaysia, Selangor, Malaysia*
[3] *National Marine Fisheries Service, Southwest Fisheries Science Center, P.O. Box 271, La Jolla, CA 92038, U.S.A. (* Corresponding author)*

**Abstract.** The role of production technology for sustainable economic growth and resource management in the multispecies renewable resources industries is a neglected issue, particularly in complex tropical ecosystems. Given the still rudimentary understanding of biological interactions among species, even in most temperate ecosystems, the importance of understanding the technological and economic interactions is heightened for sustainable economic growth and public regulation. This paper evaluates these interactions for the multiproduct gill net fisheries of Peninsular Malaysia. Standard price and quantity controls may have little promise. Gear regulations, a policy of constant escapement, and managing the entire mix of species as a single stock for economic rather than biomass yield appear the most promising management tools given the limited regulatory options.

**Key words:** Multispecies, tropical, artisanal, fisheries, public regulation, Malaysia

## 1. Introduction

Economic growth and development in the less developed countries is increasingly concerned with the issue of sustainability, the environment, and natural resource management. Primary research in this area has focused on the role of natural resources and the environment as assets or natural capital stock and a definition of sustainability itself.

One applied issue in research management in less developed countries, that has yet to receive attention, is the structure of production for producers extracting multiple fish species in a stock-flow product technology of a typical ecosystem. Regulation of this industry is critical for economic development predicated on extracting a sustainable yield from a stable natural resource stock. Public programs simply targeting total industry extraction or ad hoc regulation of individual species as separate production processes are likely to wield an excessively blunt policy instrument, failing to explicitly tailor policies to the conditions on hand. Because technological interaction between species during the resource extraction process may easily dominate the biological

*Environmental and Resource Economics* 7: 117–132, 1996.

interaction (ecosystem interaction through processes like predation and competition), knowledge of the resource extraction technology is important in multispecies resource management, and hence economic development.[1]

The complexity of these issues is exacerbated in tropical ecosystems because the diversity of species is greater than that found in temperate zones. Resource use and continued economic growth and development must account for this species diversity and the complexity it introduces into the production process by explicitly specifying a multiproduct problem.

In developing countries, such as Malaysia, the absence of well-defined and fully structured property rights for several natural resources further exacerbates the task of economic development and sustainable resource use, necessitating the requirement for public regulations. Often, fishery programs for extraction of renewable resources favor social groups with lower incomes or who are isolated, and marginal to others in the industry. Raising their incomes within the context of sustainable resource extraction and overall economic growth means sacrificing efficiency for social goals, thus compounding the challenge for optimal resource use.

Problems of species diversity and biased regulatory measures are further heightened by the limited knowledge of multispecies population dynamics and current and optimal resource abundance levels in the production systems. Continued erosion of habitats, breeding and nursery grounds (e.g., mangrove swamps), environmental degradation, and subsequent declines in environmental carrying capacities create additional pressure on policy makers and researchers alike in their search for better management options. In view of the limited biological and economic information, policies that favor marginal communities, and given the complexity of tropical ecosystems, the resource management issue is transformed from a straightforward intertemporal optimization problem of aggregate biomass into one that must explicitly recognize a number of variables.

The purpose of this paper is to evaluate the structure of production technology for a Malaysian gill net fishing industry, an industry having all the above characteristics. The paper then relates the results to some of the necessary conditions for a program of sustainable resource use, public regulation, and economic development. In the process, the paper addresses the effectiveness of some development programs, which are incidental to the overall thrust of the study. One relates to the special training programs for captains and owner-operatorship of vessels organized by the Malaysian Dept. of Fisheries, aimed at raising the productivity of their boats (proxied by their profits). The other is to test whether there is a significant difference in the profitability between two racial groups, the Malays and Chinese, who dominate the Malaysian gill net fishery but with the former getting more developmental aid from the Government.

The presentation of the paper is as follows. Section 2 offers background information. Section 3 specifies the empirical model and discusses the data. Section 4 reports empirical results and policy implications. Section 5 offers concluding remarks.

## 2. Background of Peninsular Malaysia Fisheries

Artisanal fisheries are the mainstay of the Malaysian fishing industry. Technological dualism in the form of highly commercial mechanical gears such as the trawl and purse seine coexist side-by-side in the same fishery with a large amount of traditional fishing gear such as drift/gill net, lift net, bag net, scoop net, and hooks and lines. Traditional gears account for about 62% of all fishing gear in 1991, contributing about 21% of the total marine landings (Dept. of Fisheries, 1991). The socio-economic importance of gill net fishing is apparent, since the proportion of harvesters working with it is substantially higher (37%) than their counterparts using trawlnet (22%) and seines (26%). Of the total amount of gillnetters (37%), those situated on the east coast of Peninsular Malaysia represent 13% while those on the west coast account for 24%. Alam (1991) and Ishak (1992) have provided additional background.

The structure of single-product production technology has been generally investigated by the primal approach (Jahara, 1984; Fredericks and Nair, 1985). Ishak (1984) investigated the optimal size of trawlers.

Previous studies of multiproduct fishing technologies concentrated on highly commercialized fisheries in North America, Australia, or highly migratory tuna in the Southwest Pacific. Alam (1991) first evaluated the economic production of multispecies fisheries by fully commercial and artisanal producers in tropical waters through a study of trawlers, pursue seiners, and gillnetters harvesting on the east and west coasts of Peninsular Malaysia.

## 3. Empirical Model

### 3.1. SPECIFICATION OF HARVESTING TECHNOLOGY

Gill net fishing is a traditional artisanal gear which lands over 17 species of fish. Hence, production technology is properly specified as multiproduct.

Harvesters use relatively small vessels, often of wood construction, powered by comparatively small motors resulting in fishing trips of limited duration (Tables I and II). Harvesters use variable inputs of energy (in the form of fuel and lubrication oil) and labor, conditional upon the capital stock, applied to the resource stocks in a stock-flow production technology. Gill nets are set at the beginning of the trip and the fish entangled in the mesh are extracted at the end of the trip. Ice use, and hence quality, varies. Vessel operators key production directly to the market given vessel, net, resource abundance constraints, and market information conveyed by prices. Marketing opportunities

Table I. Mean characteristics of gill net fishing.

| Boat and fishing characteristics | East coast | West coast |
|---|---|---|
| Hull length (meters) | 12.16 (14.95) | 10.50 (17.39) |
| Gross registered tones | 10.57 (34.22) | 6.33 (47.55) |
| Engine horsepower | 25.79 (34.40) | 17.35 (45.01) |
| No. of trips at sea | 19.14 (26.97) | 17.43 (28.20) |
| Total fishing days per month | 21.83 (11.88) | 21,68 (14.56) |
| Trip duration (days) | 1.14 (5.00) | 1.24 (3.20) |
| Operating distance (nautical miles) | 9.57 (53.53) | 5.32 (56.95) |
| Mean haul per day | 1.95 (42.26) | 3.23 (22.72) |
| Mean crew size | 3.16 (19.60) | 2.45 (20.57) |

*Note:* Coefficients of variation within parentheses.
*Source:* Alam (1991).

Table II. Mean monthly gill net catch, revenues, and costs.

| | East coast | West coast |
|---|---|---|
| Aggregate catch (kg) | | |
| All species | 2451.07 | 964.15 |
| Grade A | 367.76 | 162.78 |
| Grade B | 189.38 | 64.00 |
| Grade C | 1822.02 | 699.80 |
| Prawn | 71.90 | 37.58 |
| Total revenue (M$) | | |
| All species | 4451.07 | 2062.52 |
| Grade A | 1418.61 | 770.74 |
| Grade B | 582.24 | 221.49 |
| Grade C | 2057.53 | 856.28 |
| Prawn | 362.15 | 214.00 |
| Costs (M$) | | |
| Capital (investment) | 7786 | 6566 |
| Depreciation | 88.52 | 41.60 |
| Opportunity cost | 93.13 | 41.03 |
| Energy | 311.95 | 177.78 |
| Crew | 2012.88 | 1023.17 |

*Source:* Alam (1991).

vary. These include a variety of local outlets, such as petty traders (including wives), beach markets, and local "open-air" markets; state-sponsored buyers and cooperatives; and middlemen or brokers, often marketing to areas with larger populations.[2] Hence, prices are competitively formed.

Quasi-fixity of some inputs, particularly capital stock, may be observed. Adjustments in vessel size typically require different times for fishing. Among artisanal fishers, vessels can be purchased second-hand, self-constructed, or built new by professional craftspeople. New construction requires time. Even second-purchase requires some time, since local markets may be thin and even regional markets may be rudimentary, relying upon considerable personal contacts and word-of-mouth to convey information to buyers and sellers.

### 3.2. PROFIT FUNCTION

The multiproduct restricted profit function represents production technology under these conditions when producers face competitive prices, asset fixity, and outputs and variable inputs are endogenous (McFadden, 1978). The multiproduct restricted gill net profit function was specified with a translog functional form as:

$$\begin{aligned}\ln\pi = {} & \alpha_0 + \textstyle\sum_i \alpha_i \ln P_i + \alpha_z + 0.5 \sum_i\sum_j \alpha_{ij} \ln P_i P_j \\ & + 0.5\, \alpha_{zz} \ln Z \ln Z + \textstyle\sum_i \alpha_{iz} \ln P_i \ln Z + \sum_k \beta_k d_k,\end{aligned} \tag{1}$$

where $i, j = A, B, C, E, L$; $P_i$ is price of $i$; $\pi$ = restricted profit (total revenue less variables costs of energy and labor); and:

- $A$ = Grade-A species consisting of pomfret, Spanish mackerels, wolf herring, and others;
- $B$ = Grade-B species consisting of shads, horse mackerels, and others;
- $C$ = Grade-C species consisting of hardtail scad, selar scad, tuna, black kingfish, crab, marine catfish, jewfish, Indian mackerels, gizzard shads, queenfish, sharks, and others;
- $E$ = Energy (diesel fuel and lubricants and oils);
- $L$ = Implicit wage (derived from share system of distributing earning of individual vessels);
- $Z$ = Vessel size (gross registered tons), a quasi-fixed factor;
- $d_1$ = Ownership dummy (1 = owner captain and 0 otherwise);
- $d_2$ = Training dummy (1 = trained captain and 0 otherwise);
- $d_3$ = Ethnicity dummy (1 = Malay and 0 = Chinese).

The resource stocks are assumed constant in this model using cross-sectional data.

The translog form was interpreted as a second-order Taylor's series approximation around the geometric sample mean since all variables were scaled by their geometric means. Output prices were constructed as Divisia indices.[3]

The share equation for netput $i$ ($X_i$), obtained by Hotelling's Lemma, is:

$$\frac{\delta \ln\pi}{\delta \ln p_i} = S_i = \alpha_i + \textstyle\sum_j \alpha_{ij} \ln P_i + \alpha_{iz} \ln Z, \tag{2}$$

where $S_i = P_i X_i/\pi$, where $S_i$ is positive for outputs and negative for variable inputs. Without loss of generality, symmetry is imposed by $\alpha_{ij} = \alpha_{ji}$ for $i \neq j$ in Equations (1) and (2). Linear homogeneity in prices is imposed on the restricted profit function and the share equations by the econometric restrictions: $\sum_i \alpha_i = 1$, $\sum_i \alpha_{ij} = \sum_j \alpha_{ij} = \sum_i \sum_j \alpha_{ij} = 0$.

### 3.3. HYPOTHESIS TESTS

The final form of production technology can be assessed by hypothesis tests of parametric restrictions. Input-output separability implies a single aggregate input and output. The marginal rates of transformation between all output pairs are independent of factor intensities or factor prices. The firm's optimization process can also be treated as a two-stage process. The optimal combination of netputs within the subgroup is first selected, followed by a choice of the appropriate levels of the aggregate catch and aggregate variable inputs. Multispecies bioeconomic models traditionally maintain this hypothesis. From a perspective solely of the economics of public regulation, only the overall, aggregate output, not the individual outputs, requires regulation. Nonetheless, from a perspective concerning sustainable resource management alone and maintaining species and ecosystems diversity, each individual output, whether species or cohort, may require attention.

This global separability in outputs and variable inputs requires no interaction terms among all input-output combinations. This reduces the translog form to the Cobb Douglas in outputs and variable inputs, and hence imposes homogeneity, elasticities of substitution or transformation equal to one, and strong separability. The econometric restriction for input-output separability between outputs and variable inputs is (Denny and Pinto, 1978): $\alpha_{ij} = 0$; $i \neq j$; $i = A, B, C$ and $j = E, L$.

In quantitative fish stock assessments, aggregated species and cohorts treated as fish stocks, without biological interaction of species, correspond to input-output separability. This implies aggregation of species into major species groups, or even into a single aggregate, giving economic rather than biological yield. It also hopes to capture species interaction effects in the overall empirical relationship between the aggregate output and aggregate input (yield-effort) (Hilborn and Walters, 1992). This was the approach adopted by the population biologists Ralston and Polovina (1982). Hilborn and Walters suggest that this is likely to be the only alternative to the direct empirical approach for tropical fisheries with dozens of species.

Jointness-in-inputs requires all inputs used to produce all outputs. With nonjointness, there are no technological or cost trade-offs as one product is transformed into another and relative price changes or quantitative restrictions on one output do not spill over onto another output (Kohli, 1983). Hence, each production process can be separately regulated without affecting the production of the other processes; separate production processes exist for each output. Single-species bioeconomic models traditionally maintain the hypothesis of nonjointness to allow tractability in modeling, since most species inhabit multispecies ecosystems. Nonjointness helps sustainable resource management, since species or cohorts requiring special attention can receive it without adverse economic spillovers. The econometric restriction for nonjointness of outputs $i$ and $j$ is (Denny and Pinto): $\alpha_{ij} = -\alpha_i\alpha_j$, $i \neq j$; nonjointness throughout the product set requires all $i$, $j$.

The firm's capital stock (vessel size) may be in either full static equilibrium, i.e., in long-run equilibrium, or in partial static equilibrium. The full static equilibrium model can be thought of as a special case of the partial equilibrium model.

The null hypothesis of full static equilibrium is tested following Conrad and Unger (1987). The underlying restricted profit function and the variable output revenue and input cost share equations are defined as in Equations (1) and (2). Under the null hypothesis, the vessel size (capital) share equation can be differentiated with respect to vessel size to give a capital cost share equation:

$$S_z = \frac{q_z Z}{\pi} = \phi_z + \textstyle\sum_i \phi_{iz} \ln P_i + \phi_{zz} \ln Z, \qquad (3)$$

where $i = A, B, C, E, L$. The parameters of Equation (3) differ from those of the corresponding restricted profit function (1) which express that the vessel size share Equation (3) is not the result of differentiating Equation (1). Because the maintained hypothesis is the maximization of the restricted profit given vessel size, $Z$, only the restricted profit function and variable input-output share equations have common parameters. The null hypothesis is that observed vessel sizes are optimal, and the restriction imposed is: $\alpha_Z = \phi_Z$ and $\alpha_{Iz} = \phi_{Iz}$, and Equation (3) is estimated jointly with Equations (1) and (2).

The effect of captain ethnicity, whether Malay or Chinese, on relative profitability can be assessed by the $t$-ratio of the corresponding dummy variable. The effect of special training for the captain on profit can also be evaluated by the statistical significance of the corresponding dummy variable. Finally, the effect of owner-operatorship upon profit can also be assessed by the statistical significance of the corresponding dummy variable.

These tests are not nested as a group. Hence, the statistical significance of the tests is not the (approximate) sum of those of individual tests (cf. Denny and Fuss, 1977). However, Godfrey (1988) notes that when there is a high degree of dependence between the individual significance tests, the actual overall significance level may be somewhat smaller than its upper bound of $s\sigma$, where $s$ is the number of tests and $\sigma$ is the significance level of each test. Hence, the overall significance level in this case is bounded from above by 0.09, where $s = 9$ and $\sigma = 0.01$. The null hypotheses of the full static equilibrium of the capital stock, input-output separability, and nonjointness-in-inputs over all outputs and for each individual input were each tested by an $F$-test.

3.4. DATA

The cross-sectional data were collected by a multistage sampling procedure. The first and second stages selected were first states in Peninsular Malaysia and then fisheries districts within states. Eighty-two gill net vessel owners were interviewed by administering a pretested interview from August to October, 1988. Annual depreciation was calculated by the straight line method, where purchase prices and economic lives were taken from the survey. Opportunity cost of capital (interest forgone) was assumed at 7.5%. Annual values were converted into monthly values. Details have been given in Alam (1991) and summary statistics reported in Tables I and II. The catch composition reported in Table II was sorted into Grades A–C following the grading system of the Department of Fisheries.

## 4. Empirical Results and Discussion

4.1. EMPIRICAL RESULTS

The restricted profit function (1) was jointly estimated with the revenue and cost share Equations (2) for each of the east and west coasts of Peninsular Malaysia. Since the share equations summed to unity, the labor cost share equation was dropped. Estimation was by the seemingly unrelated regression method iterated to convergence, giving results equivalent to maximum likelihood.

Parameter estimates for east coast gill net vessels are reported in Table IV and for west coast gill net vessel in Table V. The ordinary least squares $R^2$ for the west (east) coast profit function was 0.90 (0.80) and for the share equations ranged from 0.21 to 0.45 (0.27 to 0.71). The system $R^2$ was 0.92 (0.80). Monotonicity was globally satisfied for east coast equations, and on the west coast for grade-B species but only for 95% of grade-A species and 93% for grade-C species. The condition for linear homogeneity in prices was satisfied for both coasts. The Hessian determinant was positive definite, satisfying the convexity condition for both coasts.

The dummy variable for Malay ethnicity of the captain was statistically insignificant at conventional levels of significance for the west coast (Table V) and negative and significant for the east coast (Table IV). Perhaps because of the greater isolation of Malay villages (kampongs) on the east coast, relative differences from ethnicity were observed. The captain training and owner-operatorship dummy variables were statistically insignificant at conventional levels of significance for both coasts (Tables IV and V). Given the apparent ineffectiveness of special captain training or owner-operatorship status upon profits, a simple approach to training or assisting operators with vessel ownership may also be ineffective in lifting the profitability of Malay captains on the east coast.

The null hypothesis that vessel sizes are the same in partial static equilibrium (observed) and in full static equilibrium was rejected at the 0.01 level of significance (Table III). Hence, vessel sizes were not in long-run equilibrium. The estimated optimal vessel size in full static equilibrium was 24 (25) GRT as against 6 (11) GRT observed mean under existing technology. The slightly larger observed and optimum vessel sizes were consistent with the greater fish abundance and wider extended economic zone on the east coast.[4]

The vessel size can be expanded about four times. This might allow vessels to harvest more offshore grounds, extend the length of fishing trips, and help fish in more difficult weather conditions. Nonetheless, unrestricted expansion may further exacerbate the open-access problem and frustrate sustainable resource management and economic development. Sustainability would be enjoyed, however, if expansion of the vessel size was accompanied by strict and effective zoning regulations to allocate fishing effort spatially according to resource abundance and yield. Because inshore waters are currently overfished but the Malaysian EEZ areas are underexplored, larger vessels may provide sustainable harvesting opportunities.

Separation of outputs and variable inputs was not rejected for gill net vessels from both coasts of Peninsular Malaysia, conditional upon capital stock (Table III). Hence an aggregate output would be formed. Nonjointness-in-inputs was also not rejected (Table III), indicating a separate production process for each output. In the context of joint cost functions, Denny (1970) and Hall

Table III. Results of hypothesis tests for gill net firms.

| Hypothesis | SSE | Degrees of freedom | | $F$ | Reject $H_0$ |
|---|---|---|---|---|---|
| | | Numerator | Denominator | | (Yes/No) |
| Linear homogenity in prices: | | | | | |
| East coast | 153.98 | 7 | 151 | 0.60 | No |
| West coast | 142.35 | 7 | 141 | 0.36 | No |
| Full static equilibrium of capital: | | | | | |
| East coast | 443.33 | 36 | 186 | 7.44 | Yes |
| West coast | 240.43 | 36 | 174 | 1.97 | Yes |
| Input-output separability: | | | | | |
| East coast | 149.12 | 10 | 151 | 0.19 | No |
| West coast | 140.67 | 10 | 141 | 0.28 | No |
| Global separability: | | | | | |
| East coast | 201.34 | 21 | 151 | 2.64 | Yes |
| West coast | 185.84 | 21 | 141 | 2.33 | Yes |
| Nonjointness in inputs: | | | | | |
| East coast | 151.25 | 3 | 151 | 1.35 | No |
| West coast | 139.27 | 3 | 141 | 0.45 | No |

Table IV. Parameter estimates: East coast gill net vessels.

| Parameter | Estimate | *t*-Ratio | Parameter | Estimate | *t*-Ratio |
|---|---|---|---|---|---|
| **Profit function** | | | | | |
| $\alpha_0$ | 0.153 | 2.742 | $\alpha_{BL}$ | 0.178 | 4.758 |
| $\alpha_A$ | 0.802 | 32.226 | $\alpha_{BZ}$ | 0.087 | 2.266 |
| $\alpha_B$ | 0.277 | 23.504 | $\alpha_{CE}$ | 0.016 | 0.445 |
| $\alpha_C$ | 0.999 | 40.188 | $\alpha_{CL}$ | 0.016 | 0.478 |
| $\alpha_E$ | -0.151 | -34.719 | $\alpha_{CZ}$ | 0.141 | 2.038 |
| $\alpha_L$ | 0.143 | 2.629 | $\alpha_{EL}$ | 0.041 | 4.032 |
| $\alpha_Z$ | 0.217 | 0.278 | $\alpha_{EZ}$ | -0.002 | 0.142 |
| $\alpha_{AA}$ | 0.277 | 1.845 | $\alpha_{LZ}$ | 0.304 | 1.926 |
| $\alpha_{BB}$ | -0.012 | -0.095 | $f_1$ | 0.011 | 0.274 |
| $\alpha_{CC}$ | 0.185 | 0.968 | $f_2$ | 0.054 | 1.352 |
| $\alpha_{EE}$ | -0.141 | -9.001 | $f_3$ | -0.094 | -2.163 |
| $\alpha_{LL}$ | -0.194 | -1.464 | | | |
| $\alpha_{ZZ}$ | 0.390 | 4.640 | **Vessel size share equation** | | |
| $\alpha_{AB}$ | -0.147 | -1.880 | $\phi_Z$ | 0.050 | 1.708 |
| $\alpha_{AC}$ | -0.272 | -1.961 | $\phi_{AZ}$ | -0.025 | -0.186 |
| $\alpha_{AE}$ | 0.039 | 1.457 | $\phi_{BZ}$ | 0.045 | 0.806 |
| $\alpha_{AL}$ | 0.431 | 5.822 | $\phi_{CZ}$ | -0.303 | -1.759 |
| $\alpha_{AZ}$ | 0.106 | 1.520 | $\phi_{EZ}$ | -0.079 | -2.368 |
| $\alpha_{BC}$ | -0.109 | -0.911 | $\phi_{LZ}$ | -0.050 | -1.116 |
| $\alpha_{BE}$ | -0.014 | -0.385 | $\phi_{ZZ}$ | 0.004 | 0.121 |

*Note:* $A$, $B$, $C$ = outputs, $E$ = energy, $L$ = labor, $Z$ = capital. Dummies: $f_1$ = captain ethnicity, $f_2$ = captain training, $f_3$ owner-operator. Estimated at sample geometric mean.

(1973) showed that input-output separability either implied jointness-in-inputs or else that the individual production functions in such a technology were identical except for a scaler multiple, implying that there was effectively only a single kind of output.

### 4.2. DISCUSSION

Short-run gill net harvesting technology is thus comprised of individual production functions for the different species harvested which are scaler multiples of one another. Targeting of individual species (movements along the product transformation frontier, PPF) is not possible since outputs are in fixed proportions (and thus form an aggregate output). Changes in product prices do not alter the species mix but can affect harvests through the level of variable inputs in the short run (expansion effects) and quasi-fixed inputs over a longer time period (shifts out of the PPF from investment).[5]

These results and interpretation are consistent with the static and indiscriminate harvesting of virtually all species, age groups, and size classes swept by currents, foraging, or migration patterns into the mesh of the gill net gear. The optimum sustainable profit-maximizing strategy is simply to extract the

Table V. Parameter estimates: West coast gill net vessels.

| Parameter | Estimate | *t*-Ratio | Parameter | Estimate | *t*-Ratio |
|---|---|---|---|---|---|
| **Profit function** | | | | | |
| $\alpha_0$ | 0.751 | 3.774 | $\alpha_{BL}$ | 0.154 | 0.776 |
| $\alpha_A$ | 0.640 | 2.479 | $\alpha_{BZ}$ | -0.015 | -0.130 |
| $\alpha_B$ | 0.173 | 3.058 | $\alpha_{CE}$ | 0.380 | 1.931 |
| $\alpha_C$ | 0.674 | 2.436 | $\alpha_{CL}$ | 0.380 | 1.931 |
| $\alpha_E$ | -0.124 | -2.549 | $\alpha_{CZ}$ | -0.639 | -1.269 |
| $\alpha_L$ | -0.439 | -3.163 | $\alpha_{EL}$ | 0.073 | 1.224 |
| $\alpha_Z$ | 0.435 | 2.652 | $\alpha_{EZ}$ | 0.127 | 1.398 |
| $\alpha_{AA}$ | 0.046 | 0.038 | $\alpha_{LZ}$ | -0.227 | -0.667 |
| $\alpha_{BB}$ | 0.732 | 0.439 | $f_1$ | -0.251 | -1.667 |
| $\alpha_{CC}$ | 1.950 | 0.904 | $f_2$ | -0.142 | -1.932 |
| $\alpha_{EE}$ | -0.231 | -3.980 | $f_3$ | -0.078 | -0.574 |
| $\alpha_{LL}$ | -1.109 | -4.987 | | | |
| $\alpha_{ZZ}$ | 0.254 | 4.579 | **Vessel size share equation** | | |
| $\alpha_{AB}$ | -0.296 | -1.170 | $\phi_Z$ | 0.435 | 1.357 |
| $\alpha_{AC}$ | -0.231 | -1.946 | $\phi_{AZ}$ | -0.043 | -0.090 |
| $\alpha_{AE}$ | 0.145 | 0.065 | $\phi_{BZ}$ | -0.015 | -0.130 |
| $\alpha_{AL}$ | 0.007 | 0.019 | $\phi_{CZ}$ | -0.694 | -1.269 |
| $\alpha_{AZ}$ | -0.043 | -0.090 | $\phi_{EZ}$ | -0.127 | 1.398 |
| $\alpha_{BC}$ | -0.281 | -0.688 | $\phi_{LZ}$ | -0.639 | -1.269 |
| $\alpha_{BE}$ | -0.053 | -0.568 | $\phi_{ZZ}$ | 0.254 | 4.579 |

*Note:* $A$, $B$, $C$ = outputs, $E$ = energy, $L$ = labor, $Z$ = capital. Dummies: $f_1$ = captain ethnicity, $f_2$ = captain training, $f_3$ owner-operator. Estimated at sample geometric mean.

sustainable yield, regardless of species type, size, or age, that corresponds to the optimal overall biomass.

This peculiar technology hinders a program of resource sustainability across all species, size classes, or cohorts in the ecosystem, since there is little scope to tailor or target regulatory policies toward individual species, age groups, or sexes. This is a particularly acute problem for those fish that are more threatened, which may grow at slower rates, are juveniles, or comprise the female spawning biomass. The problem is compounded when the harvested species vary widely in growth and recruitment rates, reproductive capabilities, natural mortality, strengths in stock-recruitment, catchability, and robustness of female spawning biomass. As is well publicized for drift gill net fishing in the North-Central Pacific, gill nets constructed of nylon or other non-degradable materials, even when loosened and swept away from their moorings, can continue indiscriminate entrapment of fish and marine mammals for considerable lengths of time.

In an economic and technological sense, only an aggregate output exists. Price or quantity controls on outputs or inputs are generally ineffective at altering the species mix and can only affect the aggregate catch level, by controlling the length of time the gear is in the water, or over a longer time period, by affecting vessel size or industry exit patterns. Hence, the only feasible and effective price or quantity controls are those that reduce fishing time (trip length and frequency) and the amount of capital in the fishery. However, these regulations, particularly price controls, may be expensive, difficult to gauge and adjust precisely, and impractical to enforce in a country with a long coastline and small artisanal producers. Nonetheless, a license limitation program may appeal to the federal government if it is tied to cooperatives and fish marketing schemes.[6] License transferability would enhance economic efficiency. Transferable quantity controls on outputs, such as individual transferable quotas, also seem inappropriate given these conditions and the complex, multispecies nature of the fisheries.

Artisanal fisheries generally harvest relatively nearshore or on inshore grounds and estuaries. These are the most accessible areas, often receiving considerable amounts of fishing effort. In addition, these areas often serve as breeding or nursery grounds, so that overfishing can diminish resource stocks both in the present and the future. Hence, traditional regulatory measures such as shutting fish seasons or areas for spawning can play an important role and are relatively simple and inexpensive. Regulatory control can also aim to restrict trawlers or large vessels from waters fished by artisanal gear as, for example, in Indonesia.

Fish migration patterns and institutional structures also play a role. Highly migratory pelagic species generally create a bigger open-access externality. When species migrate across international boundaries or along wide stretches of the coastline, fewer incentives remain to conserve a resource stock. When species are more sedentary or demersal, and situated where an institutional and political regime that that fosters low-cost, enforceable agreements among fisheries, then scope exists for self-organization and thus self-regulation (Ostrom, 1990).

Gear regulations are perhaps the most promising regulatory tool, controlling mesh size and type (e.g., diamond or square mesh), which affect escapement composition and rates.[7] In turn, this allows for further growth, sexual reproduction, or later recruitment of escaped juveniles or immature fish already recruited into the fishery. Other dimensions of gill nets that can be regulated include net size and numbers, flotation and anchoring, etc. Perhaps even more promising has been the encouragement of shifts in gear toward longline, fish pot, or other gear which are more discriminating in their output composition, and which, if properly handled, can provide a higher quality product. More selective gear also reduces incidental entrapment of marine mammals and birds and is less prone to destructive 'ghost fishing' from lost gear.

Sustainability and optimum yields in complex tropical ecosystems requires consideration of the desired or optimal levels and mix of species, sexes, age and size classes, together with such related considerations as recruitment and natural mortality. Little is known even in temperate multispecies fisheries of the long-term effects of harvesting upon these factors, whether directly through removal of the fish or more indirectly from disruption by the gear on the habitat and the relationship between recruitment, predation, or competition.[8] Even in much simpler temperate multispecies fishery ecosystems, stock-recruitment relationships (one of the cornerstones of quantitative fish stock assessments) are uncertain and may not even exist in several instances. Hence, as the population biologists Hilborn and Walters (1992, p. 448) note, ignoring biological interaction may be, '. . . a very viable alternative to spending a lot of time and effort trying to understand biological interactions, and represents a sort of default assumption.'[9]

When multiple species are harvested in the same production process, particularly one with fixed proportions in the species mix, harvesting rates of individual species do not match equilibrium yields for the corresponding stocks. Less productive stocks may be substantially diminished or even lost when harvest rates maximize total yield. In short, biological yield for each stock cannot be tailored to the stock size in a multispecies ecosystem.[10]

The harvest rate can be selected to allow the weakest stock to meet its optimum escapement. When stocks are many and some are very unproductive, the total yield and profits could be very low, unless prices are relatively high for the less productive stocks.

Since achieving optimum escapement for all stocks appears to be a difficult task, the most promising approach seems to be maintaining a constant escapement for all stocks combined, regardless of the stock composition. The constant escapement rate could be set to account for the most economically or biologically important species, or even the weaker species if the emphasis lay with species preservation or conservation. The entire mix of species would be treated as a single stock managed for economic rather than biomass yield, with the hope that species interaction effects could be captured in the overall empirical relationships between yield and effort[11] (Hilborn and Walters, 1992; Ralston and Polovina, 1982).

## 5. Concluding Remarks

Sustainable resource management and economic growth founded on natural resource extraction in complex tropical ecosystems have been challenged by a number of factors that could create greater policy challenges than those often experienced in countries with higher incomes and different latitudes. These factors have included greater species diversity, frequent involvement by social groups of a lower socio-economic status or those in isolation, incompletely structured property rights systems, pressures on environmental carrying capacities, and an extremely limited biological knowledge of these complex, often fragile ecosystems. One important consideration for policy makers is to have a thorough knowledge of the structure of production for the multiproduct resource harvesters, particularly given the very limited understanding of biological interactions among species in marine ecosystems.

This paper has shed light on this area through a case study of gill net fishing by artisanal harvesters in Peninsular Malaysia. Production technology, conditional upon existing vessel sizes of gill netters on both the east and west coasts, was comprised of individual production processes for the different species harvested which were scaler multiples of one another, so that outputs were in fixed proportions and effectively formed a single aggregate output, total catch. Little scope is offered for a program of sustainable resource management across all species, sizes, sexes, and ages in the ecosystem by price or quantity controls on outputs. License limitation, gill net mesh regulations, season and area closures, and encouragement of more selective gears such as longline or fish pot represent the most promising policy instruments consistent with the structure of production. Not surprisingly, the government programs for increasing the productivity of fishermen, through training captains or the provision of inputs were found to be ineffective.

Given the rudimentary biological knowledge of multispecies ecosystems, especially those in complex tropical waters, and the nature of gill net harvesting technology, multiple stocks might best be managed as a single stock. Sustainability coupled with optimum economic yield can be applied to the stock as a whole rather than to the individual species, tempered by a monitoring of the optimum escapement rates of the most important, or perhaps weaker, species depending upon the overall management goals.

## Notes

[1] See Hilborn and Walters (1992) for a multispecies fisheries discussion of this issue.

[2] Firth (1966) is the classic study of Malay peasant fisheries. Ishak (1992) offers a comprehensive study of the Malaysian fishing industry.

[3] The implicit wage, derived from the share system of distributing individual earnings, is specified as exogenous. Opportunity cost information for artisanal fishers, often living in relatively isolated villages, is either unavailable or essentially meaningless or unreliable. Instead, we argue that harvesters, through experience, have formed expectations of a relatively stable set of returns to labor, given a fundamentally exogenous expected value. Nonetheless, we recognize a possible source of bias with this specification and this forms a topic of needed research.

[4] The continental shelf off the east coast forms part of the shallow South China sea, so that waters are relatively shallow and fishing grounds relatively extensive. Fishing grounds on the west coast are limited by the Straits of Malacca, whose shallow waters are shared with Indonesia and Thailand in the north.

[5] Shifts out of the production possibility frontier, from either increases in the level of variable inputs or quasi-fixed factors from investment, expand production along the output expansion path. Nonrejection of input-output separability with the translog functional form reduces the translog profit function to a Cobb-Douglas function of translog aggregates, and the exact and approximate interpretations of the translog function yield the same testable hypotheses (Denny and Fuss). Because of the Cobb-Douglas form, the output expansion path is homogeneous.

[6] These have comprised much of the government's development thrust in artisanal fisheries. See Ishak (1992) for further discussion.

[7] See Sainsbury (1984) for a related discussion on optimal mesh size for tropical multispecies trawl fisheries.

[8] For example, bottom trawl gear alter not only the sex ratio, age and size compositions, and species mix, but also alter the ocean bottom. In turn, this affects the entire ocean food chain with complex and largely unknown impacts over all species, including feed-backs even from unexploited species. Fish filling certain ecological niches may be removed, allowing other species to permanently replace them, or the ecological niches may be permanently altered, in turn providing more favorable habitats to other species. Other factors which might be altered as the ecosystem itself is transformed by harvesting include predator-prey relationships, inter-species competition, larval dispersal, recruitment, and natural mortality of eggs, juveniles, and adults, which in turn feed back into species, size, and age compositions.

[9] The population biologist Ellen Pikitch (1988) notes that biological interaction is difficult and expensive to study and takes many years, whereas technological and economic interaction is much simpler and cheaper to study, and useful results can be obtained rapidly. However, see McCall (1990) for an extensive discussion of multispecies ecosystems.

[10] Writing about the Gulf of Thailand, the population biologist Pauly (1979) notes that due to species interaction, there is no single optimum level of effort simultaneously producing the maximum sustainable yield for all stocks. Pauly discusses dividing the stock into different trophic levels, determining the trophic level which maximizes economic returns, and selecting the appropriate fishery techniques.

[11] Hilborn and Walters, p. 449, state, 'This is likely to be the only alternative to the direct empirical approach for tropical fisheries with dozens of species.' An exception, however, is tuna as demonstrated by Campbell *et al.* (1992).

## References


Alam, M. (1991), *An Economic Analysis of the Production Behavior of Fishing Firms in Selected Fisheries of Malaysia*, Unpublished Ph.D. dissertation, University Pertanian, Malaysia.

Campbell, H., A. McIlgorn and R. Nicholl (1992), 'Multiproduct Tuna Fisheries in the South West Pacific', Paper presented to the Sixth International IIFET Conference, July 6–9 1992, Paris.

Conrad, K. and R. Unger (1987), 'Expost Tests for Short and Long-Run Optimization', *Journal of Econometrics* **33**, 263–284.

Denny, M. (1970), *Trade, Technology, and the Production Sector: An Exploration of Models of Multi-Product Technologies*, Unpublished Ph.D. dissertation, University of California, Berkeley.

Denny, M. and M. Fuss (1977), 'The Use of Approximation Analysis to Test for Separability and the Existence of Consistent Aggregates', *American Economic Review* **67**, 404–418.

Denny, M. and C. Pinto (1978), 'An Aggregate Model with Multiproduct Technologies', in M. Fuss and D. McFadden, eds., *Production Economics: A Dual Approach Theory and Applications*, Vol. I, North-Holland, Amsterdam.

Department of Fisheries (1991), *Annual Fisheries Statistics, 1991*, Ministry of Agriculture, Kuala Lumpur.

Firth, R. (1966), *Malay Fishermen: Their Peasant Economy*, Norton, New York.

Fredericks, L. and Sulochana Nair (1985), 'Cost Structure and Profitability of Small-Scale Fisheries in Peninsular Malaysia', in T. Panayotou, ed., *Small-Scale Fisheries in Asia: Socio-Economic Analysis and Policy*, IDRC, Ottawa, Canada.

Godfrey, L. (1988), *Misspecification Tests in Econometrics*, Cambridge University Press, Cambridge, U.K.

Hall, R. (1973), 'The Specification of Technology with Several Kinds of Outputs', *Journal of Political Economy* **81**, 878–892.

Hilborn, R. and C. Walters (1992), *Quantitative Fisheries Stock Assessment: Choice, Dynamics, and Uncertainty*, Chapman and Hall, New York.

Ishak, H. O. (1984), 'Small or Large Trawlers in a Multispecies Monsoon Affected Fisheries: A Case Study', *Malaysian Journal of Agricultural Economics* **1**, 88–99.

Ishak, H. O. (1992), *Market Power, Vertical Linkages and Government Policy: The Malaysian Fish Industry*, Faculty of Economics and Business, University Pertainian, Malaysia.

Jahara, Y. (1976), 'Some Implications of the Fishermen's Subsidy Schemes in Peninsular Malaysia', *Kajian Ekonomi Malaysia* **13**, 72–80.

Jahara, Y. (1984), 'An Economic Analysis of Fisheries Production with Specific Reference to the Multispecies Trawl Fishery of Terengganu, Malaysia', *Kajian Ekonomi Malaysia* **21**, 1–17.

Kohli, U. (1983), 'Non-joint Technologies', *Review of Economic Studies* **50**, 209–219.

McCall, A. (1990), *Dynamic Geography of Marine Fish Populations*, Washington Sea Grant Program, Seattle, Washington.

McFadden, D. (1978), 'Cost, Revenue, and Profit Functions', in M. Fuss and D. McFadden, eds., *Production Economics: A Dual Approach Theory and Applications*, Vol. I, North-Holland, Amsterdam.

Ostrom, E. (1990), *Governing the Commons: The Evolution of Institutions for Collective Action*, Cambridge University Press, Cambridge, U.K.

Pauly, D. (1979), *Theory and Management of Tropical Multispecies Stocks: A Review with Emphasis on Southeast Asian Demersal Fisheries*, ICLARM Studies and Reviews 2, 35 pp. International Center for Living Aquatic Resources Management, Manila, Philippines.

Pikitch, E. (1988), 'Objectives for Biologically and Technically Interrelated Fisheries', in W. Wooster, ed., *Fisheries Science and Management: Objectives and Limitations*, Lecture Notes on Coastal and Estuarine Studies, No. 28, Springer-Verlag, New York, Chapter 5, pp. 107–136.

Ralston, S. and J. Polovina (1982), 'An Multispecies Analysis of the Commercial Deep-Sea Handline Fishery in Hawaii', *Fishery Bulletin* **80**, 435–445.

Sainsbury, K. (1984), 'Optimal Mesh Size for Tropical Multispecies Trawl Fisheries', *J. Cons. Int. Explor. Mer.* **41**, 129–139.

# [12]

# Incentives, Regulations, and Sustainable Land Use in Costa Rica



ERNST LUTZ and HERMAN DALY
*Environment Department, The World Bank, 1818 H Street NW, Washington, DC 20433, U.S.A.*

**Abstract.** Deforestation in Costa Rica has proceeded at a rapid pace. Of the remaining 2,700 km$^2$ of virgin forests on privately-owned land, over 300 km$^2$ are being deforested each year. Pressure on National Parks, which cover about 27 percent of Costa Rica is likely to increase in the future. Preliminary information indicates that, contrary to our expectations, most of the deforestation at present is not being done by squatters, but driven by profit and asset maximization motives of the timber industry, banana companies, and large cattle ranchers. Setting aside 27 percent of the country's land as parks and reserves was a major policy decision. Aside from the removal of some "perverse" incentives operating inside park areas, the main issue there is one of sound management, including protection from intruders, strengthening enforcement, and controlled "tourism". On the remaining primary and secondary forest areas on privately-owned land outside the parks, a key question is whether public interests connected with external costs of deforestation warrant public intervention. The paper suggests that a differentiated approach to this and other questions is needed, depending on the costs and benefits involved, and it discusses incentives and regulations which influence land use, and makes proposals for reforms.

**Key words.** Incentives, regulations, deforestation, sustainable land use.

## Introduction

Deforestation in Costa Rica has proceeded at a rapid pace. From an area of 26,000 km$^2$, covering more than half of the country in 1970, primary forests have been reduced to only 16,000 km$^2$ in 1987, covering 31 percent of Costa Rica (Tschinkel, 1988). It is estimated that at the end of 1989 only about 2,700 km$^2$ of forest outside of national parks and forest reserves remained. With over 300 km$^2$ being cut each year, the domestic supply of logs from primary (virgin) forests will have been exhausted in about 7—8 years, if current rates of cutting continue.

There are valid concerns about the deforestation that has or is taking place. At times however these concerns are reflected in undifferentiated statements about its effects. Rather than over-generalizing, there is a need to differentiate, largely based on the production capability of the land that is being deforested, to whom it belongs, and whether external factors are important, which would warrant prohibiting logging, even on privately-owned land.

Preliminary information indicates that, at present, most of the deforestation is taking place by logging and other commercial interests. Squatting by smallholders appears to be insignificant in global quantitative terms, although

*Environmental and Resource Economics* **1**: 179—194, 1991.

it may be significant in specific areas. Also, most of the logging/clearing is at present being done on privately-owned land. The government has taken steps to preserve forests by designating over 13,000 km$^2$ as national parks or reserves, amounting to about 27 percent of Costa Rica's land area. On the other hand, in the past, subsidies to the livestock sector encouraged the deforestation process.

There are benefits and costs of deforestation. The timber industry is interested in obtaining logs for sawmilling; banana companies, cattle ranchers and others are interested in the use of cleared land for agricultural production. Costs — mainly external ones — of deforestation can include excessive erosion, flooding, loss of biodiversity, and loss of tourism potential. A key issue is whether these costs warrant state intervention to limit or stop deforestation on privately-owned land. A broader issue is whether and how incentives, regulations or technical assistance are influencing (or could be used to influence) land use in general.

The main objective for the country is that land be used in such a way as to maximize its long-run contribution to the nation's welfare. To the extent that current use deviates from what is considered socially optimal, steps should be taken to move the actual use closer to the desired one. The national objectives include maximization of current production subject to maintaining the productive capacity in the long run, preservation of top soil for sustained use, etc.

Between 1900 and 1990 the population of Costa Rica increased ten-fold (from 300,000 to almost 3,000,000) with more than 2 million being added after 1950. At the current population growth rate of 2.7% the number will double to almost 6,000,000 in 26 years, or roughly one generation. This is well within the life expectancy of the average Costa Rican, so the consequences of this doubling will be experienced by most of the living 3 million as well as the equal number projected to be born during this period. Whatever the hoped-for successes of family planning in reducing this growth rate, it is clear that the demands on the country's natural environment and resource base will increase, even if the per capita use of resources remained constant at its present level.

While reducing population growth is important for sustainable development in general, the information available to us shows that direct population pressure is not a major cause for the deforestation that is currently on-going. Rather, our limited information indicates that deforestation is largely driven by profit and asset maximization motives of the logging companies, other commercial enterprises and large landowners.

One could consider the opportunity cost of land use in two stages. First is the issue of expanding total economic land at the expense of wildlands. The latter are no longer perceived as infinite and their indirect services are now recognized as valuable, even if not subject to measurement by prices. Once land has been taken from wildland and incorporated in economic land, we face the second and more traditional notion of opportunity cost as the best foregone economic use, a concept approximated by prices in a well-functioning market.

Economic land should not be expanded further when the perceived (even if unmeasured) opportunity cost of converting wildland into economic land is greater than the opportunity cost involved in reallocating economic lands from less valuable to more valuable uses. The latter is now becoming the focus of land use policy in Costa Rica, and the instruments to carry out this type of policy are now evolving. To some extent the market will itself bring about this change, but its ability to do so is limited by the fact that the opportunity costs of expansion of total economic land at the expense of wildlands are generally external and long-term, while the benefits of such expansion are usually private and short-term. Consequently, the market incentives generally favor excessive expansion.

Detailed land use information is available for 1984 as shown in Table I. Noteworthy is that annual crops, where the potential for serious erosion is the greatest, covered an area of only 3.9 percent. Land under pasture, where erosion is generally less than for annual crops, amounted to 43.9 percent of

Table I. Land use in Costa Rica, 1984.

| *Land use category* | *Chorotega* | *Huetar Norte* | *Huetar Atlantico* | *Brunca* | *Pacifico Central* | *Total* | |
|---|---|---|---|---|---|---|---|
| | ha | | | | | | % |
| Urban | 9,770 | 1,140 | 400 | 200 | 15,050 | 26,570 | 0.5 |
| Agriculture | 144,600 | 17,130 | 75,960 | 65,510 | 221,960 | 525,160 | 10.4 |
| Annual Crops | 109,830 | 1,370 | 18,160 | 30,660 | 39,740 | 199,760 | 3.9 |
| Perennial Crops | 34,770 | 15,760 | 57,800 | 34,850 | 182,220 | 325,400 | 6.4 |
| Pasture | 824,160 | 328,200 | 182,070 | 424,700 | 464,900 | 2,224,030 | 43.9 |
| Forest | 271,040 | 454,210 | 690,040 | 542,310 | 275,760 | 2,233,360 | 44.0 |
| Tropical Forest | 195,730 | 308,760 | 531,190 | 397,090 | 205,700 | 1,638,470 | 32.3 |
| Other Natural Vegetation | 75,310 | 145,450 | 158,850 | 145,220 | 70,060 | 594,890 | 11.7 |
| Idle Land | 3,430 | 2,490 | 5,840 | 0 | 2,080 | 13,840 | 0.3 |
| Swamps | 5,150 | 520 | 6,020 | 1,690 | 0 | 13,370 | 0.3 |
| Waters | 660 | 420 | 400 | 420 | 1,070 | 2,970 | 0.1 |
| Other Uses | 4,190 | 7,990 | 4,590 | 7,780 | 6,890 | 31,340 | 0.6 |
| TOTAL | 1,263,000 | 812,000 | 965,220 | 1,042,610 | 987,710 | 5,070,640 | 100.0 |

*Source*: SEPSA, Land-Use Map 1:200,000, 1984.

Costa Rica's land area. Also, while deforestation has been significant, it can be noted that large primary and secondary forest areas still remained, amounting to 44 percent in 1984.

The macro level goal is to move from the actual pattern of land use towards an economically and ecologically more desirable pattern. Possible tools for accomplishing this goal include (a) a land use classification that accurately defines appropriate use categories at least in a general way (preservation, agriculture, forestry, human settlement, coastal zone uses); and (b) a coherent set of regulations and incentives. Other tools and approaches which would also be of importance in this regard include land tenure policies, wealth and income distribution, and environmental education.

**Who Is Responsible for Deforestation in Costa Rica?**

It is a commonly held view that squatters are responsible for much of the deforestation and that much or most of the land clearing is being done on government land. But the preliminary information obtained indicates that (a) most of the deforestation is done by commercial interests and enterprises with the use of heavy equipment and (b) that the deforestation/clearing, at present, is mainly happening on privately-owned land, rather than publicly-owned property. Four main groups responsible for deforestation can be identified.

*Timber Industry.* Perhaps as much as 20,000 ha annually are selectively cut by commercial loggers using heavy equipment. The operations are said to be wasteful at times, since often only higher-valued species are being cut. Most of the cutting is done on privately-owned land. According to the law, government permits have to be obtained for cutting trees. These are granted routinely where they are being sought. Because of their interest in getting out the logs with the least cost, and because of their lack of concern for local areas, roads and land tend to be damaged in the process.

*Banana and Other Companies.* In the Atlantico region, banana companies and others are expanding their plantations rapidly. One company alone expanded by 5,000 ha in 1988. Forest clearing, done by bulldozers, is generally wasteful in the sense that the wood is simply being piled on heaps and not used. It is reported that some of the wood is now being utilized, perhaps because of a rise in relative prices of valuable logs.

*Cattle Ranchers.* Cattle ranching areas have expanded rapidly during the last few decades and mainly at the expense of forested areas. But at present the conversion of forests into pasture land appears to be limited in many areas, partly because much of the land that can be sustainably used has already been cleared in many regions, and what remains are parks, reserves, or forested areas on private lands where forest cover is needed (like steep hills or areas close to waterways).

*Squatters.* Some limited squatting is taking place on both privately-owned and government land. Some of it may be for purposes of agricultural production for the squatter themselves; in other cases it is done with the intent of selling the cleared land to cattle ranchers or other land owners.

To be able to analyze the causes of deforestation more precisely, and to be able to influence the process by public policy, it is important to obtain much better information than what is currently available. Therefore, a survey should be undertaken to determine: (a) The relative importance of the various groups responsible for deforestation; (b) The land capability classes of the land that is currently being deforested; (c) A breakdown of the squatters by origin and other characteristics; (d) The percentage of deforestation on private and public land; (e) The percentage of clearing with and without a permit; (f) The relative magnitude of primary versus secondary forest being cleared and (g) How the land is being deforested/cleared (with or without burning, with or without heavy equipment, etc.); how it is used (e.g., in year 1, year 2, etc.) after the deforestation/clearing has taken place (natural regrowth, banana plantation, pasture, mixed system, etc.), and whether it is used by the person(s) who did the clearing or by others.

**Objectives of Various Groups — Private Versus Public Interests**

Understanding the various groups and their objectives is important for being able to steer or influence land use according to the priorities of public policy. Individuals and enterprises generally have income and/or asset maximization objectives. Maintaining "natural capital" can also be a goal, but this depends on the "environmental ethics" of the people involved, the extent to which natural capital directly or indirectly contributes to the financial objectives, and the extent to which the linkages are being understood and recognized. When owners of forest land consider deforestation, they compare the direct benefits from forestry with those of possible alternative uses (banana plantations, pasture, coffee, etc.). The loggers' main interest is the profitability of the logging operation itself without much consideration about future, alternative uses of the land.

A key issue is a partial divergence of private and public costs and benefits. Forests with a good understory and/or undisturbed litter keep erosion to a minimum, they regulate water flows, they support wildlife and biodiversity, they produce oxygen, absorb $CO_2$ and they can form the basis for ecotourism. Private decision-makers will seldom adequately take these benefits into account. The question then from the domestic public policy point of view is whether public interests warrant an intervention to limit the rights of land owners and restrict conversion from forestry to other uses, or force a re-conversion in critical areas either by re-planting, which is costly, or simply by mandated natural re-growth, where it is possible, such as under the Guanacaste project.

**Rationality of the Small Farmer and Sustainable Land Use**

Deforestation in some tropical areas, such as parts of Brazil, results in unsustainable cultivation. The reason is that certain soils cannot store nutrients and organic matter well (after the deforestation including the burning of biomass have taken place) and are therefore exhausted after one or two annual crops. Fertilization with chemical fertilizers, if these could be obtained at the frontier, would not be profitable for the smallholders. Since few alternatives exist for the squatters, they are forced to continue clearing forest when farming on a plot is no longer possible.

In Costa Rica, about 60 percent of the country's soils are of generally good quality (volcanic in origin) and permit use as pasture, for annual cropping, or for perennials. In some areas damage from erosion is visible, but the general impression is that farmers do not produce in obviously unsustainable ways that destroy the environment, and along with it, their own base of production. For example, "living fences" are widely used, which reduce erosion, and protective forest cover is left intact next to creeks, on contours or steep slopes, etc.

In the cases where squatters clear land legally or illegally for the main purpose of selling the land, even then, they have an interest in clearing land with as high a land capability as possible, since that will render a higher sale value. As far as the way of clearing and subsequent agricultural production is concerned, again the financial incentives for the squatters are in favor of a careful approach, since that increases the sale value of the land.

However, one incentive for deforestation and illegal occupancy is the granting of titles to illegally cleared land. When land has been deforested illegally, the land can be bought "in good faith" by a second party, e.g., by cattle ranchers who then are given formal title to the land. Also, Kauck has pointed out that inside declared park areas "perverse" incentives are at work: (a) "Currently, when property assessments are made inside of parks and reserves, soil type and climate are not taken into consideration. In other words, there is no direct relationship between suitability for agriculture and the price that the government offers to homesteaders; (b) Regardless of its suitability for agriculture and regardless of the value of the standing timber, the government pays about twice as much for cleared land as it does for forest; and (c) Typically, when a reserve is cleared, the forest service does not move with speed to defend the reserve boundaries or to determine who the occupants are at the time of the decree. Furthermore, because unregistered bills of sale and the testimony of eyewitnesses are accepted as sufficient evidence of longstanding occupation, latecomers are able to easily establish fraudulent claims to land within reserves. Consequently, the declaration of a reserve frequently elicits its invasion on the part of those who seek to establish claims and then sell out to the government."[1]

A high degree of security of tenure creates incentives for producers to make long-term investments and use production techniques that permit sustained production. Squatters are generally thought of as having very little tenure security. But examples are known of squatters (such as in the Arenal area) that have invested about US$100 per ha in barbed wire fences to delineate their land, and to keep livestock from getting out. Even without formal title to the land, such fencing, coupled with the fact that evictions are not being undertaken, in effect provides a significant level of tenure security that provides an incentive for reasonably sustainable land use. More information and research is needed on (a) what percentage of producers own their land, (b) what the tenancy arrangements are on the other land, and (c) what difference the degree of tenure security makes in terms of sustainable agricultural methods and investments, and (d) more generally what the linkages are between poverty and environmental degradation.[2]

A variety of possible methods exist which can reduce erosion and/or make land use more sustainable. Examples are: increased rotational grazing (which would relieve pressure and permit a better mix of grass varieties to be maintained or to develop); strips of grass between rows of coffee (to reduce erosion); horizontal rows of coffee (which would create less erosion than vertical ones); planting lemon grass (along contours), increased fodder production (for stall feeding), hillside ditches, grassed waterways, terracing, and the construction of stone walls.

Why some farmers adopt more conservation-oriented practices than others depends on a number of factors such as labor availability, factor prices, etc., but hard data is difficult to obtain (Anderson 1990). The discount rate issue enters here as well in the sense that farmers discount costs and benefits and therefore generally adopt conservation practices only when they are low-cost and when they have an acceptable payoff.

## Potential Use of Land Use Classificaton

A number of efforts have been made in recent years to classify land according to its biophysical use capacity (most appropriate usage) and to prepare corresponding maps. Different classifications can be made according to how much weight is given to such criteria as slope, pH, rainfall, soil depth, etc. Appropriate or optimal land use will be according to type of land classified by capability, but at an intensity usually less than maximum biological capacity, for the given type of use. Exceeding capacity results in lower future capacity and would be "optimal" only in emergency.

A classification has been developed by the Tropical Science Research Center (CCT).[3] It gives much weight to ecosystem preservation, and according to it, sizable tracts of land should be reforested. It classifies land into ten categories: (1) Very High Yield Annuals; (2) High Yield Annuals; (3) Moderate Yield Annuals; (4) Perennial or Semi-Perennial Cultivation; (5) Intensive Pasture; (6) Extensive Pasture; (7) Tree culture; (8) Intensive

Forestry; (9) Extensive Forestry; (10) Preservation. Category 10 or Preservation corresponds to maintenance as wildlands. It contains the lands that cannot be used directly for economic purposes, but can contain some land of any class, that are to be preserved for various reasons. Categories 1—9 are economic uses. Determining the size of category 10 relative to categories 1—9 is a public policy question; the apportioning of economic lands among categories 1—9 is an allocation question. Using land according to its capability will increase economic efficiency and avoid the reduction of capacity resulting from uses for which the land is unsuited.

An alternative approach to the CCT classification, recommended by McKenna[4] would be the introduction of socio-economic-agroecological zoning. It would use information on soils, vegetation, climate, slope, as well as socio-economic criteria. Seven preliminary zones have been suggested, subject to confirmation by an inter-institutional team: Zone 1, agricultural intensification; Zone 2, intensification of agro-forestry; Zone 3, intensification of livestock production (principally dairy and cheese production); Zone 4, sustainable extensive livestock production; Zone 5, sustainable commercial forestry development (on both public and private lands); Zone 6, conservation areas and permanent protection; and Zone 7, indigenous areas.

Improved ways of showing potential land capability, at the appropriate scales, is essential or can be useful for: (a) Delineation of national parks and reserve areas (aside from land capability, other factors would also have to be considered such as species diversity); (b) Delineation of building zones within which building permits can be issued; (c) Delineation of forest areas on private lands which are critical for reasons of public interest; (d) Inputs into decision-making for public projects or programs (ideally an environmental impact assessment of such projects should be done anyway, and soil capability information would be an important input); (e) Tying of credit; and (f) Land capability maps are valuable for the training of engineers and extension specialists.

However, land use mapping also has limitations for guiding land use decisions by private agents at the local level because: (a) Even the best of maps at a 1:25,000 scale cannot take into account local variations of land in terms of slope, pH, etc.; and (b) Unless compelling public interest requires land use restrictions with corresponding enforcement, private land owners or operators decide about the kind of land use based on their own objective functions.

## Actual or Potential Measures Influencing Land Use

Thousands of economic agents make decisions on a daily basis that affect land use. For policy makers, once they have accepted a desired land use classification, the issue is how to influence private or government decision makers at various levels so that their decisions move actual land use closer to the desired one. This can be done through a combination of incentives and regulations, as well as technical assistance. These are reviewed below.[5]

### OUTPUT PRICING

The question from an environmental point of view is whether one can or should intervene in output policies to encourage environmentally beneficial activities or discourage environmentally damaging ones. Because of the many objectives and pressure groups involved in pricing policy, environmental objectives can most easily be met if they coincide with other ones, and particularly when they encourage smaller distortions or more uniform tariff structures.

Erosion from land planted with coffee is generally lower than that from land planted with annual crops.[6] Therefore, based on the criteria of erosion effects, coffee production (and the production of other perennial crops such as banana, cocoa, macadamia, ornamentals, etc.) should be encouraged compared to annual crops.[7] Positive rates of protection for annual crops such as beans and maize should be gradually reduced. (Such a move would reduce food self-sufficiency slightly in return for reduced erosion, i.e., the long-run maintenance of the agricultural production potential). At the same time, to limit erosion and to encourage sustainable land use, one could argue for a removal of export taxes on perennial crops where these exist (and for raising revenues in other, more direct ways).

The 10 percent ad valorem production tax for coffee was abolished in mid-1989 at the time the International Coffee Agreement collapsed, and Costa Rican coffee producers will face a net effective export tax of about 2 percent for the 1989/90 harvest. The only other export taxes are for banana exports (50 cents per box) (World Bank, 1990).

Pricing of forestry products presents special difficulties. To encourage reforestation one may want to argue for high prices relative to agricultural products. But high prices would create even stronger incentives to deforest the standing timber that remains. Low prices on the other hand would reduce incentives for loggers but for reforestation as well.

### PESTICIDE AND FERTILIZER POLICIES

Pesticide usage in Costa Rica is high with 5 to 6 kg being used per ha annually (about the same as Japan). A large part of pesticides are being used in the production of export crops. The cost of pesticides is relatively low, generally less than 20% of production costs. To reduce risks, farmers tend to "play it safe" and apply often more than what is really needed.

The benefits of pesticide use are higher output levels (at least in the short run), and more homogeneity of the product. Costs, aside from the direct financial costs, however, include human poisonings, damage to predators, increased resistance of pests, domestic animals or wildlife, and water pollution through runoff. Some work is being done to assess these costs. There are, e.g., about 700—800 reported cases annually of human poisonings, of which an estimated 50—100 are fatal. Also, the fact that fish have been killed in waterways close to banana plantations has received considerable press attention.

Research is going on to develop integrated pest management packages that require less use of pesticides (e.g., at CATIE, a regional agricultural research center located in Turrialba, Costa Rica). Also, a project funded by German Bilateral Aid is assisting the Ministry of Agriculture to develop and strengthen its analytical and regulatory capacity. Under the project about 50 demonstration and validation plots are being used to disseminate the IPM method. More work along these lines is needed.

Highly toxic pesticides should be banned, and our impression is that this is generally done, perhaps with a certain lag. An issue is whether for pesticides of "medium toxicity" import taxes should be raised at least to the average tariff level and whether exemptions for exporters should be abolished. One study indicated a price elasticity of pesticide demand of slightly more than one. An increase in a tariff of say 10 percent would therefore reduce consumption by about 10 percent. Higher taxes would lead to more judicious usage and encourage the adoption of the Integrated Pest Management (IPM) method for the crops for which this method has been developed.

Fertilizer usage in Costa Rica is also high and concentrated heavily on export crops. Side effects from excessive or inappropriate usage are much smaller than for pesticides. However, there is a concern about possible nitrate pollution of drinking water. Import tariffs for fertilizer currently are between 5 and 11 percent, for pesticides they are between 5 and 15 percent; while the average tariff for all imports is estimated at 16.4 percent.

## CREDIT

Credit subsidies have all been removed. However, a significant distortion has arisen because of the Fodea law. This law has mainly benefitted large livestock owners, has encouraged less than careful resource management and been a drain on the country's banking system. The complex workings of this debt forgiveness scheme represent a subsidy to ranchers (some of whom have already expanded grazing operations into inappropriate land use categories, both into land that is not good enough for grazing and land that is too good to devote to grazing). Overexpansion of grazing antedates the Fodea law, so it cannot be considered an *ex ante* incentive. But it is an *ex post* incentive in the sense that it prolongs any existing inappropriate use pattern. The Fodea law also has some *ex ante* incentives for the further expansion of cattle ranching in the form of new credits, exemption from "impuesto territorial" and from import taxes on agricultural machinery, irrigation equipment, pesticides. The political strength of cattlemen relative to bankers indicated by the passage of this law makes one wonder whether the banks will be able to use selective credit as a tool for restricting expansion of herds grazing on inappropriate land.

### PROPERTY TAXES

Costa Rica has a regressive tax structure for income and property taxes. Also, resource mobilization in general depends heavily on sales and other indirect taxes. In 1968, the contribution of indirect taxes to total revenues amounted to 64.8 percent. By 1979 that figure had risen to 70 percent and may currently be higher still. Property taxes are very low. According to one source, the assessment values for tax purposes may be as low as one percent of the actual market value of property. In addition, tax evasion is a problem. One estimate is that evasion of property and income taxes currently costs Costa Rica about 100 billion colones a year (Czel, 1990).[8] Land distribution in Costa Rica is uneven, with 12,518 large owners or 13 percent of the total holding an area of 2,320,037 ha or 75.6% of the total (FAO/World Bank Cooperative Programme, 1989). At the same time, 57,827 small farmers (60 percent of the total) hold an area of 165,317 or 5.3 percent of the total. One would expect that both higher property taxation and better enforcement would induce a more intensive use of good quality land.

### REFORESTATION INCENTIVES

A set of incentives was available for reforestation on land of CCT categories 4 to 9 from 1986 until May 1990 when the Forestry Law was annulled by the Constitutional Court.[9] In earlier years, income tax credits were given, if investments were made in reforesting timber lands. This incentive reached only those wealthy enough to pay taxes. Permitting extension of reforestation incentives also to smaller operators was one of the reasons for instituting the new incentive program using certificates Certificado de Abono Forestal, CAF. Under this scheme the government granted a CAF currently worth 90.000 colones for each hectare to be reforested. The reforesting owner (or tenant with long term lease) can sell the CAF in the financial market at some market-determined discount to any person with a tax liability who can then use the full face amount of the CAF as a credit against his/her taxes.

A weak point in this system was inspection and verification to make sure that the CAF recipient really has carried out the full extent of his obligation. Officials complained of too few inspectors and vehicles, not enough gasoline, and too much bureaucracy involved in requisitioning a vehicle. Similarly, the number of park guards and forest inspectors is low relative to need. Clearly, more resources must go into enforcement or else regulations will be useless.

Some incentives for reforestation appear necessary. The question is which are the most efficient tools within the institutional setting of Costa Rica. Chile, for example, has had a successful program which financed the establishment of 1.1 million ha of fast-growing trees (World Bank, 1989). Under the program, landowners must pay for the plantation establishment themselves, often with borrowed funds. Subsequently, a cash subsidy equivalent to 75–90 percent of *documented expenses* for the first year or so is given to the landowner *after* the establishment of trees has been certified.

**Incentives for the Livestock Sector in Comparison with Those for Other Agricultural Activities**

Land used for pasture has increased from 0.8 million ha in 1950 to 2.2 million ha in 1984, while the total cattle population reached 2.3 million heads in 1982, up from 0.7 million in 1955. The expansion has taken place largely at the expense of forestry. While profitability of livestock production is low, the advantages over forestry are a shorter turnover period (yearly income) and ease of transportation in areas not accessible by roads.

Credit and credit subsidies have played an important role in the expansion of livestock. The government has actively encouraged the expansion. In 1970 credit for agriculture surpassed credit for ranching by 45%, but by 1979 credit for ranching surpassed credit for agriculture by 4% (Fallas, 1988). From 1956 to 1982 the percentage of credit for ranching from total state credit outlays rose from 13.8% in 1956 to 23.3% in 1982 (Aguilar and Solis, 1988).

Because credit tends to be given to property owners with collateral, subsidized credit has helped to cement or encourage an unequal distribution of land. According to Fallas (1988), the land concentration increased between 1963 and 1973, and the concentration process continued since then.

We lack the information to judge the total amount of subsidies given to the livestock sector and how this compared to other agricultural activities. The fact of credit subsidies themselves does not necessarily imply favored treatment since, for example, export taxes on beef, before they were abolished, partly offset the credit subsidization. The livestock sector has a naturally "built-in" advantage for obtaining credit over other agricultural activities, since cattle can be used as collateral (unlike crops in the field). This can be of special importance for those producers who do not own their land or do not have title to it.

If delinquencies are an indication of the size of subsidized credit given, they clearly are most prevalent in the livestock sector. According to Baltodano *et al.* (1988), 70 percent of all delinquent loans financed livestock activities. In comparing delinquencies of small and large ranchers one might expect a higher rate among the smaller ones. But figures by the Banco National showed that delinquency rates among large ranchers were 63.1% compared to 28.3% for small ones, and that total amounts outstanding on December 31, 1986 were colones 3.759 billion for the large livestock producers but only colones 0.252 billion for the small ones (Czel, 1990). According to various sources, one reason for the high delinquency rate among large producers is the use of loan funds for consumption purposes.

In 1987, the Fodea law was passed. It deals with various organizational and legal aspects in the agriculture sector, as well as with debt rescheduling. The intent of the original proposals was to help small and medium size agricultural producers. But as the bill moved through the parliament, large producers were also included as beneficiaries as a result of strong lobbying by the livestock association. Data from the Banco Nacional show that large livestock owners were the main beneficiaries of the debt rescheduling.[10] Not only was the Fodea law flawed from an equity point of view, it has also been costly for the banking system, and it created an atmosphere that encouraged non-payment of interest and principal on outstanding loans, particularly in the livestock sector.

Direct credit subsidies for the agriculture sector have all been abolished except for those under the Atlantico Project. Assuming that a new debt rescheduling law is not enacted, it appears that at present the incentive system no longer favors the livestock sector. However, a more in-depth analysis would be required to confirm this. Such an analysis would have to look at output prices of all agricultural products, at input prices, at taxes, and how credit decisions are actually being made by the banks.

## Summary and Conclusions

Deforestation in Costa Rica has proceeded at a rapid pace, and currently only about 2,700 $km^2$ are left outside of protected areas. There are valid concerns about the extent of deforestation. But rather than over-generalizing, there is a need to differentiate, largely based on the production capability of the land, to whom it belongs, how it is being used, and whether external factors are important enough to prohibit logging, even on privately-owned land.

According to the limited information available, most of the on-going deforestation is taking place on privately-owned land and is undertaken or driven by the timber industry, by banana companies, and by cattle ranchers. Deforestation by squatters is quantitatively limited, but may be locally significant. Some of the squatters do the clearing for purposes of selling the land to ranchers. A field survey is needed to provide more specific information on who is responsible for deforestation, how it is being done, on what kind of land, and how the deforested land is being used.

Work is needed to improve the land capability classification and to arrive at a better national consensus about it. While land use planning is limited in influencing economic decision-making by private agents, it nevertheless can be a useful guide for decision-making at various levels of government for project decisions and for designing regulations and incentives that encourage appropriate land use.

Based on the information available to us, it appears that, at present, the bias of the incentive/regulatory system in favor of deforestation in Costa Rica is not severe. Nevertheless, there is room for policy changes/improvements in a number of areas which would reduce the pressure for deforestation and also help to make land use more sustainable: (a) The laws should be changed that permit granting of titles when illegally cleared land is being sold; (b) Government should change its purchasing system of land in declared park areas; (c) According to law, the felling of any tree, even on privately owned land, requires a permit, but permits are routinely granted where these are sought. Permits should not be granted where external costs could be high, and loggers operating without permits should be fined; (d) The capacity to enforce regulations (e.g., to protect national parks) should be strengthened; (e) Land tax assessments should be increased from the current unrealistically low values, tax collection rates should be increased and tax evaders prosecuted; (f) The proposed second debt rescheduling law should not be passed, as it would not only violate government commitments under a structural adjustment agreement with the World Bank, but have a negative effect on the banking system and encourage a non-repayment attitude, particularly among large livestock owners; (g) Consideration should be given to reduce the average level of protection for maize and beans; for toxic pesticides the import tariff should be raised at least to the average tariff level; (h) Incentives for reforestation should be reviewed and an approach considered under which grants of 75—90 percent of documented expenses are given *after* the establishment of trees has been certified; (i) Since the capability to enforce existing regulations is severely limited, road construction should be limited, if possible, to areas farther than 10 km from national parks, and priority for building secondary and tertiary roads should be given where the agricultural potential is high; (j) Land use zoning should be carried out by an inter-institutional team, based on land capability maps, and discussed at a technical seminar in order to develop a consensus opinion, if possible; and (k) More generally, there is a need for research and perhaps extension of low-cost agricultural technologies that are environmentally more benign or less malign, such as in the area of integrated pest management.

**Acknowledgements**

The authors are Senior Economists in the Policy and Research Division of the Environment Department. The authors are indebted particularly to Hans Binswanger and Andres Abramovich who supported the work and made valuable comments at various stages. Also, they would like to thank Jennifer Allen, Shelton Davis, Peter Dercksen, John English, James French, David

Kauck, Barbara Lausche, Jay McKenna, Raymond Noronha, and Jan Post as well as two anonymous referees for valuable comments and/or discussions. The paper could not have been done without the valuable assistance of many individuals from the government and the private sector in Costa Rica. The views expressed, however, are those of the authors and should not be attributed to any other individual nor to the World Bank.

## Notes

[1] David Kauck, personal communication. To the extent that land purchases inside declared park areas continue at present, this should, of course, be changed and "perverse" incentives removed.

[2] It has been suggested elsewhere that there is a vicious cycle between poverty and the environment. Below a certain minimal level of income, survival is such a priority that resources are exploited without thought about long-term implications. Degraded resources later lead to more poverty. Jagannathan (1989) has provided some indications that the better the factor markets are, the less likely it is that a poverty/environment degradation cycle develops, i.e., when economic opportunities exist, migration can relieve pressures in certain areas. The efficiency of factor markets in Costa Rica could likely be increased through various means (such as through improved land taxation, more equal distribution of income and assets, etc.), but in spite of possible limitations, they appear at current to be functioning reasonably well. Together with the fact that Costa Rica has some features of a welfare state, this does not encourage squatting at the frontier.

[3] The CCT classification is based on climatic variation — on a typology of regional ecological zones based on variation in precipitation and biotemperature. Within any given climate type, ten variables are thought to condition or limit productivity. These are: depth of soil, texture, slope, pH, rockiness, risk of flooding, degree of existing erosion, micro relief, number of dry months, winds, and fogginess.

[4] See McKenna, 'Proposed Agricultural Investment Operation', Preparation Mission; Back-to-Office Report dated February 10, 1990.

[5] For a similar analysis of Brazil's incentive system, see Binswanger (1989).

[6] A rule of thumb is that erosion from land planted with coffee is about one-fourth of that from land planted with annual crops, but actual erosion may vary within a wide range, depending on the soil, crops cultivated, techniques used, etc.

[7] In addition to erosion, one should also consider other external impacts such as those of pesticides used in production and chemicals in processing.

[8] 100 colones were worth about 1 US$ in 1990.

[9] Government has re-introduced a similar law, but without the most contentious provisions.

[10] Large producers obtained 48.2 percent of benefits, medium producers 28.9 percent, and small ones 22.9 percent (Baltandao, 1988).

## References

Aguilar, Irene, and Manuel Solis (1988), 'La Elite Ganadera en Costa Rica', Editorial Universidad de Costa Rica, p. 141.

Anderson, Jock and Jesuthason Thampapillai (1990), 'Soil Conservation in Developing Countries: Project and Policy Intervention', *Policy and Research Series, No. 8*, World Bank.

Baltodano, Victor Julio, Roberto Chavez, Francisco Sequeira, and Laureano Montero (1988), 'FODEA', Universidad Nacional, Heredia, Costa Rica (mimeograph), p. 48.

Binswanger, Hans (1989), 'Brazilian Policies That Encourage Deforestation in the Amazon', *Environment Department Working Paper, No. 16*, World Bank.

Czel, Michael (1990), 'Elite Interest Groups, Political Agenda Setting, and Agricultural Subsidies in Costa Rica: FODEA, A Case Study', M. A. Thesis, Department of Political Science, University of Colorado.

FAO/World Bank Cooperative Programme (1989), 'Costa Rican Agricultural Sector Review', May 4, 1989.

Fallas, Hellio (1984), *Crisis Economica en Costa Rica: Un Analysis Economico de los Ultimo 20 Anos*, p. 94.

Jagannathan Vijay (1989), 'Poverty, Public Policies and the Environment', *Environment Working Paper, No. 24*, World Bank.

Kauck, David, and Joseph Tosi (1989), 'Public Policy Decisions and Private Sector Resource Use: Changing Patterns of Deforestation and Land Use in the Lake Arenal Basin in Costa Rica', draft prepared for the World Bank.

Tschinkel, Henry (1988), *Forestry in Costa Rica: An Overview*, USAID, San Jose.

World Bank (1989), 'Regional Forestry Strategy Paper', Report No. 7932-LAC.

World Bank (1990), 'Policy Responses to the Collapse of World Coffee Prices: The Cases of Costa Rica, Mexico, and El Salvador', Report No. 8311-LAC.

# [13]

# Conservation of Biodiversity and Economic Development: The Concept of Transferable Development Rights

THEODORE PANAYOTOU
*Harvard Institute for International Development, Harvard University, One Eliot Street, Cambridge, MA 02138, U.S.A.*

**Abstract.** For ecological and economic reasons it is more cost effective to conserve habitats rather than species, and hence biodiversity conservation becomes a land use issue. Since in developing countries, land is the most important productive asset, the opportunity costs of conservation are forgone development, while the benefits from conservation are distant and largely external to the host country. The concept of transferable development rights (TDRs), which has been extensively applied to conservation of historical buildings in urban areas, is extended and adapted here to the conservation of biodiversity, both within a country and globally. Creation of a market for TDRs makes effective the latent demand for and supply of biodiversity conservation and generates benefits for both the supplier (developing countries) and the demander (developed countries). The paper explores the conditions and public interventions necessary for the creation of an active market for TDRs. It also proposes a number of mechanisms such as credits and offsets for purchase of TDRs against domestic regulations and conservation taxes in the developed countries.

**Key words.** Biodiversity, habitats, land use, economic development, conservation, supply, demand, use value, non-use values, transferable development rights, conservation tax, credits and offsets, capital gains.

## 1. Introduction

There is a tendency in the developed countries to view tropical biodiversity as a global resource, and the host country as both a beneficiary and a custodian of this resource on behalf of humanity. The implication of this view is that the host country has a responsibility (as well as self-interest) to conserve the biodiversity within its borders regardless of opportunity costs. This misconception derives in part from exaggeration of the biodiversity conservation benefits to the host country, and in part from insufficient appreciation of the opportunity costs in terms of forgone development benefits in the complex ecology of the tropics and the resource-based developing economy of the host country. The exaggeration of the conservation benefits to the host country arise from failure to recognize differences in technology, preferences, and discount rates at different levels of development.

The present paper argues that biodiversity conservation in the tropics is a land use issue, and since land is by far the most important capital asset in developing countries, biodiversity conservation is ultimately a development rather than a conservation issue. Therefore, for biodiversity conservation in the tropics to be desirable and sustainable, the forgone development opportunities must be fully compensated. The world lacks a mechanism through which biological diversity and its opportunity costs can be valued and exchanged. The paper explores the concept of transferable development rights as a possible mechanism, forreconciling biodiversity conservation and economic development in the tropics.

The paper is organized into twelve sections. The first three sections following the introduction make a case for conserving habitats rather than species and for addressing biodiversity conservation as a development policy issue. The following three sections introduce the concept of transferable development rights (TDRs) and its potential applicability to conserving biodiversity at both the local and global levels. Sections 8 and 9 explore how credits and offsets against domestic regulations and conservation taxes can pump-prime the market for TDRs. Sections 10 and 11 discuss the appreciation of the value of TDRs over time and the conditions for and limitations of using a market approach to conserve biodiversity. The paper ends with concluding remarks.

## 2. **Conserving Habitats Rather Than Species**

Biodiversity refers to the variety and variability among living organisms and the ecological complexes in which they occur. Thus the term encompasses: species diversity, or diversity among species; genetic diversity, or diversity *within* species – the variety of genes; and ecosystem diversity, diversity among ecological systems within a given area, i.e., functional systems that include the organisms of a natural community together with their physical environment (National Research Council, 1992). The argument below is cast in terms of protection of habitats versus protection of species, but it does apply *a fortiori* to gene level as well. Just as genes can only be conserved in practice within the diversity of living species, so species depend on each other for survival and can only be conserved in a comprehensive network of representative living ecosystems, which inhabit the various physical habitats in land and in water (P. Ashton, personal communication).

The conservation of biological diversity in the tropics is largely a matter of conserving entire habitats rather than individual species of flora and fauna (Terborgh, 1992; Whitmore, 1990). First, given the multiplicity and diversity of species in habitats such as tropical forests and coral reefs, there are economies of scale in protecting several species concurrently: the opportunity cost of protecting additional species once one is protected is very low or zero if their habitat is coterminous. While some species may be more vulnerable than others and require extra protection, by and large the (marginal) costs of protecting additional species fall precipitously once a habitat is protected for the preservation of one species. Conservation of biological diversity is a public good not only from the standpoint of the beneficiaries, but also from the standpoint of the species themselves! (You cannot protect one species without protecting others which share the same habitat.) The importance of recognizing this fact is that the additional benefits from conservation of all or most species in a habitat may justify the conservation of larger areas, which increases the probability of survival under unfavorable natural conditions such as changes in temperature, rainfall, and anthropogenic impacts such as air pollution, acid rain, and encroachment.

A second reason conserving habitats is preferable to conserving species is that we are not certain which species are likely to turn out to be the most valuable or, for that matter, valuable at all. Habitat conservation has quasi-option value in that it keeps our options open until more information becomes available.

A third reason is the complexity of interactions and mutual interdependence among species in tropical habitats, and our limited understanding of these interactions, which together make it necessary to protect many species to ensure the protection of one. Thus, even if we are not interested in certain species directly as an end in themselves, we may still have to protect them as a means to protecting the species we are interested in. Since these other species are themselves dependent on yet other species for survival, soon the need for the protection of the entire habitat becomes inevitable. The conservation of biological diversity is a joint production function with many protected species as its joint inputs and outputs. The larger the number of specie's protected, the higher the probability of survival of the particular species we want to protect. At the limit, full protection of the entire habitat maximizes the probability of survival, assuming that we know enough to delineate the habitat area, and that no shifts in habitat take place due to climate changes such as global warming. The interaction of ecological and economic factors would determine the cut-off point between critical and "non-critical"[1] habitats.

A fourth reason is the relatively narrow range of habitats of several tropical species and the irreversibility of destruction of tropical habitats. Severe modification of a limited number of fragile habitats is likely to result in massive extinction of species since both the capacities of the species to adapt to a new environment and of habitats to recover their original ecosystem are severely limited (Terborgh, 1992; Whitmore, 1990). This contrasts with many temperate species which tend to have wide ranges of latitude, temperature and moisture regimes, and to exist in habitats that tend to be less fragile and easier to rehabilitate or "recreate" than tropical habitats. The implication is that for tropical biodiversity conservation, a quasi-option value should be imputed to the avoidance of irreversible destruction or severe modification of "critical" habitats rather than to the (temporary) protection of individual species from extinction. If we knew which species would become valuable and we could protect them *ex situ*, the opportunity costs would be substantially lower, but we do not have that "luxury".

A final reason for adopting a "habitat" rather than a "species" approach to the conservation of tropical biodiversity is the associated non-biodiversity benefits from habitat preservation such as watershed protection, harvesting of non-timber forest products, and attraction of recreational and scientific tourism (Panayotou and Ashton, 1992). These are joint products of habitat conservation but not of species' conservation *per se* except for the scientific tourism to some degree. These joint products are of particular importance as a source of livelihood and foreign exchange to developing countries, and hence a more compelling reason for conserving biodiversity rather than the protection of individual species. While the latter is a primary object of biodiversity conservation from the standpoint of developed countries, it is only a by-product from the standpoint of developing countries; it is an added benefit to the host country only to the extent that the ensuing global benefits can be captured through tourism, royalties, or international transfers (Panayotou, 1992). Carbon sequestration is an additional global byproduct of habitat preservation for the purpose of protecting biodiversity that may or may not be internalized to the developing country that hosts tropical forests. However, the adoption of a habitat approach to species conservation does *internalize* a significant portion of the benefits to the host country through watershed protection, sustainable production of non-timber forest products, and enhanced opportunities for local and international tourism. Consideration of these additional benefits has three implications: (a) the conservation of a larger area maybe justified; (b) a somewhat different mix of conservation areas may be chosen to include critical watersheds, tourist attractions, etc., thereby reducing the opportunity costs of conservation; and (c) the motivation of the host country to set aside and protect habitats is thereby enhanced.

## 3. **Biodiversity Conservation as a Form of Land Use**

If it is accepted that for a combination of ecological and economic reasons, biodiversity conservation in the tropics is a matter of identifying and protecting critical habitats, the issue collapses into one of land use. Setting aside land as protected habitat for the conservation of biodiversity and other associated benefits has an opportunity cost in terms of forgone benefits from alternative land uses. Assuming profit (or rather rent) maximization on the part of land owners, privately held land would be set aside as biodiversity habitat only if this is the best possible land use in the sense that it maximizes the net present value of land rents (given the landowners discount rate). This is an unlikely possibility since most of the benefits from biodiversity conservation and habitat protection are public rather than private. Therefore, without government intervention through regulations, economic incentives, or outright purchase of private land, and without sufficiently funded NGOs, very little private land is actually set aside as conservation land. Furthermore, because of wrong government intervention (e.g., distortionary agricultural and resource policies), the conversion of natural habitats to other uses is often greater and faster than it would be under a free market. This raises the question as to the type and level of intervention that can "best" internalize to the private land owner the public benefits of biodiversity conservation to induce the socially desired land use allocation.

Public land, on the other hand, is state property precisely for the purpose of the production of public goods, such as conservation of biodiversity and watershed protection. Given limited (land and non-land) resources and alternative public (and private) uses, however, there are substantial social opportunity costs to setting aside public lands as habitats for biodiversity and other environmental benefits. For example, forest land can be developed into logging or mining concessions earning foreign exchange resources for industrialization, or used as a site for an irrigation reservoir or other public project such as a road or airport. Assuming public policy that aims to maximize net social benefits, land will be set aside as protected habitat or conservation area only if this is the use that will maximize the net present value of social benefits accruing to the citizens of the country. Since the benefits from biodiversity conservation are largely global (and hence external to the host country), while the opportunity costs in terms of forgone development benefits are national and hence internal to the country, a considerably smaller area would be set aside for conservation than is required for maximization of global welfare. This raises the question as to the level and type of economic incentives that can most cost-effectively internalize to the host country the global benefits from biodiversity conservation to bring about the globally optimum land use allocation.

## 4. Biodiversity Conservation as a Development Policy Issue

In developing tropical countries with limited accumulations of physical and human capital, land is the single most valuable economic asset. Land use issues are development issues *par excellence.* Land and its associate resources of soil, water, forests, and minerals are not only the sources of employment and income for the great majority of the population, but they are also the main sources of investible surplus for industrialization. A decision to set aside land as habitat for biodiversity conservation has high opportunity costs both in terms of current income and forgone development opportunities. In private terms, alternative employment opportunities are scarce due to low levels of education and limited industrialization. If land is privately owned, compensation of land owners by the state is not a realistic option because of (a) the large land area involved in protecting habitats, and (b) the limited budgets and large deficits facing many developing country governments. If land is state property, and the state is in complete control of its use and disposal, it might be easier to set it aside for biodiversity conservation. However, the opportunity costs are equally real and must be compensated for if the society is not to be made worse off, unless conservation generates sufficient benefits internal to the country to offset such costs. The greatest difficulty arises when the status of the reserve is one of open and free access. In such a case, either secure property rights must first be established, or other institutions such as public trust funds must be created to compensate those who collectively depend on the "common" property resource for their livelihood.

In social terms, agriculture and other resource-based sectors are often the only sources of savings for investment and foreign exchange earnings for the import of producer durables. External borrowing and foreign development assistance cannot compensate for the loss of export earnings from resource-based sectors because loans must be repaid and development assistance in many countries does not even offset the outflow of foreign exchange for the service of existing foreign debt.

Thus, biodiversity conservation is perceived by both land owners and the host country government as a forgone development opportunity, one of few such opportunities available, and should be treated as such by its advocates and beneficiaries rather than as a global resource that the host country has an obligation to protect. To a tropical developing country facing limited options, a development opportunity may be as scarce and its loss as irreversible as endangered species and habitats are to the developed world. Once biodiversity conservation is viewed as a forgone development opportunity by both sides, the critical question is what would it take to compensate the host country for the lost opportunity. Theoretically, there is a demand and a supply of biodiversity conservation and an "equilibrium" price that clears the market. The demand reflects the developed world's full valuation of biological diversity (inclusive of use, option, bequest, and existence value) as reflected in their willingness to pay, which is itself a function of income level, education, environmental awareness, and other socioeconomic characteristics. The demand curve for habitats (in terms of area) is downward-sloping because of the diminishing marginal utility of saving additional species, as well as the fact that conservation of additional areas yields diminishing marginal benefits in terms of increased probability of survival and protection of additional species (Figure 1).

The supply function reflects the forgone marginal benefits of the development opportunity sacrificed in order to supply (protect) an additional unit of biological diversity by expanding the country's conservation area. The supply curve of biological diversity is upward-sloping, reflecting the rising supply price of increasingly less remote, more productive lands with higher opportunity costs (Figure 1). These opportunity costs are in turn a function of the country's level of development and the availability of alternative development opportunities. They are likely to be low at very low and very high levels of development and high at intermediate levels. Thus, while we expect the demand price of biodiversity conservation to rise over time (the demand

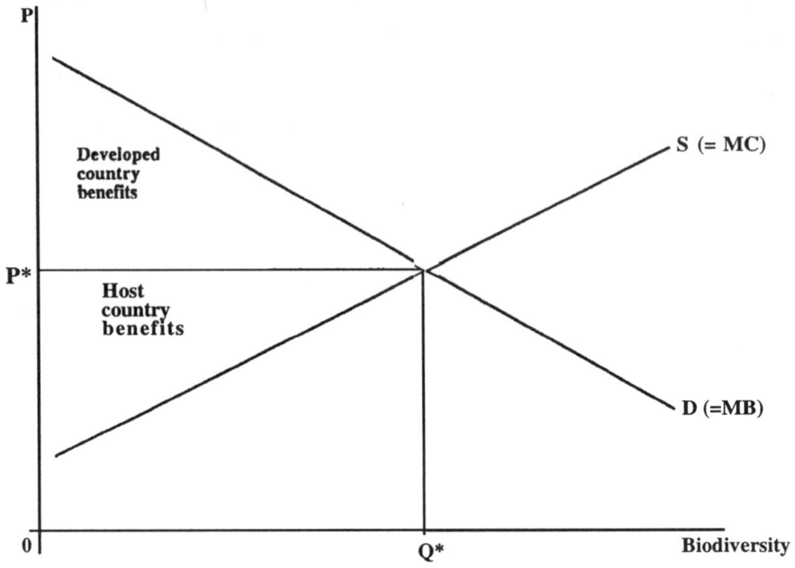


* Market-clearing price and quantity

Fig. 1. Demand and supply of biodiversity (protection).

curve shifts to the right due to rising incomes and changing tastes), the supply price of a particular host country might rise or fall depending on the country's level of development. On balance, we expect the "price" of biodiversity to rise over time due to increasing demand and shrinking supply, even as more land is freed from other uses for habitat conservation because of the irreversibility of earlier land allocation decisions.

For any market-clearing level of biodiversity, the division of the benefits from biodiversity conservation between the host country (supplier) and the developed country (demander) depends on the slopes of the demand and supply curves. The steeper the supply curve and flatter the demand curve, the larger the share of the host country. We expect the supply curve to become fairly steep as biodiversity protection moves from species-rich, low-opportunity cost habitats to species-poor, high opportunity cost habitats. The demand curve is likely to be steeper for those who "demand" biodiversity for its intrinsic or existence value and flatter for those who demand it for its use value, including its "offset" value following the introduction of transferable development rights, as discussed below.

## 5. **The Concept of Transferable Development Rights**

Much of the conflict between developed and developing countries concerning the conservation of biodiversity arises from a failure to distinguish between ownership and spatial exercise of development rights. The treatment of biodiversity as a global rather than national resource and the pressures to conserve it are perceived by developing countries as a challenge to their ownership and sovereignty over these resources. If, however, the prime purpose of efforts to protect biodiversity is conservation, not redistribution of resources, the first step is to recognize the ownership of developing countries over these resources and their right to develop them as to maximize their own benefits. The only negotiable issue is then the terms at which the development rights over critical habitats would voluntarily be transferred elsewhere in the country or abroad. Ownership of land conveys certain rights of development attenuated in some respects. Such rights can be further attenuated through sale or transfer not of the land itself, but of the right to use the land in some ways and not in others. The designation of land as conservation area is a "radical" attenuation of development rights which results in a substantial reduction of the net present value of the stream of benefits expected from the land, and hence a reduction in the market value of the land which is to a large extent the embodiment of the capitalized (net) income stream from the land. This gives rise to claims for compensation which, however, is impractical and prohibitively costly when large areas are involved, as in the case of biodiversity conservation.

The concept of transferable development rights (TDRs) makes possible the creation of conservation areas without the need for assessment of land values and compensation: it simply creates a market with demand and supply of development rights that result in an equilibrium price at which exchange or transfer takes place. The concept is being used extensively in the preservation of buildings of historical or archaeological value or areas of unique natural beauty in urban centers. For example, TDRs have been used in Chicago (Costonis, 1974) and New York City (Schnidman, 1978) for building conservation, and in Puerto Rico for coastal conservation (Costonis, 1975).

The concept of transferable development rights works as follows: the owner of a preserved building does not lose his rights to develop his property; he simply can not exercise them *in situ*; he can exercise them elsewhere where he can increase his building density and/or building coefficient by a given percentage beyond what is allowed by law in that zone; the allowable excess is specified by law (say 10% beyond what is normally allowed). Alternatively, he may sell his development rights to the highest offer. In this manner, the society benefits by preserving important cultural sites without depriving their owners of their legitimate rights and without paying astronomical sums in compensation.

The introduction of transferable development rights involves several steps toward market creation:

1) Declaration of certain areas as conservation areas and prohibition of some or all types of development in these areas.

2) Legislation permitting the transfer of development rights of land owners from the conservation area to other areas where development is permitted; this creates the supply of development rights.
3) Legislation permitting developers to exceed the area plot ratios and building coefficients by a certain pre-specified percentage through the use of owned or purchased development rights[2] since land in development areas is usually more costly than in conservation areas, developers would prefer to purchase development rights from conservation areas rather than additional land;[3] this creates the demand for development rights.
4) Since there is both demand and supply, a market for development rights would come into existence reducing transaction costs and setting a price for TDRs; the bulk of TDRs, like land, are being sold and purchased through the intermediation of real estate agencies. The equilibrium price of TDRs depends on the ratio of conservation areas to the permitted "excess" development area. TDRs have been used extensively in American and European cities for the conservation of historic buildings and other cultural heritage.

Similarly, sites of natural beauty or those rich in ecological and biological resources, both within a country and internationally, could be preserved in their natural state without depriving their owners of their development rights and without paying compensation, through the concept of transferable development rights. In principle, the total land area of a country can be divided into development areas and conservation areas. Land owners in conservation areas would retain their rights, but they would not be allowed to exercise them on the site. They would instead be allowed to sell or transfer these rights to property in the development area. Since the development area is likely to be several times the conservation area, there would be a strong demand for development rights from land owners in the development area as long as these rights can be used in lieu of land in the development area (e.g., to sidestep zoning or building regulations). Thus an active market in development rights will be created through which the land owners in the conservation areas will be fully compensated for their "frozen" development rights and they will thus share in the benefits of economic development. Here it is not assumed that buyers and sellers share similar access to information but it is precisely one of the objectives of the TDRs to make information about the value, cost, and level of protection of biodiversity more transparent and to facilitate the free flow of information between the buyers and the sellers. The price that TDRs would fetch in the market would convey information about the value (marginal benefit), the supply cost (marginal cost), and the level and value of protection of habitats from which TDRs originate, thereby internalizing the costs of mismanagement to their issuers.

Thus, the TDR is a land-management device which severs the development potential from the land and treats it as a separately marketable commodity. It is a means of providing an equitable return to property owners whose return may otherwise be lessened by regulations or restrictions of use aimed at enhancing social welfare. The transference of the development rights form the sending (conservation) area to the receiving (development) area enables the marketplace to compensate the owner of land where development is restricted in order to supply a public good (biodiversity). The buyer and holder of a TDR from a conservation area acquires the right to additional development (in the development area) beyond what non-holders are permitted. Alternatively the holder of a TDR may use it to offset other conservation obligations or environmental regulations he/she is otherwise obliged to meet.

The benefits from introducing the concept of transferable development rights are varied and substantial:

a) the critical natural habitats of a country are preserved and their species of fauna and flora protected;
b) the land owners in these areas are fully compensated; they might even become better off as a result of competition for transferable development rights, as the price of these rights would approximate the value of the land in the most developed and prosperous areas; at the same time, they would maintain some rights to the land as rural land or park land;
c) the Government would have solved the problem of conservation vs. development without the need to pay compensation and without the opposition of local land owners or environmental groups;
d) the costs of conservation and environmental improvement are widely, efficiently, and equitably distributed among the beneficiaries.

We are not aware of any tropical country applications of TDRs as a biodiversity conservation mechanism. The quotation describes a proposed application of the concept to the conservation of one of the last remaining virgin areas in the East Mediterranean. The proposal is currently under consideration and debate.

*The Akamas Peninsula:*
*A Proposed Application of TDRs in Biodiversity Conservation*

The Akamas Peninsula is 250 square kilometers and is situated in the northwest of Cyprus; it is considered to be the last virgin territory in the eastern Mediterranean. This unique area has remained almost untouched by development despite the quadrupling of the number of tourists who have visited the island in the last ten years alone.

Due to the variety of its geomorphological features and the microclimate of its individual localities, Akamas displays a large concentration of biotopes, making up a unique ecosystem. The area supports an indivisible natural resource base comprising a rich flora and fauna, beautiful beaches and landscape, and interesting historical, archeological, and cultural heritage.

The flora of Akamas includes at least twenty endemic and other rare species. About fourteen different kinds of orchids and Tuplipa Cypria (a rare endemic species) are also found in the area. Akamas also hosts the Loggerhead-Turtle (Caretta Caretta) and the Green Turtle (Chelonia Mydias), both under threat of disappearing from the Mediterranean, as well as a rare species of vulture (Griffon Vulture), a fresh water crab (Potamion Potamios), and endemic species of birds and butterflies. In addition, the area is used as a temporary stop-over by a multitude of birds when migrating from one continent to another.

The remarkably rich natural resources of Akamas are undergoing severe pressures and are threatened with degradation from a variety of sources including:

- Day visitors in the area destroying flowering plants, forests, and animal species.
- Property owners putting pressures on the government to open up the area for tourist development.
- Inhabitants in nearby villages demanding some kind of development.

The Government has responded by zoning part of the Akamas area as a non-development area, stopping short of declaring it a national park. This response has intensified the conflict. On one side, local and international environmental groups such as the Friends of Akamas and Greenpeace find this response inadequate protection for the last unspoiled part of the island and demand stricter policies and the declaration of the area as a National Park.

In the opposite camp are the inhabitants of villages surrounding Akamas, who own land in the area. They are demanding that the government provide them with roads and other infrastructure for tourist development as it has in the rest of the island. Being among the poorest people on the island, they see tourist development as their only chance for a better life; they have allied themselves with developers in lobbying the government to open the area to tourist development, and they are especially distressed because the prices of their land have dropped significantly following the government restrictions on development. Appropriation of the land by the government and compensation of land owners is out of the question because of the large amounts involved were this land to be compensated at its market value (as coastal property suitable for tourist development).

The result of these unresolved conflicts is a stalemate that neither protects biodiversity nor allows development to proceed. Akamas is neither a protected national park nor a managed tourist development zone. This uncertain situation is open to pressures for readjustments, exemptions, and relaxations that prey on nature in a silent but equally destructive way.

To resolve these development versus conservation conflicts, which are not unique to Akamas but arise throughout the island, the concept of transferable development rights has been proposed by the Enalion Environmental Management Centre (Panayotou *et al.,* 1991). The concept of transferal of development rights would ensure that areas of natural beauty be preserved in their natural state. It has been introduced in Cyprus for the first time in recent legislation for the preservation of buildings of unique cultural and historical value. It is now proposed that sites of natural beauty or those that are rich in ecological and biological resources could also be preserved through the use of this mechanism, without depriving their owners of their development rights and without paying compensation. The coastal area and, in fact, all of Cyprus could be divided into development areas and conservation areas. Land owners in conservation areas would retain their rights but they would not be allowed to exercise them on the site. They would instead be allowed to sell or transfer these rights to property in development areas, thus sharing in the benefits of development without actually developing their own land, which would remain in their hands in a natural state. It is estimated that the NPV of preservation benefits' in terms of improved quality of tourism in the development areas combined with ecotourism on the conservation area would exceed the NPV forgone earnings from not developing Akamas into a mass tourism area like other parts of the island.

## 6. International Application of TDRs

In principle, there is no reason why TDRs cannot be used internationally to transfer development rights between countries. In one sense, the debt-for-nature swaps are a form of transfer of development rights over conservation land from developing countries to international environmental NGO's in exchange for payment of a part of the national debt (e.g., Bolivia, Costa Rica, Equator, Philippines, Poland). However, these have been *ad hoc* deals with arbitrary determinations of the value of the exchange and no sustainable long-term financing sources. To the extent that a market for debt-for-nature swaps has been created, it is a very thin one in terms of the volume traded and a costly one in terms of transaction costs. Moreover, since the rate of conversion of debt into conservation is not the result of the "free" interplay of market forces of demand and supply, there have been complaints about unfairness and ambiguity about what rights have been actually transferred and what obligations have been created. Leaving aside criticism concerning their inflationary effects and implications for the country's credit-worthiness, debt-for-nature swaps have been constrained by weak demand and reluctant supply and a general lack of financial resources to effect such conversions on a large scale. Repayment of debt that is heavily discounted in secondary markets is not generally regarded by developing countries as adequate compensation for transference of development rights over large areas of tropical forest.

Another existing TDR-type of mechanism is, in some sense, the Global Environmental Facility (GEF), which is in part a collective arrangement for the "transfer" of development rights out of critical environments in developing countries with "compensation" for the foregone development opportunities provided largely by the developed countries. However, GEF is severely constrained by its limited funding and its project-by-project approach which does not benefit from the interplay of market forces.

The recent purchase of prospecting rights in a Costa Rican tropical forest by an American pharmaceutical company and the purchases of land for conservation by Nature Conservancy approximate more closely a market-based system of internationally tradable TDRs. However such transfers, like the debt for nature swaps, have been limited by a thin demand and a thin supply. The demand has been confined to a few highly publicized cases where most of the benefits accrue in the form of publicity rather than biodiversity. The supply has been similarly constrained to a few special sites of low opportunity cost or high political benefits. When markets are thin, transactions costs are high. Markets are thin partly because of the indivisibility of the good (habitat conservation) and its public good aspects. The concept of TDRs introduces divisibility and "privatization" of the good, thereby "thickening" the market and lowering transactions cost.

**7. Implementing International Tradable Development Rights (TDRs)**

Tropical countries could set aside habitats for biodiversity conservation and divide each habitat into a number of TDRs, corresponding to an area unit, say, a hectare.[4] Each TDR states the location, condition, diversity, and degree of protection of the habitat and any special rights that it conveys to the buyer/holder. TDRs could then be offered for sale both locally and internationally at an initial offer price that covers fully the opportunity cost of the corresponding land unit (i.e., the net present value of the income stream of the foregone development opportunity). It is preferable to start at a relatively high price to test the market, since undervaluation is irreversible (following sale), while overvaluation is reversible (following non-sale). If the price turns out to be too high to clear the market, i.e., to exhaust the supplied TDRs for a particular habitat, the price could be lowered to attract additional demand. Alternatively, the quality of the TDR can be enhanced by enlarging the area to include additional biodiversity values or by improving its protection and management. We do not assume here that there exists in the host country an entity that can automatically ensure the protection of biodiversity. We assume, instead, that the government of the host country is prepared to transfer sufficient revenues, obtained form the sale of TDRs, to individuals and communities that own, occupy, or simply encroach on forest land to make it in their best interest to protect rather than destroy the habitat. Another part of the revenues could be used to employ management services (including those of international management firms and/or environmental organizations) to ensure and certify the effective protection of the conserved habitats as to maintain a high and rising price for TDRs. Only when the potential revenues from the sale of TDRs under efficient management exceed the "compensation" and "management" costs will there be an economic justification for the country to forego development and issue TDRs.

The free and open access status of tropical forests, even when they are legally a state property, poses certain difficulties concerning: (a) who is entitled to compensation and for how much, and (b) how is further encroachment to be prevented after TDRs have been issued. Far from being an intractable problem, open access can be "closed" using precisely the mechanism of TDRs: the current encroachers or common users can be "grandfathered" and turned into protectors of the conserved area, paid in exchange from TDR revenues deposited into trust funds in the name of the community concerned. Payments could be linked to both individual and collective performance to induce self- and peer-group enforcement.

The potential buyers of TDRs include local and international environmental organizations, local and international foundations and corporations, developed country governments, chemical and pharmaceutical companies,[5] scientific societies, universities and research institutions, even individuals in the developed countries who are environmentally minded. The motivation for purchasing TDRs would naturally vary among prospective buyers. Some may have direct use values such as prospecting for new chemicals or pharmaceuticals. Others may be expressing their non-use values through the purchase of TDRs. Yet others might buy and hold TDRs if they expect them to rise in value as a result of decreasing supply and increasing demand due to population and income growth or change in tastes and increase in environmental awareness. Certainly every new discovery of a valuable new species, or even a new use of existing species found in a particular habitat would increase the value of the TDRs of that site.

It may be countered that if an area is already designated as a conservation area and protected against loss of biodiversity, a nature conservation organization would have no motivation to buy TDRs from land owners. The response is that designation of an area as a conservation area is provisional and contingent upon adequate demand for TDRs to compensate for the opportunity costs (potential benefits of forgone development). If demand, expressed by advanced subscription (intent of purchase), is weak, the host country has the option to cancel the issuance of TDRs and return the land to development. This would put immense pressure on nature conservation organizations and conservation-minded governments, corporations, communities, and individuals to subscribe to purchase TDRs if the habitat concerned has a significant biodiversity value. Developers, who seek low-cost offset of their environmental and conservation obligations, may also find it advantageous to buy TDRs from the tropics rather than meet stricter and more costly regulations at home. Both conservationists and developers would thus compete in the market for TDRs. The difference is that the former would buy TDRs and neutralize them, while developers would buy them and exercise them at home where their environmental impact is presumably less than at the country of origin, from a developed country or the global community perspective.

Despite the variety of increasing benefits that TDRs may confer on perspective buyers and holders, it is unlikely that there will be sufficient demand to preserve all the habitats that ecologists, or even economists, might judge worth conserving (e.g., based on contingent valuation of willingness to pay), for reasons that range from myopia to free-riding. Like charity, voluntary conservation is necessary but never sufficient. Given the public-good nature of biodiversity conservation, the government of developed countries (the main beneficiaries) could take action to stimulate the demand for TDRs (pump-priming).

There are at least two methods to enhance the demand for TDRs. One method is by providing credits or offsets against domestic regulations in exchange for purchase of TDRs from conservation areas in the tropics. The other is by introducing a conservation tax and then allowing people the option to pay this annual tax or purchase and hold TDRs from conservation areas in lieu of the tax.

## 8. Enhancing the Demand for TDRs through Credits or Offsets

One way by which developed countries can stimulate the demand for TDRs is by providing credits to domestic firms and property owners for the acquisition of TDRs from developing countries against domestic environmental regulations such as building Codes, forest harvesting and replanting regulations, environmental emission standards, $CO_2$ emissions, etc. In an analogous case recently a Connecticut utility planted trees in Guatemala as a partial offset of its $CO_2$ emissions. To the extent that the value of these credits exceeds the cost of TDRs, there will be an active demand for TDRs that will bid up their price to the value of the credit. The level of the credit per TDR would then determine the position of the demand curve for TDRs. The criticism of this method might be that the conservation of biodiversity in the tropics has been acquired at the expense of the domestic environment. One way around this problem is to tighten the environmental regulations from current levels and then provide offset credits for holding TDRs. In such a case, the demand for TDRs originating from the south would depend on how strict development regulations are in the north. To support this demand without deterioration of environmental conditions at home, the north must introduce development regulations deliberately stricter than otherwise intended. But even without such compensatory tightening of regulations in the north, the global environment and welfare would benefit more with TDRs than without them because the trade in TDRs will bring about a better match between "endowments" and "preferences". The transaction costs may be substantial, but they are offset by the absence of transport costs which "constrain" the trade in commodities.

## 9. Stimulating Demand for TDRs through a Conservation Tax

A more direct method for stimulating the demand for TDRs is the introduction of a conservation tax based on income, property, or a combination of the two for the explicit purpose of financing biodiversity in the tropics. The annual revenues from the tax (T) equals the country's total willingness to pay for habitat conservation which, given the price of TDRs ($P_{TDR}$), indicates the desired quantity of TDRs ($Q_{TDR}$). Therefore:

$$T = [(P_{TDR})(Q_{TDR})] \cdot r$$

where r is the rate of interest.

Assuming a property-based conservation tax, the tax rate $\tau$ is obtained as:

$$\tau = \frac{(P_{TDR})\ (Q_{TDR})}{V} \cdot r$$

where V is the total valuation of property in the country ($V = \Sigma v_i$). Under this formula the individual property owner would pay a tax $\tau \cdot v_i$ per year. In the first year his tax payment equals:

$$\tau_V = \frac{(P_{TDR})\ (Q_{TDR})}{V} \cdot r_{v_i}$$

If he chooses to continue paying the conservation tax rather than to purchase and hold a TDR, his tax payment would depend on the changes in the value of his property and/or his income depending on the base of the tax. If, on the other hand, he purchases and holds a TDR, he has no further tax obligation but he incurs an opportunity cost, that is the interest forgone on the funds used to purchase the TDR, minus (or plus) any appreciation (depreciation) of the value of TDR that he holds. Therefore, a land owner will be buying TDRs to defray his conservation tax obligation if he expects the value of his property to appreciate, the real interest rate to fall, the price of the TDR to rise, or some combination of the above. If he expects the reverse movement of these' variables he would be better off selling off his TDRs and paying the annual conservation tax instead. With $\tau$ and $Q_{TDR}$ fixed and the interest rate independent of the market for TDRs, a rise in the demand for TDRs would raise their price to reestablish equilibrium between their supply and demand.

## 10. Appreciation of TDRs Over Time

TDRs are nothing else but a vehicle of transformation of development values into conservation values, based on the premise that for certain resources the marginal conservation value (demand price) exceeds the marginal development value (supply price). For reasons that are analyzed in detail by Krutilla and Fisher (1985) the value of preservation benefits is likely to increase over time relative to the value of development benefits. First, the demand for environmental services including biodiversity conservation being income elastic, will increase with income growth as well as a result of population growth and increased environmental awareness. Since the supply of environmental assets is either fixed or declining, their value is likely to increase over time. In contrast, the forgone development benefits would diminish in value due to technological change and expansion of development opportunities with the growth and diversification of the economies of the host developing countries.

However, TDRs do not reflect all the environmental services and preservation values associated with conservation areas; they reflect only the global benefits from biodiversity conservation and from carbon sequestration. The rights to other services such as ecotourism, watershed protection, etc. remain with the host country, because they can be best captured locally and also because they provide a partial motivation for protection of conservation areas. Nevertheless, the growth in the value of biodiversity over time would result in appreciation of TDRs over time as scientists, biotechnologists, and pharmaceutical companies seek access to conservation areas for research and exploration for new substances and products. The owners of TDRs as shareholders in a particular habitat will be entitled to dividends and/or earn capital gains on their TDRs which will be in great demand should one or more species in the relevant habitat prove to be highly valuable. The carbon sequestration value of biodiversity habitats such as tropical forests is also likely to rise with the predicted growth in $CO_2$ emissions from fossil fuel consumption.

Thus, through appreciation of the value of TDRs, the taxpayers who, in the first instance underwrite the conservation of biodiversity, would be able to recover part if not all of their conservation tax payments and in some cases enjoy a "profit" (capital gain).

A rise in the price of TDRs would be an indication of rising demand for (and value of) biodiversity conservation and would automatically generate additional revenues for the purchase of additional TDRs from tropical countries at a rising supply price. Whether appropriate sites would be available for conservation would depend on expectations and speculation about the future price of TDRs. We anticipate that the introduction of TDRs would have at least two positive effects on future supply of conservation sites:

a) more careful land management and protection to minimize damage to existing and prospective conservation areas from development activities;
b) some additional lands rich in biodiversity that qualify as "critical" habitats ecologically but not economically as yet would be set aside for speculation purposes in anticipation of higher future conservation values due to rising demand (and falling supply elsewhere). The very existence of a TDR market that assigns a value to biodiversity internalizes future conservation benefits in non-conservation areas to the extent that the rate of expected appreciation exceeds the rate of interest.

## 11. Conditions and Limitations of a Market Approach to Biodiversity Conservation

For TDRs to be effective as a mechanism for conserving biodiversity, the revenues from the sale of TDRs must reach the local people who either own, occupy, or encroach on the land which is to be preserved. The "compensation" of forgone benefits of development (opportunity costs of conservation) must be sufficient to alter the incentive structure decisively in favor of preservation. To avoid perverse incentives and threat-making behavior to gain compensation, the local communities and individuals in and around the preservation area must be entrusted with its protection and their rewards must be linked to performance. An internationally reputable management firm or environmental organization must be recruited to monitor the protection of the habitat, to avoid adverse selection as a result of asymmetric information between buyers and sellers about the degree of protection afforded to the preserved habitat.

Another condition for the success of the market approach is clarity (if not homogeneity) of what is sold and bought. TDRs must explicitly describe the "property" rights that are being transferred. TDRs separate the right of development from the right of ownership: they freeze the unit of development *in situ* and transfer it to another location or country in exchange for compensation. The seller of TDRs maintains ownership of the physical asset (land), minus the transferred rights to certain types of development specified in the TDR, while the buyer acquires the right of "additional development" *ex situ,* and a specified share of any capital gains due to the discovery of new species or new uses for known species in the habitat from which the TDR originates. To ensure a continued benefit from the protection of biodiversity and hence a sustained interest in its protection, the issuing country should reserve for itself (or for the land owners) a share of the profits from any scientific discoveries associated with the preserved habitat. The respective shares of the seller and buyer should be clearly specified on the TDR certificate.

It should be clear by now that unlike the case of TDRs for the conservation of buildings, which are individually transferred, TDRs for habitat conservation have both private and public components. While they are also individually transferred, their value depends on the management and protection of the entire habitat of which they are a part. Therefore it is only entities with control over the entire habitat that can issue and trade TDRs. Such entities include, but are not limited to, government, communities, tribes, non-governmental organizations, and corporations. However, like other market transactions, TDRs require a basic legal framework and sanctioning by the state.

Inevitably, a market approach in general, and TDRs in particular, have their limitations as mechanisms for conserving biodiversity, as do other approaches and mechanisms. The market approach assumes that the host country governments are interested in maximizing national welfare and see TDRs as a mechanism for trading development for conservation rather than as a surrender of property rights or sovereignty. That sovereignty is not compromised can easily be seen from the fact that even private institutions, analogous to the National Conservancy in the United States, can purchase land for conservation and issue TDRs, tradable internationally, to finance the purchase. Perhaps the greatest limitation of the approach is that only habitats with rich biodiversity, high endemism, and low opportunity cost would be conserved through the market unless the TDRs are valued and demanded not only for biodiversity, but also for carbon sequestration, or governments engaged in pump-priming the market through offsets and credits.

## 12. Concluding Remarks

The proposed scheme of internationally transferable development rights differs from other related proposals such as the patent system for genetic resources (Sedjo, 1988) and the system of tradable forest protection and management obligations (Sedjo, 1991) in that it explicitly aims to reconcile the conservation of biodiversity and economic development. Another difference is that TDRs could be issued unilaterally and transferred bilaterally without the need for an international convention on biodiversity or on tropical forests. Except for a minimum level of legislation to establish the TDRs and some pump-priming to stimulate their demand, the system relies on the market to determine their value and to achieve the optimal level of biodiversity conservation. Of course, there remain many aspects to be tackled, such as the level of protection of habitats, the content of rights attached to TDRs (e.g., right of access, dividends from discoveries, etc.). Politically it is likely to be more acceptable to developing countries in that it establishes a symmetry between the biodiversity conservation and its development opportunity costs.

## Notes

[1] A "non-critical" habitat is here loosely defined as an area which is not critical directly or indirectly to the survival of valuable or potentially valuable species.

[2] This seems to imply that TDRs can work only if there are legally enforced restrictions on land-use in the non-conservation area, a strong assumption for a developing country. However, since here TDRs are proposed for global use, it is the developed countries which have the required enforcement capability.

[3] The reverse is often true in the case of urban development, but since development areas are many times larger than the conservation areas, the ratio of exchange can be set at a level which makes the purchase of TDRs less costly than the purchase of additional land.

[4] TDRs should always be issued by the host country, even if the country is poor and undeveloped. Issuing TDRs is no different than deciding to participate in international trade or to follow export-orientated industrialization. Advice and technical assistance could be sought from developed countries and the global development and environmental institutions, but the ultimate decision should be that of the sovereign state or of the institutions that have secure, exclusive, and transferable prerty rights over the area concerned.

A reviewer has raised the issue of the potential risk that "once a company owns a gene ... it may be tempted to annihilate the living source of the gene in order to exercise a monopolistic advantage." If there is such risk, it is much lower with TDRs than under the current system of open access and indiscriminate destruction of habitats. Since TDRs aim to protect habitats, they do not surrender the sovereign powers of the host state, and are held by a larger number of people around the world, it is difficult to see how a single company will be able to acquire exclusive control over species or genes and exercise control.

## References

Costonis, John J. (1974) *Space Adrift,* University of Illinois Press, Chicago.

Costonis, John J. (1975), *The Puerto Rico Plan: Environmental Protection Through Development Rights Transfer,* Urban Land Institute, Washington.

Krutilla J. and A. Fisher (1983, *The Economics of Natural Environments,* Resources for the Future, Washington D.C.

National Research Council. Board on Science and Technology for International Development (1992) *Conserving Biodiversity: A Research Agenda for Development Agencies,* National Academy Press, Washington, D. C.

Panayotou, Theodore (1992), 'Protecting Tropical Forests', Development Discussion Paper No. 416, Harvard Institute for International Development, Cambridge.

Panayotou, Theodore and Peter S. Ashton (1992), *Not by Timber Alone: Economics and Ecology for Sustaining Tropical Forests,* Island Press, New York.

Panayotou, Theodore, G. Hadjipieris, and D. Costa (August 1991), 'Recommendations and Program of Supporting Measures (Phase 2)', Enalion Environmental Management Centre, Nicosia.

Sedjo, R. A. (1988), 'Property Rights and the Protection of Plant Genetic Resources', in J. R. Kloppenburg (ed.), *The Use and Control of Plant Genetic Resources,* Duke University Press, Durham, NC, 1988.

Sedjo, R. A. (1991), 'Toward a Worldwide System of Tradable Forest Protection and Management Obligations', Resources for the Future, Washington, D.C.

Schnidman, Frank (1978), 'Transferable Development Rights', in D. Hagman and D. Misczynski (eds.), *Windfalls for Wipeouts,* American Society of Planning Officials, Chicago: 1978.

Terborgh, J. (1992) 'Diversity and the Tropical Rain Forest', Scientific American Library, New York.

Whitmore, T. C. (1990) *An Introduction to Tropical Rain Forest,* Clarendon, Oxford.

# Part III
# Valuation and Accounting of Environmental Change

# [14]

## *Evaluating Environmental Damage and Benefits*

As outlined in chapter 1, it is possible to demonstrate that economic decisions affect the environment through the intermediary role played by the flow of materials and energy. This carries the critical implication that the state of the environment can be affected by economic policy that alters economic variables. In short, if economic events have environmental impact, then so does their management. Economic policy can therefore be used as an instrument of environmental policy.

It is just as important, however, to understand that the term "environment" is an abstraction. In reality, natural environments are many, diffuse, and above all, linked to one another. Consider the example of soil erosion discussed in chapter 1. The economic impact of soil erosion is not confined to crop losses at the site of the erosion (on-site losses). The eroded soil must go somewhere. It may be picked up by high winds and cause air pollution. It may enter rivers and add to sedimentation in other parts of the watershed (which may be beneficial, as with agricultural systems that flourish on silt from rivers, or costly, as when turbidity causes fish populations to decline). Sediment in hydropower reservoirs can be very costly if it reduces the live capacity of a dam.

Tracing the environmental impact of an economic event, then, requires an understanding of the system of ecological and physical links in the environments likely to be affected. Figure 5-1 illustrates one set of links

*Figure 5-1. Ecological Effects of Deforestation*

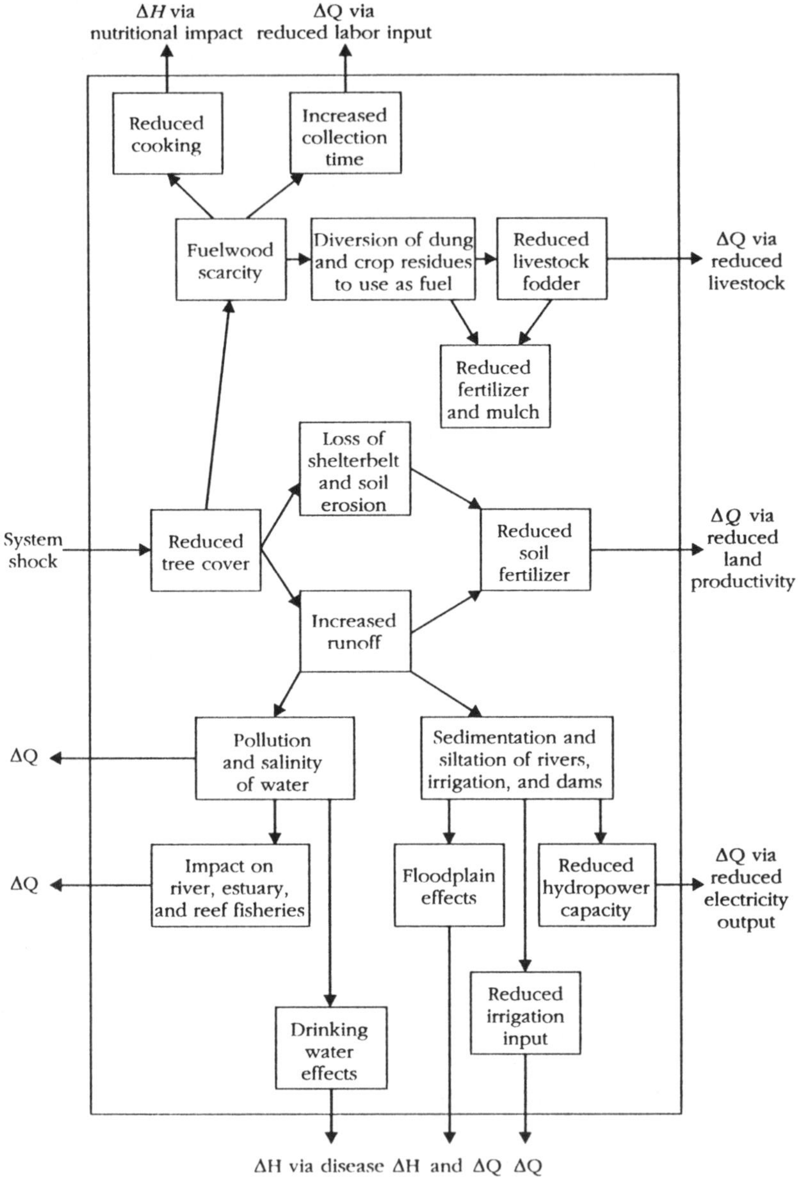


*Note:* $\Delta Q$ refers to effects that show up in measured or measurable indicators of development. $\Delta H$ refers to effects on health.
*Source:* Markandya and Pearce (1989).

related to the effects of an initial event giving rise to deforestation. Removing the tree cover affects the watershed and reduces the protective function of the forest. Sediment loads may change, affecting rivers and lakes, including hydropower reservoirs. Figure 5-1 merely scratches the surface of the complex, dynamic processes that may occur. The effects of an economic event in one location may not be replicated in another. Much depends on the nature of the ecosystems and the social responses to environmental change. Moreover, the nature of the change may not be smooth. Economics tends to assume that change takes place in a fairly continuous fashion, but change of an ecosystem may be a discontinuous response to critical loads of pollutants rather than a process of graduated change. As Myers (1988, p. 40) notes,

> Ecosystems may work in a nonlinear fashion, and across a broad expanse of space and time. The long-term and cumulative consequences of stress will be impaired functioning of the entire ecosystem and destabilization of its structures. Stress responses will appear in the form of a decline in the "natural" efficiency of resource use (nutrient losses expand as ecosystems become "leaky"), changes in energetics, an increase in parasitism, and a decrease in mutualism and other positive interactions. As human communities and their technologies continue to expand, they will exert increasing pressures on natural resource stocks and ecosystems, and ecological discontinuities will become more common.

This point is important. Predicting the environmental response to economic change can be difficult in the presence of discontinuity. Prediction is more difficult still because the various links within and between ecosystems are often unknown. Nonetheless, it is vitally important to investigate the links and likely outcomes as far as possible.

## Economic Valuation

Several times in the preceding chapters the issue of valuation has arisen. Chapter 1 reveals how important the economic cost of pollution damage and resource degradation can be when expressed as a percentage of gross national product (GNP). Such national damage estimates are obviously very crude but nonetheless show that environmental quality matters at the macroeconomic or sectoral level. Chapter 3 illustrates procedures for adjusting the national accounts to reflect such damage and the depreciation of natural resource stocks. Once again, these adjustments demonstrate the importance of environmental quality and resource conservation. Adjusting the national income accounts also shows that conventional indicators of economic progress can be very misleading. Making these adjustments is an exercise in monetary valuation.

Valuation is also important at the microeconomic and sectoral level.

Understanding the full costs and benefits of a project is essential to making investment decisions. Box 2-3 shows how important this understanding could be in afforestation projects. The same message holds for any investment that seeks to rehabilitate or protect natural resources and for any investment that has either positive or negative externalities.

Thus we have two broad reasons for engaging in valuation exercises: first, to show that environment matters for planning at the macroeconomic level and, second, to show how it matters for making efficient allocative decisions at the microeconomic level. The remainder of this chapter investigates more closely the underlying theory of valuation, the techniques for valuation, and the ways in which valuation has been used in practice. Before launching into the topic, however, it is important to understand how economists determine value. Misconceptions about the purpose and nature of economic valuation account for most of the dispute between economists and other scholars.

Value can be broadly categorized as either instrumental or intrinsic. Instrumental value refers to the capacity of something, when used, to satisfy a want or preference. Intrinsic value is regarded by ecological philosophers as being inherent to something. Opinions vary widely as to what possesses intrinsic value, in particular whether value can reside in both conscious and unconscious objects or whether only conscious objects can possess intrinsic value (see Naess 1973; Regan 1981).

Instrumental, or use value, can be divided into direct value, indirect value, and option value. Intrinsic, or nonuse, value is also referred to as existence value. An illustration using values arising in the tropical forest context is presented in table 5-1.

Direct use values are fairly straightforward in concept but not necessarily easy to measure in economic terms. Thus the output of minor forest products can be measured using market and survey data, but the value of medicinal plants is extremely difficult to measure. Indirect values correspond to the ecologists' concept of ecological functions or services and are discussed in detail below.

Option values relate to the amount that individuals are willing to pay to conserve a tropical forest for future use. That is, the forest is not used now but may be used in the future. Option value resembles an insurance premium to ensure the supply of a resource or service whose availability would otherwise be uncertain. Although option value is not necessarily positive, it is likely to be positive for tropical forests.[1]

Quasi-option value has also been identified in the literature (see Fisher and Hanemann 1987; Henry 1974). It is the value of information that arises after the choice has been made to conserve or develop now. For example, the choice may be either to conserve or to develop the tropical forest now. If conservation is chosen, the choice in the next period can also be either to conserve or to develop. If development is chosen now and irreversible change occurs, however, only development can be cho-

*Table 5-1. Total Economic Value of Tropical Forests*

| *Use value* | | | *Nonuse value* | |
|---|---|---|---|---|
| *Direct* | *Indirect* | *Option* | *Quasi-option* | *Existence* |
| Sustainable timber | None | None | None | None |
| Products other than timber | Nutrient cycling | Future uses according to direct + indirect value | None | Forests as an object of intrinsic value, a bequest, a gift to others, a responsibility (stewardship); includes cultural and heritage values |
| Recreation | Watershed protection | None | None | None |
| Medicine | Reduction of air pollution | None | None | None |
| Plant genetics | Microclimate | None | None | None |
| Education | None | None | None | None |
| Human habitat | None | None | None | None |

*Note:* Total economic value = use value, which is (direct value + indirect value + option value) (quasi-option value + existence value).

sen in the next period. In between the two periods information may arise that enhances the value of preservation, such as a scientific discovery about the flora and fauna. Quasi-option value is the value of learning about the future benefits that would be precluded if development were chosen now. It is positive if the information depends on the passage of time, which it probably would for tropical forests. Quasi-option value cannot be added to option value, which measures a different concept.

Existence value relates to valuations of the environmental asset that are unrelated either to current or to optional use. Its intuitive basis is easy to understand because a great many people are willing to pay for the existence of environmental assets through wildlife and other environmental charities. Empirical measures of existence value, obtained through questionnaires (the contingent valuation method), suggest that existence value can be a substantial component of total economic value. This finding is even more pronounced when the asset is unique, suggesting that the potential existence values are high for tropical forests and especially for luxuriant, moist forests (see Brookshire, Eubanks, and Randall 1983; Brookshire, Schulze, and Thayer 1985; Schulze and others 1983).

Typically, debates between advocates of instrumental and intrinsic value tend to assume that pursuing instrumental value is inconsistent with protecting intrinsic value. Thus using land for development is inconsistent with using it for wilderness. As we shall argue later, the inconsistency is only partial; it rests on a narrow interpretation of use values and ignores the ways in which nonuse values arise.

The pursuit of economic values as a goal is in itself a value judgment requiring a metaethical decision. It clearly implies that economic values rather than intrinsic values should be pursued.

## Total Economic Value

Total economic value, or TEV, equals direct use value plus indirect use value plus option value plus existence value. The components of TEV cannot, however, simply be aggregated: that is, before being added to the equation, components must be shown not to be mutually exclusive (for example, the benefits of clear-felling and the benefits of watershed protection). Tradeoffs exist between different types of use value and between direct and indirect use values. In practice, then, the TEV approach must be used with care. Nevertheless, exploring total economic value helps us investigate economic value.

The cost-benefit rule for adopting a policy or project is as follows:

$$\Sigma (B_t - C_t - E_t) [1 / (1 + r)^t] > 0 \quad (5\text{-}1)$$

where $B_t$ = benefits in time $t$, $C_t$ = costs in time $t$, $E_t$ = net environmental costs in time $t$, and $r$ = the discount rate.

The terms $C$ and $E$ are separated in order to focus on environmental costs and benefits. The net value of $E$ is construed to be a cost (a positive value subtracted from other net benefits), but in a number of cases $E$ may well be a benefit. Considering the specific case of land use, and the alternative of leaving land as wilderness, the constituent parts of $E$ can be partitioned as benefits forgone because of the land use sacrificed by the project and as externalities (costs and benefits) associated with a given land use.

A development that takes up land previously used for recreation, wilderness, and so forth imposes a cost in the form of benefits from the previous land use that are lost. Such costs would typically encompass aesthetic externalities such as damage to buildings or unsightly development near a historic monument or wilderness area. The principles underlying the valuation of positive and negative $E$ are no different.

### *A Deterministic Model for Land Use Benefits Forgone*

Consider first a deterministic world in which no uncertainty exists. We are interested in environmental damage (benefits) and consider first the category of land use benefits forgone. Then we can write

$$\text{TEV} = \text{TUV} + \text{TEXV} \tag{5-2}$$

where TEV = total economic value, TUV = total use value, and TEXV = total existence value.

If TEV is sacrificed because of a development, then equation 5-2 is substituted into equation 5-1, and we can accept a project if

$$\Sigma_t \, [B_t - C_t - (\text{TUV} + \text{TEXV})] \, [1 \, / \, (1 + r)^t] > 0. \tag{5-3}$$

Similarly, TUV + TEXV is added to net benefits if the policy or project improves the environment.[2] Since the impact of pollution has been omitted so far, equation 5-3 is an incomplete model for choice.

Imagining a hypothetical project will help us probe the TUV and TEXV components further. Imagine that a new road is scheduled to pass through an environmentally valuable area. Environmentally valuable means either that it has been officially scheduled as valuable or that its potential damage excites significant protest. The damage to the environmentally valuable site is thus a component of $E$ in equation 5-1 and is subject to being decomposed according to equation 5-2 (as yet, no uncertainty exists). Use values for the site tend to be confined to two classes of people: residents and visitors. The use value in question might be for recreation, for example. Persons who are neither residents nor visitors do not have use values since they neither live in nor visit the area.

Each of the three classes of people may have existence values for the site. Residents and visitors may value it whether they use it or not. Persons who are neither residents nor visitors may also have existence values if they learn about the asset and wish to conserve it even though, by definition, they neither visit nor reside near it. In order, therefore, to uncover TEV in the deterministic context, we must identify the three mutually exclusive categories of individuals who value the resource and, if possible, uncover both their existence and their use values.

### *An Uncertainty Model for Land Use Benefits Forgone*

We now need to relax the assumption of a certain world and introduce uncertainty. If relevant, uncertainty affects all components of TEV by turning them into ex ante concepts. An ex ante valuation involves judgments about expectations for the future based on what is known now, at the time of valuation. The literature on environmental economics tends to distinguish two kinds of uncertainty with regard to environmental assets.

Supply uncertainty concerns the continued availability of the environmental asset in question. Supply tends to be the most relevant source of uncertainty in the environmental context because the stock of environmental assets is perceived to be diminishing rather than increasing over time. In industrial countries, the disappearance of species and the reduction of wildlife habitat tend to support this presumption. Improvements in air quality tend to point in the other direction. Supply uncertainty thus appears to be somewhat important for evaluating projects and policies with environmental consequences. The implications of supply uncertainty for valuation are addressed shortly.

Demand uncertainty relates to uncertainty that an individual expressing a valuation will, in fact, demand the commodity at the time of use in the future. Demand uncertainty can arise because either future incomes or preferences are uncertain.

The two types of uncertainty are relevant because they modify equation 5-2 and therefore equation 5-3. The literature has yet to agree on the most desirable procedure. Some authors retain equation 5-2 but alter the meaning of the terms so that they become ex ante concepts that depend on probabilities about the state of the world (independent of policy) and on the way policy alters the environment (this procedure is used by Randall 1987, 1990). More popular has been the concept of option value, which was introduced by Weisbrod (1964) and followed by an extensive literature (for important material on option value, see R. Bishop 1982; Freeman 1985; Plummer and Hartman 1986; V. K. Smith 1987). Option value (OV) is the difference between the amount someone is willing to pay in order to retain the option of using an environmental asset in the future (the option price, OP) and the expected value of the ex post consumer surplus, $E(CS)$.[3] That is, we can write

$$\text{OP} = E(CS) + \text{OV}. \tag{5-4}$$

Since $E(CS)$ is the equivalent of TUV in equation 5-2, the component OV has been added to the deterministic model to reflect uncertainty. In other words, equation 5-3—the deterministic cost-benefit model with land use forgone—now must be modified to become

$$(5\text{-}5)\quad \Sigma_t \{B_t - C_t - [E(CS) + \text{OV} + \text{TEXV}]\} [1 / (1 + r)^t] > 0.$$

A great deal of the literature is occupied with the sign of OV. Although the sign of OV is generally indeterminate, an important case is when demand is certain, but supply is uncertain. In this case, the valuer knows what he or she wants in the future but cannot be sure that the object of value will be available, and OV tends to be positive. When future demand is uncertain because future income is uncertain and future supply is certain, OV is negative for individuals who are averse to risks. If the uncertainty of future demand is a result of uncertain future preferences (state-dependent preferences), the sign of OV is ambiguous. This implies that normal cost-benefit analysis, which simply computes $E(CS)$, overstates the benefits of conservation if OV is, in reality, negative.

Few empirical studies claim to have separated option value from the overall willingness-to-pay concept of option price. That is, most studies tend to estimate option price itself without further decomposition. A number of studies in the United Kingdom and United States (see the section of this chapter on recent valuation experience) have found that option and nonuse values can be very significant indeed in relation to use values, particularly when unique assets are concerned (endangered species, unique habitats, heritage).

### *Total Economic Value and Pollution*

We can now complete the cost-benefit model by incorporating the various effects of pollution. These effects may be negative or positive, depending on the project or policy in question. The cost-benefit model is simply extended to account for pollution as follows:

$$(5\text{-}6)\quad \Sigma_t \{B_t - C_t [E(CS) + \text{OV} + \text{TEXV}] - \text{TEC}\} [1 / (1 + r)^t] > 0$$

where TEC refers to damage costs from pollution. Such damage would normally be estimated using techniques such as hedonic property prices, contingent valuation, and indirect procedures involving dose-response functions (see appendix). Land-use benefits forgone can be estimated using the same techniques, but existence and option values can only be derived using contingent valuation approaches.

## Recent Valuation Experience

Table 5-2 shows some of the recent estimates of environmental values secured in the United Kingdom. The use of different measures of willingness to pay (WTP; per visit, per household, per hectare) makes any de-

*Table 5-2. Valuation Studies in the United Kingdom*
(British pounds per household or person a year, unless otherwise stated)

| *Study and source* | *Valuation* | *Method* |
|---|---|---|
| Button and Pearce (1989) | | |
| Canal amenity | 517,000 | HPM, aggregate value |
| Green and Tunstall (1991) | | |
| Green and others (1988, 1989, 1990) | | |
| River quality, 1987–88 | 9.6 | CVM, user values |
| Beach amenity, 1988–89 | 14.0–18.0 | CVM, user values |
| Coastal sites, 1989 | 21–25 | CVM, nonuse values |
| Hanley (1988) | | |
| Straw burning | WTP, 5.2<br>WTA, 9.6 | CVM, user values |
| Hanley (1989) | | |
| Forest recreation | 0.34–15.1 per trip | TCM, user values |
| | 1.2 per trip | CVM, user values |
| Harley and Hanley (1989) | | |
| Nature reserves | 1.2–2.5 per visit | CVM, user values |
| | 2.0–3.5 | TCM, user values |
| Turner and Brooke (1988) | | |
| Coastal amenity | 15 | CVM, local users |
| | 18 | CVM, nonlocal users |
| Willis and Benson (1988) | | |
| Nature reserves | 46–251 hectares a year | TCM, all users |
| | 6–34 hectares | TCM, wildlife visitors only |
| | 25 hectares a year | CVM, nonuse values |
| Forest recreation | 1.9 per visit | TCM |

*Note:* WTP, willingness to pay; CVM, contingent valuation method; WTA, willingness to accept; TCM, travel cost method; HPM, hedonic price method.

tailed comparison difficult. The broad impression is that values cluster in the range of £10 to £25 per household a year for river quality, beach erosion, and coastal recreation; £25 corresponds to approximately 0.2 percent of the average income. For forest recreation, trip values appear to range widely, although the extent of the range depends on one study (Willis and Benson 1988). Other environmental services have been the subject of too little study to discern any possible tendency for clustering.

Table 5-3 presents some nonuse values in the United States. Insofar as they have actually been estimated, they appear to be significant.

## Environmental Valuation in the Developing World

Chapter 1 provides examples of broadbrush attempts to value environmental damage at the national level in developing countries as well as several more sophisticated attempts to value resource depreciation. A

*Table 5-3. Estimates of Nonuse Value in the United States*
(U.S. dollars per household a year)

| *Study* | *Total* | *Preservation* | *Use* | *Option*[a] | *Existence* |
|---|---|---|---|---|---|
| Bishop, Boyle, and Walsh (1987) | | | | | |
| Striped shiners | — | — | — | — | 1–6 |
| Bowker and Stoll (1988) | | | | | |
| Whooping cranes | 5–149 | — | — | — | — |
| Boyle and Bishop (1987) | | | | | |
| Bald eagles | 6–75 | — | — | — | 5–28 |
| Brookshire, Eubanks, and Randall (1983) | | | | | |
| Grizzly bears | | | | | |
| Hunters | — | — | — | 10–21[b] | — |
| Observers | — | — | — | 21–22[b] | — |
| Nonusers | — | — | — | — | 15–24 |
| Bighorn sheep | | | | | |
| Hunters | — | — | — | 11–23[b] | — |
| Observers | — | — | — | 18–23[b] | — |
| Nonusers | — | — | — | — | 7 |
| Desvousges, Smith, and Fisher (1987) | | | | | |
| Water quality | — | — | — | 54–118[b] | — |
| Edwards (1988) | | | | | |
| Groundwater quality | — | — | — | 285–1,436[b], 3–14[c] | — |
| Schulze and others (1983) | | | | | |
| Visibility | | | | | |
| Grand Canyon only | — | 45–62 | — | — | — |
| Southwest parklands | — | 79–116 | — | — | — |
| Plume removal | — | 34–51 | — | — | — |
| Stoll and Johnson (1984) | | | | | |
| Whooping cranes | — | 2–3 | — | 29–42[c] | 0–39 |
| Sutherland and Walsh (1985) | | | | | |
| Water preservation | — | 8 | — | 3[b] | 5 |
| Walsh, Loomis, and Gillman (1984) | | | | | |
| Wilderness | 107 | 32 | 76 | 9[c] | 11 |

— Not available.

*Note:* Option prices are reported in present values and converted to annual values. Preservation values are use plus existence values, but use values are smaller than existence values. User values per recreation day have been converted to values per household a year using average trips a year.

a. Some studies estimate option price, some estimate option value.

b. Option price.

c. Option value.

review of the valuation techniques might give the impression that they have limited relevance in the developing world (see the appendix to this chapter). Hedonic property price approaches rely on housing markets that function fairly well. Wage premia models require labor markets that function equally well. Contingent valuation models require reasonably sophisticated interview techniques that collect willingness-to-pay responses from individuals. Production function approaches are less problematic since, as we have seen, the costs of soil erosion, for example, should show up in market responses through reduced crop yields. Although applying all valuation techniques to developing countries is in its infancy, enough evidence exists to show that the techniques can be applied. The following section illustrates various approaches through case studies.

### *Production Function Approaches*

Production function approaches have perhaps the greatest potential for valuation in the context of developing countries. Numerous studies underline this. Table 5-4 looks at the issue of logging versus fishing and tourism in an area of the Philippines. Logging operations commenced in 1985 in Bacuit Bay, Palawan. The bay supports two other industries that earn foreign exchange: tourism and marine fishing. The logging produced high rates of sedimentation in the bay, damaging coral reefs and the fishery. A valuation study was undertaken principally to evaluate gross revenues with and without a hypothesized ban on logging. The study concluded that a logging ban was clearly preferable to no ban, and this finding was not greatly affected by either raising the discount rate or assuming different sedimentation-damage rates.

Table 5-5 looks at another study in the Philippines (Briones 1986). In this case, a multipurpose dam was to be built on the Lower Agno River to supply hydroelectricity, irrigation water, and flood control as well as improve water quality. At the same time, however, the reservoir was expected to trap tailings from gold and copper mines in the watershed, despite the existence of tailing dams for trapping the mine waste. The study evaluated a watershed management plan designed to reduce reser-

*Table 5-4. Revenues Generated by Fishing and Tourism with and without a Ban on Logging, Bacuit Bay, Philippines, 1987–96*
(millions of 1987 U.S. dollars at present value given a 10 percent discount rate)

| *Activity* | *Option 1: ban on logging* | *Option 2: no ban on logging* | *Option 1 minus option 2* |
|---|---|---|---|
| Fisheries | 17.2 | 9.1 | 8.1 |
| Logging | 0.0 | 9.8 | −9.8 |
| Tourism | 25.5 | 6.3 | 19.2 |
| Total | 42.7 | 25.2 | 17.5 |

*Note:* If logging is banned, gross revenues from tourism and fishing would be \$43 million. If logging is not banned, tourism and fishing would continue, but at reduced rates because of damage from sedimentation. Gross revenues from logging, tourism, and fishing would then be \$25 million. Clearly, it pays to ban logging and maintain the fishery.

*Source:* Hodgson and Dixon (1988).

*Table 5-5. Benefits of Watershed Management in the Context of a Multipurpose Dam, the Philippines*
(billions of U.S. dollars in present value given a 10 percent discount rate)

| *Cost or benefit of management scheme* | *Low erosion* | *High erosion* |
|---|---|---|
| Cost | 5.33 | 7.34 |
| Benefit | 14.50 | 30.36 |
| Net benefit | 9.17 | 23.02 |

*Note:* Introducing a watershed management scheme that involves afforestation, controls soil erosion, and protects the forest reduces by $14 million to $30 million the costs of sedimentation damage caused by mine tailings in the dam reservoir. Because its costs are much lower, the scheme shows net benefits.
*Source:* Briones (1986).

voir sedimentation. Sedimentation was shown to reduce the originally forecast net benefits of $2.97 billion to $2.60 billion–$2.67 billion over a fifty-year period. The issue, then, was whether the $0.30 billion–$0.37 billion loss could be reduced, at a net gain, by investing in watershed management. Watershed management was found to have positive net benefits: the costs of introducing a management scheme were less than the expected costs of sediment damage (other studies on production function valuation can be found in Bojo, Mäler, and Unemo 1990; Dixon and others 1988).

Table 5-6 looks at a forest development project in Nepal (Dixon and others 1986). The production function approach was used, but this time several alternative market values were adopted to value the effects of the project. The project was concerned with improving the use of land, the quality of 7,000 hectares of timber stand, and the management of 16,000 hectares of scrubland; with building additional fencing to stop livestock damage; and with establishing 4,000 hectares of forest for fodder, fuelwood, and fencing timber. Its goals, or outputs, were to increase the amount of fuelwood and fodder, raise productivity of the land, and reduce soil erosion. To find the incremental productivity arising from the management program, it was necessary first to estimate what the value of output from the land would be without the project.[4] As an example, grazing land produces two products, milk and animal dung, which is used as fertilizer. Each animal produces 15 kilograms of nitrogen equivalent and 2 kilograms of phosphorus equivalent a year. Nitrogen is valued at NRs6 per kilogram and phosphorus at NRs18 per kilogram, so that one animal produces (15 kilograms x NRs6) + (2 kilograms x NRs18) of fertilizer a year, or NRs126. Each hectare supports 0.0857 of an animal, so fertilizer production per hectare is 0.0857 x NRs126 = NRs11 per hectare.

Scrubland and unmanaged forest produce fertilizer, milk, and fuelwood. Fuelwood is valued three ways. First, it is sold on the market, and

*Table 5-6. Valuing the Benefits of a Hill Forest Development Project in Nepal*
(millions of rupees of output for total land area)

| *Year of the project* | *Output with project* | *Output without project* | *Output with project minus output without it* |
|---|---|---|---|
| 1 | 12.5 | 7.5 | 5.0 |
| 2 | 5.3 | 7.2 | −1.9 |
| 3 | 10.8 | 6.9 | 3.9 |
| 4 | 5.8 | 6.6 | −0.8 |
| 5 | 9.9 | 6.4 | 3.5 |
| 40 | 21.7 | 1.6 | 20.1 |

*Note:* The forest management project involved changes in land use, so the output from each type of land use had to be valued and then the changes arising from differences in value due to differences in land use and increased productivity on a given land use had to be examined. The discounted value of the net benefits was then compared with the discounted value of the costs. The result was expressed as an internal rate of return of 8.5 percent.
*Source:* Dixon and others (1988).

the market price net of collection costs was NRs280 per cubic meter. Second, animal dung is a substitute for fuelwood. Dung could, in turn, be valued several ways, but the method chosen was to look at crop responses. Thus, 1 cubic meter of wood equals 0.6 tons of dried manure, which equals 2.4 tons of fresh manure. Maize yields were estimated to rise 15 percent because 6 tons of fresh manure are applied to a 0.5-hectare plot each year. Thus a hectare that currently produces 1.53 tons of maize would produce 1.8 tons. Since maize output is worth NRs1,200 per ton, the productivity gain would be NRs1,200 x (1.80 tons − 1.53 tons) = NRs324. Hence the value of a cubic meter of wood is (324 rupees x 0.5 hectares) / 6 tons = NRs27 per hectare for fresh manure = NRs27 x 2.4 tons = NRs65 per cubic meter. Third, fuelwood can be valued by the time taken to collect it. Each family spends 132 days a year collecting 7.92 cubic meters. Since NRs5 per day is the alternative income that could be earned from other activity, each cubic meter of wood costs (132 days x NRs5) / 7.92 cubic meters = NRs83.

Thus output can be calculated by looking at each type of land. When project interventions are envisaged, output should be estimated for the new use of land under the project and compared with output without the project.

Valuation of environmental effects is not only relevant to investment decisions, but also to social cost pricing (see chapter 8). The basic idea is that the price of a product should reflect not just the private costs of production, but also any environmental costs attributed to its production. This basic principle can also be applied to a resource. Oil products, for example, should be priced to reflect the costs of extraction, transportation, and processing and the impact of any pollution that can be attributed to their production. Box 5-1 outlines a study that analyzes fuelwood pricing in Haiti in this context (Hosier and Bernstein 1989). The basic rule used is marginal opportunity costs = marginal costs of harvesting + marginal external costs + marginal user costs, or MOC = MC + MEC + MUC.

MEC is the value of any environmental damage arising from the use of the resource. MUC is the value of future benefits forgone as a result of using one unit of the resource today. If a resource is genuinely renewable, its use today should not involve a cost in the future because the resource can regenerate. Many renewable resources are not used this way, however, so it may be legitimate to speak of a user cost component of the overall true cost (the MOC) of the resource (for more on the concept of MOC, see Markandya and Pearce 1989). Hosier and Bernstein's study found that actual prices for fuelwood in Haiti are too low. MOC is from 1.5 to 10.0 times greater than MC, which, in this study, is approximated by the actual market price. Effectively, fuelwood is underpriced in the marketplace. The low price partly explains the overuse of fuelwood in Haiti and its associated environmental impact.

### *Discrete Choice Valuation*

Discrete choice valuations are derived by comparing actual choices to see what they imply for the value of the good chosen and its attributes. For example, consider how households choose their source of water in developing countries. A study was conducted of the choices facing households in a village in Kenya. In that village, water can be obtained from vendors who deliver it to the house, from kiosks where it is sold to members of the household, who then must carry it to the dwelling, or from wells, where it is collected directly by the household (Mu, Whittington, and Briscoe 1991; Whittington, Mu, and Roche 1990; Whittington and others 1989).[5] Each option presents a different set of prices, from zero for the open well to the market price for the kiosk and the vendor. Each also presents a different amount of time needed to collect the water, from none for the vendor to significant amounts for the open well and the kiosk. The results of the analysis indicated that households buying water from vendors placed a particularly high value on the time that would otherwise be spent in collecting water. Overall, the implied value of time for those who purchased from water vendors or kiosks was roughly equal to the average wage rate. This kind of valuation procedure has evident uses for planning investments in a water supply. Connecting villages to a water supply will save the households' time spent collecting the water, and a value of the time saved should appear as a benefit of the connection scheme. The procedure shows how such benefits might be estimated.

Discrete choice approaches can estimate the willingness of all consumers to pay for a supply of water. On the assumption that consumers

### *Box 5-1. Determining the True Price of Fuelwood in Haiti*

Fuelwood is bought and sold in markets in Haiti, but the market price does not reflect the true cost of harvesting it. At least three external costs are associated with the use of fuelwood. First, trees contribute to soil nutrients. One ton of dry firewood in Haiti produces some 760 kilograms of dry foliage, which, in turn, is equivalent to 17 kilograms of nitrogen. The market price for nitrogen fertilizer is some G150–G250 a ton. Converted to tons of oil equivalent, the value of fuelwood in relation to its contribution to fertilizer is G12.0–G19.8 a ton. This value is lost by harvesting, so it appears as a fertilizer externality in the estimates below. Second, trees reduce soil erosion. In Haiti soil erosion is associated with a 2 percent reduction in farm income. Allowing for the number of trees per farm, their weight, and the amount used as fuelwood, the soil erosion externality is G45 a ton. Third, soil erosion is associated with reservoir sedimentation. Reservoir sedimentation reduces the generation of electricity, which has a direct market cost. On this basis, around G$10 per ton of oil equivalent of fuelwood must be debited as the sedimentation externality.

In addition to external costs, user costs exist if the resource is thought of as depletable rather than renewable. A formula for estimating the marginal user cost is MUC $= (P_b - C) / (1 + r)^T$, where $P_b$ is the price of the substitute technology (kerosene, say), $C$ is the cost of harvesting fuelwood, $r$ is the discount rate, and $T$ is the time at which fuelwood is exhausted (see D. W. Pearce and Turner 1989, chap. 18). This, then, is the basis for obtaining values of G10–G290 per ton of fuelwood.

*Table B5-1. True Price of Fuelwood in Haiti, by User, 1985*
(value in gourdes)

| *Marginal opportunity cost* | *Rural household* | *Rural industry* | *Urban industry* |
|---|---|---|---|
| Market price | 18.5 | 37.3 | 129.0 |
| Externality | | | |
| Fertilizer | 20.0 | 20.0 | 20.0 |
| Soil erosion | 45.0 | 45.0 | 45.0 |
| Sedimentation | 10.0 | 10.0 | 10.0 |
| User costs | 69.5 | 66.2 | 50.0 |
| Total | 163.0 | 178.5 | 254.0 |

*Source:* Hosier and Bernstein (1989).

If marginal external costs alone are allowed for, the ratio of marginal opportunity cost to marginal cost of harvesting is 1.6 to 5.0. Allowing for marginal user cost, which is debatable, the ratios are much greater. All the estimates are subject to considerable uncertainty, but the analysis illustrates a further role for valuation procedures.

perceive the benefits of supply as not just time savings but also health and convenience, such a measure would indicate the overall benefit of a given water supply. This could then be compared with the costs of supplying the water. Such a procedure would contrast with current rules of thumb used to develop water supply projects, which frequently assume that willingness to pay is equal to between 3 and 5 percent of household income. This assumption has no firm empirical basis. Box 5-2 shows the results of a discrete choice model for supplying connections to public water systems in the Punjab, Pakistan. The procedure used to estimate willingness to pay was based on observations in five villages, all of which had a system of piped water. Some households chose to connect to the piped system, others did not. In general, households who did not connect to the system used indoor hand or electric pumps to collect groundwater. The benefits of a piped system are that it generally improves the quality of water, allows indoor plumbing to be installed, and makes the water supply more reliable.

The decision to connect is influenced by three prices: a one-time connection fee, a monthly tariff unrelated to consumption, and the costs of connecting the specific household, which tend to vary with distance from the water line. Other factors influencing the decision to connect were assumed to be income, socioeconomic characteristics of the household, the availability of women and children to collect water from other sources, and household attitudes to water quality. The relation that exists between these factors and the decision to connect or not allows us to construct a demand function for being connected to the piped system. A demand function is, in fact, a willingness-to-pay function. The area under the demand curve is the total or gross willingness to pay, and the area under the curve but net of the actual payment made is the net willingness to pay, or consumer surplus (see figure B5-2). This example demonstrates that determining the value of the benefits of water supply is feasible in developing countries. Given the enormous magnitude of the investments in water supply, and the rules of thumb used to justify many of them, valuation procedures should be developed.

### *Contingent Valuation*

Contingent valuation methods (CVM) ask people whether they are willing to pay for a benefit. Applied to developing countries CVM could be an important component of project appraisal since, frequently, the output of a project is not marketed. This is the case, for example, with water supply investments, which absorb a substantial amount of donor funds. The presumption has been that people will pay up to approximately 5 percent of their income for piped water. In practice, however, this is not always the case. People often retain their old sources of supply even when

*Box 5-2. Willingness to Pay for Piped Water in the Punjab, Pakistan*

The benefits of an improved supply of water tend to be assumed rather than demonstrated. A study in the Punjab (Altaf and others 1990) showed how a demand function for piped water could be estimated by looking at the relation of past decisions to connect or not connect with various factors: connection prices, income, socioeconomic factors such as education, and attitudes to water quality. The study estimated a simplistic demand function of the kind presented in figure B5-2 and showed that the gross willingness to pay was always positive but that the consumer surplus for some households was negative (they were willing to pay less than the ruling effective tariff). For others the consumer surplus was positive. If aggregated, the benefits could be compared with the costs of providing the connections for piped water, greatly improving the basis on which decisions about water supply are made.

*Figure B5-2. Willingness to Pay*

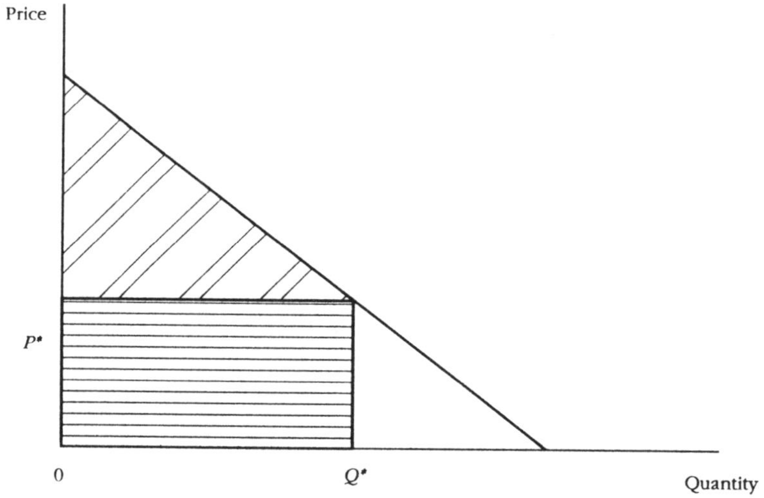


At price $P^*$ the quantity $Q^*$ of water is purchased. The crosshatched area is the consumer surplus, the lightly shaded area is the actual payment made. Con-

(*continued on next page*)

the new supply is provided. For this reason, it is important to find the value of supplying water to a specific village or town.

A contingent valuation study of water supply was conducted in Haiti (see MacRea and Whittington 1988; Whittington and others 1990). Tests for strategic and starting point bias were conducted by varying the questions given to different respondents. By and large, no evidence of sumers with valuations less than $P^*$ have a negative consumer surplus. Those with valuations above $P^*$ have a positive consumer surplus.

Table B5-2 shows the estimates of consumer surplus per household (for one of the models used by the authors). The actual prices were PRs102 in the sweet water area and PRs119 in the brackish water area. The consumer surplus must be added to these prices to estimate gross willingness to pay. For many households, willingness to pay is less than the tariff, which explains why they do not connect. Others do not connect for reasons other than price.

*Table B5-2. Consumer Surplus per Household in Punjab, Pakistan, by Type of Area, 1985*
(consumer surplus per household in 1985 rupees)

| *Consumer surplus per household* | *Sweet water* | | *Brackish water* | |
|---|---|---|---|---|
| | *Connected* | *Not connected* | *Connected* | *Not connected* |
| Mean | 78 | 26 | 43 | 19 |
| Minimum | −1 | −38 | −21 | −94 |
| Maximum | 282 | 107 | 133 | 54 |

*Source:* Altaf and others (1990).

these biases was found. The mean bid—the average willingness to pay—for public standpipes was Gs5.7 (about $1) a month, or about 1.7 percent of household income. This is significantly lower than the 5 percent rule referred to above. The mean WTP for private connections was Gs7.1, or around 2.1 percent of average income. Whittington and others (1990) concluded that it was possible to obtain reasonable consistent answers from a contingent valuation survey among a very poor, illiterate population.

## Ecosystem Valuation of Tropical Forests

The idea of total economic value (TEV) has already been introduced for valuing both resources and pollution damage. The subsequent case studies looked at the costs of pollution damage and other externalities arising from the misuse of natural resources. TEV can also be applied to the choice of land use. This section takes an extended look at one major, controversial issue of land use: the use of tropical forest land.

Various options exist for using the land in tropical forests. It could be left alone. If humans are not allowed to use forest land at all, this option might be seen as preservation. Maintaining the forest stock in broadly its original state, but allowing humans to use it, could be defined as conservation. There is also a broad spectrum of conservation options. Limited, selective logging might be permitted if it is followed by natural or managed regeneration of the removed timber. The harvesting of forest products, such as the production of latex or the gathering of rattan, might be accomplished without removing timber stock. Agricultural clearance using shifting cultivation might be practiced with the forest being allowed to regenerate fully as a new plot is exploited. Some experts do not regard shifting cultivation as a conservation option, and the terminology is not universally accepted. The basic idea remains that conservation involves use without significant destruction of the forest ecosystem. Above all, any option for use that produces irreversible effects is not a conservation use of the land. Development options would then include clearing land for agricultural use without any intent to secure regeneration, clear-felling timber without regeneration, or removing the forest to use the land for infrastructure, such as a road or a mining or industrial development. By and large, development options preclude the regeneration of the forest because development programs damage forest soils. This is not inevitable, but it is very likely.

The issue, then, is how the framework of total economic value can help policymakers and others choose between land use options.

## *The Rate of Deforestation*

Global concern about the rate of tropical deforestation accelerated in the 1980s. Data for all types of forests are approximate, and different sources use different definitions of tropical forest and deforestation. However, annual rates of deforestation at the end of the 1980s were apparently somewhere between 14 million and 17 million hectares (table 5-7). Depending on how forest area is defined, this rate of deforestation may equal 1.8 to 2.1 percent of the remaining area of tropical forest (taken to be some 8 million square kilometers, or 800 million hectares). Although comparisons are difficult because of changing definitions, deforestation rates may have been much lower, around 0.6 percent a year, in the late 1970s.

Attention has focused on tropical forests because they serve so many diverse functions, the primary forest has unique evolutionary and ecological characteristics, and the threat to their existence is accelerating. In the briefest of terms, tropical forests

- Are the homeland of many indigenous peoples, some of whom practice shifting cultivation
- Provide the habitat for extensive fauna and flora (biodiversity), which are considered to have inherent value, educational value, value for breeding crops, and medicinal value
- Supply hardwood timber
- Supply other forest products such as fruit, nuts, latex, rattan, meat, honey, resins, and oils
- Provide recreation (ecotourism)
- Protect watersheds by retaining and regulating the flow of water and cleansing water pollution and organic nutrients

*Table 5-7. Preliminary Estimates of Tropical Forest Area and Rate of Deforestation for Eighty-Seven Tropical Countries, 1981–90*

(thousands of hectares)

| Regions or subregions | Number of countries studied | Total land area | Forest area, 1980 | Forest area, 1990 | Area deforested annually, 1981–90 | Annual rate of change, 1981–90 (percent) |
|---|---|---|---|---|---|---|
| *Latin America* | 32 | 1,675,700 | 923,000 | 839,900 | 8,300 | −0.9 |
| Central America and Mexico | 7 | 245,300 | 77,000 | 63,500 | 1,400 | −1.8 |
| Caribbean subregion | 18 | 69,500 | 48,800 | 47,100 | 200 | −0.4 |
| Tropical South America | 7 | 1,360,800 | 797,100 | 729,300 | 6,800 | −0.8 |
| *Asia* | 15 | 896,600 | 310,800 | 274,900 | 3,600 | −1.2 |
| South Asia | 6 | 445,600 | 70,600 | 66,200 | 400 | −0.6 |
| Continental Southeast Asia | 5 | 192,900 | 83,200 | 69,700 | 1,300 | −1.6 |
| Insular Southeast Asia | 4 | 258,100 | 157,000 | 138,900 | 1,800 | −1.2 |
| *Africa* | 40 | 2,243,400 | 650,300 | 600,100 | 5,000 | −0.8 |
| West Sahelian Africa | 8 | 528,000 | 41,900 | 38,000 | 400 | −0.9 |
| East Sahelian Africa | 6 | 489,600 | 92,300 | 85,300 | 700 | −0.8 |
| West Africa | 8 | 203,200 | 55,200 | 43,400 | 1,200 | −2.1 |
| Central Africa | 7 | 406,400 | 230,100 | 215,400 | 1,500 | −0.6 |
| Tropical Southern Africa | 10 | 557,900 | 217,700 | 206,300 | 1,100 | −0.5 |
| Insular Africa | 1 | 58,200 | 13,200 | 11,700 | 200 | −1.2 |
| *Total* | 87 | 4,815,700 | 1,884,100 | 1,714,800 | 16,900 | −0.9 |

*Source:* World Resources Institute (1992).

- Act as a store of carbon dioxide
- Fix carbon in secondary forests and reforested areas
- Serve a possible regional microclimatic function.

These are economic functions because they contribute to human welfare either directly or indirectly.[6] How should the total economic value of a tropical forest be determined? The issue is important because decisions about the use of tropical forest land are made all too often with an imperfect understanding of the total functions of the forest. Even when they are broadly understood, only some of the functions enter into the economic calculus that determines land use. In particular, the direct use values (for timber or agriculture) dominate decisions about land use, and the wider environmental values are neglected. The resulting asymmetry of values explains much deforestation, and analyzing it can indicate policy instruments for improving the management of forests.

### *Calculating Total Economic Value*

One approach to making decisions about the use of tropical forests is the cost-benefit approach. Under this, decisions to develop a tropical forest must demonstrate that the net benefits from development exceed the net benefits from conservation. Development is taken to mean a use that is inconsistent with keeping the forest close to its natural state.

Conservation could have two dimensions: preservation, which would be formally equivalent to outright nonuse of the resource, and sustainable conservation, which would allow limited uses of the forest that are consistent with retaining the natural forest. The definitions are necessarily ambiguous. Some people would argue, for example, that ecotourism is not consistent with sustainable conservation; others would argue that it may be. Accepting the lack of precise lines of differentiation, the rule of the cost-benefit approach would be to develop the forest if and only if DEVBEN − DEVCOST > CONSBEN − CONSCOST. That is, the development benefits minus the development costs must be greater than the benefits of conservation minus the costs of conservation. Rearranging this inequality, we have DEVBEN − DEVCOST − Net CONSBEN > 0. It is not sufficient, therefore, for the net benefits of development to be positive. The forgone net benefits of conservation must also be subtracted from the net benefits of development (Pearce 1989; Pearce and Turner 1989, chap. 20).

Typically, the benefits and costs of development can be fairly readily calculated because of the attendant cash flows. Timber production, for example, tends to be undertaken for commercial markets and thus is associated with market prices. Conservation benefits, however, are associated with a mix of cash flows and nonmarket benefits, and this association imparts two biases. The first bias is that the components of the first inequality that are associated with cash flows appear more real than those not associated with such flows. Concreteness is misplaced, and decisions are likely to be biased in favor of the development option because the benefits of conservation cannot be calculated easily. The second bias follows from the first. Unless incentives are devised so that the nonmarket benefits are internalized into the mechanism for choice of land use, conservation benefits will automatically be downgraded. Very simply, those who stand to gain from, say, timber extraction or agricultural clearance cannot consume the nonmarketed benefits. This asymmetry of values imparts a considerable bias in favor of the development option.

In both inequalities, CONSBEN is measured by the total economic value of the tropical forest, which is explained in table 5-1.

### *Direct Use Values in the Tropical Forest*

Direct use values may be classified broadly as timber and nontimber uses. Nontimber products include fruits, nuts, rattan, latex, resins, honey, and wild meat.

TIMBER. Logging for timber can be consistent with conservation if the regime for managing timber practices sustainable forestry. Sustainable forestry, which leaves the original ecosystem broadly intact, effectively requires the management of natural forests: selective cutting combined with natural regeneration. Traditionally, natural management regimes have been regarded as producing losses unless

- Biological growth rates are very high
- Stumpage prices (log prices) are high
- Management is effective and at minimum cost
- The discount rate is low compared with typical commercial and even official government levels (Leslie 1987).

This bias explains the general absence of sustainable natural management systems in tropical forestry.[7] Inefficiency arising from government interference is of considerable importance for high-cost, unsustainable management.

Table 5-8 presents estimates of the financial profitability of six forestry systems in Indonesia. TPI is a selective cutting system that takes only the largest commercial trees (over 50 centimeters in diameter at breast height). The management of TPI is crucial since careless selective cutting can damage the residual stock, reducing future harvests. In its ideal form, however, it is a sustainable system. Complete harvesting and regeneration (CHR) is a system where all merchantable trees are harvested, followed by natural or enriched regeneration. INTD is an intensive dipterocarp system in which heavily managed plantations are located on clear-felled land. PULP refers to plantations of fast-growing species for pulp. SAW refers to sawtimber plantations at rotations of ten and twenty years. Environmentally, TPI should be ranked above CHR.[8] INTD is an untried system that may or may not be environmentally better than CHR. At first view, SAW and PULP seem to be environmentally undesirable since they typically involve uniform plantings of nonindigenous species on cleared land. Locating such plantations on currently unforested land could, however, be important for carbon-fixing purposes.

Table 5-8 suggests that rapid-growth plantations for producing pulp are most financially desirable at an interest rate of 6 percent but are also desirable at a rate of 10 percent. Of the systems involving the least management, the selective cutting system is not favored except at the low discount rate of 5 percent. Typically, the discount rates used to appraise projects in developing countries are 10 percent and above. Table 5-8 therefore bears out the general presumption that natural management systems based on selective cutting are less profitable than managed intensive systems and, perhaps, clear cutting systems with some natural regeneration.

Many caveats must, however, be attached to this conclusion. First, the results are likely to be specific to the location. Second, they relate to financial profitability, not economic worth. An economic assessment would allow for shadow pricing, or a valuation procedure that reflects the worth of the investment to the economy as a whole rather than to a forest concessionaire.[9] Third, the discount rate is crucial. Shadow pricing may dictate a lower rate depending on the nature of the rationale used for discounting (Markandya and Pearce 1988). Nonetheless, appealing directly to timber benefits is clearly a risky defense for the sustainable use of tropical forests.

PRODUCTS OTHER THAN TIMBER. Products other than timber can be important sources of revenue. In Indonesia, for example, exports of

*Table 5-8. Financial Profitability of Forest Management Systems in Indonesia, by Discount Rate, 1986*
(net present value in 1986 U.S. dollars per hectare)

| *Regime* | *5 percent* | *6 percent* | *10 percent* |
|---|---|---|---|
| TPI | 2,705 | 2,409 | 2,177 |
| CHR | 2,690 | 2,593 | 2,553 |
| INTD | — | 2,746 | 2,203 |
| PULP | — | 2,926 | 2,562 |
| SAW10 | — | 2,165 | 2,130 |
| SAW20 | — | 2,419 | 2,278 |

— Not available.

*Note:* TPI, selective cutting; CHR, complete harvesting and regeneration; INTD, intensive dipterocarp system; PULP, plantations of fast-growing species for pulp; SAW10, sawtimber plantations at ten-year rotations; SAW20, sawtimber plantations at twenty-year rotations. Net present value includes revenues from the initial harvest of standing stock.

*Source:* Pearce (1987). The base data come from Sedjo (1987a, 1987b).

nontimber forest products rose from \$17 million in 1973 to \$154 million in 1985, comprising 12 percent of the export earnings of forest products (D. W. Pearce, Barbier, and Markandya 1990, chap. 5). They rose to \$238 million in 1987 (de Beer and McDermott 1989). Exports of rattan alone earned \$80 million in 1985. Tropical forests also supply essential oils such as camphor, cinnamon, clove, and nutmeg, a trade worth some \$1 billion a year (Myers 1983). It cannot be assumed that the exploitation of nontimber products is itself free of environmental damage. The management record for many nontimber products is hardly better than that for tropical timber.[10] Analysis of fruit and latex yields on a 1-hectare plot of rain forest in the Peruvian Amazonia suggests that revenues generated by nontimber products may actually exceed those generated by timber (Peters, Gentry, and Mendelsohn 1989; table 5-9).

The implication of table 5-9 is that tropical forest conservation might be achieved simply by appealing to financial profitability. Much forest may be damaged unnecessarily because alternative management regimes are not investigated for alternative crops. Several dangers are, however, inherent in extrapolating from a 1-hectare plot to an entire forest. First, markets for nontimber products are very unlikely to be that large. As production of nontimber products expands, their price is likely to fall. Second, the Peruvian case considers a plot of land located near to markets, whereas most tropical forest areas are located far from the marketplace, which increases the cost of transportation. The analysis also raises an important question: if exploiting forests for nontimber products is privately profitable, why are so few forests used for this purpose? Put another way, why does the exercise of market forces fail to produce this result?

The answer to this question reveals some of the most important policies for conserving tropical forests. A great deal of deforestation would be avoided if markets were allowed to function more efficiently. Direct government interference distorts price signals, making the extraction and, more important, the clearance (usually by fire) of timber for agriculture profitable. This interference takes well-established forms. In the case of Brazil, for example,

*Table 5-9. Timber and Nontimber Revenues from a Rain Forest in Iquitos, Peru*
(U.S. dollars per hectare)

| *Activity* | *Net present value at 5 percent* |
|---|---|
| Fruit and latex | 6,330 |
| Selective logging | 490 |
| Subtotal | 6,820 |
| Clear-felling timber | 1,000 |

*Source:* Southgate, Sierra, and Brown (1989).

- Tax credits are passed that allow farmers to use the costs of clearing forest land for cattle ranching to offset income in the tax regime
- Subsidized credit is available to develop crops and livestock
- Road infrastructure is built to establish political boundaries (Binswanger 1989; Mahar 1989; Repetto and Gillis 1988).

Equally important in the bias toward clearance is the status of land tenure. Forest dwellers rarely hold secure rights to the land, so outsiders can readily establish rights through clearance. Indeed, in many cases, the land must be cleared in order to claim land rights (Southgate, Sierra, and Brown 1989). Agricultural colonists invariably win the competition for land rights. Ensuring secure land tenure for indigenous peoples may be one of the most important ways of conserving tropical forests. Conferring security of tenure on colonists, however, acts like a magnet for outsiders wishing to clear land for agriculture.

Clearing forests for ranching is socially irrational: without subsidies, revenues from Brazilian beef cattle ranching cover only one-third of the costs of setting up the ranches, as table 5-10 shows (Browder 1988a, 1988b). The subsidy system explains why an activity that is privately profitable is socially unprofitable. The combined costs of tax credits, subsidized credit, and the timber revenues forgone because a forest is

*Table 5-10. Cost Structure of a Typical Beef Cattle Ranch in the Brazilian Amazon, 1979–84*
(U.S. dollars per hectare)

| *Expenses* | *Amount invested* | *Percentage of the total* |
|---|---|---|
| *Capital investment* | | |
| Land cost | 31.7 | 13.1 |
| Forest clearance | 66.0 | 27.3 |
| Pasture planting | 26.4 | 10.9 |
| Fencing | 19.4 | 8.0 |
| Cattle acquisition | 90.9 | 37.6 |
| Other | 7.4 | 3.1 |
| Subtotal | 241.8 | 100.0 |
| *Operating costs* | | |
| Labor | 26.2 | 15.2 |
| Herd maintenance | 21.0 | 12.1 |
| Pasture maintenance | 47.3 | 27.3 |
| Infrastructure | 74.3 | 43.0 |
| Other | 4.2 | 2.4 |
| Subtotal | 173.0 | 100.0 |
| Total costs | 414.8 | 100.0 |
| Total revenues | 112.5 | 100.0 |
| Revenues as a percentage of costs | n.a. | 27.1 |

n.a. Not applicable.
*Source:* Ruitenbeek (1989).

destroyed are estimated to have been $4.8 billion between 1966 and 1983. Both market forces and government price distortions seem to explain why the forest was cleared for agriculture and livestock. While large ranches collected subsidies, small ranches did not. Yet small ranches expanded rapidly, which suggests that financial returns to smaller ranches may be quite high.

ECOTOURISM VALUES. Tropical forests are attracting a growing number of tourists searching for adventure or a place to appreciate nature. Ecotourism promises to be a major development capable of generating substantial revenues such as those earned in African countries from wildlife viewing and game drives. European package explorer holidays to the Peruvian Amazon, for example, cost around $2,300 per person for twenty days.[11] In Costa Rica, Ecuador, the Philippines, and Thailand, tourism ranks among the top five industries and brings in more foreign exchange than exports of timber and timber products (Gradwohl and Greenberg 1988, pp. 66–67). Thus Costa Rica earned $138 million in 1986 in what was mainly nature-based tourism. The number of tourists arriving in Manaus, Amazonas, Brazil, increased from 12,000 in 1983 to 70,000 in 1988. Tourism is expected to be the largest single source of income in Brazil's Amazonas State in the 1990s (quoted in Dogse 1989). The potential for tourism in Central America and Latin America remains largely untapped (Dourojeanni 1985; Leonard 1987). Obviously, not all tourism to these countries can be credited to forest areas, but some unquestionably is. Additionally, tourism brings its own external costs in the form of pollution, overexposure of wildlife to tourist vehicles, and so on.

Ruitenbeek (1989) suggests tentative values for tourist benefits in the Korup Forest in Cameroon. On the basis of assumptions about the rates charged both tourists and researchers, annual net income to Cameroon would, once rates were stabilized, be an estimated $180,000.

Of course, not all tourists originate from other countries. As real income per capita increases, so does the incipient demand for recreation in the developing countries. In Tunisia, for example, Lake Ichkeul and its associated marshes, which have been designated a national park, are particularly rich in wildlife, especially birds. A visitor survey in 1988 showed that, on a single day, 1,500 persons visited the park, and only 200 of them were from overseas. Tunisians were also prepared to travel long distances to visit the park: 60 percent of the visitors had come from Tunis, and 4 percent had traveled more than 350 kilometers (Thomas, Ayache, and Hollis 1989).

USES OF WILD FLORA AND FAUNA. Tropical forests act as the habitat for an enormous variety of species. The production of meat from wild animals in Peru amounted to some 13,000 tons in 1976 (Dourojeanni

1985, p. 420); fish and game comprise 80 to 85 percent of all animal protein intake in the lowland Amazon region outside urban centers. Legal exports of hides and skins from Peru amounted to 5 million and 0.5 million, respectively, between 1965 and 1976 (Dourojeanni 1985, p. 423). The trade in live animals is significant and, sadly, unsustainable due to excessive exploitation. As with tourism, fine distinctions frequently separate what is and is not sustainable.

Tropical forests act as the source of genetic material for modern food crops. Crossbreeding with wild varieties is essential for producing crops that resist diseases and pests. Myers (1983) suggests that such crossbreeding has already saved sugarcane, banana, and cocoa from major damage. Tropical forests are home to many insects that are the natural enemies of plant-damaging pests and to plant chemicals that are used as insecticides. No reliable estimates of willingness to pay for genetic material from tropical forests are available, and the informational needs for securing such estimates may be substantially greater than the information that exists in codified form (Brown 1986). Certainly, a valuation exercise should not be confused with simply looking at the value of the final product.

Placing value on the pharmaceutical use of tropical forest species is another formidable task. One out of four beginning materials for prescribed drugs originates in tropical forests, and the market value of drugs based on plants has been estimated.[12] But calculations of the market value of the prescriptions bought for a particular plant-based drug are not good estimates of the value of the plant used to manufacture the drug. What is required is the price drug manufacturers are willing to pay for the plant material plus a measure of consumers' net gains from using such drugs compared with those from using a substitute. The role of substitutes for plant-based drugs is thus crucial. Many modern drug manufacturers tend to focus more on the production of synthetic drugs using recent advances in molecular biology and biotechnology (Principe 1987). Put another way, their willingness to pay for retaining tropical forests as repositories of potential pharmaceuticals could be very low.

One study (Ruitenbeek 1989) has approached the value of genetic information in the Korup Rain Forest, Cameroon, by assuming that the value of patents can be applied to a guesstimated number of research discoveries in the forest area. Assuming ten such discoveries a year and an average patent value of $8,000, the annual benefits could equal $80,000, of which Cameroon would, of course, capture only a fraction.

### *Indirect Use Values*

Tropical forests have many ecological functions. Valuation procedures tend to focus on either damage done or cost of replacement. Thus removing a tropical forest that protects a watershed can result in soil erosion, downstream sedimentation, and increased floods. This damage would then be a measure of the value of the watershed protection function, since such damage would have been avoided by conserving the forest. Alternatively, if the damage occurs, the amount spent reconstituting the affected area would be a measure of the protection function. If the damage cannot be reconstituted, it may be necessary to replace the protection function.

Although replacement cost approaches are useful because they provide an upper limit to the value of the resource or service to be replaced, they must be used with caution. Implicitly, they assume that making the replacement is worthwhile, which means that the benefits from replacement exceed the costs of replacement. Replacement costs are being used, however, to value the benefits of replacement, and this procedure automatically produces benefit-cost ratios of unity.

WATERSHED EFFECTS. The nature and extent of ecological functions that are lost from deforestation are disputed. Hamilton and King (1983) provide a survey, summarized in table 5-11, of claimed watershed effects and the empirical evidence for their existence; others, such as Myers (1983), dispute their assessment. Ecological impact depends on the use to which deforested land is put—that is, the nature of the agricultural system if deforested land is converted to agriculture, the nature of the logging regime, and so on. The argument is that forests are not unique in their watershed protection functions, and hence deforestation per se does not produce adverse effects. Rather the nature of the succeeding land use is what matters. In theory, forest clearance can have limited or negligible

*Table 5-11. Assessment of the Ecological Impact of Tropical Deforestation*

| *Impact* | *Assessment* |
|---|---|
| Reduced rainfall | No evidence supports this claim, with the possible exception of recycling in the Amazon rain forest if permanent and large-scale deforestation occurs. Fog and cloud forests increase rainfall. |
| Reduced water supplies and reduced floods | Claim is based on the idea of forests as a sponge absorbing water in the wet season and releasing it slowly in the dry, but forests act more like a pump than a sponge. Cutting tends to increase the supply of water, but conversion to agriculture can lower the water table and reduce the river's flow during the dry season. |
| Soil erosion and sedimentation | Both effects are the result of conversion to unstable agricultural systems. Traditional shifting agriculture is not implicated in such damage, but modern slash-and-burn techniques (forest farming) are unstable. |

*Source:* Hamilton and King (1983); Myers (1983); Salati and others (1979).

watershed effects if, for example, soils are allowed to secure a cover of grasses and shrubs. In reality, the forest clearer is often the same agent who subsequently uses the forest soils in an environmentally damaging way, such as cattle ranching or agriculture.

Ruitenbeek (1989) estimates the present value of forest protection for inshore fisheries in the Korup region of Cameroon as £3.8 million at an 8 percent discount rate. The benefits of flood control are an estimated £1.6 million.

*Figure 5-2. Distribution of Inorganic Nutrients in Tropical Rain Forests above and below the Surface*

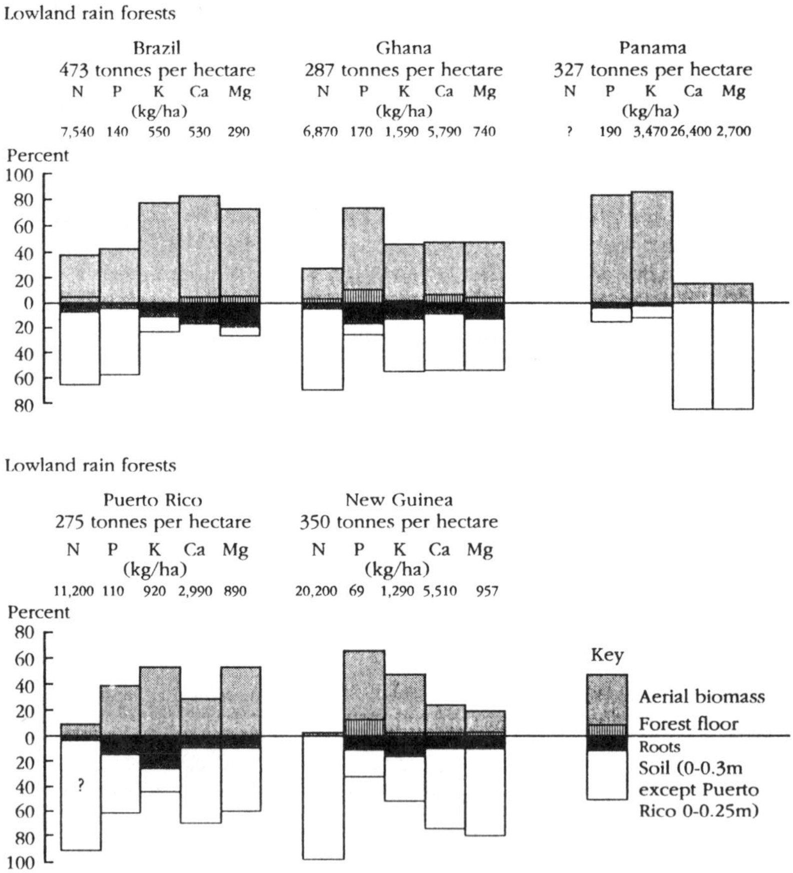


*Source:* Whitmore (1990), p. 137.

Nutrient Cycling. Figure 5-2 shows a typical nutrient cycling diagram for a tropical forest. The nutrients in question include calcium, magnesium, and potassium, which are bound to soil and water, and elements such as nitrogen, which are interchanged with the atmosphere. Nitrogen, phosphorus, potassium, and, to some extent, calcium are stocked in the biomass. The carbon and sulfur cycles are considered separately below. Contrary to some discussions, we show that nutrients lie both below the surface and in the biomass.

The significance of nutrient cycling for valuation is twofold. First, disturbing the forest system releases nutrients into aquatic systems. In tropical forests, drainage water in the aquatic system is typically low in nutrients. Deforestation and, more generally, opening of the canopy cause a nutrient outflow, which itself can pollute river and coastal ecosystems (Furtado 1978; Furtado and Ruddle 1986). Second, and far more significant, however, the outflow of nutrients from deforestation drastically reduces the productive capacity of the area that had been forest. Forest soils are low in nutrients, and this explains why cleared forest land often sustains only limited livestock and crop production unless substantial amounts of artificial fertilizer are added. In short, nutrient lockup tends to impose irreversibility on the spectrum of land uses possible after deforestation.

Carbon Cycling and the Greenhouse Effect. In the process of photosynthesis, growing forests fix carbon dioxide and give off oxygen. Once grown, forests no longer accumulate carbon from the atmosphere. Mature forests are said to be in a state of (approximate) carbon equilibrium, which means that they release as much carbon dioxide as they absorb. (The northern hemisphere's temperate and boreal forests may actually exhibit a slight net fixation of carbon, but tropical forests are in carbon equilibrium if they are mature, as is the case for the remaining primary forest.) Although their rate of carbon exchange with the atmosphere is zero, mature tropical forests lock up or sequester carbon as a stock. This distinction is important since it means that deforestation releases carbon dioxide into the atmosphere and thus contributes to the greenhouse effect. Indeed, deforestation releases other greenhouse gases such as methane. Tropical forests are major stores of carbon, and hence the use made of tropical forest land, and of the timber on the land, is an important factor in global warming.

It is important to distinguish what is being valued when talking of the carbon-fixing value of a tropical forest. The context is best viewed as one of the costs and benefits of alternative land use. Consider two basic options: to conserve tropical forest or clear it for agriculture.

- Conserving a mature forest in carbon equilibrium avoids the release of any carbon associated with the alternative land use (agriculture) and hence avoids the damage associated with that carbon release as well. The forest, then, has a carbon credit equal to the avoided damage.

- By clearing the forest for agriculture, deforestation occurs and carbon (and other pollutants) is released. The damage associated with that carbon release is, therefore, a carbon debit to that particular use of forest land.

However, it is not legitimate both to ascribe a credit to the conservation option and a debit to the clearance option. That would be double counting since credit and debit are the obverse of each other. Either conservation is credited with damage avoided or the agriculture option is debited with the damage done by deforestation.

A further complication is that the credit or debit depends on how the timber is removed, how it is subsequently used, and how the deforested land is subsequently managed.[13] Clearance by burning is associated with a total release of carbon dioxide and has no offsetting credits for the use made of the timber. If the land is subsequently managed so that carbon is once again fixed (for example, if it is converted to grassland), then that rate of fixation has to be offset against the loss of carbon from deforestation. Typically, forests contain 20–100 times more carbon per unit of area than agricultural lands. Thus, the offset due to subsequent land use will be much less than the loss from deforestation through clearance. The same goes for any downstream reappearance of carbon: by far the greatest portion of released carbon goes into the atmosphere.

If the forest is clear-felled and all the timber is used to make long-lived wood products (housing timbers and furniture, for example), the act of deforestation may release very little carbon because the carbon remains locked up in the timber products; this is known as product carbon offset. Subsequent land use may then fix some carbon, so that the overall effect of deforestation on the release of carbon could be very small: zero or even negative. This second kind of offset is land use carbon offset.

Most deforestation occurs through direct clearance or incidental damage. The estimates of deforestation in the early 1980s suggested that some 11.1 million hectares of tropical forest were being lost each year. Of this, 7.3 million hectares were being cleared directly for agriculture, usually by burning, and a further 3.8 million hectares were being cleared for a combination of agriculture and fuelwood. Selective logging was taking place on another 4.4 million hectares, and although selective logging is, in principle, consistent with regeneration (and hence with little change in the store of carbon over time), in practice it tends to be associated with extensive damage to the remaining tree stocks and produces carbon release (Repetto 1990). Although the extent of net carbon released by deforestation is specific to the location, little product carbon offset occurs overall. Both the land use offset and the product offset tend to be allowed for in the better studies of carbon release (such as Houghton 1990).

Taking the various offsets into account, carbon emissions due to deforestation in 1980 were estimated to be in the range of 0.4–2.5 x $10^{15}$ grams, which equals 0.4–2.5 gigatons a year ($10^{15}$ grams = 1 billion metric tons = 1 gigaton), with a mean figure of 1.8 gigatons a year (Houghton 1990; Houghton and others 1985). This compares with releases of fossil fuel carbon dioxide, which equaled 5.3 gigatons in 1984. Of this total (1.8 + 5.3 = 7.1 gigatons), around half remains in the atmosphere while the rest is absorbed by the oceans and other sinks. The net accretion is approximately 3.6 gigatons in the atmosphere. Tropical deforestation may therefore contribute about 25 percent of carbon dioxide emissions, which, in turn, contribute perhaps half of the total greenhouse gases. Tropical deforestation would therefore contribute 10–13 percent of all emissions of greenhouse gases. More recent estimates suggest that rates of deforestation have increased, and the amount of carbon released could be some 2–3 gigatons each year (Houghton 1990).

Two issues arise. First, what carbon credit should be given to tropical forests for their contribution to avoiding the global warming impact of deforestation (in other words, what is the carbon credit for conservation and hence the carbon debit for clearance)? Second, what contribution could afforestation make to containing the greenhouse effect?

In line with the valuation of damage avoided, a tropical forest should be credited with the value of global warming damage avoided by its conservation. Estimates of global warming suggest that the damage done, mainly the rising level of the sea, could equal $13 per ton of carbon (in 1989 dollars; Nordhaus 1991). Given the uncertainty regarding the speed, extent, and physical impact of global warming, these estimates must be regarded with care.

Table 5-12 shows some recent estimates of rates of deforestation and the resulting carbon releases for a single year, 1989. Most of the carbon is released in the first five years following deforestation. Focusing on a

*Table 5-12. Rate of Deforestation and Release of Carbon, 1989*

| *Country* | *Rate of deforestation (millions of hectares)* | *Release of carbon (millions of tons)* | *Carbon release per deforestation (tons of carbon per hectare)* |
|---|---|---|---|
| Bolivia | 0.15 | 14 | 93.3 |
| Brazil | 5.00 | 454 | 90.8 |
| Guyanas | 0.05 | 4 | 80.0 |
| Indonesia | 1.20 | 124 | 103.3 |
| Viet Nam | 0.35 | 36 | 102.9 |
| Thirty-four countries | 13.86 | 1,398 | 100.9 |

*Source:* Adapted from Houghton (1990).

single year therefore understates the total amount of carbon lost since release occurs beyond that year. The analysis helps illustrate the magnitude of the costs involved.

Table 5-12 indicates that, on average, deforestation of 1 hectare of land contributes some 100 tons of carbon to the atmosphere in a single year. At some $13 per ton, deforestation causes damage at a rate of $1,300 per hectare. Again, given the uncertainty of the estimated damage caused by global warming, this figure should be treated as a rough approximation. In reality, of course, the damage is higher than this because carbon continues to be released after the first year. Such carbon debits greatly outweigh the revenues generated by cattle ranching in Amazonia (table 5-10).

Sedjo (1989) has suggested that 1 hectare of new forest on a good site in the Pacific Northwest or southern United States could sequester 6 x 10 million grams of carbon each year (6 tons). If, hypothetically, afforestation programs were designed to take up, say, 3 of the 3.6 gigatons net accretion of carbon, 470 million hectares of new plantation would be needed, or around 10 percent of the current area of forest in the world. Given the obvious problems of such a massive taking of land for forestry, effort might be better devoted to raising the biomass of standing crops. The figures suggest that crop biomass would have to be raised 50 percent.

Myers (1990) suggests that a working mean sequestration rate of 10 tons of carbon per hectare a year is appropriate for tropical forests, making the required hectarage of afforestation around 300 million hectares. At 10 tons per hectare a year, the annual carbon credit would be $130 per hectare.

Sulfur Cycling. The nature of sulfur cycling in tropical forests is imperfectly understood. Some authorities suggest that tropical forests contribute to acid rain (Samples, Gowen, and Dixon 1986). Others regard tropical forests as net scrubbers of sulfur.

Conclusions. The nature of the ecological functions of tropical forests is uncertain. In fact, the physical assessment of the impact of environmental damage or protection is often a greater problem than is economic valuation. Forests clearly generate positive economic value in this respect. Moreover, given the uncertainty, deforestation is inconsistent with risk-averse behavior since deforestation of closed canopy primary forest cannot be reversed. That is, the secondary forest that replaces primary forest, if the land is not converted to alternative uses after deforestation, is not the same as the primary forest. Nonetheless, irreversibility should not be exaggerated. Many of the protective functions of forests may be conserved by the land uses that succeed deforestation. As the secondary forest grows, much of the original biodiversity may be

*Table 5-13. Nonuse Values for Unique Natural Assets, Mid-1980s*
(U.S. dollars per adult)

| *Asset* | *Value* |
|---|---|
| *Animal species* | |
| Bald eagle | 11 |
| Emerald shiner | 4 |
| Grizzly bear | 15 |
| Bighorn sheep | 7 |
| Whooping crane | 1 |
| Blue whale | 8 |
| Bottlenose dolphin | 6 |
| California sea otter | 7 |
| Northern elephant seal | 7 |
| *Natural amenities* | |
| Water quality (South Platte river basin) | 4 |
| Visibility (Grand Canyon) | 22 |

*Source:* C. W. Clark (1980); Herrera (1985).

reintroduced. Rational behavior under uncertainty would dictate taking a very cautious attitude to deforestation.

### *Nonuse Values*

The final category of value is nonuse value, the inherent value attached to the existence of tropical forests. The motivations for existence value need not concern us unduly.[14] Efforts to estimate existence value are based on contingent valuation studies, which use a questionnaire on willingness to pay. No study has been carried out for tropical forests, but table 5-13 reports estimates of average annual values per person taken from contingent valuation studies for selected animal species and natural amenities. Although limited in number, these studies offer consistent values. The animal values cluster in the $5–$8 range, with American national symbols—the grizzly bear and the bald eagle—in the $10–$15 range. The Grand Canyon similarly has a higher valuation as a major national heritage than, for example, cleaning up a river.

Could such values be borrowed for tropical forests? Tropical forests are unique assets, but they are generally located in developing countries. Allowing for this distance between the valuer and the object of value (which applies to the blue whale as well, for example), and the substantial global interest in tropical deforestation, a figure of $8 per adult a year seems very conservative. Allowing only for the valuations of the richest nations of the world, with some 400 million adults (Australasia, North America, and Western Europe), the valuation would be $3.2 billion a year. Of course, the $8 million may capture some of the indirect benefits of tropical forests, although it mainly captures existence value.

The opportunity costs of forest conservation are the development benefits forgone. As we have seen, these may not, in fact, be greater than the benefits of sustainable use of tropical forests. In order to assess the back-of-the-envelope guesstimate of existence value, however, one might look at the developmental uses of tropical forests to see what benefits accrue. If we take Amazonia as an example, the entire GNP of classical Amazonia is about 6 percent of Brazil's GNP, which was $200 billion in 1986. Thus Amazonia contributed $12 billion to the total. If each adult in wealthy countries would be willing to contribute $8 a year to an Amazon Conservation Fund, the resulting $3.2 billion would enable the people responsible for more than 25 percent of the economic output of Amazonia to be compensated for ceasing their activities.

### *Conclusions*

The concept of total economic value offers a comprehensive framework within which to value tropical forests. Total economic value comprises use values, option values, and existence values. Direct use values include timber and nontimber products and ecotourism. Indirect use values include the ecological functions of tropical forests: their watershed protection and mineral cycling functions. Existence value relates to the intrinsic value of the forest unrelated to its use. Since all these values are given by people, the total economic value approach is totally anthropomorphic. It does not deny other rationales, such as natural rights, for conserving tropical forests. Resorting to such moral arguments may not be necessary. Economic arguments alone could justify a dramatic reduction in deforestation. A major issue, however, is that any mobilization of existence value must result in flows of cash or technology targeted to the people who make the decisions about resource use. If those individuals are small colonist farmers, for example, this fact would have formidable implications for the way in which any transferred funds are used in the receiving country.

Use values alone may favor forest conservation. Clearing forests for livestock agriculture, in particular, appears to have limited rationale. Doing so depends on substantial subsidies, which themselves introduce major economic distortions. Using forests as a source of products other than timber, such as minor forest products, appears to give higher financial rates of return than using them as a source of timber in some areas. Markets fail to allocate forests to their best uses because government intervention is inefficient, notably in the areas of subsidies and land tenure. The recreational use of tropical forests is only now beginning to be realized.

Indirect use values must be estimated. As yet, little effort has been made to value these indirect functions. Some of them are disputed, but there is no question that deforestation followed by unsuitable land use causes significant damage. Additionally, tropical forests should be given carbon credits for their role in containing the greenhouse effect. For existing forests the credit would relate to damage avoided by choosing not to pursue the development option, which is the benefit of conservation. This might total $1,000 per hectare for a single year, with similar benefits for about five years. For new forests, values might be $130 per hectare a year.

Existence values could be substantial and might dominate the use and indirect values. That would be consistent with other findings in the literature on total economic valuation. Assuming that the Amazon forest is valued at an average of $8 per adult in the advanced economies of the world, existence value could readily amount to $3 billion, or one-quarter of the entire contribution of classic Amazonia to Brazil's gross domestic product—including mineral extraction, timber, and agriculture.

## Environment and Health

Environmental quality produces direct and indirect benefits. As a source of amenity, environmental quality is an important provider of direct benefits. It is tempting to think that this is only so in the industrial world, where amenity plays a large role in meeting the rapidly growing demand for recreation and wilderness. It is important in many developing countries, too, and as real income per capita increases, so does the incipient demand for recreation. The popular image that recreation does not matter in the developing world has to be resisted.

Arguably the most important and immediate consequences of environmental degradation in the developing world take the form of damage to human health. Not only is health an end in itself, but a healthy work force is essential to the development process as a whole. The economic effects of impaired health can be formidable. Diarrhea is a common occurrence in many developing countries, where 3 billion–5 billion cases are recorded every year. Each case is estimated to involve 3–5 days lost, so that 9 billion–25 billion working days could be lost in a single year. At a nominal $0.50 a day, the output lost could be $4.5 billion–$12.5 billion a year from this one disease (these are clearly guesstimates; see Meybeck, Chapman, and Helmer 1990). Table 5-14 provides data on the incidence of waterborne diseases. In Sri Lanka, 5.7 times as many males die from infectious and parasitic diseases, and 7.2 times as many females, as die in the United States. Similar ratios for other countries are 2.5 and 2.8 for Chile and 2.1 and 2.1 for Mauritius (data from the World Health Organization, which were reported in World Resources Institute 1990).

### *Costing Health Damage*

An extensive literature exists on the economic cost of health damage from environmental degradation, most of it relating to the industrial world. The procedures used for valuation are often sophisticated. Those

*Table 5-14. Morbidity and Mortality from Waterborne Diseases in Africa, Latin America, and Asia, 1977–78*

| Type of disease and infection | Number of infections (thousands per year) | Number of deaths (thousands per year) | Average number of days lost per illness | Relative disability |
|---|---|---|---|---|
| *Waterborne* | | | | |
| Amebiasis | 400 | 30 | 7–10 | Able to work |
| Diarrhea | 3,000–5,000 | 5,000–20,000 | 3–5 | Able to function some |
| Polio | 80 | 10–20 | 3,000+ | Able to function some |
| Typhoid | 1 | 25 | 14–28 | Able to function some |
| *Water hygiene* | | | | |
| Ascariasis (roundworm) | 800–1,000 | 20 | 7–10 | Able to work |
| Leprosy | 12 | Very low | 500–3,000 | Able to function some or able to work |
| Trichuriasis (whipworm) | 500 | Low | 7–10 | Able to work |
| Hookworm | 7,000–9,000 | 50–60 | 100 | Suffers minor effects |
| *Water habitat with water-related vectors* | | | | |
| Schistosomiasis (bilharziasis) | 200 | 500–1,000 | 600–1,000 | Able to work or suffers minor effects |
| African trypanosomiasis (sleeping sickness) | 1 | 5 | 150 | Bedridden |
| Malaria | 800 | 1,200 | 3–5 | Able to function some |
| Onchocerciasis (river blindness) | 30 | 20–50 | 3,000 | Bedridden or able to function some |

*Note:* The number of infections and deaths = $(10^3 \cdot a^{-1})$.
*Source:* Walsh and Warren (1979).

relating to morbidity tend to be different from those relating to mortality, but both tend to be part of a more general model known as a dose-response model or, sometimes, the damage function approach. This model traces a pollutant from its emission to its ambient concentration, which is called the dose. The response consists of a health impact, such as respiratory illness, that shows up as days lost from work, restricted activity days, and death. The valuation exercise only takes place when the epidemiological response is estimated. Statistics on diseases related to the environment offer a first-stage measure of the potential importance of the link between environment and health. It is not always easy, however, to distinguish the causes of disease. Lung cancers might, for example, be induced by airborne toxic substances, cigarette smoking, or a host of other factors. If the link can be established, the value of the health damage done—its monetary cost—becomes a second-stage environmental indicator. Rising monetary costs (in real prices) might indicate a path of unsustainable development.

As yet, monetary estimates of national health damage are few and far between. Freeman (1982) suggests that in 1978 the United States received a health benefit of \$3 billion–\$41 billion, with a best estimate of \$17 billion, from policies on clean air and perhaps another \$1 billion from improvements in the quality of water. Since the estimates relate to one year only, little can be said about trends.

Morbidity might be valued as a measure of the economic cost of a working day lost using the ruling wage rate. Mortality requires the use of what is misleadingly known as a value of human life. These values are, in fact, measures of willingness to pay for reducing risk or willingness to accept payment for increased risk. For example, such values might be taken from analyses of the extent to which wage rates in risky jobs compensate for the risks involved. Box 5-3 illustrates the dose-response approach for the United States. The example chosen uses what is known as macroepidemiology; that is, it relates large data sets on mortality and morbidity to factors thought to influence those rates.

## *Pollution and Health in the Developing World*

Can the economic approaches to assessing health damage from environmental degradation be applied to developing countries? In principle they can, with two qualifications. First, data are usually not available to the extent required to model damage functions in the manner suggested. Second, valuation is more complex, particularly for mortality because wages and health risks may not be linked in the labor markets of developing countries in the same way they appear to be in the richer world. Thus many studies of industrial countries value health damage by looking at the implicit valuation of risks in the labor market: the higher the risk of occupational accident or disease, the higher is the risk premium in wage rates expected to be. Labor markets in many developing countries will not adjust this way, and second-best valuation techniques, such as wages per day lost, may have to be used to value morbidity and perhaps lifetime income forgone for mortality.[15]

A further issue applies equally to the literature for industrial countries. The multiple regression approach relates a given measure of health damage to various indicators of factors that might be associated with that damage. That is, an equation is estimated of the general form: health damage = $f(V1, V2, V3 \ldots Vn)$. $V1 \ldots Vn$ are the variables thought

*Box 5-3. Air Pollution and Health Damage in the United States*

A 1976 data base covering 50,000 households was matched to pollution data and other information (Ostro 1983). Morbidity was measured by days off work—work lost days (WLD)—and restricted activity days—RAD, days in which activity was restricted because of ill health. Then WLD and RAD were regressed on various variables: indicators of chronic disease, race, marriage, temperature, population density, rainfall, cigarette consumption, and work status. There were no variables for air pollution other than sulfur oxides and suspended particulates nor any for water quality or diet. The results, showing just the estimates for the two air pollution variables, were as follows:

$$\text{RAD} = -0.83 + 0.00282\,\text{TSP} - 0.00008\,\text{SULF} + \ldots \text{ and}$$
$$\text{WLD} = -0.47 + 0.00145\,\text{TSP} - 0.001\,\text{SULF} + \ldots.$$

In these equations, the sulfur coefficients were not significant, which means that sulfur concentrations were not implicated in morbidity. This bears out earlier studies. The coefficients for TSP were significant and can be translated into elasticities, showing the percentage increase in morbidity for each percentage point increase in air pollution. The coefficients were 0.45 for WLD and 0.39 for RAD when expressed as elasticities. Thus a 1 percent improvement in air quality would reduce the number of working days lost 0.45 percent. Ostro did not estimate the monetary value of days lost or days of restricted activity.

A similar regression study (Kneese 1984) looked at mortality benefits. The regressions found that TSP was linked to deaths from pneumonia and influenza and that sulfur oxides were linked to early infant disease. Extrapolating these relationships to all 150 million urban dwellers at risk in the United States (experiencing similar exposure levels) and using a value of life of $0.34 million–$1.0 million based on wage-risk studies, the following results were obtained.

*Table B5-3. Link between Air Pollution and Select Diseases, United States*
(billions of 1978 U.S. dollars a year)

| *Disease* | *Pollutant* | *Value of a 60 percent reduction in air pollution* |
|---|---|---|
| Pneumonia | Particulates | 4.4–13.7 |
| Early infant disease | Sulfur dioxide | 0.7–2.2 |
| Total | All | 5.1–15.9 |

*Source:* For morbidity, see Ostro (1983), pp. 371–82. For mortality, see Kneese (1984). For a general discussion, see Pearce and Markandya (1989).

to influence health damage, and they include pollution indexes. The pollution measures usually refer to concentrations, for example, *X* parts per million of sulfur dioxide. A further stage—exposure—exists between ambient concentrations and dose that is determined by the period of time an individual spends in the polluted area. People actually spend a great

Table 5-15. *Air Pollution Emissions Produced by Different Fuels*
(kilograms of pollutants per 1 trillion joules delivered, unless otherwise indicated)

| *Type of fuel* | *Percentage efficiency* | *Fuel equivalent to 1 trillion joules* | *Total particulates* | *Sulfur oxides* | *Nitrogen oxides* | *Hydro-carbons* | *Carbon monoxide* |
|---|---|---|---|---|---|---|---|
| *Industrial boilers* | | | | | | | |
| Wood | 70 | 89[a] | 500 | 53 | 400 | 400 | 450 |
| Bituminous coal | 80 | 43[a] | 2,800 | 820 | 320 | 22 | 45 |
| Residual oil | 80 | 33,000[b] | 94 | 1,310 | 240 | .. | 20 |
| Distillate oil | 90 | 31,400[b] | 8 | 1,120 | 83 | .. | 19 |
| Natural gas | 90 | 28,200[c] | 7 | .. | 99 | 2 | 8 |
| *Residential heating stoves* | | | | | | | |
| Wood | 50 | 130[a] | 2,700 | 30 | 100 | 6,800 | 17,000 |
| Anthracite | 65 | 49[a] | 46 | 200 | 250 | 100 | 1,000 |
| Bituminous coal | 65 | 53[a] | 550 | 1,100 | 270 | 530 | 5,300 |
| Distillate oil | 85 | 32,900[b] | 11 | 1,170 | 71 | 4 | 20 |
| Natural gas | 85 | 30,000[c] | 7 | .. | 38 | 4 | 10 |
| *Residential cooking stoves* | | | | | | | |
| Tropical wood | 15 | 420[a] | 3,800 | 250 | 300 | 3,200 | 34,000 |
| Hawaiian cow dung | 15 | 530[a] | 10,000 | 3,200 | — | — | 44,000 |
| Indian coal | 20 | 220[a] | 280 | 2,200 | 460 | 2,200 | 27,000 |
| Coconut husks | 15 | 480[a] | 17,000 | — | — | — | 54,000 |
| Natural gas | 80 | 32,000[c] | 0.5 | — | 10 | 5 | 250 |

— Not available.

.. Negligible.

*Note:* Actual efficiences and emissions vary greatly according to the quality of the fuel and the combustion conditions. Combustion-derived particulates and hydrocarbons contain complex mixtures of hundreds or thousands of organic chemicals, many of which are mutagenic or toxic. Residential heating stoves were measured under conditions in the United States. Biomass and coal cooking stoves were measured under rural conditions in India.

a. Metric tons.

b. Liters.

c. Cubic meters.

*Source:* V. K. Smith (1987).

deal of their time indoors rather than outdoors, yet the pollution measures tend to be outdoor concentrations. For example, the major sources of exposure to air toxins such as benzene and chloroform are found inside, not outside. Even for traditional pollutants, the main source of exposure is often at home: for particulates, it is cigarette smoke; for nitrogen dioxide, it is gas stoves (these important findings are summarized in Smith 1988b).

This focus on exposure rather than ambient concentration is just as important in the developing world. Three-quarters of the world's population lives in the developing countries, and two-thirds of those persons live in rural areas. Yet rural dwellers in developing countries spend 60 percent of their time indoors, not outdoors. Assuming that rural dwellers are not exposed to air pollution is therefore wrong, since indoor pollution from open-hearth fires or stoves, for example, can be significant (table 5-15). The influence of cooking stoves using wood, dung, and crop residues is enormous. Formidable policy implications arise from this finding. Suppose the issue is whether or not to install particulate control technology in a coal-fired power station or how much of this technology to introduce (how much particulate matter is to be removed). It may be far cheaper to launch a program for cleaning up household stoves than to introduce controls at the power station. Smith (1988a) suggests that the same reductions in total exposure (individual exposure multiplied by the number of people at risk) could be achieved at only one-ninth the cost.

What are the risks from exposure to pollution in the developing world? In Mexico City deaths attributed to cancer, influenza, and pneumonia have increased sixfold since 1956, and deaths due to cardiovascular disease have quadrupled. Deaths to people over sixty-five years of age due to bronchitis, emphysema, and asthma increased 12 percent between 1978 and 1984. People suffering long-term mental impairment could double over the next few decades due to high concentrations of lead in newborns. Nor are the risks just from air pollution alone. Mexico City and the surrounding areas have 2,100 chemical plants. In November 1984 a gas storage plant exploded, killing some 650 people. Although disasters of this kind are perhaps extreme examples of pollution, chemical leaks in cities such as Mexico City are not unusual. Perhaps more than 70 percent of populations in urban areas live with unacceptable levels of air pollution (unpublished estimate of the World Health Organization and the United Nations Environment Programme, quoted in Weil and others 1990, chap. 4).

## Appendix: Methodologies for Eliciting Economic Values

Numerous surveys now exist on the kinds of methodologies that may be used to elicit economic values (Bentkover and others 1986; Cummings, Brookshire, and Schulze 1986; Feenberg and Mills 1980; Freeman 1979, 1982; Johansson 1987; Kneese 1984; Mitchell and Carson

1989; Pearce and Markandya 1989; Smith and Desvousges 1986). Three broad categories of valuation techniques may be distinguished.[16] This appendix briefly reviews the main techniques and assesses their usefulness for the valuation of materials damage.[17]

### *Surrogate Markets Techniques*

The surrogate markets technique involves finding a market in a good or service that is influenced by the nonmarketed good. The hedonic property price approach is based on this idea. Environmental quality affects the decision to purchase a particular house, and the price of the house should be influenced by the environmental attributes of the property. The price of the property, $Hp$, is dependent on site variables, $S$, accessibility, $A$, neighborhood characteristics, $N$, and environmental lack of quality, $Q$. Then,

$$Hp = f(S, A, N, Q). \tag{5A-1}$$

The specific form of this equation is important, but if it is specified in log linear terms, a regression equation of the form

$$\ln \cdot Hp = a(\ln \cdot S) + b(\ln \cdot A) + c(\ln \cdot N) + d(\ln \cdot Q) \tag{5A-2}$$

enables a direct estimate of the effect of $Q$ on $Hp$ to be determined independent of the absolute levels of $Q$ and $HP$. The marginal willingness to pay to reduce $Q$ is then

$$dHp \;/\; dQ = w. \tag{5A-3}$$

Many hedonic price studies stop at estimating $w$, but theory technically requires that $w$ should then be regressed on a set of household characteristics, such as income and family size, and environmental quality:

$$w = g(H, Q). \tag{5A-4}$$

The area under this inverse demand function, between the relevant environmental quality levels, is an estimate of the benefit of improved environmental quality.

The travel cost method identifies the expenditures made by travelers as the surrogate market. A household's utility, $U$, depends on recreation, $R$, and other goods, $E$:

$$U = U(R, E). \tag{5A-5}$$

The recreational services of site $i$ are dependent on the number of visits to the site, $Vi$, the time taken to get there, $Ti$, and the attributes of the site, $Ai$:

$$Ri = R(Vi, Ti, Ai). \tag{5A-6}$$

The household's budget constraint is

$$Y = wH + N + L = E + \{[Di + (Q \cdot Ti)] \cdot Vi\}. \tag{5A-7}$$

Its time constraint is

(5A-8) $$T = H + (Ti \cdot Vi)$$

where $Y$ = potential income, $N$ = nonwage income, $L$ = income forgone due to recreation, $Di$ = monetary cost of traveling to site $i$, $Q$ = opportunity cost of recreational travel time, $w$ = hourly wage, and $H$ = hours worked. If

(5A-9) $$Pi = Di + (Q \cdot Ti)$$

the demand function for $R$ becomes

(5A-10) $$R = R(P1, P2 \ldots Pi; Y).$$

From equation 5A-6, and assuming that the relationship between $Vi$ and $Ri$ is strictly increasing, we have

(5A-11) $$Vi = Vi(Ti, Ai, Ri).$$

Next, assume $Vi$ consists of two parts, one depending on $Ti$ and $Ri$ only, the other depending on $Ai$ only. Then,

(5A-12) $$Vi = G(Ti, Ri) \cdot H(Ai).$$

Equation 5A-12 says that the services of each site can be transferred into units $H(Ai)$ that are comparable across sites. An equal expenditure on two sites $i$ and $j$ will lead to visit rates $Vi$ and $Vj$ such that

(5A-13) $$Vi \;/\; Vj = H(Ai) \;/\; H(Aj)$$

where $Vi \;/\; H(Ai)$ is now the attribute-adjusted number of visits.

Households are assumed to minimize the cost of securing a given level of recreational services, $R$. This means that the approach will equalize the unit costs per visit to each site:

(5A-14) $$Pi \;/\; H(Ai) = Pj \;/\; H(Aj).$$

We can now write the minimum cost of securing $R$ as $C$, where

(5A-15) $$C = C[Pi \;/\; H(Ai), R].$$

The demand function for $Vi$ given $R$ is now $dC \;/\; dPi$. $R$, in turn, can be written as a function of attribute-adjusted prices and income (see equation 5A-10). Substituting this for $R$ in equation 5A-15 gives

(5A-16) $$Vi = V\,[Pi, H(Ai), Y].$$

This equation needs to be estimated:

(5A-17) $$\ln \cdot Vi = a(Ai) + b(Ai)Pi + c(Ai)Y$$

where the coefficients $a$, $b$, and $c$ are functions of the site attributes. Estimation tends to take place in two stages.

The hedonic wage approach also uses a surrogate market, the labor market, to value risks to life and limb. The assumption is that such risks will attract wage premia. A regression of the form

$$W = W(S, I, J) \tag{5A-18}$$

can be established, where $S$ refers to site-specific variables such as air pollution and crime; $I$ refers to individual-specific variables such as race, sex, education, and job experience; and $J$ refers to job-specific variables such as injury rates. Hedonic wage approaches have been widely used to value occupational risks of injury and death (for a survey of the findings of hedonic wage models, see Viscusi 1986).

Discrete choice techniques look at situations in which an implicit price is expressed for a nonmarketed good through the choice of a marketed good. The most notable example of valuation through discrete choice is the valuation of time. Someone using a travel mode A, say, and paying $Pa$ for a journey time of $Ta$, may have chosen this mode over an alternative mode B with price $Pb$ and journey time $Tb$. If $Pa > Pb$ and $Ta < Tb$, the implied value of time saved $Tb - Ta$ is $Pa - Pb$, and the value of a unit of time is

$$Vt = (Pa - Pb) / (Tb - Ta). \tag{5A-19}$$

*Market Creation Techniques*

With market creation techniques individuals are asked directly about their willingness to pay (or be compensated) for a change in environmental quality. Such techniques are known as contingent valuation methods, although variations, including contingent ranking, exist.

Contingent valuation is founded directly on the theory of consumer behavior. Thus an individual is assumed to have a utility function:

$$U = U(a1, a2 \ldots an; Q1, Q2 \ldots Qn; X) \tag{5A-20}$$

where $a1$ and so forth are activity levels, $Q1$ and so forth are environmental quality levels, and $X$ is a composite commodity. The individual's expenditure is given by

$$E = (Pi \cdot ai) + X \tag{5A-21}$$

where $Pi$ is the price of a unit of activity $ai$. The minimum level of expenditure needed to achieve a utility level $Uo$ is $Mo$, and this equals $Y$ for the consumer's initial equilibrium. Thus,

$$Y = Mo = g(P1o \ldots Pno; Q1o \ldots Qno; Uo). \tag{5A-22}$$

The valuation of an improvement in environmental quality $Q$ that takes the consumer from $Uo$ to $U1$, a higher level of utility, is then one of two measures: willingness to pay (WTP) to go from a lower level of utility to a higher level or willingness to accept (WTA) compensation for the improvement not to take place.

Contingent valuation techniques have been widely used to obtain measures of both WTA and WTP. Typically, they should diverge only slightly as long as the ratio of WTP or WTA to income is small. In practice, WTA estimates have often been much higher than WTP estimates. Ratios of 2–5 are not uncommon (see the discussion in Pearce and Markandya 1989, p. 26). Explanations for the differences range from statistical artefact (because contingent valuation experiments do not repeat valuations in the same way that consumers do when purchasing goods in a real marketplace) to prospect theory (in which consumers are regarded as having kinked valuation functions at a given endowment of environmental quality). Under prospect theory, increments in quality are valued lower than decrements since a decrement removes an entitlement to the initial endowment.

Much of the literature on contingent valuation methods is devoted to determining biases, which may be summarized as follows.

Strategic bias relates to the incentive to undervalue a public good that, if provided to one person, is provided to all. Individuals, it is assumed, understate their preference in the hope that the price charged for the good will be related to their stated maximum willingness to pay. The provision of the good depends on the aggregate willingness to pay that exceeds the cost of provision. This is the classic free rider problem.

Design bias relates to issues in the design of the willingness-to-pay questionnaire. Starting point bias arises when the initial bid is suggested by the interviewer, which biases the respondent's answers. Clearly, if the mean maximum willingness to pay is close to the questioner's starting point, this is a sign of potential starting point bias. Vehicle (or instrument) bias relates to the hypothetical means of payment: answers should not vary significantly according to the means of payment. In the same way, the degree of information given to the respondent affects the valuation. This is not clearly a bias, however, since valuations are influenced by the provision of information in real marketplaces.

Hypothetical bias is clearly a risk when a questionnaire poses hypothetical questions; in this case, the answers may not correspond to the amount that individuals are willing to pay when the time comes to express real values by paying up. Modern analysts discuss hypothetical bias in content, criterion, and construct validity (the definitive volume on contingent valuation is Mitchell and Carson 1989). Content validity relates to asking the right questions in an appropriate manner and can be assessed only as a matter of expert judgment. Criterion validity relates the hypothetical value to some real value, or market price. Some studies have sought to measure criterion validity by relating expressed WTP to WTP when actual money changes hands. Construct validity is the extent to which different measures of WTP agree with one another, none of which, however, is close to the criterion validity measure (convergent validity) or to theoretical expectations (theoretical validity).

Contingent ranking requires respondents to order outcomes for combinations of goods and payment requirements. Rather than directly asking for WTP, it infers WTP from the rankings. Thus a combination of environmental quality level *Q*1 and a price tag of *P*1 is compared to a combination of *Q*2 and *P*2, and so on. Respondents are then asked to rank the combinations (for a detailed discussion of contingent ranking, see Smith and Desvousges 1986; unfortunately, few studies of comparative ranking exist on which to base an empirical assessment). The rankings are then used to determine a valuation. It is not clear, however, whether attitude or behavioral intent is being measured.

### *Dose-response Relationships*

Dose-response relationships, or production function approaches, are perhaps the most familiar valuation technique. Essentially, a link is established between, say, a pollution level and a physical response, for example, the rate at which the surface of a material decays. The decay is then valued by applying the market price (costs of repair) or by borrowing a unit valuation from nonmarket studies. Notable examples include the valuation of health damage. Once air pollution is linked to morbidity and morbidity is linked to days lost from work, the days lost can be valued, perhaps using a market wage rate. The main effort of the analysis is devoted to identifying the link between the dose and the response. Valuation itself tends to be fairly secondary to the research effort.

## Notes

1. The literature on option value is extensive (see Bishop 1982, 1988; Freeman 1985; Johansson 1988; Plummer 1986). The sign of option value is indeterminate but may be expected to be positive if the future demand for the asset in question (the tropical forest, in this case) is certain and the supply is uncertain.

2. We do not dwell on the way in which TEV is derived here, but Hoehn and Randall (1989) have shown that estimating the component parts separately, and then summing them, is not formally identical to TEV estimated by a sequential procedure in which, say, existence value is estimated first, followed by site experience value, and then by activity-related values at the site. This is because the consumer surplus for a bundle of goods is not the same as the sum of consumer surpluses on individual goods.

3. Option value must be distinguished from quasi-option value (QOV). Arrow and Fisher (1974) introduced QOV to deal with the issue of project choice under conditions of uncertainty and irreversibility, where efficiency in decisionmaking may be influenced by the acquisition of additional information. Supply uncertainty, on the one hand, assumes that the valuer can control probabilities of the state of the environment in the future. QOV, on the other hand, relates to situations in which new information can be generated that will affect the assessment of costs and benefits. QOV would be relevant, for example, for assessing deforestation when genetic assets have unknown, or imperfectly known, economic value due to lack of research.

4. Dixon and others (1988) use land values for these outputs. This is misleading, however; whereas land values refer to the market price of the land, these outputs refer to the

value of output from the land. They are linked, of course, in that, under competitive conditions, the land value should equal the discounted value of the net profits from the land.

5. The scale of water vending in the developing world is substantial and perhaps unappreciated. In a study of Onitsha, Nigeria, Whittington, Lauria, and Mu (1989) found that households were paying $28,000 per day for 3 million gallons of water in the dry season to vendors who collected water from wells and resold it to other vendors, businesses, and households. In comparison, the public utility sold 1.5 million gallons per day for just $1,100.

6. Economic value should not be confused with financial or commercial value. Anything contributing to human welfare is deemed to be an economic function, and the flow of services may or may not be associated with a cash flow. Most of the functions of tropical forests do not have evident cash flows.

7. A detailed survey of systems for managing tropical moist forests concluded that only 1 percent of the 828 million hectares of productive forest is under sustained-yield management (Poore 1989, chap. 7). Sustained-yield management is consistent with two regimes that follow the completion of logging. One involves intensive silvicultural treatment. The other involves leaving the forest to regenerate on its own because the returns to silvicultural treatment are uncertain. Large areas of Malaysian forests are subject to this nonintervention approach, as are those of the forests of Cameroon, the Central African Republic, Congo, and Gabon. On this second basis, then, sustained-yield management is far more widespread. We are indebted to Jeff Sayer for this point.

8. For the view that sustained forest management should be based on clear-cutting and the maximum use of biomass, see Hartshorn, Simeone, and Tosi (1987). The analysis tends to assume that market conditions are right, which means that timber production takes place near to markets.

9. Leslie (1988) suggests that shadow pricing favors the more natural management systems.

10. We are indebted to Simon Reitbergen for this point.

11. One company advertises a tour with a two-day excursion into Amazonia. The excursion costs an additional $250 to the basic charge of $2,300. As a very rough guide, therefore, each visitor day could be worth $125.

12. Farnsworth and Morris (1976); Farnsworth and Soejarto (1985). A figure of $8 billion is quoted as the value of prescribed plant-based drugs for the United States. Principe (1987) calculates a figure for all countries in the Organisation for Economic Co-operation and Development of $43 billion in 1985, including over-the-counter drugs.

13. We are indebted to Jack Ruitenbeek for his assistance in clarifying the argument in this section. Much of the literature on the carbon value of tropical forests is misleading because it fails to take into account uses of the timber culled from deforestation and the subsequent use of the land. For an exercise in calculating carbon credits for temperate forests, see Pearce (1990a).

14. Some economists are concerned, however, that such valuations may be counterpreferential (inconsistent with the preference of individuals) in the same way that acts of duty or obligation are counterpreferential. If true, this may have implications for the underlying structure of the welfare economics used to evaluate resource worth. See Brookshire, Eubanks, and Sorg (1986).

15. These are second-best procedures because the measure required is the willingness to pay for a reduced risk. In fact, the link between the wages received for a day's work and willingness to pay to avoid losing that day is ambiguous. For further discussion, see chapter 6.

16. Some writers add other techniques, such as the use of expert assessments or values implied by past government decisions. These are not strictly valuation techniques, however, since they are rooted in the need to determine the valuations of individuals rather than those of representatives or experts. In the same vein, several authors regard opportunity cost as a valuation technique. This involves looking at, say, a development and valuing its benefits. The conservation sacrificed by the development is then valued as the benefits of the development. This is obviously circular reasoning.

17. This section is presented in formal terms. Readers wishing for more intuitive explanations of the various procedures should see an explanatory text on valuation, such as Pearce and Markandya (1989).

# *References*

Altaf, M. A., H. Jamal, J. Liu, V. K. Smith, and D. Whittington. 1990. "Prices and Connection Decisions for Public Water Systems in Developing Countries: A Case Study of the Punjab, Pakistan." Applied Economics Research Centre, Karachi, Pakistan. Processed.

Arrow, Kenneth J., and Anthony Fisher. 1974. "Environmental Preservation, Uncertainty, and Irreversibility." *Quarterly Journal of Economics* 88: 312–19.

Bentkover, Judith D., and others. 1986. *Benefits Assessment: The State of the Art.* Dordrecht, Netherlands: D. Reidel Publishing Company.

Binswanger, Hans P. 1989. "Brazilian Policies That Encourage Deforestation in the Amazon." Working Paper 16. World Bank, Environment Department, Washington, D.C. Processed.

———. 1982. "Option Value: An Exposition and Extension." *Land Economics* 58 (1): 1–15.

———. 1988. "Option Value: Reply." *Land Economics* 64: 88–93.

Bishop, Richard C., Kevin J. Boyle, and Michael Walsh. 1987. "Towards Total Economic Valuation of Great Lakes Fishery Resources." *Transactions of the American Fisheries Society* 116: 339–45.

Bojo, Jan, Karl-Goran Mäler, and Lena Unemo. 1990. *Environment and Development: An Economic Approach.* Dordrecht, Netherlands, and Boston, Mass.: Kluwer Academic Publishers.

Bowker, J. M., and John R. Stoll. 1988. "Use of Dichotomous Choice Nonmarket Methods to Value the Whooping Crane Resource." *American Journal of Agricultural Economics* 70: 372–81

Boyle, Kevin J., and Richard C. Bishop. 1987. "Valuing Wildlife in Benefit-Cost Analysis: A Case Study Involving Endangered Species." *Water Resources Research* 23: 943–50.

Briones, Nicomedes. 1986. "Estimating Erosion Costs: A Philippine Case Study in the Lower Agno River Watershed." In K. William Easter, John Dixon, and Maynard Hufschmidt, eds., *Watershed Resources Management: An Integrated Framework with Studies from Asia and the Pacific.* Singapore: Institute of Southeast Asian Studies.

Brookshire, David, Larry Eubanks, and Alan Randall. 1983. "Estimating Option Prices and Existence Values for Wildlife Resources." *Land Economics* 59: 1–15.

Brookshire, David S., Larry Eubanks, and Cindy F. Sorg. 1986. "Existence Values and Normative Economics: Implications for Valuing Water Resources." *Water Resources Research* 22 (11): 1509–18.

Brookshire, David S., William Schulze, and M. Thayer. 1985 "Some Unusual Aspects of Valuing a Unique Natural Resource." University of Wyoming, Department of Economics, Laramie. Processed.

Browder, John O. 1988a. "Public Policy and Deforestation in the Brazilian Amazon." In Robert Repetto and Malcolm Gillis, eds., *Public Policies and the Misuse of Forest Resources.* Cambridge, Eng.: Cambridge University Press.

———. 1988b. "The Social Costs of Rain Forest Destruction: A Critique and Economic Analysis of the 'Hamburger Debate.'" *Interciencia* 13 (3): 115–20.

Brown, Gardner. 1986. "Preserving Endangered Species and Other Biological Resources." *The Science of the Total Environment* 56: 89–97.

Button, Kenneth, and David W. Pearce. 1989. "Infrastructure Restoration as a Tool for Stimulating Urban Renewal: The Glasgow Canal." *Urban Studies* 26: 559–73.

Cummings, Ronald G., David S. Brookshire, and William Schulze. 1986. *Valuing Environmental Goods*. Totowa, N.J.: Rowman and Allanheld.

de Beer, Jenne H., and Melanie J. McDermott. 1989. "The Economic Value of Non-timber Products in South-east Asia." International Union for the Conservation of Nature, Netherlands Committee, Amsterdam, Netherlands. Processed.

Desvousges, William H., V. Kerry Smith, and Anne Fisher. 1987. "Option Price Estimates for Water Quality Improvements: A Contingent Valuation Study for the Monongahela River." *Journal of Environmental Economics and Management* 14: 248–67.

Dixon, John, and others. 1988. *Economic Analysis of the Environmental Impacts of Development Projects*. London: Earthscan Publications in association with the Asian Development Bank.

Dogse, Peter. 1989. "Sustainable Tropical Rain Forest Management: Some Economic Considerations." Paper prepared for Unesco, Division of Ecological Sciences, Paris. Processed.

Dourojeanni, Marc J. 1985. "Over-Exploited and Under-Used Animals in the Amazon Region." In Ghillean T. Prance and Thomas E. Lovejoy, eds., *Key Environments: Amazonia*. Oxford: Pergamon.

Edwards, Steven F. 1988. "Option Prices for Groundwater Protection." *Journal of Environmental Economics and Management* 15: 475–87.

Farnsworth, Norman R., and R. Morris. 1976. "Higher Plants: The Sleeping Giant of Drug-Development." *American Journal of Pharmacy* 147 (2): 46–52

Farnsworth, Norman R., and Djaja Doel Soejarto. 1985. "Potential Consequence of Plant Extinction in the United States on the Current and Future Availability of Prescription Drugs." *Economic Botany* 39 (3): 231–40.

Feenberg, Daniel, and Edwin Mills. 1980. *Measuring the Benefits of Water Pollution Abatement*. New York: Academic Press.

Fisher, Anthony C., and W. Michael Hanemann. 1987. "Quasi Option Value: Some Misconceptions Dispelled." *Journal of Environmental Economics and Management* 14: 183–90.

Freeman, A. Myrick. 1979. *The Benefits of Environmental Improvement*. Baltimore, Md.: Johns Hopkins University Press.

———. 1982. *Air and Water Pollution Control: A Benefit-Cost Assessment*. New York: Wiley.

———. 1985. "Supply Uncertainty, Option Price, and Option Value in Project Evaluation." *Land Economics* 61; 176–81.

Furtado, Jose I. 1978. "The Status and Future of the Tropical Moist Forest in South East Asia." In Colin MacAndrews and Lin Sien Chia, eds., *Developing Economies in South East Asia and the Environment.* New York: McGraw Hill.

Furtado, Jose I., and Kenneth Ruddle. 1986. "The Future of Tropical Forests." In Nicholas Polunin, ed., *Ecosystem Theory and Application.* New York: Wiley.

Gradwohl, Judith, and Russell Greenberg. 1988. *Saving the Tropical Forests.* London: Earthscan Publications.

Green, Colin H., and S. M. Tunstall. 1991. "The Evaluation of River Water Quality Improvements by the Contingent Valuation Method." *Applied Economics* 23: 1135–46.

Green, Colin H., S. M. Tunstall, A. N'jai, and A. Rogers. 1988. "Evaluating the Benefits of River Water Quality Improvements." Middlesex Polytechnic Flood Hazard Research Centre, Middlesex, Eng. Processed.

———. 1989. "Water Quality: The Public Dimension." In David Wheeler and others, eds., *Watershed 89: The Future for Water Quality in Europe.* Oxford: Pergamon.

———. 1990. "The Economic Evaluation of Environmental Goods." *Project Appraisal* 5(2): 70—82.

Hamilton, Lawrence S., and Peter N. King. 1983. *Tropical Forested Watersheds: Hydrologic and Soils Response to Major Uses or Conversions.* Boulder, Colo.: Westview Press.

Hanley, Nick. 1988. "Using Contingent Valuation to Value Environmental Improvements." *Applied Economics* 20: 541–51.

———. 1989. "Valuing Rural Recreational Benefits: An Empirical Comparison of Two Approaches." *Journal of Agricultural Economics* 40 (Part III, September): 361–74.

Harley, David C., and Nick Hanley. 1989. "Economic Benefit Estimates for Nature Reserves: Methods and Results." Discussion Paper in Economics 89/6. University of Stirling, Scotland. Processed.

Hartshorn, G., R. Simeone, and J. Tosi. 1987. "Sustained Yield Management of Tropical Forests: A Synopsis of the Palcazú Development Project in the Central Selva of the Peruvian Amazon." Tropical Science Center, San José, Costa Rica. Processed.

Henry, C. 1974. "Option Values in the Economics of Irreplaceable Resources." *Review of Economic Studies* 41: 88–93.

Herrera, R. 1985. "Nutrient Cycling in Amazonian Forests." In Ghillean Prance and Thomas E. Lovejoy, eds., *Key Environments: Amazonia.* Oxford: Pergamon.

Hodgson, Gregor, and John Dixon. 1988. *Logging versus Fisheries and Tourism in Palawan.* Occasional Paper 7. Honolulu, Hawaii: East-West Environment and Policy Institute.

Hoehn, John P., and Alan Randall. 1989. "Too Many Proposals Pass the Benefit-Cost Test." *American Economic Review* 79: 544–51.

Hosier, R., and M. Bernstein. 1989. "Woodfuel Use and Sustainable

Development in Haiti." University of Pennsylvania, Center for Energy and Development, Philadelphia, Penn. Processed.

Houghton, R. A. 1990. "The Future Role of Tropical Forests in Affecting the Carbon Dioxide Concentration of the Atmosphere." *Ambio* 19 (4): 204–09.

Houghton, R. A., and others. 1985. "Net Flux of Carbon Dioxide from Tropical Forests in 1980." *Nature* 316 (August): 617–20.

Johansson, Per-Olov. 1987. *The Economic Theory and Measurement of Environmental Benefits*. New York: Cambridge University Press.

———. 1988. "On the Properties of Supply-Side Option Value." *Land Economics* 64: 86–87.

Kneese, Allen V. 1984. *Measuring the Benefits of Clean Air and Water.* Washington, D.C.: Resources for the Future.

Leonard, H. Jeffrey. 1987. *Natural Resources and Economic Development in Central America: A Regional Environmental Profile.* New Brunswick, Canada: Transaction Books.

Leslie, Alan J. 1988. "A Second Look at the Economics of Natural Management Systems in Tropical Mixed Forests." *Unasylva* 39 (155): 46–58.

MacRea, Duncan, and Dale Whittington. 1988. "Assessing Preferences in Cost-Benefit Analysis: Reflections on Rural Water Supply Evaluation in Haiti." *Journal of Policy Analysis and Management* 7 (2): 246–63.

Mahar, Dennis J. 1989. *Government Policies and Deforestation in Brazil's Amazon Region.* Washington, D.C.: World Bank

Markandya, Anil, and David W. Pearce. 1988. "Environmental Considerations and the Choice of Discount Rate in Developing Countries." Working Paper 3. World Bank, Environment Department, Washington, D.C. Processed.

———. 1989. "Marginal Opportunity Cost as a Planning Concept in Natural Resource Management." In Gunter Schramm and Jeremy Warford, eds., *Environmental Management and Economic Development.* Baltimore, Md.: Johns Hopkins University Press.

Meybeck, Michel, Deborah V. Chapman, and Richard Helmer. 1990. *Global Freshwater Quality; A First Assessment.* Oxford: Blackwell Reference for the World Health Organization and the United Nations Environment Programme.

Mitchell, Robert Cameron, and Richard T. Carson. 1989. *Using Surveys to Value Public Goods: The Contingent Valuation Method.* Washington, D.C.: Resources for the Future.

Mu, Xinming, Dale Whittington, and John Briscoe. 1991. "Modelling Village Water Demand Behaviour: A Discrete Choice Approach." *Water Resources Research* 26 (24): 521–29.

Myers, Norman. 1983. "Tropical Moist Forests: Over-Exploited and Under-Utilized?" *Forest Ecology and Management* 6: 59–79.

———. 1988. "Natural Resource Systems and Human Exploitation Systems: Physiobiotic and Ecological Linkages." Working Paper 12. World Bank, Environment Department, Washington, D.C. Processed.

———. 1990. "The Greenhouse Effect: A Tropical Forestry Response." *Biomass* 18: 73–78.

Naess, Arne. 1973. "The Shallow and the Deep Long-Range Ecology Movement: A Summary." *Inquiry* 16 (1): 95–100.

Nordhaus, William D. 1991. "To Slow or Not To Slow: The Economics of the Greenhouse Effect." *Economic Journal* 101 (July).

Ostro, Bart D. 1983. "The Effects of Air Pollution on Work Loss and Morbidity." *Journal of Environmental Economics and Management* 10: 371–82.

Pearce, David W. 1987. "Forest Policy in Indonesia." World Bank, Indonesia Department, Washington, D.C. Processed.

———. 1989. "Economic Incentives and Renewable Natural Resource Management." In OECD, *Renewable and Natural Resources: Economic Incentives for Improved Management.* Paris.

———. 1990a. "Assessing the Returns to the Economy and to Society from Investment in Forestry." *Forestry Expansion.* Edinburgh, Scotland: Forestry Commission.

Pearce, David W., Edward Barbier, and Anil Markandya. 1990. *Sustainable Development: Economics and Environment in the Third World.* London: Earthscan Publications.

Pearce, David W., and Anil Markandya. 1989. *The Benefits of Environmental Policy: Monetary Valuation.* Paris: OECD.

Pearce, David W., and R. Kerry Turner. 1989. *Economics of Natural Resources and the Environment.* London: Harvester-Wheatsheaf.

Peters, Charles M., Alwyn H. Gentry, and Robert O. Mendelsohn. 1989. "Valuation of an Amazonian Rain Forest." *Nature* 339 (June): 65–56.

Plummer, Mark L. 1986. "Supply Uncertainty, Option Price, and Option Value." *Land Economics* 62: 313–18.

Plummer, Mark L., and Richard C. Hartman. 1986. "Option Value: A General Approach." *Economic Inquiry* 24: 455–71.

Poore, Duncan. 1989. *No Timber without Trees: Sustainability in the Tropical Forest.* London: Earthscan Publications.

Principe, Peter. 1987. *The Economic Value of Biological Diversity among Medicinal Plants.* Paris: OECD.

Randall, Alan. 1987. "Total Economic Value as a Basis for Policy." *Transactions of the American Fisheries Society* 116: 325–35.

———. 1990. "Nonuse Benefits." Ohio State University, Columbus. Processed.

Rauscher, Michael. 1991. "Foreign Trade and the Environment." In Horst Siebert, ed., *Environmental Scarcity: The International Dimension.* Tubingen, Germany: J. C. Mohr.

Regan, Trevor. 1981. "The Nature and Possibility of an Environmental Ethic." *Environmental Ethics* 3: 19–34.

Repetto, Robert. 1990. "Deforestation in the Tropics." *Scientific American* 262 (4); 36–42.

Repetto, Robert, and Malcolm Gillis, eds. 1988. *Public Policies and the Misuse of Forest Resources.* Cambridge, Eng.: Cambridge University Press.

Ruitenbeek, H. Jack. 1989. *Social Cost-Benefit Analysis of the Korup Project, Cameroon.* London: Worldwide Fund for Nature.

Salati, Eneas, and others. 1979. "Recycling of Water in the Amazon Basin: An Isotopic Study." *Water Resources Research* 15: 1250–58.

Samples, Karl C., Marcia Gowen, and John Dixon. 1986. "The Validity of the Contingent Valuation Method for Estimating Non-Use Components of Preservation Values for Unique Natural Resources." Paper presented to a meeting of the American Agricultural Economics Association, Reno, Nevada. Processed.

Schulze, William D., and others. 1983. "Economic Benefits of Preserving Visibility in the National Parklands of the Southwest." *Natural Resources Journal* 23; 149–73.

Sedjo, Roger. 1987a. "The Economics of Natural and Plantation Forests in Indonesia." Resources for the Future, Washington, D.C. Processed.

———. 1987b. "Incentives and Distortions in Indonesian Forest Policy." Resources for the Future, Washington, D.C. Processed.

———. 1989. "Forests to Offset the Greenhouse Effect." *Journal of Forestry* 87: 12–14.

Smith, Kirk R. 1988a. "Air Pollution: Assessing Total Exposure in Developing Countries." *Environment* 30 (10): 16–20, 28–35.

———. 1988b. "Air Pollution: Assessing Total Exposure in the United States." *Environment* 30 (8): 10–15.

Smith, V. Kerry. 1987. "Nonuse Values in Benefit Cost Analysis." *Southern Economic Journal* 54: 19–26.

Smith, V. Kerry, and William H. Desvousges. 1986. *Measuring Water Quality Benefits.* Boston, Mass.: Kluwer-Nijhof.

Southgate, Douglas Dewitt, Rodrigo Sierra, and Lawrence A. Brown. 1989. "The Causes of Tropical Deforestation in Ecuador: A Statistical Analysis." Paper 89–09. London Environmental Economics Centre, London. Processed.

Stoll, John R., and L. Johnson. 1984. "Concepts of Value, Non-Market Valuation, and the Case of the Whooping Crane." *Transactions of the North American Wildlife and Natural Resources Conference* 49: 382–93.

Sutherland, Ronald J., and Richard G. Walsh. 1985. "Effects of Distance on the Preservation Value of Water Quality." *Land Economics* 61: 281–91.

Thomas, D., F. Ayache, and T. Hollis. 1989. "Use Values and Non-Use Values in the Conservation of Ichkeul National Park, Tunisia." University College London, Department of Geography. Processed.

Turner, Jan, and J. Brooke, 1988. "A Cost-Benefit Analysis of the Aldeburgh Sea Defence Scheme." Environmental Appraisal Group, University of East Anglia. Processed.

Viscusi, W. Kip. 1986. "Valuation of Risks to Life and Health: Guidelines for Policy Analysis." In Judith Bentkover and others, eds., *Benefits Assessment: The State of the Art.* Dordrecht, Netherlands: D. Reidel Publishing Company.

Walsh, Julia A., and Kenneth S. Warren. 1979. "Selective Primary Health

Care: An Interim Strategy for Disease Control in Developing Countries." *New England Journal of Medicine* 301 (18): 967–74.

Walsh, Richard G., John B. Loomis, and Richard A. Gillman. 1984. "Valuing Option, Existence, and Bequest Demands for Wilderness." *Land Economics* 60: 14–29.

Weil, Diana E., and others. 1990. *The Impact of Development Policies on Health: A Review of the Literature.* Geneva, Switzerland: WHO.

Weisbrod, Burton. 1964. "Collective Consumption Services of Individual Consumption Goods." *Quarterly Journal of Economics* 78: 471–77.

Whitmore, Timothy Charles. 1990. *An Introduction to Tropical Rain Forests.* Oxford: Clarendon Press.

Whittington, Dale, Donald T. Lauria, and Xinming Mu. 1989. "Paying for Urban Services: A Study of Water Vending and Willingness to Pay for Water in Onitsha, Nigeria." World Bank, Infrastructure and Urban Development Department, Washington, D.C. Processed.

Whittington, Dale, Xinming Mu, and Robert Roche. 1990. "Calculating the Value of Time Spent Collecting Water: Some Estimates for Ukundu, Kenya." *World Development* 18 (2): 269–80.

Whittington, Dale, and others. 1989. "Water Vending Activities in Developing Countries." *Water Resources Development* 5 (3): 158–68.

———. 1990. "Estimating the Willingness to Pay for Water Services in Developing Countries: A Case Study of the Use of Contingent Valuation Surveys in Southern Haiti." *Economic Development and Cultural Change.*

Willis, Kenneth G., and John Benson. 1988. "Valuation of Wildlife: A Case Study on the Upper Teesdale Site of Special Scientific Interest and Comparison of Methods in Environmental Economics." In R. Kerry Turner, ed., *Sustainable Environmental Management: Principles and Practice.* London: Belhaven Press.

World Resources Institute. 1990. *World Resources 1990–91.* Oxford: Oxford University Press.

———. 1992. *World Resources 1992–93: A Guide to the Global Environment.* New York: Oxford University Press.

# [15]

# *Wasting assets: natural resources in the national income accounts*

***Robert Repetto, William Magrath, Michael Wells, Christine Beer and Fabrizio Rossini***

## THE NEED FOR NATURAL RESOURCE ACCOUNTING

### Overview and recommendations

Whatever their shortcomings, and however little their construction is understood by the general public, the national income accounts are undoubtedly one of the most significant social inventions of the twentieth century. Their political and economic impact can scarcely be overestimated. However inappropriately, they serve to divide the world into "developed" and "less developed" countries. In the "developed countries," whenever the quarterly gross national product (GNP) figures emerge, policy-makers stir. Should they be lower, even marginally, than those of the preceding three months, a recession is declared, the strategies and competence of the administration is impugned, and public political debate ensues. In the "developing" countries, the rate of growth of GNP is the principal measure of economic progress and transformation.

The national accounts have become so much a part of our life that it is hard to remember that they are scarcely fifty years old. They were first published in the United States in the year 1942. It is no coincidence that the period during which these measures have been available, with all their imperfections, has been the period within which governments in all developed and most developing countries have taken responsibility for the growth and stability of their economies, and during which enormous investments of talent and energy have been made in understanding how economies can be better managed. Forecasting the next few quarterly estimates of these statistics has become, with no exaggeration, a hundred million dollar industry.

The aim of national income accounting is to provide an information framework suitable for analyzing the performance of the economic system. The current system of national accounts reflects the Keynesian macroeconomic model that was dominant when the system was developed. The great aggregates of Keynesian analysis – consumption, savings, investment, and government expenditures – are carefully defined and measured. But Keynes and his contemporaries were preoccupied with the Great Depression and the business cycle; specifically, with explaining how an economy could remain for long periods of time at less than full employment. The least of their worries was a scarcity of natural resources. Unfortunately, as Keynesian analysis largely ignored the productive role of natural resources, so does the current system of national accounts.

**Wasting assets**

In fact, natural resource scarcity played little part in 19th century neo-classical economics, from which traditional Keynesian and most contemporary economic theories are derived. Gone were the dismal predictions of Ricardo, Malthus, Marx, and other earlier classical economists that industrial economies would stagnate or collapse because of rising rents and subsistence wages. In 19th century Europe, steamships and railroads were markedly lowering transport costs while foodgrains and raw materials were flooding in from North and South America, Australia, Russia, and the imperial colonies. What mattered to England and other industrializing nations was the pace of investment and technological change. The classical economists had regarded income as the return on three kinds of assets: natural resources, human resources, and invested capital (land, labor, and capital, in their vocabulary). The neo-classical economists virtually dropped natural resources from their model and concentrated on labor and invested capital. When these theories were applied after World War II to problems of economic development in the Third World, human resources were also left out on the grounds that labor was always "surplus," and development was seen almost entirely as a matter of savings and investment in physical capital.

As a result, there is a dangerous asymmetry today in the way we measure, and hence, the way we think about, the value of natural resources. Man-made assets – buildings and equipment, for example – are valued as productive capital, and are written off against the value of production as they depreciate. This practice recognizes that a consumption level maintained by drawing down the stock of capital exceeds the sustainable level of income. Natural resource assets are not so valued, and their loss entails no debit charge against current income that would account for the decrease in potential future production. A country could exhaust its mineral resources, cut down its forests, erode its soils, pollute its aquifers, and hunt its wildlife and fisheries to extinction, but measured income would not be affected as these assets disappeared. Ironically, low-income countries, which are typically most dependent on natural resources for employment, revenues, and foreign exchange earnings are instructed to use a system for national accounting and macroeconomic analysis that almost completely ignores their principal assets.

Underlying this anomaly is the implicit and inappropriate assumption that natural resources are so abundant that they have no marginal value. This is a misunderstanding. Whether they enter the marketplace directly or not, natural resources make important contributions to long-term economic productivity and so are, strictly speaking, economic assets. Many are under increasing pressure from human activities and are deteriorating in quantity or quality.

Another misunderstanding underlies the contention that natural resources are "free gifts of nature," so that there are no investment costs to be "written off." The value of an asset is not its investment cost, but the present value of its income potential. Many companies valued by the stock market as worth many billions of dollars have as their principal assets the brilliant ideas and inventions of their founders: the Polaroid Camera, the Apple Computer, the Lotus Spreadsheet, for example. These inspired inventions are worth vastly more than any measurable costs to their inventors in developing them and could also be regarded as the products of genius – free gifts of nature.

Common formulas for calculating depreciation by "writing off" investment costs (e.g., straight line depreciation) are just convenient rules of thumb, or artifacts of tax legislation. The true measure of depreciation, which statisticians have tried to adopt for fixed capital in the national accounts, is the capitalized value of the decline in the future income stream because of an asset's decay or obsolescence. (Usher 1980, pp. 104–105) Thus, in the same sense that a machine depreciates, soils depreciate as their fertility is diminished since they can produce only at higher costs or lower yields.

Codified in the United Nations system of national accounts closely followed by most countries, this difference in the treatment of natural resources and other tangible assets provides false signals to policymakers. It reinforces the false dichotomy between economy and the "environment" that leads policymakers to ignore or destroy the latter in the name of economic development. It confuses the depreciation of valuable assets with the generation of income. Thus it promotes and seems to validate the idea that rapid rates of economic growth can be achieved and sustained by exploiting the resource base. The result can be illusory gains in income and permanent losses in wealth.

Indeed, natural resource assets are legitimately drawn upon to finance economic growth, especially in resource-dependent countries. The revenues derived from resource extraction finance investments in industrial capacity, infrastructure, and education. A reasonable accounting representation of the process, however, would recognize that one kind of asset has been exchanged for another, which is expected to yield a higher return. Should a farmer cut and sell the timber in his woods to raise money for a new barn, his private accounts would reflect the acquisition of a new asset, the barn, and the loss of an old asset, the timber. He thinks himself better off because the barn is worth more to him than the timber. In the national accounts, however, income and investment would rise as the barn is built, but income would also rise as the wood is cut. The value of the timber, less that of any intermediate purchases (e.g., gas and oil for the chainsaw) would be credited to value added in the logging industry. Nowhere is the loss of a valuable asset reflected. This can lead to serious miscalculation of the development potential of resource-dependent economies by confusing gross and net capital formation. Even worse, should the proceeds of resource depletion be used to finance current consumption, then the economic path is ultimately unsustainable, whatever the national accounts say. If the same farmer used the proceeds from his timber sale to finance a winter vacation, he would be poorer on his return and no longer able to afford the barn, but national income would only register a gain, not a loss in wealth.

Many countries now heavily burdened with debt are resource-dependent: Mexico, Venezuela, and Nigeria are oil exporters, for example. Their national balance sheets before the debt crisis deteriorated substantially as they drew down national resource assets and piled up external debt, using the proceeds of both to finance consumption and subsidize investments of little or no economic value. A national accounting system that drew attention to their deteriorating asset positions might have alerted policy-makers to the need for policy changes and international lenders to the growing risks of further exposure.

The fundamental definition of income encompasses the notion of sustainability. In accounting and in economics textbooks, income is defined as the maximum amount that the recipient could consume in a given period without reducing the amount of possible consumption in a future period (Edwards and Bell 1961; Hicks 1946). Business income is defined as the maximum amount the firm could pay out in current dividends without reducing net worth. This income concept encompasses not only current earnings but also changes in asset positions: capital gains are a source of income, and capital losses are a reduction in income. The depreciation accounts reflect the fact that unless the capital stock is maintained and replaced, future consumption possibilities will inevitably decline. In resource-dependent countries, failure to extend this depreciation concept to the capital stock embodied in natural resources, which are such a significant source of income and consumption, is a major omission and inconsistency.

This is not academic hairsplitting. For resource-based economics, evaluations of economic performance and estimates of macroeconomic relationships are seriously distorted by failure to account for natural resource depreciation. In this report, Indonesia is used as an example. Over the past 20 years, Indonesia has drawn heavily on its considerable natural resource endowment to finance development expenditures. Revenues from production of oil, gas, hard minerals, timber, and forest products have offset a large share of government development and routine expenditures. Primary production contributes more than 43 percent of gross domestic product, 83 percent of exports, and 55 percent of total employment. Indonesia's economic performance over this period is generally judged to have been successful: per capita GDP growth averaging 4.6 percent per year from 1965 to 1986 has been exceeded by only a handful of low and middle-income countries, and is far above the average for those groups. Gross domestic investment rose from 8 percent of GDP in 1965, at the end of the Sukarno era, to 26 percent of GDP (also well above average) in 1986, despite low oil prices and a difficult debt situation (World Bank 1988).

Estimates derived from the Indonesian country case study, presented in more detail in Part II of this report, illustrate how much this evaluation is affected by "keeping score" more correctly. Table 25.1 and Figure 25.1 compare the growth of gross domestic product at constant prices with the growth of net domestic product, derived by subtracting estimates of net natural resource depreciation for only three sectors, petroleum, timber, and soils. It is clear that conventionally measured gross domestic product substantially overstates net income and its growth after accounting for consumption of natural resource capital. In fact, while GDP increased at an average annual rate of 7.1 percent from 1971 to 1984, the period covered by this case study, our estimate of net domestic product rose by only 4.0 percent per year. If 1971, a year of significant additions to petroleum reserves, is excluded, the respective growth rates from 1972 to 1984 are 6.9 percent and 5.4 percent per year, for a gross and net domestic product.

The overstatement of income and its growth may actually be considerably more than these estimates indicate since only petroleum, timber, and soils in Java are covered. Other important exhaustible resources that have been exploited over the period, such as natural gas, coal, copper, tin, and nickel have not yet been included in the accounts. The depreciation of other renewable resources, such as non-timber forest products and fisheries, is also unaccounted for. When complete depreciation accounts are available, they will probably show a greater divergence between growth in gross output and net income.

Other important macroeconomic estimates are even more badly distorted. Table 25.2 and Figure 25.1 compare estimates of gross and net domestic investment, the latter reflecting depreciation of natural resource capital. This statistic is central to economic planning in resource-based economies. Countries such as Indonesia that are heavily dependent on exhaustible natural resources *must* diversify their asset base to preserve a sustainable long-term growth path. Extraction and sale of natural resources must finance investments in other productive capital. It is relevant, therefore, to compare gross domestic

**R. Repetto *et al.***

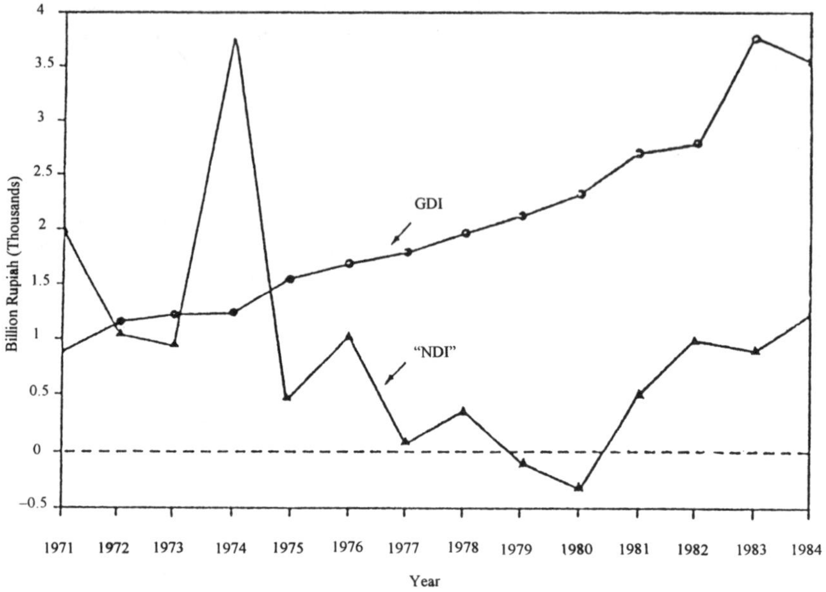


**Figure 25.1** GDI and "NDI," in constant 1973 Rupiah.

**Table 25.1** Comparison of GDP and "NDP" in 1973 Rupiah (billions).

| | | Net change in natural resource sectors[b] | | | | |
|---|---|---|---|---|---|---|
| Year | GDP[a] | Petroleum | Forestry | Soil | Net change | NDP |
| 1971 | 5,545 | 1,527 | –312 | –89 | 1,126 | 6,671 |
| 1972 | 6,067 | 337 | –354 | –83 | –100 | 5,967 |
| 1973 | 6,753 | 407 | –591 | –95 | –279 | 6,474 |
| 1974 | 7,296 | 3,228 | –533 | –90 | 2,605 | 9,901 |
| 1975 | 7,631 | –787 | –249 | –85 | –1,121 | 6,510 |
| 1976 | 8,156 | –187 | –423 | –74 | –684 | 7,472 |
| 1977 | 8,882 | –1,225 | –405 | –81 | –1,711 | 7,171 |
| 1978 | 9,567 | –1,117 | –401 | –89 | –1,607 | 7,960 |
| 1979 | 10,165 | –1,200 | –946 | –73 | –2,219 | 7,946 |
| 1980 | 11,169 | –1,633 | –965 | –65 | –2,663 | 8,506 |
| 1981 | 12,055 | –1,552 | –595 | –68 | –2,215 | 9,840 |
| 1982 | 12,325 | –1,158 | –551 | –55 | –1,764 | 10,561 |
| 1983 | 12,842 | –1,825 | –974 | –71 | –2,870 | 9,972 |
| 1984 | 13,520 | –1,765 | –493 | –76 | –2,334 | 11,186 |
| Average Annual Growth | 7.1% | | | | | 4.0% |

a. In constant 1973 Rupiah, billions. From the Indonesian Central Bureau of Statistics.
b. The flow of resources in each sector is elaborated in the sections on the specific resource later in the text. Positive numbers imply a growth in the physical reserves of that resource during the year.

**Wasting assets**

investment with the value of natural resource depletion. Should gross investment be less than resource depreciation, then, on balance, the country is drawing down, rather than building up, its asset base, and using its natural resources endowment to finance current consumption. Should net investment be positive but less than required to equip new labor force entrants with at least the capital per worker of the existing labor force, then increases in output per worker and income per capital are unlikely. In fact, the results from the Indonesian case study show that the adjustment for natural resource asset changes is large in many years relative to gross domestic investment. In 1971 and 1973, the adjustment is positive, due to additions to petroleum reserves.[1] In most years during the period, however, the depletion adjustment offsets a good part of gross capital formation. In some years, net investment was negative. A fuller accounting of natural resource depletion might conclude that in many years depletion exceeded gross investment, implying that natural resources were being depleted to finance current consumption expenditures.

**Table 25.2** Comparison of GDI and "NDI".

| Year | GDI[a] | Resource depletion[b] | NDI |
|---|---|---|---|
| 1971 | 876 | 1,126 | 2,002 |
| 1972 | 1,139 | − 100 | 1,039 |
| 1973 | 1,208 | −279 | 929 |
| 1974 | 1,224 | 2,605 | 3,829 |
| 1975 | 1,552 | −1,121 | 431 |
| 1976 | 1,690 | −684 | 1,006 |
| 1977 | 1,785 | −1,711 | 74 |
| 1978 | 1,965 | −1,607 | 358 |
| 1979 | 2,128 | −2,219 | −91 |
| 1980 | 2,331 | −2,663 | −332 |
| 1981 | 2,704 | −2,215 | 489 |
| 1982 | 2,783 | −1,764 | 1,019 |
| 1983 | 3,776 | −2,870 | 906 |
| 1984 | 3,551 | −2,334 | 1,217 |

a. In constant 1973 Rupiah, billions. From the Indonesian Central Bureau of Statistics.
b. In constant 1973 Rupiah, billions. Includes depletion of forests, petroleum and the cost of erosion on the island of Java. These figures are explained fully in Part II.

Such an evaluation should flash an unmistakable warning signal to economic policy-makers that they were on an unsustainable course. An economic accounting system that does not generate and highlight such evaluations is deficient as a tool for analysis and policy in resource-based economies and should be amended.

The same holds true with respect to evaluation of performance in particular economic sectors, such as agriculture. Almost three-quarters of the Indonesian population live on the fertile but overcrowded "inner" islands of Java, Bali, and Madura, where lowland irrigated rice paddies are intensively farmed. In the highlands, population pressures have brought steep hillsides into use for cultivation of maize, cassava, and other annual crops. As hillsides have been cleared of trees, erosion has increased, now averaging over 60 tons per hectare per year, by our estimates.

Erosion's economic consequences include loss of nutrients and soil fertility from thin soils, and increased downstream sedimentation in reservoirs, harbors, and irrigation systems. Increased silt concentrations affect fisheries and downstream water users. Although crop yields have improved in the hills because farmers have used better seed and more fertilizers, the estimates imply that the annual depreciation of soil fertility, calculated as the value of the lost farm income, is about 4 percent of the value of crop production, which is as large as the annual production increase. In other words, these estimates suggest that current increases in farm output in Indonesia's uplands are being achieved almost wholly at the expense of potential *future* output. Since the upland population is unlikely to be smaller in the future than it is now, the process of soil erosion represents a transfer of wealth from the future to the present. By ignoring the future costs of soil erosion, the sectoral income accounts significantly overstate the growth of agricultural income in Indonesia's highlands.

A considerable and growing body of expert opinion has recognized the need to remove this anomaly from the accounting framework by accounting for depreciation of natural resource assets like depreciation of other physical capital. In the words of a recent treatise on the measurement of economic growth, "Policy-makers need, among other types of information, a set or sets of accounts which describe the significant dimensions of the system for which they are responsible . . . a cogent argument can be made for the view that the present set of national accounts provides an increasingly deficient representation of the substantive economic activities taking place within the system, and that many of these deficiencies are capable of being remedied by using available data" (Juster 1973, pp. 26–27).

In June 1985, the member governments of the OECD adopted a "Declaration on Environment: Resources for the Future." They declared that they will "ensure that environmental considerations are taken fully into account at an early stage in the development and implementation of economic and other policies by . . . [*inter alia*] . . . improving the management of natural resources, using an integrated approach, with a view to ensuring long-term environmental and economic sustainability. For this purpose, they will develop appropriate mechanisms and techniques, including more accurate resource accounts." (OECD, 1986)

*Our Common Future,* the 1987 report of the World Commission on Environment and Development, stated, "Thus, figuring profits from logging rarely takes full account of the losses in future revenue incurred through degradation of the forest. Similar incomplete accounting occurs in the exploitation of other resources, especially in the case of resources that are not capitalized in enterprise or national accounts: air, water, and soil. *In all countries, rich or poor, economic development must take full account in its measurements of growth of the improvement or deterioration in the stock of natural resources" (Our Common Future,* p. 52).

Similarly, academic experts (Stauffer, 1983) and such international agencies as the OECD have recommended that capital consumption allowances be extended to natural resource assets, such as mineral deposits (OECD, 1986). The World Bank and the United Nations Environment Programme have emphasized the deficiencies in the current accounting system and have sponsored work on improvements. According to a recent Bank publication, "GDP is essentially a short-term measure of economic activity for which exchange occurs in monetary terms. It is of limited usefulness to gauge long-term sustainable growth, partly because natural resource depletion and degradation are being ignored under current practices." (Lutz and El-Sarafy 1988)

A number of OECD member governments, including Canada, France, Netherlands, Australia, and Norway, have carried out substantial statistical work programs to compile accounts on natural resource stocks and stock changes. France and Norway have made perhaps the most extensive official estimates, France's patrimony accounts have emphasized the development of physical accounts (Weber 1983). Norway's resource accounts for energy and other significant economic resources have stressed integration with macroeconomic models and budgets (Alfsen, Bye and Lorentsen 1987). There is a detailed estimate of the national balance sheet of the United States that includes values for timber and subsoil assets, and an important study of national balance sheets covering twenty countries by the same scholar (Goldsmith, 1982, 1985).

Within the last few years, governments in developing countries, recognizing their natural resource dependence, have become interested in a more adequate accounting framework. The World Resources Institute is collaborating on pilot studies with government research institutes and statistical agencies in Indonesia, Costa Rica, and the People's Republic of China. Other governments considering new work programs in natural resources accounting include Thailand, the Ivory Coast, and Argentina. Policy-makers in these countries recognize the need for a planning tool that more effectively integrates economic and ecological considerations.

In filling this need, the United Nations Statistical Office has an important role to play. The U.N. System of National Accounts provides a standard and model that, at least in its core flow accounts, is closely followed by most countries. The U.N. Statistics Office is also a worldwide source of expertise and guidance in the development of national income and other statistical systems.

The system of national accounts (SNA) published by the United Nations Statistical Office (United Nations 1968) is more complete with respect to natural resource accounting than are the accounting systems actually implemented by most national governments. The SNA provides for balance sheets that record opening and closing stocks, and sources of increase and decrease. Such accounts are included for reproducible tangible assets, such as tree plantations, and non-reproducible tangible assets, such as agricultural land and subsoil minerals. The criterion for inclusion in the SNA is whether the assets are privately owned and used in the commercial production of goods and services so that economic values can be established. Natural resources in the public domain, such as surface water, atmosphere, and wilderness, are excluded on the grounds that the SNA deals with the market economy and that the economic values of natural resources outside the market system cannot readily be established.

For natural resource assets included in the SNA, the accounting framework provides for "reconciliation accounts" that link balance sheet and flow accounts. These revaluation accounts encompass changes in opening stocks due to changes in prices during the period, and due to physical changes such as growth, discoveries, depletion, extraction, and natural losses. The valuation principle endorsed by the United Nations for use in these accounts is market asset value, when possible. When direct asset value cannot be established, the U.N. guidelines endorse the economic asset-valuing principle discussed above: the present value of the expected future income stream obtainable from the resource is the measure of the resource's asset value.

**R. Repetto *et al.***

The U.N. Statistical Commission, advised by a number of expert working groups, is currently considering changes in the SNA, as it does periodically. Dissatisfaction stems from many inconsistencies and omissions in the current system. For example, production of goods and services outside the enterprise sector, notably by households, is largely omitted. Also, along with natural resources, other kinds of capital assets, such as knowledge and the stock of skills possessed by the workforce are ignored. Furthermore, in the government sector, the goods and services produced are not directly measured, but are valued at their factor cost. These and many other deficiencies have led to a long agenda of suggested improvements.

Although deliberations will continue until 1991, the U.N. Statistical Commission has evidently already reached the decision that there should be no fundamental changes in the existing SNA. The existing accounting methodology is protected, in a sense, by its very inadequacy; wholesale reform is a large task, and improvement limited to just one aspect is hard to justify when so many other problems would still remain. Moreover, both at the national and international level, decisions regarding the accounting system are in the hands of the *producers* of statistics, not the users. The national income accounts are like sausages: there are many consumers, but few who want to know how they are put together. Partly for this reason, decisions are dominated by the concerns of national income statisticians, who are typically handicapped by shortages of staff, budgets, and raw data. These statisticians are resistant to recommending changes when so much work remains to be done before the *existing* SNA can be fully implemented.

With respect to depreciation accounts for natural resources, therefore, the expert committees of the U.N. Statistical Office have taken the position that countries should be encouraged to implement balance sheet accounts for reproducible and non-reproducible tangible assets and link those to conventional national income measures through "satellite accounts," as indicated in the present system. In other words, their position is that depletion accounts for natural resources should be calculated, but kept apart from the main tables. The measure of depreciation in the national income accounts should not be extended to include natural resources, and the present misleading indicators of economic performance should be maintained.

The rationale for this position is pragmatic: until more national statistical offices are capable of estimating depreciation accounts for natural resource assets, the core national income accounts should not be modified. Any estimates of natural resource balance sheets and depreciation should be displayed in ancillary tables, so that users can make their own evaluations.

Therefore, from the statistician's perspective, the amount of effort required to implement national resource accounts is important. The Indonesian country case study was implemented partly to obtain first-hand information about the level of effort needed to prepare numerical estimates. The accounts presented in this report were prepared almost entirely by pre-doctoral and master's level graduate students. Enough information to make reasonable estimates was found to be already available, so that compilation and reorganization of data were the main tasks. In this pilot study, without prior experience, working solely with existing data (no fresh field surveys were conducted), without the access to data a government statistical office would have, researchers spent approximately 12 person-months mostly in the United States. This modest input generated estimates that shed substantial new light on Indonesia's growth performance over more than a decade.

**Wasting assets**

The importance of bringing such estimates into the main national income accounts, rather than relegating them to "satellite" or "reconciliation" accounts, is demonstrated by events of the past decade. While virtually all countries calculate national income accounts, few have implemented the United Nation's recommendations with respect to ancillary tables in the SNA because with limited resources they have had to "stick to the basics." Similarly, despite their recognized deficiencies, politicians, journalists, and even sophisticated economists in official agencies continue to use GDP growth as the prime measure of economic performance. (In the first statistical table of the World Bank's annual *World Development Report,* for example, entitled, "Basic Indicators," the economic indicators are GDP, GDP growth per capita, and the rate of inflation.) Only if the basic measures of economic performance, as codified by the official national accounting framework, are brought into conformity with a valid definition of income will economic policies be influenced toward sustainability.

There is ample time before the revisions to the SNA are announced for the U.N. Statistical Office to explore fully the implications of extending the concept of depreciation to natural resource assets. It should use this time to prepare for that change. At the same time, key international economic institutions, such as the World Bank, other multilateral development banks, the IMF, and the OECD, should begin to compile, use, and publish revised estimates of net national product and national income, as this report has done. All these institutions should ready themselves to provide technical assistance to the growing number of national statistical offices that wish to adopt these changes and make such estimates for themselves.

## CURRENT NATIONAL INCOME ACCOUNTING

### Imputations and the treatment of depreciation

The market economy – goods and services exchanged for financial consideration – broadly limits the scope of national income accounts. For this reason, intra-household production and exchanges are excluded, except for subsistence agricultural production. Nonetheless, the accounts often do impute values to important economic activities that take place without any market transaction. For example, the rental value of owner-occupied housing is treated as if the owner rented the premises to himself. The criteria used to judge whether nonmarket activities should be included in national accounts are (1) whether they are directly comparable to production taking place in the market, and (2) whether their value can be reliably measured, given the statistical resources.

An imputed value of particular concern here is for the consumption of capital stock. The value of capital goods, such as structures and equipment, declines over time with use because of physical wear and obsolescence. This gradual decrease in the future productive potential of capital goods is reflected in the national accounts by a depreciation allowance that amortizes the asset's value over its useful lifetime. There are markets for some used capital goods, such as vehicles, from which depreciation factors can be estimated. Otherwise, amortization is a surrogate measure for the loss of income-generating capacity of older assets. Straight-line depreciation and other formulas are imputations for the loss of value.

Depreciation of tangible producible capital is subtracted from gross national product (GNP) in calculating the net national product (NNP) and national income. A nation must invest enough in new capital goods to offset the depreciation of existing assets if the future income-producing ability of the entire capital stock is to be preserved. Therefore, according to the definition of income given above, this capital consumption allowance must be excluded from total production. However, this procedure is applied only to structures and equipment, not to natural resources or other types of assets. NNP should provide a more useful measure of economic performance than GNP but generally receives less attention in economic policy planning. As currently defined and estimated to include only buildings and equipment assumed to depreciate at fixed rates, gross and net product tend to move closely together. However, ignoring or underestimating the deterioration or depletion of the capital stock can lead to economic policy errors with serious, long-term consequences.

## Income statements and balance sheets

A complete system of financial accounts consists of two parts, one (the *income statement*) dealing with transaction flows over a period of time, and the other (the *balance sheet*) with stocks of tangible and financial assets at different points in time. The concepts of production, consumption, revenues and costs relate to transaction flows within accounting periods. The national economic accounts in which they appear are comparable to income statements in business accounting. In contrast, balance sheets comprise stocks or levels of assets, liabilities and net worth at the end of accounting periods. Flows and stocks are linked, in that flows are equal to differences between stocks, and the stocks are equal to accumulated past flows.

National balance sheets provide a picture of a country's tangible and financial wealth at different points in time, facilitating intertemporal and international economic structural comparisons. The evaluation of a nation's future potential for sustained income generation can be enhanced by the detailed analyses of national assets and liabilities, through the preparation of national balance sheets. In the United Nations' SNA, the importance of balance sheets and wealth estimates for economic analysis are fully recognized, and the SNA includes models and an explicit recommendation to construct national balance sheets. However, while neither business firms nor households would ignore significant changes in their balance sheets, few national governments even calculate theirs.

At least in concept, the United Nations has endorsed accounting for certain natural resources. SNA specifically includes forests and subsoil assets (e.g., oil and gas reserves) in model national balance sheets. Two principal approaches to valuing assets have been endorsed for application to natural resources. These are (1) the use of values derived from market transactions in assets, and (2) the use of the discounted present value of estimated future income flows derived from the assets to be valued. For example, the SNA guidelines (United Nations 1977) suggest that the value of timber tracts should be based upon market data if available, taking account of timber type and the situation and character of the land. If there have been insufficient market transactions in timber to provide estimates, standing timber should be valued by discounting the future proceeds of selling the timber at current prices after deducting management and harvesting costs. An identical approach is suggested with respect to subsoil assets, using as a discount rate a rate of return "expected by investors in mining or quarrying enterprises."

Neither the United Nation's SNA nor the national income accounts of any country now integrates the treatment of natural resource between income and balance sheet accounts. Final sales to consumers are included on the product side; on the income side, the value added from resource extraction is included in wages and salaries, in rental incomes and in company profits. In other words, the *total* value of current production, net of purchased inputs, is imputed to current income.

There are no accounting entries in the flow accounts for depletion, growth (in the case of forests), discoveries (in the case of subsoil assets) or asset revaluation due to price changes. Only capital investments in durable structures and equipment used in the industry are subject to depreciation, not the resources themselves. There is no depreciation factor in the flow accounts to represent the loss of forests, the depletion of minerals, the erosion of soils, or the deterioration of water resources, even though these user costs impair the future income-generating capacity of those assets.

The U.N. recommends instead that these balance sheet valuation adjustments should flow through reconciliation accounts and not the current income accounts. The SNA guidelines suggest, for example, that reductions in the market value of land due to erosion be reflected in the reconciliation accounts (United Nations 1977). An expert group of the United Nations has expressed general support for a calculation of the change in the value of proven subsoil mineral reserves that would include allowances for both depletion and new finds, as well as the effects of price changes. This group recommended that the resulting adjustments also flow through the reconciliation accounts (United Nations 1980), leaving GNP and NNP unadjusted.

In arguing for keeping such asset revaluations in satellite accounts, the U.N. guidelines pointed out that large and sudden revaluations of subsoil asset values as a result of (1) extensive new discoveries; (2) changes in technology increasing the range of exploiting reserves; or (3) changes in market conditions could markedly affect estimates of current income if admitted into the flow accounts. This position ignores the fact that changes in technology or market conditions can equally affect the reproducible capital stock. Energy price shocks, for example, first made most older heavy industrial equipment economically worthless because at high energy prices those plants could not produce at a profit. The same fluctuations in energy markets led to drastic inflation, then deflation, in real estate values in oil-producing regions, such as Texas. The income accounts were insulated from these changes in asset values only because depreciation rates are estimated at constant "book" values, a procedure equally applicable to natural resource assets. The impact of capital consumption allowances for natural resources on the national income accounts would depend, as it should, entirely on the importance of natural resources to the particular economy.

In essence, reconciliation accounts provide a means of recording changes in the value of net assets between successive measurement dates *without having to show any effect on the income of the intervening period*. Recording these adjustments in reconciliation accounts is likely to minimize their consideration in national policy analysis. Therefore, while it is significant that the United Nations has specifically endorsed the principle of valuing natural resource assets and asset changes in the system of national accounts, the procedure they have recommended would still leave the income account seriously biased as an estimate of economic performance.

**R. Repetto *et al.***

## THE SCOPE OF NATURAL RESOURCE ACCOUNTING

A number of developed countries have proposed to set up systems of environmental accounts, including Norway, Canada, Japan, the Netherlands, the United States, and France. These systems have been reviewed in detail and evaluated for the United Nations Environment Programme by Weiller (1983) and Friend (1983). While natural resources take priority in Norway and France, pollution and environmental quality have been the focus in the United States and Japan. The approaches of Canada and the Netherlands combine elements of both approaches.

In both Norway and France, extensive systems of resource accounting have been established to supplement their economic accounts. The Norwegian system of natural resource accounting and the past decade's experience with it has recently been described (Alfsen, Bye, and Lorentsen, 1987; Garnasjordet and Saebo, 1986). Accounts have been compiled for "material" resources, such as fossil fuels and other minerals, such "biotic" resources as forests and fisheries, and such "environmental" resources as land, water, and air. The accounts are compiled in physical units of measurement, and not integrated with the national income accounts. However, resource accounts, especially those for petroleum and gas, have been expressed in value terms for use in macroeconomic planning and projection models maintained by the Central Bureau of Statistics.

The French natural patrimony accounts are intended as a comprehensive statistical framework to provide the authorities with the facts and data they need to monitor the state and changes in "that subsystem of the terrestrial ecosphere that can be quantitatively and qualitatively altered by human activity" (Corniere, 1986). They are conceptually broader than the national income accounts: material and energy flows to and from economic activites form only a subset of the accounts (Commission Interministerielle des Comptes du Patrimoine Naturel, 1983). Methodology and empirical estimates have been under development since 1971, and they now cover the same range of resources as Norway's: non-renewables, the physical environment, and living organisms. The basic accounting units are physical, with provision for monetary valuation of stocks and flows that are marketed or contribute directly to market production (Weber, 1983).

The construction of such frameworks for the compilation of environmental statistics may well encourage decision-makers to consider the impact of specific policies on the national stock of natural resources. However, a physical accounting approach *by itself* has considerable shortcomings. On the one hand, it does not lend itself to useful aggregation. Aggregating wood from various species of trees in physical units (cubic meters) obscures wide differences in the economic value of different species. Aggregating reserves of a mineral in physical units (tons) obscures vast differences in the value of different deposits, due to grade and recovery cost. On the other hand, maintaining physical accounts in disaggregated detail results in a mountain of statistics that are not easily summarized or used.

A further problem is that accounts maintained in physical units do not enable economic policy-makers and planners to understand the impact of economic policies on a nation's natural resource and environmental considerations into economic decisions – presumably, the main point of the exercise. While the information from the physical resource accounts undoubtedly facilitates the assignment of monetary values to balances and transaction flows (as will be described in this paper), from the perspective of *economic* policy, it is only an intermediate step (Theys, 1984). Yet, there is no conflict between accounting in physical economic units because, as the Indonesian study shows, physical accounts are necessary prerequisites to economic accounts. If the measurement of economic depreciation is extended to natural resources, physical accounts are inevitable by-products.

Notwithstanding these points, there are limits to monetary valuation, set mainly by remoteness of the resource in question from the market economy. Some resources, such as minerals, enter directly. Others, such as surface water, are extensively used as input market production, and although they are rarely bought and sold, values can be readily imputed. Others, however, such as noncommercial wild species, do not contribute directly to production and can be valued in monetary terms only through quite roundabout methods involving numerous, somewhat questionable assumptions. While methodological and empirical research into the economic value of resources that are remote from market processes is to be encouraged, common sense suggests that highly speculative values should not be included in official accounts.

In industrialized countries experiencing increasingly acute problems of pollution and congestion while becoming less dependent on agriculture, mining, and other forms of primary production, the focus of attention has been on "environmental" rather than natural resource accounting. Since Nordhaus & Tobin (1973) proposed their "measure of economic welfare" as an alternative to GNP, several different approaches to the development of more comprehensive systems of national income accounting have been described that go well beyond the scope of natural resource accounting described above. An excellent recent survey of these approaches is available (Eisner, 1988). Each reflects their authors' particular concerns (e.g., Daly, in press; Hueting 1980, 1984; Peskin 1980; Peskin & Peskin 1976, 1978). For example, Herfindahl & Kneese (1973) considered how GNP might be modified by the costs and benefits associated with pollution and its abatement. Others have proposed general systems to account for the impacts of economic activities on the quality of the environment more broadly defined.

Problems with the current framework are obvious since they lead to bizarre anomalies. If toxic substances leak from a dumpsite to pollute soils and aquifers, measured income does not go down, despite possible severe impairment of vital natural resources. If the government spends millions of dollars to clean up the mess, measured income rises, other things equal, because such government expenditures are considered to be purchases of final goods and services. If industry itself undertakes the cleanup, even if under court order, income does not rise because the same expenditures are considered to be intermediate production costs if carried out by enterprises. If the site is not cleaned up, and nearby households suffer increased medical expenses, measured income again rises because household medical expenses are also defined as final consumption expenditures in the national income accounts.

Although the system that gives rise to such results is widely regarded as faulty, there is little consensus on the remedy. Suggested approaches can initially be classified into those involving physical accounting and those that attempt to establish monetary values. The physical approach rests on a straightforward extension of input–output analysis to keep track of "deliveries" of various material from various resource stocks to producing and consuming sectors, and "deliveries" of materials from producing and consuming sectors to various receiving bodies in the environment (Leontief, 1970; Kneese, Ayres, & d'Arge, 1970). Thus, for example, each industrial sector's discharges of waste materials to water, land, and air are estimated, along with each sector's use of water, primary raw materials, land, and other natural resources.

This approach, conceptually straightforward and empirically feasible, has the virtue of bringing common economic models of "production" and "consumption" into approximate accord with the physical laws of nature. Moreover, the data thus organized provides an important intermediate step toward approaches that do involve estimation of monetary values. However, the plausible assumption of approximate linearity in the relation of waste generation to production and consumption activities cannot be carried over to the effects of emissions on environmental quality, or to the effects of environmental quality on human welfare. Both of these linkages are often highly non-linear, due to thresholds and chemical or biological interactions.

Establishing monetary accounts for changes in environmental quality is by no means so straightforward. While all would agree in principle that a good environment yields a continuing flow of beneficial goods and services, valuing those benefits is complex. For one thing, the existing accounts already reflect some of those values, but not others, so that there is the danger of double-counting along with that of omitting important elements of income. Agricultural output, yields, and income, for example, already reflect the environmental inputs of sunshine and precipitation, which make purchased inputs more productive. Increased concentrations of ozone and other air pollutants reduce agricultural yields and thus diminish measured income in the existing accounts. Environmental deterioration, insofar as it raises current production costs or reduces productivity, is already reflected in the accounts of the enterprise sector.

The glaring omission is the direct value of environmental quality or quality changes to the household. In principle, the damages to individuals from increasing pollution, congestion, and noise can be estimated by measuring willingness to pay, lost productivity, or needed defensive expenditures. Despite a large body of research literature on methodology and statistical problems, the task would be formidable if attempted on a national scale and remains in the realm of research rather than accounting.

On the other side of the ledger, there are problems – although perhaps not so serious – in improving the accounting of expenditures undertaken to prevent or remedy environmental damages. These problems can be brought into focus by assuming that households and enterprises are forced to spend more and more as the economy grows to maintain a constant level of environmental quality (Juster, 1973). One anomaly might be addressed by treating such expenditures as intermediate purchases when undertaken by households and governments, as they now are when undertaken by enterprises. However, this immediately raises the broader question of treating as intermediate expenses a wide range of outlays by governments and households that have the basic function of maintaining productivity (including, for example, traffic control, health maintenance, and so on). The notion of "defensive" expenditures is elusive, since spending on food can be considered a defence against hunger, clothing a defence against cold, and religion a defence against sin.

Another difficulty is in establishing the boundary between outlays to maintain environmental quality and those undertaken for other purposes. A household's purchase of a water filter, or a firm's installation of a water treatment plant, might be readily identified. However, a household's move to another region with a superior environment, or a firm's adoption of an intrinsically low-residuals process technology would probably not.

There has been little consensus on the principles or quantification of proposals for broader environmental quality accounting so far, though the discussion has helped highlight the importance of incorporating environmental protection and effective natural resource management in national economic planning. However, for most developing countries and other resource-based economies, it is more relevant to think of natural resources as productive assets than as consumer goods. The first priority is to account for those disappearing assets in a way that gives due emphasis to the costs.

## SETTING UP NATURAL RESOURCE ACCOUNTS

### Physical accounts

Natural resource physical stocks and any changes in those stocks during an accounting period can be recorded in physical units appropriate to the particular resource. The basic accounting identity is that opening stocks *plus* all growth, increase or addition less all extraction, destruction, or diminution *equals* closing stocks. Although the following discussion refers to oil and gas reserves and timber stocks as examples, the principles are applicable to many other resources.

Oil and natural gas resources, the former measured in barrels and the latter in barrel-equivalents, consist of identified reserves and other resources and identified reserves can be divided into proven reserves and probable reserves. Proven reserves are the estimated quantities of oil and gas that geological and engineering data indicate with reasonable certainty to be recoverable from known reservoirs under existing market and operating conditions – that is, prices and costs as of the date the estimate is made. Probable reserves are quantities of recoverable reserves that are less certain than proven reserves. Thus, one limit on the stock of reserves is informational. Additional proven reserves can usually be generated by drilling additional test wells or undertaking other exploratory investments to reduce uncertainty about the extent of known fields. The boundary between reserves and other resources is basically economic. Vast quantities of known hydrocarbon deposits cannot be extracted profitably under current conditions. They are thus known resources, but cannot be counted as current reserves, though price increases or technological improvements might transform them into reserves in the future.

For other mining industries, geological characteristics tend to be known with more certainty, so there is less distinction between proven and probable reserves but a sharp division between economic reserves and total resources. Many minerals are present at very low concentrations in the earth's crust in almost infinite total amounts (Goeller & Weinberg, 1984). Technological changes in mining and refining processes have markedly reduced the minimum ore concentrations that can profitably be mined, correspondingly expanding mineral reserves.

A similar framework is applicable to sub-soil deposits of water in available aquifers, except that accounting for changes in stocks must take into consideration the annual recharge. Accounting for water *quality* changes encounters problems that illustrate the limitations of physical accounting. Quality changes can be reflected in economic valuation rather readily, if they affect treatment costs or the economic uses to which water can be put. However, the numerous dimensions of quality, reflecting contamination by many other substances in varying concentrations and combinations, makes the construction of discrete physical categories difficult.

Changes in oil and gas stocks may be classified under various headings. Landefeld & Hines (1982) include under additions to reserves: "discoveries," the quantity of proven reserves that exploratory drilling finds in new oil and gas fields or in new reservoirs in oil fields; "extensions," increases in proven reserves because of subsequent drilling showing that discovered reservoirs are larger than originally estimated; and, "revisions," increases in proven reserves because oil and gas firms acquire new information on market conditions or new technology. Extensions of and revisions to oil and gas reserves have historically been significantly larger than new discoveries. Landefeld & Hines (1982) point out that reserve statistics generally produce very conservative estimates of the total resource stocks that will ultimately enter the economic system. Soladay (1980) estimated that actual production from new U.S. fields and reservoirs was over seven times the amount initially reported as discovered.

Reserve levels fall because of extraction and downward revisions. In the United States, oil and gas companies are required by the Securities and Exchange Commission to disclose net annual changes in estimated quantities of oil and gas reserves, showing separately opening and closing balances; revisions of previous estimates (from new information); improved recovery (resulting from improved techniques); purchases and sales of minerals in place; extensions and discoveries; and, production (FASB 1977).

The accounting framework for timber resources in physical units could be expressed in hectares, in tons of biomass, or in cubic meters of available wood (Weber 1983), though the last is probably the most important economic measure. As in the case of minerals, the total resource is larger than the economic reserve since a substantial part of the total stock of standing timber in any country cannot be profitably harvested and marketed with current technologies and market conditions.

Additions to the timber stock can originate from growth and regeneration of the initial stock, and from reforestation and afforestation. Reductions can be classified into production (harvesting); natural degradation (fire, insect infestations, etc); and, deforestation by man. Separate accounts might be established for different categories of forests – for example, virgin production forests, logged (secondary) forests, protected forests, and plantations. In temperate forests, where species diversity is limited, timber stocks are further disaggregated by species.

Physical accounts can be constructed along similar lines for agricultural land. Land and soil maps and classification systems are used to disaggregate land into productivity categories. Changes in stocks of each land category within a period reflect various phenomena: conversion to non-agricultural uses; conversion to lower productivity classes through physical deterioration by erosion, salinization, or waterlogging; and conversions to higher productivity classes through physical improvements by irrigation, drainage, and other investments. A set of physical accounts for agricultural land would record stocks of land at each accounting date by productivity class, and flows among classes and to other land uses according to cause.

Similarly, physical accounts can be set up for other biological resources, such as wildlife or fish populations. The principles are essentially those of demography. Additions to initial populations are attributed to fertility, estimated from reproduction rates and the size of the breeding population, and immigration. Subtractions from stocks are attributed to natural mortality, estimated from age-specific or general mortality rates, harvesting operations, other special sources of mortality, and outmigration.

### Valuation principles

The concept of economic rent is central to natural resource valuation. Economic rent is defined as the return to any production input over the minimum amount required to retain it in its present use. It is broadly equivalent to the profit that can be derived or earned from a factor of production (for example, a natural resource stock) beyond its normal supply cost. For example, if a barrel of crude oil can be sold for $10 and costs a total of $6 to discover, extract, and bring to market, a rent of $4 can be assigned to each barrel.

Rents to natural resources arise from their scarcity and from locational and other cost advantages of particular stocks. These rents are distinct from monopoly rents, which increase returns to a factor of production beyond its opportunity cost by restricting supply through market power or government action. In principle, rents can be determined as the international resource commodity price less all factor costs incurred in extraction, including a normal return to capital but excluding taxes, duties and royalties. Thus, the economic rent is equivalent to the net price.

This is the same concept of rent that appears in a Ricardian-scarcity model, which assumes that resources from different "deposits" will be supplied at a rising incremental cost until profit on the marginal source of supply is completely exhausted. In this Ricardian model, rents arise on relatively low-cost, infra-marginal sources of supply.

It is also equivalent to a user cost in a Malthusian scarcity model, which assumes that a homogeneous exhaustible resource is exploited at an economically efficient rate, such that the profit on the marginal amount brought to market is equal to the expected return derived from holding the asset in stock for future capital gain (Hall & Hall 1984). In such a Malthusian model, if the resource is being extracted at an efficient rate, the current rent on the last unit of resources extracted is thus equal to the discounted present value of future returns from a unit remaining in stock.

As Ward (1982) has pointed out, the gross operating surplus of the extractive sector in the SNA, represented by the sum of the profits made by all the different enterprises involved in resource extraction activities, does not represent true rewards to factors of production alone but also reflects rents from a "one time only" irredeemable sale of a non-renewable natural asset. By failing to measure an appropriate depletion allowance, conventional national accounting procedures allocate a disproportionate share of current income flows to present generations at the expense of future generations. The basic definition of income as the amount that can be consumed without becoming worse off is clearly being infringed as the value of the asset base declines.

Ward presents the sad exemplary tale of Kiribati, the small atoll republic of the Solomon Islands, which depended throughout the 20th century on its phosphate mines for income and government revenues. While the mines ran, gross domestic product was high and rising, but the mining proceeds were treated as current income rather than as capital consumption. When the deposits were mined out in the 1970s, income and government revenues declined drastically because far too little had been set aside for investment in other assets that would replace the lost revenues.

It would seem reasonable to apply this argument, not only to all soil and subsoil assets, but also to tropical forests which, though theoretically renewable, are being removed without adequate provision being made for their replacement in many areas. In forest economics, the concept of "stumpage value" is very close to that of economic rent. Stumpage value represents timber sale proceeds, less the costs of logging, transportation, and processing. Better quality and more accessible timber stands will command a higher stumpage value.

Asset transactions in natural resources, such as competitive auction sales of rights to extract timber or minerals, closely follow estimated stumpage values or rents, with allowance for risk. Because holders of those rights can usually hold the resources in stock or bring them to market immediately, the current rent or stumpage value tends to reflect the present value of expected future net income that can be derived from them.

This principle is readily extended to other resources: agricultural land can be valued directly on the basis of its current market worth, or indirectly as the present value of the future stream of net income, or annual rent, that can be derived from it. The value of sub-surface irrigation water deposits can be estimated from market transactions in water rights, or by comparing the value of agricultural land overlaying a usable, known, aquifer with that of otherwise equivalent land without subsurface water. Alternatively, it can be estimated as the present value of future rents, calculated as the difference between the costs (per cubic meter) of supplying the water for irrigation and the incremental net farm income attributable to the use of the water for irrigation. The value of a fishery could be estimated, in principle, as the maximum amount of revenue that a government authority could collect in bids from potential fishermen for the rights to participate in the catch. Alternatively, it could be estimated as the present value of the net income fishermen could derive from the catch under optimal regulation. In a world of frictionless, competitive markets, these valuation methods would yield the same results.

If adjustments to national income accounts for natural resource stock changes are to attain broad acceptance, a credible standard technique for valuing natural resources must be adopted that can be applied to various resources by statisticians in different countries. That method must be as free as possible from speculative estimates (about future market prices, for example) and must depend on underlying data that is reasonably available to statistical agencies.

Landefeld & Hines (1985) have recently compared the three principal methods discussed above for estimating the value of natural resource stocks: 1) the present value of future net revenues; 2) the transaction value of market purchases and sales of the resource *in situ*; and 3) the net price, or unit rent, of the resource multiplied by the relevant quantity of the reserve.

The present value method requires that future prices, operating costs, production levels, and interest rates be forecast over the life of, for example, a given oil field, after its discovery. The present value of the stream of net revenue is then calculated, net revenue representing the total revenue from the resource less all extraction costs. Soladay (1980) extends the present value method by attempting to take into account the upward revisions in estimates of reserves that typically occur subsequent to the initial discovery. The United Nations Statistical Office has recommended use of the present value method when market values for transactions in resource stock are not available (United Nations 1979).

The net price method applies the prevailing average net price per unit of the resource (current revenues less current production costs) to the physical quantities of proved reserves and changes in the levels of proved reserves. Landefeld & Hines make the important point that while the net price method requires only current data on prices and costs, it will be equivalent to the other two methods if output prices behave in accordance with long-run competitive market equilibrium. "Equilibrium in natural resource markets (where the net price rises in accordance with the rate of return on alternative investments) produces the interesting result that depletion as measured by changes in the present value of the resource equals depletion as measured by the net price method" (Landefeld & Hines 1985, p.14). The assumption here is derived from the theory of optimal depletion of exhaustible resources, that resource owners will tend to arbitrage returns from holding the stock into future periods with returns from bringing it immediately to market, adjusting current and future supplies until price changes equate those returns. (Dasgupta, 1982) When expected future increases in the net price take place at a rate equal to the return on alternative investments, these increases would therefore be eliminated in the calculation of the net present value of future cash flows (Miller & Upton, 1985).

A number of recent studies (Boskin et al. 1985; Landefeld & Hines 1982, 1985; Soladay 1980; Ward 1982; Lutz and El-Sarafy 1988, Devarajan and Wiener 1988) have considered the issues associated with valuing the discovery and use of depletion of exhaustible natural resources in measures of national income and wealth.

In the private sector, financial accounting and reporting for petroleum- and mineral-producing companies has been debated for many years in the United States by the accounting profession, regulatory agencies, industry groups, and the companies themselves. The U.S. Securities and Exchange Commission (SEC) and Financial Accounting Standards Board (FASB) have given extensive consideration to the appropriate accounting and financial reporting for publicly traded corporations involved in extractive activities. The debate was initially focused on the two widely different methods of reserve valuation used by companies, the full cost method and the successful efforts method (FASB 1977). Each was based upon the costs of exploration and development actually incurred, but without reflecting the market value of reserves or annual changes in reserves to which the company has rights of ownership. Believing with ample justification that neither method provided sufficient information to stockholders, the SEC proposed a new method of reserve recognition accounting (SEC 1978) that valued proven oil and gas reserves according to the discounted present value of the stream of future income at current prices and costs. Following further debate on the issue, however, SEC abandoned this method of accounting since the burden of producing the information was considered to outweigh its usefulness to users of financial statements (SEC 1981).

The FASB recently considered means by which companies could provide information about future cash flows from oil and gas reserves as supplemental information, outside the financial statements (FASB 1982). They evaluated the alternatives of fair market value, discounted future net cash flows, and a "standardized measure" of discounted net cash flows. Fair market value was rejected on the basis that relatively few exchanges of oil and gas mineral interests take place, and the geological characteristics of each property are unique and thus incomparable. The use of discounted future net cash flows, based on estimated future prices and costs, production timing, and an enterprise-specific discount rate as a surrogate for fair market value, was also rejected since such subjectively based calculations could not provide sufficiently comparable and verifiable information for financial reporting. The Board settled on a standardized measure of discounted net cash flows. Future net cash flows result from subtracting future development and production costs (and tax expenses) from future cash inflows relating to proved oil and gas reserves, using prices and unit costs as of the end of the reporting year. A discount rate of 10 percent is specified. The FASB points out that the standardized measure cannot be considered an estimate of fair market value but should reflect some of the key variables that affect fair market value – such as changes in reserve quantities, selling prices, production rates, and tax rates. Thus, the private accounting profession, after lengthy consideration, has adopted a valuation method based on the net price approach.

## INTEGRATING NATURAL RESOURCES INTO THE NATIONAL ACCOUNTS

Income accounts for natural resources can be developed directly from accounts expressed in physical units by assigning appropriate monetary values to stock levels and changes. Net changes in the value of stocks are attributed to current year additions (discoveries, net revisions, extensions, growth or reproduction) less deductions (degradation, deforestation, or depletion) plus any price changes of the resource during the year, as illustrated in Table 25.3. This framework is applicable with suitable specification to a wide variety of resources.

If the primary objective were only the national balance sheet presentation of natural resource accounts, the example shown in Table 25.3 would be relatively straightforward. The net value of the resource increased by $155 ($255–$100) during the year and net national wealth also increased by $155.

To adjust gross national product to a net basis, economists have a number of options. If the only desired adjustment to income were to reflect resource *depletion*, then net national product would be reduced by $32, using the average valuation rate of $1.60 per barrel. If *all* the physical changes in the resource base were netted, yielding a decrease of 15 physical units, NNP would be reduced by $24, at the same average valuation. However, if the gain in value of the opening stock due to price changes were also treated as current income, NNP would be increased by $155, the difference between the two balance sheets.

In other words, alternative adjustments are possible, depending on the objective. Treating unrealized capital gains and losses due to price changes as income is inconsistent with the definition of income given above, since the capital gain during the year could be consumed without reducing future potential consumption below what it would have been at the original price level. However, accounting conventions now in use for physical plant and equipment value assets at "book value" rather than replacement cost: they *do not* reflect changes in asset values in current income accounts.

The United Nations (1977, 1980) has suggested that all changes in the value of natural resource stocks due to new finds, price changes, and depletion should be excluded from the income accounts. At the opposite extreme, Eisner (1980, 1985) has argued that capital revaluations in excess of those generated by general price

**Wasting assets**

**Table 25.3** Example of resource inclusive national accounting system.

| | Physical units | Unit value | Value ($) | Basis of calculation |
|---|---|---|---|---|
| Opening Stock | 100 | 1.00 | 100 | |
| Additions: | | | | |
| Discoveries | 20 | 1.60 | 32 | |
| Revisions (Net) | (30) | 1.60 | (48) | |
| Extensions | 15 | 1.60 | 24 | |
| Growth* | 0 | 1.60 | 0 | |
| Reproduction* | 0 | 1.60 | 0 | |
| Reductions: | | | | |
| Production | (20) | 1.60 | (32) | |
| Deforestation* | 0 | 1.60 | 0 | |
| Degradation* | 0 | 1.60 | 0 | |
| Net Change | (15) | 1.60 | (24) | |
| Revaluations: | | | | |
| Opening stock | – | – | 200 | 100 × (3.00–1.00) |
| Transactions | – | – | (21) | 15 × (3.00–1.60) |
| Closing stock | 85 | 3.00 | 255 | |

*Note:* Example of a natural resource account as it might appear in national economic accounts. The resource unit value (based on international commodity prices less factor costs incurred in extraction or production) is assumed to be $1.00 at the beginning of the year, $3.00 at the end of the year, and to average $1.60 during the year.

The total increase in the value of the resource over the period shown is equal to $155 ($255–$100). The methodology recommended in this paper would result in a downward adjustment to net national product of ($24). The remaining net change in total value of $179 ($155 + $24 or $200 – $21) would be recorded in a revaluation reserve and have no impact on income of the current period.

Items marked * are specific to forest resources; all other categories are applicable to subsoil minerals, e.g., oil and gas.

rises should be included in measures of income and capital accumulation. Accordingly, the money value of all capital gains in excess of those necessary to keep the real value of capital intact should be included in income. Eisner (1980) extends this argument to propose the inclusion of capital gains arising from the discovery of new resources in income, and the exclusion of resource depletion from income.

International resource commodity prices are subject to dramatic fluctuations over comparatively short time periods because price elasticities of demand and supply are often small in the short run. Including unrealized capital gains from natural resource price changes in current income could lead to significant swings in income between successful periods in resource-dependent countries. However, natural resource price swings (such as the energy price shocks) also markedly affect the value of plant, equipment, and real estate that are specific to those natural resource sectors.

The procedures illustrated here, which incorporate the net price method (Landefeld & Hines 1982, 1985), include only the value of *physical* resource stock changes in national income. This procedure is consistent with current asset-accounting practices. In addition, it is more readily implemented since, for most natural resources, information on stock changes due to extraction or discovery is more accurate than information on the size and composition of the total stock. At the end of each accounting period, the physical units comprising the opening balance of natural resource stocks have been revalued at the net price prevailing at the end of the period. The revaluation adjustment (which, in the example shown in Table 25.3, equals $200) has been recorded in a revaluation reserve and therefore has no effect on the current period's income. The net physical change (15 units) is valued at the average net price prevailing during the period and is used to adjust NPP downwards by $24. The remaining revaluation adjustment, which arises from the difference between average and closing prices applied to the net physical change in resource stocks ($21) is recorded in the revaluation reserve as an unrealized capital gain, with no impact on income.

If national accounts are adjusted to show income at constant prices, thereby eliminating the effects of general inflation, the adjustment to income ($24) should be deflated by an appropriate price index. As a result, only real wealth increases or decreases will be reflected in measured national income.

Preliminary resource accounts in physical and value terms for tropical timber, petroleum, and soil resources in Indonesia from 1970 to 1984 illustrate this methodology. The net charges in resource values from physical sources (for example, excluding price revaluations) implied by these tables were reflected in the summary tables and figures presented earlier to illustrate the usefulness of such calculations in macroeconomic evaluation. The resource accounts are preliminary, in that they have not been endorsed by official Indonesian statistical or economic agencies, but represent a non-governmental research effort that drew on published and some unpublished statistical sources. Efforts are currently under way in cooperation with the Ministry for Environment and Population and a consortium of universities in Indonesia to revise these accounts and to extend the methodology to other resource sectors.

## NOTE

1. It may seem anomalous that in 1971 and 1973 depreciation was a negative number, that is, net capital consumption was *added* to gross domestic product and investment. The reason for this is that the value of additions to petroleum reserves in these years were considerably larger than all categories of depletion combined, leading to "negative" depreciation.

   One way of resolving this apparent anomaly would be to account separately for additions and subtractions from natural resource assets. Real capital gains (as distinct from those resulting from price changes) can be accounted for as gross income and gross capital formation. This is consistent with our earlier definition of income, because additions to resources during the current year augment the amount that *could* be consumed currently without reducing potential consumption in future years. This is obvious in the case of forest growth, but less obvious for mineral discoveries, since current discoveries may leave less to be discovered later on. However, insofar as additions to mineral reserves reflect advances in the technology of exploration or extraction, the total potential resource base will have expanded.

## REFERENCES

Alfsen, Knut H., Torstein Bye and Lorents Lorentsen, 1987. Natural Resource Accounting and Analysis: The Norwegian Experience 1978–1986. Oslo, Norway: Central Bureau of Statistics of Norway.

Boskin, Michael J., Marc S. Robinson, Terrance O'Reilly, and Praveen Kumar, 1985. New

## Wasting assets

Estimates of the Value of Federal Mineral Rights and Land. *American Economic Review* (December): 923–936.

Commission Interministerielle des Comptes du Patrimoine Naturel, (1983). *Les Comptes du Patrimoine Naturel.* Paris: Institut National de la Statistique et des Etudes Economiques.

Corniere, P., (1986). Natural Resource Accounts in France. An Example: Inland Water. In Organisation for Economic Cooperation and Development, *Information and Natural Resources.* Paris: OECD.

Dasgupta, Partha, (1982). *The Control of Resources.* Cambridge: Harvard University Press.

Devarajan, Shantayanan and Robert J. Weiner, (1988). Natural Resource Depletion and National Income Accounts. Unpublished. Harvard University, John F. Kennedy School of Government, Cambridge, Massachusetts.

Edwards, E.O. and P.W. Bell, (1961). The Theory and Measurement of Business Income. Berkeley: University of California Press.

Eisner, R., (1980). Capital gains and income: real changes in the value of capital in the United States, 1946–77. In Usher, D. (ed.), *The Measurement of Capital. Studies in Income and Wealth,* Vol. 45. Chicago: University of Chicago Press.

Eisner, R., (1985). The total incomes system of accounts. *Survey of Current Business.* Vol 65 (1): 24–28.

Financial Accounting Standards Board , (1977). Financial accounting and reporting by oil and gas companies. Statement of financial accounting standards no. 19. Accounting Standards Board. Stamford, California.

Friend, Anthony. Natural Resource Accounting: International Experience. Paper presented at Consultative Meeting of United Nations Environment Programme. Geneva, February 23–25, 1983.

Garnasjordet, P.A. and H. Viggo Saebo, (1986). A System of Natural Resource Accounts in Norway. In Organisation for Economic Cooperation and Development, *Information and natural resources.* Paris: OECD.

Goeller, H.E. and A. Zucker, (1984). Infinite resources: the ultimate strategy. *Science.* Vol. 223, (February): 456–62.

Goldsmith, R.W., (1982) *The national balance sheets of the United States,* 1952–1975. Chicago: University of Chicago Press.

Goldsmith, R.W., (1985). Comparative national balance sheets. A study of twenty countries, 1688–1978. Chicago: University of Chicago Press.

Hall, Darwin C. and Jane V. Hall, 1984. Concepts and Measures of Natural Resource Scarcity with a Summary of Recent Trends. *Journal of Environmental Economics and Management.* Vol 11: 363–379.

Hicks, John R., (1946). *Value and Capital: An Inquiry into Some Fundamental Principles of Economic Theory.* Oxford: Oxford University Press.

Hueting, R., (1980). *New Scarcity and Economic Growth.* Amsterdam: North-Holland Publishing Company.

Hueting, Roefie, (1984). Economic Aspects of Environmental Accounting. Paper prepared for the Environmental Accounting Workshop, organized by UNEP and hosted by the World Bank, Washington, D.C., 5-8 November, 1984.

Juster, F. Thomas, 1973. The framework for the measurement of economic and social performance. In: M. Moss (ed.), *The Measurement of Economic and Social Performance. Studies in Income and Wealth.* Vol. 38. National Bureau of Economic Research, New York.

Kneese, A. Ayres, R. & d'Arge, R., (1970). Economics and the Environment: A Materials Balance Approach. Resources for the Future, Washington, D.C.: Johns Hopkins Press.

Landefeld, J.S. & J.M. Hines (1982). Valuing non-renewable natural resources: the mining industries. In: *Measuring Nonmarket Economic Activity: BEA Working Papers,* Bureau of Economic Analysis.

Leontief, W., (1970). Environmental Repercussions and the Economic Structure. *Review of Economics and Statistics,* August.

Lutz, Ernst and Salah El Serafy. Environmental and Resource Accounting: An Overview. Environment Department Working Paper No. 6, World Bank, Washington, D.C.: June 1988.

Miller, Merton H. and Charles W. Upton, (1985). A Test of the Hotelling Valuation Principle. *Journal of Political Economy*. Vol. 93, No. 1: 1–25.

Organisation for Economic Cooperation and Development, (1986). Declaration on environment resources for the future. In OECD, *OECD and the Environment*. Paris: OECD.

Peskin, Henry M. and Janice Peskin, (1978). The Valuation of Nonmarket Activities in Income Accounting. *Review of Income and Wealth*. Vol. 24, March: 41–70.

Peskin, Henry M., (1980). Two papers on national accounting and the environment. Discussion Paper D-71, Resources for the Future, Washington, D.C., October.

Securities and Exchange Commission, (1981). Financial reporting by oil and gas producers. ASR No. 259, Securities and Exchange Commission, Washington, D.C.

Soladay, J., (1980). Measurement of Income and Product in the Oil and Gas Industry. In: D. Usher (ed.), *The Measurement of Capital Studies in Income and Wealth*. Vol. 45. University of Chicago Press.

Stauffer, Thomas R. Accounting for "wasting assets": Income Measurement for Oil and Mineral-Exporting Rentier States. Paper presented to Eighteenth General Conference International Association for Research in Income and Wealth, Luxembourg, 1983.

Theys, J., (1984). Environmental accounting and its use in development policy. Proposals based on the French experience. Unpublished manuscript.

United Nations, Department of Economic and Social Affairs, (1968). A System of National Accounts. Statistical Papers, Series F, No. 2, Rev. 3. United Nations, New York.

United Nations, Department of Economic and Social Affairs, (1977). Provisional international guidelines on the national and sectoral balance-sheet and reconciliation accounts of the system of national accounts. Statistical Papers, Series M, No. 60. United Nations, New York.

United Nations, Statistical Office (1979). Future Directions for Work on the System of National Accounts. United Nations, New York.

United Nations, Economic and Social Council, Statistical Commission, (1980). Future Directions for Work on System of National Accounts.

Usher, Dan, (1980). *The Measurement of Economic Growth*. New York: Columbia University Press.

Ward, Michael, (1982). Accounting for the Depletion of Natural Resources in the National Accounts of Developing Economies. Paris, France: Development Centre, Organisation for Economic Cooperation and Development, June.

Ward, Michael. The Impact of Resource Depletion on the National Accounts. Paper presented to Conference on "National Accounts and their Uses in Development Planning in the Arab Countries," Kuwait, May, 1984.

Weber, J.L., (1983). The French Natural Patrimony Accounts. *Statistical Journal of the United Nations*. ECI 1:419-444.

Weiller, Edward, (1983). The Use of Environmental Accounting for Development Planning. Report to the United Nations Environment Programme, New York, January.

World Bank, (1987). Indonesia, The Outer Islands: Issues in the Sustainable Use of Land and Forest Resources. Main Report. Unpublished paper.

World Bank, (1988). *World Development Report, 1988*. Oxford: Oxford University Press.

World Commission on Environment and Development, (1987). *Our Common Future*. Oxford: Oxford University Press.

# [16]

# *Environmental and Natural Resource Accounting*

*Salah El Serafy and Ernst Lutz*



Most production and consumption activities have some impact on the physical environment. As economic growth and population expansion have occurred, they have increasingly put pressure on the environment and the natural resource base. Years ago, when the pressure was still light, there may have been some justification for economists to ignore the contribution to economic activities made by the environment, both as a resource base and as a "waste sink," receiving the residues of the production and consumption process. But there is little justification for this now.

Side effects of production and consumption activities have been considered by economists as external effects. But they are external only if a narrow view is taken with no consideration of the impact on the resource system as a whole, which although large, is nevertheless finite and in certain respects subject to great stress. We are now beginning to understand that we have done and are still doing enormous harm to our environment, treating it with disdain as if it were infinite, and that eventually those "external" costs will have to be borne by someone. If a broader view is taken, environmental costs would be internalized within the production processes. In this connection, it is essential to attribute costs and benefits properly, and to distinguish clearly between the true generation of income and the drawing down of capital assets through resource depletion or degradation.

### *Shortcomings of the Current Measures of National Income*

If properly done, income accounting is a crucial tool for economic analysis and policy prescriptions. It can indicate the level of economic activity, its variations from year to year, the size of savings and investments, the limits to what society can consume out of its current receipts, factor productivity, industrial structure, comparative performance, and many other things. Development planners, economists, and politicians thus make frequent use of the national income measure of gross national product (GNP) and variants such as gross domestic product (GDP), net domestic product (NDP), and net national product (NNP) for a variety of purposes. GDP, the most commonly used variant of aggregate income, is essentially a measure of total economic activity for which exchange occurs in monetary terms within a given year. It is valuable mostly for indicating short- to medium-term changes in the level of economic activity, and it is widely used for demand management and stabilization policies. As calculated at present, however, GDP is less useful either for measuring year to year variations in economic activity or for gauging long-term sustainable growth, partly because natural resource depletion and degradation are being ignored. Furthermore, GDP is often used inappropriately as an indicator of economic welfare, frequently without any cautioning about its shortcomings for that purpose. The concept of welfare is much broader than that of a money income measure, and covers many dimensions of subjective well-being other than those involving market transactions and those that can be measured in money terms, particularly for people whose basic material needs have been met.

As most economists know, controversial issues with regard to current practices of national income accounting include the treatment of leisure, household and subsistence production and other nonmarket transactions, and services of long-lived consumer durables. This chapter will not deal with any of those issues; we address only certain environmental and natural resource issues that relate to the proper measurement of income and variations in assets. Because of two key shortcomings in national accounting, GDP, as measured at present, does not adequately represent true, sustainable income. These shortcomings are the treatment of environmental protection costs and the degradation and depletion of natural resources. The fact that these issues are not properly dealt with under the current United Nations System of National Accounts (SNA) represents a serious accounting flaw. As a result, policy advice based on measurements produced under the SNA can be faulty.

### *The Objective: Measurement of Sustainable Income*

True income is sustainable income. This is a key point stressed by Daly (1989) and El Serafy (1981, 1989). True income may be thought of as the maximum amount a recipient can consume in a given period without reducing possible consumption in a future period. This concept encompasses not only current earnings but also changes in the asset position of the income earner: capital gains are a source of income; capital losses reduce income. The essence of the concept of income has been stated by Sir John Hicks (1946:172) as the maximum amount that a person can consume during a certain period and still be as well-off at the end of the period as he or she was at the beginning.

Prudent national economic management thus requires that governments should know the maximum amount that can be consumed by a nation without running down its environmental capital. It is important, therefore, that national income be measured correctly to indicate sustainable income. Adjustments of the SNA appear to be necessary in the two areas noted because they are currently not dealt with satisfactorily: the costs of environmental protection (defensive expenditures) and the depletion and degradation of natural resources.

## *Defensive Expenditures*

Actions are often taken to defend the environment against encroachment by economic activities, and the SNA treats their costs as generating income. Defensive expenditures can be large or small depending on where we draw the boundaries. For the purpose of this chapter we are considering only defensive expenditures against the unwanted side effects of production and consumption (such as pollution), but not those relating to national security, even though similar arguments would apply to the latter. Another possible category would be car repair and medical expenses incurred as a result of traffic accidents. Leipert (1986) has listed yet other costs that might be included, and produced a paper (1987) that measures environmental defensive expenditures for the Federal Republic of Germany.

When expenditures are incurred to redress some or all of the negative consequences of production or consumption, incorporating them in the stream of income generated by economic activity does not make sense. It has been proposed that such outlays should be counted not as final expenditures, as is currently the case, but rather as intermediate expenditures. There are counterarguments against doing this. National defense expenditure, which is one type of defensive expenditure, is much more important in terms of size, but is currently counted as final expenditure. In the case of other production and consumption activities such as those involving tobacco, drugs, and alcohol, one could also justifiably argue for their exclusion from national income aggregates. If environmentally defensive expenditures are defined as intermediate so that they can be deducted from the national income aggregates, national accountants would resist the idea because those definitions would not be consistent with current definitions and conventions under the SNA.

A conceptually different approach looks at resources such as water, air, and soil as natural capital. When such capital is being drawn down or degraded, this should show up as consumption when measuring national income. It should be reflected irrespective of whether or not defensive expenditures are actually incurred either to redress the negative effects or to restore the drawn-down natural capital. The difference between the defensive expenditures actually incurred and the depreciation of the environmental capital would be reflected in the net domestic product. This approach has been proposed by Harrison (1989). A similar conceptual approach has been developed by Peskin (1989), who advocates the introduction of a "nature account" in addition to the standard accounts for households, industry, and government. Aside from the difficulty of reaching a consensus on how natural capital is to be treated conceptually, there is the difficulty of attaching a value to the level of natural capital and environmental services and damages.

### *Some Aspects of Measuring Pollution within the SNA Framework*

Pollution is the discharge of wastes in ways that raise the cost of later activities, harm people, or reduce the enjoyment people get from their surroundings. National accounts can be used to improve environmental policymaking in this important area. Blades (1989) distinguishes four aspects of pollution and considers the extent to which it is possible and useful to measure them within the framework of the national accounts. These are the output of pollutants, the damage of pollution, the costs of abatement, and the benefits derived from such abatement.

Although it may be feasible to use national accounts to measure the output of pollutants, the information so obtained may be too general to be useful for environmental policymaking. With regard to pollution damage, Blades notes that although there are conceptual and practical difficulties in estimating the total costs involved, it would be possible and helpful to identify some of the main costs already included in the national accounts, but not shown separately at present. The costs of pollution abatement are a part of defensive expenditures. They have been measured in several countries and have been incorporated in macroeconomic models in order to show the impact of abatement policies on prices, output, and employment. In this area national accounts would be a valuable tool for environmental policymaking, and Blades considers in detail the conceptual and practical problems of measuring abatement costs. Finally, Blades notes that although it would be interesting to measure the market value of the benefits of pollution abatement, the practical difficulties involved are enormous and it would not generally be feasible to incorporate such data in the national accounts on a regular basis.

Hueting (1989) discusses several ways to deal with defensive expenditures and lists the pros and cons of the various options. He is skeptical about the willingness-to-pay method and advocates that environmental standards be set by considerations of health and sustainable development. The costs of achieving such standards would indicate how far a country has drifted away from sustainable economic development. Although this approach has intuitive appeal, it would be difficult to implement, given the uncertainites about the linkages between production and consumption on the one hand and the environment on the other.

In general, the treatment of defensive expenditures for national accounting assumes greater significance the higher the degree of industrialization of the country concerned. In contrast, depletion and degradation are not directly related to the level of industrialization, but are particularly important for countries that base their economic activities on the exploitation of their natural resources.

## *Depletion and Degradation of Natural Resources*

Under the SNA, there is an evident asymmetry in the treatment of man-made assets and natural resources. Man-made assets—buildings and equipment, for example—are valued as productive assets and are written off against the value of production as they depreciate. Natural resource assets are not so valued or adequately accounted for in most instances, and their loss entails no charge in the national accounts against current income to reflect the decrease in potential future production. A country may be exhausting its renewable or nonrenewable natural resources, and its current income will thus be inflated by the sale of natural assets that will eventually disappear. Differences in recording under the SNA may arise depending on whether a resource is publicly or privately owned. Private companies that take a long view of the natural assets they own often make provisions for the decrease in the capital stock of their natural resources, and in certain countries tax legislation permits the exclusion of such provisions from taxable income. No such exclusion is effected in developing countries where natural resource exploitation is carried out in the public sector.

Underlying this asymmetry is the implicit and inappropriate assumption that natural resources are so abundant that they are costless or have no marginal value. Historically they have been regarded as gifts of nature—a bias that has provided false signals for policymakers. This approach confuses the depletion of valuable resources with the generation of income. Thus it promotes and seems to validate the idea that rapid rates of economic growth can be obtained by exploiting a diminishing resource base. The growth can be illusory and the prosperity it engenders transitory if the apparent gain in income means permanent loss in wealth, that is, if at least part of the receipts is not redirected into new productive investments. As income is inflated, so often also is consumption, and the country concerned becomes complacent about its economic performance. Necessary adjustment to economic policy is then delayed by the seeming prosperity. For natural resource-dependent countries, failure to account for the depletion of the capital stock embodied in natural resources represents a major flaw in the accounting process.

Existing natural capital of geological (nonrenewable) and biological (renewable) resources is needed for agricultural, industrial, and other production. New geological discoveries, as well as recycling and conservation, do not reverse the process of depletion of existing stocks. The newly discovered stocks come from a finite source and they merely extend the time span over which depletion can continue. Depletion of renewable natural resources can have serious indirect effects because a reduction in the stocks or populations of plants and animals may in turn reduce the sustainable flow of resource inputs and ecosystem services. Similarly, crop production at the expense of soil erosion cannot be sustained. Only careful husbandry of environmental capacities can ensure sustainable and potentially larger income flows in the future. The optimistic argument that human ingenuity is bound to find substitutes for the natural resources being depleted may be generally valid, but it would be imprudent for society to base its behavior on such optimism and wrong for economists and accountants not to take rational precautions in case substitution does not occur.

Two main conceptual approaches—the use of depreciation and user cost—have been proposed to deal with the depletion and degradation of natural resources. The principle of depreciation of man-made capital can be applied straightforwardly to the consumption of renewable and nonrenewable resources (Daly 1989; Harrison 1989). Because geological and ecological information on depletion or degradation comes in physical units, these units must be priced or valued in some way before the gross national product can be adjusted to arrive at a corrected net product. Valuation could be based either on the principle of replacement cost where replacement is possible or on the discounted value of the willingness to pay. Present conventions would value the depleted or degraded resources at current prices. If such a correction is effected, based on the full value of depletion, the gross product will remain unadjusted, but the net product will reflect the depreciation of environmental capital that has taken place during the accounting period.

Because the full-value depreciation approach would leave the GDP unadjusted and would eliminate from the net product the entire proceeds from natural resource sales, the user cost approach has been proposed as a way of properly taking into account the depletion of mineral resources. Possession of a natural resource conveys on its owner an income advantage that is denied to those without a natural resource, and a measurement of zero net income, as produced by the full-value depreciation method, is therefore not satisfactory. The user cost approach avoids the difficulties of putting a value on the stock of the resource and relies instead on the conscious assessment of current rates of extraction of the total available stock measured in physical terms. Depending on the rate of depletion and on the discount rate, the gross revenue from the sales of a depletable resource—net of extraction cost—can be split into a capital element or user cost, and a value-added element equal to true income. The capital element represents asset erosion. It has been proposed that capital should be hypothetically (El Serafy 1981) or actually (Ward 1982) reinvested in alternative assets so that it can continue to generate income after the resource had been totally exhausted. Unlike the full-value depreciation method, the user cost approach would alter the reckoning of GDP itself, not just NDP. This method uses current market prices for valuation purposes and is in harmony with accounting principles, but it requires a rule-of-thumb discount rate to convert the capital sales into a sustained income stream. In addition, it is rooted in a proper understanding of the economic meanings of value added and rent, which should not be confused with asset sales. A less satisfactory compromise would combine the two approaches so that GDP would be left inflated with the user cost, whereas depreciation for reckoning NDP would be not at the full value of the resource degradation but at the value of the user cost.

How the net revenue can be split into user costs and true income is explained in El Serafy (1989). One first must decide on a discount rate $r$, for example, 5 percent. Then one has to determine the number of periods over which the resource is being liquidated. This is simply read from the ratio between total reserves and whatever amount is extracted in the current period. Next, the formula developed by El Serafy (1981) can be used to calculate the ratio of true income $X$ to net receipts (exclusive of extraction costs) $R$:

$$X/R = 1 - \frac{1}{(1 + r)^{n+1}}$$

$R - X$ would be the "depletion factor" (or user cost) that should be set aside and allocated to capital investment and excluded from GDP, while $X$ would represent true, or sustainable, income.

This method is flexible enough to handle changing levels of extraction, movements in the discount rate, and alterations in reserve estimates. Such alterations would include new discoveries, which would change the reserve-to-extraction ratio. In the above formula, alterations in reserve estimates are denoted by $n$—the life expectancy of the reserve measured in years at the current period's extraction rate. The method is not concerned with the valuation of total reserves, but only with the fraction of the resource being liquidated in the current accounting period, which is valued at current prices. That fraction relies entirely on physical quantities because the price is the same in the nominator and denominator. The method can be adapted to deal with mineral extraction under conditions of deteriorating quality of the product and rising extraction cost, inasmuch as resource owners usually mine the richer deposits first and leave inferior deposits for later extraction, thereby inevitably raising the cost of future extraction.

Like all accounting methods, this method does not indicate an ex ante optimal rate of depletion, but merely mirrors decisions already taken by the resource owner regarding the liquidation of his natural resource. The owner usually determines his extraction rate in the light of many factors, including his expectation of future price changes. If he decides to extract 20 percent of his reserves in one year, then $n$ in the above formulation is equal to 5, and the income content of his net receipts, with a 5 percent discount rate, would be 25 percent and the user cost to be reinvested would be 75 percent. If, however, he extracts only 10 percent of his reserves—that is, over ten years—then he needs to set aside 58 percent of his net receipts for reinvestment, and can enjoy 42 percent as current income. The correction needed to reckon true income out of natural resource sales is higher the closer the resource is to exhaustion and lower the longer its life expectancy at current extraction rates. Were the resource to last 100 years at current extraction rates, only a 1 percent reduction would be necessary in net receipts to arrive at true income with a 5 percent discount rate. The choice of the discount rate materially affects the calculation. A high discount rate, which depresses future against current valuation, raises the ratio of true income in current receipts. But note that alternative investments must be found in which to sink the depletion factor $(R - X)$ so that it can yield that much as a return.[1]

Table 3-1 shows the percentage of net receipts—gross sales minus extraction cost—that represents true income at selected levels of discount rates and years of life expectancy of a natural resource.

## *Resource Accounting*

For resource accounting, data need to be collected on renewable and nonrenewable natural resources, primarily for the purpose of planning long-run exploitation in pursuit of sustainable economic activity. Several industrial countries—among them Canada, France, Japan, Norway, and the United States—have developed resource accounts that are tailored to their specific resource availabilities and policy priorities.

**Table 3-1. *True Income (X) as a Percentage of Net Receipts (R)***

| *Life expectancy of the reserve (years)* | *Discount rate (r) (percent)* | | |
|---|---|---|---|
| | *2* | *5* | *10* |
| 2 | 6 | 14 | 25 |
| 5 | 11 | 25 | 44 |
| 10 | 20 | 42 | 65 |
| 20 | 34 | 64 | 86 |
| 50 | 64 | 92 | 99 |
| 100 | 86 | 99 | 100 |

*Source:* Based on El Serafy (1981).

Instead of the expression "resource accounting" the French use the term "patrimonial accounting," which could be described as "accounting for the national environmental heritage" (Theys 1989). The concept is broader than resource accounting because it covers cultural heritage in addition to natural resources. The French resource accounting approach is intended ultimately to relate economic growth to the quantities of natural resources that have to be used up or imported to make economic growth possible. Such a system would also enable a country to optimize the economic value of available natural resources, determine the fraction of GDP that should be set aside for the efficient protection of the environment, and orient economic growth so that it does not threaten ecosystems.

The system when fully developed would be versatile and serve various ends. It could be used to (1) make optimal the use of natural resources as factors of production (for example, through the inversion of a quantitative input-output table that would indicate the intermediate use of natural resources in the productive process); (2) to describe the economic aspects of resource use (for example, by determining which resources would be marketed and in what quantities and values, how to improve the productivity of processing industries to optimize the use of natural resources, and the opportunity costs of alternatives); (3) to treat resources as environmental goods (by taking into account changes in the quality of the environment, costs and benefits of environmental policies, the economic consequences of alternative environmental policies); and (4) to take stock of the national environmental heritage and define the long-term implications of its transformations, so that the environment could be preserved for future generations. Because resources to develop such a system are limited, stress is placed on satisfying the needs of policymakers. Although it would be easier to collect environmental data in the form of flexible reports on the state of the environment and country profiles, the paramount need is to develop a system of environmental accounts so that the information is standardized, exhaustive, summed up in physical and monetary terms, and comparable in time and space. The long-term goal is to match the standards already reached by national (economic) accounting, which make the SNA such a powerful planning tool for economic management.

The French approach is only one among several being pursued in developed countries. (Norway, for example, has been using resource accounts for several years; see Alfsen, Bye, and Lorentsen 1987.) The thrust of the French approach is to build up balance sheets for resources and monitor their change from year to year with emphasis on physical measurements. Such measurements are clearly indispensable; accounting in money terms cannot be undertaken without them. The French approach requires that a comprehensive physical inventory system be in place before any changes can be proposed in national accounting methodology. This is a point of view shared by many, but there are others who want to see national accounting methods adjusted gradually as measurements of parts of the physical environment become feasible.

### *Linking Environmental and Resource Accounts to the SNA*

The SNA does not contain an explicit environmental dimension. The current revisions to SNA were mandated by the U.N. Statistical Commission to simplify and clarify the existing system rather than to propose radical changes in it. This position is being justified by a desire to maintain consistency-in-time series, even if those series contain conceptual shortcomings.

Environmentalists and economists with environmental and resource concerns support several schools of thought about the best approach to the accounting problem. Some advocate environmental accounting in physical terms and have little interest in establishing any linkage with the SNA. Their aim is to use indicators of physical change to influence public opinion and environmental policies. At the other end of the spectrum are those who feel that environmental accounting would not have the same impact unless the accounts were monetized and integrated into the SNA to give an adjusted national income that is more sustainable. We take a middle position: we believe that environmental accounting in physical terms is essential, particularly because the data collected would indicate the speed with which the quantity and quality of natural resources are changing and the direction of change. At the same time, we recognize that monetization, to the extent possible, is also important, and that a linkage with the SNA and an adjustment of the current income measurements are urgently needed. Given the current state of the art, we believe that more work, both conceptual and empirical, is needed before GDP and NDP in the core of the SNA can be replaced by a more sustainable GDP and NDP. That is why, as an interim step, we would encourage the construction of satellite accounts, linked with the SNA, where the adjustments can be made. In other words, the user can compute sustainable GDP and NDP in satellite accounts, which would not threaten the historical continuity of GDP and would have a fair chance of being adopted, particularly to guide policy analysis and prescriptions. If such environmental accounts are adopted, national accountants are bound to take the issues discussed here more seriously and might eventually be willing to adjust the core of the SNA.

### *Developing Environmental and Resource Accounts for Developing Countries*

To ensure that resource concerns are eventually reflected in the SNA and in policymaking, it is necessary to proceed at an operational level so that government officials, national accountants, and economists alike see how, in practice, one can include environmental and resource concerns in the calculations. Certain factors might even facilitate resource accounting work in developing countries, because environmental problems in most developing countries tend to be concentrated and easily perceived. In addition, benefits can be derived from progress made in developed countries and from remote sensing methods of surveying.

Environmental and resource accounting, however, demands a great many data and a great deal of effort, and a plurality of disciplines is required for working on these accounts. The problems are compounded in developing countries by the still limited political demand for this type of activity, because short-run problems are more pressing and the relevant human resources needed are acutely scarce. It is therefore clear that the development of environmental and resource accounts will take time. This fact, however, should not keep statistical and planning officials in developing countries from initiating relevant work now, especially on minerals and forestry, where data are already available.

In the case of Indonesia, Peskin (1989) argues that a local research effort should start right away, supported initially with periodic input from consultants. He also proposes that, ideally, not only environmental but also other important nonmarket factors be considered in an expanded accounting structure.

Repetto and others (1987) have applied resource accounting to fuel and forestry activities in Indonesia. For forestry they estimated the harvesting, deforestation, and degradation net of regrowth; valued the estimates at certain rent factors; and suggested that degradation be treated like depreciation of man-made assets. That is, they proposed reducing the NDP by the estimated amount of depletion. The proposed reductions amounted to over US$3 billion annually for 1979–82, which represents more than 3 percent of the GDP. A similar approach was followed for valuing the depletion of fuel reserves (reservations about this approach and an alternative proposal can be found in El Serafy 1989).

Another empirical study (Magrath and Arens 1987) estimated the costs to the economy of soil erosion in Java. The annual amount estimated was US$350 million to US$415 million, which is somewhat less than 4 percent of the GDP of Java's dryland agriculture. Over 95 percent of these costs are on-site costs of declining productivity. These two studies have made valuable contributions, but it is clear that further empirical work is needed.

### A Variety of Approaches but a Common Theme

Some of the papers presented at the Joint United Nations Environment Programme–World Bank series of Workshops on Environmental Accounting over the past few years have put forward incompatible propositions for amending the SNA. This incompatibility should not detract from the central theme (argued in Ahmad, El Serafy, and Lutz 1989) that in their present form the guidelines for income calculation under the SNA leave out extremely important aspects of economic development that should be brought into the accounts. Under present practices the accounts produce readings activity and growth over time that often lead to mistaken policy advice. Such readings frequently exaggerate income, encourage consumption, and promote habits of behavior that cannot be sustained over the longer term.

An interesting argument over what kind of adjustment is desirable and practical is highlighted by the approaches of Harrison (1989) and El Serafy (1989) regarding depletable resources. Both are in fundamental agreement about what constitutes sustainable income and what does not. Harrison would work within the existing framework of the SNA by preserving the definition of final demand used at present, but she would include consumption of natural capital as a parallel entry to consumption of man-made capital with appropriate adjustments to NDP. Further, she argues that income measures should exclude all capital consumption and that net products should therefore be used as indicators of the level of economic activity and its development over time. In contrast, El Serafy would redefine the distinction between intermediate and final demand, maintaining that the sale of natural capital must not be viewed as generating value added and that at least part of that should be excluded from the GDP, as well as from the net product, so that the GDP measurement can continue to be used to describe performance and guide economic policy.

At the other extreme, Norgaard (1989) is altogether skeptical about environmental economists and accountants ever being able to agree on a set of corrections that would simply rectify and fill in gaps in the existing SNA, so that they can end up with one aggregate figure expressed in money terms. He claims that existing SNAs contain contradictions because they are based on conventions and reflect consensus rather than being built on deductive reasoning. Unlike both Daly (1989) and El Serafy (1989), Norgaard does not view sustainability as implicit in the definition of income, but as an "ethical" goal, representing a "separate objective of objective strategies." He sees the concerns of future generations as being undervalued because future generations do not participate in the capital markets of today.

A more conventional view would ascribe such undervaluation not to the absence of future generations from the marketplace, but to the use of too high a discount rate, which has the effect of reducing the value of future net benefits to almost nothing the farther one projects into the future. Because future generations will never be in a position to participate in today's capital markets, the best way to reflect their preferences is to use lower discount rates. The main thrust of Norgaard's argument, however, is against the economic approach to "sustainability of development" based on accounting that relies on market valuations. He espouses "methodological pluralism" in the belief that a multiplicity of perspectives would ensure that "all values are respected" so that decisionmakers have information alerting them to "as many aspects of environmental and resource phenomena as possible" (Norgaard 1989). Norgaard, however, never spells out how such alternative value systems can be established or used, nor does he speculate on the sort of solutions they would bring about.

Various papers in Ahmad, El Serafy, and Lutz (1989) present other areas of disagreement, but the main message of this work is the urgent need to recognize explicitly the shortcomings of current measurements of income and to work toward better measurements and a more sustainable concept of income—common threads in virtually all the contributions.

### *SNA Expert Group Meeting*

In the context of deliberations over whether and in what direction the SNA should be revised, the World Bank presented a discussion note to the SNA Expert Group meeting in Vienna, March 21–30, 1988. The note focused on the two major concerns already elaborated: defensive expenditures and the depletion and degradation of natural resources. With regard to defensive expenditures, the Bank recommended (1) that the experts discuss and decide as a matter of urgency which expenditures are to be included under this category; (2) that they show these expenditures as a separate line item; and (3) that the Group decide where the adjustments are to be made and whether the adjusted aggregates are to be shown in satellite accounts or in the main system of production, consumption, and accumulation accounts.

With regard to depletion and degradation, the Bank (1) urged the adoption of SNA-linked satellite accounts where adjustments for resource depletion and degradation can be made; (2) recommended that the Expert Group warn countries in which a significant portion of GNP derives from the depletion and degradation of natural resources, and that their current income, as calculated at present, overestimates sustainable income (policymakers should particularly be alerted to this fact); and (3) requested that the Group encourage work on estimating costs and benefits related to the exploitation of depletable natural resources.

The Expert Group acknowledged the importance of the two issues raised and expressed concern about the way the environment was being accounted for under the SNA. Although the experts were not yet ready to advocate changes in the core accounts, they were prepared to support the construction of satellite accounts to be linked to the SNA. Rearranging the core accounts would require a conceptual consensus that was not likely to materialize during the ongoing revision, which has to be finalized by 1991. To attain that consensus, it would be necessary to undertake a functional breakdown in the central framework of such activities as health and research and development in addition to considering the environment. Rearranging the core accounts for just one function would not be justified even if such rearrangement would be beneficial from an analytical as well as an accounting point of view. The experts stressed that valuation issues were very difficult and required further work before standard valuation techniques were agreed upon.

Among the many points made during the discussion were that (1) shortcomings of the GDP as currently measured should be emphasized in the revised SNA manual known as the "Blue Book"; (2) national accountants and environmental economists should tackle the problem jointly; and (3) approximations required for environmental accounting might not be any worse than some conventional estimate methods already sanctioned by the SNA. Such issues and others related to them merit further discussion: a possible venue for this might be the SNA Expert Group meeting scheduled for January 1989, which would deal with inventories and physical assets and their treatment in balance sheets and reconciliation accounts. As a concession to the environmental community the Expert Group chairman stated that if and when adequate experience had been gained with satellite accounts and various conceptual and valuation issues had been resolved, an SNA revision would be called for even if that proved to be much sooner than envisaged.

## Ongoing and Projected Work

Although efforts are being exerted to refine concepts and develop approaches to take care of environmental concerns in national income accounting, some of the principles proposed need to be applied to a set of case studies before they can be generally accepted. Environmental concerns are already being integrated into the World Bank's country economic and sector work. Gone are the days when natural resources could be treated as extraneous to economic activity. Resource issues must be integrated in macroeconomic analysis and policies so that resources can be managed efficiently in the service of sustainable development.

The integration of environmental and resource concerns into the SNA, albeit initially via satellite accounts, is an important part of this endeavor. An in-depth review is also planned of the resource accounting done by industrial countries (such as Canada, France, Japan, Norway, and the United States) so that lessons can be drawn from that work. As the case studies are undertaken, perhaps over a two- to three-year period, parallel work should proceed to produce internationally standardized methodologies, perhaps in a handbook on environmental accounting within the series of the SNA. At the March 1988 meeting the Expert Group stated that it would be invaluable as an interim measure if an international organization were to piece together what is known about environmental and resource accounting, with emphasis on problems capable of solution, in order to minimize the duplication of effort and resources that would result from individual countries pursuing the subject independently.

## Note

1. J. M. Keynes (1936:ch. 6) first introduced the concept of user cost—in relation to capital equipment—defining it as the "maximum net value which might have been conserved . . . if it [the equipment] had not been used." He described user cost as "one of the links between the present and the future." Project analysis of depletable minerals has also made use of the concept of user cost at the micro level (see, for example, Schramm 1986).

## References

Ahmad, Yusuf J., Salah El Serafy, and Ernst Lutz, editors. 1989. *Environmental Accounting and Sustainable Income.* Washington, D.C.: World Bank.

Alfsen, Knut, Torstein Bye, and Lorents Lorentsen. 1987. *Natural Resource Accounting and Analyses: The Norwegian Experience, 1978–1986.* Social and Economic Study 65. Oslo: Central Bureau of Statistics of Norway.

Blades, Derek W. 1989. "Some Aspects of Measuring Pollution within the SNA Framework." In Ahmad, El Serafy, and Lutz (1989).

Daly, Herman. 1989. "Toward a Measure of Sustainable Social Net Product." In Ahmad, El Serafy, and Lutz (1989).

El Serafy, Salah. 1981. "Absorptive Capacity, the Demand for Revenue, and the Supply of Petroleum." *Journal of Energy and Development* 7(1):73–88.

———. 1989. "The Proper Calculation of Income from Depletable Natural Resources." In Ahmad, El Serafy, and Lutz (1989).

Harrison, Anne. 1989. "A Possible Conceptual Approach to Introducing Natural Capital into the SNA." In Ahmad, El Serafy, and Lutz (1989).

Hicks, John. 1946. *Value and Capital*, 2d ed. Oxford, U.K.: Oxford University Press.

Hueting, Rofie. "Options for Dealing with Defensive Expenditures." In Ahmad, El Serafy, and Lutz (1989).

Keynes, John Maynard. 1936. *The General Theory of Employment, Interest and Money.* London: Macmillan.

Leipert, Christian. 1986. "Social Costs as a Factor of Economic Growth." *Journal of Economic Issues* 2(1):109–31.

———. 1987. "Defensive Ausgaben in der Bundesrepublik Deutschland 1970 bis 1985: Absolute Werte und Relations zahlen mit dem BSP." Berlin. Processed.

Magrath, William, and P. Arens, 1987. "The Costs of Soil Erosion on Java—A Natural Resource Accounting Approach." World Resources Institute, Washington, D.C. Processed.

Norgaard, Richard. 1989. "Issues Related to the Linkage of Environmental and National Income Accounts." In Ahmad, El Serafy, and Lutz (1989).

Peskin, Henry. 1989. "Environmental and Non-Market Accounting with Some References to Indonesia." In Ahmad, El Serafy, and Lutz (1989).

Repetto, Robert, Michael Wells, Christine Beer, and Fabrizio Rossini. 1987. "Natural Resource Accounting for Indonesia." World Resources Institute, Washington, D.C. Processed.

Schramm, Gunter. 1986. "Practical Approaches for Estimating Resource Depletion Costs." In *Natural Resources Economics and Policy Application,* edited by E. Miles, R. Pealy, and R. Stokes. Seattle: University of Washington Press.

Theys, Jacques. 1989. "Environmental Accounting and Its Use in Development Policy." In Ahmad, El Serafy, and Lutz (1989).

United Nations. 1968. *A System of National Accounts.* U.N. Publication Sales no. E.69.XVII.3. New York.

Ward, Michael. 1982. *Accounting for the Depletion of Natural Resources in the National Accounts of Developing Economics.* Development Centre Publication CD/R(82)3010. Paris: Organisation for Economic Co-operation and Development.

# [17]

## Risk and Uncertainty in Dryland Development and Management

John A. Dixon, Paul B. Sherman
David E. James



### Handling risk and uncertainty

Risk and uncertainty are unavoidable aspects of decisions concerning the development and management of dryland areas. Questions that need to be answered in addressing the problem of risk and uncertainty include:

- How can risk and uncertainty be defined and measured?
- How should the land user evaluate risk and uncertainty in managing resources at his/her disposal and balance the prospect of production failure against the need to produce physical or economic returns?
- In benefit – cost assessments of public policies, programmes and projects, how should the analyst take risk and uncertainty into account and present meaningful information to public decision-makers?
- How should public decision-makers, acting in the best interest of the community, deal with the problem of risk and uncertainty in formulating and implementing improvement policies, programmes and projects?

Decisions on dryland development schemes and land management practices typically involve both the private and the public sector. Private decision-makers can be expected to deal with the problem of risk and uncertainty to maximize their own economic welfare. The "best" options for private decision-makers will be influenced by their perceptions of and attitudes towards risk and uncertainty. Public decision-makers must accept responsibility for dealing with risk and uncertainty on behalf of society as a whole. There may be major divergencies between private and social valuations of risk.

In many benefit – cost analyses, the problem of risk and uncertainty is ignored. The "best estimate" of net benefits is usually the one that the assessment team regards as being most appropriate. It is compiled from the "best estimates" of all the components of the analysis. In practice, a decision-maker often has no way of knowing how the assessment team arrived at its "best estimate". Any subjective combination of the level of net benefits and probability may have been used.

Where the distribution of values for any variable or for net benefits is known, the most commonly used "best estimate" is the mean value or arithmetic average of the distribution, also known as the expected value. It is unfortunately only a single figure and reveals very little about risk. "Best estimates" of the net benefits of policies, programmes and projects give no indication of the likelihood of success or failure.

Several courses of action are available to a decision-maker, private or public, forced to consider the results of an economic analysis presenting only "best estimates" of net benefits, with no information on the significance of risk and uncertainty:

(1) The decision-maker may make an *ad hoc* decision based on the available information. Subjective judgements by the decision-maker him-/herself are inevitable if this approach is adopted. Threshold values may be prescribed, such as a minimum level of net benefits or minimum internal rate of return, to allow for risk and uncertainty.
(2) The information base and underlying analysis can be improved to facilitate a decision. Such improvement may be carried out to varying degrees (Mar *et al.*, 1987). A decision may be reached with considerable uncertainties remaining in the information base. Better information may be obtained through such methods as sensitivity analysis, scenario construction, reliance on expert opinion and the use of decision-analysis techniques.
(3) The analysis can be carried through to a full risk assessment. Risk assessment involves a number of separate steps. The first is identification of the nature and sources of risk. In economic terms, this would refer to factors possibly leading to low net benefits or major losses. Second is the measurement of risk. To carry out this step, the pathways and processes creating risk must be identified. Probability distributions for stochastic factors are needed. Values for other inputs to the analysis must be specified. Through appropriate computational or modelling procedures, the probability distribution for net benefits can be derived. Finally, an evaluation of risk must be undertaken. Actions can then be formulated based on risk assessment. Such strategies can be described as risk management (Whyte and Burton, 1980).
(4) The decision-maker may decide to abandon the original proposal and proceed on an entirely different basis. A possible approach is adaptive environmental assessment and management

(AEAM), under which the decision-maker deliberately attempts to keep management options open as development proceeds, generating information from the experience gained as a guide to subsequent action. Other defensive strategies, specifically designed to cope with risk and uncertainty, might also be tried. An important strategy, aimed especially at the problem of critical zones and irreversibility, is the safe minimum standard (SMS).

*Sources of risk and uncertainty in dryland decision-making*

Changes in dryland environments are typically difficult to predict. The economic effects of existing land-use practices, the introduction of new practices and the application of investment funds to land improvements cannot be readily determined. In any economic analysis of management options, a range of possible values for benefits and costs is often obtained.

There are many sources of risk and uncertainty in the dryland context. Consider a dryland production system such as a communal farm or grazing plot, as shown in Figure 8.1. General social, economic and political factors can influence the decisions and behaviour of land users and the general community. Land tenure and financial conditions may be poorly defined.

Natural events affecting production include rainfall, drought, windstorms, floods, fire, lightning, hail, frost and freezing. Animal and plant diseases, plagues and pests are common. Other environmental processes may also be important such as erosion, salinization and devegetation.

Changes in physical yields, damages to property and shifts in the productivity of the resource base are some of the on-site effects that can be expected. Another class of effects is off-site environmental impacts imposed on other producers and members of the community. Pathways linking all these activities may not be known or clearly specified.

As explained in previous chapters, methods are available to value on-site and off-site effects. Such methods, however, are often subject to error. In addition, the prices selected to value inputs to production, outputs and environmental impacts are often uncertain or subject to wide fluctuation.

The dryland production system example is an appropriate vehicle for classifying all variables into three separate categories for analysis. Some variables may be known with *complete certainty*. A good example is a predetermined stocking rate. Other inputs might be known only in *probabilistic terms*, such as rainfall or the occurrence of insect plagues. Finally, in some situations, events may be

Figure 8.1: Dryland production system

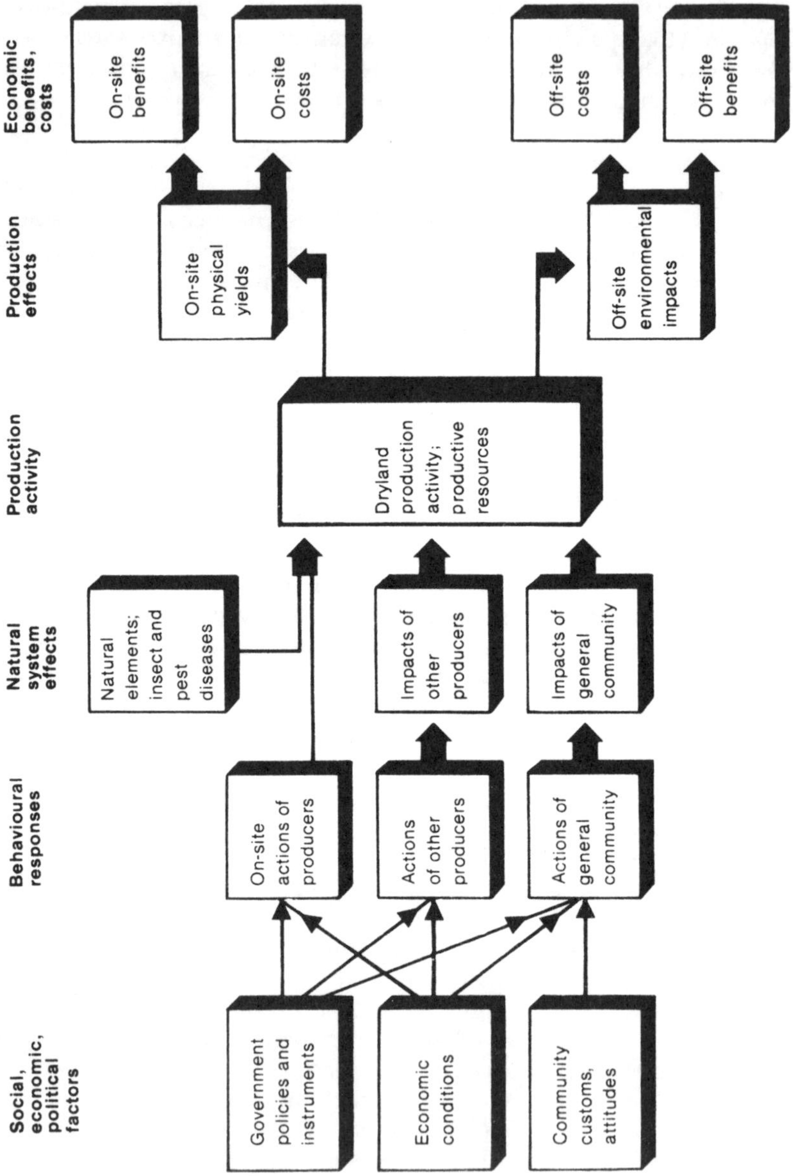

*totally unpredictable* (for example, social upheaval or natural disasters). Variables that are known with certainty can be described as deterministic. Randomly occurring variables are stochastic. The techniques used to handle these different types of variable in an economic analysis rely heavily on mathematical and statistical methods. The main concepts are presented in this chapter. Further details can be found in the recommended references.

*Definitions of risk and uncertainty*

The terms "risk" and "uncertainty" are commonly used interchangeably, but a distinction is drawn for economic analysis. With risk, the probability distributions for the variables are known. (A probability distribution reflects the probability associated with each possible value of the variable.) With uncertainty, the probability distributions are not known.

Probability distributions for stochastic (random)variables such as precipitation can be obtained from historical data, either directly as relative frequency distributions, or as fitted theoretical distributions (see Box 8.1). Such distributions are said to be objectively derived. Alternatively, where data are scarce, probability distributions may be obtained from subjective judgements by experts, assessment teams or decision-makers themselves (see Box 8.2).

---

**Box 8.1: Objective probability distributions based on historical data**

A frequency distribution is a tabular arrangement of historical data in classes. The frequency distribution can be described in graphical form as a *histogram* or a *frequency polygon*. A frequency histogram consists of a set of rectangles with areas proportional to class frequencies. The total area of the histogram is the total number of frequencies multiplied by the width of the class intervals. A frequency polygon is obtained by connecting the mid-points of the tops of the rectangles in the histogram. The area under the polygon is equal to the area of the histogram. A frequency distribution for rainfall is shown in Figure 8.2 based on forty yearly values.

A *relative frequency distribution* is found by dividing the class frequencies by the total number of frequencies (number of data items). A relative frequency distribution can be described by a histogram or polygon. The sum of the relative frequencies is 1. The total area of the histogram or area under the polygon is thus also equal to 1.

The normal or Gaussian distribution is a theoretical distribution which can be fitted to data sets with a large number of values – in practice, more than thirty. The graph of a normal distribution is shown in Figure 8.3. The normal distribution is symmetrical, and the mean, mode and median coincide. With any normal distribution, 68.27 per cent of the frequencies lie within + and – 1 standard deviations on either side of the mean, and 95.45 per cent within + or – 2 standard deviations.

The normal distribution is not always appropriate in dryland applications because of its symmetry. In reality, the probability distributions best representing stochastic variables in dryland projects are often strongly skewed. Distributions allowing for skewness, such as the log-normal distribution, would generally be more appropriate.

Special theoretical distributions are available to predict the occurrence of rare events (Rowe, 1981). The most commonly used distributions are the binomial distribution and the Poisson distribution. The binomial and Poisson distributions have very similar properties. Both approach the form of a normal distribution as their means increase in size.

---

The techniques used to deal with risk and uncertainty also differ. Risk is handled through the techniques of risk assessment, risk – benefit analysis, and risk management. Uncertainty requires the use of decision analysis techniques.

*Risk*. Risk is usually viewed as an adverse factor in economic decisions. Rowe (1981), for example, defines risk as the chance of harm. In other contexts, risk is conceived as a hazard or danger (Whyte and Burton, 1980). In economic analysis, risk is usually specified in terms of the probability of an adverse event and its magnitude. In monetary terms, it is measured as the product of the probability and the associated monetary value of the event.

To assess the risk associated with a particular policy, programme, project or resource management action, the probability distribution for net benefits must be specified. If the probability distribution is known, it will be possible to measure the likely occurrence of above-average net benefits, as well as low net benefits or serious losses. Whether the odds favour high or low values depends on the form of the relevant probability distribution.

*Uncertainty*. Uncertainty is said to exist when the probability distribution for net benefits is unknown. As is evident from even a simple case such as that shown by Figure 8.1, there are many reasons why the probability distribution might not be known, ranging from incomplete data to inadequate methods of prediction and analysis.

Decisions designed to overcome the problem of uncertainty by postulating arbitrary values or by using *ad hoc* predictive procedures are necessarily subjective. Measurement of risk is

**Figure 8.2: Frequency distribution for annual rainfall (forty years of observations)**

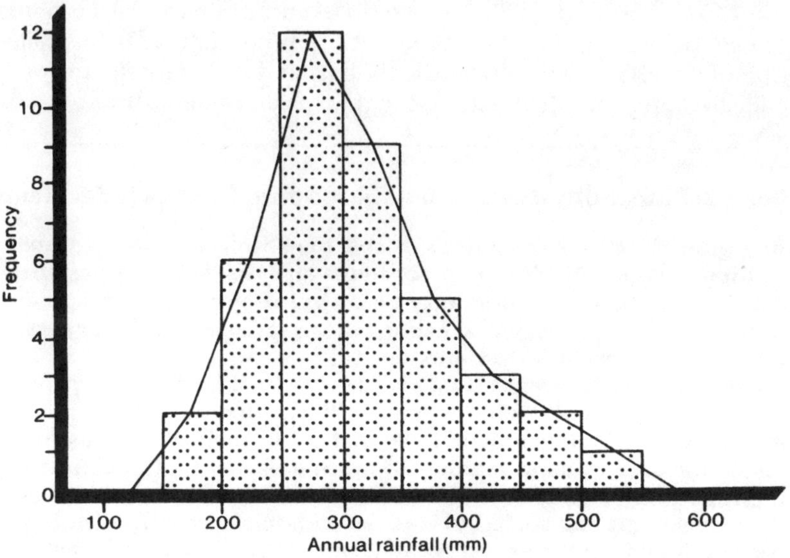


**Figure 8.3: Normal distribution**

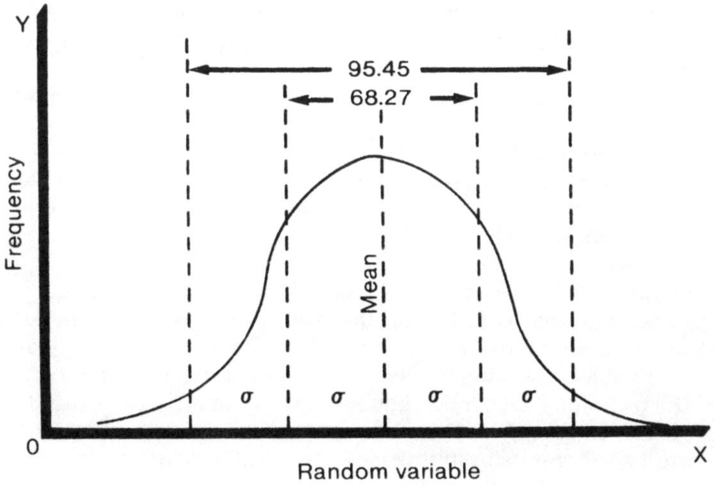

supposedly objective, since it is based on known probability distributions. For example, probabilities of rainfall are often based on historical records. However, subjectivity is still involved in measuring risks from such data, as certain assumptions must be made. These include the assumptions that the time period for the collection of data has been sufficiently long, that data have been properly collected and that the past is a reliable guide to the future.

---

**Box 8.2: Probability distributions based on subjective judgements**

As historical data are often not available to use in estimating probability distributions of variables in an economic analysis, subjective estimates may have to be used. These may be provided by the project appraisal team, where economic and scientific experts provide their best guess for the relevant probability distributions.

Alternatively, the project team may consult local farmers, independent experts or individuals with extensive field experience. In such a process, it is important for two criteria to be met. First, it should be possible to obtain the data without creating too much difficulty for those providing the information; otherwise, the process may become too complicated, time-consuming and subject to bias. Second, the form of the distribution chosen should, on theoretical grounds, match the kind of probability distribution that could be expected if proper historical data were in fact available.

The triangular distribution is very easy to use, as shown by North (1981). It requires subjective judgements on a lower limit ($a$), an upper limit ($b$) and the mode ($m$). One theoretical property of interest is that the distribution can be skewed, as often occurs with environmental variables in dryland situations. The graph of a triangular distribution for wheat prices is shown in Figure 8.4. In this case the distribution is positively skewed; that is, it has a larger number of observations to the right of the mode.

The step-rectangular distribution is described by Pouliquen (1970). To derive this distribution, experts are asked in a series of steps to divide the probabilities of various outcomes into successively smaller intervals. An example is shown in Figure 8.5, for the probability of crop yields in a dryland area.

Pouliquen claims several advantages for the step-rectangular distribution. The approach is based on the concept of preference ranking; the appraisal team is able to freely specify the size and number of class intervals; in practical use, the distribution has proved to be extremely reliable; and the technique gave much better results than attempts to arbitrarily fit theoretical probability distributions to limited data. Pouliquen also reported good results from the use of triangular distributions.

**Figure 8.4: Triangular distribution**

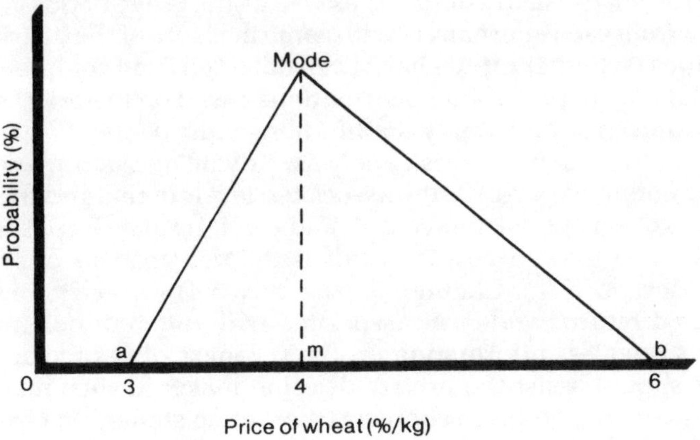


**Figure 8.5: Step-rectangular probability distribution for crop yield**

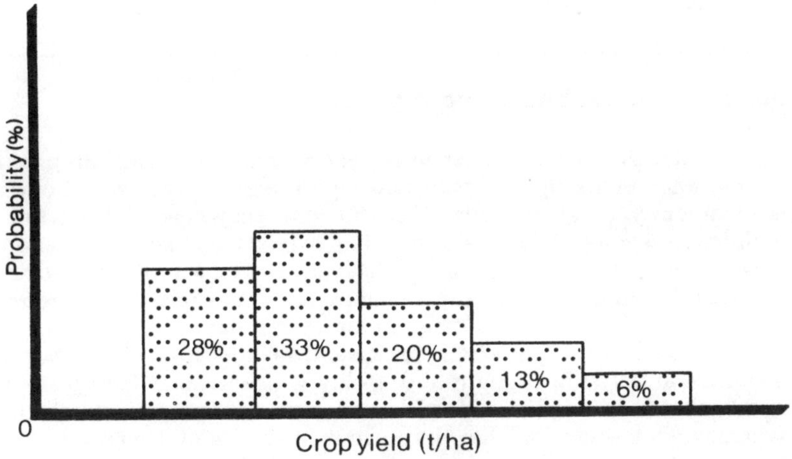


## Risk analysis

*Applications of risk analysis*
Risk analysis forces the analyst to obtain more detailed information on the consequences of alternative actions and rigorously examine the different elements underlying final economic assessments.

More specifically, the probabilistic properties of inputs to the analysis will be clearly defined, as well as the range of possible outcomes from each alternative, with some measure of the distribution of values. Whether inputs have been obtained from completely certain data, from probability distributions based on historical data or from subjective probability distributions must be clearly specified.

Given the results of a risk analysis, private decision-makers can assess potential pay-offs, the associated levels of risk and their willingness to accept risk or avoid it, and can formulate a specific plan of action. A good example of this is the risk analysis of stocking rates described in Chapter 5 (see Box 5.4), which shows the expected returns and costs associated with different risk management strategies. Information on the riskiness of particular alternatives should assist the private decision-maker in such matters as debt financing, crop selection and marketing strategies. Groups of private producers may institute special arrangements to offset risk, such as drought insurance or income stabilization schemes. Government assistance may also be appropriate, but some precautions may need to be observed (see Box 8.3).

---

**Box 8.3: Land use and drought relief**

While arid regions are characterized by low average rainfall resulting from their location in the high-pressure subtropical subsidence zones, drought is a temporary, irregular event which can occur anywhere, and is defined in different regions of the world according to land usage and expectations of water users. Apart from rainfall, other variables which contribute to the different definitions of drought are temperature, precipitation at ground level, evaporation, effective evaporation (precipitation minus evaporation), runoff, sub-surface water storage and soil moisture. Often there is a confusion between drought and aridity which enables land users to redefine arid or semi-arid land as "drought stricken" for government relief schemes. This is facilitated in the Australian system of drought declaration, which is based not on rainfall data or soil moisture measures, but on percentage crop loss or percentage of animals to be moved or slaughtered.

---

In the public investment arena, Pouliquen (1970) has identified four important applications of risk analysis to project evaluations:

(1) The first is in marginal projects, where net benefits are just

positive or where the internal rate of return is very close to the prescribed minimum level. An analysis of the riskiness of the project may determine whether to accept or reject the project.

(2) Another case is where there are unusual uncertainties, such that there is a strong possibility that the project will not earn a satisfactory rate of return. Many dryland development projects are of this nature.

(3) Risk analysis can assist in the design of projects, by isolating the main components and their probabilities influencing the rate of return. Changes in projects can be made in terms of scale, timing and design characteristics.

(4) Finally, in identifying new projects to be considered, risk analysis can increase the scope for action. Uncertain elements in the specification phase can be dealt with at an early stage, and inputs of time, effort and analysis can be minimized by an early rejection of projects with undesirable risk characteristics.

*A framework for risk analysis*

A general framework for risk analysis is described in Figure 8.6. When applied by land users, the aim of the analysis is to derive a probability distribution of the net benefits of a particular investment or land management strategy. The same procedure is applied to public decision-making to obtain a probability distribution of the net benefits of a policy, programme or project.

In the first step, raw data must be obtained. From the raw data, inputs to a predictive model or analytical framework are then prepared. Such inputs can be divided into three distinct categories: deterministic variables, which are known with certainty; stochastic variables with probability distributions obtained from historical data; and variables with probability distributions obtained from subjective judgements. These inputs are then introduced to a predictive model to determine the physical and social impacts of the proposed action. Economic values are placed on predicted effects to obtain estimates of benefits and costs. Finally, a probability distribution for net benefits is generated. This process can be carried out through explicit mathematical analysis or, more commonly, through computer-assisted methods such as Monte Carlo simulation (see Box 8.4).

Despite the difficulties introduced by incomplete knowledge and forecasting ability, it is important to be as objective as possible in the collection and analysis of information, and to present the results to decision-makers in the clearest and most meaningful way. Where subjective judgements have been made, these should be explicitly stated. An interpretation of the results of the analysis should be provided.

**Figure 8.6: General framework for risk analysis**

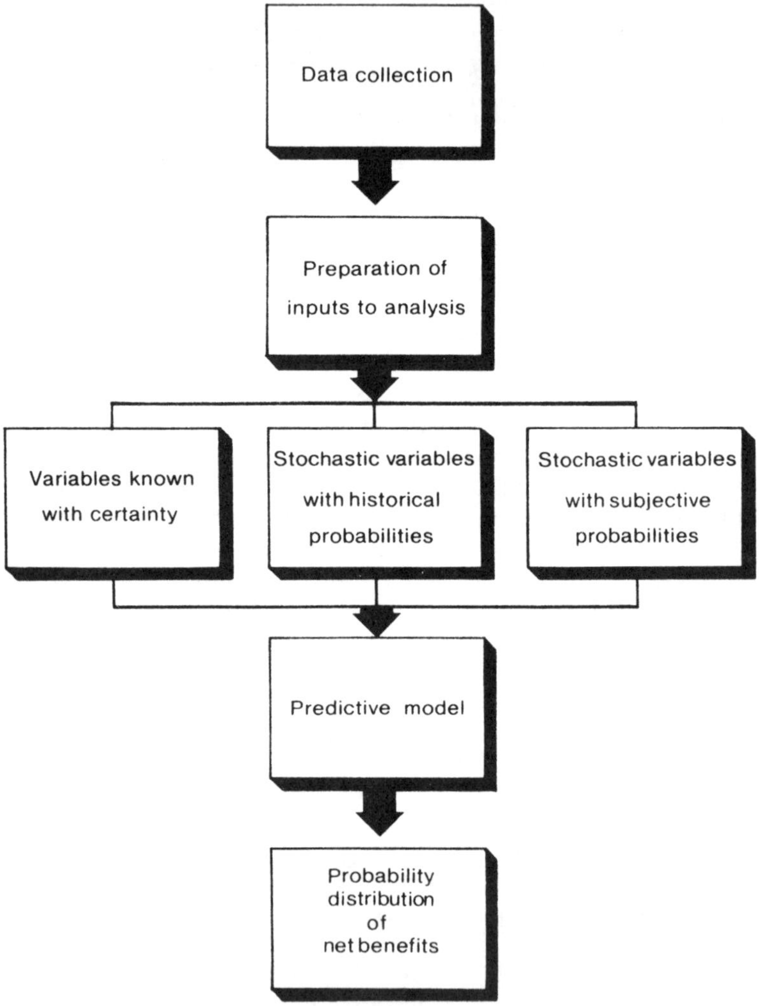


*Interpretation of results of risk analysis*

*Properties of probability distributions.* An example of a probability distribution for the net benefits of a dryland development project is given in Figure 8.8. The range of possible values for net benefits is measured on the horizontal axis, and the probability of each value occurring is measured on the vertical axis. The area under the curve is equal to 1, reflecting the fact that the total probability of all possible net benefit values occurring in reality is 100 per cent. The *expected value* of the distribution is the mean value or arithmetic average of all the values.

---

**Box 8.4: Monte Carlo simulation**

The Monte Carlo technique involves computer simulation of the entire economic analysis. Inputs to the analysis, together with their probability distributions, are fed into the predictive model. Net benefits, with a corresponding probability distribution, are then generated for consideration by the decision-maker. The procedure is shown in diagrammatic form in Figure 8.7; for wheat production where production costs are known with certainty, annual rainfall depends on historical probabilities, and wheat prices are given in terms of subjective probabilities.

Monte Carlo simulation involves a large number of iterations, possibly several hundred. Before beginning the calculations, the probability distributions for rainfall and wheat prices are required in cumulative relative frequency or cumulative probability form. A random number selection procedure must also be established, with random numbers varying from 0 to 1, representing cumulative probabilities for the stochastic variables in the analysis. This is easily achieved with a simple computer program.

To carry out a single iteration, values are randomly selected for each of the stochastic inputs and treated as if they were deterministic variables. The necessary calculations within the predictive model are then performed. A single value will be obtained for estimated net benefits.

The same process is repeated for a second iteration, giving a second estimate of net benefits. By carrying out a large number of iterations, a set of computed values will be obtained for the net benefits of wheat production. From the results, a frequency distribution can be derived. The information is then presented to the decision-maker for his or her evaluation of the relevant risks.

Monte Carlo simulation has a number of advantages (Environmental Resources Ltd, 1985). The technique is flexible and simple and can be understood by the non-expert or non-mathematician. It can be applied by people with limited training, as compared with the use of fitted theoretical distributions which require more highly skilled and costly staff. Any probability distribution can be used and may be specified to the degree of completeness required. Accuracy of the technique depends on the reliability of the predictive model and the number of iterations. It is particularly

**Figure 8.7: Procedure for Monte Carlo simulation**

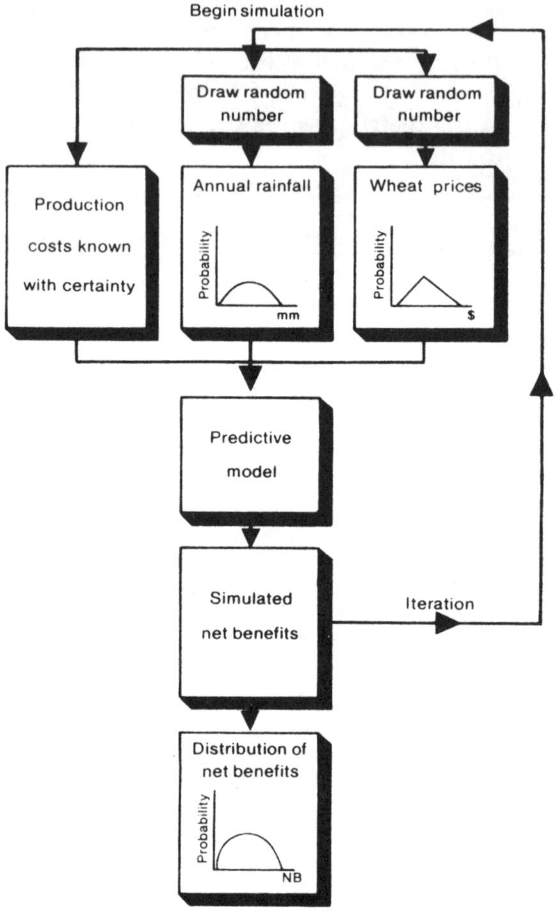


useful for non-linear models. One limitation of the technique is that it becomes much more complicated if the input variables are in any way correlated.

---

The main properties of a probability distribution of relevance to an analysis of risk are measures of central tendency, dispersion and skewness. The *central tendency* of a distribution is most commonly measured by the *mean* (or arithmetic average), the *mode* (the most commonly occurring or most likely value) or the *median* (the value above which and below which half of the probabilities lie). In a symmetrical distribution the mean, mode and median coincide; but if the distribution is skewed, the mean, mode and median have different values. In Figure 8.8 the distribution is positively skewed. For this particular distribution, rare events will tend to have a high rather than a low value. Various statistics are available to measure the *dispersion* of values in the distribution. In general, the greater the dispersion of net benefits, the riskier is the project.

In some applications of risk analysis, cumulative probability distributions are required. Cumulative probability indicates the total probability of all values less than or equal to a particular value. A cumulative probability distribution for rainfall is shown in Figure 8.9. It has the typical S-shape of an ogive.

**Figure 8.8: Probability distribution for net benefits**

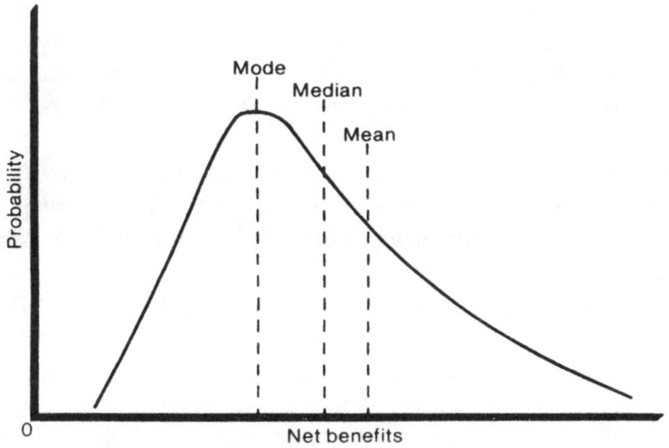


*Attitudes towards risk*. Individuals may be risk averters, risk takers or risk neutral. A simple example illustrates the difference. Consider a new dryland farming technique that is estimated to yield a net benefit of \$1,000 with a probability of 80 per cent, giving expected net benefits of \$1,000 × 0.8 or \$800 (this implies a 20 per cent chance of complete failure with a net benefit of zero). A second technique has a yield of \$4,000 with a probability of 20 per cent, giving the same expected net benefits, calculated as \$4,000 × 0.2 or

**Figure 8.9: Cumulative probability distribution for rainfall**

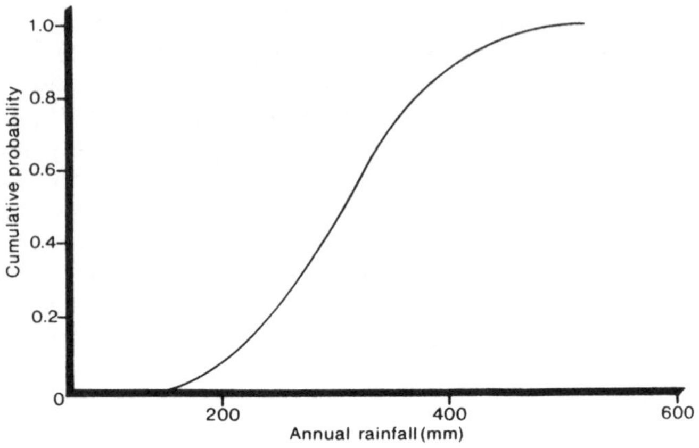


$800 (this alternative has an 80 per cent chance of failure with net benefits equal to zero).

Farmers who regard the two alternatives as equally desirable (that is, who are indifferent between the two outcomes) because they both have expected net benefits of $800 are said to be risk neutral. Those preferring the first technique and who would insist on a higher level of net benefits from the second before judging it equal are described as risk averse. Those who prefer the second technique because of its potentially higher pay-off are said to be risk takers.

A benchmark for assessing the welfare implications of risk is the certainty equivalent, which measures the guaranteed benefit that would make an individual as well off as a risky benefit. The individual's risk preference can be measured by the amount of benefit he/she is willing to trade off to make him-/herself indifferent between a risky benefit and the certainty equivalent. If this amount is positive, he/she will be risk averse; if negative, he/she will be a risk taker; and if zero, he/she will be risk neutral (Norton, 1984).

*Social valuation of risk.* For formulating policies, programmes and projects, societal valuation of risk must be taken into account. Public decision-makers should be aware that their own perception of risk may influence their approach to the formulation of policies, programmes and projects. Community attitudes to risk, whether judged rational or irrational by public decision-makers, are important and can significantly affect the workability of improvement measures in dryland areas. Public decision-makers must nevertheless determine whether they will accept community preferences based on perceived risk, or whether to introduce policies specifically designed to change community attitudes and behaviour. For example, private land users in dryland areas may be reluctant to plant potentially high-yielding crops or adopt new productive technologies because of risk aversion. Through various kinds of economic incentives, land users may be encouraged to adopt improved production methods for the benefit of themselves and the whole community.

It can be generally presumed that, especially in dryland areas with widespread degradation and human suffering, people will be risk averse. In such situations, projects should be selected that minimize exposure to risk. As an example, consider two alternative development opportunities, *A* and *B*. The distributions of net benefits for *A* and *B* are shown in Figure 8.10. Both distributions are symmetrical and have the same mean or expected value. Project *B* is riskier in the sense that there is a greater chance that low net benefits might eventuate, although large net benefits might also accrue. Project *A* is less risky, as the dispersion of values around the mean is smaller. A low value for net benefits is less likely to occur for project *A*. To minimize the probability of an adverse outcome, project *A* should be selected.

To pursue socially risk-averse development strategies within the context of benefit – cost analysis, a risk premium should be

**Figure 8.10: Alternative probability distributions for net benefits**

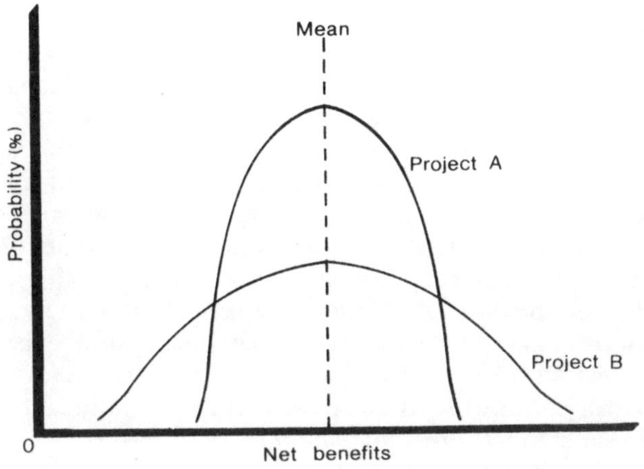

subtracted from expected values to derive estimates of the social value of risky benefits, and added in the case of risky costs. Empirical methods for obtaining measures of risk trade-offs appear to be lacking. It is possible to say only that the cost of risk bearing will be positive in policies and programmes affecting people that are risk averse. A conservative approach to risk bearing in resource management is accordingly suggested.

*Voluntary and involuntary risk.* An important consideration for policy purposes is the distinction between voluntary and involuntary risk. Most individuals insist on safer standards for goods and services provided by governments or large-scale enterprises than they apply to a substitute supplied by themselves. For example, farmers may willingly accept high levels of health risk by using pesticides, but insist on stringent pollution control measures for factories creating an environmental hazard.

New development projects such as the construction of new electric power-stations, intended to relieve pressure from fuelwood extraction in dryland areas, may not contribute significantly to general social welfare because of the community's resistance to the health risks associated with air pollution generated by the power-stations. Such risks are largely involuntarily borne. Even though the objectively estimated risks may be low and the investment shows a high expected rate of economic return, the disutility associated with the perceived health risks may offset the apparent gains.

## Decision-making under conditions of uncertainty

*Decisions based on available information*

The most direct way for a decision-maker to proceed in the absence of information on probabilities is to make an *ad hoc* decision based on available information. Paradoxically, there may be certain advantages, especially for public decision-makers, in this approach. As pointed out by North (1981), many public decision-makers will not accept probabilistic information because it may suggest weakness in the analysis. They may feel uncomfortable about making decisions involving a range of values, rather than a single figure.

Another political problem is associated with risk analysis. If public decision-makers know in advance that harm, however unlikely, can be expected from a particular policy or action, they may have to face a hostile community if an adverse event actually takes place. In some circumstances, ignorance may be preferred.

If uncertainty prevails, one approach is to insist on a higher level of net benefits or higher internal rate of return from public investments in dryland programmes and projects. Some economists have advocated adding a risk premium to the rate of discount, giving a "risky discount rate". This procedure, however, is not advisable. Altering the discount rate is equivalent to deliberately distorting community time preference and capital productivity, which are quite distinct from community attitudes towards risk. The range of uncertainty typically varies for different components of a benefit – cost analysis, and this cannot be properly measured by applying a risk-adjusted discount rate uniformly to all benefits and costs. Instead, the range of uncertainty applicable to different components of the analysis and the attitudes of the community or decision-maker to that uncertainty should be explicitly taken into account.

*Sensitivity analysis*

The information base can be improved through sensitivity analysis or the construction of scenarios. Arbitrary assumptions are made for key inputs to the analysis, generating net benefits ranging from the most optimistic to the most pessimistic values. This approach unfortunately does not indicate the probability of occurrence of the upper and lower estimates, or of values in between. Sensitivity analysis does have the advantage, however, of determining which variables have the most pronounced effect on benefits and costs and which are therefore the most critical in reaching a decision.

*Decision analysis techniques*

*Applications of decision analysis.* Decision analysis is a useful approach to the evaluation of alternative policies, programmes, projects and land-use practices under conditions of uncertainty. Decision analysis has been applied specifically to dryland management by Norton and Walker (1985). The approach assists a decision-maker in making the best decision, but only after allowing for the decision-maker's own attitude towards uncertainty in defining acceptable planning and management strategies. Two important tools of decision analysis are pay-off matrices and decision trees.

*Pay-off matrices.* Pay-off matrices are an extension of sensitivity analysis and can usefully be applied to the ranking of alternative strategies, actions or options which are mutually exclusive. Choice of one alternative automatically precludes choice of another. By conducting sensitivity analysis, the effects of different states of nature (for example, environmental factors or economic conditions) on the net benefits of each alternative can be assessed. The results can then be displayed in a matrix, with strategies as the rows, and different states of nature as the columns. Each element, $NB_{ij}$, indicates the estimated net benefit of the *i*th strategy under the *j*th set of conditions. Such a matrix is called a "pay-off matrix".

An example of a pay-off matrix in a drylands context is given in Table 8.1. It is assumed that a particular section of land may be used for wheat, cattle or sheep. One of these alternatives must be chosen. Net benefits are affected by rainfall which may be high, low or moderate. The net benefits predicted for each alternative under different rainfall conditions are displayed in the pay-off matrix. The problem is to determine which of the land uses is best.

**Table 8.1: Pay-off matrix of net benefits ($000) under different land uses and rainfall conditions**

| | *Rainfall* | | |
|---|---|---|---|
| *Strategy* | *High* | *Low* | *Moderate* |
| Wheat | 170 | 14 | 30 |
| Cattle | 100 | 10 | 70 |
| Sheep | 80 | 20 | 50 |

If the probability of each net benefit value is known, conventional risk analysis can be applied. Objective probabilities are assigned to each outcome, and the best strategy is selected according to expected value, calculated as the net benefit multiplied by the corresponding objective probability (Norton, 1984).

For example, if the probabilities of high, low and moderate rainfall are 0.25, 0.25 and 0.5, respectively, the expected pay-off for each land use can be calculated as

wheat: $0.25(170) + 0.25(14) + 0.5(30) = 61.0$;

cattle: $0.25(100) + 0.25(10) + 0.5(70) = 62.5$;

sheep: $0.25(80) + 0.25(20) + 0.5(50) = 50.0$.

The cattle strategy has the highest level of expected net benefits and is the preferred alternative. The drawback with this approach, as previously explained, is that it assumes that the decision-maker is risk neutral. It does not allow for the effects of specific events on human welfare. In the preceding example, if any level of net benefits below 15 resulted in starvation, the outcomes might be evaluated quite differently.

Where probabilities are not known, arbitrary or subjective judgements must be made about the outcomes in the pay-off matrix. The "best" management strategy can be identified only when additional decision criteria are introduced (Pearce and Nash, 1981).

An acceptable trade-off between exploiting a dryland system and avoiding adverse consequences can be achieved by applying Wald's maximin criterion. This approach is based on caution. Wald advocates listing the worst pay-off for each strategy, then choosing the strategy with the highest of these minimum values. When the outcomes in the pay-off matrix are costs or losses rather than benefits, the Wald criterion leads to the minimization of the highest costs. Under these conditions, the Wald criterion is described as the minimax criterion. It is especially appropriate when a bad year would result in starvation or economic crisis and no defences, such as drought insurance, are available.

The lowest values for the pay-off matrix in Table 8.1 are 14 for wheat, 10 for cattle and 20 for sheep. The largest minimum value is 20, indicating that sheep would be the best choice.

*Decision trees.* In complex resource management situations, outcomes of decisions can be studied by means of a decision tree (Norton, 1984). Decision trees describe the possibilities open to decision-makers and the implications of alternative decision sequences.

A simplified decision tree for the management of land suitable for wheat or sheep production is given in Figure 8.11. The net benefits from each sequence of decisions can be estimated to inform the decision-maker of the economic consequences of his/her actions. In this respect, decision trees are similar to pay-off matrices. The advantage of decision trees is that they clearly describe the options available. They also indicate which options are foreclosed once a particular sequence of decisions has been commenced. Another virtue of decision trees is that they can show where further data collection and analysis are likely to be of value.

*Uncertainty associated with irreversible damage to resources*

*Concepts of irreversibility.* The problem of irreversibility has already

**Figure 8.11: Decision tree for dryland production**

been raised in earlier chapters. In the dryland context, two important categories of response were delineated. First, fallowing or "passive repair" may be practised to reverse past damage. As the required time period must be extended, the more accurately the damage may be classified as permanent. In the second category, positive actions are taken, possibly involving significant investment, to restore the productivity of the resource. Again, as the cost of restoration increases, so can the degree of damage be described as irreversible.

Irreversibility can be viewed as a narrowing of options, and thus the effect of decisions with irreversible consequences is potentially to reduce future economic welfare. A constrained optimal decision cannot be superior to an unconstrained one. The welfare implications and the need for society to take a conservative approach to resource utilization where irreversible effects are imminent have been stressed by economists in the case of stock resources (Hotelling, 1931) for natural species (Ciriacy-Wantrup, 1952) and natural environments (Krutilla and Fisher, 1975).

*Option value*. Irreversibility can be appraised in terms of an "option value" which has been defined by Cicchetti and Freeman (1971) as the difference between an option price and the expected value of consumer's surplus for the use of a particular resource. The option price is the maximum price someone would be prepared to pay to preserve future choices in use of the resource. Alternatively, it may be conceived as the value, in addition to consumer's surplus, of retaining an option to a good or service for which the future demand is uncertain (Fisher and Krutilla, 1975). Option value is similar to a risk premium and would be positive for risk-averse people.

A related concept is "quasi-option value", which represents the benefits obtained by delaying a decision when one of the alternatives involves an irreversible choice and the benefits of other alternatives are uncertain. The policy implications of this concept are that it should be worthwhile reducing pressure on a resource and incurring a short-term reduction in economic benefits to offset uncertainty about future options. Quasi-option value can be associated with delaying a decision to generate better information (Conrad, 1980) and with management of development to reduce uncertainty and improve the information base. These applications are similar to those of adaptive environmental assessment and management (AEAM), which has its origins in ecology rather than economics.

*Problems of irreversibility in the drylands.* The fragility of dryland environments makes them particularly vulnerable to irreversible degradation if improperly used, with serious implications for the welfare of dryland inhabitants. The issue of uncertainty revolves around the economic value of these lands in the future. As agricultural land is in relatively fixed supply, its value will tend to increase as populations grow and as other activities, such as industrialization and urban development, expand. If the opportunity cost of preserving land for agriculture is presently low, options should be preserved. Indeed, any delay in implementing resource protection or rehabilitation measures may simply result in the later generation of massive rectification costs.

## Defensive strategies to cope with risk and uncertainty

*Overcoming the effects of risk*

Various approaches to the management of risk are available. Where risk itself cannot be reduced or avoided, policies can be implemented that mitigate the effects of risk (Little and Mirrlees, 1974). For example, the effects of drought can be mitigated by early warning systems (see Box 8.5), famine relief schemes, emergency cattle fodder reserves and flexible transport systems to move stock and people out of drought-affected areas. Some of these strategies have already been discussed in Chapter 5. Financially, stochastic effects can be buffered through market stabilization schemes, flexible lending arrangements and farm insurance (Ray, 1981). Little and Mirrlees suggest that exposure to risk can be reduced by substituting less risky projects for risky ones.

---

**Box 8.5: Early warning systems**

The advent of drought requires immediate action to reduce the demand for animal feed (by moving or reducing animal numbers) and to find other sources of feed. An early response permits a more gradual transition and reduces the level of the crisis compared to that which occurs when action is delayed until the full force of the drought is felt.

The possibility of early warning rests on the fact that rainfall and forage growth follow somewhat regular patterns. Any marked departure during the early part of the pattern makes it more likely that the pattern as a whole will be affected.

If the data required for the early warning were used only to anticipate drought, gathering it might be too expensive relative to the benefits. However, knowing the state of range production is essential for management during all years, good or bad. In fact, the best possibilities of improving the range and optimizing production may occur only during the more favourable years. Therefore the good years should also be anticipated as early as possible in order to take maximum advantage of them.

An early warning system requires an adequate network for data gathering and sufficient long-term observations so that estimates of variability can be obtained. The network may pose problems of cost where there is a high rainfall variability because the greater the variability the more observation points are necessary. Nevertheless, such a system provides a rational approach to both grazing management and coping with drought.

Remote-sensing data from satellites can show rainfall distribution and vegetative cover. If correlated properly with ground data, this method could vastly increase the area sampled and would be much cheaper than full ground sampling. Indeed, this is a case where the most advanced technology is one that can do the job properly.

(Child *et al.*, 1987 pp.162 – 3. Reprinted by permission of the publisher.)

---

Howe (1979) points out that risk can be handled by risk pooling and risk spreading. Pooling refers to the ability of a centralized agency to undertake a large number of independent projects and combine the total costs and benefits. The expected (mean) return of the pool rises faster than the variance as the number of independent projects increases. Risk spreading involves splitting the burden of risk from a given project among a large number of individuals. Such a policy can be pursued in countries which have diversified economic systems. Potential drought victims can be supported by other members of society. Where the drylands are dominant in the economy, however, the whole society may suffer from adverse outcomes, as is the case in much of the Sudanese – Sahelian region. Under these conditions, risk-averse strategies and development programmes should be followed.

*Investment in information*

As already explained, if excess pressure on dryland resources leads to effects that cannot easily be predicted, future options may be eliminated. Long-run economic benefits may be maximized by delaying development and investing in better information instead (Dasgupta, 1982).

Such investment may take the form of an opportunity cost (that is, the short-term benefits forgone by doing nothing).

Information can be obtained by monitoring the behaviour of dryland ecosystems. Investment in information may also consist of directly sponsoring research programmes and field experiments.

*Use of expert systems*

Expert systems are computer programs that use expert knowledge to assist management decisions. Originating from research into artificial intelligence, expert systems have been widely used in mineral exploration, medicine and organic chemistry, and recently have been applied to natural resource and environmental management problems (Kessell, Good and Hopkins, 1984; Davis and Nanninga, 1985).

Expert systems are particularly useful in situations where decision-makers have only limited time and information to explore management strategies. The computer program is designed to function like an expert adviser and can be operated interactively by the decision-maker.

Unlike traditional simulation models that require detailed numerical data, expert systems focus on the main parameters and causal relations within a system. Moreover, they are more concerned with answering specific questions about the effects of particular environmental conditions and management options. "What if" scenarios are described mainly in terms of the kind of outcome that an expert would predict. Traditional simulation models frequently generate output that is irrelevant to specific management issues, in unnecessarily detailed numerical form. Expert systems are not designed to replace traditional simulation models and, in some situations, could be a valuable precursor to a traditional model-building exercise.

Expert systems are constructed by specialists with skills in computer programming and an ability to elicit and organize information from experts. Considerable time is needed to obtain the relevant bits of information and assemble the program. Special computer languages emphasizing relational operators are used. Once established, the main advantage of an expert system is its flexibility and ease of application. Most programs can be run on a portable personal computer.

Expert systems could greatly assist decision-making in the management of dryland resources. Possible applications include land-use practices, cropping techniques, stocking patterns and rehabilitation measures. They represent an effective way of transferring research results from one country or agency to another and of overcoming problems of deficient knowledge and management expertise in field situations.

*Adaptive environmental assessment and management*

Adaptive environmental assessment and management (AEAM) is an approach to natural-resource management originating in the Institute of Resource Ecology at the University of British Columbia, the Canadian Department of Environment and the International Institute for Applied Systems Analysis in Austria (Holling, 1978; Environment Canada, 1982; Walters, 1986).

AEAM is based on the assumption that uncertainty is an inevitable aspect of natural-resource management. Uncertainty cannot be eliminated, and any attempts to reduce uncertainty should be carefully scrutinized. Such attempts frequently involve significant economic costs. According to the proponents of AEAM, a superior approach is one that explicitly recognizes uncertainty and leads to more resilient strategies that create opportunities to benefit from ecological change. A wide range of alternative management strategies should be explored.

Ecological considerations should be incorporated at an early stage, rather than as an afterthought, so that management strategies can benefit from an enhancement of natural systems. The opportunity to benefit from change should be part of the design goal. Management plans should contain a trial-and-error component. In this way, information will be generated. Monitoring and remedial mechanisms should be part of the management approach. Holling (1978) argues that it is impossible to assess all possible impacts of development. Detailed surveys and descriptive studies are of only limited value, and scientific studies are useful only if focused through policy concerns.

A key feature of the AEAM process is the staging of professional workshops to formulate and explore management strategies. The workshops are led by a small core group of analysts with technical expertise and with skills in integrating information and co-ordinating people. Synthesis of information, specification of management alternatives and communication of results are accomplished through systems analysis modelling. An initial workshop is held with the core group and participating specialists. A crude model is developed reflecting expert opinion, available data and management alternatives. A consolidation phase follows, during which the model is refined. Subsequent workshops explore management options and the implications of uncertainty in greater detail.

AEAM does not rely on any particular type of model. Applications of the method have been based on cross-impact (Leopold) matrices, qualitative simulation models (GSIM and KSIM) and numerical simulation models. Selection of a model depends on available time and data, the system under study and the management options. The technique has considerable potential for applications to the management of dryland resources.

*Critical zones and safe minimum standards*

*The critical zone*. The safe minimum standard (SMS) approach is based on the concept of a critical zone, which defines the limits within which the effects of depletion on the flow of renewable resources are economically reversible. It suggests a benchmark from which the economic desirability of further conservation practices can be gauged. The idea has been developed largely by Ciriacy-Wantrup (1952) and Bishop (1978).

Critical zone resources can be defined in terms of a sustainable flow of renewable products or services. The capacity of the resource is usually an operational measure based on conservation practices such as a permissible rate of soil erosion, maximum stocking rate or maximum harvesting rate. If the critical zone for a particular use has been passed, consideration of a standard for a "lower" use is encouraged. There is little point trying to implement a standard which has already been passed.

*The economic rationale for the SMS*. The basic assumption of the SMS is that the costs of maintaining the SMS are small in comparison with the possible losses accompanying irreversible depletion of land resources. The SMS is specified in physical terms to allow for uncertainty about the process of irreversibility.

As developed by Bishop (1978), the approach uses a pay-off matrix to assess whether the SMS is worthwhile in specific situations. Applied to dryland problems, the rows of the matrix would describe two basic options: adoption of the SMS, or allowing the land to continue to degrade. The columns of the matrix would reflect two possible states: sustainable use of the land, or loss of that option. The elements of the matrix would be social costs.

Wald's minimax rule is then applied to the pay-off matrix. According to the rule, the best option is that which minimizes the maximum cost. Unless the SMS leads to very high levels of social cost, it is preferable to the other alternative. The approach is, as previously explained, based on an attitude of caution towards resource management.

It is important to note that the social costs of adopting a standard in one particular area may be vastly different from those associated with the same standard in some other area. Conclusions on an SMS cannot be transferred between regions or nations.

## References

Bishop, R. C. (1978),
"Endangered species and uncertainty: the economics of a safe minimum standard", *American Journal of Agricultural Economics*, vol.60, no.1, pp.10 – 18.

Child, R. D., H. F. Heady, R. A. Peterson, R. D. Pieper and C. E. Poulton (1987),
*Arid and Semi-Arid Rangelands: Guidelines for Development* (Morrilton, Ark.: Winrock International).

Cicchetti, C. J. and A. M. Freeman III (1971),
"Option demand and consumer surplus: further comment", *Quarterly Journal of Economics*, vol.85, no.3, pp.528 – 39.

Ciriacy-Wantrup, S. V. (1952),
*Resource Conservation* (Berkeley, Calif.: University of California Press).

Conrad, J. (1980),
"Quasi-option value and the expected value of information", *Quarterly Journal of Economics*, vol.94, no.4, pp.813 – 20.

Dasgupta, P. (1982),
*The Control of Resources* (Oxford: Blackwell).

Davies, J. R. and P. M. Nanninga (1985),
"GEOMYCIN: towards a geographical expert system for resource management", *Journal of Environmental Management*, vol.20, no.4, pp.377 – 90.

Environment Canada (1982),
*Review and Evaluation of Adaptive Environmental Assessment and Management* (Ottawa: Environment Canada).

Environmental Resources Ltd (1985),
*Handling Uncertainty in Environmental Impact Assessment* (The Hague: Netherlands Ministry of Public Housing, Physical Planning and Environmental Protection).

Fisher, A. C. and J. V. Krutilla (1975),
"Resource conservation, environmental preservation, and the rate of discount", *Quarterly Journal of Economics*, vol.89, no.3, pp.358 – 70.

Holling, C. S. (1978),
*Adaptive Environmental Assessment and Management* (New York: Wiley).

Hotelling, H. (1931),
"The economics of exhaustible resources", *Journal of Political Economy*, vol.39, no.2, pp.137 – 75.

Howe, C. W. (1979),
*Natural Resource Economics* (New York: Wiley).

Kessell, S. R., R. B. Good and A. J. M. Hopkins (1984),
"Implementation of two new resource management information systems in Australia", *Environmental Management*, vol.8, no.3, pp.251 – 69.
Krutilla, J. V. and A. C. Fisher (1975),
*The Economics of Natural Environments* (Baltimore, Md:Johns Hopkins University Press).
Little, I. M. D. and J. A. Mirrlees (1974),
*Project Appraisal and Planning for Developing Countries* (New York: Basic Books).
Mar, B. W., W. S. Mitter, R. N. Palmer and R. A. Carpenter (1987),
*Cost-Effective Data Acquisition*, Workshop Report No.1 (Honolulu: East – West Environment and Policy Institute).
North, R. M. (1981),
"Risk analyses applicable to water resources program and project planning and evaluation", in Y. Y. Haimes (ed.) *Risk Benefit Analysis in Water Resources Planning and Management* (New York: Plenum Press).
Norton, G. A. (1984),
*Resource Economics* (London: Edward Arnold).
Norton, G. A. and B. H. Walker (1985),
"A decision analysis approach to savannah management", *Journal of Environmental Management*, vol.21, no.1, pp.15 – 31.
Pearce, D. W. and C. A. Nash (1981),
*The Social Appraisal of Projects: A Text in Cost – Benefit Analysis* (London: Macmillan).
Pouliquen, L. Y. (1970),
*Risk Analysis in Project Appraisal* (Baltimore, Md: Johns Hopkins University Press).
Ray, P. K. (1981),
*Agricultural Insurance: Theory and Practice and Application to Developing Countries* (Oxford: Pergamon).
Rowe, W. D. (1981),
"Methodology and myth", in Y. Y. Haimes (ed.), *Risk Benefit Analysis in Water Resources Planning and Management* (New York: Plenum Press).
Walters, C. (1986),
*Adaptive Management of Renewable Resources* (New York: Macmillan).
Whyte, A. V. and I. Burton (eds) (1980),
*Environmental Risk Assessment*, SCOPE Report No.15 (Chichester: Wiley).

# Part IV
# Environmental Policy Instruments

[18]

# POLICY INSTRUMENTS FOR POLLUTION CONTROL IN DEVELOPING COUNTRIES

*Gunnar S. Eskeland*
*Emmanuel Jimenez*

*What are appropriate strategies for protecting the environment in developing countries that also seek to promote growth and reduce poverty? This article reviews the literature on cost-effective intervention, comparing regulatory and fiscal instruments that can be attuned to the purpose of reducing pollution. The authors look at what happens when developing country ingredients are introduced into the standard policy problem, and show how indirect instruments can be effective when monitoring and enforcement are costly. They discuss distributive concerns for two reasons: the effect on the poor may need particular consideration for equity reasons, and the effect on groups with vested interests can determine whether reforms are likely to stand or fall.*

Rigorous studies of pollution control in developing countries do not exist, but there is convincing casual evidence that regulations to protect the environment are ineffective or unnecessarily costly. Often, there are no regulations or they are badly designed or enforced (see Bernstein 1991). In addition, economic policies seemingly unrelated to the environment—subsidies for water consumption, pesticides, fertilizers, and energy use—nevertheless affect it, often for the worse (Schramm and Warford 1989). Evidence on the damage that pollution is doing to human health and productivity is starting to accumulate (see Thomas 1981 and 1985 on São Paulo; Hertzman 1990 on Poland; Margulis 1992 on Mexico).

*The World Bank Research Observer*, vol. 7, no. 2 (July 1992), pp. 145–169

This article reviews the design of cost-effective interventions to protect the environment from excessive pollution in developing countries. The focus is deliberately limited to domestic policies to control pollution. We do not treat policies to address other environmental problems, such as soil erosion, deforestation, biodiversity, or desertification; nor do we deal explicitly with transnational problems (acid rain) or the global consequences of pollution (climate change; ozone depletion). Many of the principles we present, however, relate broadly to correcting for externalities, or spillover effects, and can be applied to these other problems as well (see Binswanger 1989; Mahar 1989; Repetto and Gillis 1988; Schramm and Warford 1989).

The analysis concentrates on policy instruments that have traditionally been in the realm of public finance, such as taxes, prices, and subsidies, comparing these with regulations and other instruments traditionally used to reduce pollution or ameliorate its damage. The interventions can be categorized as (a) market-based incentives (MBIs) that affect the incentives of private agents, (b) command and control (CAC) instruments that regulate activity through constraints on the source of pollution, and (c) government spending on cleanup or enforcement (table 1). In this article we focus on (a) and (b), because the principles guiding the decisions regarding (c) are fairly well established in the cost-benefit literature. We also distinguish between instruments directly associated with the amount of damage created or pollutants emitted, and those addressing pollution indirectly via related variables such as inputs and outputs.

The analysis begins by examining the rationale for government intervention and goes on to look at the relative merits of the policy instruments traditionally prescribed for that intervention in industrial countries. The arguments for these standard policy prescriptions are based on several simplifying assumptions—

**Table 1.** *A Taxonomy of Policy Instruments to Reduce Pollution*

| *Policies* | *Direct instruments* | *Indirect instruments* |
|---|---|---|
| Market-based incentives | Effluent charges; tradable permits; deposit refund systems | Input/output taxes and subsidies; subsidies for substitutes and abatement inputs |
| Command and control measures | Emission regulations (source-specific, nontransferable quotas) | Regulation of equipment, processes, inputs, and outputs |
| Government production or expenditure | Regulatory agency expenditures for purification, cleanup, waste disposal, and enforcement | Development of "clean" technologies |

competitive markets, costless transfers, certainty, full information. These assumptions may be less applicable in developing countries. The remainder of the article investigates what happens to policy prescription when the standard assumptions are relaxed to take conditions in developing countries into account.

## The Rationale for Government Intervention

The efficiency argument for public intervention to mitigate pollution problems is well established in the theoretical literature (see Baumol and Oates 1979, 1988; Tietenberg 1988b). Pollution is an example of a negative external effect; it imposes harmful effects and costs on people other than the polluters. The free market offers the polluters no inducement to reduce the damage, since the costs are largely paid by others. The market, if left to itself, is consequently not the most effective mechanism for keeping pollution at reasonable levels. Optimal control of pollution would occur if the marginal costs, including damages from pollution, were low enough to be balanced by the marginal benefits from the activity.

Is public intervention in fact essential to correct for such externalities? According to Coase (1960), there is no efficiency reason for a government to be involved except to help enforce property rights. Coase's proposition is that if those affected by pollution hold the rights to an unpolluted environment, polluters will "bribe" them to allow some level of pollution. (Member states of the Organization for Economic Cooperation and Development [OECD] and many other countries have, in principle, given property rights to victims through the "polluter pays" principle.) Similarly, if polluters have the right to pollute, victims will bribe them to pollute less. In either case, as long as negotiations are not costly, the resulting amount of pollution would be optimal.

When polluters and victims are few and the number of beneficiaries from an agreement is fixed, the Coase proposition may indeed be valid: negotiations can provide for the internalization of externalities. Such a negotiated solution seems feasible in a situation such as in the Philippines, where soil sediments caused by a single logger threatened the development of tourism in a bay (Dixon and Hodgson 1988). When rivers run from one jurisdiction to another (as the Paraíba does between São Paulo and Rio de Janeiro), the parties involved are easily identified, and they could agree on pollution loads through negotiation. In Turkey, farmers have been awarded damages in court when emissions from factories have hurt their crops; here the established right to an unpolluted environment did provide incentives to abate. Thus, when stakeholders are easily identified and law enforcement is assured, a case can be made that government intervention is unnecessary for efficient outcomes.

But, for the Coase proposition to hold, the costs of negotiating and enforcing agreements must be zero or negligible. In practice, the costs will increase with the number of polluters and victims. In Mexico City, for example, there are

20 million consumers, 2.5 million motor vehicles, and 30,000 industries; it seems hardly feasible that the economic agents concerned will conduct efficient negotiations without an intervening authority. In private negotiation, parties have an incentive to free-ride, either by not revealing willingness to pay or by breaking the agreement. Moreover, to be efficient in the long run, the agreement must accommodate the entry of newcomers into the market and the exit of others.[1] Public intervention will often be the only efficient solution to these coordination problems.

## Standard Policy Prescriptions

Given that intervention is required, what form should it take? Policies aim either to regulate the level of pollution at the source or to change prices or regulations to increase the private costs of polluting. To facilitate comparison, discussion of the standard policy instruments that follows starts out with some restrictive assumptions: (a) pollution is uniformly dispersed—that is, the external costs to society are independent of the location of the source; (b) transferring revenue to or from the public sector is not in itself costly; (c) the costs of monitoring damage and emissions are low; (d) there is no uncertainty about the costs and benefits of pollution control; and (e) a competitive market structure prevails. Toward the end of this section we refine the comparison of instruments by relaxing the first assumption—uniform dispersion. The subsequent section will relate the argument to developing country conditions by relaxing each of the remaining assumptions in turn and adding the issue of distributive objectives.

### *Uniform Dispersion of Pollutants*

When pollutants are uniformly dispersed, ambient quality can be improved or protected only by curbing emissions overall. Command and control policies constrain emissions from each source and do not allow sources to trade the right to pollute. Most industrial countries have relied predominantly on CAC methods, setting and enforcing standards for equipment, processes, or emissions (Opschoor and Vos 1989; Bernstein 1991). Emerging experience from developing countries does not appear to break this trend. With market-based incentives, by contrast, constraints are not source-specific; they provide equal incentives to all by increasing the marginal costs of polluting. Tradable permits, subsidies for abatement, and emission taxes are examples of such instruments. All let the market distribute abatement to where it is cheapest.

CAC VERSUS MBIs IN GENERAL. Command and control and market-based incentives can achieve the same ambient quality, but market-based incentives are generally more cost-effective. CAC can possibly minimize the cost to society if the regulator tailors the abatement costs to each firm, so that no polluter is asked to reduce emissions if another can do so at lower costs. The policy is feasible if polluters are few and readily identified—for example, power plants emitting sulfur oxides in some cities. CAC by a strong regulatory agency may then be quite cost-effective. But generally, and especially in situations with many heterogenous polluters, a large informal sector, and weak public administration, command and control policies will not work so well. Furthermore, in practice, source-specific constraints allow marginal costs to vary among polluters, so that total costs of abatement are not minimized.

In contrast, market-based incentives generally require the regulator to estimate only aggregate (rather than individual) costs of abatement to minimize cost. A regulator would, for instance, issue enough tradable permits for the marginal benefits and costs of abatement to be equated overall; a polluter whose abatement costs are high would purchase permits, whereas one with cheaper abatement options would prefer to reduce emissions (Dales 1968 is an early proponent of this point). A pollution tax can also achieve cost-effective abatement. It allows each polluting source to decide whether to pay the tax or to undertake additional abatement, with the result that low-cost abatement is selected since each source will abate only if the marginal costs of abatement do not exceed the tax rate.

Empirical investigations have strongly supported the theoretical case for market-based incentives: cost saving is reported to be significant over the command and control alternative. Tietenberg (1988b) reviews nine studies in which market-based incentives are calibrated to reach the same ambience level as applied command and control methods. In seven of these studies, the ratio of MBI to CAC costs is 1:4 or lower; in two of them, the ratio is 1:14 or lower. Thomas's (1981) findings from São Paulo, with vastly differing abatement costs between firms and sectors, indicate that savings from market-based incentives would be high.

Market-based incentives are sometimes used in combination with command and control instruments to obtain some of the advantages of a more flexible approach without going to a full MBI system. In the United States, for example, some limited opportunities to "trade" the right to pollute within a command and control framework have been allowed in an attempt to gain some of the savings possible with market-based incentives (see Hahn 1989; Opschoor and Vos 1989). Expanded provisions for emission trading are among the amendments to the United States Clean Air Act (U.S. Government 1990). Some of the manifestations of emission trading have been netting, offsets, bubbles, banking, and lead trading.

- *Netting* allows for internal trades within a firm: a firm can avoid the stringent emission requirements for a new source if it reduces emissions from existing sources.
- *Offsets* are used in areas where the establishment of new polluting activities is banned because air quality standards are not met. Through the offset

provision, a new source may be created if it will reduce more emissions from another source than it will create itself. Germany and the United States have offset provisions.

- *Bubbles* place an imaginary "bubble" over a factory. This allows a firm to combine emissions from its various sources and comply with the general rather than the particular requirements.
- *Banking* allows a firm to earn credits if its emissions are under the legal limit; credits can be used later or sold to others.
- *Lead trading* between refineries in the United States was allowed in order to reduce the costs of a major program to phase out lead in gasoline (1982–87).

The savings from limited opportunities to trade within bounds like these are substantial if the trade allowed is between sources that would otherwise abate at vastly differing marginal costs. Hahn (1989) estimates that the savings related to netting, offsets, bubbles, and lead trading have been considerable.

PRICE-BASED VERSUS QUANTITY-BASED INCENTIVES. As long as there is no uncertainty about abatement costs, price-based incentives (such as taxes) and quantity-based incentives (such as tradable permits) have exactly the same effect. The same level of emissions and economic costs should result. A uniform emission tax will have the same incentive effects as emission permits, because the market will distribute them within the industry according to willingness to pay. Both minimize abatement costs overall, because high-cost abaters will either pay the tax or outbid low-cost abaters for permits.

But although taxes and permits that can be traded freely are conceptually equivalent, some analysts have argued that, for administrative reasons, tradable quotas may be preferable to tax or price instruments (Baumol and Oates 1988). First, adjustment of the tax rate to reach appropriate environmental goals may be costly, particularly in inflationary environments. Second, permits may be easy to implement, because they make it possible to introduce controls without increasing the costs for existing firms. But in some cases, tax-like instruments may be easier to administer than quotas. For example, an indirect pollution tax on fuel consumption may fit more easily into existing administrative processes than a quota (Anderson 1990). In most developing countries, input taxes to curtail emissions would be easier to implement than a completely new scheme such as permit trading.

Unless permits are auctioned, their distributive implications differ from those of taxes. Nonmarket distribution of permits, as well as other compensation schemes, must be designed with caution so as to avoid creating undesirable incentives.

SETTING PRICE-BASED INCENTIVES. Governments using a pollution tax to protect ambient quality should select a base and rate so that the external cost of the activity is internalized. Such an instrument is often called a Pigouvian tax.[2]

The appropriate base for the tax should be the damage caused or a close proxy for damage, such as the volume of emissions. An example might be a carbon tax, which has lately been proposed as a tool for efficient reduction of the emissions that cause global warming. Other examples are taxes applied on air pollution in France, on discharges into water in Germany, and on solid waste in Denmark (Whalley and Wigle 1991; Opschoor and Vos 1989).

The Pigouvian incentive can be either a tax on pollution or a subsidy for abatement. In the short term, the incentive effects can be the same. In the long term, when market entry and exit can be affected, a tax is normally preferable because it does not give firms incentives to enter a subsidized polluting industry.

What determines the rate of the tax? The general rule is to set taxes or public prices of commodities that produce externalities at a rate equivalent to marginal cost of production plus the incremental value of the externality (see Eskeland and Jimenez 1991 for a full discussion). There is no need to tax complements or to subsidize substitutes when the tax on the polluting good fully internalizes the externality. In practice, many polluting activities are subsidized, being priced at less than marginal cost (Schramm and Warford 1989; Repetto and Gillis 1988; Anderson 1990). In such cases, raising prices or taxes closer to marginal cost will already be an improvement over the present situation; emissions can be reduced with no cost at all.

## *Nonuniform Dispersion of Pollutants*

The preceding discussion of policy instruments, for the purposes of comparison, has assumed uniform dispersal of pollutants. Greenhouse gases, such as carbon dioxide, *are* uniformly dispersed. But often pollutants are concentrated in some pattern around the source and downwind or downstream. Removing the assumption of uniform dispersal does not affect the general argument about the relative merits of command and control policies versus market-based incentives, but it does have implications for the details of policy design.

The damage (per unit of emission) caused by a polluting activity will vary, depending on location, on the dispersion characteristics of emissions (determined, for air pollution, by such variables as stack height or speed and temperature of flow), and on the site being polluted. For many major air pollutants, reducing emissions has few benefits over vast rural areas, so that applying uniform emission charges (or one-for-one tradable emission permits) in zones comprising both urban and rural areas would not be cost-effective. The rural/urban dimension illustrates differences in marginal damages per unit of emissions. The principle, and the need for differentiated instruments, is valid for any pattern of nonuniform damages (or, equivalently, benefits). Area A may be vulnerable, but less important to protect than area B if higher present pollution loads in B make the marginal damage there higher. Similarly, for water pollutants such as those characterized by biological oxygen demand, marginal damage from discharges may be high where discharges are high but lower both upstream and downstream. Uniform emission charges might require unnecessary abatement from many sources whose emissions do not pollute the "hot spots." In these cases, the most cost-effective program would require abatement for each source according to whether its emissions pollute vulnerable locations or not. For example, emission charges could vary by location to reflect the ratio of damages to emissions.

In essence, differences in damages per unit of emissions mean that unlimited trading of emission permits is not a good idea. If zoning is in effect, permits need to be distributed carefully among zones, since sources are barred from solving problems of misallocation through trades.

If the polluters in a region display very different ratios of damages to emissions, differentiating instruments accordingly can yield significant cost savings. By the same token, the costs of applying uniform emission charges or permits without zoning will also be high. Atkinson and Tietenberg (1982) calculate that a market-based scheme for particulate emissions in St. Louis would save 83 percent of the costs of a command and control scheme if charges were fully differentiated. The savings would be lower if geographical differentiation of emission charges were limited, and would be only 50 percent if charges were uniform throughout. Seskin, Anderson, and Reid (1983), modeling control strategies for nitrogen oxides in Chicago, find that savings of 93 percent relative to command and control fall to 50 percent if instruments have to be uniform within industries, whereas a scheme with completely uniform instruments would cost twice as much as the command and control strategy. The regulators, not surprisingly, have had an eye on the geographical dimension when designing the command and control scheme, and thus it did better than a market-based scheme that ignored geography.

## Efficient Pollution Control Policy in Developing Countries

How are the standard results just discussed affected when we change the standard assumptions? Let us assume a public revenue constraint, inability to monitor emissions and damages, uncertainty, and a market structure that is not competitive—constraints that confront policymakers in many developing countries.

### *Pigouvian Taxes under a Public Sector Revenue Constraint*

Public budgets are often tight in developing countries. Raising additional revenue through existing tax structures can injure resource allocation, as firms and households adapt to a distorted price regime. And such distortions can be immense: estimates from the United States assess costs at 17 to 56 cents for every additional dollar of tax collected (Ballard, Shoven, and Whalley 1985). In developing countries, where the tax base is often narrow and rates high, distortionary costs are likely to be higher (World Bank 1991).

One attraction of pollution taxes is that they can raise revenue while improving efficiency, by persuading firms and households to reduce negative externalities. Taxing commodities with negative externalities will thus reduce not only the efficiency losses arising from the externality itself (say, damage from pollution) but also the efficiency losses related to generating revenue, since the proceeds may allow other rates to be reduced.

How much can be raised by such efficient taxes? Sandmo (1975) shows theoretically that pollution taxes belong in an optimal tax structure, adding to the rates on polluting goods. Some empirical studies indicate that revenues from efficient pollution control policies will be of the same order of magnitude as total control costs. In a simulation of particulate control in St. Louis, Atkinson and Tietenberg (1982) found that proceeds from permit charges would be in the same range as abatement costs. The study of control strategies for nitrous oxides in Chicago (Seskin, Anderson, and Reid 1983) also found charges in the same range as control costs.

So far, charges have not made an impressive contribution to general revenue in OECD countries. At less than a third of 1 percent of gross national product (GNP) in the Netherlands and at 0.04 percent or less of GNP in the other countries surveyed, the revenues were found to be of no importance for the general budget (Opschoor and Vos 1989). The OECD study further showed that charges were rarely effective in changing behavior because rates were too low and the base was usually insufficiently responsive to individual behavior. But proceeds from pollution charges were an important mechanism for funding selective environmental expenditures in countries where they were earmarked for that purpose. Indirect taxes, such as fuel taxes, could be important in generating revenue: for countries such as Pakistan, the Republic of Korea, and Turkey, a 20 percent increase in the tax on fossil fuels could raise an additional 3–5 percent of revenue. Gil Diaz (1987) found that energy subsidies in Mexico from 1977 to 1984 amounted to $100 billion—equal to the total amount of foreign public debt. Clearly, the budgetary implications of energy pricing can be immense.

Pollution charges may yield more or less than what is needed for environmental expenditures, so the benefits of earmarking should be examined in the broader context of public expenditure analysis (see McCleary 1991 on the pros and cons of earmarking).

### *Monitoring Damages or Emissions: A Role for Indirect Instruments*

The theory reviewed earlier implies that the efficient economic policy (whether market-based or command and control) is to address the external effect directly—for instance, by taxing a polluter or regulating emissions according to the environmental damage caused. In practice, monitoring damages or even emissions at the source may be costly, particularly in developing countries, for technological and institutional reasons. The emissions of many pollutants can only be imperfectly monitored, and the fact that the results of monitoring may cost the polluter money does not make the task easier. In the United States the Environmental Protection Agency (EPA) has 14,000 federal employees, and even so, it monitors very few sources continuously. Russell (1990) notes that the EPA largely trusts corporations in matters of compliance and self-reporting, even though experience with motor vehicles has shown that active tampering (not only inadequate operation and maintenance) is prevalent (see also Hamrin 1991). The monitoring problem is likely to be worse for regulatory agencies in developing countries, since the agencies are often inadequately funded and have less access to technology and trained labor. In Mexico only three plants are scheduled to install equipment for continuous monitoring of emissions; the rest of the 300 most-polluting firms report their own emissions.

To be credible, regulatory agencies must be able to design and administer new schemes; behavior will change only if a threat to penalize noncompliance is seen to have teeth. Even in industrial countries, sophisticated schemes, such as permit trading, have run afoul of implementation issues (Hahn 1989). And even when monitoring is technically feasible, institutions may be too weak to enforce the taxes or regulations based on the monitoring.

When environmental damage or emissions cannot be tackled directly because monitoring and enforcement costs are too high, the regulator will use indirect instruments aimed at the outputs and inputs of the polluting industry or substitutes and complements to its outputs. Indirect pollution taxes applied to fuels such as coal and gasoline—presumptive Pigouvian taxes—are an example. How would the use of such instruments affect the policy choices discussed earlier? With indirect instruments, the "tradability" results apply, in that actions that reduce (increase) emissions by an equal amount should receive an equal subsidy (tax). Indirect instruments, however, typically specify physical actions (such as installation of catalytic converters) rather than emission reductions, and they often yield more emission reductions at one place than another. Investments that reduce emission coefficents for vehicles, for instance, yield highest benefits for the vehicles that are used most intensively. For this reason, indirect instruments will often need to be applied with stronger inducements to specific polluters and, consequently, will have aspects of command and control. An example in which this principle is applied: In Mexico City, high-use vehicles such as taxis and minibuses are required to be cleaner than vehicles in general. Presumptive emission taxes on fuel will thus be effective if emission coefficients for one fuel are the same across users, but they should otherwise be differentiated, if possible. The cement industry, for instance, which does not discharge the sulfur of its fuels, should ideally be refunded presumptive sulfur taxes on fuels.

In assessing the desirability of indirect instruments, the reduced cost of the externality must be compared with the distortions the instruments themselves create through their effect on other choices. A fuel tax, for instance, is efficient if the relationship between consumption and emissions is fixed, if nonpolluting fuel use will be unaffected, and if fuel consumption can be monitored relatively easily. A fuel tax is relatively inefficient, however, for fuel used in polluting as well as nonpolluting activities. Furthermore, other effective abatement measures (such as catalytic converters and scrubbers) are not triggered by fuel economy and thus require instruments other than fuel taxes. Deposit refund systems, similarly, can be attractive when unsafe disposal, rather than use, causes damages (Bohm 1981).

Indirect instruments are blunter tools for tackling pollution in that they may also have undesirable effects on behavior. How can such side effects be minimized?

OUTPUTS AND INPUTS AS A BASE. If a polluter's emissions are fully determined by the consumption of one good, then taxing the good according to marginal external costs is equivalent to an emission tax. Carbon taxes on fuels are an example, because the external effects are independent of both source location and combustion process. But if a polluting good cannot be fully taxed, a related good should be taxed if it is a complement to the polluting good, and subsidized if it is a substitute good. For example, suppose that private vehicle use in urban areas is polluting but cannot be taxed sufficiently (or only at a prohibitive cost). A clean substitute such as a subway should be subsidized, but a clean complement such as central parking facilities should be taxed. This holds unambiguously as long as demand for subway service is unrelated to demand for parking space.

Wijkander (1985) shows that taxation of complements and subsidization of substitutes are efficient under fairly general assumptions, but counterintuitive results can take place depending on own-price and cross-price elasticities of demand. These occur when the indirect instruments bring unintended distortions. In our motor vehicle example, if public transport and central parking facilities are sufficiently strong substitutes for each other, subsidizing subways and taxing parking spaces may lead to overutilization of subways. If this problem arises, parking space should not be taxed so much and may even have to be subsidized.

Sandmo (1976) presents another situation in which indirect instruments are useful. A commodity is used by consumers for two purposes, only one of which has negative external effects. Gasoline use, for example, can be said to be "innocent" when used for countryside driving, but it has negative external effects in terms of pollution and congestion when used in cities. A commodity tax to address the externality is then itself distortionary in relation to the innocent use, and the question is whether an additional instrument on a related good can reduce the costs of that distortion. Sandmo concludes that a related good should be taxed if it is a complement to the polluting activity and a substitute for the "innocent" activity, and subsidized if it is a complement to the "innocent" activity while a substitute for the polluting activity. Intuitively, supplementing gasoline taxes with taxes on central parking and central road use, and subsidizing parking at peripheral metrorail and bus stations, would fit in this picture. If the related good is a complement to *both* uses, it should be taxed if it is more complementary to the polluting use, but subsidized if it is more complementary to the "innocent" use. Likewise for a substitute good: it should be subsidized if it is more substitutable to the polluting use, but taxed if it is more substitutable for the "innocent" use. For instance, if bus services are substitutes for polluting cars, but also for "innocent" bicycles, then one would subsidize buses only to the extent that the former effect is stronger. (See Sandmo 1975 and Balcer 1980 for further illustration of this point.)

There are several possible bases for pollution taxes:

- *Taxing the damage created* makes it possible to differentiate between polluters according to the amount of damage caused per unit of emission. Each source balances marginal abatement costs equally against individual differentiated marginal benefits. No such taxes have yet been applied. Other damage-related instruments are used, however. Liability rules hold polluters accountable for accidents, such as oil spillage (a market-based incentive). Offsets, bubbles (market-based), and zoning policies (market-based and command and control) give some consideration to the location of the source and thereby to the amount of damage it creates. Ambience permit systems are markets in damage quotas and have been simulated but not tried in practice.
- *Taxing emissions* minimizes the costs of abatement by equalizing marginal abatement costs across sources but does not differentiate between sources according to damages. Emission charges thus fail to provide incentives to relocate within a region. Examples include France's tax on emissions to air, water charges in Germany, waste charges in Denmark, manure taxes in the Netherlands, and carbon taxes in Norway.
- *Taxing inputs and outputs of polluting activities* mimics an emission or damage tax (imperfectly) but fails to give incentives to minimize emissions or damages for a given level of inputs or outputs. As an example, lead in gasoline is taxed in Norway and Germany. Many countries also tax fossil fuels in general.
- *Taxing (or subsidizing) fixed inputs of polluting activities* can provide some abatement incentive, but fails to influence how carefully and frequently the equipment is maintained and used. Tax differentiation is applied according to emission characteristics of cars in Germany, the Netherlands, Norway, and Sweden. Many countries tax noise characteristics of aircraft and subsidize or mandate the installation of "clean" equipment or processes.
- *Taxing complements and subsidizing substitutes* are alternatives if the polluting activity is untaxable; they can also be valuable supplementary instruments. Apart from complementary inputs (vehicles), complements are

not otherwise known to have been taxed. As a substitute for private transport, urban mass transport is subsidized almost everywhere.

- *Taxing unreturned items*. Depending on cost relationships, many materials will be recycled without government intervention, particularly if labor is cheap. When additional incentives to recycling are desirable because of external costs, a deposit refund system may be efficient. Such systems have been proposed for batteries and are in place for car hulks and beverage containers in Scandinavia.

FIXED INPUTS. If one cannot monitor emissions or variable inputs and outputs, one can still achieve something by targeting fixed inputs, such as equipment and installations. When it is difficult to observe what people do and earn, governments have often resorted to presumptive taxation to raise revenue, basing the taxes on observable proxies for income such as land ownership or house size. To correct for externalities, the analogous approach would be to tax pollution-generating equipment as if it were used (when use is unobservable) and to tax cleaner equipment at a lower rate. Unlike presumptive taxes used for revenue collection, presumptive taxes on pollution make sense only if they affect behavior.

Technical standards can thus be regarded as indirect instruments under monitoring costs. In the United States the costs of monitoring emissions continuously are prohibitive not only for mobile sources, but often for stationary sources as well (Hamrin 1991). In the United States, Mexico, and many other countries, emissions from mobile sources are controlled through testing of new sources (and in some places through annual testing), even though the results are imperfectly correlated with actual emissions.

Technical standards have been heavily criticized by economists because they tend to be applied in a mandatory, uniform, and thus excessively costly way—and generally in the form of command and control policies, instead of through selective taxes or subsidies on equipment that are differentiated according to presumed emissions. Often, regulations are applied only to new sources, failing to exploit abatement opportunities among other sources. Another problem with this "new-source bias" is that it may increase the market power of incumbents.

Many developing countries now follow the United States's example in lowering vehicle emissions mainly by setting strict tailpipe standards for new vehicles. Thus the major instrument for control is a source-specific constraint applied to equipment, as opposed to emission taxes or taxes on variable inputs such as fuels and road use. The strategy certainly reduces emissions per kilometer traveled. It would be more productive, however, when combined with fuel taxes or other instruments that encourage people to buy smaller vehicles or use their vehicles less.

The effects of indirect instruments are often subtle, because they are frequently a stopgap device, instituted to compensate for the lack of first best instruments. Take, for example, the interaction between standards for new vehicles and a proposed presumptive Pigouvian tax on fuels in Mexico City. As new cars are purchased, the vehicle fleet will become cleaner *and* larger. Whether the Pigouvian tax should decline over time as the fleet becomes cleaner on average depends on whether the air pollution situation overall deteriorates or not.

### *Charges and Permits under Uncertainty*

Even under perfect monitoring, the effects of environmental policies may be uncertain. The benefits from abatement may be subject to events that are inherently difficult to predict. For example, the effects of air pollution can depend on the health of the affected population—about which there is little information in developing countries. Furthermore, the costs of abatement depend on how easily polluters adjust, which a regulator cannot know with certainty.

The standard recommendations about the choice of instruments are affected by uncertainty in three ways: (a) the equivalence of price-based versus quantity-based instruments may no longer hold; (b) in an uncertain environment, flexible instruments are better; and (c) liability rules may be an attractive option.

PRICE-BASED VERSUS QUANTITY-BASED INSTRUMENTS UNDER UNCERTAINTY. When the marginal costs of pollution abatement are known to the regulatory agency, uncertainty about the benefits does not favor one type of instrument over the other. Firms' abatement response depends only on costs and on the policy instrument, which are both known to the firm. So, even if the benefits deviate from expected levels, the abatement level and the efficiency losses will be exactly the same whether the price or the quantity instrument is used.

When abatement costs are uncertain to the agency, producers are assumed to have information that the agency does not have (Weitzman 1974). The quantity instrument, which can guarantee an emission level, is better if unexpected emission loads are costly. This would occur if marginal damages from unexpectedly high emissions are steep (as with leaks from nuclear facilities). Correspondingly, the price instrument, which guarantees that marginal abatement costs do not exceed the tax rate, is better when marginal damages are relatively flat.

In an empirical study, Kolstad (1986) evaluated policies to control sulfur emissions from power plants, where abatement costs were uncertain because of uncertainty about future electricity demand. He found that if marginal benefits were constant, a price instrument would be slightly preferable, but that a mild slope would be enough to make permits the more desirable option. Lyon (1989) argues that tradable permits are particularly attractive to developing countries because they provide certainty about ambient quality in a dynamic context, and they also allow implicit property rights to be changed gradually.

However, if marginal benefits are seen as fairly flat, then price instruments do have the attraction of placing a definite upper bound on control costs.

A combination of instruments may be the solution. Roberts and Spence (1976) suggest a permit to be accompanied by a (high) fee for further emissions and by a promise to repurchase unused parts of the permit (as a subsidy for additional abatement) at a (low) price. As they explain, "The subsidy provides a residual incentive for firms to clean up even more when costs are low. The finite penalty provides an escape valve if costs are very high" (page 203).

FLEXIBILITY OF INSTRUMENTS. What if the planner can adjust policy instruments when information is revealed? The results just mentioned may change if some instruments are more easily adjusted than others. Bawa (1988) suggests a mixed policy under the assumption that a regulatory policy (command and control) can be put into effect faster and more flexibly than a charge (or a tradable permit).

Suppose, for example, that stochastic changes (such as weather) make the ambient quality resulting from a steady flow of emissions worse in some periods than others, but the periods are too short for the effluent charge to be adjusted. An emission tax can then be complemented by a command and control instrument—for instance, factories are closed down under a "smog alert" (see Plourde and Yeung 1989). In practice, pollution control authorities are often authorized to shut down polluting activities selectively on short notice. In several cities in Brazil and also in Mexico City, industries are shut down during crisis periods (Sebastian forthcoming). Both Mexico City and Santiago close central areas to traffic when air pollution reaches threshold levels.

LIABILITY RULES. If monitoring of actions to avoid causing damage is expensive but the source of discharges or spills can be identified, a liability rule might usefully substitute for a regulation (Bohm and Russell 1985). This view of liability is similar to the Coasean proposition about negotiation—that negotiation between polluters and victims can take the place of government intervention—but it explicitly requires support from a legal system. Liability rules will usually distribute property rights, for instance, by postulating that everybody has the right not to be harmed by others. Liability rules can be seen as a complement to other regulations (Posner 1986; Farrel 1987) and will then undoubtedly allow for more flexible case-by-case damage assessment. Incidents such as the Bhopal catastrophe and the Prince William's Sound oil spillage (with sizable damage awards and losses of reputation for the responsible firms) warn firms of their potential liability and thus induce them to take more precautions.

But there are many potential problems that might limit the usefulness of liability rules: low likelihood that offenders will be detected, high costs to victims for representation and litigation, the unpredictability of an underdeveloped judicial process, and the potential insolvency of the liable party. Ringleb and Wiggins (1990) find that in the United States, where liability is generally unlimited, industries prone to litigation are increasingly being dominated by small, independent firms. Shell, for instance, pulled out of oil transport in U.S. waters in 1990. This pattern could indicate that less wealth is backing the potential liabilities, in which case the incentives given may be less powerful, since owners have little to lose. Bohm and Russell (1985) note that the liability instrument may encourage people not to protect themselves against pollution, since the price paid by the polluter is actually passed on to the victims. Kolstad, Ulen, and Johnson (1990) add that uncertainty about liability assessment gives a rationale for supplementing ex-post liability with ex-ante regulatory standards.

### *Noncompetitive Market Structure*

The rules of policy intervention generally assume that markets are competitive. But often that assumption is untenable. In industrial countries, utilities are prime examples of monopolies; they are often subject to controls on both pricing and emissions. In developing countries, many markets may be small; entry barriers, tariffs, and transportation costs high; and access to credit, technology, and law enforcement limited. Utilities and some industries are often public and loss-making, and profit maximization—or even cost minimization—may not be a primary objective.

How do the recommendations for policy intervention change when the polluting firm is also a monopoly (such as a utility) whose market power permits it to supply less than optimal output? In such a case there are two sources of market failure—pollution externalities and market power. Indeed, it is theoretically possible (since output is lower from a monopoly than from a competitive firm) that the exercise of monopoly power may partially address the pollution externality (Buchanan 1969). There would be efficiency gains with two instruments to address each source of market failure. But, if a tax to address the externality directly were infeasible, an output tax would address both problems and would be the sum of a Pigouvian tax and a subsidy to output (Baumol and Oates 1988).

Market power introduces a more serious problem if abatement is to be regulated within a market for pollution permits. If the permit market does not result in competitive pricing, abatement will not be efficiently distributed, even if the number of permits available is optimal. That permit markets will often be fragmented and interdependent may be an additional argument for using price instruments. If polluters behave strategically to manipulate the charge, however, problems similar to those in permit markets will emerge (see Jack 1990).

Different policies may affect firms' entry into and exit from markets, and thereby the extent of their market power (Dewees 1983; Kohn 1988; Spulber 1985). This intuitive conclusion runs counter to the finding in short-term static models that nonmarginal rewards are neutral. The most important consideration is probably that quotas and standards, if they raise the costs of entry, could provide for collusion among existing firms. Assuming competitive behavior, Spulber (1985) shows that an optimal effluent charge (or number of tradable permits) will yield the efficient number of firms and efficient output even if there are economies or diseconomies of scale in production and abatement.

There are many claims that industries in industrial countries (paper and pulp, for example, and copper smelting) have become more concentrated as a result of environmental control policies. This may, however, be a response to excessive concentration on mandated equipment, or a reflection of the fact that abatement requirements usually favor incumbents, thereby discouraging new entrants. (As noted earlier, abatement activities that rely on equipment and fixed installations may justifiably be preferred to other, equally cheap abatement options if they are less costly to monitor.) There are also examples, such as fossil-fueled power generation and steel production in the United States, where pollution control policies have eroded some economies of scale, thus giving a boost to small plants (Gollop and Roberts 1983).

In developing countries, small firms in the informal sector are often major polluters. Restructuring and concentration in an industry could lower the costs of monitoring and enforcement, but using flexible instruments such as taxes and regulation of inputs may also save on those costs. This may be a way to curb emissions from small firms without forcing them underground or out of business.

## Distributive Effects: Welfare and Political Economy

The distributive effects of alternative pollution control policies are important for two reasons. First, an increase in income may be valued more highly for the poor than for others. Second, the government should know who gains and who loses so that it can judge whether a particular reform will have sufficient political support.[3]

### *Environmental Policies and the Poor*

The distribution of the benefits of pollution control is an empirical issue, and the evidence on the differential health effects of reducing pollution is mixed. Several authors have noted that the poor are likely to benefit more (see Anderson 1990; Asch and Seneca 1978), because they tend to live in unhealthy, unsanitary conditions in polluted urban areas and cannot afford to protect themselves or move. Some U.S. studies (see Christiansen and Tietenberg 1985 for a review) support this view—they show that air pollution is worse in cities with many poor residents and, within cities, in the areas where the poor live. Theoretical arguments and some empirical evidence, however, indicate that wealthier people may be more willing to pay for environmental improvement than the poor. This could make the wealthy the principal beneficiaries of control policies (Johansson 1987; Christiansen and Tietenberg 1985).

Most of the researchers comparing the incidence of costs assume the distribution of benefits to be uniform. An exception is Harrison (1975), who notes that the policies to control air pollution from motor vehicles in the United States have affected the rural poor badly—their car ownership rates (and thus control costs) are necessarily high because they have no public transportation alternatives, and the environmental benefits in their areas are modest. In the 1990 Clean Air Act Amendments (U.S. Congress 1990), emission standards for vehicles were made stricter only in the most polluting cities, and this could somewhat reduce the costs to households that derive only minor benefits. Such differentiation makes pollution control harder to administer but perhaps more efficient, if damages per unit of emissions are lower in less polluted areas. As for water pollution in developing countries, it is clear that the wealthy can protect themselves from exposure. Private wells, piped water, and bottled water are available to households that can afford them, leaving the poorer families most vulnerable to surface water conditions.

The incidence of the costs of alternative pollution policies depends on the ability of polluters to pass on the costs to customers, to other producers (if intermediate goods are produced), and to workers. Thus, the elasticities of demand and supply in production and consumption must be analyzed along with the amount that poor households spend on the polluting goods. A higher gasoline tax, for example, may have very little effect on slum dwellers who own no cars and do not use public transport. A diesel price hike may affect commuters and rural communities; vulnerability will depend on the availability of substitutes. Regulatory intervention can also have distributive effects because it affects the cost of doing business, which can be shifted forward to prices or backward to labor and capital. The poor may be especially vulnerable to selective price increases and at greater risk of unemployment if an industry becomes uncompetitive (Yu and Ingene 1982; Yohe 1979).

In industries for which environmental regulations are very costly, changes in costs and practices may affect incidence. For example, if labor is a substitute for polluting inputs (labor and energy are often substitutable), abatement policies can lead to increased labor-intensity in production and can thus increase employment or remuneration of labor. Another situation arises when abatement does not change input combination but simply raises costs in the industry. Assuming flexible prices, Forster (1983) uses a simple theoretical general equilibrium framework to show that the factor most intensively used in the polluting sector will lose remuneration, while the other factors will earn more. Alternative assumptions, such as the introduction of price/wage rigidities (and possible unemployment) or immobile factors would affect the results.

Most empirical studies incorporating the incidence of costs do not explicitly compare alternative instruments. Pearson and Smith (1990) find that carbon taxes sufficient to reduce carbon emissions in the United Kingdom by 20 percent would raise £8 billion in the short run and would be highly regressive, reducing the real income of the very poor by up to 2.7 percent compared with only 0.4 percent for the very rich.[4] They do find, naturally, that if all the proceeds from the carbon tax were redistributed to the poor, the scheme could end up being progressive.

Because the poor most likely spend more of their income, price increases generally tend to have a regressive effect (Gianessi, Peskin, and Wolff 1979; Dorfman 1975), although this may be seen as a transitory phenomenon. Over and above this, Yan and others (1975) found no pattern of regressiveness or progressiveness arising from the specific prices that increased as a result of environmental policies. Water pollution treatment, which is typically partially financed through charges and taxes, appears to have been progressive in some cases and regressive in others.

Lessons about presumptive Pigouvian taxes on marketed goods and services can be derived from empirical studies in developing countries. An internal World Bank study on Indonesia found that the average household spends 4.2 to 4.5 percent of its income on fuels and 0.2 to 0.3 on transport. Among manufacturing industries, no industry had an elasticity to costs of fuel prices higher than 9 percent (most are in the range of 1–3 percent), and labor was assumed to be a substitute for energy. Another internal World Bank study, on Mexico, found that wealthy households spend a higher share of their budgets on transport and communication, suggesting a good tax base for distributive purposes.

## *Political Economy and Implementation*

If some instruments are so much better than others (for instance, market-based incentives rather than command and control, direct rather than indirect), why are they not applied more in practice? Many researchers have shown that policy outcomes are influenced not so much by net gains to society as by who gains and who bears the burden of different strategies. (See Hahn 1989 for a brief review and interpretation; see also Baumol and Oates 1979, 1988; Dewees 1983; Buchanan and Tullock 1975.) If a group that prefers one instrument over another can influence policy decisions, it is likely that a policy will be chosen that does not minimize costs. For example, Buchanan and Tullock (1975, pp. 141–42) compare regulation to an effluent tax, and note:

> Regulation is less desirable on efficiency grounds...but this instrument will be preferred by those whose behavior is subjected to either one or the other of the two policy instruments.... [In] their own

> private interests, owners of firms in the industry along with employees will oppose the (effluent) tax. By contrast, under regulation firms may well secure pecuniary gains from the imposition of direct controls that reduce total industry output.... This political choice setting is...the familiar one in which a small, concentrated, identifiable and intensely interested group may exert more influence on political choice making than the much larger majority.

Thus, a tax on emissions is unpopular among influential polluting industries that, for any given level of abatement effort, strongly prefer not to pay for the remaining emissions. The regulatory agency, for its part, is likely to settle for any solution that is consistent with its ambient quality goals. Those who pay the additional costs of inefficient intervention are citizens at large, who are often badly organized compared to the industry in question. In addition to the inefficiency problems already mentioned, real-world command and control policies tend to be selective and thus very susceptible to rent-seeking behavior.

Political economy—the study of how distributive effects affect decisions—can also be important in setting priorities among environmental problems. Dixon (1991) argues that the wealthy can privately avoid the consequences of water pollution to a greater extent than they can avoid the consequences of air pollution, and that as a result, water pollution control will lag in the policy process.

## Implications for Policy Reform

Which policy instruments are more efficient, practical, and equitable under the constraints that developing country governments confront? What research must be done to provide better answers to the questions we have raised?

The stringent budgetary restrictions in developing countries probably strengthen considerably the case for price-based versus quantity-based interventions, particularly if the instruments are related only indirectly to damages or emissions.

Even though quantity-based interventions (such as tradable permits) can incorporate aspects of market-based incentives, they will in most cases require new administrative systems. For indirect instruments, many governments already have ways of charging for or taxing relevant commodities, and the administrative capacity to manipulate domestic relative prices is generally well established. What price-based interventions and permits have in common is that they can generate revenue. But the potential revenues from pollution control instruments are likely to be small in relation to the overall needs of the treasury—except in the case of fuel taxes, which can generate vast revenues.

In an uncertain world, price-based instruments provide greater certainty about abatement costs. Such instruments are superior when there are concerns that underestimating costs would yield controls that are "too strict" and environmental quality that is "too high"—concerns that arguably trouble policymakers in many developing countries.

The costs of monitoring individual emissions and enforcing their abatement can be high, particularly in developing countries, for technological and institutional reasons. Indirect taxes or subsidies for marketed inputs and outputs are desirable alternatives because they depend less on vulnerable and costly monitoring and enforcement functions. But these instruments also imply additional costs because they can only imperfectly mimic taxes on monitored emissions and damages. The choice of which commodities to tax and at what rates should be sensitive to demand relationships, which play a role in emission reduction and in the probable incidence. These empirical issues should be the subject of future research.

The considerations raised in this article do not mean that instruments such as tradable permits should not be tried out, but that less sophisticated instruments should be considered wherever they can potentially do much of the job in an easy-to-implement, low-cost way. Then, monitoring and enforcement capacity can be developed and priorities set for remaining problem sectors or pollutants. Schemes that encourage self-compliance, such as deposit refund systems, should also be considered.

## Notes

Gunnar Eskeland is an economist in the Country Economics Department of the World Bank. Emmanuel Jimenez is a division chief in the Bank's Population and Human Resources Department.

1. On the long-term efficiency of the negotiated solution with well-defined property rights, see Frech (1973) and Tybout (1972, 1973). Efficiency can be the result if firms that leave or enter a market can charge or be charged for doing so. For a discussion of incentive-compatible demand revelation, see Groves and Ledyard (1977) and Green and Laffont (1979). Farrel (1987) uses a simple approach to show that an intervening bureaucrat may be more efficient than negotiations, even when the bureaucrat is limited by poor information and there are only two agents.

2. Since A. C. Pigou's (1920) seminal contribution, the expression "Pigouvian taxes" has been used for taxes intended to discourage activities with negative externalities. The "polluter pays" principle, as defined by OECD guidelines (OECD 1975; Opschoor and Vos 1989) is not a "true" Pigouvian instrument, because it usually requires payment for abatement but not for damages from emissions.

3. The perspective of this article is policy analysis under a well-defined welfare objective. In this context, insights from public choice models are relevant mostly for problems of policy adoption and implementation. See Buchanan and Tullock (1975) and Hahn (1989) for applications to environmental policies.

4. This calculation is a rough approximation using Roy's identity and a money measure of utility.

## References

The word "processed" describes informally reproduced works that may not be commonly available through libraries.


Anderson, Dennis. 1990. "Environmental Policy and the Public Revenue in Developing Countries." Environment Department Working Paper 36. World Bank, Washington, D.C. Processed.

Atkinson, Scott E., and T. H. Tietenberg. 1982. "The Empirical Properties of Two Classes of Designs for Transferable Discharge Permit Markets." *Journal of Environmental Economics and Management* 9: 101–21.

Asch, Peter, and Joseph J. Seneca. 1978. "Some Evidence on the Distribution of Air Quality." *Land Economics* 54: 278–97.

Balcer, Yves. 1980. "Taxation of Externalities, Direct Versus Indirect." *Journal of Public Economics* 13: 121–29.

Ballard, C. L., J. B. Shoven, and John Whalley. 1985. "General Equilibrium Computations of the Marginal Welfare Costs of Taxes in the United States." *American Economic Review* 75: 128–38.

Bawa, V. S. 1988. "On Optimal Pollution Costs of Policies." In Baumol and Oates 1988.

Baumol, William J., and Wallace E. Oates. 1979. *Economics, Environmental Policy and the Quality of Life*. Englewood Cliffs, N.J.: Prentice Hall.

———. 1988. *The Theory of Environmental Policy.* Cambridge and New York: Cambridge University Press.

Bernstein, Janis D. 1991. "Alternative Approaches to Pollution Control and Waste Management: Regulatory and Economic Instruments." Urban Management Program Discussion Paper 3. World Bank, Washington, D.C. Processed.

Binswanger, Hans P. 1989. "Brazilian Policies That Encourage Deforestation in the Amazon." Environment Department Working Paper 16. World Bank, Washington, D.C. Processed.

Bohm, Peter. 1981. "Deposit-Refund Systems: Theory and Applications to Environmental, Conservation, and Consumer Policy." Published for Resources for the Future. Baltimore and London: The Johns Hopkins University Press.

Bohm, Peter, and C. S. Russell. 1985. "Comparative Analysis of Alternative Policy Instruments." In Allen V. Kneese and James L. Sweeney, eds., *Handbook of Natural Resource and Energy Economics*. Vol. I. Amsterdam: North Holland.

Buchanan, James M. 1969. "External Diseconomies, Corrective Taxes and Market Structure." *American Economic Review* 59, no. 7 (March): 174–77.

Buchanan, James M., and Gordon Tullock. 1975. "Polluters' Profit and Political Response: Direct Controls Versus Taxes." *American Economic Review* 59, no. 7 (March): 139–47.

Christiansen, G. B., and T. H. Tietenberg. 1985. "Distributional and Macroeconomic Aspects of Environmental Policy." In Allen V. Kneese and James L. Sweeney, eds., *Handbook of Natural Resource and Energy Economics*. Vol I. Amsterdam: North Holland.

Coase, Ronald. 1960. "The Problems of Social Costs." *Journal of Law and Economics* 3: 1–44.

Dales, J. H. 1968. *Pollution, Property and Prices*. Toronto: University of Toronto Press.

Dewees, Donald N. 1983. "Instrument Choice in Environmental Policy." *Economic Inquiry* 21 (January): 53–71.

Dixon, J. A. 1991. "The Social Costs of Urban Pollution in Latin America: Incidence and Implications." World Bank, Latin America Technical Department, Washington, D.C. Processed.

Dixon, John, and G. Hodgson. 1988. "Logging Versus Fisheries and Tourism in Palawan: An Environmental and Economic Analysis." EAPI Occasional Paper 7. East/West Center, Honolulu, Hawaii. Processed.

Dorfman, N. S. 1975. "Who Will Pay for Pollution Control? The Distribution by Income of the Burden of the National Environmental Protection Program, 1972–1980." *National Tax Journal* 28: 101–15.

Eskeland, Gunnar, and Emmanuel Jimenez. 1991. "Choosing Policy Instruments for Pollution Control: A Review." Policy, Planning, and Research Working Paper 624. World Bank, Country Economics Department, Washington, D.C. Processed.

Farrel, Joseph. 1987. "Information and the Coase Theorem." *Journal of Economic Perspectives* 1, no. 2: 113–29.

Forster, Bruce A. 1983. "The Backward Incidence of Pollution Control: A Dual Approach." *Journal of Environmental Economics and Management* 11: 14–17.

Frech, H. E., III. 1973. "Pricing of Pollution: The Coase Theorem in the Long Run." *The Bell Journal of Economics and Management Science* 4, no. 1: 316–19.

Gianessi, L. P., Henry M. Peskin, and Edward Wolff. 1979. "The Distributional Effects of Uniform Air Pollution Policy in the United States." *Quarterly Journal* 91: 654–74.

Gil Diaz, Francisco. 1987. "Debt Accumulation and Distorted Growth through Subsidized Public Sector Prices." Banco de Mexico. Processed.

Gollop, Frank M., and Mark J. Roberts. 1983. "Environmental Regulations and Productivity Growth: The Case of Fossil-Fueled Electric Power Generation." *Journal of Political Economy* 91, no. 4: 654–74.

Green, Jerry, and J. J. Laffont. 1979. *Individual Incentives in Public Decision Making.* Amsterdam: North Holland.

Groves, Theodore, and John O. Ledyard. 1977. "Optimal Allocation of Public Goods: a Solution to the 'Free Rider' Problem." *Econometrica* 45: 783–809.

Hahn, Robert W. 1989. "Economic Prescriptions for Environmental Problems: How the Patient Followed the Doctor's Orders." *Journal of Economic Perspectives* 3, no. 2 (Spring): 95–114.

Hamrin, Robert. 1991. "Monitoring and Enforcement of Pollution Control—Lessons from the U.S. Experience." World Bank, Country Economics Department, Washington, D.C. Processed.

Harrison, David, Jr. 1975. *Who Pays for Clean Air: The Cost and Benefit Distribution of Automobile Emission Standards.* Cambridge, Mass.: Ballinger.

Hertzman, Clyde. 1990. "Poland: Health and Environment in the Context of Socioeconomic Decline." Internal Document 13. University of British Columbia, Vancouver. Processed.

Jack, W. G. 1990. "Power Sharing and Pollution Control: Coordinating Policies among Levels of Government." Policy, Planning, and Research Working Paper 887. World Bank, Country Economics Department, Washington, D.C. Processed.

Johansson, Per-Olov. 1987. *The Economic Theory and Measurement of Environmental Benefits.* Cambridge: Cambridge University Press.

Kohn, Robert E. 1988. "Efficient Scale of the Pollution-Abating Firm." *Land Economics* 64, no. 1 (February): 53–61.

Kolstad, Charles. 1986. "Empirical Properties of Economic Incentives and Command-and-Control Regulations for Air Pollution Control." *Land Economics* 62, no. 3 (August): 250–68.

Kolstad, C. D., T. S. Ulen, and G. V. Johnson. 1990. "Ex Post Liability for Harm Versus Ex Ante Safety Regulation: Substitutes or Complements?" *American Economic Review* 80 (September): 888–901.

Lyon, Randolph M. 1989. "Transferable Discharge Permit Systems and Environmental Management in Developing Countries." *World Development* 17, no. 8: 1299–1312.

Mahar, Dennis J. 1989. *Government Policies and Deforestation in Brazil's Amazon Region.* Washington, D.C.: World Bank.

Margulis, Sergio. 1992. "Back-of-the-Envelope Estimates of Environmental Damage Costs in Mexico." Working Paper 824. World Bank, Latin America and the Caribbean—Country Department II, Agriculture Operations Division, Washington, D.C. Processed.

McCleary, William. 1991. "The Earmarking of Government Revenue: A Review of Some World Bank Experience." *World Bank Research Observer* 6, no. 1: 81–104.

OECD (Organization for Economic Cooperation and Development). 1975. *The Polluter Pays Principle.* Paris.

Opschoor, J. P., and Hans Vos. 1989. *The Application of Economic Instruments for Environmental Protection in OECD Member Countries.* Paris: Organization for Economic Cooperation and Development.

Pearson, M., and Smith S. 1990. "Taxation and Environmental Policy: Some Empirical Evidence." Commentary 19. Institute for Fiscal Studies, London. Processed.

Pigou, A. C. 1920. *The Economics of Welfare.* London: Macmillan.

Plourde, Charles, and David Yeung. 1989. "A Model of Industrial Pollution in a Stochastic Environment." *Journal of Environmental Economics and Management* 16: 97–105.

Posner, Richard A. 1986. *Economic Analysis of Law.* 3rd ed. Boston: Little, Brown.

Repetto, Robert, and Malcolm Gillis, eds. 1988. *Public Policies and the Misuse of Forest Resources.* Cambridge and New York: Cambridge University Press, with World Resources Institute.

Ringleb, Al H., and Steven N. Wiggins. 1990. "Liability and Large-Scale, Long-Term Hazards." *Journal of Political Economy* 98, no. 3: 574–95.

Roberts, Marc J., and Michael Spence. 1976. "Effluent Charges and Licenses under Uncertainty." *Journal of Public Economics* 5: 193–208.

Russell, Clifford S. 1990. "Monitoring and Enforcement." In Paul R. Portney, ed., *Public Policies for Environmental Protection,* Washington, D.C.: Resources for the Future.

Sandmo, Agnar. 1975. "Optimal Taxation in the Presence of Externalities." *Scandinavian Journal of Economics* 77: 86–98.

———. 1976. "Direct versus Indirect Pigouvian Taxation." *European Economic Review* 7: 337–49.

Schramm, Gunter, and Jeremy J. Warford, eds. 1989. *Environmental Management and Economic Development.* Baltimore: Johns Hopkins University Press.

Sebastian, Iona. Forthcoming. "Issues in Urban Air Pollution: Mexico City Diagnostic Study." Environment Department Working Paper. World Bank, Washington, D.C. Processed.

Seskin, Eugene P., Robert J. Anderson, Jr., and Robert O. Reid. 1983. "An Empirical Analysis of Economic Strategies for Controlling Air Pollution." *Journal of Environmental Economics and Management* 10: 112–24.

Spulber, Daniel F. 1985. "Effluent Regulation and Long-Run Optimality." *Journal of Environmental Economics and Management* 12: 103–16.

Thomas, Vinod. 1981. *Pollution Control in São Paulo, Brazil: Costs, Benefits and Effects on Industrial Location.* Staff Working Paper 501. Washington, D.C.: World Bank.

———. 1985. "Evaluating Pollution Control: The Case of São Paulo, Brazil." *Journal of Development Economics* 19: 133–46.

Tietenberg, T. H. 1988a. *Emissions Trading: An Exercise in Reforming Pollution Policy.* Washington, D.C.: Resources for the Future.

———. 1988b. *Environmental and Natural Resource Economics.* 2nd ed. Glenview, Ill.: Scott, Foresman.

Tybout, R. A. 1972. "Pricing Pollution and Other Negative Externalities." *The Bell Journal of Economics and Management Science* 3, no. 1 (Spring): 252–66.

———. 1973. "Pricing of Pollution: Reply." *The Bell Journal of Economics and Management Science* 4, no. 7: 320–21.

U.S. Congress. 1990. *Clean Air Act Amendments.* Report S.1630. 101st Cong., 2nd sess.

Weitzman, Martin L. 1974. "Prices vs. Quantities." *Review of Economic Studies* 41: 477–91.

Whalley, John, and Randall Wigle. 1991. "Cutting $CO_2$ Emissions: The Effects of Alternative Policy Approaches." *Energy Journal* 12, no. 1 (January): 109–24.

Wijkander, Hans. 1985. "Correcting Externalities through Taxes on/Subsidies to Related Goods." *Journal of Public Economics* 28: 111–25.

World Bank. 1991. *Lessons of Tax Reform.* Washington, D.C.

Yan, Chiou-Shuang, Ah-Min Chung, Edward C. Kaziara, and Andrew G. Verzilli. 1975. "Air Pollution Control Costs and Consumption Pattern Effects: A Regional Analysis." *Journal of Environmental Economics and Management* 2: 60–68.

Yohe, Gary W. 1979. "The Backward Incidence of Pollution Control—Some Comparative Statics in General Equilibrium." *Journal of Environmental Economics and Management* 6: 187–98.

Yu, E. S. H., and C. A. Ingene. 1982. "The Backward Incidence of Pollution Control in a Rigid Wage Economy." *Journal of Environmental Economics and Management* 9: 304–10.

408-430

[96]

# [19]

*Environment and Development Economics* 1 (1996): 41–63


O13
Q25
H23

## Carbon abatement costs: an integrated approach for India*

SUJATA GUPTA
*Tata Energy Research Institute, India Habitat Place, Lodi Road, New Delhi 110003, India*

STEPHEN G. HALL
*London Business School, Sussex Place, Regent's Park, London, NW1 4SA*

ABSTRACT. Economic models for assessing costs of greenhouse gas abatement can be classified as macroeconomic (top-down) models or micro (bottom-up) models. As yet little attention has been focused on the modelling of developing countries. This paper proposes a methodology for integrating the two approaches and illustrates it with the example of India. The results show that a carbon tax would have limited effectiveness in controlling carbon emissions. Investing carbon tax revenues in carbon-abating technologies can give substantial carbon savings. The costs of carbon abatement using the integrated model are higher than those predicted by other global models with India as a sub-region.

### 1. Introduction

Developing countries (DCs) presently account for approximately 25 per cent of energy-related carbon dioxide ($CO_2$) emissions. It has been projected by a number of studies (e.g. World Bank, 1992; Grubler *et al.*, 1993) that this percentage will almost double by the year 2020. Despite the growing importance of the role of DCs, little attention has been focused on issues specific to their economies. Rather, methodologies and estimates made for the industrialized countries (ICs) are applied to developing economies to arrive at reduction scenarios and cost estimates for the latter. Many global models have been developed to estimate the costs of greenhouse gas abatement. In some of these, DCs are not represented at all (e.g., the DICE model is globally aggregated with parameters based on data for the USA; see Nordhaus, 1990). Most global models are regionally disaggregated to account for regional differences and to model the inter-regional interactions (see, e.g., the IEA model with ten regions (International Energy Agency, 1992); Global 2100 with five regions (Manne and Richels, 1992); and the GREEN model with seven regions (Burniaux *et al.*, 1991)). However, the different regions are modelled with or with reference to data from the OECD (Organization for Economic Cooperation and Development) regions. This limits the models' ability to analyse the effectiveness of different policy instruments in developing regions. Given the structural dissimilarities and

* The authors would specially like to thank Scott Barrett who was responsible for initiating this paper. The paper has improved much with his astute and constructive comments. We would also like to acknowledge the useful comments made by three anonymous referees. This research was carried out with the aid of a grant from the UK Economic and Social Research Council (No. L320 25 3010).

the differences in the objectives of DCs and ICs, developing economies have to be studied within a framework appropriate to these economies.

Single-country models are more useful from the policy planners' point of view as these can be structured according to the specific requirements and characteristics of an economy. A number of country models have been developed, e.g., CBO (1990), Jorgenson and Wilcoxen (1990), Manne and Richels (1990) for the USA; Boonekamp *et al.* (1989) for the Netherlands; Blitzer *et al.* (1990) for Egypt; Blitzer *et al.* (1992) for India; Marks *et al.* (1990) for Australia; Barrett (1990), Ingham and Ulph (1990), Barker and Lewney (1991), Sondheimer (1991) and Symons *et al.* (1994) for the UK. Most of these studies focus on the ICs. Comparing the results from both the country studies and the different regions in the global models surveyed by Boero *et al.* (1991) (pp. 51–3), it is apparent that developing regions incur higher costs for carbon abatement. In the study by Anderson and Bird (1990), the cost of a 68 per cent global reduction in $CO_2$ emissions by 2050 is a 2.8 per cent loss in global GDP, the cost for industrialized economies being a 1.4 per cent loss, and for developing economies a 4.8 per cent loss in GDP.

The estimation of costs for different strategies to control $CO_2$ emissions can be made using either macroeconomic models or micro analysis of technological options to reduce carbon emissions. Few micro level studies have been carried out to assess the technological potential at the global level. Goldemberg *et al.* (1987) attempted a global bottom-up study; other examples of bottom-up studies are Williams (1990) and Lovins and Lovins (1991). UNEP (1992) provides a comprehensive review of both top-down and bottom-up models.

Macro models are based on aggregate macroeconomic relationships and provide a framework for studying macroeconomic impacts of and responses to different policies, in the short as well as the long term. These models lack technological detail, and typically overestimate costs since technological responses to the emission constraint are not adequately modelled. Micro, or engineering, models are based on engineering relationships, and contain the necessary technical information to assess technologies and abatement potential. They have limited interactions with the rest of the economy. In micro models, costs are underestimated, since indirect costs of implementing specific strategies are overlooked and economic and physical barriers preventing full realization of technological potential are ignored. Each approach has strengths and limitations. Wilson and Swisher (1993) report a wide gap between the cost estimates from the two approaches. Using both models complementarily can remove the limitations which are inherent when an approach is used in isolation. As yet, few attempts have been made to integrate top-down and bottom-up modelling. Grubb (1993) reviews the various modelling approaches, and comments that 'we are still missing an adequate model for the technical-behavioural-econometric interface'.

In this paper, a methodology for integrating the two types of models is proposed and illustrated with the example of India. For the success of a global initiative on global environmental issues like greenhouse warming it is important to appraise DCs, like India, with high anticipated population and economic growth rates.

The next section examines the characteristics of the Indian energy situation and of factors contributing to the increasing emissions of energy-related $CO_2$. The third section of the paper presents the integrated micro and macro model, and section 4 discusses some of the results for India. The final two sections compare the results with other studies and draw some conclusions.

**2. Overview of the energy situation in India**

From the energy consumption point of view, the evolution of an economy can be categorized in three stages. In the initial stage of development, the level of per capita income and commercial energy consumption is low and there is heavy reliance on traditional forms of energy. In stage two, the pace of economic development accelerates. There is a change in the composition of GDP towards more energy-intensive output, an increased level of urbanization, a growth in per capita income levels and greater availability of and preference for commercial energy. In the third stage, commercial energy intensity starts to decline with development and growth in the economy. The share of energy-intensive goods in total output declines and technological advancement makes production more efficient and less energy-intensive. Eventually, total commercial energy consumption may start to decline. India is in the second stage. Because of subsidized energy prices, constrained energy supply and lack of reliable time series data on traditional energy sources for India, it is difficult to predict when its energy consumption pattern will move from stage two to stage three.

Commercial energy consumption in India is increasing rapidly and is projected to grow in future. An evaluation and review of past energy consumption patterns provides useful directions and insights for formulating future energy scenarios. As shown in Table 1, between 1971 and 1991, commercial energy consumption increased at an average rate of 5.5 per cent and that of fossil fuels at 5.6 per cent per annum. The share of coal has remained consistently high, and accounts for more than 55 per cent of commercial energy consumption. The share of natural gas has increased and that of oil has fluctuated around 30 per cent, seeming to decline from 1989 onwards. The share of non-fossil commercial energy, i.e. hydro and nuclear power, is also falling. Given India's large coal reserves and past trends and recent developments in its economy, coal can be expected to

Table 1. *Percentage share of different sources of primary commercial energy*

| *Year* | *Coal (%)* | *Oil (%)* | *Natural (%)* | *Hydropower and nuclear (%)* | *Fossil fuels (Mtoe)* | *Total commercial energy (Mtoe)* |
|---|---|---|---|---|---|---|
| 1971 | 57 | 30 | 1 | 12 | 58.2 | 65.8 |
| 1976 | 59 | 28 | 1 | 12 | 74.5 | 84.4 |
| 1981 | 56 | 30 | 1 | 12 | 94.2 | 107.9 |
| 1986 | 56 | 30 | 3 | 11 | 130.4 | 145.8 |
| 1991 | 57 | 28 | 5 | 10 | 179.2 | 198.2 |

*Source:* International Energy Agency (1993).
*Note:* For converting hydro and nuclear power in terms of primary energy equivalent, a conversion efficiency of 33 per cent was assumed.

Table 2. *Energy intensity and per capita energy consumption*

| *Year* | *Annual per capita GDP (1987 Rs)* | *Energy intensity(kgoe/ 1000 Rs)* | | | *Annual per capita energy availability (kgoe)* | | |
|---|---|---|---|---|---|---|---|
| | | *Carbon energy* | *Total commercial energy* | *Total energy* | *Carbon energy* | *Total commercial energy* | *Total energy* |
| 1971 | 2823 | 36.8 | 41.6 | 96.2 | 103.8 | 117.4 | 271.6 |
| 1976 | 2931 | 40.5 | 45.9 | na | 118.7 | 134.5 | na |
| 1980 | 3084 | 41.6 | 47.7 | 97.6 | 128.3 | 147.1 | 301.0 |
| 1987 | 3691 | 47.6 | 52.2 | 90.4 | 175.7 | 192.8 | 333.8 |
| 1991 | 4243 | 48.7 | 53.9 | na | 206.8 | 228.8 | na |

*Source:* World Bank (1993); Government of India (1991) and International Energy Agency (1993) for non-commercial energy consumption.
*Note:* na indicates non-availability of data for non-commercial energy sources.

remain a major source of commercial energy, and the share of natural gas is likely to increase.

Two important energy indicators are per capita energy consumption and the energy intensity in the economy. These are estimated in Table 2, with respect to carbon energy, commercial energy and total (commercial and traditional) energy. The main conclusions are:

1. Total energy intensity is decreasing.
2. Total commercial energy and carbon energy intensities in the economy are increasing.
3. Per capita consumption of carbon energy, of commercial energy and of total energy is increasing rapidly.

The increasing rate of growth of carbon energy and of carbon energy intensity indicates that carbon emissions will continue to grow. However, the decline in total (commercial and traditional) energy intensity and the decreasing rate of increase in commercial energy intensity indicate that a reduction in the rate of growth of carbon emissions is possible in the future.

In the past, all energy sectors have been at least partially subsidized. Subsidization of certain energy products is not uncommon worldwide and the opportunity cost principle is not always followed. In India, subsidized prices prevent consumers and producers of energy from receiving appropriate signals from the market, and energy markets are often in disequilibrium. As energy is priced below its opportunity cost, the demand for it is not affected by a small rise in prices. On the supply side, with low prices, producers do not receive an adequate incentive or generate surpluses to invest in production expansion. Energy markets are thus supply constrained. This results in a very low responsiveness to prices; price elasticities for energy demand are very low and sometimes positive.

Some comparative statistics at the international level are presented in Table 3 and in Figure 1. A positive correlation between per capita income level and per capita energy consumption is evident (Figure 1). At low levels of per capita incomes the increase in per capita commercial energy consumption is more than the proportionate increase in per capita income,

Table 3. *International comparison (1992)*

| *Country* | *Per capita income (1992 $)* | *Commercial energy intensity (kgoe/1992 $)* | *Per capita commercial energy consumption (kgoe)* |
|---|---|---|---|
| Germany | 23030 | 0.1818 | 4358 |
| Japan | 28190 | 0.1220 | 3586 |
| UK | 17790 | 0.2083 | 3743 |
| USA | 23240 | 0.3330 | 7662 |
| Brazil | 2770 | 0.2632 | 681 |
| China | 470 | 1.4286 | 600 |
| India | 310 | 0.8330 | 235 |

*Source:* World Bank (1994).

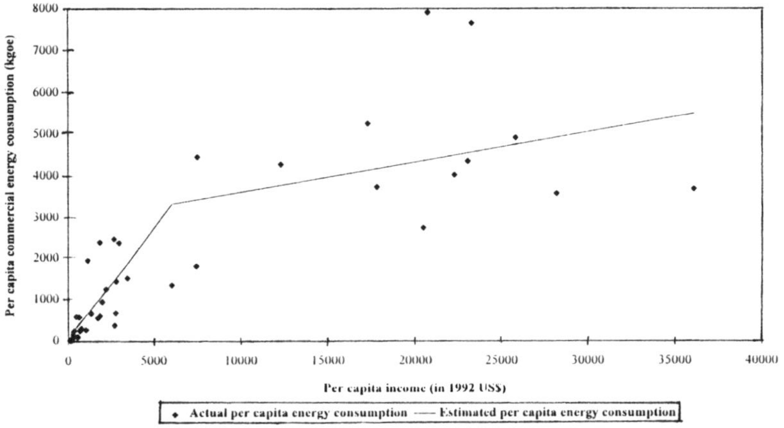


Figure 1. *International comparison.*

implying that energy intensity increases with economic growth. At higher per capita income levels, changes in per capita energy consumption are less than the proportionate changes in per capita incomes, indicating decreasing energy intensity with growth. India's very low per capita incomes are expected to rise, and a more than proportionate increase in per capita energy consumption is likely. Energy intensity in the economy is negatively related to the per capita income level. Developing countries like India and China have very high energy intensities and have substantial scope to improve the efficiency of their energy use. Thus, with increasing per capita incomes there are two opposite forces in operation, one which is likely to increase and the other to reduce energy consumption. The former is likely to predominate in India for the next two to three decades.

The main characteristics of the energy situation in India are: traditional energy sources comprise a large proportion of energy consumption; coal is the main commercial energy source; there are distortions in the energy markets, the correction of which would have positive impacts on energy demand and supply; and commercial and carbon energy intensities are high and increasing, and, combined with rapid growth and increasing per capita income in the economy, will increase commercial energy consumption.

*Carbon emissions*

Energy-related $CO_2$ emissions have increased from 56.52 MtC (million tonnes of carbon) in 1971 to 171.76 MtC in 1991, an average annual growth rate of 5.56 per cent. Population, per capita GDP, energy intensity, the share of fossil fuels in total energy and the composition of fossil fuels (which determines the carbon intensity of fossil fuels) are the factors which explain the change in carbon emissions. The following identity (Equation (1)) gives a decomposition of different factors contributing to $CO_2$ emissions.[1]

$$CO_2 = POP * \frac{GDP}{POP} * \frac{TCE}{GDP} * \frac{FF}{TCE} * \frac{CO_2}{FF} \qquad (1)$$

where $CO_2$ is the total of $CO_2$ emissions in the economy (in MtC) per year; *POP* is the total population (in millions); *GDP* is the gross domestic product (in million 1987 rupees) per year; *TCE* is the total commercial energy (in Mt oil equivalent (Mtoe)) per year; and *FF* is the fossil fuel energy (in Mtoe) per year. Annual growth rates are calculated for each of the contributing factors, and the sum of the percentage changes for these factors explains the total change in carbon emissions.

In Table 4, the figures in parentheses show the contribution of each factor to the growth in carbon emissions. Carbon emissions from the energy sector are increasing at an increasing rate (Table 4, column 7). This pattern is consistent over the past twenty years. Population growth is a significant factor in the increase in carbon emissions, but its relative role has been steadily declining (from 45.4 per cent to 32.7 per cent). The contribution of per capita GDP has increased from 15 per cent to over 50 per cent. The

Table 4. *Annual rate of growth (%) in factors contributing to carbon emissions*

| *Period* | *Population* (*POP*) | *Per capita GDP* (*GDP/POP*) | *Commercial energy intensity* (*TCE/GDP*) | *Fossil fuel share* (*FF/TCE*) | *Carbon intensity of fossil fuels* ($CO_2/FF$) | *Carbon* ($CO_2$) |
|---|---|---|---|---|---|---|
| 1971–76 | 2.27 | 0.75 | 1.97 | –0.04 | 0.05 | 5.00 |
| | (45.4) | (15.0) | (39.4) | (–0.8) | (1.0) | (100) |
| 1976–81 | 2.26 | 1.75 | 0.90 | –0.21 | 0.40 | 5.08 |
| | (44.5) | (34.4) | (17.7) | (–4.2) | (7.6) | (100) |
| 1981–86 | 2.13 | 2.45 | 1.42 | 0.50 | –0.60 | 5.86 |
| | (36.4) | (41.9) | (24.3) | (8.4) | (–10.9) | (100) |
| 1986–91 | 2.05 | 3.20 | 0.90 | 0.21 | –0.70 | 6.29 |
| | (32.7) | (50.9) | (14.2) | (3.3) | (–1.1) | (100) |

[1] Ideally the change in carbon emissions should be studied by specifying energy intensity in terms of primary energy. However, given the data limitations associated with traditional energy use, the analysis is based on Equation (1).

growth rate for commercial energy intensity has fluctuated, and is diminishing, as is its contribution to growing carbon emissions. The share of fossil fuels in total commercial energy decreased in the first half of the period, but has grown in the second half. Since 1981, despite the decline in the share of non-fossil energy in commercial energy, the carbon intensity of fossil fuel has started to decrease; this is explained by the higher share of natural gas in fossil fuel consumption (Table 1).

The above analysis suggests that the main driving force behind the increase of carbon emissions in the Indian economy is increasing per capita incomes. A declining rate of growth in carbon intensity of fossil fuels is not sufficient to reduce or stabilize the growth in carbon emissions. Given India's large coal reserves, this factor has limited scope to decrease $CO_2$ emissions substantially in the future. Analysis of past data and of factors contributing to growing energy-related carbon emissions indicates that commercial energy intensity will increase in the near future. This conclusion contradicts the assumptions made in most studies examining $CO_2$ emissions and their abatement for India and other developing regions, which assume that commercial energy intensities will decline (e.g. the 12RT model; L. Schrattenholzer (International Institute of Applied System Analysis), personal communication, 1993). With increasing per capita incomes and with the switch from traditional sources of energy to commercial energy, such a decline seems unlikely for India in the next twenty to thirty years.

**3. The integrated micro–macro model for India**

As noted in the introduction, two extremes in modelling approaches are being used to study the economics of global warming: macro models which oversimplify technological development and assume that economic choice operates at the technical optimum (Grubb, 1993); and engineering models which evaluate technology in great detail but exclude all the macroeconomic linkages and economic barriers that prevent the full realization of technological potential. Most of the energy environmental models developed are either macroeconomic (top-down) or engineering (bottom-up) models. Integrating the two approaches can improve the quality of analysis considerably. Though the importance of synthesizing these two approaches is well recognized, the actual integration has rarely been attempted. The UNEP (1992) study on greenhouse gas abatement costs does not find a model which is a mixture of both approaches. An integrated model would enable a better estimation of costs of policy options for carbon abatement. Manne and Richels (1992) use an Energy Technology Assessment model where energy is divided into electric and non-electric, with a simplified technology representation for both. Anderson and Bird (1992) use a global model which allows renewable energy technologies to expand at different rates and at costs which reduce with economies of scale. The macroeconomic part of their model is not very developed. A methodology to integrate micro and macro analysis within a single framework has been developed by Gupta (1995) and is briefly summarized below.

*Micro analysis*

A range of technological options which would reduce emissions of $CO_2$ is examined by Mathur *et al.* (1992) and Gupta (1995). For each carbon-abating technology identified, its potential in the Indian economy, the investment required to achieve this potential and the resultant saving in $CO_2$ emissions are estimated. The investments are annualized to account for the different operating lifetimes of the investments. The ratio of annualized investments to annual carbon savings gives the specific *investment* cost per tonne of carbon saved. The technologies are ranked in order of increasing investment requirements per unit of carbon saved. Cumulatively adding the investment requirements and the carbon savings (in order of increasing specific investment requirements), a relationship between the level of investments and carbon savings in the economy is estimated. The resultant carbon abatement–investment curve for the Indian economy is shown in Figure 2, where cumulative annual carbon savings are plotted on the $x$ axis and cumulative annualized investments on the $y$ axis. From the investment–abatement curve it is possible to determine the level of annual carbon savings if the level of annualized investments in carbon-abating technologies is known.

*Macroeconometric model*

Developing economies are not in equilibrium, and given our interest in the near and medium term, rather than in the very long term, a macroeconometric model is more suitable than a general equilibrium framework. Macroeconometric models are able to model market imperfections and disequilibria like unemployment and capital shortage. They are based on economic data and give fairly robust economic predictions. These models are therefore appropriate for the study of the adjustment period and adjustment costs. However, econometric models can identify welfare only with aggregate consumption or with GDP, as these are based on National Accounts data and not on explicit optimization behaviour at the individ-

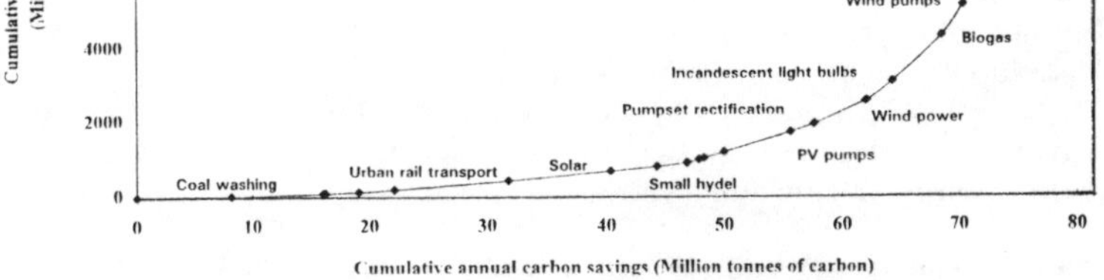


Figure 2. *Investment abatement curve.*

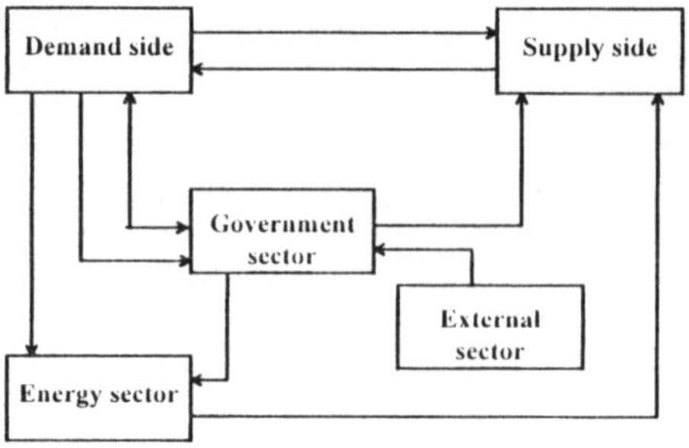


Figure 3. *Macroeconometric model for India.*

ual level. A detailed comparison of the two approaches is contained in Gupta (1995).

The macroeconometric model estimated for India is a Keynesian demand model with a fully specified supply side. The supply side of the economy is modelled through prices in the economy. The model has twenty-five behavioural equations and forty-three other equations (link equations, identities and conditions). Figure 3 represents the model schematically. In estimating the model for India, cointegration analysis and two-step error correction modelling techniques,[2] separating the long-run relationship from the short-run dynamics, have been used. This made the model suitable for longer-term analysis (up to the year 2020) than conventional econometric models. In the Appendix, the key equations for the energy sector are given.[3] The energy sector in the model is discussed here to explain the integration of the micro and macro approaches.

Carbon energy demand is modelled as a function of real carbon energy prices, GDP and a trend term. The long-run equation for carbon energy demand has the following functional form which has been used to model the long-run fossil energy demand for nine OECD countries in Boone *et al.* (1992).

$$CE_t = A.CEPR_t^{\alpha}.YD_t.e^{\gamma T} \quad (2)$$

where $A$ is a constant; $CE_t$ is carbon energy demand; $CEPR_t$ is the real weighted price of carbon fuels; $T$ is trend; $YD_t$ is gross domestic product; $\alpha$ is price elasticity of carbon energy demand; and $\gamma$ is a parameter relating to the trend term.

The technological response to policy changes and to other non-price factors (for example, the shift from non-commercial forms of energy to commercial energy) is represented by the trend term. The parameter $\gamma$ is related to the factors capturing the trend in energy intensity.

In the model a unitary income elasticity for carbon energy demand is assumed, i.e., carbon energy demand is scaled to the level of output. This assumption assists in determining the price elasticity, irrespective of the

[2] A review of these techniques is given in Cuthbertson *et al.* (1992).
[3] The full model is available from the authors on request.

size of the economy, and in isolating the pure price effect. The changes in carbon energy demand with a change in the level and composition of output, discussed by Hodgson and Miller (1995), are accounted for by the trend term. Energy scaled to the size of the economy avoids spurious regressions that would result from an identification problem. This is analogous to the approach adopted by Davidson *et al.* (1978) in explaining the long-run relationship between consumption and income. They found that different researchers modelling similar theories with the same data set arrived at different estimates. The solution to this range of 'spurious estimates' was a model with a unitary income elasticity of consumption. Imposing a unitary income elasticity also avoids the problem of multicollinearity between GDP and the real price of carbon energy.

The long-run price elasticity for fossil energy demand, $\alpha$, was found to change from negative to positive with change in the estimation period and with varying of the lag length specified in the Johansen procedure. The price elasticity is expected to be negative. The largest, estimated significant negative value for $\alpha$, $-0.028$, implies a very low price responsiveness. This is not unexpected, as in the Indian economy the supply side factors have dominated the demand for fossil energy.

The value estimated for the $\gamma$ coefficient was found to be positive. In the energy demand models for the OECD countries (Boone *et al.*, 1992), this parameter was negative for all the countries and could be interpreted as a proxy for the technological innovation parameter. For India, this parameter was positive, indicating that energy intensity would increase, as would be expected for a developing economy. However, the increase would be at a declining rate. Thus, for the future the trend term is modelled such that the rate of increase is not constant but declining. The trend term $T$, is defined as

$$T = T(-1) + 1 - Be^{rt} - \lambda *(\ln CEPR_{simu} - \ln CEPR_{base}) \qquad (3)$$

where $t$ = time. The term $Be^{rt}$ accounts for the less than constant increase in energy intensity over time. Therefore, $T$ is not a simple time trend, but a trend which increases by a decreasing amount over time.

In a policy simulation, the trend is further affected by the policies undertaken. Equation (3) assumes that policy-induced price changes, through carbon taxes, will have effects on technological innovation and energy intensity in the economy that will be permanent and cumulative over time. For example, if increasing energy prices through taxation resulted in an improvement in the efficiency of energy utilization, removing the tax would not return the economy to the earlier path of inefficient energy consumption as in the business-as-usual scenario (where no policy is undertaken). The last part of Equation (3) models this effect caused by a change in energy prices between the base case ($CEPR_{base}$) and the policy simulation ($CEPR_{simu}$). The difference in the logs of energy prices in the simulation and the base case, multiplied by $-\lambda$, models the technological response to policy. This response persists in future as the specification of $T$ includes its lagged value. This effect is permanent and cumulative over time, thereby incorporating price-induced technical progress in the model.

This specification of the trend term endogenizes the impact of a policy on the carbon energy intensity.

The parameter measuring the technological (permanent) response to price changes, $\lambda$, was estimated for nine ICs using Kalman filter techniques (C. Smith, personal communication, 1994; Smith *et al.*, 1995). The parameters for all the ICs were found to be fairly close. It is not possible to directly estimate this parameter for India, given the imperfect energy markets and lack of other relevant information. In the model for India, the value for $\lambda$ is based on the estimates for the ICs. It is possible that the value of $\lambda$ for India would be higher given the lower level of technological development (Gupta, 1995).

*Integrated framework*

In a capital-constrained economy, from the macro point of view, the level of total investment is very important. The level of total investment in carbon-abating technologies determines the extent of implementation of these technologies and the resulting carbon savings in the economy. At the micro level, lack of investment capital prevents the implementation of carbon-abating technologies.

A relationship between the level of investment in carbon-reducing technologies and the carbon savings is derived from the micro analysis of carbon-abating technologies. The investment–abatement relationship is obtained by regressing the annualized investment against the annual carbon savings. The value of annualized investments in carbon-abating technologies ($ACARINV_t$) depends on the total investments in carbon-abating technologies ($TCARINV_t$) and the operating life of these technologies:

$$\ln(ACARINV_t) = constant + \omega \ln(TCARINV_t) \quad (4)$$

Carbon savings in the economy are a function of investments in carbon-abating technologies undertaken in the past. It has been assumed that the policy-related investments in carbon-abating technologies are different from the business-as-usual scenario for ten years. In other words, after ten years it is assumed that the carbon-abating technology under consideration becomes the standard level of technology in the economy. Therefore, in the model, investments in carbon-abating technologies are first annualized, then in order to determine the 'effective' level of investments ($CARINV$) which reduce $CO_2$ emissions, the annualized investments in carbon-abating technologies over the past ten years are aggregated. These aggregated annualized investments determine the level of carbon abatement:

$$CARINV_t = \sum_{i=t-40}^{i=t} ACARINV_t \quad (5)$$

The investment–abatement curve based on current carbon-abating technologies is the best estimate for the future investment–abatement relationship, given the uncertainty. The investment–abatement relationship represents the different carbon-abating technologies that would be operational at various points in future. The investment–abatement curve for India is relatively flat at first, but beyond a certain level of carbon abatement it is very steep (Figure 2). We approximate this by fitting two different functional forms, one for the more elastic part and the second for the relatively inelastic portion:

$$\ln(CARSAV_t) = constant + \tau \ln(CARINV_t) \qquad (6a)$$

$$CARSAV_t = constant + \chi \ln(CARINV_t) \qquad (6b)$$

Total carbon savings are translated into carbon energy saved (*CESAV*) by using the carbon intensity of fossil energy in the previous time period. The ratio of carbon energy savings to GDP is subtracted from the carbon energy intensity of GDP (i.e. *CE / GDP*) in the long-run equation for energy demand in the macro model. In the base case scenario, total carbon investment will equal zero, whereas in a policy scenario with a policy initiative to invest in carbon-abating technologies, carbon savings would result:

$$\ln(CE_t/GDP_t) - (CESAV_t/GDP_t) = constant + \alpha \ln(CEPR_t) + \gamma T + v_t \qquad (7)$$

Equation (7) incorporates in the long-run equation for carbon energy demand the impact of micro level investments in carbon-abating technologies. The price-induced technological response and the declining energy intensity over time are included through the trend term, *T*. All the above equations are part of the macro model, but the parameters in Equations (4), (5) and (6) have been estimated from the micro level analysis.

It is important to stress that the price-induced technological effect on carbon energy intensity is different from the effect on carbon energy intensity due to investment in carbon-abating technologies. Investments in carbon-abating technologies represent a movement along the investment–abatement curve and are not price-induced. The price-induced technological effect is analogous to a shift in the investment–abatement curve due to a greater penetration of efficient technologies and an irreversible and higher level of technological innovation.

The integrated model incorporating micro level information within a macro framework, has the capability of studying policy scenarios where, besides macroeconomic policies, additional efforts are undertaken to reduce $CO_2$ emissions.

## 4. Results

*Base case*

The base case run provides a basis for comparing different scenarios and for analyzing the impact of different policies. A scenario approach has been adopted: i.e., cases with different policy initiatives are considered and the model is used to determine their impact on the economy and its energy-related $CO_2$ emissions. The impact of a policy simulation is measured as a deviation from the base case. Analysing the results under different 'what if' cases gives useful insights into the likely effect of different initiatives undertaken to control $CO_2$ emissions and the performance of the

Table 5. *Growth rates (%) for GDP, carbon energy and $CO_2$ emissions in the base case*

| | *1976–1990* | *1991–2000* | *2000–2010* | *2010–2020* | *1991–2020* |
|---|---|---|---|---|---|
| GDP | 4.9 | 4.6 | 3.9 | 4.0 | 4.1 |
| Carbon energy demand | 5.9 | 5.7 | 4.7 | 4.4 | 4.9 |
| Real price of carbon energy | 1.4 | 0.7 | 0.5 | 0.5 | 0.5 |
| Carbon energy price | 9.0 | 6.0 | 4.4 | 4.3 | 4.9 |
| Carbon energy intensity | 0.9 | 0.9 | 0.8 | 0.4 | 0.7 |
| Carbon emissions | 5.8 | 5.6 | 4.6 | 4.3 | 4.9 |

economy under these changed circumstances. The model for India gives results for the economy till the year 2020.

In the base case the economy grows at an average rate of 4.1 per cent per annum from 1990 to 2020. An overall average annual growth rate of 4.1 per cent over thirty years is not unlikely, given that the economy has grown at nearly 5 per cent in the past twenty-five years.

Carbon energy demand grew at 5.9 per cent per annum from 1976 to 1990, and in future grows at 4.9 per cent per annum for the base case. There is a decrease in the average annual growth rate for each decade (Table 5). $CO_2$ emission growth rates are marginally lower than those for carbon energy demand. This is because over time the share of natural gas, a less carbon-intensive fuel, increases and the share of coal, a more carbon-intensive fuel, decreases.

The carbon energy intensity in the economy in the base case increases at an average annual rate of 0.7 per cent per year over the period 1990–2020. The rate of growth is much slower in the last ten years at only 0.4 per cent. The model predicts a growth in carbon energy intensity, albeit at a declining rate. Stabilization of energy-related carbon emissions at a pre-2020 level is unlikely in the absence of policy initiatives undertaken to reduce these emissions. We examine the impact of a carbon tax on carbon emissions and growth in the economy.

*Description of the scenarios*

The following two scenarios were compared with the base run.

1. *Low carbon tax:* In this scenario a carbon tax of Rs200 per tonne of carbon, in real terms, is levied on fossil fuels from the year 2000 onwards. This tax is equivalent to approximately 10 per cent of the real average price of carbon energy in the early 1990s.
2. *High carbon tax:* A carbon tax of Rs600 per tonne of carbon, in real terms, is imposed from the year 2000 to 2020. This tax is equivalent to approximately 30 per cent of the average real price of carbon energy in the early 1990s. This scenario signifies a stronger initiative from the government to control $CO_2$ emissions compared with scenario 1.

Three different cases were considered for each scenario:

(A) All carbon tax revenues add to government revenue, thereby reducing the government budget deficit. This case measures the direct as well as indirect price effects of a change in energy price through taxation.

(B) Fifty per cent of the carbon tax revenues add to government revenue (as lump sum tax revenues) such that the government budget deficit is reduced. Fifty per cent of the tax revenues are invested in carbon-abating technologies. In this case, control of carbon emissions is more important than in case A.

(C) All carbon tax revenues are invested in carbon-abating technologies. There is no reduction in the government budget deficit as a result of this tax. Cases B and C examine the combined impact of the price effect and specific policies aimed at technological upgrading to reduce $CO_2$ emissions.

*Scenario results*

The results for these scenarios are given in detail by Gupta (1995), and are summarized in Tables 6 and 7.

*Scenario 1:* The real price of carbon energy increases by approximately 11 per cent. The higher price of energy increases the price level in the economy (the consumer price index, CPI) in each case. The change in the CPI increases from case A to case B to case C. The cost of carbon abatement is measured as the average loss in GDP in the last ten years, i.e. from 2011 to 2020, over the base case. This loss in GDP is approximately 2.3 per cent in all three cases (Figure 4).

Three factors reduce demand for carbon energy: the 2.3 per cent decrease in GDP; the direct and indirect price effects; and in cases B and C, the investments in carbon-abating technologies. The decrease in carbon energy demand is smallest in case A, where there are no investments in carbon-abating technologies (Figure 5). Case C has the highest investments in carbon-abating technologies, and gives the largest carbon energy savings (Table 7).

Carbon savings increase from 157.2 million tonnes in case B to 168.2 million tonnes in case C for the year 2020, an increase of only 11 million tonnes (6.8 per cent), despite a near-doubling of investment in carbon-abating technologies (Table 7). This result can be explained by the non-linear relationship between investment in carbon-abating technologies and the carbon saved. In the initial stages, large carbon savings can be produced from relatively small investments in carbon-abating technologies, but once the cheaper options are exercised (corresponding to Equation (6a)), further investments in carbon-abating technologies bring about less than proportionate increases in carbon savings (corresponding to Equation (6b)). The non-linearity also explains the decrease in the percentage of carbon saved over the base case, over time. Increasing investment in carbon-abating technologies for cases B and C brings about larger absolute savings in carbon emissions, but smaller savings relative to the base case (Tables 6 and 7). Investing in carbon-abating technology can increase carbon savings significantly; the limitation is that, as investment increases, its efficiency in reducing carbon emissions declines.

Carbon energy intensity, relative to the base case, reduces from case A

Table 6. *Percentage change in selected variables over base case for scenarios 1 and 2*

| *Variable* | *Case A* | | *Case B* | | *Case C* | |
|---|---|---|---|---|---|---|
| | *2010* | *2020* | *2010* | *2020* | *2010* | *2020* |
| Real price of carbon energy: | | | | | | |
| Scenario 1 | 11.1 | 11.1 | 11.0 | 11.2 | 11.0 | 11.3 |
| Scenario 2 | 32.4 | 32.8 | 32.4 | 32.9 | 32.4 | 33.4 |
| GDP: | | | | | | |
| Scenario 1 | −2.3 | −2.3 | −2.3 | −2.3 | −2.3 | −2.3 |
| Scenario 2 | −5.8 | −6.0 | −5.8 | −5.8 | −5.8 | −5.8 |
| Carbon energy: | | | | | | |
| Scenario 1 | −3.5 | −4.5 | −29.2 | −22.8 | −31.9 | −24.4 |
| Scenario 2 | −8.8 | 11.5 | −38.2 | −31.8 | −40.5 | −33.3 |

Table 7. *Selected variables for scenarios 1 and 2*

| *Variable* | *Case A* | | *Case B* | | *Case C* | |
|---|---|---|---|---|---|---|
| | *2010* | *2020* | *2010* | *2020* | *2010* | *2020* |
| Carbon tax revenue (billion 1987 Rs): | | | | | | |
| Scenario 1 | 87 | 132 | 64 | 107 | 62 | 105 |
| Scenario 2 | 246 | 366 | 166 | 282 | 160 | 276 |
| Total investment in carbon-abating technologies (billion 1987 Rs): | | | | | | |
| Scenario 1 | 0 | 0 | 32 | 53 | 61 | 104 |
| Scenario 2 | 0 | 0 | 82 | 139 | 158 | 272 |
| Carbon emissions (Mt C): | | | | | | |
| Base case | 452 | 693 | 452 | 693 | 452 | 693 |
| Scenario 1 | 435 | 660 | 319 | 535 | 308 | 524 |
| Scenario 2 | 410 | 609 | 277 | 469 | 267 | 459 |
| Carbon energy intensity of GDP (kgoe/Rs): | | | | | | |
| Base case | 0.051 | 0.053 | 0.051 | 0.053 | 0.051 | 0.053 |
| Scenario 1 | 0.050 | 0.051 | 0.037 | 0.042 | 0.035 | 0.041 |
| Scenario 2 | 0.049 | 0.049 | 0.033 | 0.038 | 0.031 | 0.037 |
| Total carbon savings (Mt C): | | | | | | |
| Scenario 1 | 16.7 | 32.2 | 132.7 | 157.2 | 143.7 | 168.2 |
| Scenario 2 | 41.7 | 83.6 | 174.7 | 223.6 | 184.7 | 233.6 |

to case B to case C. In case A, given the decrease in GDP and the small decline in energy demand, the carbon energy intensity is close to the base case values. In cases B and C, the values of carbon energy intensity for 2020 are lower than in the base case by 21 per cent and 22.5 per cent, respectively. Policies to put carbon energy intensity on a lower growth path are available, but stronger policies are required to stabilize and reduce carbon energy intensity and to decouple growth in the economy and the demand for carbon energy.

*Scenario 2:* The rate of carbon tax is three times that in scenario 1. The impact of a higher tax is similar to the results in scenario 1, but with a

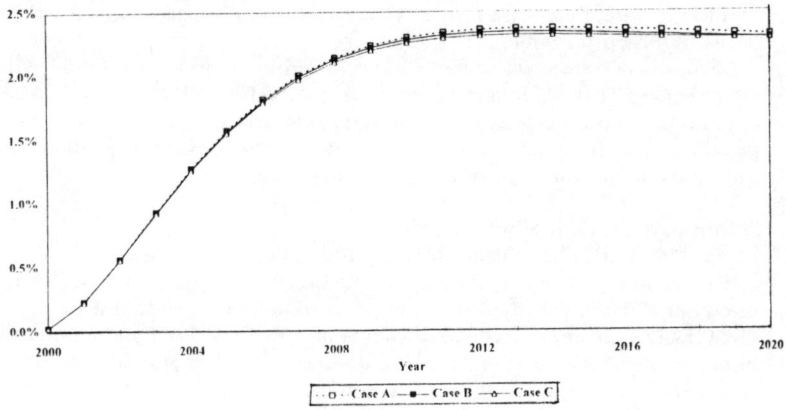


Figure 4. *Loss in GDP.*

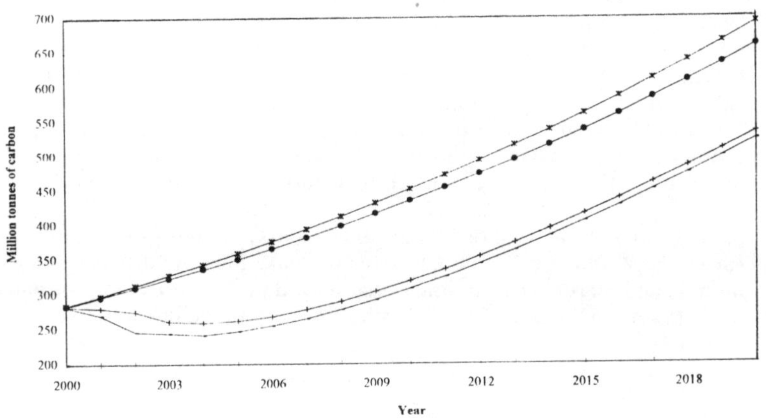


Figure 5. *Carbon emissions: scenario 1.*

difference in the magnitude of the results. Loss in GDP is higher at 5.9 per cent over the base case. Carbon energy demand declines in each case; the observations made in scenario 1 are repeated here and can be explained on a similar basis. As expected, the carbon energy savings are larger, with carbon energy intensity of GDP lower by 6.3 per cent, 38 per cent and 41.1 per cent for cases A, B and C, respectively, for the year 2020.

Comparing scenarios 1 and 2, we find that in cases B and C the percentage reductions in carbon energy demand in scenario 2 are 1.4 times the values for scenario 1. Total investments in carbon-abating technologies increase by a factor of 2.6 for both cases B and C. The less than proportionate change in carbon energy demand can be explained by the non-linear relationship between the level of investment in carbon-abating technologies and the resultant carbon savings. This effect is not apparent for case A, as here only the price effect is operating.

Beyond a certain level of investment in carbon-abating technologies the effectiveness of these investments declines. Additional savings in carbon emissions require very large investments. Different policies, aimed at improving the technological response and at structural changes, would be required to stabilize and/or reduce carbon emissions.

**5. Comparison with other studies**

Few other studies have been done for India, despite the strong likelihood of its becoming a major contributor to greenhouse gases in the future. Blitzer *et al.* (1992) studied the combined reduction of $CO_2$ and methane. The OECD's GREEN model and Manne and Richels' 12RT model include India as one of their regions (L. Schrattenholzer (International Institute of Applied System Analysis), personal communication, 1993). These and the results from this study are shown in Table 8.

For the GREEN model (Table 8) a policy scenario with a carbon tax of $200 per tonne of carbon reduces carbon emissions by 78 per cent over the base case with a loss in GDP of 1.8 per cent. The results for the 12RT model for the same policy are a 56 per cent reduction in carbon emissions and a loss in GDP of 3.4 per cent over the base case. The results from GREEN and 12RT indicate that carbon emissions for India can be reduced below the 1990 level by 2020. Results from this study are presented as an average percentage change in GDP and carbon emissions over the base case for the last ten years of the forecast period. In this study, a 27.7 per cent reduction in carbon emissions over the base case is possible with a loss of 2.3 per cent in GDP. At a higher cost of 5.9 per cent loss in GDP, it is possible to reduce carbon emissions by 37 per cent over the base case. As different types of models with very different time horizons and policies are being compared, the ratio of percentage loss in GDP to the percentage of carbon savings is

Table 8. *Comparison with other studies*

| *Model* | *1990* | *Base case 2020* | *Policy scenario 2020* | *Loss over base case 2020* | *Ratio of loss in GDP to carbon savings* |
|---|---|---|---|---|---|
| GREEN: | | | | | |
| GDP (index ) | 100 | 375.5 | 368.9 | 1.8% | |
| Carbon (Mt C) | 151.2 | 613.9 (4.7) | 135.7 | 78% | 0.023 |
| 12RT: | | | | | |
| GDP (Index) | 100 | 371.7 | 359.4 | 3.4% | |
| Carbon (Mt C) | 158 | 260.5 (1.7) | 115.7 | 56% | 0.061 |
| This study, scenario 1: | | | | | |
| GDP (index) | 100 | 347.1 | 339.1 | 2.3% | |
| Carbon (Mt C) | 161.5 | 692.6 (4.9) | 524–660 | 4.3–27.6% | 0.535–0.083 |
| This study, scenario 2: | | | | | |
| GDP (index) | 100 | 347.1 | 326.8 | 5.9% | |
| Carbon (Mt C) | 161.5 | 692.6 (4.9) | 459–609 | 10.9–36.8% | 0.541–0.160 |

*Note:* Figures in brackets give rate of growth in the business-as-usual case for carbon emissions.

a better measure to compare results from different studies. The costs from this study are much higher. This indicates that assumptions for DCs based on OECD data often underestimate the costs of reducing carbon emissions in developing regions.

There are a number of reasons for the differences between the various studies, such as: the values of the behavioural parameters; the time-frame under consideration; the structure and type of the model; the level of aggregation; interactions with the rest of the world; and the treatment of backstop technologies.

The main reason for the difference in costs of carbon abatement is the price elasticity for carbon energy demand. This model uses an estimated value of –0.028, whereas other studies impose a much higher price elasticity. For example, in the 12RT model the implicit price elasticity is –0.3.

Another reason for the difference in costs is the type of model. From the developing economies' point of view, the next few decades are more important than the very distant future. Also, DCs' economies are far from an equilibrium position, and a small shock to the system affects their stability. In view of these considerations, econometric models are better suited to assess the costs of policies to control $CO_2$ emissions. This model is an econometric, non-optimization model with myopic foresight. The time-frame of the model is the near-medium term, that is 2020. Other studies adopt an optimizing general equilibrium framework with a much longer time horizon.

Weyant (1993), reporting on the analysis of comparison of costs for reducing global carbon emissions from different models, undertaken by the Energy Modeling Forum 12 (EMF 12), concluded, 'it is easier to reach a more stringent annual emissions target over a longer period of time than a less stringent one over a shorter period of time'. As the important time horizon for developing countries is the medium term, the costs over this time-span are more relevant.

In this study, there is no offsetting of other distortionary taxes against the carbon tax revenues, as the government is in a perpetual deficit. This gives cost estimates on the high side. The perpetual government budget deficit is a realistic feature of the model. If the model were more disaggregate and the offsetting of other distortionary taxes had been modelled, the loss in GDP might have been lower.

Results from the general equilibrium type of model indicate that to control emissions for developing countries below 1990 levels by the year 2020 is relatively inexpensive. Total energy consumption in 2020 at a lower level than that in 1990 with a growing population implies a lower per capita availability of energy with higher per capita incomes. This seems an implausible scenario, given the very low levels of per capita energy consumption in 1992. Transferring global models with features suitable to study ICs gives results for DCs which are not very likely.

**6. Conclusions and directions for further research**

This study bridges some of the gaps in the research on costs and benefits of controlling greenhouse emissions for DCs. There is scope for further refinements to and expansions of the analysis in this study. For example, in the micro analysis, only the investment costs have been addressed. A more complete study would assess the incremental costs associated with these technologies. This was not done in the present study, due to limited data availability. The crucial micro–macro link has been achieved through investments. When sufficient data are available to carry out a complete analysis of incremental costs for the carbon-abating technologies, the existing links in the macro framework can be expanded to include all categories of costs. As the new technologies would be more efficient, lower operating, maintenance and fuel costs could be expected. The expansion to include all types of costs would most likely reduce the costs of carbon abatement in the economy.

At the macro level, there is scope for refinement through further disaggregation, both in the energy sector and in the non-energy sectors. In the energy sector, only carbon energy has been modelled explicitly, because of its relevance to global warming and its importance in the country's commercial energy consumption. Non-carbon energy is modelled through the trend term. Including non-carbon commercial energy and further disaggregation in the non-energy sectors will increase the substitution possibilities and work towards reducing the costs of carbon abatement. The availability of backstop technologies is a question beyond the time-frame of this model. Another refinement in the model would be to develop the international linkages.

The main contributions of this study are:

- developing a model to study the medium-term costs of carbon abatement for India, a region not adequately represented in modelling efforts so far;
- developing a methodology for synthesis of micro and macro modelling approaches and its illustration for India; and
- application of new econometric estimation techniques to a developing economy.

The results from the integrated model for India indicate that macroeconomic policies have limited effect in controlling emissions, given the constrained energy markets. In the next three decades, technological options will play an important role in reducing carbon emissions. However, the effectiveness of investments in carbon-abating technologies declines beyond a certain level of investment. Models based on assumptions relevant to ICs underestimate the costs of carbon abatement for DCs. Therefore, specific models for developing regions are required.

## APPENDIX

**Energy sector in the econometric model**

| *Variable* | *Variable description* |
|---|---|
| CARTAX | Carbon tax |
| CE | Carbon energy |
| CEPR | Real carbon energy prices |
| CEYD | Carbon energy intensity of GDP |
| CLPR | Coal price |

*Sujata Gupta and Stephen G. Hall*

| | |
|---|---|
| CLSHR | Percentage share of coal in CE |
| CPI | Consumer price index |
| CRTXREV | Carbon tax revenues |
| GSPR | Gas price |
| GSSHR | Percentage share of gas in CE |
| OLPR | Oil price |
| OLSHR | Percentage share of oil in CE |
| T | Trend term |
| WDPO | World price of oil |
| YD | Gross domestic product |

*Notes:*

| | |
|---|---|
| B–J statistic | Bera–Jarque normality test (chi-squared (2)) tests the null hypothesis that the residuals are normally distributed (Cuthbertson *et al.*, 1992) |
| SE | Standard error of the regression |
| ADF | Augmented Dickey Fuller statistic |
| Variable (–*n*) | Variable lagged *n* time periods |

In equations where the Johansen method has been used to estimate the cointegrating vector, the significant eigenvector is determined using the likelihood ratio test.

**Carbon energy demand**
Significant cointegrating vector: long-run
Price elasticity of –0.028

*158.8 + 49.01*ln(CEYD) + 1.38*ln(CEPR) – 0.1431 T = 0*

Estimation method: Johansen procedure; lag length: 4;
Likelihood ratio test of maximum *r* significant cointegrating vectors: *r* = 1
Small sample LR test = 8.233 (critical value = 9.24);
Standard error of the dynamic specification: 0.01

*Fossil fuel share*
Figures in brackets are the T-ratios

*OLSHR =*
*27.07 – 0.06*TIME –2.46*ln(OLPR) + 1.63*ln(GSPR) + 3.23*ln(CLPR(-1))*
*(9.8) (-5.0) (5.3) (5.8) (4.5)*

Estimation period: 1978(3)–1990(4); Estimation method: OLS; *R*-squared: 0.92; SE: 0.25;
B–J statistic: 0.21; ADF(1): –5.1

*GSSHR = 0.085752*TIME –2.899322*
*(28.4) (–14.0)*

Estimation period: 1978(4)–1991(1); Estimation method: OLS; *R*-squared: 0.94; SE: 0.31;

B–J statistic: 5.5; ADF(1): –3.3

$$CLSHR = 100 - OLSHR - GSSHR$$

*Fossil fuel prices*

$$\ln(OLPR) = 1.97 + 1.09*\ln(CPI(-1)) + 0.34*\ln(WDPO(-1)) + CARTAX*0.87*CPI/100$$

*(11.2) (41.1) (13.7)*

Estimation period: 1978(4)–1989(4); Estimation method: OLS; *R*-squared: 0.98; SE: 0.04;
B–J statistic: 0.54; ADF(1): –3.54

$$\ln(CLPR) = 0.68 + 0.74*\ln(CPI(-1)) + 0.24*\ln(OLPR(-1)) + CARTAX*1.04*(1-.24)*CPI/100$$

*(1.5) (5.8) (2.1)*

Estimation period: 1978(3)–1990(4); Estimation method: OLS; *R*-squared: 0.98; SE: 0.049;
B–J statistic: 0.40; ADF(1): –2.97

$$\ln(GSPR) = 5.56518 + 0.056*\ln(TIME) + 0.42*\ln(WDPO(-1)) + CARTAX*0.65*CPI/100$$

*(15.8) (1.9) (9.5)*

Estimation period: 1978(2)–1990(4); Estimation method: OLS; *R*-squared: 0.66; SE: 0.102;
B–J statistic: 2.35; ADF(1): –2.96

**Exogenous variable**

Assuming world price of oil (nominal) increases by 3% per annum

$$\ln(WDPO) = \ln(WDPO(-1)) + 0.0074$$

**References**

Anderson, D. and C. Bird (1990), 'Carbon emissions and carbon fixing from an economic perspective', University College, London, and St Antony's College, Oxford.

Anderson, D. and C. Bird (1992), 'Carbon accumulation and technical progress—a simulation study of costs', *Oxford Bulletin of Economics and Statistics* **54**(1): 1–29.

Barker, T. and R. Lewney (1991), 'A green scenario for the UK economy', in T. Barker, ed., *Green Futures for Economic Growth: Britain in 2010*, Cambridge Econometrics.

Barrett, S. (1990), 'Pricing the environment: the economic and environmental consequences of a carbon tax', *Economic Outlook* **14**(5): 24–33.

Blitzer, C.R., R.S. Eckaus, S. Lahiri and A. Meeraus (1990), 'A general equilibrium analysis of the effects of carbon emissions restrictions on economic growth in a developing country', *Workshop on Economic/Energy/Environmental Modeling for Climate Policy Analysis, 22–23 Oct.*, The World Bank, Washington, DC.

Blitzer, C.R., R.S. Eckaus, S. Lahiri and A. Meeraus (1992), 'How restricting carbon dioxide and methane emissions would affect the Indian economy', *Policy Research Working Papers*, The World Bank.

*Sujata Gupta and Stephen G. Hall*

Boero, G., R. Clarke and L.A. Winters (1991), *The Macroeconomic Consequences of Controlling Greenhouse Gases: A Survey*, London: HMSO.

Boone, L., S.G. Hall and D. Kemball-Cook (1992), 'Fossil fuel demand for nine OECD countries', Discussion Paper No. 21-92, Centre for Economic Forecasting, London Business School.

Boonekamp, P.G.M., T. Kram, P.A. Okken, M. Rouw and D. Tiemersma (1989), *Baseline and $CO_2$-Response Scenarios for the Netherlands*, Energy Study Centre, Petten, The Netherlands.

Burniaux, J.M., J.P. Martin, G. Nicoletti and J. Oliveira Martins (1991), 'The costs of policies to reduce global emissions of $CO_2$: initial simulation results with GREEN', *OECD Economics Department Working Papers*, No. 103.

CBO (Congressional Budget Office) (1990), *Carbon Charges as a Response to Global Warming: The Effects of Taxing Fossil Fuels*, Washington, DC: The Congress of the United States.

Cuthbertson, K., S.G. Hall and M.P. Taylor (1992), *Applied Econometric Techniques*, Hemel Hempstead: Harvester Wheatsheaf.

Davidson, J.E.H., D.F. Hendry, F. Srba and S. Yeo (1978), 'Econometric modelling of the aggregate time-series relationship between consumers' expenditure and income in the United Kingdom', *Economic Journal* **88**: 661–692.

Goldemberg, J., T.B. Johansson, A.K.N. Reddy, and R.H. Williams (1987), *Energy for a Sustainable World*. New Delhi: Wiley-Eastern.

Government of India (1991), *Sectoral Energy Demand in India*, New Delhi: Planning Commission.

Grubb M. (1993), 'Policy modelling for climate change. The missing models', *Energy Policy* **21**(3): 203–208.

Grubler A., S. Messner, L. Schrattenholzer and A. Schafer (1993), 'Emission reduction at the global level', *Energy* **18**(5), 539–581.

Gupta S. (1995), 'Carbon dioxide abatement costs in an empirical model of the Indian economy—an integration of micro and macro approaches', PhD thesis, London Business School, University of London.

Hodgson, D. and K. Miller (1995), 'Modelling UK energy demand', in T. Barker, P. Ekins and N. Johnstone, eds., *Global Warming and Energy Demand*, London and New York: Routledge.

Ingham, A. and A. Ulph (1990), *Market-based Instruments for Reducing $CO_2$ Emissions —The Case for U.K. Manufacturing*, University of Southampton.

International Energy Agency (1992), *IEA Model*, Paris: OECD.

International Energy Agency (1993), *Energy Statistics and Balances*, Paris: OECD.

Jorgenson, D.W. and P.J. Wilcoxen (1990), 'The costs of controlling U.S. carbon dioxide emissions', *Workshop on Economics/Energy/Environmental Modeling for Climate Policy Analysis, 22–23 Oct.*, The World Bank, Washington, DC.

Lovins, A.B. and H.L. Lovins (1991), 'Least cost climatic stabilisation', *Annual Review of Energy and Environment* **16**.

Manne, A.S. and R.G. Richels (1990), '$CO_2$ emission limits: an economic cost analysis for the USA', *Energy Journal* **11**(2): 51–74.

Manne, A.S. and R.G. Richels (1992), *Buying Greenhouse Insurance: The Economic Costs of $CO_2$ Emission Limits*, Cambridge, MA: MIT Press.

Marks, R.E., P.L. Swan, P. McLennan, R. Schodde, P.B. Dixon and D.T. Johnson (1990), *The Cost of Australian Carbon Dioxide Abatement*, Sydney: Australian Graduate School of Management, University of New South Wales.

Mathur, A., S. Gupta and N. Khanna (1992), 'India country paper', in R.K. Pachauri and P. Bhandari, eds., *Global Warming Mitigation Strategies and Perspectives from Asia and Brazil*, New Delhi: TATA McGraw-Hill Publications Ltd.

Nordhaus, W.D. (1990), 'An intertemporal general equilibrium model of economic growth and climate change', *Workshop on Economics/Energy/Environmental*

*Modeling for Climate Policy Analysis, 22–23 Oct.*, The World Bank, Washington, DC.
Smith, C., S. Hall and N. Mabey (1995), 'Econometric modelling of international carbon tax regimes', *Energy Economics* **17**(2): 133–146.
Sondheimer, J. (1991), 'Macro-economic effects of a carbon tax', in T. Barker, ed., *Green Futures for Economic Growth: Britain in 2010*, Cambridge Econometrics.
Symons, E., J. Proops and P. Gay (1994), 'Carbon taxes, consumer demand and carbon dioxide emissions: a simulation analysis for the UK', *Fiscal Studies* **15**(2): 19–43.
United Nations Environment Programme (1992), 'UNEP greenhouse gas abatement costing study', UNEP Collaborating Centre on Energy and Environment, Riso National Laboratory, Denmark.
Weyant (1993), 'Costs of reducing global carbon emissions', *Journal of Economic Perspectives* **7**(4): 27–46.
Williams, R.H. (1990), 'Low cost strategies for coping with $CO_2$ emissions limits', *Energy Journal* **11**(4): 35–59
Wilson and Swisher (1993), 'Exploring the gap. Top-down versus bottom-up analyses of the cost of mitigating global warming', *Energy Policy* **21**(3): 249–263
World Bank (1992), *World Development Report 1992: Development and the Environment*, New York: Oxford University Press.
World Bank (1993), *World Bank Tables*, New York: Oxford University Press.
World Bank (1994), *World Development Report 1994: Infrastructure for Development*, New York: Oxford University Press.

431-67
[97]

# [20]

*Environmental and Resource Economics* **10:** 63–99, 1997.


Q28
Q25
R48

# Using Tradeable Permits to Achieve Sustainability in the World's Large Cities

## *Policy Design Issues and Efficiency Conditions for Controlling Vehicle Emissions, Congestion and Urban Decentralization with an Application to Mexico City*

Mexico

HAYNES C. GODDARD
*Instituto Tecnológico Autónomo de México, Río Hondo 1, Colonia San Angel Tizapán, 01000 México D.F. México (present address: Department of Economics, University of Cincinnati, Cincinnati, Ohio 45221-0371 USA) (e-mail: Haynes.Goddard@uc.edu)*

Accepted 18 September 1996

**Abstract.** Many large cities in the world have serious ground level ozone problems, largely the product of vehicular emissions and thus the argued unsustainability of current urban growth patterns is frequently blamed on unrestricted private vehicle use. This article reviews Mexico City's experience with vehicle use restrictions as an emissions control program and develops the conditions for optimal quantitative restrictions on vehicle use and for complementary abatement technologies. The stochastic nature of air pollution outcomes is modelled explicitly in both the static and dynamic formulations of the control problem, in which for the first time in the literature the use of tradeable vehicle use permits is proposed as a cost-effective complement to technological abatement for mobile emissions control. This control regime gives the authorities a broader and more flexible set of instruments with which to deal more effectively with vehicle emissions, and with seasonal and stochastic variation of air quality outcomes. The market in tradeable vehicle use permits would be very competitive with low transactions costs. This control policy would have very favorable impacts on air quality, vehicle congestion and on urban form and development. Given the general political resistance to environmental taxes, this program could constitute a workable and politically palatable set of policies for controlling greenhouse gas emissions from the transport sector.

**Key words:** energy and environment, urban transport, emissions trading, vehicular emissions, sustainable development, traffic control, planning and administration

## 1. Introduction[1]

The literature detailing humanity's impacts on environmental and natural resource systems is growing exponentially, with new academic societies and journals created apace dedicated to examining the proposition that the scale and composition of our consumption and population growth paths are unsustainable. Perhaps nowhere is this perception more acute than when examining the problems of the world's largest cities, of which Mexico City seems to be one of the most frequently mentioned as an example of the problems that result when policies are inconsistent with the ecologically sustainable scale of human activity and concentration. For many years Mexico City residents have complained of the unlivability of the city. These complaints have been centered especially on the high levels of air pollution, congestion and noise, problems caused principally by private automobiles.

It has long been clear to many observers that the private automobile is a major determinant of urban form and structure and that its unrestricted use is largely responsible for many of the inefficiencies of urban spatial structure and the loss in amenity caused by air pollution and vehicular congestion. Both are known to inflict large and growing losses on the urban economy and well being of city inhabitants. One recent estimate for Mexico City calculates that the total economic losses associated with the unrestricted use of the private auto exceed $7.1 billion annually (Pedrero Nieto). Neither unhealthful exposure to primary and secondary pollutants nor congestion are any longer just peak hour problems in Mexico City, a problem created by population growth and concentration and income growth.

Further, instruments are urgently needed in urban areas to redirect and curb growth where ecological space is threatened. For example, in Mexico City sprawl has major impacts on the loss of ecological areas and services, such as the loss of groundwater recharge areas as urbanization spreads to the surrounding State of Mexico. Yet for all that has been written about what to do about the problem, only in recent years have a few governments around the world attempted to curtail the unrestricted use of private vehicles in recognition that the auto places unsustainable demands on the air shed to receive emissions and on the capacity of road systems to provide efficient transportation services. It is the unrestricted use of vehicles that is the root cause of the unsustainability of urban growth and structural patterns.

Around the globe various transportation control measures have been experimented with in recent years. Access bans, or partial and total vehicle bans, have been widely used in Italy, and in such cities as Athens, Amsterdam, Barcelona, and Munich. Traffic cells, pie-shaped wedges of urban areas, have been employed in Sweden, Germany, Holland, and France, as a way to limit through traffic and to encourage use of public transport. Some other incentive-based policy options being given consideration for discouraging vehicle use are: urban road pricing as conducted in Singapore; employer incentives to employees to share rides (U.S.); taxation of the imputed income from employer provided free parking (U.S.) and closure of central cities to vehicles. The Intermodal Surface Transportation Efficiency Act of 1991 (ISTEA) in the U.S. specifically directs local planning authorities to examine trip and congestion reduction measures in transportation planning as measures to reduce vehicular emissions and avoid additional highway construction. These moves do seem to reflect a newfound political determination to confront the unrestricted use of the private vehicle, and with the growing recognition of the unsustainability of many consumption practices, this may represent the beginning of a trend.

While there is a growing recognition that demand side management policies that are efficient, cost-effective and equitable are needed, what the policies should be is not clear. Congestion pricing has received the most attention in the literature, but from a political economy perspective, 'winning political approval is the most serious obstacle to congestion pricing' (Gómez-Ibáñez and Small 1994: 3).[2] In the literature on urban transportation economics, there is not much in the way of guidance to urban decision makers for designing efficient and *equitable* mechanisms for stimulating reduced use of the auto. The need is great, as the developed countries have agreed to stabilize greenhouse gas emissions at 1990 levels, but it is not clear how the U.S., for example, will meet the goal without effective controls on auto use in urban areas.

This paper seeks to make a contribution to the search for effective and efficient demand side management (DSM) policies for making urban areas sustainably viable and for reducing the sector's carbon emissions, and is organized in three parts. Section 2 provides a description of several aspects of the problem of controlling vehicle use in large cities using Mexico City as an example and explains an innovative proposal to deal with it cost-effectively. Section 3 is a technical discussion of the static and dynamic efficiency conditions for using quantitative restrictions on vehicle use as part of a cost-effective program for controlling vehicle emissions. For the first time in the literature the use of tradeable vehicle use permits is proposed as a cost-effective complement to technological abatement for mobile emissions control. The conditions for the permit market equilibria are presented in Section 4. The policy described here is applicable to any large U.S. city that cannot achieve ozone attainment status.

## 2. Control of Vehicle Emissions in the World's Large Cities

A number of the world's large cities suffer from severe air pollution and congestion caused by private vehicles,[3] and a significant percentage of the world's total emissions of greenhouse gases come from vehicles, most notably in the U.S. and Europe. The International Energy Agency and the OECD (IEA/OECD) have reported that the transport sector in the member countries contributes 30% of all carbon emissions, of which road transport contributes 75%. A full 90% of CO emissions emanate from light duty gasoline engines (mainly passenger vehicles) and 50% of $NO_x$ emissions come from gasoline engines. Fuel use for road transport in OECD countries tripled between 1960 and 1990. In the judgment of these agencies, it is unlikely that a carbon tax will be adopted in the near future as a method of discouraging carbon emissions. This pessimistic observation suggests that the identification of alternative controls on vehicles that will be viewed as equitable becomes all the more important.

Policy recommendations for controlling urban traffic congestion in the large literature on urban transportation economics are nearly completely focused on the use of road pricing techniques. Indeed, with advances in electronic technologies, there are experiments and applications underway in which road authorities collect toll charges with the use of these new technologies. These are viewed mainly as cordon pricing technologies for rationing access to the central business districts

(CBDs) of central cities. The cost-effectiveness of such pricing techniques in the world's megacities, however, is not clear, as their emissions and congestion problems are not confined to the CBDs; in the U.S. it is frequent today to find the most serious congestion in suburban areas along circumferential expressways. Thus, as an instrument to control area wide congestion such as in Mexico City or as an emissions control measure for mobile sources, road pricing would have to be extended over an entire urban area, raising its cost. At our current level of understanding of the economics of such mechanisms, it is not clear that they represent an economically feasible method of controlling urban vehicle use. Mexico City officials, realizing that technology would have virtually no short-term impact in controlling the very serious air quality problem of the area in the late 1980s, opted to follow an environmental group's (the Movimiento Ecologista Mexicano) rather insistent suggestion that a no driving day program be instituted during the inversion season, roughly November through March. How well this program has functioned will be discussed below.

It is not difficult to envision, however, that completely generalized road pricing schemes will encounter popular resistance, and therefore may well be politically infeasible.[4] The reason is the same as that for which the economist's most often recommended emissions control incentive, emissions charges, has proven unacceptable to decision makers, industry and the public: it would generate large transfers from the public to the government because of the relatively inelastic demand for transportation. While economists consider an emissions charge to be a 'green tax' *par excellence*, only in substituting such a green tax for other existing taxes in order to offset the large financial cost of the policy does it seem that politicians would have a chance of selling this to the public. Without fiscal neutrality, these incentive schemes are usually met with considerable skepticism, if not hostility. Given that offsetting lump sum transfers are difficult if not impossible to devise, such proposals have met with a singular lack of success.

During the early part of the decade the World Bank conducted a large project in Mexico City on the air quality problem there. Eskeland (1994) produced evidence that the steeply rising marginal cost of reducing vehicular emissions through technology alone would make a policy of stimulating reduced vehicle use part of an overall cost-effective emissions control policy. Eskeland recommended the usual, and at least in Mexico politically unacceptable, policy of instituting an increase in the price of gasoline for the metropolitan area, to be placed in effect only when the cost (lost welfare) would be less than that of the least cost technological alternative, especially so when considering the refining of higher grades of gasoline. Such a policy would also have the effect of reducing congestion, although these benefits were not included in his analysis – if they were, the indicated increase in gasoline prices would be greater. Mexico City officials have rejected the World Bank's advice, a position we think correct.

There are at least two reasons for suspecting that raising gasoline prices will not be the solution to vehicular emissions and congestion in the world's large cities.

First is the matter of political economy. We observe that nowhere to our knowledge have gasoline prices been employed to control a regional air quality problem.[5] Conversations with public officials confirm that the large financial transfers that the policy would engender make it politically infeasible in Mexico, and perhaps in most regions. Secondly and more importantly, the use of higher gasoline prices in this matter would be spatially inefficient and ineffective. To implement the policy, it would be necessary to establish a gasoline price frontier around the metropolitan area to be controlled, within which prices would be higher than outside. The long-run effects of this policy are readily apparent: those living near the border need only to cross it to buy at the lower price, returning to the metropolitan area to use their vehicles as usual, causing no reduction in emissions. Further, for a gas price differential sufficiently high to have an impact on consumer behavior, over time the frontier would create a strong incentive to locate near it, thus reducing population density in the metropolitan area and increasing the use of vehicles in these areas less well served by mass transit. To counteract the effect, the frontier would have to be moved periodically as the urban area became larger, a spatial growth caused by the price differential itself. In short, the policy would create spatial price disequilibria, and the resulting arbitrage would have perverse effects, leading to a less compact urban area and to more vehicle use. Although apparently political considerations were the determining factor in the decision, Mexico's rejection of the gasoline price policy seems well placed.[6]

Mexico City has opted for a vehicular emissions policy that relies on technology for reduced emissions per kilometer travelled as the long-run solution, with vehicle use restrictions ('Hoy No Circula', HNC) as a fill-in policy. For reasons detailed in the next section, most independent observers think that this policy has been perverse and has led to more vehicles on the road and therefore increased emissions over what they would have been without the intervention. Congestion has consequently increased and is now a completely generalized problem throughout the metropolitan area. This is a dramatic case of 'intervention failure' (Opschoor 1994). The problem with the current policy is that simple command and control restrictions that do not alter the incentive structure surrounding the vehicle use decision will at best make the cost of control unnecessarily high, or in the case of Mexico City, fail completely, and make the problem more serious. This leaves us with the question: what then is the urban air quality manager to do about controlling vehicles?

### 2.1. A NEW INCENTIVE MECHANISM FOR CONTROL OF MOBILE EMISSIONS

In recent years a new mechanism for the cost-effective control of emissions has been developed, that of tradeable emissions permits (Tietenberg 1985). It is now being implemented for sulfur emissions control for fixed sources in the eastern half of the U.S. and limited variants are being employed in the South Coast Air Quality Management District (Los Angeles). While this technique has received attention primarily as an incentive mechanism for reducing emissions from fixed sources, an initial examination suggests that it may be an effective mechanism to control vehicle emissions and congestion, at least partially, as well as slow if not stop the uneconomic decentralization of economic activity observed in many of the world's large cities and especially in North America.[7]

As we shall detail below, Mexico City's flawed experiment with restricting vehicle use can nonetheless be seen to contain some of the elements that would likely constitute a successful application of a tradeable permit system for vehicle use. The fact that such permits would be a homogeneous commodity means that the resulting market would be very competitive due to the large number of potential participants and that the associated transactions costs be would relatively low. 'Thin' markets (few participants) as well as high transactions costs are problems in the existing markets for emissions trading for fixed sources, but preliminary analysis is suggestive that this would not be true for a vehicle use market.[8]

### 2.2. Vehicle emissions and air quality in Mexico City[9]

Mexico City's air pollution problems are notorious for their severity, sometimes characterized as the worst in the world. These problems stem from (a) its high altitude location (2200 meters, 7200 feet) which causes incomplete fuel combustion, increased ultraviolet radiation and ozone formation; (b) location in a valley where the air circulation is impeded by mountain ranges; (c) a fleet of approximately three million vehicles with an average age of nine years; and (d) introduction of catalytic converters only recently in the 1991 model year. The one hour ozone standard of 0.11 ppm is regularly violated as is that for carbon monoxide in virtually all parts of the metropolitan area.

Ozone is viewed as the most serious mobile emissions problem. Ozone exceedences occurred 88% of the time in the southwestern part of the city in 1988 and have exceeded the standard by as much as 400% (0.44 ppm), although the trend in the last three years has been downward. The exceedences are particularly severe in the winter months when temperature inversions and multiple day calms occur regularly, but the worst month is May when solar radiation is at its highest. Total energy use has been projected until the year 2010 to increase at an annual rate of 4.9%. Forty five percent of the energy consumed in the area is in the transport sector. Of the 29.5 million trips made daily, 39% are in private autos.

### 2.3. Policy responses to air quality trends

In the mid 1980s, monitoring was improved and confirmed the trend of increasing deterioration in air quality for most of the indicators; as a consequence, heightened citizen awareness and concern have motivated the government to move more aggressively to control the problem. As a developing country with many pressing economic concerns, the thrust of policy decisions made in Mexico over the past twenty years has been to defer pollution control in favor of a traditional economic development agenda, in particular not to require vehicular and industrial emissions controls. The effect of this economic policy is that the environmental authorities today find themselves quite restricted in the choice of technological emission control options in the short to medium run to meet the new demands for increased air quality.

The technical emissions control actions for vehicles taken to date have been to require catalytic converters starting in 1991, good engine tuning verified with automated emissions testing, the installation of reduced particulate emitting diesel engines in the bus fleet and a program to convert the minibuses in the public transport fleet to LP. These actions should have a significant impact on emissions but are unlikely to lead to attainment of Mexico's ambient air standards.

The public pressure to do something about emissions has meant that essentially the only available policies in the short run for controlling vehicle emissions have been those command and control actions involving quantitative restrictions on the use of vehicles during the day and the weekend, and partial shutdowns of local industry.

### 2.4. No driving day program and effects

This command and control program mandates not driving one day during the week (weekends excepted) and two days during serious pollution episodes. On the weekends, odd and even license plate numbers are used, causing one half of the fleet to be parked during air pollution emergencies. It was conceived as an emissions control program and was instituted in November of 1989 for the winter inversion season; it effectively removed 20% of the vehicles from the streets in its first few months of operation. Air pollution monitoring data did show a small improvement on most of the measured indices, although measured ozone levels increased nonetheless.

The authorities liked the results and public reception of the program so much that they decided to make it permanent. But once the program was made permanent, it led to unexpected consumer behavior. The driving public, now faced with a long term restriction on driving, apparently found the public transport system a very imperfect substitute and adjusted to the restriction by purchasing additional autos in order always to have at least one vehicle available on any given day. The result of the program quite likely is that there are more vehicles on the road than there would have been without the program.

The indirect evidence that the NDD program may have worsened the air pollution problem can be seen from the data on gasoline use (Asesoría). As Mexico slowly grew out of the debt crisis of the 1980s, gasoline consumption followed a slow upward trend, but the slope of the trend increased markedly in 1990. Similarly, the moving average of peak ozone measurements showed an even greater increase in the slope of the trend, and the number of days in which the ozone readings exceeded 200 points on the pollution index (IMECA) grew (1988, 67 days; 1989,

19 days; 1990, 86 days; and 1991, 192 days). Additionally, CO concentrations have dramatically increased, although the rising percentage on controlled vehicles, as well as favorable ventilation patterns, are beginning to offset that trend. Since the restriction does not apply to the weekends (except during alerts), congestion has risen on the weekends over what it used to be. In practical terms, the apparent failure of the NDD program has forced authorities to place more the required emissions reduction for episodic control on industry and commerce, causing great but unmeasured economic cost. It is an easy hypothesis that the cost of episodic control is greater with the NDD than without it, although these measurements remain to be undertaken. The available evidence then is suggestive that not only has the no driving day program not reduced total vehicle emissions in the long term, it has actually raised them and moved the area *away* from improved air quality (Eskeland 1994).

### 2.5. Reasons for NDD difficulties

In general terms, this 'unexpected consequence' of the NDD program can be traced to a near universal belief among the general public and public authorities everywhere that restrictions on choices are less 'costly' than monetary instruments such as taxes or fees because they do not involve financial transfers. Further, these quantitative restrictions are typically viewed as substitutes for rather than complements to economic incentives. Being focused on the understandable unpopularity of taxes and prices with their financial transfers (the fiscal unneutrality), decision makers usually ignore or discount consumer and producer adjustments that restrictions engender when they are not accompanied by monetary inducements to cause the restrictions to be chosen and sustained as an equilibrium. In the case in point, it is precisely the consumer adjustment to the NDD restriction used in isolation that has made the no driving policy an apparently perverse one.

More specifically, the problem can be traced to two facets of the particular form of the NDD program adopted, that of a fixed ratio of one vehicle/one day off or one vehicle/one decal, and no restriction on the total number of permitted vehicle/days. Since the number of driving days permitted was made a function of the number of vehicles in a fixed proportion, the only consumer adjustments possible under the circumstances were to elect alternative transport modes (the policy makers' expectations) or to increase the number of vehicles per household. This policy induced rigidity or lack of flexibility between vehicles and driving days then led to an increased supply of eligible vehicle days (four days per vehicle times the growth in the fleet) because the policy induced consumers to purchase more vehicles than they would have chosen in the absence of the restriction. This is the source of the consequently increased congestion and emissions. Since there are typically more drivers in a household than vehicles, the increased supply of potential vehicle use days has quite likely led to increased, not decreased, overall use.

Also, more importantly from the standpoint of the efficiency and health of the local economy, the no driving day program made no distinction among the relative *values* of the various use-days–this means that commuting, shopping, recreational and commercial/industrial delivery use-days are treated as if they are of equal value. Since they are not in fact equal in value, economic activity is (unnecessarily) reduced over what a more flexible externality internalizing program would cause. In point of fact, a very disproportionate 41% of all the vehicles cited for violating the restriction in the first year of operation were commercial delivery vehicles (Dirección). Whereas a more flexible internalizing program would unambiguously lead to improved welfare (counting the benefits of improved air quality), the program chosen has most probably reduced it by causing more emissions, more congestion and households to purchase more vehicles than they otherwise would have.

## 3. The Theory of Optimal Restrictions on Vehicle Use

Economists have long focused on the analysis of the net benefits of alternative pollution control programs in the search for efficient rules for guiding the decision-making processes of the control authorities. When measures of the benefits of pollution control are lacking, as they frequently are, economists have devised market-based cost-effectiveness measures, such as emissions trading, that are based on a broad conception of cost-effectiveness which goes well beyond the typical engineering approach of selecting the least cost combination of technologies to meet some pollution control target.

The identification of the least cost combination of *technological* controls is a necessary but *not sufficient* condition to minimize the cost of pollution control, as it ignores the possibility that the total costs of control can be lower by reducing the consumption of the polluting good or service. With emissions charges, in a competitive industry such a reduction in output will be an eventual and natural result of incurring emissions control costs.

The objective of this paper is to model the conditions under which demand reduction or DSM policies employing quantitative restrictions will enter in the optimal set of cost-effective emissions controls in both static and dynamic control settings, applying the model to the case of mobile sources in Mexico City. In particular, we analyze the conditions to identify the optimal combination of emissions reductions achieved per unit of vehicle use (kilometers travelled, the standard engineering measure) and that achieved by simply using vehicles less. This is completely overlooked in the non-economic mobile source control (engineering) literature. In addition, we model the permit market.

As a general proposition, demand reduction as a complementary emissions reduction policy will be preferred to an *exclusive* reliance on technology based controls (reduced emissions per kilometer) for high levels of emissions reduction. The implementation mechanism analyzed here for assigning efficiently the demand reductions is that of tradeable permits. The only previous work similar in intent to this paper is that by Eskeland (1994), although he focuses on the conditions to calculate the gasoline surcharge to generate optimal or cost-effective demand reductions.

The paper is focused on the identification of the optimality and market conditions for controlling mobile emissions cost-effectively when demand reduction is an explicit policy option but emissions charges are not. The design, institutional and administrative aspects of implementing a demand reduction policy through a tradeable vehicle system are discussed briefly in the last section.

### 3.1. Nature of the Problem

What follows is an application of an idea that has long existed in the literature today known as 'ecological economics': an objective function consistent with exogenous ecological constraints requires us to minimize material flows subject to a constraint on population and a desirable standard of living, rather than the standard maximization of material flows as implied by growth models and even the standard application of utility and profit maximization models that do not take account of ecological constraints (Daly 1973: 19). The form we give the idea here is that of cost-effectiveness subject to an explicit environmental constraint.

The basic decision rule is fairly straightforward: for each emission abatement technology with a positive cost, (a) compute the level of operation at which technological abatement will generate a unit of emissions reduction (ER) and the associated costs; (b) compute the level of demand reduction (reduced vehicle use in this case) that will generate the same units of ER; and (c) compute the cost of the demand reduction, i.e., the lost consumer's welfare. Make all pairwise comparisons over the emissions reduction schedules and implement demand reduction policies at that point in the emissions reduction programs where the loss in consumer welfare occasioned by reduced vehicle use is less than the cost of technology for an equal reduction in emissions. The resulting optimal program in general will be a mixed program of technologies and demand reduction measures. The optimal set of policies of course must contain the least expensive of all possible *alternative* demand reduction policies, and just as the least cost combination of technologies is an convex envelope of all possible control technologies, so it will be for demand controls.

### 3.2. General Formal Structure

The problem then is to choose the combination of abatement technologies and demand reduction policies that minimizes the overall cost of reaching exogenously given emissions reduction objectives, normally expressed in terms of tons of pollutants reduced, often weighted by their respective toxicities. In this paper, we assume that the emissions reduction target is set as a function of the scarce and variable dispersive capacity of the local airshed, and therefore is exogenous to the problem posed here. In order to focus on the essentials of the argument, the following exposition is in terms of emissions reduction only.

The objective function is simple: minimize the total cost of emissions reduction subject to a constraint on allowable emissions. This cost function is simply $C(V_p,K)$ where $C$ is total cost, $V_p$ is passenger vehicle use and $K$ is investment in abatement technologies for mobile sources which reduce emissions per kilometer travelled. The general problem is given in Equation (1):

$$\min_{V_p,K} C_{ER} = C(V_p, K) \text{ s.t. } e(V_p, K) = e_0. \tag{1}$$

While this is cost-effectiveness analysis – choosing the least cost combinations of abatement technologies and demand reduction policies – the proper definition of cost here is opportunity cost. This means that the problem is to minimize cost in all of its dimensions – the two in question here are (a) reductions in consumer welfare as the result of reduced vehicle use and (b) the cost of technological resources assigned to abatement of vehicle emissions per unit of vehicle use. This identification of costs means that $C(V_p,K)$ is strongly separable in its major arguments: cost to the consumer and cost of technology, respectively. We denote consumer cost as lost utility or the total negative value of being restricted in choosing the individually preferred amount of vehicle use (the distance between two indifference curves), given the absence of Pigouvian prices on vehicle use. As we shall see, an efficient control program means that we should seek to minimize any losses, i.e., reduce consumer welfare by only the optimal amount. As a result, $C(V_p,K)$ can be written as:

$$C(V_p, K) = -U(Y, V_p, e_0) + C^K_{ER}[ER(K)]. \tag{2}$$

Note that the second cost term on the right now bears a superscript '$K$' to refer to technology alone (ER is emissions reduction). Because this is cost-effectiveness analysis, we have written the consumer cost attributable to reduced vehicle use as a negative benefit or negative utility and have written the utility function to include the usual arguments of a composite good $Y$ and an environmental quality variable, proxied here with the emissions target $e_0$. The air quality variable $e_0$ is not a choice variable in this analysis, but is chosen by the authorities based on health and other considerations and so can be ignored for present purposes. As improved air quality would have income effects on the demand for vehicle use, it would be a factor in the measurement of changes in consumer utility. The air pollution control authority's problem is then:

$$\min_{V_p,K} C_{ER} = -U(Y, K, e) + C^K_{ER}[ER(K)] + \lambda_p[e(V_p, K) - e_0]. \tag{3}$$

If we multiply this equation by (–1), the control authority's problem becomes:

$$\max_{V_p,K} W_{ER} = U(Y, V_p, e_0) - C^K_{ER}[ER(K)] - \lambda_p[e(V_p, K) - e_0]. \tag{4}$$

This transformation converts the authority's cost minimization problem into a constrained welfare maximization or net benefits problem. Although formally the analysis is still one of cost-effectiveness, the definition of cost utilized here (minimizing opportunity costs in all dimensions) makes it also a legitimate net benefit (constrained) problem. The only new aspect is the explicit ecological constraint.

The discussion to this point has been general only. Two issues to be clarified are (a) the relevant decision dimensions of the problem and (b) a more accurate specification of the emissions constraint. For the first issue, we note that this formulation of the control authority's problem is focused on emissions reduction (ER), while it is vehicle use, $V_p$, that appears in the cost functions and constraint. Thus we need a collateral relation that gives the change in emissions as vehicle use changes, or $\partial e/\partial V_p$. From the emissions control function $e = e(V_p,K)$, we will know $\partial e/\partial V_p$ from engineering measurements.[10] Emissions reduction (ER) is the value of this function when $\delta V_p < 0$, a relationship which needs to be estimated. Thus, from a starting point of zero control of vehicle use, the relevant decision domain for $V_p$ is all $V_p$ for which $\delta V_p < 0$. For abatement technology, $\delta K > 0$ implies $\partial e/\partial K < 0$, i.e., increases in abatement technology reduce emissions. In sum, for a situation in which $e_0$ is violated, the set of control actions analyzed here is restricted to $\{\delta V_p < 0; \delta K > 0\}$.

### 3.3. Specification of the Constraint[11,12]

For the second issue, since this is applied analysis focused on periodic decision making, emissions measurement necessarily will rely on the air pollution monitoring network and the data it generates on ambient concentrations. The air pollution index (I) in Mexico is the IMECA (Indice Metropolitano de la Calidad del Aire). Thus it is necessary to define and measure the relationship $I = f(e)$, no small undertaking. This will change the nature of the earlier constraint in Equation (4) to $I = f[e(V_p,K)]$ or $I = I(V_p,K)$, and where we further define the target index as a function of emissions, $I_0 = f(e_0)$.

Using the index of air quality ($I$) as the guide to the success of control measures, we note that because $I$ is a stochastic variable, the previously formulated constraint needs to be redefined to reflect this fact. Therefore, the operational constraint would be one in which the authority would seek to keep the measured index $I_t$ ($t$ = time index) from exceeding the objective $I_0$ more than $\alpha$ percent of the time, where the paired combination $\{I_0,\alpha\}$ must be feasible with some feasible combination of $\{V_p,K\}$, given the stochastic process that generates air quality outcomes, $I_t$.

The problem is then to choose levels of $V_p$ and $K$ to control, but not eliminate, the exceedences of the air quality norms as given by $I_0$. In other words, if $I_t > I_0$, then $I^E = I_t - I_0 > 0$ where $I^E$ is the level of the exceedence. These exceedences are stochastic due to the probabilistic nature of ventilation patterns and levels, cloud cover, and temperature gradients. Therefore $P(I_t^E) = P(I_t - I_0)$ and this probability is given by:

$$P(I^E) = \int_{I_0}^{\infty} f(I)\mathrm{d}I, \tag{5}$$

where $f(I)$ is the density function of the IMECA's. Since an air pollution control program to guarantee $I_t < I_0$ at all times would not be cost-effective (it implies a zero risk preference for exceedences), the stochastic constraint is:

$$\int_{I_0}^{\infty} f(I)\mathrm{d}I \leqslant \alpha \tag{6}$$

where $\alpha$ is the probability of an exceedence. This is chosen exogenously to this analysis, as it would have to be in practice given the inadequate state of knowledge concerning the benefits of emissions reduction and the consequent difficulty of making the relevant benefit–cost comparisons. As formulated here, these exceedences are weighted only by their densities, but weights derived from health or visibility impacts could be introduced as well. With the above reasoning, the control authority's problem is restated as:

$$\max_{V_p,K} W_{ER} = U(Y, V_p, e_0) - C_{ER}^K[ER(K)] - \lambda_p \left[\int_{I_0}^{\infty} f(I)\mathrm{d}I - \alpha\right], \tag{7}$$

where

$$\mathrm{Prob}\{I \geqslant I - I_0\} = G(V_p, K) = \int_{I_0}^{\infty} (I; V_p, K)\mathrm{d}I. \tag{8}$$

Equation (8) specifies that the cumulative distribution of the $I_t$, $G(V_p,K)$, is a function of $V_p$ and $K$ and which means that the distribution parameters, the mean $\mu$ and variance $\sigma^2$, are therefore functions of $V_p$ and $K$ also. There is evidence (Larsen) that pollutant concentrations for all averaging times are distributed approximately lognormally as $\ln N(\mu,\sigma^2)$.[13] Equation (8) implies that $I_t = I(V_p,K)$ and therefore the density of the $I_t$ (observed air quality index readings) can be written as $f[I(V_p,K)]$ in which $\mu = \mu(V_p,K)$ and $\sigma^2 = \sigma^2(V_p,K)$. Thus we can rewrite the density function as $f[I(V_p,K)] = g[\mu(V_p,K), \sigma^2(V_p,K)]$. The cost-effectiveness problem for the control authorities is (a) to choose the combinations of $V_p$ and $K$ such to shift the mean $\mu$ of this two-parameter distribution to the left and (b) to reduce the systematic part of the variance so that $I_0$ is not exceeded more than $\alpha$ percent of the time. This is illustrated in Figure 1. Two density functions are shown: the one labelled $\ln N(\mu_1)$ is the pre-control distribution for air quality index outcomes. If the air quality norm is $I_0$ and the uncontrolled distribution of outcomes has a mean of $\mu_1$, for example, then the norm $I_0$ is violated ($\alpha$ + $\beta$) percent of the time (area under the density function labelled $\ln N(\mu_1)$ and to the right of $I_0$) rather than the target frequency of exceedences of $\alpha$ percent (area under the curve labelled $\ln N(\mu_0)$ to the right of $I_0$). To meet the probabilistic standard, the control authorities choose and implement reductions in vehicle use $V_p$ and investments in abatement technologies $K$ that will

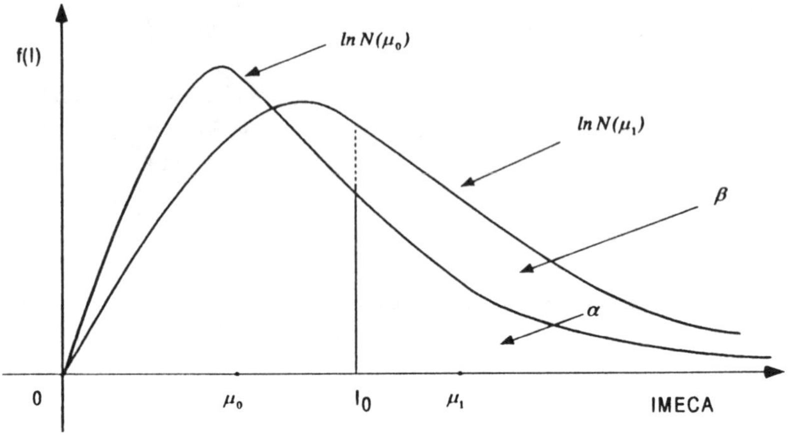


*Figure 1.* Air quality density before and after control.

shift the density function to that labelled ln $N(\mu_0)$ so that $I_0$ is not exceeded more than $\alpha$ percent of the time. Since both $\Delta V_p$ and $\Delta K$ are costly, they must be chosen in a fashion to minimize the cost of shifting the density function, an objective to which we turn next.

### 3.4. Conditions for Cost-Effectiveness

We find the cost minimizing combinations of $V_p$ and $K$ by maximizing Equation (7) with respect to these arguments, the results of which are shown in the following equations, where the function $g(\cdot)$ was defined above as $g[\mu(V_p,K), \sigma^2(V-p,K)]$.

$$V_p : \frac{\partial W}{\partial V_p} = \frac{\partial U}{\partial V_p} - \lambda_p \left[ \int_{I_0}^{\infty} \left( \frac{\partial g}{\partial \mu}\frac{\partial \mu}{\partial V_p} + \frac{\partial g}{\partial \sigma^2}\frac{\partial \sigma^2}{\partial V_p} \right) \mathrm{d}I \right] \leqslant 0. \tag{9}$$

$$K : \frac{\partial W}{\partial K} = -\frac{\partial C_{ER}^{K}}{\partial ER}\frac{\partial ER}{\partial K} - \lambda_p \left[ \int_{I_0}^{\infty} \left( \frac{\partial g}{\partial \mu}\frac{\partial \mu}{\partial K} + \frac{\partial g}{\partial \sigma^2}\frac{\partial \sigma^2}{\partial K} \right) \mathrm{d}I \right] \leqslant 0. \tag{10}$$

$$\lambda_p : \frac{\partial W}{\partial \lambda} = \int_{I_0}^{\infty} g[\mu(V_p, K), \sigma^2(V_p, K)]\mathrm{d}I - \alpha \leqslant 0. \tag{11}$$

The bracketed term in Equation (9) measures the decrease in the probability of exceedence of the norm $I_0$ caused by using an appropriate demand reduction incentive to stimulate a reduction in vehicle use, $V_p$. Figure 2 depicts this case, where

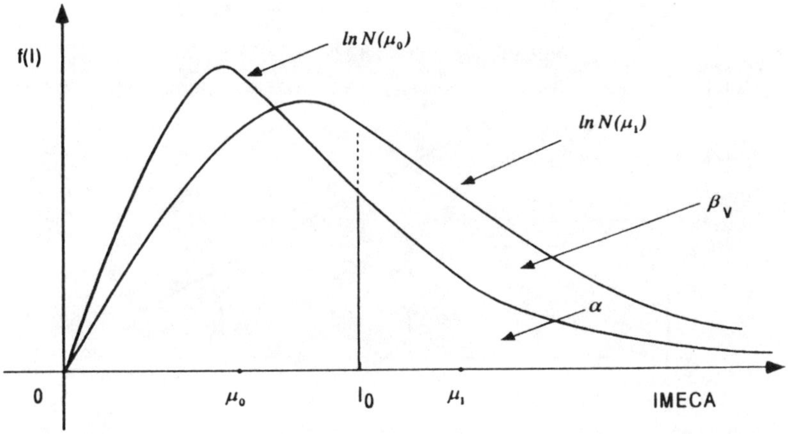


*Figure* 2. Impact of demand reduction measures of probability of exceedence.

the area labelled $\beta$ in Figure 1 is relabelled as $\beta_V$, showing how the probability of exceedence is reduced when only demand reduction measures are implemented, i.e., for $\partial V_p < 0$. The bracketed term in Equation (10), renamed as $\beta_K$, similarly would measure the reduced probability of an exceedence for an increase in investment in abatement.

The expression $\partial W/\partial\alpha = -\lambda_p$. This represents the change in welfare (consumer and resource cost) caused by relaxing or tightening the constraint. For example, for a small relaxation of the constraint (increasing $\alpha$ by $\delta\alpha$), the norm will be exceeded by a small increment in frequency of $\delta\alpha$ percent. This will increase welfare as defined here (reduce cost) by permitting increased vehicle use and reduced investment in abatement, from which we conclude that $\partial W/\partial\alpha > 0$ or that $-\lambda_p > 0$ which implies that $\lambda_p < 0$. Recall that in the circumscribed scope of this cost-effectiveness problem, the external cost of the air pollution itself (health and visibility effects, e.g.) do not appear in the utility function. The argument would be similar for a tightening of the constraint.

Simplifying Equations (9) and (10) by equating them to $\lambda_p$, yields Equations (12) and (13) which represent the optimality conditions on which to predicate decision rules for determining how much of the emissions targets ($e_0$ and its measurement analogue $I_0$) are to be met through (a) a reduction in vehicle use ($V_p$) and (b) investments in abatement (K).

$$\frac{\frac{\partial U}{\partial V_p}}{\int_{I_0}^{\infty}\left(\frac{\partial g}{\partial \mu}\frac{\partial \mu}{\partial V_p} + \frac{\partial g}{\partial \sigma^2}\frac{\partial \sigma^2}{\partial V_p}\right)\mathrm{d}I} = \lambda_p. \tag{12}$$

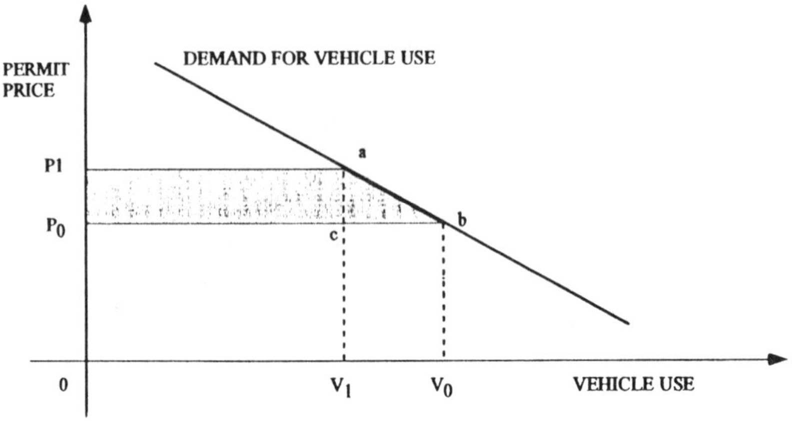


*Figure 3.* Welfare effects of demand reduction.

$$\frac{-\frac{\partial C^K_{ER}}{\partial ER}\frac{\partial ER}{\partial K}}{\int_{I_0}^{\infty}\left(\frac{\partial g}{\partial \mu}\frac{\partial \mu}{\partial K}+\frac{\partial g}{\partial \sigma^2}\frac{\partial \sigma^2}{\partial K}\right)\mathrm{d}I}=\lambda_p. \tag{13}$$

As indicated above, the denominator in condition (12) measures the *reduction* in probability that the norm ($I_0$) will be exceeded as vehicle use is reduced. The area labelled $\beta_V$ in Figure 2 represents this reduction in the probability an exceedence, i.e., $\partial P(I > I_0)/\partial V_p$, and is negative.

The numerator of Equation (12) is positive: $\partial V_p$ is negative as a policy action and causes a reduction in utility to the vehicle owner – therefore $\partial U/\partial V_p > 0$. This term is shown in Figure 3 where the demand curve shown there is derived from the consumer's utility maximization problem where $D$ is simply the demand curve for vehicle use, and $P$ is the price of that use (gasoline, maintenance, etc.).

View the initial price $P_0$ as the private marginal cost of vehicle use, and $V_0$ as the initial unrestricted private equilibrium. Purely for the sake of illustration, suppose the restriction on vehicle use results in a market price of $P_1$ (the market in tradeable driving permits is discussed below) and that after all adjustments to the restriction (including the initial endowment of vehicle use permits), this owner chooses $V_1$ of vehicle use at the market price $P_1$. The welfare loss of the restriction is measured by area $V_1ab\,V_0$, but the reduced vehicle expenses are $V_1cb\,V_0$, so the net welfare loss is the usual welfare triangle *abc*. Area $P_1acP_0$ is the value of the endowment of vehicle use (also discussed below) and is not a welfare cost.

Analyzing the signs of Equation (13), increased abatement means that $\partial K > 0$. In the denominator, $\partial K > 0$, and the partial changes in $\mu$ and $\sigma^2$ are negative with the lognormal distribution (density increases when mean and variance decrease), and therefore the two chained partials are positive, so that $\beta_K > 0$. The numerator is negative and so the entire expression is negative.

### 3.5. Decision Rules for Implementing Demand Reduction Programs

If we relabel the denominators in Equations (12) and (13) as $\beta_{V_p}$ and $\beta_K$ respectively (the partial shifts in the probability of exceedence for unit changes in the choice variables) and equate the equations, we have Equation (14):

$$\frac{\frac{\partial U}{\partial V_p}}{\beta_{V_p}} = -\frac{\frac{\partial C^K_{ER}}{\partial ER}\frac{\partial ER}{\partial K}}{\beta_K}. \tag{14}$$

This equation gives the fundamental decision rule or condition for efficient allocation of control between demand reduction policies and technical abatement measures. It says that the control authorities should choose the levels of vehicle use and investment in technological controls so as to equate the incremental costs *per unit of reduced probability of exceedence of the norm*. The unit of probability is just percentage units. The numerators of the expression are marginal costs of emissions reduction, and each side of the equation represents the marginal cost of exceedence reduction. This condition lends itself to a rather standard graphical representation, as shown in Figure 4 (see Eskeland 1994 for a similar representation). The efficient or cost-effective division of control is shown at the intersection of the two marginal cost curves where MOC denotes the marginal opportunity cost to the consumer for alternative levels of vehicle use, the partial $\partial U/\partial V_p$ in Equation (14). Area A is total abatement cost using technological controls to reduce emissions per kilometer travelled; area B is the opportunity cost of the vehicle use restriction, net of other costs (gasoline, etc.), and area C is the net savings in avoided expenditure on technological controls.

Reduced driving and technological abatement are complementary controls and therefore are not mutually exclusive. Thus, in moving from one level of emissions reduction to another, reduced vehicle use may be the optimal choice, but as the emissions reduction target is increased (the length of the lower horizonal axis in Figure 4), the technology not chosen at the earlier or previously considered target level of control will now become cost-effective. In general, we would find that the marginal cost of emissions reduction curve that incorporates both reduced driving and abatement will have shifted down in relation to the curve that measures the marginal costs of technological controls only. In more technical terms, the marginal cost function computed with the information in Equations (7) and (14) will follow a lower trajectory, as shown in Figure 5, where DR denotes driving restrictions.

The precise location of $ER_V$ (the point where vehicle use restrictions enters in the set of controls) will depend on the relative elasticities of the demand for vehicle use and of the marginal cost of abatement with technological controls. Using the empirical information for the case of Mexico City in Eskeland (1994), a policy of cost-effective demand reduction extends over virtually the entire range of emissions reduction targets, as would be expected.

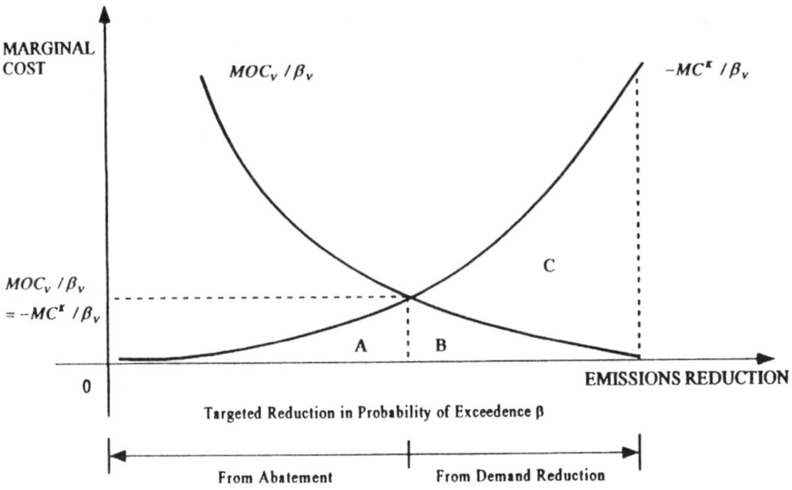


*Figure 4.* Optimal abatement and reduction in vehicle use.

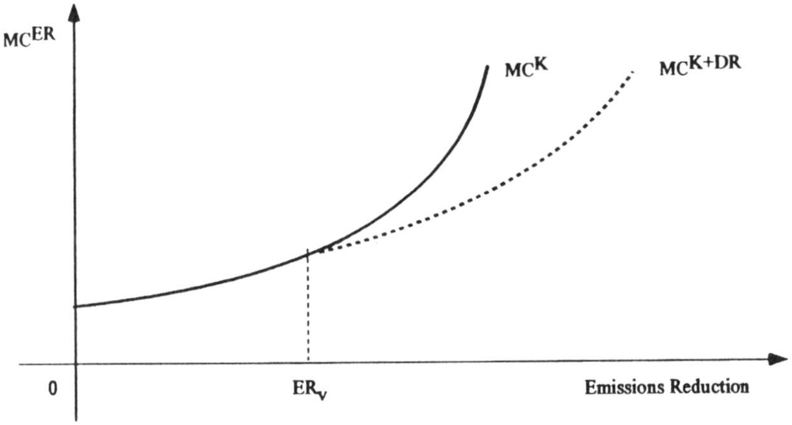


*Figure 5.* Marginal emissions reduction costs with optimal combination of controls.

With a little manipulation, we have Equation (15):

$$\frac{\frac{\partial U}{\partial V_p}}{-\frac{\partial C^K_{ER}}{\partial ER}\frac{\partial ER}{\partial K}} = \frac{\beta_{V_p}}{\beta_K}. \tag{15}$$

The right-hand side measures that rate at which demand reduction and technical abatement measures can be substituted for one another (the marginal rate of transformation) and still satisfy the constraint that the norm ($I_0$) not be exceeded more than $\alpha$ percent of the time. In Figure 1, there is no a priori reason to expect that $\beta_{V_p}$ and $\beta_K$ will be equal for unit changes in $V_p$ and $K$ respectively because they will not in general affect the density of $I_t$ in the same way. In other words, they are not perfect substitutes, simply because abatement only reduces emissions, but demand reduction eliminates them over the entire gasoline production, distribution and use system, with different implications for the relevant atmospheric chemistry and the pollutant concentrations measured by $I_t$. It follows then that the left-hand side also measures the rate at which $V_p$ and $K$ can be substituted for one another, while always minimizing the cost of meeting the emissions target.

## 4. Market Features and Efficiency Conditions

What is a desirable set of institutions to achieve an ecologically sustainable use of private vehicles? As indicated earlier, we shall choose private markets for pollution rights as the institution, and use tradeable vehicle use permits in this case as the control instrument. We next describe the nature of the good to be traded, and then develop the market equilibrium conditions needed to achieve the cost-effectiveness conditions described in Section 3.

### 4.1. Vehicle use trading: basic design features

The current Mexico City program works by using license plates coordinated with color coded decals to determine the particular day per week that vehicles are not allowed to circulate. This proposal would change this system to one in which vehicle owners would have to display similarly colored coded, but removable, cards in the windscreen for the days they *could* use their vehicles. This would introduce flexibility into the vehicle use control program, reducing costs and eliminating the incentive to acquire additional vehicles just to cover the day of required non-use under the current program. It would have the desirable collateral effect of reducing vehicular congestion and would additionally be a useful tool for slowing the rapid population growth in the State of Mexico surrounding the Federal District.

### 4.2. Permit issuance

The basic idea is to set the total supply of permits to achieve specified targets for ambient air quality and congestion reduction (average vehicle speed). The shift over to the new tradeable regime would occur by making a free, *one-time* grant of, say, three daily permits per week, to each of all currently registered vehicles in the air shed to be controlled. These permits would be perpetuities and the grandfathering of existing vehicles avoids serious political resistance to the mechanism that would result if some group were favored over another. Being a one-time grant or endowment will reduce any perverse behaviors to acquire additional permits through the purchase of additional vehicles for example. As mentioned, the quantity of pollution mitigation and therefore the total number of permits made available would be determined by the air quality objectives and by how much of total emissions control would be allocated to reduction in emissions from the vehicle fleet, as opposed to fixed sources. It would require substantial modeling of the variable (probabilistic) relationship between measured air quality indices and vehicular emissions.

Basically there are three air pollution control margins on which the authorities need instruments to control vehicular emissions cost-effectively. They need an instrument for controlling the overall level of vehicle emissions (the base load of emissions), an instrument for incremental base (episodic) control during the inversion season (December through April), and an instrument to provide complete flexibility to the driving public for unanticipated vehicle use. We envision three types of permits for these control margins:

- a perpetual base permit which allows vehicle use on the designated day under any air quality circumstances;
- a perpetual interruptible permit which differs slightly from a base permit in that it can be declared unusable during air pollution episodes;[14]
- a temporary permit to permit unanticipated vehicle use and to facilitate traffic to and from areas outside of Mexico City.

A possible initial endowment consistent with these control margins would involve the granting of two base permits and one interruptible permit, per existing vehicle.[15] The reduction in the endowment from the current four days to three in the proposed program would be used to provide a pool of driving days to be issued under the temporary permit program consistent with air quality targets. Drivers with excess permits or desirous of more base permits would need to go the market to make their exchanges. Permits could be bought and sold, leased, rented and lent. The authorities could change the number of outstanding base and interruptible permits by entering the market, either buying or selling them. The temporary permits would be issued by the authorities at widely dispersed locations such as gasoline stations, banks, supermarkets, etc., and at all entrances to the metropolitan area as well as in other cities for those travelling to the controlled area. Even credit card operated vending machines could be used to dispense the permits. The quantity demanded of these temporary permits would be rationed by price, set by the authorities as a function of present and expected pollutant concentrations.

The addition to the analysis of three types of permits does not change the basic nature of the preceding theoretical analysis. It yields three optimality conditions for vehicle restrictions, one for each type of permit, which are not presented here for reasons of space limitations and because it is treated next in the market analysis.

### 4.3. Permit markets

The preceding analysis details the conditions for determining optimal restrictions on vehicle use in a cost-effective set of abatement policies. Next we examine the associated market behavior and structure that will give rise to market prices with the same optimality properties.

We begin by reviewing the consumer's choice problem, which is straightforward. The representative consumer maximizes a utility function with arguments for three types of vehicle-use permits mentioned above, $V_i$, other goods and services and the level of air quality chosen by the authorities. As before, air quality or emissions targets are exogenous to this analysis. The consumer's problem is given in Equation (16) in which the initial vehicle day endowment is shown as $\overline{V}_j$.

$$\max_{V_j} L_\gamma = U(X, V_B, V_{IN}, V_T, e_0) - \gamma\left[\sum_i^N P_i X_i + \sum_j^J (V_j - \overline{V}_j) - \overline{M}\right], \tag{16}$$

where $X$ is other goods and services and $j = \{V_B, V_{IN}, V_T\}$. A typical first order condition for the choice of permits is:

$$\frac{\partial U}{\partial V_j} = \gamma P_j. \tag{17}$$

Comparing this market condition for consumer choice in Equation (17) and with the optimality conditions for minimal welfare loss Equations (9) and (10), we have for any given permit type:[16]

$$\lambda = \frac{\gamma}{\beta_{V_p}} P_j = -\frac{\frac{\partial C^K_{ER}}{\partial ER}\frac{\partial ER}{\partial K}}{\beta_K} \tag{18}$$

or

$$\frac{P_j}{\beta_{V_p}} = -\frac{\frac{\partial C^K_{ER}}{\partial ER}\frac{\partial ER}{\partial K}}{\gamma\beta_K} = \frac{\lambda}{\gamma}. \tag{19}$$

This condition indicates that for a permit market to generate the socially optimal (minimal opportunity cost) amount of vehicle use as a complementary emissions control policy (as identified by the condition in Equation (14)), the ratio of the LaGrangean multipliers will be the same as the marginal opportunity costs of the reductions in the probability of exceedence of the air quality norm engendered by the two abatement instruments, adjusted by the marginal utility of income. For the market condition in Equation (17) to generate those same levels of instrument use of permits and abatement as indicated by the optimality conditions in Equation (14) we need to assume that the marginal utility of income, $\gamma$, must be equal to one. This assumption would imply that Equation (19) equals $\lambda$, the change in the net opportunity cost of altering the probability of exceeding the norm $\alpha$.[17]

### 4.4. Permit Price Relationships

Because the trading scenario we envision contains three types of permits, we hypothesize that the following relationships will hold among them in a market situation: $P_T > P_B > P_{IN}$. Temporary permits on average should always be priced by the authorities at a premium over the base permits so that they do not become perfect substitutes with the base permits; otherwise they would lose control of the permit instrument. Further, we would expect that the demand for temporary permits to be relatively inelastic because this demand would be comprised of mainly unanticipated and therefore unplanned vehicle usage. Interruptible permits will trade at a discount from the base permits because of the nonzero probability that they will be periodically declared unusable – they are really base permits with less than a probability of one that they can be used at any time. Taking the base permit as the numeraire permit, i.e., $P_j = P_B$ in Equation (19), these relationships can be represented as:

$$\begin{aligned} P_{IN} &= \frac{P_B}{1+g_{IN}} \Rightarrow P_B = P_{IN}(1+g_{IN}) \\ P_T &= P_B(1+g_T) \Rightarrow P_B = \frac{P_T}{(1+g_T)}, \end{aligned} \tag{20}$$

where the discount factors, $g_j$, are greater than one. The $g_{IN}$ will be probabilistic and the associated price $P_{IN}$ as well. This price should reflect the underlying objective variabilities of air quality outcomes, but of course this price formation will depend on the information provided by the government and the confidence that the information is reliable.

To examine the static equilibrium properties of these prices we substitute these relationships alternatively into the basic market efficiency condition in Equation (19) (with the assumption that $\gamma = 1$). Solving them for the prices of the different permits, we have:

$$\begin{aligned} P_T &= -\frac{\beta_V}{\beta_K}\left(\frac{\frac{\partial C^K_{ER}}{\partial ER}\frac{\partial ER}{\partial K}}{1+g_{IN}}\right) = -\frac{\beta_V}{\beta_K}\left(\frac{MC^{ER}_K}{1+g_{IN}}\right) \\ P_B &= \frac{\beta_V}{\beta_K}(MC^{ER}_K) \\ P_{IN} &= -\frac{\beta_V}{\beta_K}MC^{ER}_K(1+g_T). \end{aligned} \tag{21}$$

The second line in this set of equations is a repetition of Equation (19), the equality of the MRS and MRT. The first and third lines are similar expressions for the market prices for the interruptible and temporary permits, and are also functions of the MRS and MRT, as adjusted by the discount factors.

What can we say about the relative reliance the authorities should make of each type of permit? Since the basic problem the authorities face is time dependent, this static model is not adequate to answer this question. We need to know what the expected frequency of air pollution episodes is, as well as their intensity and duration, as a function of the exogenously chosen $\alpha$. The higher the acceptable or planned probability of exceedences, the lower the need for interruptible permits. In such a circumstance, dealing with exceedences could be handled by an appropriate choice of $V_B$ and $V_T$. Other things equal, interruptible permits are a more flexible instrument for authorities and for consumers – thus in part their lower value ('cost') in the market. This would mean that the authorities should make *relatively* greater use of this instrument than the others, but in the final analysis, we need to know the size and variability of the airshed capacity to be allocated among them, an issue to which we now turn.

## 4.5. AIR QUALITY VARIABILITY AND STOCHASTIC CONTROLS[18]

Although the above model does incorporate stochastic variability in the emissions constraint, the model is basically static in nature, as it does not permit analysis of multiple day episodes nor of the manner in which the stochastic nature of the problem impacts on the choice of the relative permit endowments. An episode results when there is incomplete dispersal of a previous day's emissions and pollutant concentrations. The basic stochastic influences are weather related, in particular wind velocity or ventilation, and additionally cloud cover and daily mean temperature in the case of ozone formation. We shall use 'dispersability' to refer to these factors. The following builds on the static model above.

A simple definition of dispersability, or more precisely 'non-dispersability' can be seen in the following relationship:

$$\mathrm{d}_t = \frac{A_t - e_t(V, K)}{A_{t-1}}, \tag{22}$$

where $A_t$ and $A_{t-1}$ are respectively today's and yesterday's ambient pollutant concentrations and $\mathrm{d}_t$ is the percentage of yesterday's concentration not dispersed by today. This can be rewritten as:

$$A_t = d_t A_{t-1} + e_t(V, K). \tag{23}$$

This equation is a first order difference equation with a stochastic coefficient. Next we add background sources (which include fixed sources in the present treatment), switch notation to the air quality index, IMECA or I, as the measure of ambient concentrations, and make explicit the three controls on vehicle usage:

$$I_t = \mathrm{d}_t I_{t-1} + \bar{e} + e_t(\mathbf{V}, K) \tag{24}$$

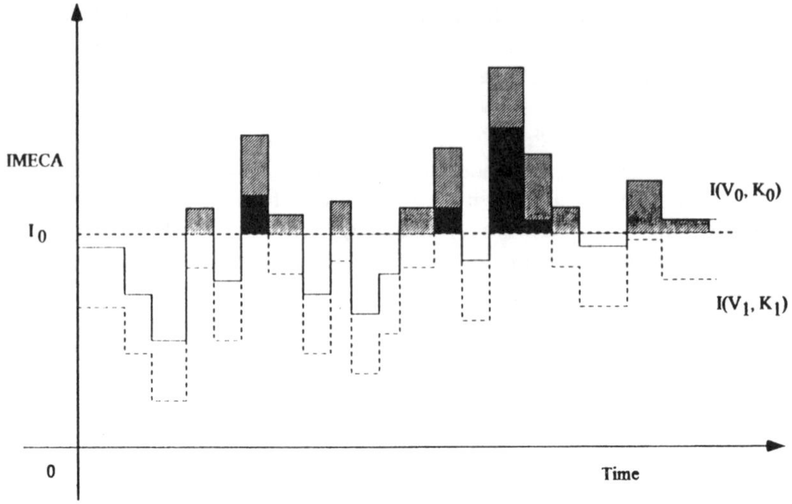


*Figure 6.* Time profile of air quality.

where **V** is a $3 \times 1$ vector with elements ($V_B$ $V_{IN}$ $V_T$). A multiple day episode would be given by:

$$I_t = \sum_{s=0}^{S} \mathrm{d}_{t-s} I_{(s+1)} + \bar{e} + e_t(\mathbf{V}, K), \tag{25}$$

where $s$ is the lag index. The $\mathrm{d}_t$ can be estimated empirically from meteorological data and together with predictions of weather conditions (wind velocity and cloud cover) this relationship can be used as a forecasting tool by which to predict pollution episodes as many days ahead as current techniques will permit.

The basic control problem facing the air quality managers is to choose the cost-effective combination of vehicle controls and abatement technologies that will reduce both the base load of emissions (the annual average) and the variance of the exceedences. The variances are a function of the acuteness and duration of the episodes. As a control relationship, $I_t$ would be set to $I_0$, the air quality norm, and in the long run the number of base and interruptible permits, as well as the predicted *average* number of temporary permits, would be chosen in order not to exceed the air quality target more than $\alpha$ percent of the time. Declaring the interruptible permits temporarily suspended and controlling the demand for the $V_T$ through temporary permit price changes would be used to control that portion of the variance of the exceedences not already controlled through a reduction in the base number of vehicles circulating.

This problem of stochastic controls can be illustrated with Figure 6 adapted from Baumol and Oates (1988). Two profiles are shown. The upper profile of air quality outcomes labelled I($V_0$,$K_0$) shows the realizations with no or insufficient controls, leading to exceedences greater than $\alpha$ percent of the time; the shaded area above the standard $I_0$ in the figure corresponds to the area ($\alpha + \beta$) shown in Figure 1 above. The overall profile of outcomes is lowered to I($V_1$,$K_1$) by employing base emissions controls (abatement technology and the general level of vehicle usage). The reduces the number of exceedences in the planning period to the darkly shared area. If the frequency of the remaining exceedences still exceeds $\alpha$ percent, the stochastic controls of interruptible and temporary permits can be employed to achieve that level. The cost-effectiveness argument is that one should *not* employ base controls to achieve the $\alpha$ percent target over the entire period as such controls are too blunt. In short, it is obviously less expensive to use an occasional control to deal with an occasional problem rather than a permanent control to deal with an occasional problem, another reason why gasoline taxes would not be a cost-effective control. The decision problem is to balance off the controls and the displacement in the entire profile in order to minimize the cost of control over all control dimensions.

To illustrate the nature of the physical control problem further, let us first assume that the nondispersability index 'd' is non-stochastic. With this assumption, Equation (24) is changed and its solution is:

$$\begin{aligned} I_t &= dI_{t-1} + \bar{e} + e_t(\mathbf{V}, K), \\ I_e &= \frac{\bar{e} + e_t(\mathbf{V}, K)}{1 - d}, \end{aligned} \tag{26}$$

where $I_e$ is the now stable long run level of air quality. The term $(1 - d)$ is the dispersability index. Next we make the additional simplifying assumption (still for illustration) that the relationship among $e_t$, $V_t$ and $K$ is linear.[19] Then we have $e_t = aV + bK$ ($V$ is vector) with the corresponding change in Equation (24). The authorities' problem is to chose $V$ and $K$ to achieve the target air quality index, $I_0$, cost-effectively (for the moment there are no stochastic outcomes), as given in:

$$I_e = \frac{\bar{e} + a\mathbf{V} + bK}{1 - d} = I_0. \tag{27}$$

Assuming that choices of vehicle use are made optimally (cost-effective combination with $K$ as given in Equation (14)), we can solve the relationship for the base number of vehicles to satisfy the air quality norm (ignoring interruptible and temporary permits for the moment). This solution is:

$$\mathbf{V}_e = -\frac{1}{a}(\bar{e} + bK) + \frac{I_0}{a}(1 - d) \tag{28}$$

and is represented in Figure 7 adapted from Baumol and Oates (1988). The variable of interest is the dispersability index, $(1 - d)$. The slope of the outcomes is given by $(I_0/a)$. When dispersability is high, then a larger number of permitted vehicles in use is consistent with the air quality norm, $I_0$; conversely, low dispersability implies that vehicles must be taken out of service until dispersability increases again. The difference between $V_{\text{high}}$ and $V_{\text{low}}$ is the required adjustment in vehicle use to satisfy the constraint. As a planning problem, the authorities need to predict the dispersability index and when the index is predicted to be low, declare suspended the use of those vehicles with interruptible permits, as well as raise the price of the temporary permits. Using a nonlinear emissions control function would yield similar qualitative results but different quantitative effects.

In terms of the given process for air quality outcomes, we have $P(I_e > I_0 \leqslant$ or $P(I_e - I_0 > 0) \leqslant \alpha$. As analyzed earlier in the static model (Equation (6)), the problem is to choose the control instruments such that

$$P\left(\frac{\bar{e} + a\mathbf{V} + bK}{1 - d} - I_0\right) \leqslant \alpha \tag{29}$$

or in general,

$$P\left(\frac{\bar{e} + e_t(\mathbf{V}, K)}{1 - d} - I_0\right) \leqslant \alpha. \tag{30}$$

This probably distribution will be known once the distribution for $d$ or $(1 - d)$ is known, a distribution that can be determined from historical data.

### 4.6. Implementing the Controls

As discussed earlier, the decision rule requires choosing the level of technological and vehicle use controls to satisfy the condition that the marginal opportunity cost of the instruments (prices of permits and marginal cost of abatement) divided by their respective reductions in the probability of exceedences (the $\beta$s) be equal. The prices of the permits are not likely to be known with much certainty until after some experience with the program. As a result, satisfying the efficiency conditions will be a matter of successive approximations. A major practical and political advantage of quantity based controls is that the authorities can have more certainty and control over the effects of the instruments and the predictability of these approximations than is the case with price-based instruments.

A possible way to structure the implementation of the program initially would be to use a two-step recursive approach. Since the air quality management problem in Mexico City is principally a seasonal one (as in many large cities), a possible recursive program would be to compute the number of vehicles that can circulate during the non-inversion season without exceeding the norm with the established frequency $\alpha$. In this period the base and interruptible permits would be virtually indistinguishable in that the probability of interruption would be very low. The price charged for temporary permits would be relatively low also compared to the

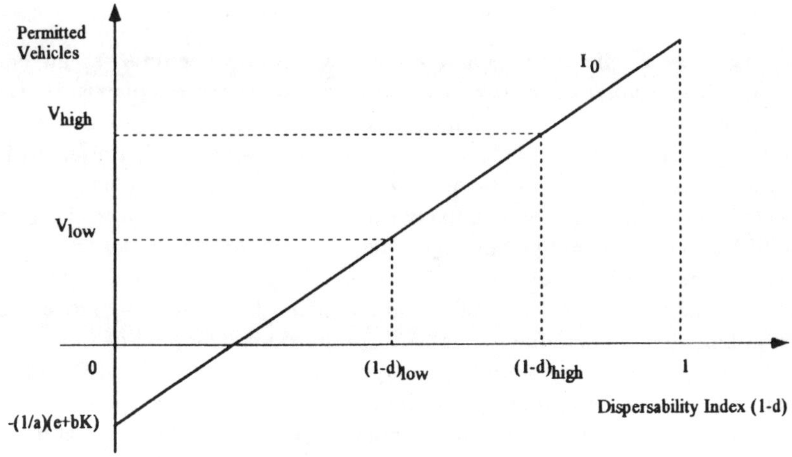


*Figure 7.* Time profile of air quality.

inversion season, but could be varied to deal with those days of low dispersability that do occasionally occur in the non-inversion season. Interruptibility still remains a control option for rare events in this non-inversion season.

For the pollution season, the authorities must calculate the proportion of the perpetual permits (base and interruptible), $P_{IN}/(P_{IN} + P_B)$, that must be available for suspension in order to meet the air quality constraint during inversion episodes. The greater the number of the interruptible permits, the lower will be their relative price in the secondary market. The secondary market for permits will determine the price relative for these permits, and therefore the floor for the price of the temporary permits.

After the markets have begun to stabilize, there will be sufficient data on prices and exchanges available to allow estimation of the permit demand relationships, and with these estimates the relevant opportunity costs for vehicle users can be computed. With this information and that of the marginal costs of abatement, the authorities can set the level of abatement technology indicated and also enter the permit market, buying or selling permits as appropriate in order to approximate successively the cost-effectiveness conditions identified earlier. Attaining the cost-effectiveness conditions may be a matter of a few years as the indicated complementary investments in abatement technologies require more time.

In terms of close substitutes for privately owned vehicles, taxis and leased vehicles in particular, failure to include these alternatives in the permit program would greatly diminish its effectiveness. They would have to be included in the initial endowments and subsequent operation of the program.

### 4.7. Speculative behaviors and the initial allocations

It is to be expected that the typical household will need some time to plan its long-term vehicle use with its endowment of permits, and that there will exist substantial uncertainty concerning both the future value in use and the exchange value of the permits. In such a situation, the rational consumer response in the presence of such uncertainty would be to retain the permits and not offer them on the market, as the expected reservation value would likely exceed current market prices. This implies that initial markets would be thin and subject to perhaps substantial volatility.

This market will be characterized by spatially differentiated demands and supplies. One would expect that the initial demand for permits by those residing in suburban areas to be quite strong. A disproportionate amount of the secondary supply would likely come from those residing at more central locations which are better served with mass transit. Via the argument above, this secondary supply will may well be thin initially. This situation would drive up the market price, but as these permits are perpetuities, expectations of high prices will lead to further speculative retention on the part of the potential suppliers. The result could be substantial price instability in the secondary market.

All of which raises the question of how to start up the market and to encourage voluntary permit exchanges. At least a partial autonomous startup will occur as there is an already established institution in Mexico City for matching buyers and sellers of various kinds of permits. For example, due to the excess demand for telephone lines, it has been customary to advertise these lines (and other kinds of permits) in the Mexico City newspapers, and so it can be expected that a primary market for secondary permit sales will take this form. In addition, the authorities could encourage and license permit brokers who will match buyers and sellers and arrange for exchanges, as well as buy and sell for their own accounts, thus introducing stabilizing behaviors in the market. Finally, the authorities should be prepared to make the market (sell permits) initially if it fails to start adequately, and once established, re-enter it with purchases to bring down gradually the stock of outstanding endowments in order to satisfy the emissions constraint.

### 4.8. Demand reduction via prices or quantity controls

In an earlier paper (Goddard 1992) we analyzed from a public policy perspective three alternative mechanisms for stimulating reduced vehicle use: )1) a fuel tax, (2) tradeable vehicle use permits as analyzed here and (3) tradeable gasoline coupons. The first is of course a pure price incentive, while the latter two present mixed regimes of quantity controls with price incentives. It was concluded there that the tradeable permits policy offers the best combination of cost-effectiveness, administrative flexibility and distributional fairness. As was discussed above, an important provision of a tradeable permit system for vehicles is that there be a one-time distribution of permits in order to minimize speculative behavior (acquiring more vehicles or registering vehicles from outside of the control region in order to increase one's endowment of permits). Gasoline coupons would have to be distributed periodically, and thus would give rise to the speculative behavior. Eskeland (1994) focuses on using an optimally calculated price incentive, gasoline taxes, to stimulate reduced driving. Aside from the spatial inefficiency that a gasoline tax would generate, an additional shortcoming to using the price of gasoline for ozone control is that it cannot be made stochastic, and therefore can deal only with the base load of emissions. As a result, it would be a very blunt instrument for dealing with a time varying pollution problem. A quantity control mechanism using tradeable permits, however, can provide the necessary flexibility to deal with the base load of emissions, acute pollution episodes and seasonal variation.

### 4.9. Practical Matters

The effectiveness of the permit program would be very dependent on the details of implementation and operation, and as all policy designers know, here is where the devil resides. This obviously is a large topic and so can be treated only briefly here. We discuss two important matters: market organization and market operation.

As indicated earlier, we envision a free, one-time, distribution of permits to the eligible public. The resultant stock of permits can be freely traded, bought, sold, leased, rented, lent, and unfortunately also stolen, as they will be valuable. On this last point, since the permits are a form of currency or financial asset, they could be carefully printed, with serial numbers and even holograms to reduce counterfeiting. As with any illicit activity, a judicious combination of fines and a probability of being caught should reduce this problem to manageable levels.

The market would likely take two principal forms. Most formal exchange would likely occur through the use of newspaper advertisements, as with other consumer assets (houses, vehicles, etc.) and through a series of brokers that would be licensed by the authorities. These brokers could match buyers and seller for a brokerage fee and also buy and sell for the own accounts.

How should the outstanding supply of permits be managed? It would seem that an independent body of technical experts, operating under broad guidelines established by law, would best ensure smooth operation without political interference. Here the analogy to a central bank's operation is very close. The group of technical experts to run the market would be composed of economists, statisticians, operations researchers, financial experts and atmospheric specialists, among others. Their function would be to determine what size and composition of the stock of permits should be that would satisfy the constraint on ambient concentrations and would also set the daily price for the temporary permits.

For traffic into the controlled region, permits would be sold both in cities of origin as well as at establishments near the frontier of the controlled region. Permits could be sold at peripheral brokerage branches, banks, gasoline stations, supermarkets, etc.

With respect to enforcement, a judicious choice of the magnitude of fines and a reasonable probability of being caught should be enough to encourage substantial compliance, as is the case with all traffic signs in many parts of the world, for example. In Mexico City, enforcement of the current program is handled by the traffic police widely stationed on street corners throughout the city. The enforcement has been very effective, for were it not, the purchase of extra vehicles to avoid the driving restriction would not have occurred.

The current proposal applies only to private passenger vehicles, and could be extended to commercial vehicles. This aspect, however, is more complex because of the greater variability of engine sizes and fuels. A complete scheme would increase cost-effectiveness by allowing trading across vehicle classes. What the transactions costs of extending the concept to commercial vehicles would be is a matter to be investigated.

### 4.10. Implications and Comments

While the focus of the scheme is on vehicle emissions, it is readily apparent that the program would operate on several margins relevant to achieving urban sustainability. It would likely have a dramatic impact on road congestion, controlling both the base weekday flow of vehicles and diminishing the peak congestion problem. These benefits would be quite substantial. It is not, however, designed to be a rationing mechanism for peak hour use of the road system. That margin would have to be controlled directly, if still a problem, but depending on how tight the air quality constraint is, it is quite possible that the mechanism described here would make even peak hour congestion costs non-Pareto relevant when the transactions costs of internalizing them are included, thus removing the need for congestion pricing. In addition, there would have to be complementary investments made in mass transit systems to accommodate transport mode shifting. There would of course have to be a large public informational component to a shift to the trading program.

The fact that the initial endowment is free greatly enhances the political acceptability of the program. The program would actually enhance the distribution of income, since although it is true that, as always, the wealthy would be little inconvenienced by the program, acquiring all the permits they desire from lower income groups, the flow of money would be in the opposite direction, from the wealthy to the less so, thereby actually improving the distribution of income. In addition, the program would favor those who tend to buy new vehicles (again the wealthy), thereby reducing the average age of the fleet and altering its composition toward vehicles with more pollution control equipment, thus providing an incentive toward adoption of cleaner vehicles. If the non-vehicle owning public were not a direct participant in this control program, it would nonetheless benefit from the air quality improvements, the increased capacity of the public transit systems and reduced travel times. Alternatively, permits could also be distributed beyond the vehicle-owning public, but this would raise considerable problems of identifying the targeted group, the residents of the control region only.

This program would not suffer from a shortcoming that characterizes the current sulfur dioxide trading program in the U.S., that of few participants or 'thinness'. In the case of Mexico City, the market for vehicle use permits has potentially more than three million participants in a geographically small area. Further, trading of uniformly mixed vehicle emissions would not suffer from the localized exposure problems ('hot spots') resultant from nonuniformly mixed pollutants that characterizes trading among fixed sources.

The program would have a number of favorable effects on city growth and form. Recalling that only existing vehicles at the time of program commencement are grandfathered, all purchasers of additional vehicles after the permit distribution date would have to enter the permit market to buy them. This has the effect of keeping the total fleet size consistent with the air quality targets. The same applies to those moving from other cities with their vehicles. Thus, the program could become an cost-effective and *decentralized* method of controlling unsustainable urban growth.

Since fringe urban areas everywhere are less well served by public transport, those inhabiting those areas will have greater demands for purchasing permits to allow vehicle use each day. This raises the cost of fringe locations, creating an appropriate and effective disincentive for urban sprawl. Conversely, the program creates increased demand for more centralized locations and for making residential location decisions more consistent with workplace and school locations. It would be a strong impetus for urban renewal and for raising the tax bases of central urban areas. The program would also create positive incentives for decentralization of economic activity to other regions of the country where such restrictions are not in place, thus slowing the growth of the world's megacities, already considered by many to be evidence of the unsustainability of urban development patterns. On this account, it appears to us that the scheme would have applicability in virtually any large urban area that wants to control growth patterns.

A further potential advantage of this system is that the permit holders will have a vested interest in maintaining the value of their property. Thus an interest group is created with an interest in ensuring that air quality does not deteriorate at the hands of excessive issue of permits. To the extent that permit holders treat this asset as any other financial asset, then the asset holders will want the value to grow at least at the rate of interest. This correspondence is not perfect, however, for the market value of the asset could grow at a rate greater than the interest rate due to population and income growth in the region. This would allow the authorities to issue more permits, causing air quality to diminish, without causing the rate of asset depreciation to fall below the interest rate. They might especially be tempted to sell permits as a revenue measure, and so for this reason the program would require an independent body to manage the program. There are many important lessons in central bank and money supply management of particular relevance here.

In terms of caveats, an important one would be that the program would cause vehicle owners to intensify the use of their vehicles on days for which they possessed a permit. To the extent that this represents trip shifting, there would be no gain or loss in air quality (except for those periods in which the shift turned out to be from a potentially good air quality day to a poor one, or vice versa). But there would be a cost. Certainty trip shifting and intensification of use will occur, and these are matters to be investigated. However, some of the intensification might in fact represent increased efficiency of vehicle use, resulting in fewer cold starts, thus offsetting the emissions associated with intensification. Further, there is a time cost to shifting, which would place a limit on intensified use.

Another small caveat is that this program does not provide an incentive to choose more fuel-efficient vehicles with their lower emissions rates and the derivative incentive for manufacturers to improve both fuel and emissions efficiency. It would seem that this shortcoming could be accommodated by awarding more permits to those owners of greatly reduced emissions rates. In fact, authorities in Mexico are contemplating relaxing the current no driving day restriction for those vehicles that meet a very stringent emissions test. In the proposal described here, however, since the margin of control is a day's worth of vehicle use, the extra permit could be used on any vehicle, thus potentially vitiating the program. Here we would argue for the use of a CAFE (corporate average fuel economy) program to deal effectively with this margin. We note that the two programs together would diminish or eliminate the inefficiency of the U.S. CAFE program described by Nivola and Crandall (1995). Further, while space has not permitted extension of the discussion to the potentially great advantages this systems brings to the management of road congestion and urban form (planning) and the entire matter of urban sustainability, we think they are great, and so would argue that viewing this permit system as simply an air quality management places a much too narrow perspective on the matter.

### 4.11. Needed Research

While the proposal would seem to possess a number of potentially useful characteristics as an efficient and equitable mechanism for controlling mobile emissions, there are a number of important issues that need to be studied. Paramount among them are the administrative requirements of the program; measurement of the opportunity cost of enforced reduced driving; the degree of intensification of vehicle use on days for which a permit is owned stimulated by the program; the at least initial potential for speculative holding of permits rather than active participation in the market; and methods for managing it.

On the technical side, the non-convex relationship between ozone, $NO_x$ (nitrogen oxides) and HC (hydrocarbons) means a balance needs to be struck between the reduced concentrations of $NO_x$ from reduced vehicle use and the other sources of HC. Complementary controls of HC sources would have to be put in place. In our model above, these would be captured in the marginal control cost terms.

## 5. Conclusions

Problems of sustainability in urban growth are already quite apparent in a number of the world's cities, and it is clear that the current unrestricted use of the private automobile is at the center of this problem. It is a reasonable supposition that the world will soon have to confront this unrestricted use, and yet there is no consensus about what practical instruments are available to achieve this objective efficiently, effectively and in a politically feasible manner. The analysis presented here indicates that optimal use of demand reduction strategies should be part of a comprehensive mobile source control program.

The argument presented here is that a no driving day program seems to possess a sufficient number of characteristics to warrant a thorough examination of its advantages and disadvantages, especially in the face of the sobering realities of political economy surrounding the use of price instruments such as gasoline taxes for regional or even global emissions control. Using Mexico City as a case study, it seems that the current no driving day program can be modified to allow the implementation of a tradeable vehicle use program to introduce flexibility and cost-effectiveness in attaining emissions targets for the Mexico City metropolitan area.

This control policy would have substantially favorable impacts on air quality, vehicle congestion and uncontrolled suburban development, and given the general political unacceptability of environmental taxes, could form part of a workable and politically palatable set of policies to control greenhouse gas emissions from the transport sector.

## Notes

1. I would like to thank Benjamín Contreras of the Instituto Tecnológico Autónomo de México for his most helpful assistance, Alan Radford of Glasgow Caledonian University for his extensive comments and suggestions, and Thomas Tietenberg, Wallace Oates, Henk Folmer, Kenneth Small, Gregory W. Characklis and two referees for their constructive suggestions. This work was supported with funds from the Pemex Chair in Economics at ITAM, made possible by a grant from Petróleos Mexicanos. Alan Radford's assistance was made possible through a grant made by the British Council. Finally, this line of research was made possible by the award of a Senior Fulbright Fellowship in 1991 by the U.S.-Mexico Fulbright Commission to spend a year at ITAM.
2. For a full and sobering discussion of the political difficulties in forging rational gasoline vehicle use policies in the U.S., see Nivola and Crandall (1995), Chapter 5, 'The American Experience'.
3. To mention a few: Mexico City, São Paulo, New York City, Los Angeles, Cairo, Bangkok and Athens. Virtually all large cities make important contributions to the production of greenhouse gases due to their large fleets.
4. As an example of the political infeasibility, even in the very environmentally conscious Netherlands, a proposal in 1989 for an environmental tax that had strong negative consequences for long distance commuters led to the breakup of an political coalition and the calling of new parliamentary elections. (Rietveld 1995)
5. Ignoring the spatial implications to be discussed in the text, technical infeasibility is not the problem, as even with inelastic demands for gasoline, there could be a price high enough to generate the targeted reduction in gasoline use. Not that the elasticity is that low, as one extensive

review (Goodwin 1988) indicates that the long run price elasticity of gasoline is −0.73, based on a review of eighty-five separate studies. However, taking into account that high gasoline prices stimulate a shift in vehicle size and fuel efficiency, this review indicates that the impact on *traffic levels* (a measure of vehicle trips) is only −0.39, considerably more inelastic. The elasticity for gasoline consumption would imply that there would be a reasonably favorable effect on emissions, but the traffic elasticity suggests that there would not be a proportional impact on congestion.

6. Other policies such as differentially high taxes on older and more polluting vehicles are frequently suggested, but as these vehicles tend to be owned by lower income individuals, the adverse implications for the income distribution make this a politically unacceptable policy as well, probably in most countries. The same difficulty applies to raising the general vehicle licensing fee. The lack of fiscal neutrality of these mechanisms in general makes them unacceptable to policy makers.
7. We know this decentralization (urban sprawl) to be uneconomic (marginal costs exceed marginal benefits) because both congestion and emissions are unpriced and therefore the perceived transportation costs are lower than what they would otherwise be with a program to make the costs explicit. It is known from many studies of the determinants of urban density that transportation costs are a major determinant of choice of residential location, measured as distance from the central city. In other words, the rent bid function for land is higher at fringe locations that it would otherwise be. See Muth (1969). For a recent review of the effects of congestion pricing on urban form, see Deakin (1994). What the relative effects on urban form are for the trading scheme proposal here compared to congestion pricing is a matter to be investigated.
8. The use of purchased licenses for controlling urban congestion has been used extensively in Singapore. In contrast to the proposal described here which involves a free endowment of vehicle use permits, Singapore's program sells the permits for entering the controlled area as well as for vehicle ownership. As will be seen, our proposal has several advantages on distributional grounds and for controlling emissions as well. For a recent survey of congestion pricing schemes in Singapore and elsewhere, see Gómez-Ibáñez and Small (1994).
9. The data mentioned in the following paragraphs come from various unpublished governmental reports.
10. A demand reduction policy will also reduce congestion and lead to reduced emissions. The emissions function $e(V,K)$ is already defined to include those emissions reductions created by reduced congestion.
11. There is an important aspect of this constraint (and the cost function) which requires mention but which we do not model here in order to keep the complexity down. There is a well known relationship between the ambient concentration *ratio* of ozone precursors (hydrocarbons and nitrogen oxides) and subsequent ozone formation as contained in EKMA (empirical kinetic modeling approach) and three dimensional grid models (see National Research Council 1991). A policy that reduces one of the precursors without reducing the other proportionally will have little to no impact on ozone formation over an important range. For the policy examined in this study, the emissions relation, $e(V_p,K)$, and the cost function need to include those controls that preserve the ratio, but is not modelled here. For a useful discussion involving integration of this physical relationship and economic variables, see Repetto (1987).
12. Only after all of the theoretical modeling for this paper was long completed did I become aware of a partial antecedent in the literature written by Charles Howe and Dwight Lee (1983). Although this work was developed completely independently of theirs, there are some gratifying similarities involving the use of stochastic outcomes. They also do anticipate that their work could be applied to mobile sources.
13. The general form for the lognormal density function is $f(x) = 1/[x(2\pi\sigma)^{1/2}] \exp[-(\ln x - \mu)^2/2\sigma^2]$. The mean and variance for this application are given in the Appendix.
14. This suggestion was made by Thomas Tietenberg. For a discussion of episodic control with trading among fixed sources, see Tietenberg (1985: 163–164).
15. We choose three permits under the assumption that a real 20% reduction in vehicle use, from five days to four *on average*, would be sufficient to achieve the vehicle emissions targets. This is of course an empirical question and a matter of choice for the control authorities.

16. These results are found by equating the marginal utility terms in Equations (9) and (18), solving for $\lambda$ and in turn equating the result to Equation (10) once solved for $\lambda$ as well.
17. The orthodox result in comparisons of optimality and market conditions in the context of general equilibrium analysis is that the multipliers are equal to one another and thus cancel out, a result which occurs because both restrictions are expressed in terms of market or resource equilibria. We do not get that result here because of the dissimilarity of the restrictions on the two objective functions and because this is not general equilibrium analysis. What the loss of generality is for assuming that $\gamma = 1$ is a matter to be explored.
18. The intellectual antecedents to much of the analysis in this section can be found in Baumol and Oates (1988, Chapter 13, 'Stochastic Influences, Direct Controls and Taxes': 190–210), and in Tietenberg (1985).
19. Whether the relationship is linear or not for ozone control depends on the average ratio of $NO_x$ to VOC emissions for each vehicle removed for use in relation to the overall ratio for the airshed to be controlled and to the nature of the impacts caused by abatement technologies on the same emissions. See note 10 and (National Research Council 1991, Chapter 6, 'VOC's and $NO_x$: Relationship to Ozone and Associated Pollutants'.
20. See Mood et al. (1974: 540–541).

## Appendix

In this appendix we analyze the impact on the variance of $I^0$ with respect to changes in vehicle use and abatement investment for the case of lognormally distributed air pollution outcomes as measured by the air quality index $I^0$. The index $I^0$ is composed of a systematic component $I^s = f(V,K)$ and a stochastic component $\epsilon$ which is assumed to be independently and identically distributed as $\epsilon \sim \ln N(\mu_\epsilon, \sigma_\epsilon^2)$. Since pollution indices are distributed approximately lognormally, a functional form which fits these facts is a multiplicative one, i.e., $I^0 = I^s \cdot \epsilon$ and therefore $\ln I^0 = \ln I^s + \ln \epsilon$. Recalling that $I^s = f(V,K)$ and $\epsilon \sim \ln N(\mu_\epsilon, \sigma_\epsilon^2)$, this means that $\ln \epsilon \sim N(\mu_\epsilon, \sigma_\epsilon^2)$ and that with the functional form chosen, $\ln I^0 \sim N(\mu_\epsilon + \ln I^s, \sigma_\epsilon^2)$ (because $\ln I^0 = \ln I^s + \ln \epsilon$ and $\mu_\epsilon$ is the mean of $\epsilon$, not of $I^0$). Then for this functional form[20] the antilogs are distributed as:

$$I \sim \ln \left[ e^{\mu_\epsilon + \ln I^s + 0.5\sigma_\epsilon^2)}; e^{2(\mu_\epsilon + \ln I^s + \sigma_\epsilon^2)} - e^{2(\mu_\epsilon + \ln I^s) + \sigma_\epsilon^2} \right]. \tag{A1}$$

The stochastic elements in this analysis are basically two: (a) meteorology or the weather and (b) those elements of randomness in vehicle use $V$ and economic activity. Since we expect that $\partial I^s / \partial V > 0$, this implies that $\partial I^0 / \partial V > 0$ also. The impact on reduced vehicle use on the variance of the observed air quality index is given by:

$$\frac{\partial \text{var}(I^0)}{\partial V_P} = \frac{2}{I^s} \frac{\partial V^s}{\partial V_P} \left[ e^{2(\mu_\epsilon + \ln I^s + \sigma_\epsilon^2)} - e^{2(\mu_\epsilon + \ln I^s) + \sigma_\epsilon^2} \right]. \tag{A2}$$

This expression is the specific form for the terms $\partial \sigma^2 / \partial V$ in the text, as in Equations (9) and (12) and is positive as a result of the policy action (concentrations decline as vehicle use diminishes). The term in the brackets is positive as the first term within is larger than the second. This means that $\partial(\text{var } I^0)/\partial V > 0$ and for $\delta V < 0$, the variance of the $I^0$ declines. Thus we conclude that the variance of the $I^0$ will decrease as a result of the policy actions of (a) stimulating less use of vehicles and (b) of increasing abatement expenditure, $K$, that is, $\partial(\text{var } I^0)/\partial K < 0$. Technically this occurs because the mean of the lognormal distribution for the observed $I$, the $I^0$ is contained in the expression for the variance in Equation (A1): this is $\mu + \ln I^s$. Intuitively, the usual explanation applies: demand reduction and abatement measures push the density function to the left and given the fact that $I$ is non-zero and that there is a new restriction ($\alpha$) on the probability of an exceedence, the variance must decline. Inspection of the mean in Equation (A1) indicates via similar reasoning that $\partial\mu/\partial V_p > 0$ also and so the mean declines for reductions in $V_p$.

## References


Asesoría Ecológica del Jefe del Departamento del Distrito Federal (January 1992), *Reporte Anual Sobre la Calidad del Aire en la Ciudad de México*. Mexico City: Departamento del Distrito Federal.

Baumol, W. and W. Oates (1988), *The Theory of Environmental Policy*, second edition. Cambridge University Press.

Daly, Herman, ed. (1973), *Toward A Steady-State Economy*. Boston: W. H. Freeman.

Deakin, Betty (1994), 'Urban Transportation Congestion Pricing Effects on Urban Form', in National Research Council, *Curbing Gridlock: Peak-Period Fees to Relieve Urban Congestion*, Volume I. Washington, D.C.: National Academy Press, Washington.

Dirección de Prevención y Control de la Contaminación (1990), *Informe de Evaluación del Programa "Hoy No Circula"*. Mexico City: Departamento Del Distrito Federal.

Dix, M. C. and P. B. Goodwin (1992), 'Petrol Prices and Car Use: A Synthesis of Conflicting Evidence', *Transport Policy and Decision Making* **2**(3).

Eskeland, Gunnar (1994), 'A Presumptive Pigouvian Tax: Complementing Regulation to Mimic an Emissions Fee', *The World Bank Economic Review* **8**(3), 373–394.

Eskeland, G. and T. Feyzioglu (1994), 'Is Demand for Polluting Goods Manageable?: An Econometric Study of Car Ownership and Use in Mexico', *Policy Research Working Paper 1309*, The World Bank.

Goddard, Haynes C. (1992), *Emissions Trading for Mobile Source Control in Mexico City: Part I: An Exploratory Policy Analysis*, unpublished manuscript, Instituto Tecnológico Autónomo de México, Mexico City.

Gómez-Ibáñez, J. and K. Small (1994), *Road Pricing for Congestion Management: A Survey of International Practice*, Washington: Transportation Research Board, National Research Council, National Academy Press.

Goodwin, P. B., 'Evidence on Car and Public Transport Demand Elasticities', unpublished manuscript, Reference 427 (revised), Transport Studies Unit, Oxford University, June, 1988.

Howe, C. and D. Lee (1983), 'Priority Pollution Rights: Adapting Pollution Control to a Variable Environment', *Land Economics* **59**(2), 141–149.

International Energy Agency/OECD (1993), *Car and Global Climate Change*. Paris.

Larsen, R. I. (1969), 'A New Mathematical Model of Air Pollutant Concentration Averaging Time and Frequency', *Journal of the Air Pollution Control Association* **1**(1), 24–30.

Mood A., F. Graybill, and D. Boes (1974), *Introduction to the Theory of Statistics*, 3rd. edition. New York: McGraw-Hill.

Muth, Richard (1969), *Cities and Housing: The Spatial Pattern of Urban Residential Land Use*. Chicago: University of Chicago.

National Research Council (1991), *Rethinking the Ozone Problem in Urban and Regional Air Pollution*. Washington, D.C: National Academy Press.

Nivola, P. and R. Crandall (1995), *The Extra Mile: Rethinking Energy Policy for Automotive Transportation*. Washington: The Brookings Institution.

Opschoor, J. (October, 1994), 'Institutional Change and Development Towards Sustainability', paper presented at Third Meeting of International Society for Ecological Economics, Costa Rica.

Pedrero Nieto, R. (1993), *Administración Estratégica del Tráfico Urbano* (*Costo económico y ecológico del tráfico urbano en el área metropolitana de la Ciudad de México*): Alternativas de solución. Mexico City: Instituto de Investigación Económica y Social Lucas Alamán, A.C.

Repetto, R. (1987), 'The Policy Implications of Non-convex Environmental Damages', *Journal of Environmental Economics and Management* **14**(1), 13–29.

Rietveld, P. (February 1995), 'Political Economy Issues of Environmental Friendly Transport Policies'. Amsterdam: paper presented at VSB International Symposium on Transport and the Global Environment.

Tietenberg, T. (1985), *Emissions Trading: An Exercise in Reforming Pollution Policy*. Washington, D.C.: Resources for the Future.

# Part V
# Adjustment, Trade and the Environment

# [21]

## *The Environment as a Factor of Production: The Economic Growth and Trade Policy Linkages*

*Ramon Lopez*

A large number of developing countries have recently embarked on profound economic reforms with the aim of increasing economic efficiency and stability. Among these reforms, trade liberalization has been emphasized. Trade reform in most developing countries has involved a rather drastic realignment of relative prices. One consequence of the reforms that is present in a large number of cases is a significant improvement of the domestic relative prices of agriculture vis-a-vis the manufacturing sector. In many cases the decrease of the anti-export biases induced by trade liberalization has entailed a reduced protection of the manufacturing sector (typically the major import substitution sector) and a concomitant reduction in the effective taxation of agriculture, in most cases the key export sector.

The increased economic efficiency associated with trade liberalization leads to once-and-for-all income gains. Empirical measurement of these static gains have been in most cases shown to be rather small. However, several empirical studies have concluded that increasing the degree of openness of the economy induces dynamic income gains that are much larger than the static gains (Balassa, 1982; Kavoussi, 1984; Ram, 1985). These growth effects apparently arise from an acceleration of investment and an increase in the rate of adoption of new technologies that an export-oriented trade strategy seems to bring about.

Several authors have addressed different aspects of the relationships between environmental degradation and economic growth (Anderson, 1990, Uimonen and Whalley, 1991). The connection between trade policies and the environment has also been the object of recent analysis (Sutton, 1988; Schuh, 1990; Lutz, 1991; Uimonen and Whalley, 1991). In general there is very little agreement on the nature of the linkages among trade reform, growth and environmental degradation.[1] This is not surprising in view of the complexity of the issues and given the large number of environmental factors that one can consider and the variety of mechanisms by which growth, relative prices and environmental change can interact.[2]

The objective of this paper is to reconsider the growth/trade policy/environment analysis but within a substantially more modest and limited framework: (i) Instead of focusing on the interactions between economic growth and environmental developments we consider only a one-way connection from growth to environmental degradation. To do this we define growth as increases in the conventional factors of production

---

[1]See Dean (1991) for an excellent survey of this literature.

[2]Some authors have even questioned the relevance of the analysis because whatever the environmental effects are, the analysis needs to focus on the externality/public goods aspects of the environment. Since these issues have been thoroughly explored in the theoretical literature, it is argued that there is little new in the debate on growth/trade/environment relationships. See Uimonen and Whalley (1991) for an analysis of these issues and for a discussion of why this simple Pigouvian view of the world needs to be qualified in important ways.

and technological change rather than as output growth.[3] (ii) Instead of focusing on liberalization of trade at a world scale we consider only unilateral trade liberalization in a small open developing country, where liberalization is defined as a reduction in tariffs that protect the manufacturing sector. (iii) We try to provide a systematic analysis of polar cases using highly simplified models. The fact that we concentrate on polar cases and the simplistic nature of the models used obviously subtract "realism" from the exercise but at the same time it may be useful to introduce a degree of systematicity to the analysis and serve as a departing point to consider more "realistic" aspects.

The idea is to reconsider the growth/trade policy/environment relationships using a neoclassical model that incorporates the more or less standard assumptions that have been most widely used in conventional general equilibrium and growth analyses. These assumptions include: (i) the existence of an aggregator function of capital (K), labor (L) and technology (t), f(K, L, t), that in the conventional models is called "output"; (ii) the production technology exhibits constant returns to scale in the factors of production; (iii) preferences are homothetic.[4] The basic question is what such a standard and well-accepted neoclassical model would have to say when the environmental factor is inserted in this framework.

We suggest that in the analysis of the impact of growth and trade policy on the environment there are two important distinctions to be made that may significantly alter the effects. On the one hand it is necessary to distinguish whether the natural resource has or has not stock feedback productive effects. That is, whether the changes in the stock of the environmental factor play a role on output. Examples of environmental factors that have productive stock feedback effects are the forest resource, the fish stock and agricultural soil depth. In these cases production can expand in the short run by more intense exploitation of the resource but at the cost of a gradual reduction in the stock which eventually may decrease productivity in the respective industries. An important example where the productive stock feedback effects are negligible is air quality. Expansion of industrial production may increase air pollution but greater air pollution is unlikely to significantly affect industrial production.[5] Moreover, at least on a local basis the stock effect of air pollution is very short lived. A reduction in emissions is likely to cause a fast recovery of air quality in the local (city) framework and thus the stock effect is quite negligible.[6]

A second essential distinction is whether producers and consumers internalize temporal and intertemporal externalities whether through private ownership, contractual community arrangements à la Coase or government policies. It turns out that the impact of economic growth and trade policy are crucially dependent on the internalization of the environmental effects by individual producers in the case where productive stock feedback effects are present. However, internalization is of no consequence for the qualitative effects of growth/trade policy on the environment in the absence of productive feedback effects.

---

[3]Output growth is necessarily affected by environmental change while capital expansion or technical change may allow us to at least conceptually consider them as independent of environmental changes.

[4]Practically all neoclassical growth models use the first two assumptions. The exception is the more recent "endogenous" growth literature (see Lucas (1988) and Romer (1985) among others). General equilibrium trade models traditionally use the three assumptions. Examples are Van Wijnbergen (1987), Johnson (1958), Dornbusch (1980), Razin and Svensson (1983) and many others.

[5]Air pollution, however, does have a negative direct effect on welfare, but not through income.

[6]This is ignoring global stock effects related to climatic warming and ozone depletion.

The remainder of the paper is organized as follows: The first section considers the case of resources that exhibit little stock productive effects, while the next section discusses the opposite case. Then we devote a section to the relative price effects of trade liberalization, consider available empirical evidence, and finally draw conclusions and discuss the policy implications of the analysis.

## Resources that do not have Stock Feedback Effects in Production

Here we consider environmental resources that affect output and/or utility essentially through a flow effect. That is, the environmental factor can recover quite rapidly as soon as its exploitation rate is reduced There are no important stock accumulation effects. An example of this is air pollution. Air quality tends to improve very fast when the rate of air emissions is reduced. Moreover, air pollution does not have directly negative effects on production although it does have a negative utility effect.

We assume that the economy is comprised of two sectors. Consistent with the conventional neoclassical assumption we assume that we can define an aggregator function of capital, labor and technology for each industry of the form

(1) $$f^i = f^i(K_i, L_i; t), \quad i = 1, 2,$$

where $K_i$ and $L_i$ are capital and labor in industry i, respectively and t is an index of technology. The function $f^i(\cdot)$ are assumed increasing and linearly homogenous in $K_i$ and $L_i$. The functions $f^i(\cdot)$ are of course, the production functions, typically specified as independent of the environmental factors.

To consider the environment as a factor of production we simply extend (1) to specify that total industry output is also a function of the environmental factor of production,

(2) $$y_i = G^i[f^i(K_i, L_i; t), x_i; \tau], \quad i = 1, 2,$$

where $y_i$ is output of industry i, $x_i$ is the environmental factor used by industry i[7] and $\tau$ is an index of technology. $G(\cdot)$ is increasing and concave in $f^i$ and $x_i$. Technical change may generate changes in $\tau$ that could affect the marginal rate of substitution between the conventional factors $f^i$ and the environmental factor $x_i$. Consistent with the conventional neoclassical specification of technology we assume that $G^i[\cdot]$ is also linearly homogenous in $f^i$ and the level of air pollution, $x_i$. This implies that the macro production function $G^i[\cdot]$ is characterized by constant returns to scale in $K_i$, $L_i$ and $x_i$.

The specification (2) assumes weak separability between the conventional factors of production and the environmental factor. This is quite consistent with the neoclassical specification. Weak separability a in (2) is a condition for the production function defined only in terms of conventional factors of production to make sense when factors other than the conventional ones change. Moreover, this assumption simplifies the algebra substantially by allowing us to consider the interactions between one aggregate conventional factor and the environmental resource. The robustness of the results to relaxing this assumption will be discussed

Assuming that the total capital and labor endowments are fixed and mobile across sectors we can define a revenue function as follows,

[7]For the case of air as an environmental factor, $x_i$ are air emissions produced by industry i.

(3) $$R[p; f(K, L, t), x, \tau] \equiv \max_{K_i, x_i, L_i} \left\{ \sum_i p_i G^i[f^i(K_i, L_i; t), x_i; \tau] : \Sigma K_i = K, \ \Sigma L_i = L, \ \Sigma x_i = x \right\},$$

where p is a vector of output prices, K and L are total capital and labor endowments, $x \equiv \Sigma x_i$ is the total utilization of the environmental factor (i.e., the total level of air emissions) and $f(\cdot)$ is an aggregator of the total conventional factors of production. The revenue function is homogenous of degree one in p. Moreover, because of the constant returns to scale assumption $R(\cdot)$ is also linearly homogenous in K, L and x. We note that in contrast with K and L, the total use of the environmental factor, x, is not fixed. In the absence of any internalization of the environmental externality, presumably firms would use $x_i$ until its marginal product is zero. If the air quality effects are internalized (through policy), firms would be forced to pay a price for their emissions. In either case as long as the price paid by firms is identical, we can use well-known aggregation theorems to define $R(\cdot)$ in terms of x rather than of the individual $x_i$.

Apart from being a factor of production, x has a direct effect on the societal welfare function, $\mu(\cdot)$. We assume that $\mu(\cdot)$ is a function of total consumption and x. Total consumption, in turn, is assumed equal to the revenue. The welfare function is then increasing and concave in R and decreasing and concave in x. Moreover, for simplicity we assume that preferences are homothetic. Thus, the welfare function is,

(4) $$\mu = \mu[R[p; f(K, L; t), x; \tau], x].$$

Maximization of $\mu(\cdot)$ with respect to x yields the optimal level of air emissions under the assumption that the air quality externality is completely internalized. The first order condition of such maximizations is,

(5) $$\mu_1(\cdot)\, R_3(\cdot) = -\mu_2(\cdot)$$

where $\mu_1(\cdot)$ and $\mu_2(\cdot)$ stand for the marginal utility of the consumer good and emissions, respectively and

$$R_3 \equiv \frac{\partial R}{\partial x}.$$

First we consider the growth effect, i.e., an increase in $f(\cdot)$ caused, for example, by capital accumulation (of course $\partial f/\partial K > 0$) or by a combined increase in capital and employment and the technical change t, that is, of an increase in output as defined in conventional models. We examine here two polar cases, namely, a case where no policies are in effect to affect the externality arising from the fact that firms' emissions have a detrimental effect for consumers, and the other extreme case that occurs when there is full internalization of the externality as in (5). The first case may occur either because of lack of policies to internalize the externality or simply because $\mu_2(\cdot)$ is about negligible. In this case we have,

(6) $$R_3(\cdot) = 0$$

and, hence, that

$$\frac{dx}{df} = -\frac{R_{32}}{R_{33}},$$

which is necessarily positive by concavity of R ($R_{33} < 0$) and by the fact that $R_{32}$ is positive under the constant returns to scale assumption. In general, without constant returns to scale, $R_{32}$ is positive under the plausible assumption of cooperant factors of production, i.e., that the marginal product of one factor increases when the level of the other factor rises. Thus, the level of pollution emissions necessarily rises with growth in conventional factors of production. This result is not dependent on the constant returns to scale assumption. Furthermore, it can be easily seen that an increase of any conventional factor of production (say K) or technology t, will have an unambiguously positive effect on air pollution even if the separability assumption is not imposed. All that matters is that the marginal revenue product of x be increasing in the conventional factor that expands. Under constant returns to scale and separability (6) can be written as,

$$\frac{x}{f} = g(p, \tau) > 0, \qquad (6')$$

where g(•) is a positive function. From (6') it is clear that the factor ratio x/f is fixed for given p and $\tau$. Hence, any increase in f(•), whether originated in increasing levels of factor endowments or technical change t, will be followed by a proportional increase in air pollution.

In the second polar case we use (5) which given constant returns to scale in production and homothetic preferences can be written as follows,

$$R_3\left[p;\ 1,\ \frac{x}{f(\cdot)}\right] = -\frac{\mu_2[1,\ x/R[p,\ f(\cdot),\ x;\ \tau]}{\mu_1[1,\ x/R[p,\ f(\cdot),\ x;\ \tau]} \qquad (7)$$

$$= \psi\left\{\frac{x}{f(\cdot)\ R\left[p,\ 1,\ \frac{x}{f};\ \tau\right]}\right\},$$

where $\psi(\cdot)$ is a well defined function. Note that the constant returns to scale assumption implies that $R_3(\cdot)$ is homogenous of degree zero in x and f(•). Hence, $R_3(\cdot)$ is a function of the x/f ratio. Similarly, the assumption of homothetic preferences also implies, without loss of generality, that $\mu(\cdot)$ is linearly homogenous and, hence, that the right hand of (7) can also be written as a function of the ratio x/f.

Thus, from (7) we can solve for the x/f ratio as,

$$\frac{x}{f(K,\ L;\ t)} = \phi(p;\ \tau) > 0, \qquad (8)$$

where $\phi(p)$ is some function of the vector of output prices. To see the effect of f on x we, therefore, do not require any specific knowledge of the function $\phi(p)$ except that it is positive. This is enough to allow us to know that an increase in f(•) will necessarily cause the level of emissions x to proportionally increase.

Differentiating (8) with respect to time and assuming that factors are paid their marginal value products, we obtain

$$\hat{x} = s_k\ \hat{K} + s_L\ \hat{L} + A + \eta, \qquad (9)$$

where a ^ indicates rate of growth, $s_k$ is the share of capital and $s_L$ the share of labor in total revenue, $A \equiv f_t/f$ is the rate of (conventional) factor enhancing technical change and $\eta \equiv \phi_t/\phi$ is the rate of technical innovation that changes the pollution intensity. A negative value for $\eta$ reflects technical change that is environmental saving and $\eta > 0$ implies conventional factor saving technical change. Coefficient A is of course non-negative under normal conditions. That is, technical change if anything increases the efficiency of the conventional factors of production, $A \geq 0$.

From (9) it is clear that growth based on capital accumulation or increased employment necessarily causes increases in pollution. If growth is based purely on technological change the effect on pollution would be ambiguous. To the extent that technical change is environmentally saving, i.e., $\eta < 0$, the net effect will depend on the strength of this effect relative to $A > 0$.

The positive relationship between factor endowments and pollution is robust to the separability assumption to the extent that the capital/labor ratio is constant as in the long-run neoclassical growth model. Without imposing separability it can be shown that (7) implies,

$$\frac{x}{L} = \psi(p, K/L, \tau, t) > 0, \tag{10}$$

where $\psi(\cdot)$ is some positive function. In this case a simultaneous increase in K and L that preserves the capital labor ratio will unambiguously increase pollution x. That is, as in the neoclassical growth model, steady state factor ratios do not change (unless non-neutral technical change occurs); this is true for the pollution/labor and pollution/capital ratios. Therefore, any increase in factor endowments will necessarily imply a corresponding increase in the third factor of production, x.

Another important implication of the above analysis is that the degree of pollution intensity (x/f) can be affected by the price level p and will depend on whether the externality is internalized or not. It can be shown that $g(\cdot) > \phi(\cdot)$ in (6′) and (8); that is, the pollution intensity is less when the negative consumption effects of the externality are taken into consideration in the production decisions than when they are not. The growth effects, however, are identical in both cases! That is, the elasticity of pollution with respect to f is equal to one whether the externality is internalized or not.

The cost of pollution controls for firms in industrialized economies have been shown to be very small, less than 1 percent of total costs (Low, 1991). Hence, one would expect that the research and development efforts of the private sector in developed countries (the originator of most new technologies) to generate environment-saving innovations are not likely to be large. Given the small private cost share of pollution controls, environment saving technical change is not likely to generate very significant increases in profits for firms while the large costs of conventional factors, particularly labor, imply that the bulk of the research effort in the private sector is likely to continue to be oriented to conventional factor saving technical change. All this implies that the factor A in (9) is still very large while $\eta$ may not yet be sufficiently negative to induce a negative $\hat{x}$ even if growth were entirely based on technological change.

If growth is originated in both conventional factor accumulation and productivity growth, the possibility of a net negative value for $\hat{x}$ is even more remote. In summary, growth based on factor expansion necessarily increases pollution. Growth based on factor accumulation and technological change is likely to also increase pollution. It is important to emphasize that this happens in the best possible situation, when firms are forced to fully pay for the pollution externalities.

## Resources that have Stock Feedback Productive Effects

In this section we consider resources that have both flow and stock effects on production. We will consider here only the effects of changes in the conventional factors of production (and of t). We ignore here $\tau$, but all the caveats about $\tau$ discussed in the previous section apply. An example of the stock feedback effects in production of environmental resources can be found in agriculture. Agriculture production under shifting cultivation in tropical areas is dependent not only on the cultivated land area (i.e., the amount of deforestation) but also on the stock of forest (biomass) itself because soil quality and fertility are dependent on an adequate stock of forest or biomass.[8] This permits us to write the production function in agriculture as

(11) $$y^A = F^A(K^A, L^A, z, s),$$

where $y^A$ is agricultural output, z is cultivated land and s is the stock of forest or biomass. $F^A(\cdot)$ is thus increasing and concave in the four factors of production. Moreover, we also assume that $F^A(\cdot)$ exhibits constant returns to scale in the four factors of production. The assumption of constant returns to scale in all factors including the stock of the resource was tested by Lopez (1991) for agriculture in Côte d'Ivoire. He could not reject this hypothesis, finding that the estimated returns to scale fluctuated between 0.92 and 1.01.

For a given total availability of land the stock of biomass depletion is proportional to the level of cultivated area.[9] Hence, assuming that the natural rate of biomass growth is $\alpha > 0$ and that biomass extraction is $\beta z$, where $\beta$ is a positive constant, the time evolution of the stock of biomass is,

$$\dot{s} = \alpha s - \beta z.$$

The revenue function for an economy comprised of two sectors, agriculture and the rest of the economy, under the assumption of weak separability between the conventional and the environmental factor can be written as,[10]

(12) $$R = R[p_A, p_N; f(K, L), z, s],$$

where $p_A$ is the price of the agricultural good, $p_N$ is the price of the nonagricultural output, and K, L are the total resource endowments of capital and labor in the economy.

We assume that the nonagricultural sector is also characterized by constant returns to scale and, hence, $R(\cdot)$ is linearly homogenous in f, z, and s. Also $f(\cdot)$ itself is homogenous of degree one in K and L. Given that only agriculture uses the environmental factor we have that $R_{14} \equiv \frac{\partial^2 R}{\partial p_A \partial z} > 0$, $R_{24} < 0$, $R_{15} > 0$, $R_{25} < 0$.

The socially optimal level of z would then be determined by,

(13) $$\max_z \int_0^\infty R(p_A, p_N; f(K, L), z, s)e^{-rt}dt$$

---

[8]The level of forest itself plays an important role in preventing flooding and soil erosion. Also in the context of shifting cultivation the fertility of the land periodically cleared for cultivation depends on the forest density. For details on the stock/flow effects see Lopez and Niklitschek (1991). Another example is in the context of soil conservation. Agricultural output depends on both the extent of soil loss (the flow) and on soil depth (the stock of the resource) (McConnell, 1983).

[9]The larger the cultivated area the shorter the fallow periods and, hence, the shorter the period allowed for regeneration of the forest.

[10]Here for notational simplicity we are ignoring the factor x used in the nonmanufacturing sector. This does not, however, affect any of the results below.

$$\text{s. t.} \qquad \dot{s} = \alpha s - \beta z$$

$$s(0) = \bar{s}_0,$$

where r is the discount rate and s(0) is the initial level of biomass stock. The first order necessary conditions are

(14) (i) $R_4(\cdot) = \lambda,$

(ii) $\dot{\lambda} = (r-\alpha)\lambda - R_5(\cdot),$

(iii) $\dot{s} = \alpha s - \beta z,$

(iv) $s(0) = \bar{s}_0; \ \lim_{t \to \infty} e^{-rt}\lambda(t)s(t) = 0,$

where $\lambda$ is the current value co-state variable measuring the shadow value of s.[11]

First we consider the case when individual producers do not internalize the stock effect of the resource on society's wealth. This may happen when the stock of biomass is public or common property and the community for whatever reason has not developed the necessary contractual arrangements that would have led to a solution like (14). We first analyze a polar case where producers totally ignore the shadow value of biomass in their decisions. That is, they behave as if $\lambda = 0$, and hence equation 14(ii) would not form part of the solution and equation 14(iii) will simply take the role of an accounting identity. Thus, the effect of economic growth is in this case entirely ruled by the condition $R_4(\cdot) = 0$.

Figure 9-1 considers the effect of an increase in f for the case when the initial equilibrium is stable. Before f increases, the stock of biomass is $s_0$ and the cultivated area is $z_0$. A rise in h will increase the marginal revenue product of cultivated land for any given level of the stock. Hence, the $R_4 = 0$ schedule will shift upwards. This will cause an instantaneous increase in the area cultivated to $z^1$ which, in turn, will cause the stock s to decline. As s is reduced the marginal revenue product of cultivated land is gradually reduced, thus causing z to decline. This process is shown by the arrow lines. The new steady state will occur at a lower stock and service flow of the resource. That is, under stability, capital expansion or more generally, an increase in the conventional factors of production will necessarily cause a higher rate of deforestation.[12]

Next we examine the other polar case, individual producer decisions take full account of the social value of the stock of biomass. In this case the behavior of the system is ruled by the complete system of equations (14). First we consider the steady state, i.e., we assume $\dot{\lambda} = \dot{s} = 0$. In this case we have

(15) $$R_4(p_A, p_N; f(K, L), \frac{\alpha}{\beta}s^*, s^*) = \frac{1}{r-\alpha} R_5(\cdot),$$

---

[11]An additional assumption is that $r > \alpha$.

[12]The unstable case occurs when the slope of the $R_4 = 0$ schedule is flatter than the $\dot{s} = 0$ schedule. In this case an increase in h will lead to complete extinction of the resource.

145

Figure 9-1

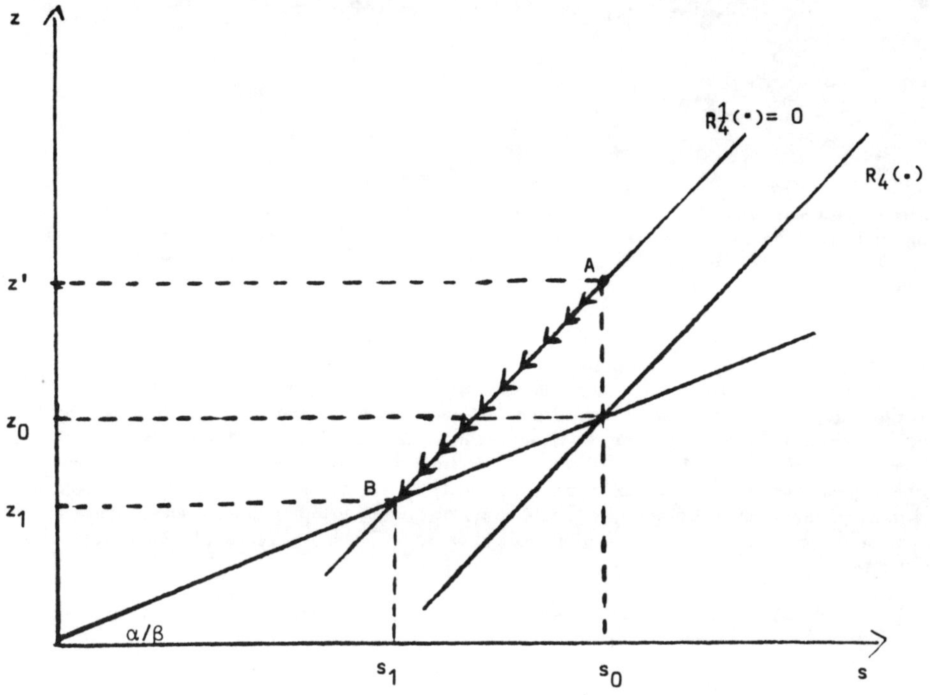

where $s^*$ is the steady state level of biomass stock. Individual producers fully consider the social shadow price of the stock of biomass (the right-hand side of (15)) and also they are fully aware that in the long run the flow of resource extraction is proportional to the long run level of the stock, in the long run $z = \frac{\alpha}{\beta} s^*$.

Under constant returns to scale both $R_4(\cdot)$ and $R_5(\cdot)$ are homogenous of degree 0 in h, z, and s and, hence, (15) can be expressed as,

$$(16) \qquad R_4[p_A, p_N; \frac{f(K, L)}{s^*}, \frac{\alpha}{\beta}, 1] = \frac{1}{r-\alpha} R_5[p_A, p_N; \frac{f(K, L)}{s}, \frac{\alpha}{\beta}, 1].$$

Thus, (16) can be solved for $\frac{f}{s^*}$,

$$(17) \qquad \frac{f(K, L)}{s^*} = \epsilon \left[ p_A, p_N, \frac{\alpha}{\beta}, \frac{1}{r-\alpha} \right] > 0,$$

where $\epsilon(\cdot)$ is some unspecified function of the exogenous variables. Since $\epsilon(\cdot) > 0$ we have that the optimal long-run level of the stock of biomass, $s^*$, is necessarily increasing in $f(\cdot)$ and, therefore, in K and L. That is, in contrast with the case when producers do not internalize the biomass externality, now deforestation will decrease as economic growth takes place.

An expansion in the level of conventional factors of production increases the value of biomass as a factor of production. The marginal productivity of the resource extracted from the forest also increases, and hence producers would like to extract more biomass from the forest. However, producers are aware that in order to extract a greater flow of resources from the forest stock on a sustainable basis they need to allow the stock of biomass to expand. In contrast with the previous case, now individual producers have incentives to increase the stock because they will directly benefit from their investment in the resource stock. In the previous polar case, because of lack of private property or lack of adequate contractual arrangements, an individual producer may not necessarily benefit in the long run by investing in the resource stock, and hence has no incentives in allowing the stock of biomass to expand. This is the crucial difference between the two polar cases.

The dynamic of the system can be represented by the following two differential equations derived from (14),

$$(18) \quad \text{(i)} \qquad \dot{z} = \frac{1}{R_{44}}[(r-\alpha) R_4(\cdot) - R_5(\cdot) - R_{45}(\alpha s - \beta z)]$$

$$\text{(ii)} \qquad \dot{s} = \alpha s - \beta z.$$

From (18) we obtain the slopes of the $\dot{z} = 0$ and $\dot{s} = 0$ schedules. The slope of the $\dot{s} = 0$ schedule is positive with slope $\alpha/\beta$ (Figure 9-2). The slope of the $\dot{z} = 0$ may be positive or negative but stability requires

147

**Figure 9-2a**

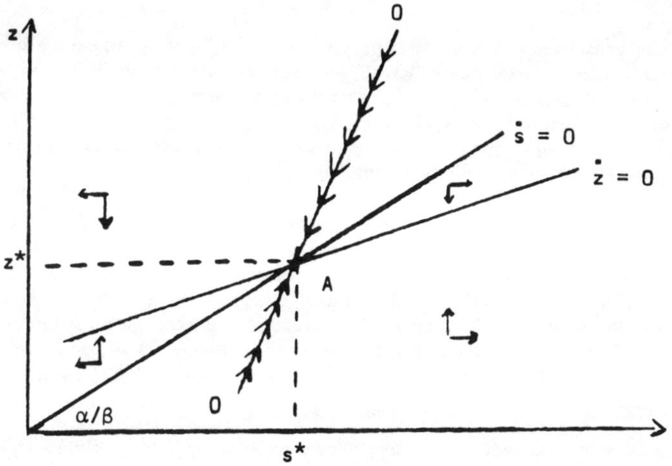

that its slope be less than the slope of the $\dot{s} = 0$. Figure 9-2a shows the case when the slope of the $\dot{z} = 0$ schedule is positive and Figure 9-2b shows it when is negative. Also Figures 9-2a and 9-2b show with the arrows the motion of the system in the neighborhood of the steady state shown by the points A in the figures. Stability thus requires that the adjustment shown as line 00 in Figure 9-2 to be steeper than the $\dot{s} = 0$ schedule.

Figure 9-3 shows the adjustment toward equilibrium when f(•) increases. A rise in h will not affect the $\dot{s} = 0$ schedule. Since we know from (17) that the new steady state occurs at a higher s, it is clear that the schedule $\dot{z} = 0$ must shift to the right (from $\dot{z} = 0$ to $\dot{z}' = 0$ in Figure 9-3). The adjustment path from the old steady state A to the new one at C is depicted by the arrow line BC. That is, first the rate of extraction is reduced from $z^*$ to $z_1$ and then gradually increases to the new steady state level $z^{*\prime}$ which is above the original extraction level $z^+$.

We have so far considered two polar cases of resource control, namely, where the stock effect is not considered at all in producers' decisions and alternatively when the complete shadow value of the resource stock is considered in the allocation decisions. In cases where the resource is privately owned the second polar case would be valid. There are, however, important examples, particularly in LDCs, where natural resources are owned in communal form rather than individually. In this case it is most likely that neither of the two polar cases analyzed would be entirely appropriate.

A recent study by Lopez (1991) using data from Côte d'Ivoire has empirically tested the hypothesis that social controls in the context of communal ownership are sufficient to induce individual producers to fully internalize the value of the resource stock in their decisions. Lopez found that, in fact, although the communities do exert some control on individual producers these controls are far from being sufficient to cause socially optimal allocation. The biomass stock is overexploited although some internalization of the stock value does occur. Lopez found that on average producers consider about 30 percent of the social value of the resource stock in their decisions, i.e., the value of λ actually considered is about one third of the true λ in (14).

Thus if $\lambda^a$ is the actual value of the resource stock considered by producers, then $\lambda^a = \Omega\lambda$, where Ω in the case of Côte d'Ivoire is about 0.3. If the Ω coefficient does not change with f, i.e., if the actual distortion does not change with economic growth, one would expect the analysis of the second polar case to be valid for this intermediate situation. If, however, Ω does change with growth, the analysis would become more complicated. Presumably, if $\Omega'(f) > 0$, that is, if growth induces a greater resource control, the result of increased resource conservation as growth occurs would be reinforced. If $\Omega'(f) < 0$, on the other hand, the net effect of growth on the resource stock would be ambiguous. In general, unless economic growth causes an increase in the rate of distortion affecting resource valuation, resource degradation will decrease with growth.

## The Relative Price Effects of Trade Liberalization

In this section we consider the effects of trade liberalization in a typical developing country on the environment. We focus here on the effects that take place through the changes in relative prices as well as through the static income effect induced by trade liberalization.

149

**Figure 9-2b**

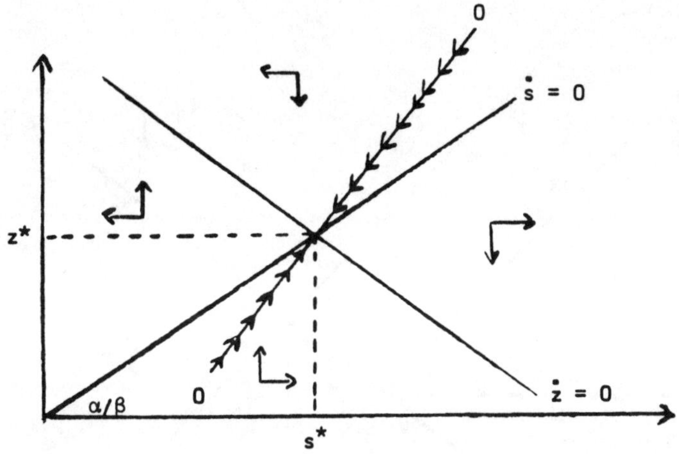

150

**Figure 9-3**

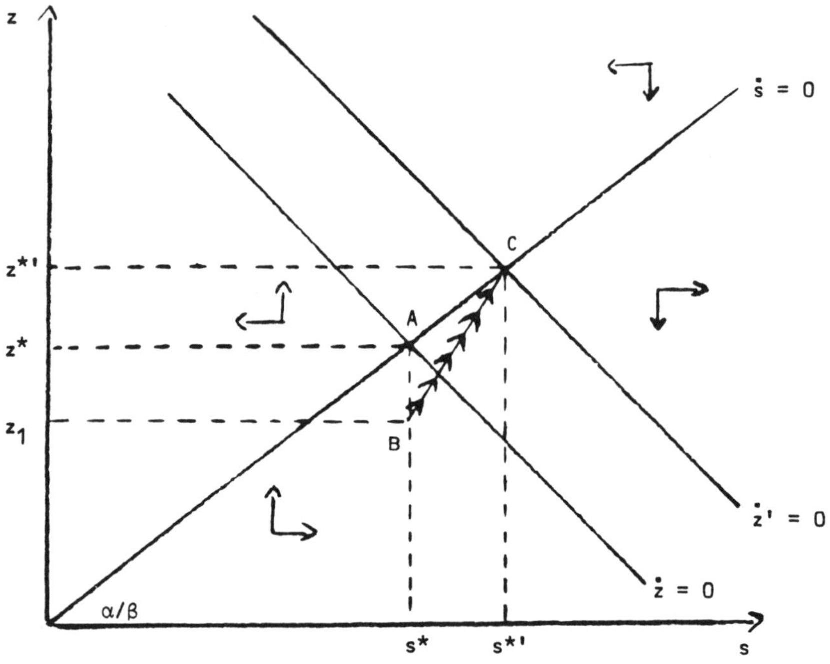

151

We assume that the economy is small and open. It produces two tradable outputs, an agricultural good which is exportable and a manufactured good which is a substitute for imports. Both production and consumption of the manufactured good generates air pollution. Neither production nor consumption of the agricultural good, on the other hand, causes air pollution. The pollution effect at the consumer level has not received nearly as much attention in the literature as the production generated pollution. However, consumption pollution appears to be quite important particularly in the consumption of durable (manufactured) goods. Pollution from the operation of cars, refrigerators, air conditioners, etc., appear to be a major source of air contamination in many middle and high income countries. On the other hand, consumption of food and other agricultural products does not appear to be nearly as polluting as the manufactured good.

We assume that initially the manufacturing import substitution sector is protected to the detriment of the agricultural export-oriented sector. We assume that neither the production nor the consumption air pollution externalities are internalized. Revenue function for this economy is thus,

(19) $$R = R(p_A,\ 1 + m,\ f(K, L),\ x_1),$$

where we normalize the world price of the manufactured good to 1, m is the ad valorem tariff rate, $p_A$ is the price of the agricultural good (1 + m is therefore its domestic price) and $x_1$ is now industrial production pollution. As before, constant returns to scale implies that $R(\cdot)$ is linearly homogenous in $f(\cdot)$ and $x_1$, and $R_i > 0$ for i = 1, 2, 3, 4.

Moreover, due to the fact that only the manufacturing sector emits production pollution, $R_{14} < 0$ and $R_{24} > 0$. In the absence of pollution controls firms will drive the marginal revenue product of $x_1$ to zero,

(20) $$R_4(\cdot) = 0,$$

which implies that

(21) $$\frac{\partial x_1}{\partial m} = -\frac{R_{24}}{R_{22}} > 0$$

That is, trade liberalization, i.e., a reduction in $\tau$, necessarily decreases production pollution.

To consider consumption pollution we need to incorporate the consumption sector in a general equilibrium framework. We define $x_2 = x_2(c_2)$, with $x_2'(c_2) > 0$ as consumption pollution. The level of $x_2$ is an increasing function of the consumption of the manufactured good $c_2$. The (dual) expenditure function is,

(22) $$E = E(p_A,\ 1 + m;\ \mu,\ x_1 + x_2(c_2)),$$

which is increasing and concave in $p_A$ and 1 + m and increasing in $\mu$. $E(\cdot)$ is of course also increasing in $x_1 + x_2$. The economy wide budget constraint implies that,

(23) $$E(p_A,\ 1 + m;\ \mu,\ x_1 + x_2(c_2)) = R(p_A,\ 1 + m;\ f,\ x_1) - m[E_2(\cdot) - R_2(\cdot)].$$

Next to specify the consumption of the manufactured good, $c_2$, we can use Shephard's lemma,

(24) $$c_2 = E_2(p_A,\ 1 + m;\ \mu,\ x_1 + x_2(c_2)).$$

By differentiating (23) and (24) using (21) it can be shown that the effect of a decrease in m is to increase the consumption of the manufactured good. This, in turn, would cause an increase in consumer originated air pollution.

Thus, the net effect of trade liberalization on air pollution is ambiguous. Lowering protection reduces production generated pollution but at the same time increases consumer generated pollution. The strength of the production effect will depend on the supply elasticity of the manufactured good and on the pollution intensiveness of manufacturing production. Empirical studies suggest (Michaely et al., 1991) that the manufacturing sector has a large degree of flexibility to respond to decreased protection. Thus, the level of economic activity in manufacturing tends to be only slightly affected by trade liberalization in most cases. Moreover, given that developing countries tend to have relatively more lenient environmental regulations than developed countries, it is likely that trade liberalization would bring about changes in the composition of industrial output toward more pollution-intensive activities. Thus, one would expect that the effect of decreased industrial protection will cause a relatively minor reduction in production generated pollution.

The consumption effect is likely to be greater. The consumption effect depends on the demand elasticity for the manufacturing goods and on the degree to which pollution increases with an expansion in the consumption of industrial goods. Demand for manufactured goods in developing countries appears to be very elastic with respect to both price and income. Hence, the decrease in price of import substitutes and increase in income associated with trade liberalization is likely to cause a large expansion in demand for manufactured goods, particularly automobiles and other durables. The experience of certain Latin American countries is illustrative. After a period of adjustment, trade liberalization has been followed by a strong expansion in the demand for durables. In Chile, for example, after the trade reform of 1975, the automotive park increased almost three times in six years in part because of the drastic reduction in the domestic price of motor vehicles. Thus, it appears that the consumption effects of trade reform are likely to dominate the production effects causing a net increase in air pollution.

Finally, we consider the effect of trade liberalization on deforestation. If there is no internalization of the stock effect of biomass and assuming that agriculture is a more intensive user of biomass than manufacturing, the effect of trade liberalization on the stock of forest biomass is unambiguously negative. A decrease in protection of manufacturing in this case causes a flow of capital and labor toward agriculture which now is relatively more competitive. This, in turn, increases the marginal value product of the biomass extracted from the forest (i.e., increases the marginal value product of cultivated land) inducing greater deforestation.[13]

If farm producers do internalize the stock value of the forest, trade liberalization induces an increase in the forest stock. The effect of a reduction in m on agriculture is entirely captured by an increase in f. As m is reduced factor returns in the manufacturing sector temporarily fall thus inducing capital and labor to flow from industry to agriculture, thus increasing f in agriculture. From this point the analysis is, therefore, identical to the growth effect in the first section of this paper. The net effect is to increase the long-run forest stock. The key thing to understand is that the complete effect of a reduction in m is through an expansion in the $f_1(K_1, L_1)$ for agriculture.

---

[13]See Lopez and Niklitschek (1991) for details about the adjustment dynamics in this case.

## Empirical Evidence

Empirical evidence on the effect of growth and the trade regime on environmental degradation is quite scarce. Two recent empirical studies have focused on air pollution generated in the manufacturing sector using developing and developed country data for 1960-88 (Lucas, Wheeler and Hettige, 1991; Birdsall and Wheeler, 1991). Both studies conclude that toxic intensity of GDP (i.e., air pollution emissions/GDP) does not decline with income.

Lucas et al. find that pollution intensity remained constant throughout the 1960s being independent of income. During the 1970s and 1980s the pollution-intensity effect of income is on average also zero or rather negligible. However, the effect of income on pollution intensity tends to be negative in more open countries while it is positive in closed economies. Even in the most open countries, however, the absolute level of pollution increases with income despite the fact that pollution intensity declines. These effects are quantitatively more important during the 1980s than in the 1970s. In fact, the strength of the openness effect in the 1980s is more than twice that effect in the 1970s.

These findings are highly consistent with the results that emerged from the theoretical model in the first section of this paper. The absolute constancy of the pollution-intensity indexes during the 1960s and their constancy when evaluated at average values of the explanatory variables in the last two decades suggest that the elasticity of total pollution with respect to income is equal to one. A major result in the first section is that this elasticity is indeed about 1 (equation (8)).

Another theoretical result is that increasing economic openness should cause a once-and-for-all decrease in production pollution intensity. The empirical results by Lucas et al. indicate that air pollution intensity during the 1970s and 1980s decreased with openness. The openness effect, however, appears to be dynamic rather than once-and-for-all as our model suggests. It is possible, however, that Lucas et al. are effectively capturing a purely static effect of openness on pollution intensity in their data for the 1970s and 1980s. Several developing countries experienced significant increases in their degree of openness during the 1970s and, particularly, the 1980s. So countries that show a greater degree of openness during each decade are also the countries that have liberalized their economy more in the same decade. Hence, it is possible that Lucas et al. are capturing the one-and-for-all effects of liberalizing trade on pollution intensity that spread over a few years. This is consistent with the fact that the effect of openness is much greater during the 1980s than in the 1970s. In fact, trade liberalization episodes were more intensive and were implemented by more countries in the 1980s than in the 1970s.

## Conclusions

The major implication of the previous analysis is that the effects of economic growth and relative price changes on the environment critically depend on the nature of the resource stock effects on production and/or whether individual producers internalize such stock effects. It is shown that for resources that have a productive stock feedback effect, economic growth and trade liberalization in a typical developing country decrease degradation both in the short run and long run if individual producers internalize the stock effect. This is valid whether the internalization is induced by government policy, contractual arrangements among producers or because individual private property on the resource prevails. Also, the effect of trade liberalization is dependent on two assumptions, namely, that initially the manufacturing sector is protected vis-a-vis the primary sectors and that the productive stock effects of the resource occur entirely in the primary sectors. On the other hand, the effects of economic growth and trade liberalization on the resource stock are unambiguously negative if individual producers do not internalize the productive stock effects of the resource.

For environmental factors that do not have stock effects on production (i.e., air quality), economic growth originated by the accumulation of conventional factors is necessarily detrimental whether individual producers (are forced to) consider the environmental externality or not. Moreover, policies (i.e., trade policy, price policy, taxation of pollution, etc.) can affect pollution intensity (pollution per capita or per unit of capital) in a once-and-for-all form but will not affect the relationship between pollution change and (conventional) factor accumulation. The elasticity of environmental degradation with respect to factor accumulation is identical in the long run whatever the policy mix. In the absence of environmentally biased technical change the elasticity is equal to one.

The effect on air pollution of growth based on technical change is in principle ambiguous. Technical change has two effects: (i) it increases the efficiency of conventional factors of production, and (ii) it may generate biases toward more or toward less environment-intensive technologies. Insofar as (i) is effectively equivalent to conventional factor accumulation, its effect on the environment is negative. The effect of (ii) is to decrease environmental degradation if technical change is environment saving. Given that environmental control costs are a very small fraction of the total cost in developed countries, it is likely that the bulk of the R & D efforts by the private sector are still oriented more toward the development of conventional factors saving techniques rather than to environmental saving techniques. Hence, it is likely that the effect (i) of technical change dominates the effect (ii), implying that growth, even if generated by technological change only, will lead to increased pollution. Finally, the effect of trade liberalization in a typical developing country for the latter type of resources is ambiguous: production pollution tends to decrease but consumption pollution is likely to increase in response to trade liberalization.

The policy implications of the analysis are quite clear. Policies that provide internalization of the full social value of the resources that have stock productive effects can be very effective in inducing resource conservation. These policies not only cause a once-and-for-all decrease in the rate of extraction of the resource but also lead to a positive dynamic relationship between resource conservation and economic growth.

Thus, to a large extent the fate of resources such as biomass, fishing, forestry, soil quality, etc., so vital for many developing countries, will depend crucially on the ability of the developing countries to implement and enforce an adequate regulatory framework. This implies provision of the legal and institutional infrastructure to support socially efficient commercial exploitation of resources in some cases, provision of individual private property rights for resources in others, and implementation of adequate taxation systems (i.e., stumpage fees, etc.) to internalize the true social costs of the resources in still others. An important issue here is that many developing countries, particularly the poorest, do not seem to have sufficient institutional capability to implement these first-best type policies. In these cases an important question is the extent to which governments should use second- or even third-best policies, such as trade policy, which are usually easier to use than the first-best policy. Although these policies can be enforced more easily, they require a lot of fine-tuning and flexibility to assure that their benefits are greater than the efficiency losses that they cause in the allocation of other resources. It is unlikely that the poorest developing countries will have sufficient expertise to achieve this.

For environmental factors that do not have productive stock effects things are quite different. Efforts by developing countries to introduce policies to force individuals to fully pay the social cost of the environmental factors can cause static once-and-for-all reductions in environmental degradation, but the dynamic effects of growth are still likely to be negative. The negative relation between environmental conservation and economic growth can only be broken if the biases of technological change become more environmentally saving and less labor (and other conventional factors) saving. Since most new technologies are developed in the industrialized world, what developing countries do in terms of policy will matter very little in this respect. If the induced innovation hypothesis is a reasonable theory of endogenous technical change, one can conclude that such technological change will take place only if developed countries force firms to fully pay for any environmental losses that they cause.[14] To the extent that this will cause environmental costs to become a sizable component in the total cost, firms will orient a greater proportion of their R&D resources to generate these new technologies. Thus, by implementing policies to fully internalize the social cost of environmental resources, developed countries can achieve not only static gains but also dynamic gains by altering the relationship between economic growth and environmental degradation. Given the technological dependence of the developing countries, these dynamic gains may have strong spillover effects in the less developed countries as well.

[14]For an early account of endogenous technical change, see Hayami and Ruttan (1971). The authors not only present an insightful analysis of endogenous technical change in the context of the induced innovation hypothesis but also provide convincing empirical evidence of it for the United States and Japan. It is unfortunate that the recent literature on endogenous growth has not paid any attention to this important pioneering work.

# References


Anderson, Anthony B. 1990. "Smokestacks in the Rainforest; Industrial Development and Deforestation in the Amazon Basin." *World Development*, vol. 18, no.9, pp. 1191–205.

Balassa, Bela A. 1982. "Development Strategies and Economic Performance." In B. Balassa (ed.) *Development Strategies in Semi-industrialized Economies.* London, Oxford; University Press.

Birdsall, N. and D. Wheeler. 1991. Openness Reduces Industrial Pollution in Latin America: The Missing Pollution Haven Effect. Paper presented at the Symposium on International Trade and the Environment. Washington, D.C.: World Bank (November).

Dean, Judith. 1991. Trade and the Environment: A Survey of the Literature. Background paper for the World Development Report 1992. Washington, D.C.: World Bank.

Dornbusch, R. 1980. *Open Economy Macroeconomics.* New York: Basic Books.

Hayami, Y. and V. Ruttan. 1971. *Agricultural Development: An International Perspective.* Baltimore, MD: Johns Hopkins University Press.

Johnson, H. G. 1958. "Towards a General Theory of the Balance of Payments." In H. Johnson (ed.) *International Trade and Economic Growth.* London: George Allen and Unwin.

Kavoussi, R. 1984. "Export Expansion and Economic Growth: Further Empirical Evidence." *Journal of Development Economics*, 14, pp. 241–50.

Lopez, Ramon. 1991. Resource Degradation and Agricultural Productivity in Poor Tropical Areas: The Effectiveness of Community Controls of Common Property Resource. University of Maryland, College Park, unpublished.

——— and M. Niklitschek. 1991. "Dual Economic Growth in Poor Tropical Areas." *Journal of Development Economics*, no. 36, pp. 189–211.

Low, Patrick. 1991. Trade Measure and Environmental Quality: The Implications for Mexico's Exports. Washington: World Bank, mimeo.

Lucas, Robert. 1988. "On the Mechanics of Economic Development." *Journal of Monetary Economics*, 22 pp. 3–42.

———, D. Wheeler and H. Hettige. 1991. Economic Development, Environmental Regulation and the International Migration of Toxic Industrial Pollution: 1960–1988. Paper presented at the Symposium on International Trade and the Environment. Washington, D.C.: World Bank (November).

Lutz, E. 1991. "Agricultural Trade Liberalization, Price Changes and Environmental Effects." *Journal of Environmental Economics and Management*, forthcoming.

McConnell, K. 1983. "An Economic Model of Soil Conservation." *American Journal of Agricultural Economics,* no. 65, pp. 83–89.

Michaely, M., D. Papageorgiou and A. Choksi. 1991. *Liberalizing Foreign Trade: Lessons of Experience in the Developing World.* Oxford: Basil Blackwell.

Ram, R. 1985. "Exports and Economic Growth: Some Additional Evidence." *Economic Development and Cultural Change*, vol. 33, pp. 415–25.

Razin, A. and L. Svensson. 1983. "An Asymmetry between Imports and Export Taxes." *Economics Letters*, vol. 13, pp. 33–57.

Schuh, E. 1990. International Economic Policies and Sustainable Development. Paper presented at the Workshop on the Economics of Sustainable Development, Washington, D.C.

Sutton, J. (ed.) 1988. *Agricultural Trade and Natural Resources: Discovering the Critical Linkages.* Boulden and London: Rieumer Publishers.

Uimonen, P. and J. Whalley. 1991. Trade and Environment. Washington, D.C.: World Bank, unpublished.

Van Wijnbergen, S. 1987. "Tariffs, Employment and the Current Account: Real Wage Resistance and the Macroeconomics of Protectionism." *International Economic Review*, vol. 28, pp. 691–706.

# [22]

*Environment and Development Economics* 1 (1996): 149–163




## Macroeconomic policies, second-best theory and the environment

KARL-GÖRAN MÄLER
*Beijer International Institute of Ecological Economics, Royal Swedish Academy of Sciences, Box 50005, S-104 05, Stockholm, Sweden*

MOHAN MUNASINGHE
*Colombo University, Colombo, Sri Lanka*



ABSTRACT. This paper seeks to develop a basic analytical framework that can be used to trace the environmental impacts of macroeconomic policies, and especially to identify where unforeseen negative environmental effects may occur and design remedial measures. The framework is based on a formal mathematical model which shows the second-best nature of macroeconomic policies in the presence of environmental externalities. The model confirms the empirically observed and intuitively appealing conclusion that it is the *combination* of macroeconomic policies and subsidiary imperfections (policy, market or institutional), rather than macroeconomic policies alone, that leads to environmental degradation. Several illustrative examples are presented from case studies in selected developing countries.

### 1. Introduction

In recent times, environmental degradation has emerged as a major threat to economic development and sustained improvements in human welfare. For industrial countries, where the quality of life has hitherto been measured mainly in terms of growth in net material output, pollution in particular is recognized as a serious threat. For developing countries, where economic development and poverty alleviation take centre stage, both pollution and natural resource degradation are seen as serious impediments.

Decision-makers worldwide are searching for sustainable development strategies that will permit continuing improvements to the present quality of life at a lower intensity of resource use, thereby protecting productive assets for future use. Sustainable development necessarily involves the pursuit of economic efficiency, social equity and environmental protection. In particular, it requires policies and projects to be designed and implemented in such a way that environmental degradation (much of which hits the poor the hardest) is anticipated and minimized, rather than just reacted to after the damage has occurred. To the extent that macroeconomic policies have major economic and social impacts, it is particularly important to understand the linkages that give rise to such effects.

As the scale of human activities has grown in modern times, the evidence of environmental degradation has also increased, forcing recognition of the problem by the development community. In 1989 for example, the World Bank issued its guidelines for environmental impact assessment (including social aspects), thereby elevating environmental analysis to the same level of importance as the three existing aspects of project evaluation: financial, economic and technical analyses. Cost–benefit analysis (CBA), which seeks to assess project costs and benefits, is the key element in economic evaluation. Benefits are defined by how a project enhances human welfare. Project costs are measured in terms of opportunity costs: the benefits foregone by not using scarce resources in the best alternative present or future application. In particular, recent advances in valuation of environmental (and social) impacts permit these concerns to be incorporated more effectively into project decisions, in the World Bank's cases potentially affecting an annual pipeline of more than 200 investment projects worth over $11 billion. Continued progress in this area is extremely important, given that conventional development projects often have serious environmental effects.

However, economy-wide policies (both macroeconomic and sectoral) frequently have much more powerful environmental effects than mere project level investments. Some progress has been made in tracing the environmental consequences of sectoral policies involving, for example, energy, water or agricultural pricing. However, the impacts of broad macroeconomic reforms (such as exchange rate devaluation, trade liberalization, privatization and other fiscal and monetary stabilization policies) on natural resource and pollution management are far more difficult to trace, thereby hampering efforts to design better sustainable development strategies. A key case in point is the World Bank, where the general lack of knowledge about links between economic policies and the environment has impeded attempts to better incorporate environmental concerns into economy-wide or policy-based lending—the second largest use of Bank resources (about $5.8 billion annually, or 27 per cent of total lending). This lack of knowledge has also hampered efforts to develop more effective national Environmental Action Plans (these are prepared by borrowing countries, with Bank assistance, to help determine priority activities to address national environmental issues).

A recent empirically based study of economy-wide policies and the environment (Munasinghe and Cruz, 1994) indicates that the effects of such policies on the environment vary, since they were originally intended to address non-environmental issues (e.g. economic growth or poverty alleviation). Its authors conclude, further, that the removal of major price distortions, promotion of market incentives, and relaxation of other constraints (which are among the main features of adjustment-related reforms aimed at improving economic efficiency and productivity) will generally lead to environmental gains. For example, reforms to improve the efficiency of industrial or energy-related activities could reduce both economic waste and environmental pollution. Similarly, addressing the problems of land tenure and access to financial and social services not only yields economic gains but also promotes better environmental stewardship.

More interesting, however, is another broad conclusion of this study, supported by extensive empirical evidence, that unintended side-effects may damage the environment when economy-wide reforms are undertaken in some areas while subsidiary policy, market or institutional imperfections persist elsewhere. Therefore, specific additional measures are required to remove such policy, market and institutional difficulties; these measures are not only generally environmentally beneficial in their own right, but also critical complements to broader economy-wide reforms. A typical *policy distortion* might involve an underpriced or subsidized natural resource (such as low stumpage fees for logging) that could result in excessive extraction and deforestation, following the introduction of export promotion and trade liberalization policies. An example of *market failure* would be where the external environmental effects of economic activities (like pollution) were not adequately reflected in market prices, and led to excessive environmental damage following an economic expansion induced by successful economy-wide policy reforms. Finally, *institutional constraints* would include poor accountability of state-owned enterprises, inadequate land titling, or weak financial intermediation, that may negate the environmental and economic benefits of economy-wide reforms. Other recent studies provide more *ad hoc* evidence linking macroeconomic policies with the environment (see, e.g., Persson and Munasinghe, 1995; Munasinghe, 1996).

There has been much less effort devoted to developing a consistent and systematic theoretical model to analyze such linkages. Accordingly, in this paper we seek to develop a basic analytical framework that can be used to trace the environmental impacts of macroeconomic policies, and especially to identify where unforeseen negative environmental effects may occur and design remedial measures. A formal mathematical model is described in the Appendix. The analysis confirms the empirically observed and intuitively appealing conclusion that it is the combination of macroeconomic policies and subsidiary imperfections (policy, market or institutional), rather than macroeconomic policies alone, that leads to environmental degradation. We show that the first-best remedy would be to eliminate the subsidiary imperfections without changing macroeconomic policies. As a corollary, we argue that many policy, market or institutional imperfections may remain unnoticed in a relatively stagnant economy, because the resultant environmental damage is minor. However, once economic growth is induced by macroeconomic policy reforms, the environmental damage will rapidly worsen, and the underlying subsidiary imperfections can no longer be ignored. Finally, the paper shows that if real-world constraints prevent or delay the correction of policy, market or institutional problems, then a second-best situation will arise. In such a case, there is justification for modifying or fine-tuning the intensity of macroeconomic policy reform, to reduce environmental harm. The extent of such a trade-off between achieving broad macroeconomic objectives and minimizing more specific environmental damage will need to be determined on a case-by-case basis. There is also a dynamic element, to the extent that the relevant macroeconomic policies could be progressively intensified over a period of time, as the subsidiary imperfections were gradually eliminated by appropriate environmental reform. Illustrative examples are presented from case studies in selected developing countries. Mathematical details are provided in the Appendix.

## 2. Macroeconomic policies and general equilibrium theory

We begin with a brief review of the relevant theory. In microeconomic textbooks it is often argued that environmental degradation occurs because of market failures—the prevalence of negative externalities. However, during the last five to ten years it has become evident that government policies have in many countries contributed to an accelerating degradation of environmental resources. Perhaps the most obvious example of this is the devastation of the environment in the former Soviet Union. One can hardly blame markets for the mismanagement of resources in a country where markets did not play an important role. Instead, decision-makers must be blamed for this allocation failure. But this is true in many other countries too, even if the basic resource allocation mechanism is the market mechanism. Thus, we can talk about policy distortions as another source of allocation failures. We may extend this list of reasons underlying allocation failures to include institutional constraints: for example, the inability of governments to define property rights adequately, or to enact and enforce environmental legislation to protect the environment.

Another idea that has been discussed more during recent years is the idea of *macroeconomic policy failures*. The idea here is that macroeconomic policies may have unintended side-effects, positive as well as negative, on the environment (as described earlier), and that these should be considered when policies are designed. This is the issue that will be analyzed and discussed in this paper. We will start with a theoretical discussion in which we explore the reasons underlying the existence of such macroeconomic policy failures.

### *2.1. A simple example involving monetary policy and wage stickiness*

The first fundamental theorem of welfare economics may be elucidated basically as follows: In an economy that is perfectly competitive and in which all goods and services can be assigned property rights and therefore be traded on markets, the resulting equilibrium is Pareto efficient. This means that in a market equilibrium, with all goods and services tradeable, it is impossible to improve the welfare of any economic agent without impoverishing someone else. However, this result is less interesting than it seems since we do not know whether a competitive equilibrium exists or not. Furthermore, the resulting distribution of goods and services among the households may be very inequitable. Both these remarks are answered by the second theorem of welfare economics: If all goods and services are tradeable, if the economy is convex,[1] and if the

[1] That is, the production possibilities are characterized by returns to scale and decreasing returns to individuals and to individual production factors, and the consumption preferences can be characterized by indifference curves, convex towards the origin.

economy is continuous,[2] then any Pareto-efficient allocation of resources can be obtained as a competitive equilibrium after the initial endowments have been redistributed in a socially acceptable way.

Obviously, these theorems do not depict reality, but they are immensely useful in discussing the consequences of macroeconomic policies. First, note that given the strict assumptions of the second theorem there is no role for macroeconomic policies, except possibly in redistributing initial endowments. As we will not investigate distributional issues in this discussion, let us neglect this otherwise potentially very important role. However, the economy described by the assumptions in the theorems is really a barter economy. To make macroeconomic policies meaningful, let us assume that there is a good called money that is accepted as a means of payment in all transactions.[3] Furthermore, we assume that the money supply is controlled by the government. Still, there is no role for the government in carrying out macroeconomic policies. Since all the markets function perfectly, the only thing that the government should do is keep the money supply constant (but even if the money supply changed, that would not matter as all transactions are in real terms).

However, let us now assume that one central market does not operate smoothly enough; e.g., the labour market is characterized by sticky wages. It is of no concern to this discussion what the reasons are for these sticky wages. They may be due to union monopsonies or to insider/outsider relations or to any other realistic cause. But the existence of sticky wages means that this single market in an otherwise perfect economy will not equilibrate automatically, and there may be unemployment or excess demand for labour with ensuing inflationary pressures.

With sticky wages, there is now a clear role for macroeconomic policies. For example, if the initial situation is one with unemployment, an increase in money supply would tend to increase all monetary prices of goods and services outside the labour market, while nominal wages would remain unchanged. The result would be a fall in the real price for labour, and if the increase in the money supply were adjusted until the real wage rate reached the competitive equilibrium level, full employment would be restored.[4] Exactly the reverse procedure, of decreasing money supply, would be the appropriate macroeconomic policy response if the economy was starting from a situation of excess demand for labour.

Thus, in this simple model, by using monetary policies, the government can always maintain full employment, by increasing or decreasing the money supply. Furthermore, this managed full employment equilibrium will correspond to a Pareto-efficient allocation. The monetary policy will

[2] That is, the production possibility sets are closed and consumer preferences can be described by continuous utility functions.

[3] There is no need to discuss here all the problems connected with introducing money in general equilibrium models. For an early attempt, see Patinkin (1965), and for a critical discussion, see Arrow and Hahn (1971).

[4] This is obviously a drastic oversimplification of macroeconomic theories, but as we have repeatedly stressed, this is not a discussion of macroeconomic politics *per se*, but of their relationship to environment failures.

be neutral *vis-à-vis* the allocation of resources (yielding the same outcome as in the case where the labour market equilibrates automatically).

Let us now introduce another distortion in the economy, one that affects the use of environmental resources. This distortion may be a traditional externality of the kind that is discussed in elementary or intermediate microeconomic textbooks. For example, plants may be allowed to emit pollutants into the air without having to compensate the victims of the ensuing air pollution. Such externalities are basically due to the absence of well-defined property rights.[5] Let us assume, therefore, that there is at least one environmental resource for which property rights are not well defined. This situation may arise for several reasons. First, it could be due to the inherent difficulty or impossibility of defining individual property rights. For example, since clean air in a town is shared by all inhabitants living there, it is impossible to define individual rights to clean air (which is now a public good). Second, the government may be unwilling to define property rights for the resources. This latter situation is quite common. For example, in many countries, the land tenure system is such that an individual landowner cannot reap all of the benefits from his own land, but has to share it with others. The land tenure regime also may not ensure that the tenant has the rights to the land in the future, which will reduce his incentives to manage the land efficiently. In some cases, the land may originally have been managed collectively by the village or the tribe (that is, as a common property resource), in an efficient manner. Subsequently, this management system may have eroded because of instabilities and external pressures so that either the social norms controlling the use of the resource weakened or the system turned into an open access common property resource. The result is that after having been efficiently managed the resource now becomes overexploited because of poorly defined rights. These issues are exemplified in the case studies of Botswana and Ghana discussed below.

We now face a situation where there are (at least) two deviations from full optimality or first-best allocation of resources: labour market failure and resource failure. This is the classical case of a second-best situation. Should we try to manage the money supply so that full employment is restored, assuming that we can do nothing about the environmental resource failure? According to the theory of second best,[6] it is not socially optimal to equilibrate the labour market, given the failure to allocate the environmental resource efficiently. Assuming then that the government can do nothing with the failure characterizing the environmental resource, it is not socially desirable to use monetary policy to equilibrate the labour mar-

[5] See Coase (1960) for an illuminating discussion of the case when property rights are well defined.

[6] Lancaster and Lipsey (1956) were the first to investigate the problem of second best. They posed the question: if one of the marginal condtions for Pareto optimality cannot be achieved, is it desirable to achieve all other marginal conditions? They found that the answer was no. In fact, in order to achieve the best allocation when one of the marginal conditions cannot be satisfied, the best policy would be to violate *all* marginal conditions!

ket! This is what we mean by the concept of macroeconomic failure: *A macroeconomic environmental policy failure occurs when macroeconomic policies, aimed at correcting one allocation failure (usually unrelated to the environment) result, at most, in a second-best allocation because of an accompanying deterioration of the environmental resource base.*

**3. Effects of taxes**

There are many other similar situations in which macroeconomic policies can have consequences for the environment even though the root of the problem is not directly connected to the environmental resource. It is widely recognized, when fiscal policies for macroeconomic stabilization are designed, that such policies will carry dead-weight burdens. An increase in taxes to reduce effective demand and generate government revenues generally creates distortions in the economy, especially in the case of taxes unrelated to real resource costs; such a tax increase cannot be implemented as a lump sum tax. The conventional view is that the resulting dead-weight burden is due mainly to distortions in the labour and capital markets. But taxes also affect location patterns and the structure of production, which in general will also affect the environmental resource base. In this case the root of the problem is that taxes will have incentive effects, and an increase in taxes (to solve a macroeconomic problem) will therefore have a dead-weight burden which will include environmental deterioration. It is obvious that the dead-weight burden will sometimes be negative: for example, when the environmental resources are underpriced and the tax increase takes the form of pricing these resources. Here there are three distortions: the general macroeconomic distortion, the distortion from tax increases and the lack of environmental pricing. With environmental taxes, the macroeconomic policy objectives can be achieved by taxes that improve upon the existing allocation of resources.

This situation has given rise to the idea of a 'green' tax reform. As taxes on conventional factors of production—labour and capital—and commodity taxes are distortive, while taxes on underpriced environmental resources improve the efficiency of resource allocation and provide tax revenues, it is thought that such a tax reform should have a 'double dividend'. The first dividend would be the improvement in the environment, and the second would be the reduction of dead-weight burden from existing taxes. However, recent theoretical and empirical work has cast serious doubt on the existence of the second dividend. In fact a 'green' tax may increase the excess burden from existing taxes with more than the corresponding reduction from lowering these taxes.

The same arguments obviously apply also to changes in expenditure patterns. Expenditures for ensuring increased effective demand will certainly have allocation effects, and we have to argue as above. What are the effects of increased government expenditures on the exploitation of environmental resources? They may be positive or negative; it is impossible to say a priori. But it is necessary to take these effects into account when designing the fiscal and expenditure policies.

The natural and obvious solution to these problems is, of course, to try to reduce the market failure that gives rise to the environmental degradation, and thereby improve upon second-best solution. In Botswana, this result can be achieved by introducing appropriate property rights, by introducing effective environmental legislation that is enforced, etc. Whenever possible, this is the route that should be followed, yet in many cases it is not possible. For example, the root of the problem may lie in old cultural patterns which cannot be changed in the short run (as in Ghana), or it may be difficult to monitor property rights or enforce environmental protection legislation.

Furthermore, as lump sum taxes are not feasible, it follows that there will always be dead-weight burdens. Ideally, the tax system should be designed to minimize the total dead-weight burden (taking due account of distributional impacts). However, it is then important to include effects on the environment in the measurement of the dead-weight burden. The model in the Appendix shows how that can be done in simple cases.

## 4. Developing-country case studies

Three recent case studies from the developing world are summarized below to illustrate how macroeconomic policies might combine with more local imperfections to harm the environment.

### *4.1. Botswana*

A recent study of Botswana (Unemo, 1993) provides an interesting example. The author studies the effect of changing world market prices on various domestic environmental assets. One such asset is grazing land. The dominant export commodity in Botswana is diamonds, and their world market price determines (more or less) the terms of trade of Botswana. One could therefore ask what would happen to grazing behaviour if the world price for diamonds fell. On the face of it, a change in diamond prices should be of no consequence for grazing behaviour. However, taking the general equilibrium effects into account, it seems that such a change may have a non-negligible effect. Unemo analyzed this in the context of a computable general equilibrium (CGE) model, with which she carried out a number of policy experiments. One of these involved a change in world market prices for diamonds. Although such a change is not a deliberate policy action, we could instead specify changes in government export subsidies which would result in effectively the same change in terms of trade.

Unemo found that a fall in diamond prices would increase overgrazing in Botswana, thereby imposing increased environmental costs. The intuitive reason for this is that a worsening in terms of trade would reduce the profits of industry and therefore the return on capital. But if the return on capital goes down, capital becomes cheaper and this will encourage more investment in cattle which, in turn, leads to overgrazing.

Note that if there had been effective private property rights to land (or communal ownership with strict social control over the number of cattle that members of the community were allowed to graze), this would not be a problem. Each landowner would make a comparison of costs and benefits, taking into account the damage to grazing from increasing the herd. In fact each cattle owner would bring cattle to his grazing land up to the point where the selling price of the cattle equalled the marginal cost, including the environmental damage. Thus, he would balance the environmental damage with the increased profits from cattle herding. The change in terms of trade would not lead to macroeconomic policy failure.

However, in large parts of Botswana, the grazing areas are under open access common property regimes. Thus, each cattle owner will bring as many cattle to the commons as is profitable only to him. Since he will not consider the damage he is inflicting on others, he will continue to add cattle up to the point where price equals average cost. The average cost curve is less steep than the marginal cost curve, and the result is therefore a bigger increase in the number of cattle brought to the grazing land than would take place with private property rights. Here we would have a macroeconomic policy failure. It is important to note that it is now the lack of private property rights that is basically responsible for this failure, rather than the original fall in diamond prices (or reduction in export subsidies).

*4.2. Ghana*

The role of institutional constraints in programmes of macroeconomic reforms is examined in a recent case study of Ghana (Lopez, 1993). In this example, trade liberalization, by reducing the taxation of agricultural exports, leads to increased production incentives. At the same time, efforts to reduce the government wage bill tend to increase the pool of unemployed (the interaction of wage stickiness, unemployment and environmental damage is examined in the Appendix). Thus, the adjustment process helps to stimulate production of export crops, and combines with rapid population growth and lack of employment opportunities outside the rural sector to create increasing pressure on land resources, encroachment onto marginal lands, and soil erosion. This effect on resource use is influenced by the allocation of property rights. Whether in relation to the security of land tenure of peasant farmers, or to the right of logging companies to extract timber, uncertainty normally results in environmental degradation. In Ghana, as in many regions in Africa, agricultural lands are governed by traditional land use institutions, and farms are communally owned by the village or tribe. These common property regimes may have been sufficient to allow sustainable use of agricultural lands when populations were much smaller and sufficient fallow periods could allow land to regain its fertility. However, such traditional arrangements would be overwhelmed ultimately by economy-wide forces, resulting in reduced fallowing, loss of soil fertility and environmental decline. The best remedy would be to revise the land tenure regime to resist externally induced pressures.

In this study, socio-economic and land-mapping data were combined to analyze the effects of ongoing trade liberalization and public employment reduction on agricultural productivity and land use in the country's western region. A key empirical result underlying the policy simulations is that the main source of supply response in agriculture is the expansion of cultivated area rather than agricultural intensification. It was estimated that biomass, measured in terms of the proportion of land under forest cover, is an important factor of production, contributing 15–20 per cent of the value of agricultural output. This compares with the contribution of 'conventional' factor inputs: 26 per cent for land cultivated, 25 per cent for labour, and 26 per cent for capital. Since the share of agricultural output in national GDP is about 50 per cent, this means that the contribution of biomass to national income is about 7.5 per cent. Thus the stock of biomass is an important determinant not only of agricultural production but also of GDP.

In the agricultural system prevalent in the area, a large proportion of the land available in the village is reserved exclusively for the use of villagers. The system is consistent with shifting cultivation, since the individual has exclusive rights to the land actually being cultivated, but once the land is left idle in fallow it can be reallocated by consensus and consent of the village chief. Under these conditions, biomass is already being overexploited through a more than optimal level of land cultivated. Fallow periods appear to be too short, and the stock of the environmental resource is below socially optimal levels. The study found that an increase in agricultural prices or reduction in wages causes an expansion in the cultivated area, with the direct effect of increasing output. For example, a 10 per cent increase in land cultivated leads to a 2.7 per cent increase in the direct output effect. However, such an increase in cultivated area leads to a reduction in fallowing, and total biomass declines by 14.5 per cent. This, in turn, leads to a 2.5 per cent loss in sustainable agricultural productivity. Thus, the net effect of expanding area cultivated (2.7 per cent direct output effect less 2.5 per cent biomass loss effect), though still positive, is only 0.2 per cent, many times smaller than the direct effect alone. In addition to policy changes, other factors contribute to expansion of cultivated area: large family size, availability of capital and the presence of migrant populations in the area.

The results suggest that, in general, economy-wide price and wage policy reforms that do not include changes in land management practices will have very limited impact on national income, once the existence of land quality effects is considered. For example, the effects of further reducing implicit taxation of agriculture are in general ambiguous while the effects of import liberalization are perverse. However, reducing the fiscal deficit (through reducing public employment or wages) has an unambiguously positive effect on agriculture and national income.

If agricultural price responsiveness relied less on land expansion and more on intensification, the policy implications of trade liberalization would be more favourable. Currently, Ghana is gradually improving its agricultural research and extension service, and this could result in future yield increases. However, it is likely that without institutional reforms, and with land still available for cultivation, a significant component of the supply response will continue to be based on agricultural area expansion. This would have unfortunate implications for sustainable agricultural development. Indeed, in the area studied in the west of the country, the economy-wide policy reforms lead to an expansion of cultivated area and thus a decline in fallowing. Environmental and socio-economic data indicate that, in terms of contribution to agricultural production, fallowing (measured in terms of the ratio of forest biomass to cultivated land) is comparable to other more conventional inputs, such as area cultivated, labour, and capital. Explicitly incorporating the effect of this environmental change reduces the otherwise substantial positive effect of the reform on agricultural output. The assessment concludes that complementary institutional reforms will be needed to ensure that the current income improvements from adjustment reforms will be sustainable.

*4.3. Morocco*

The Morocco study focuses on the linkages between macroeconomic policies and how the existing water allocation system has led to sub-optimal and unsustainable patterns of water use (Goldin and Roland-Host, 1994). Specifically, low water charges (coupled with ineffective collection of these charges) have artificially promoted production of water-intensive crops such as sugarcane. Thus, rural irrigation water accounts for 92 per cent of the country's marketed water use. At the same time, irrigation charges cover less than 10 per cent of the LRMC, and the corresponding figure for urban water tariffs is less than 50 per cent. Given these policies, it is not surprising that a water deficit is projected for Morocco by the year 2020, notwithstanding the fact that by that year water sector investments would be high.

The study, however, goes beyond the traditional sectoral remedy of proposing an increase in water tariffs. It links sectoral policy reforms with ongoing macroeconomic adjustment policies, namely the complete removal of nominal trade tariffs, and analyzes the overall effects of both sets of reforms. As a consequence of the trade reforms, prices of sugar, cereals, oilseeds, meat and dairy products, among other things, would decline to world levels from their current protected levels. Further, a *simultaneous* introduction of trade and water-pricing reforms would imply increased input prices and a decline in output prices. As in the Botswana case, a CGE model is used to trace the impact of these reforms on output, consumption, imports, exports and the use of factors of production (including water) by the different sectors in the economy.

To separate out the effects of the sectoral and macroeconomic reforms, the study considers three scenarios: trade reform only, water pricing reform only, and a combination of the two. In the first scenario the only policy change is a complete removal of nominal tariffs (which in 1985 averaged 21 per cent for the whole economy and 32 per cent for agriculture). Similarly, in the second scenario the only change is a doubling in the price of rural irrigation water. In the final scenario the two policy reforms are combined.

In the first scenario, liberalization of trade alone has several positive effects: there is a marginal rise in real GDP, while household incomes and consumption post significant gains as import barriers are reduced, exports become more competitive, domestic purchasing power rises and resources are allocated more efficiently across the economy. The two major drawbacks are that elimination of tariffs leads to budgetary deficits, and domestic water use increases substantially due to the expansionary effects of liberalization, resulting in increased environmental pressures.

In the second scenario, the results indicate that, other things being equal, reform of water prices alone reduces water use significantly: by 34 per cent in rural areas and by 29 per cent for the economy as a whole. This is as would be expected. Associated changes in GDP and real consumption are minimal.

In the final scenario, the expansionary effects of trade liberalization are retained, but reform of water prices still induces substantial reductions in agricultural (and economy-wide) water use. Moreover, this reduction in water consumption occurs against a backdrop of growth in real GDP in contrast to the scenario involving price reform only. Thus, the combination of trade reforms and improved water pricing provides both economic and environmental gains.

## 5. Summary and conclusions

Too often, economists have assumed that we live in a first-best world, and have based policy recommendations on that assumption. But in fact, we live in a second-best world and it is this fact that gives rise to macroeconomic policy failures *vis-à-vis* the environment. Macroeconomic policy reforms should take this into account. If it is found that the environmental side-effects will be substantial, either the root causes (market failures or property rights problems) should be addressed or, if that is not feasible, the macroeconomic policy should be appropriately modified in order to reduce losses.

Most often, the impacts on the environment of changes in macroeconomic policies are channelled through rather complex and less direct mechanisms in the economy. In the identification of these side-effects, general equilibrium analysis has proven to be quite valuable. In spite of the rather severe problems with numerical accuracy in CGE models, they are at the present the only tools available that can help us identify relevant second-best problems when macroeconomic policies are developed. It therefore seems to us that an active programme of amalgamating macroeconomic objectives with environmental objectives in the context of general equilibrium models could yield useful insights.

The difficulties of analyzing the potential environmental impacts of proposed economy-wide reforms should not be underestimated. Linking specific causes with particular effects is especially problematic in countries where many conditions are changing simultaneously and data is scarce. Nevertheless, this paper indicates that many direct linkages may be traced using existing methods, and the potential gains from integrating environmental aspects into policy reform discussion are substantial.

## References

Arrow, K.J., and Hahn, F.H. (1971); *General Competitive Analysis*, San Francisco: Holden-Day Inc.; Edinburgh: Oliver and Boyd.

Coase, R.H. (1960), 'The problems of social cost', *Journal of Law and Economics* **3**: 1–44.

Goldin, I. and D. Roland-Host (1994), 'Economic policies for sustainable resource use in Morocco', paper prepared for the Joint Meeting on Sustainable Economic Development: Domestic and International Policy, sponsored by the OECD Development Centre and CEPR, Paris, 24–25 May 1993.

Lancaster, K. and R.G. Lipsey (1956), 'The general theory of second best', *Review of Economic Studies* **24**(1): 11–36.

Lopez, R. (1993), 'Economywide policies, agricultural productivity, and environmental factors: the case of Ghana', Workshop on Economywide Policies and the Environment, The World Bank, Washington DC, December 1993.

Munasinghe, M. (1996), *Environmental Impact of Macroeconomic and Sectoral Policies*, Washington, DC: The World Bank.

Munasinghe, M. and W. Cruz (1994), *Economywide Policies and the Environment*, Washington, DC: The World Bank.

Patinkin, D. (1965), *Money, Interest, and Prices*, New York: Row, Peterson and Company.

Persson, A. and M. Munasinghe (1995), 'Natural resource management and economywide policies in Costa Rica: a CGE modeling approach', *World Bank Economic Review* **9**: 259–285.

Unemo, L. (1993), 'Environmental impact of government policies and external shocks in Botswana: a CGE-model approach', *Beijer Discussion Paper Series* No. 26, The Beijer International Institute of Ecological Economics, Stockholm.

## APPENDIX

In this appendix, a mathematical model is presented to show the second-best nature of macroeconomic policies when there are environmental externalities that are not internalized. As the purpose is only to exemplify the second-best nature, the choice of macroeconomic model has been made solely on the grounds of simplicity. Thus, the macroeconomic model is basically the general equilibrium model analyzed by Patinkin (1965). In this model, it is assumed that individuals value real balances for various reasons (mainly to reduce transaction costs) and that the demand for such balances is determined by prices, wealth and initial balance. Patinkin further assumes (at least in one chapter) that wages are sticky. Thus we will consider a disequilibrium model, in spite of the fact that such models are now not considered adequate (basically because they do not explain the stickiness of wages).

Let there be a representative consumer with a utility function

$$U = U(x, E, L^s, \frac{M}{p})$$

where $x$ is demand for the consumption good, $E$ is a vector of emissions of pollutants to the environment, $L^s$ is the desired supply of labour, $M$ is the demanded nominal money balance, and $p$ is the price for the consumption good. Thus $1/p$ is the 'price' of money. The inclusion of money in the utility functions has been severely criticized (see, e.g., Arrow and Hahn, 1971). However, this is not the place to discuss that criticism.

The budget constraint for the representative consumer can be written as:

$$px + M + T = wL^d + M_0$$

where $w$ is the wage rate, $L^d$ is the demand for labour (which in the case of wage stickiness may be different from the desired supply), and $T$ is the lump sum tax paid by the consumer. With a fixed wage rate, the demand $L^d$ for labour must be smaller than or equal to the supply of labour $L^s$.

Utility maximization subject to the budget constraint (and to the constraint that labour supply must not exceed labour demand) yields the following net demand functions for goods and money:

$$x = x^d (p, E, M_0, w)$$
$$M = M^d (p, E, M_0, w).$$

Let us now turn to the supply of goods and services. We assume that production of all goods and services is characterized by constant returns to scale. The production follows the following production functions:

$$x = f(L^d, E).$$

Note that emission of pollutants is regarded as a factor of production. Let us assume that the government is internalizing the emissions by charging the firms with $q$ per ton emitted. The profit is then

$$\pi = pf(L^d, E) - wL^d - qE.$$

Maximizing profits yields the following demand and supply functions:

$$x = x(p, w, q)$$
$$L_i^d = L^d(p, w, q)$$
$$E = E(p, w, q).$$

Let us now consider the public sector. The government is responsible for taxing individuals, for controlling the money supply and for controlling emissions to the environment. The budget in the public sector looks like

$$T + M + qE = 0.$$

If the government has determined the marginal willingness to pay for environmental improvements and has set the emissions charge equal to this marginal willingness to pay, then:

$$q = -p\frac{\partial U/\partial E}{\partial U/\partial x} = \phi(p, E, M_0, w).$$

Here, $\phi$ gives the marginal willingness to pay for the public good as a function of the variables determining the budget constraint for the individual. By this assumption, we are assured that there will always be an optimal level of pollution.

Assume for the moment that wages are flexible so that the labour market clears. Then it follows from the model that money would be neutral, and a change in the money supply would have no real consequences. Furthermore, the resulting allocation of resources would be efficient. However, the point to be made has to do with sticky wages. Therefore, assume that the wage rate is exogenously given

$$w = \overline{w}.$$

If $\overline{w}$ is high enough, the total demand for labour will be less than the exogenously given supply $L^s$ and there will be unemployment. Now there is room for government macroeconomic policies. An increase in the money supply will now have effects on the real economy. The mechanism is the conventional one. After an increase in the money supply, each individual will find themselves with too high real balances, which will increase their net demand for goods and services. This will increase the prices of goods and services in general, thereby reducing the real money balance held by individuals and increasing the output and therefore the demand for labour. It follows that the real wage rate will fall and in the end it would be possible to reach a situation with full employment. However, in the process the emissions have probably increased and the environment has therefore probably deteriorated. This is as it should be, because the polluters are paying the marginal social cost of pollution. The gains from increasing employment exceed the loss in environmental quality.

If the marginal social cost of pollution rose very sharply with increases in pollution, the end result would be only marginal increases in emissions, and monetary expansion would cause reallocations between different sectors so that less polluting sectors would expand and more polluting sectors would contract. In the end, full employment would in general be reached.

Obviously, if the marginal willingness to pay for environmental quality is inelastic with respect to emissions and if the emissions per ton of output are very high, there may not exist a full employment equilibrium. However, we will disregard that possibility as plants always have other ways of abating emissions than reducing production.

In order to study this more closely, let us depart from the assumption that the emission charge is optimal. On the contrary, assume that $q$ is less than the marginal willingness to pay for pollution abatement. In such a situation, what would be the effect of an increase in money supply? Differentiating the utility function yields

$$\begin{aligned} dU &= U_x dx + U_E dE + U_L dL + U_M d\frac{M}{p} \\ &= p dx - q dE + w^s dL + Y d\frac{M}{p} \\ &= (\overline{w} - w^s) dL - (q - \overline{q}) dE + Y d\frac{M}{p}. \end{aligned}$$

The first parenthesis indicates that an increase in the demand for labour increases welfare as the fixed wage rate exceeds the reservation wage $w^s$. The second parenthesis indicates, however, that the increase in pollution will reduce well-being as the marginal willingness to pay exceeds the emission charge. If the emission charge had been equal to the marginal willingness to pay, then it would obviously have been optimal to increase the money supply until the reservation wage rate equalled the fixed wage rate. However, in the face of an inadequate pollution charge, this will not be optimal. In fact, the formula above says that the increase in money supply should be smaller than what would correspond to full employment. Thus, *if it is not possible to optimize the allocation rule regarding the environment, it is not optimal to try to achieve first-best macroeconomic policies.*

# [23]

*Environment and Development Economics* 1 (1996): 183–202




## Bretton Woods intervention programmes and sustainable development

J.B. OPSCHOOR
*Institute of Social Studies, P.O. Box 29776, 2502 LT, The Hague, Netherlands*
*email: opschoor@iss.nl*

S.M. JONGMA
*Department of Spatial and Environmental Economics, Free University of Amsterdam, De Boelaan 1105, HV Amsterdam, Netherlands*

ABSTRACT. Since the beginning of the 1980s the Bretton Woods institutions (World Bank and International Monetary Fund) have introduced structural adjustment loans and stabilization programmes to correct balance-of-payments distortions and to realize the conditions necessary for economic growth in developing countries. In the course of the 1980s, the concept of sustainable development was launched which asked for a qualitatively different orientation of growth. This paper presents a summary of what has been learned with respect to the relationship between Bretton Woods intervention programmes and development. Adjustment programmes appear to have evolved through three different stages, with attention for environmental aspects of sustainable development emerging in the third stage. A sectoral analysis is presented of the possible environmental impacts of the various components of intervention programmes. Recommendations are made regarding possible improvements of WB and IMF adjustment strategies in the light of sustainable development, without fully translating them into actual changes at the level of specific programmes.

'The question is not whether there should be continued economic growth. There must be. Nor is the question whether the impact on the environment must be respected. It has to be. Nor—least of all—is it a question of whether these two are interlocked. They are'.

Robert McNamara, Stockholm 1972.

### 1. Introduction

The Bretton Woods institutions—the International Bank for Reconstruction and Development (or World Bank, WB hereafter) and the International Monetary Fund (IMF hereafter)—were established in 1944, basically in order to enhance postwar economic recovery and development. These objectives required a strategy based on a stable international monetary system and trade liberalization on a global scale.

The term development then was almost synonymous with 'economic growth' defined as rising per capita gross domestic product, or income. Since 1987, the concept of sustainable development became *en vogue*. With this is meant 'development that meets the needs of the present without compromising the abilities of future generations to meet their own needs' (WCED, 1987).

At the beginning of the 1980s—after about thirty-five years of only project financing—the World Bank introduced structural adjustment loans aiming at restructuring entire national economies or specific economic sectors. At the same time IMF developed an interest in growth-stimulating policies as a precondition for achieving macroeconomic balances. The two institutions have developed close working relationships in the field of furthering growth, as well as a set of practices implying conditions imposed on the economic and other domestic policies of countries soliciting assistance or requiring stabilization. This set of measures and conditions (adjustment loans, stabilization support and the associated conditional reform policies) we refer to below as the 'Bretton Woods interventions'. Assuming that these interventions have stimulated economic growth and development (over which there is still debate but this is beyond the scope of this paper), one may ask whether this has had repercussions for environmental quality and natural resources, and whether this growth is sustainable.

In the next section we will briefly review the development of the concept of stabilization and structural adjustment in the light of the policies of both institutions, and the role of environmental considerations in this. Section three investigates to what extent the various types of interventions do have predictable environmental impacts, on the basis of a survey of empirical studies. In section four, recommendations will be made for adjusting WB and IMF intervention programmes to realize a more sustainable development. Section five presents our conclusions.

## 2. IMF, World Bank and intervention programmes

This section will first outline the original mandates of the Bretton Woods institutions and developments in their policies, in so far as these are relevant in the light of the questions addressed here. It proceeds by presenting our synthesis of these developments, in terms of a description and analysis of the adjustment programmes as undertaken until now.

### 2.1 *Institutional roots of intervention programmes*

International Monetary Fund

The IMF is the main multilateral institution in the international monetary system. Its objectives as laid down in Article I of the Fund's Charter include: (i) to promote international monetary coordination and foreign exchange stability, (ii) to facilitate the expansion and balanced growth of international trade and in this way contribute to the promotion and maintenance of high levels of employment and real income and to the development of productive resources, as primary objectives of economic policy,

(iii) to give confidence to members by providing them with opportunities to correct maladjustments in their balance of payments, without resorting to measures destructive of national or international prosperity.

For decades, the Fund has been preoccupied with problems of balance-of-payments equilibrium. In the light of this paper, the most important activity has been the Fund's support for correcting short-term balance-of-payments distortions, also named stabilization programmes (SPs). In the 1980s it became clear that there has been a lack of attention for the 'primary objectives' of employment, income and resource development and a tendency has evolved in IMF to pay more attention to these wider interests (see e.g. Akyuz and Dell, 1987; Denters, 1993). Growth-based stability is needed to achieve these objectives, and the IMF has at its disposal the instruments of stand-by arrangements and extended fund facilities for periods up to three years, with strict conditionalities on macroeconomic policies attached to them. Only in exceptional cases may conditions relate to micro variables, i.e. in situations in which these have strong impacts at the macro level (see e.g. Denters, 1993). In 1990 about 28 extended fund facilities were supporting 25 countries. These adjustment programmes were developed in close cooperation with the World Bank. Some other agencies (e.g. UNCTAD, 1987) felt they had to remind IMF that disequilibria in the balance of payments are to be corrected 'without resorting to measures destructive of national or international prosperity', to use the phrase from Article I.

World Bank

The primary objective of the World Bank is stimulating development by means of financing productive investments in member states through specific development projects and programmes. The idea behind this policy is that it contributes to improved standards of living and to increased productivity of the economies of member states. The World Bank annually approves some two hundred projects at a total cost of US$20 billion.

At the beginning of the 1980s the World Bank realized that its development projects quite often were ineffective as a consequence of defective physical or administrative infrastructure or price mechanisms. Also the occurrence of the international debt crisis at the beginning of the 1980s led to general doubts about the effectiveness of project financing (Mosley *et al.*, 1991). As a reaction to this situation, the World Bank introduced a new type of development programmes, the structural adjustment programmes (SAPs) (see section 2.2). These programmes should contribute to economic growth in the medium term. Two types of loans are issued in relation to this: structural adjustment loans (SALs) and sectoral adjustment loans (SECALs). In 1991 SAP-related financial allocations accounted for 26 per cent of total World Bank loans (Denters, 1993).

Since the early 1980s many WB projects have been criticized for their environmental and social aspects. This has led to various adaptations in WB policies and structures (see section 4), including the financing of environmental projects. In 1993 $2 billion in new loans and credits was given for 23 projects with explicit environmental objectives (World Bank, 1993). This paper deals with WB's structural adjustment programmes primarily, as economy-wide policies frequently have much more powerful environmental impacts than projects (Persson and Munasinghe, 1994). However, some attention will be given to project activities in section 4.

*2.2 Adjustment programmes*

We start by sketching the skeleton of the development 'philosophy' underneath the original mandates and policies of the Bretton Woods institutions; this is the precursor of the adjustment approach. Then, we shall identify the main economic assumptions underlying the adjustment approach, based on a series of documents and evaluations of these interventions (Akyuz and Dell, 1987; Mosley, 1987; World Bank, 1988, 1989; Sebastian and Alibuscan, 1989; McCleary, 1991; Mosley *et al.*, 1991; Corbo *et al.*, 1992; Reed, 1992; Denters, 1993; Singer, 1994). In fact, we shall distinguish three stages in the development of the adjustment approach.

Initially WB stimulated projects aimed at developing the physical capital base in developing countries; this was seen as a direct stimulus to economic growth in terms of GDP and national incomes. IMF directed its efforts to financially relevant imbalances (primarily between variables affecting the exchange rate: exports and imports). This would directly influence the import/export ratio, and indirectly contribute to stable exchange rates, with trade-stimulating effects. Stable exchange rates and balances of payments and an enhanced capital base all contribute to increased production growth, for both domestic and foreign markets, and this economic development would potentially result in other social improvements as well. Meanwhile, sectoral projects (quite often initiated by specialized international organizations such as UNDP, FAO, UNESCO) were directed towards changes at the sectoral level in agriculture, health, education, etc.

Macroeconomic 'imbalances' (regarding the current account, government budget and high inflation), microeconomic distortions (market rigidities, price distortions and imperfect competition) and weak economic political institutions present impediments to economic growth and development (World Bank, 1990; Jansen, 1991; Corbo *et al.*, 1992). In many countries this had become painfully manifest when they were hit by external shocks such as the fluctuations in oil prices, interest rates and commodity prices of the 1970s and 1980s. Thus, in the course of the histories of both Bank and Fund, the underlying economic conditions for growth were increasingly recognized to be essential preconditions for both stability and development. This led to a situation in which activities of both institutions coincided in mutually agreed structural adjustment programmes (SAPs) and the related structural adjustment loans aim at diminishing macroeconomic distortions through growth stimulation and increased efficiency, e.g. by means of price reforms, trade political measures such as liberalization and devaluation, reduced government expenditures as well as removal of institutional obstructions to flexible responses of the private sector (Mosley, 1987; Sebastian and Alicbusan, 1989). The normal procedure is that Bank, IMF and the relevant countries draw up 'Policy Framework Papers' with structural adjustment priorities and objectives for the next three years. The measures proposed could affect price structures, collective investment programmes, institutions—including property rights. SAPs thus imposed conditionalities that influence the micro- and macroeconomic policies of countries involved.

In the initial stage (the 1980s) the focus clearly was on boosting the dynamics in the subsystem capital–GDP–income. The main difference with the pre-adjustment period was the introduction of policies in addition to projects and stabilization activities, and a shift to causal elements to boost the dynamics underlying growth and stability. Critics of the early SAPs pointed at the neglect of developing longer-run potentials of the economies involved (UNCTAD, 1990: 9; see also Reed, 1992: 33; Denters, 1993: 104; Ramirez, 1993: 115; Singer, 1994):

i. structural adjustment often rests on short-term strategies that are not always suitable to solve long-term problems;
ii. due to its focus on income growth there is lack of attention for capital formation. Moreover, the cutting down of government expenses required in SAPs often results in neglect of infrastructure maintenance, which even reduces the capital base. The role of the public sector is heavily underestimated;
iii. quite often, deindustrialization turned out to offset industrialization developments, resulting in economic contractions;
iv. there have been negative effects on human capital (e.g. reduced expenditure on welfare, health, nutrition and education facilities).

These criticisms have led especially the WB to recognize that the effective capital base of an economy includes human capital. Organizations such as FAO, WHO, UNDP, and UNESCO primarily operate in that area. It was recognized that programmes and projects adversely affecting human assets would reduce the capital base, as well as reductions in physical infrastructure and industrial capital. Moreover, stabilizing the national economies may have adverse economic repercussions in the short run which the WB SALs may attempt to mitigate by growth-stimulating corrections also at the level of institutions, sectoral policies and markets. Sustainable growth within this 'philosophy' requires: (i) stable macroeconomic conditions; (ii) a well-functioning system of markets and incentives in order to improve the allocation of resources; (iii) a sufficient level of savings; and (iv) institutions capable of converting savings into physical and human capital (Corbo and others, 1992: 11). Thus, compared with the initial adjustment philosophy, which was biased strongly towards growth of GDP and the dynamics of investment in physical capital and infrastructure, in this second stage the approach was widened to include other elements into the capital base and to also address institutional features of the economic processes in the countries concerned, including the functioning of markets. One could refer to this as a socially and institutionally conscious adjustment philosophy.

Meanwhile, in a third stage, WB is developing a policy perspective in which there is a growing attention for the environmental aspects of its activities (see e.g. World Bank 1992, 1993), in response to criticism as summarized by Abaza (1995) on the neglect in economy-wide policies of resource use and environmental protection. The position in this perspective of environmental considerations can be characterized as follows. Both macroeconomic stability and the removal of price distortions are assumed to contribute positively to environmental conservation, almost automatically and by definition. Market failures—quite often associated with ill-defined property rights regarding environmental goods and natural resources—and lack of environmental policy are considered as important sources of price distortions leading to unsustainable development. As long as market imperfections and price distortions exist, substitution, technical progress and structural change are seen as difficult to realize. Moreover, macroeconomic adjustment policies implemented in a situation of market and policy failures might even aggravate environmental degradation. Missing or inefficient markets would give rise to waste of resources and lasting external environmental effects, in spite of a good environmental policy. Efficient markets are expected to result in less waste of environmental resources and, provided that good environmental policies are implemented, external environmental effects will diminish. Thus, in this third, environmentally conscious extension of the adjustment philosophy, an explicit recognition of the importance of environmental assets and an associated increase in environmental projects are added. We will elaborate on this in section 4; in the next section we shall review evidence with respect to the impacts of SAPs and stabilization-related interventions on the environment.

**3. A review of environmental impacts of IMF/WB interventions**

We now turn to empirical observations on the links between intervention programmes and the environment. If these turn out to be significant, we may have to come back to the intervention philosophy and suggest changes at that level. In this section, existing empirical evidence is reviewed (for another review, see Young and Bishop, 1995). A distinction will be made between stabilization policies and adjustment policies. In analyzing the effects of interventions, the following problems emerge:

i. Various evaluation methods exist (before–after comparisons; actual–target comparisons; control-group approach; Mosley and others, 1991) and are being developed (e.g. general equilibrium-based simulation models) and there are methodological problems associated with comparing results from these different approaches.
ii. Intervention programmes have been implemented only since the beginning of the 1980s. This means that long-term effects cannot yet be assessed (World Bank, 1988; McCleary, 1991).
iii. In assessing environmental effects of intervention programmes one should take into account whether the programme was implemented fully—this is often not the case (World Bank, 1989).
iv. Intervention programmes are integrated packages of various policy measures; this makes it hard to judge which environmental effect is caused by which policy measure (World Bank, 1988).

*3.1 Stabilization policies and environmental impacts*

Stabilization measures focus on issues related to a country's current account, employment and inflation—mainly by combining 'expenditure reduction' with 'expenditure switching', to be realized through interventions such as increased market orientation, liberalization and institutional changes. An important aspect of stabilization policies is a reduction of national demand for import products in order to reduce the demand for foreign currency. This subsection reviews studies on the environmental impacts of stabilization programmes (Jansen, 1991; Mearns, 1991; Bishop, 1992; George, 1992; Reed, 1992; Young, 1993; Daly, 1994); we will discern direct and indirect effects on the environment of stabilization-oriented measures.

The direct environmental consequences of stabilization strongly depend on the impact of the intervention on investments and levels of production in specific economic sectors. IMF loans are intended to stimulate exports, often favouring or promoting crops and farming methods that possibly lead to soil degradation, deforestation and overexploitation of non-renewable natural resources (George, 1992). In the medium term, the environmental effects of stimulated economic growth most probably are negative and have to be compared with the advantages of development. Effective environmental policies might compensate for the negative environmental impacts of increased export-oriented production growth, but governments may not be ready yet to adopt these.

Balance-of-payments support programmes may also have indirect environmental consequences when the conditionalities for intervention imply policy adjustments that are in themselves environmentally significant. In this respect, the most relevant policies are public expenditure reduction and export promotion.

Cutbacks of government expenditures may result directly in a reduction of investments in economic infrastructure. This might have positive short-term environmental consequences, as long as these cuts are effective—albeit that this can be associated with sometimes severe medium-term economic repercussions (such as larger expenditure for maintenance and investments later). Cutbacks, however, quite often also result in reduced expenditures on human capital (education and health facilities). This may lead to a more unequal distribution of incomes, contributing to long-term negative environmental effects; more people will have to live on the marginal lands in the countryside, since the fertile land is in use for growing cash crops. Reduced government expenses most likely will mean cutbacks in expenses on environmental management programmes, with evidently negative environmental consequences.

Another indirect effect has to do with stabilization-related decreases in economic activities. The idea behind stabilization programmes is that economic growth will return after about two years of recession caused by control of national demand. The initial short-term decline of economic activities might be environmentally beneficial when polluting or resource-intensive sectors are concerned.

Finally, there may be export-related indirect effects. Export promotion might decrease future development potentials (increased exports nowadays at the cost of future export possibilities). In other words, short-term 'selling out' (at prices not reflecting full social costs—including environmental costs) of natural resources (e.g. fishery, forestry, mining sector) might take place, entailing negative external environmental costs that are shifted forward through time. Costs of environmental degradation may also be shifted on to poorer population groups (e.g., by taking land away from them for the production of export crops). Moreover, since benefits of natural resources to the poor are not or incompletely accounted—and do not manifest themselves via markets—they have an extra disadvantage when their ecological infrastructure deteriorates, if that forces them to less sustainable production processes (as in the case of Mexico; Reed, 1992: 89).

Another environmental consequence of balance-of-payments stabilization has to do with the reduction or abolishment of export levies and their replacement by product levies, or with the abandonment of subsidies. In many countries this resulted in price increases for fertilizers and pesticides. The environmental consequences of this, however, may not be generalized since changing price structures might induce cultivation of alternative products, with different environmental impacts. High prices for agricultural products are likely to result in increased values of agricultural land (Jansen, 1991); this makes investments in soil conservation and good maintenance more attractive. The opposite may happen in case of a price decrease for agricultural products as a result of price liberalization: less incentives for environmental conservation (see e.g. Thailand: Reed (1992)). This effect may be reinforced when also the national currency devaluates. Stabilization then results in a shift from demand for resources needed for production of the 'non-tradables' towards demand for resources of the relatively more profitable 'tradables'. The environmental consequences of this shift depend on both the size of this shift and the types of products involved.

In conclusion: stabilization measures may indeed have environmental impacts, many of which are indirect and/or long-run effects. But these impacts tend to be unpredictable with respect to their sign and depend on the period that is taken into consideration. More direct impacts may exist as well but they too cannot always be quantified unambiguously; in principle policies can be envisaged that would mitigate these and very often the costs of such policies would be outweighed by their long-term benefits (Markandya, 1994); nevertheless, they are not always implemented by national authorities.

### 3.2 *Adjustment policies and environmental impacts*

In most countries SAPs have had two major effects: a shift towards export-oriented production and a strong distributional effect due to expenditure cuts and changes in relative prices; both may result in increased environmental damage (Abaza, 1995). Structural adjustment programmes consist of combinations of exchange rate policies, fiscal policies, trade policies, etc. The policy objectives can be realized through changes in exchange rates, tariffs, quota, public expenses, taxes, prices, regulations and institutions. Below, these different types of economic policy measures are disentangled and related to potential environmental effects, drawing on Mosley (1987), Sebastian and Alicbusan (1989), Jansen (1991), Reed (1992), Heering and Kuyvenhoven (1993) and Young (1993) (see also Young and Bishop, 1995).

For this purpose, interventions are roughly classified into six categories: (i) fiscal, subsidy and price policies; (ii) public sector policies; (iii) monetary and interest policies; (iv) exchange rate policies; (v) trade policies; (vi) institutional policies. Furthermore, the environmental effects are classified according to the main economic sectors in which they manifest themselves: agriculture, forestry/fishery and industry.

i. Fiscal policy, subsidy and price policies

These policies affect relative prices, which may operate on environmental pressure directly (by changing demand) or indirectly (by changing activity patterns or substitution). Examples of such policy measures are taxes and excise duties on products such as fuel and pesticides.

In the agricultural sector such interventions may lead to changes in crop cultivation patterns. In cases where this entails a shift from one-year crops to perennial crops the environment will often be better off, since perennial crops imply less soil degradation. At the same time, the removal of subsidies makes inputs more expensive. On the one hand, this may cause a decrease in the use of agricultural chemicals; on the other hand, insufficient use might cause soil degradation, resulting in a decreased soil productivity (e.g. Heering and Kuyvenhoven, 1993). The outcomes of price policies depend to a large extent on the existing price elasticities. Jansen (1991) finds that in some countries the price elasticity of fertilizer use is fairly low.

In the forestry and fishery sector, prices often do not (fully) reflect the total of socio-economic functions of forests and water, specifically not those functions it supplies the poor with. This situation may lead to overexploitation of the resource base. Moreover, if the products of exploiting the resource are exported, low prices may mean a competitive advantage. In the short run this may appear beneficial, but in the long run this may effectively mean a far from optimal and unsustainable selling out of natural resources. 'Getting prices right' (i.e. internalizing social and environmental externalities) will contribute significantly to sustainable development.

Removing price subsidies on energy sources will certainly lead to energy price rises in the industrial sector. This price rise might encourage the development of energy-saving techniques and the introduction of new energy sources (e.g. solar energy). Also, perceptible energy reductions might result if changes in relative prices affect sectoral levels of production. In general, lower prices may domestically appear to have social advantages and could give rise to competitive advantages on international markets, but if they result in lower levels of profitability, they could adversely affect the propensity of firms to invest in environmentally friendly equipment and processes.

ii. Public sector policies

A cutback of public expenses may have environmentally relevant consequences in several respects; these have already been outlined in the above subsection on stabilization programmes.

iii. Monetary and interest policies

Monetary policies do not have a straightforward and direct impact on the quality of the environment. Indirectly, removing credit facilities and subsidized interest rates may affect environmental quality if it leads to changes in the sectoral composition and if these changes are not environmentally neutral. Monetary and interest reforms will contribute positively to environmental quality in so far as credits and subsidies benefited environmentally damaging activities. An example of the latter can be found in Costa Rica: relatively cheap loans made it possible that large areas of land were used for large-scale cattle farming on largely unsuitable land (Foy and Daly, 1989). In so far as credits and subsidized loans support environmentally beneficial activities, the opposite effect will result.

iv. Exchange rate policies
In so far as currency devaluation results in higher export prices, this might encourage producers of export goods—in many developing countries these are typically agricultural products and primary commodities—to use natural resources in a more sustainable way. At the same time, production levels of export goods will go up, and this may increase environmental pressure. So the question becomes whether the environmental losses caused by increased output volumes fully offset the environmental benefits from increased efficiency in the production process.

In the agricultural sector, a currency devaluation will probably lead to a shift from production of 'non-tradables' (food crops) to 'tradables' (cash crops). 'Tradables' are quite often perennial crops, causing less soil erosion compared to one-year crops. On the other hand, agricultural inputs such as pesticides and fertilizers are mainly import products, which become more expensive. This will result in reduced use of chemicals on the land with probably positive environmental effects, but with an increased risk of soil degradation. In the forestry and fishery sector, a currency devaluation might result in a situation of overexploitation of these resources, since export prices have become relatively higher.

In the industrial sector, the production of export products will rise. Many developing countries have an apparent comparative advantage in industries for which nature is the most important production factor, sometimes due to the absence of effective environmental policies that internalize environmental costs. In such situations a rise in production of export goods means more pressure on the environment, which may eventually entail overexploitation and environmental degradation.

v. Trade policies
These too have in essence been dealt with above. In the context of SAPs trade policy is in fact trade liberalization, the environmental effects of which can be both positive and negative. What the overall outcome will be in a specific country depends largely on national and local circumstances. An important factor is the extent to which the natural environment is affected by the production of 'tradables' and 'non-tradables'. This, in turn, depends on the production location and the environmental policy that is pursued in the specific regions. A policy of export stimulation certainly influences the exploitation level of natural resources (e.g. forests). Increasing sales on the world market can best be realized at relatively low prices and this may induce a shift of environmental costs towards other actors and to future generations. From a range of country case-studies (Reed, 1992;

Markandya, 1994) the conclusion is that trade liberalization did not systematically damage the environment, and where it did, mitigating policies could be identified. In general, the environmental effects of trade liberalization in the three economic sectors will be largely analogous to those of exchange rate devaluation.

vi. Institutional policies

In the agricultural sector, an important institutional reform is the introduction of property rights. Land ownership may contribute to a more sustainable use of this resource. Improved access to credit facilities is another institutional reform, which may increase the use of machinery and other industrial products (e.g. agricultural chemicals). In the short run, these forms of intensification might decrease pressure on land and indirectly such changes in farming systems might even prevent marginal lands being cultivated. In the long run, lavish use of chemicals would lead to soil degradation, resulting in increased pressure on marginal land.

The environmental effects of institutional policies in the forestry and fishery sector are largely the same as in the agricultural sector. More specifically, institutional reforms in these sectors mean the introduction or extension of logging permits and fishing quotas. In this way expanding the time horizon of the lumberjack/fisher makes investments in conservation of their resource more attractive.

Liberalization of financial markets means rising real interest rates. This means a disincentive for investment—both environmentally harmful and environmentally sound investment. As discount rates also rise, time horizons will be shortened and this will affect resource conservation behaviour.

Finally, SAPs often result in a more skewed income distribution. Quite often, although not generally, this has induced negative environmental effects (e.g. in the case of Thailand; Reed, 1992: 127).

In conclusion, the environmental consequences of SAPs (though frequently more direct than those of stabilization) are difficult to predict in terms of signs and magnitudes as well. Secondly, there is no proof that export stimulation generally implies a selling out of natural resources. Thirdly, adjustment measures have to be assessed in terms of their environmental effects, on the basis of environmental impact studies. It seems plausible that environmental consequences of stabilization and structural adjustment measures differ between countries, depending on the economic structure, the 'tradables' and 'non-tradables' that are produced—including the cash and food crops that are grown—and the government policies that are pursued regarding economic, environmental and social issues. More systematic, empirical research is needed to indicate the relationships between specific SAPs and stabilization programmes and the net environmental pressure they entail. More systematic *ex ante* research is needed to identify administrative, technical and economic options to avoid, mitigate or compensate these effects. On balance: good macroeconomic policy may be a necessary condition for development, but it certainly is not a sufficient condition for sustainable development; adjustment programmes explicitly designed to correct institutional failures (both in the market and in the policy area) with respect to environmental goods and services may be expected to further both economic and ecological interests even more efficiently than environmentally retrofitted adjustment policies. The latter considerations lead us to reconsider the growth-oriented adjustment philosophy as outlined in section 2.

**4. Intervention programmes and sustainable development**

Section 3 showed that there may be serious environmental problems associated with narrowly focused stabilization and adjustment programmes; even if there is no one-to-one relation between adjustment and environmental degradation, these potential problems warrant a rethinking of the original philosophy. In this section recommendations will be made (in 4.3) towards adjusting WB and IMF policies—more specifically their intervention strategies—in an effort to contribute to sustainable development. This notion is elaborated in 4.1, and related to current practices of the Bretton Woods institutions in 4.2.

*4.1 Sustainability and accountability*

The World Commission on Environment and Development (1987: 43) has defined sustainable development as 'development that meets the needs of the present without compromising the ability of future generations to meet their own needs'. Given this definition, a process of change is needed with respect to: (i) nature and level of exploitation of natural resources, (ii) technology, innovation and investment patterns, and (iii) the institutional context of the economic process (WCED, 1987: 46).

Sustainability thus defined entails the requirement that per capita incomes should show non-negative change over time (Bojo *et al.*, 1992) and this implies that the total capital base at least remains intact (Solow, 1992). The World Bank has in fact adopted this definition of sustainable development: 'What matters is that the overall productivity of the accumulated capital ... more than compensates for any loss from depletion of natural capital' (World Bank, 1992: 8). This is called 'weak sustainability', since it implicitly assumes a welfare-production function with variable technical coefficients. From an ecological perspective, substitution is not always possible. Technical coefficients in terms of environmental, financial and human capital inputs may be fixed, at least in part. In such circumstances, and when irreversible large-scale changes are to be avoided, sustainability may require that the level of environmental capital at least remains constant; this is called 'strong sustainability'. An intermediate position seems appropriate, as at least partial substitutability may be assumed. This would nevertheless reinforce the case for safe and effective standards and zoning where appropriate—which underlines the need for strong institutions in addition to the market.

Sustainability implies a policy of 'merging environment and economics in decision making' (WCED, 1987: 49). This has to do with: (i) bringing environmental and resource costs to bear on prices, and (ii) proper accounting systems at the macro level. This should be done at the level of national governments and may be the subject of multilateral negotiation; in the next section we shall explore what this may mean for IMF and WB.

We proceed with the pricing aspect. Especially in developing countries, the economic process may lead to inefficient use or even exhaustion of natural resources, due to—*inter alia*—missing or malfunctioning markets. Policies and interventions directed at market failures are necessary to address this. But they are likely to be insufficient, especially when market failures are pervasive throughout the economy. Moreover, even when it is possible to value specific natural resources and to set up systems of property or access rights to provide incentives for their sustainable use, valuation of the underlying environmental infrastructure—the aggregate of regeneration system, ecosystem processes, etc. (James *et al.*, 1989)—is extremely difficult, if not impossible. The introduction of safe (minimum) standards and zoning in order to protect minimum qualities and quantities of the environmental infrastructure might be the best solution for this problem. Market forces may help in achieving more efficient solutions, but only if the setting or domain in which they have to work are safeguarded by other institutions and policies. In this respect achieving sustainable allocative efficiency goes far beyond the removal of distortions and the clarification of property rights; institutional structures must be developed for imposing *appropriate* (individual and communal) property and access rights as well as for generating *adequate* incentives for sustainable use, and disincentives for and controls on unsustainable use.

Secondly, we look at the accounting aspect. In a broad economic perspective, the economic process can be considered to be a process of transformation of factors of production such as capital, labour and natural resources, into goods and services. Theoretically this puts all production factors on an equal footing, including environmental capital. Under the conditions prevailing in developing economies, consumption possibilities are often considered to be the main aspect of welfare; a higher income gives the opportunity to consume a larger amount of goods and services, that is, a higher level of welfare. In terms of economic policy, a higher level of economic activity in terms of gross national product should be pursued in order to generate higher net national incomes. According to Hicks' definition of sustainable income, welfare and income run parallel only if: (i) income is corrected for depreciation in all stocks of resources, and (ii) income fully reflects the externalities of production and consumption processes. From the point of view of sustainable development, these two conditions are not fulfilled in prevailing accounting systems. Use of natural resources and external effects such as pollution often are not (fully) taken into account as production costs. Negative mutations in the stock of natural resources should be compensated for by depreciation, but valuation problems make this correction difficult to put into practice. As a result, even net national income structurally overestimates sustainable income.

Thus, policies for which GNP is used as a welfare indicator may be incompatible with, or unconducive towards sustainable development. These shortcomings of GNP as welfare indicator should be taken into account by WB, IMF and member state when drawing up intervention programmes. If external effects and opportunity costs can be valued, net measures of income should be applied as yardsticks. As long as they cannot be valued properly, indicators other than economic ones (i.e. a system of social and environmental indicators) should be used to get an impression of the environmental depreciations and externalities that are involved in intervention programmes.

*4.2 Bretton Woods institutions and sustainability*

What can be said about the position IMF and WB should take regarding sustainable development? Should both organizations stick to their original mission, that is stimulating economic growth and economic development, and leave concerns over sustainability to other institutions? Or should sustainable development be integrated into their (intervention) programmes? The first option is no real option since there is no alternative international organization capable of effectively stimulating sustainable development; nor is the emergence of such an institution likely, as UNCED has demonstrated. The second option is conceivable, and may in fact be unavoidable in the absence of other institutions. We will assume that this latter course will be taken in reality.

Economic development cannot successfully and sustainably be pursued by IMF and WB without these institutions paying (more) attention to the state of the natural environment. In fact, the original mandates of both institutions warrant their being concerned over national and even international prosperity as well as resource endowments and development, which goes beyond mere stabilization and production growth, as was shown in section 2.

In the early 1970s, the World Bank was one of the very first international organizations to recognize the importance of environmental issues for the process of development (Warford and Partow, 1989). Since the early 1980s many WB projects have been criticized for their environmental and social aspects (in 1994 an independent Inspection Panel was established to investigate projects). Shortly after the WCED conference on sustainable development in 1987, the rather small environmental unit of the World Bank was replaced by the Environmental Department (Falloux and Talbot, 1993). In 1993 attention to environmental issues was further institutionalized by establishing a Vice Presidency for 'Environmentally Sustainable Development' (Serageldin, 1993). Meanwhile, WB policy statements indicate that it wishes to adhere to—at least—weak sustainability. In general terms, the WB's environmental agenda consists of: (i) assisting countries in their environmental stewardship (through loans, assistance in policy development and institution building), (ii) mitigating adverse environmental impacts of all bank-financed projects, (iii) developing human capital and promoting the efficient use of resources, and (iv) addressing global environmental challenges. The WB analysis of environmental degradation hinges, as we saw in section 2, on the recognition of environmentally relevant market imperfections and institutional weaknesses. The WB has developed a therapy for sustainable development which is composed of the following measures:

- removal of price distortions and impediments for market forces;
- clarifying property rights on environmental goods;
- introduction of incentives for sustainable use of natural resources.

Moreover, the WB displays a growing awareness of the environmental repercussions of macroeconomic and sectoral policies. Not all economic reforms are claimed to benefit the environment, and economic growth without environmental policies may accelerate environmental damage (World Bank, 1993: 96). The WB proposes that such damage can be mitigated or compensated by 'complementary policies' (World Bank, 1993: 97; Persson and Munasinghe, 1994), but this has yet to become effective.

In terms of its project-related activities the WB has undergone a change, in that environmental impact assessments are now increasingly guiding project development, though there still are serious problems with this (World Bank, 1993: 57ff). Moreover, environmental projects have become more important. In 1993, 23 environmental projects were approved with a value of some $2 billion, or 10% of project activities; with GEF-related projects ($70 million) this amounted to explicit environmental activities worth $2.054 billion in 1993 (see Table 1). This still has to be compared with a total of approximately $5 billion worth of projects in general, with potentially adverse environmental repercussions. Of all environmental activity of the Bank in 1989–93, that of 1993 accounted for 40%, thus indicating an upswing in the wake of the UNCED conference of 1992 (Table 1). Originally these funds were spread almost evenly over the low, the lower middle and the upper middle income countries; the 1993 allocations benefited particularly the lower income and upper middle income ones. Data on 1994 confirm the trend set in in 1993 (25 environmental projects involving commitments of $2.5 billion).

Yet it has correctly been observed that up till now economy-wide policy reforms designed to promote growth and liberalization have been encouraged with little regard to their environmental consequences (e.g. Arrow *et al.*, 1995), due to the presumption that these effects could be ignored or could be dealt with separately (and by others). Section 3 above has led to

Table 1. *Environmentally relevant financial commitments of World Bank, 1989–93 (millions US$)*

| | *1989–92* | | | | *1993* | | | |
|---|---|---|---|---|---|---|---|---|
| | *LI* | *LMI* | *UMI* | *Total* | *LI* | *LMI* | *UMI* | *Total* |
| Environmental project | | | | | | | | |
| pollution | 396 | 708 | 336 | 1440 | 440 | 130 | 720 | 1290 |
| resources | 548 | 469 | 371 | 1388 | 293 | 146 | 82 | 521 |
| institutions | 104 | 18 | 167 | 289 | 79 | 35 | 60 | 173 |
| GEF | n.a. | n.a. | n.a. | n.a. | 48 | 19 | 3 | 70 |
| Total environmental | 1048 | 1195 | 874 | 3117 | 860 | 330 | 865 | 2054 |
| WB projects cat. A and B | n.a | n.a. | n.a. | n.a. | 2043 | 510 | 1330 | 3883 |

*Source*: Calculated from World Bank (1993)
*Notes*: LI = Low Income Countries
LMI = Lower Middle Income Countries
UMI = Upper Middle Income Countries

the conclusion that serious environmental impacts should be anticipated and checked for *ex ante*. Such impacts can indeed often be dealt with separately as we saw earlier. The WB suggestion to develop 'complementary policies' is one way of dealing with this. However, this would amount to an approach that can at best be characterized as 'retrofitting' economy-wide reforms where an integrated sustainability-oriented intervention might have long-run efficiency benefits.

The IMF should take into account the need for adjustment programmes to avoid measures with negative impacts on either national or international prosperity (UNCTAD, 1987). Recently, the IMF has become interested in the possible environmental consequences of policy measures that are part of the intervention programmes (e.g. Bishop, 1992). One reason for this change in attitude is the notion that a healthy environment contributes positively to macroeconomic developments. Secondly, the Environmental Action Plans that are now required of countries applying for adjustment or stabilization loans may have fiscal as well as financial repercussions that are relevant to IMF's concerns and activities. It seems that the IBM staff does increasingly feel inclined to go beyond that and develop a more proactive approach in its field missions. If prosperity is to include an adequate endowment of environmental capital and amenities, then at least IMF should develop an interest in the proper assessment of the environmental impacts of its interventions. In case the latter requirement is extended to welfare-threatening environmental changes, the IMF might consider taking a position in favour of at least weak sustainability as the appropriate welfare measure. Interventions that in themselves would lead to reductions in the overall capital base would then have to be complemented by compensatory activities or programmes, for which it or other institutions could be made financially responsible.

Another general observation concerns some strategic foci that are embedded in the current stabilization and adjustment strategies. One may question whether fostering unrestricted trade liberalization and unconditionally enhancing export-led growth is always the fastest road towards sustainable development (Daly, 1994). Strengthening economies by developing domestic and regional markets might be more prudent and even more effective from a long-term point of view. This observation, however, does not directly rest on the evidence reviewed in section 3.

In reviewing this and the previous section, several suggestions emerge. As a first point we suggest that the trend in WB project development is apparently in a direction that is favourable to enhancing sustainability; these may be regarded as elements of a strategy of improving economy-wide reforms by retrofitting them—an 'end-of-pipe' approach, in environmentalists' jargon. However, given the overriding importance of macroeconomic policies, more integrated adjustment programmes are needed that are developed with sustainability in mind from the very onset (cf. Abaza, 1995). Adjustment-oriented interventions should become much less exclusively geared towards income and capital as traditionally defined; the significance for welfare generation of managing environmental capital must substantially be taken into account and micro conditionalities as well as non-market interventions will have to be made use of more intensively. Until that is realized, that is, as long as adjustment programmes remain macroeconomic in focus, they are to be accompanied by effective and adequate complementary environmental programmes and projects so that at least the weak-sustainability criterion is met, analogous to the 'social sector project loans' as a remedy for adverse social externalities of interventions (World Bank, 1990: 8), and this so far has not effectively been done.

Secondly, the general objective of intervention programmes should be sustainable development. Both WB and IMF should indicate what kind of sustainability they aim for—strong, weak or a compromise—and what that entails in principle, in terms of: (i) maximum levels of exploitation of existing natural resources, (ii) conservation of the environmental infrastructure as a basis for regeneration processes, (iii) maximum levels of degradation of environmental capital, and (iv) types of conditionality. Given the importance for the environment of economy-wide policies it is recommended that WB take a position in support of strong sustainability with respect to irreversible losses of essential and unique infrastructural environmental components and of weak sustainability in case substitution of natural capital for man-made capital is proved to be viable—on the condition that the total stock of capital goods remains the same. This still provides developing countries with possibilities to benefit from their natural and environmental comparative advantages.

Thirdly, even though the World Bank policy is formally oriented towards 'weak sustainability' the next operational step of translating this into the structures, procedures and the culture at all operational levels has yet to be accomplished (World Bank, 1993: 36ff).

Fourthly, monitoring economic performance and assessing policies, programmes and projects, should be done on a broad basis capturing more elements of prosperity than GDP. Traditional welfare measures should ideally be corrected for depreciations in natural capital and relevant environmental externalities, but in practice well-defined and comprehensive environmental indicators should be used to correct for economistic biases (Weterings and Opschoor, 1994).

In the fifth place, changes of property rights and markets are necessary to correct for market and government failures (Reed, 1992). This involves the introduction of institutions and conditions for realization and maintenance of sustainability. It must be realized that incomplete institutional reform may be worse than no reform (cf. Abaza, 1995). Intervention measures should be tested for their consequences in terms of environmentally relevant institutional impacts. And in relation to claims on essential life support systems multilateral agreement on standards of minimum environmental qualities should be aimed at, in order to safeguard future development options. Even better would be to pursue safe minimum standards, which requires a more stringent environmental policy. Realizing standards for strong sustainability, let alone imposing them, will probably turn out to be unfeasible for the majority of developing countries. Industrialized countries may assist those countries in their efforts with transfers of money and know-how, and/or joint implementation strategies. The Global Environmental Facilities (GEF), administered by the WB, may be a financial vehicle for this, although the amount of money it contains now is far from sufficient and its field of work would have to be extended.

**5. Conclusion**

The fields of activity of both IMF and World Bank have evolved over time. Traditionally, the WB was mainly involved in the financing of development projects, whereas the IMF was involved in correcting balance-of-payments distortions. Over the years, economic growth became recognized to be an ever more important precondition for the success of both project financing and stabilization. This resulted in co-operation between WB and IMF through mutually agreed, growth-oriented adjustment programmes. These interventions affect macro- and microeconomic policies, economic structures and social and environmental conditions in borrowing countries.

From the perspective of sustainable development it is clear that the traditional growth-oriented policies present environmental risks, and many of these would in the longer run turn out as economic risks as well. Macroeconomic policies may be a necessary, but they certainly are not a sufficient condition for sustainable development.

The environmental consequences of stabilization programmes are mostly indirect, unpredictable in direction and dependent on the period during which the programmes are carried out. However, because of the long-term risk that is involved, the environmental effects cannot be ignored. The same holds for the environmental effects of SAPs. No general statements can be made, since they entail (positive and negative) direct consequences but also various indirect environmental consequences (e.g., through changing income distributions). Empirical research is necessary to assess the relationship between specific interventions and their overall effects in terms of environmental pressure.

Formally, the World Bank aims at weak sustainability, but in practice traditional ideas on economic growth and development still play an important role in both WB and IMF policies. In designing SAPs and SPs, WB and IMF orientation is on traditional economic indicators such as GNP. These indicators do not give sufficient information on sustainable income, so using them as criteria may threaten future sustainable development. A solution to this might be the use of social and environmental indicators in addition to the economic indicators. In this way WB and IMF could work with corrections on the GNP in terms of reduced environmental capital or quality. In case the WB develops its concept of sustainability in relation to the 'precautionary principle', this might result in a concept of sustainability somewhere in between weak and strong sustainability.

The IMF has not yet taken a position regarding the concept of sustainable development, but one may assume that at least it should intend not to induce (further) unsustainability as an impediment to international prosperity.

Sustainable development will certainly benefit from adjustment policies that pursue the removal of price distortions through the elimination of market and government failures. However, this is far from implying that sustainability can be achieved through market forces alone. Institutional changes such as introduction of property rights are necessary to correct for market and government failures that hamper the realization and maintenance of sustainability. Effective environmental policy at least should protect the most essential parts of 'environmental infrastructure'. The changes required by intervention programmes should at least not entail a decreased institutional capacity in the area of environmental policy.

To safeguard future development potentials, long-term maintenance of absolute minimum environmental qualities and resources should be aimed at. Financial and technical support of industrialized countries will be indispensable in going beyond bare minimum levels of environmental protection.

Macroeconomic adjustments should trigger and stimulate sustainable developments, but at least they should not further unsustainability. Implementation of complementary environmental projects might provide a short-term retrofitting option. In the long run, our analysis suggests the need for a more integrated approach.

**References**

Abaza, H. (1995), 'UNEP/World Bank Workshop on the Environmental Impacts of Structural Adjustment Programmes', *Ecological Economics* **14**(1): 1–5.

Akyuz, Y. and S. Dell (1987), 'The role of the International Monetary Fund', *in* UNCTAD (1987).

Arrow, K., B. Bolin, R. Costanza, P. Dasgupta, C. Folke, C.S. Holling, B. Jansson, S. Levin, K. Maler, C. Perrings and D. Pimentel (1995), 'Economic growth, carrying capacity and the environment', *Ecological Economics* **15**(2): 91–97.

Bishop, J.T. (1992), *Structural Adjustment and the Environment*, London Environmental Economics Centre.

Bojo J. Maler and L. Unemo (1992), *Environment and Development: An Economic Approach*, Dordrecht/Boston: Kluwer Ac. Publ.

Corbo, V., S. Fisher and S.B. Webb, eds. (1992), *Adjustment Lending Revisited: Policies to Restore Growth*, Washington D.C.: World Bank.

Daly, H.E. (1994), 'Fostering environmentally sustainable development: four parting suggestions for the World Bank', *Ecological Economics* **10**: 183–187.

Denters, H.M.G. (1993), 'IMF Conditionaliteit', Ph.D. dissertation, VU Amsterdam.

Falloux, F. and L.M. Talbot (1993), *Crisis and Opportunity: Environment and Development in Africa*, London: Earthscan Publishers Ltd.

Foy, G. and H.E. Daly (1989), 'Allocation, distribution and scale as determinants of environmental degradation: case studies of Haiti, El Salvador and Costa Rica', Environment Department Working Paper no. 19, The World Bank, Washington D.C.

George, S. (1992), *The Debt Boomerang*, London: Pluto Press.

Heering, N.B.M. and A. Kuyvenhoven (1993), 'Macro economic policy reform and sustainable agriculture in West Africa', *in* A. Huijsman and A. van Tilburg, eds., *Agriculture, Economics and Sustainability in the Sahel*, Amsterdam: Royal Tropical Institute.

James, D.E., P. Nijkamp and J.B. Opschoor (1989), 'Ecological sustainability and economic development', *in* F. Archibugi and P. Nijkamp, eds., *Economy and Ecology: Towards Sustainable Development*, Dordrecht/Boston: Kluwer Ac. Publ.

Jansen, K. (1991), *Structural Adjustment and Sustainable Development*, Internationale Spectator, November 1991.

Markandya, A. (1994), *Reconciliation of Environment and Trade Policies: Synthesis of Country Case Studies*, Geneva: UNCTAD.

McCleary, W.A. (1991), 'The design and implementation of conditionality', *in* V. Thomas, *et al.*, eds., *Restructuring Economies in Distress: Policy Reform and the World Bank*, Oxford University Press.
Mearns, R. (1991), 'Environmental implications of structural adjustment: reflections on scientific method', IDS-Discussion Paper no. 284, Institute of Development Studies, Sussex.
Mosley, P. (1987), *Conditionality as Bargaining Process: Structural Adjustment Lending, 1980–1986*, Princeton University Press.
Mosley, P., J. Harrigan and J. Tage (1991), *Aid and Power, the World Bank and Policy-based Lending*, London: Routledge.
Persson, A. and M. Munasinghe (1994), 'Economywide policies and deforestation: the case of Costa Rica', Paper prepared for the 3rd international meeting of the International Society for Ecological Economics, San José, Costa Rica, 24–28 October 1994. Environmental Economics Division, The World Bank, Washington DC.
Ramirez, M.D. (1993), 'Stabilization and adjustment in Latin America: a neostructuralist perspective', *Journal of Economic Issues* **27**(4): 1015–1040.
Reed, D. (1992), *Structural Adjustment and the Environment*, London: Earthscan Publishers Ltd.
Sebastian, I. and A. Alicbusan (1989), *Sustainable Development: Issues in Adjustment Lending Policies*, World Bank, Environmental Department, Policy and Research Division.
Serageldin, I. (1993), 'The Vice-Presidency for Environmentally Sustainable Development', mimeo.
Singer, H.W. (1994), 'Structural adjustment programmes: evaluating success', *in* J.W. Gunning *et al.*, *Trade, Aid and Development*, New York: St Martin's, 172–185.
Solow, R. (1992), *An Almost Practical Step Toward Sustainability*, Washington, D.C: Resources for the Future.
UNCTAD (1987), *Compendium of Selected Studies on International Monetary and Financial Issues for the Developing Countries*, United Nations, New York.
UNCTAD (1990), *The Least Developed Countries 1989 Report*, UN, New York.
Warford, J. and Z. Partow (1989), *Evolution of the World Bank's Environmental Policy*, Finance and Development, December 1989.
Weterings, R. and J.B. Opschoor (1994), 'Environmental utilisation space and reference values for performance evaluation', *Milieu* **9**: 221–229.
World Bank (1988), *The World Bank's Lending for Structural Adjustment: an Interim Report*, The World Bank, Washington D.C.
World Bank (1989), *Adjustment Lending, an Evaluation of Ten Years of Experience*, The World Bank, Washington D.C.
World Bank (1990), *Adjustment Lending Policies for Sustainable Growth*, World Bank, Country Economics Department Policy and Research Series No. 14, Washington D.C.
World Bank (1992), *World Development Report 1992: Development and the Environment*, Oxford University Press.
World Bank (1993), *The World Bank and the Environment*, Washington D.C.
World Commission on Environment and Development (WCED) (1987), *Our Common Future*, Oxford University Press.
Young, C.E.F (1993), *Adjustment Policies and the Environment: A Review*, University College London.
Young, C.E.F. and J. Bishop (1995), 'Adjustment policies and the environment: a critical review of the literature', CREED Working Papers No. 1, IIED, London.

# Part VI
# Distributional Issues

# [24]

Partha Dasgupta

# Population, Resources, and Poverty



This article applies the theory of resource allocation to rural households in poor countries to see what one may mean by a population problem. It is argued by an appeal to evidence that there is a serious population problem in these parts, and that it is related synergistically to poverty, and possibly also to an erosion of the local environmental resource base. The problem lies in that very high fertility rates are experienced by women bearing risks of death that should now be unacceptable. An argument is sketched to show how the cycle of poverty and high fertility rates can perpetuate within a dynasty. The one general policy conclusion which may be novel is that an integrated population policy in these parts would include standard measures for the alleviation of poverty, such as increased female education and outside-work oppor-tunities, improved credit and savings markets, and a ready availability of basic household needs, such as water and fuel.

## INCOME, FERTILITY, AND FOOD: THE ENVIRONMENTALIST'S ARGUMENT

Excepting for sub-Saharan Africa over the past 25 years or so, gross income *per head* has grown in nearly all poor regions since the end of the Second World War. Moreover, growth in world food production since 1960 has exceeded the world's population growth rate; by an annual 0.8% during 1960–1970, by an annual 0.5% during 1970–1980, and by an annual 0.4% during 1980–1987 (1, 2). This has been associated with increases in the value of a number of indicators of well-being, such as the infant survival rate, life expectancy at birth, and literacy. In the late 1980s, total fertility rate in the World Bank's list of low income countries (excluding China and India) was 5.6. The figures for China and India were, 2.4 and 4.2, respectively (1). (*Total fertility rate* is the number of live births a woman would expect to give were she to live through her childbearing years and to bear children at each age in accordance with the prevailing age-specific fertility rates. The measure pertains to the number of live births, not pregnancies.) To place international figures in perspective, we should observe that in western industrial countries today, total fertility rates lie between 1.5 and 1.9.

Cross-sectional curve-fitting on data from 98 so-called developing countries displays a declining relationship between the fertility rate and national income per head (see figure). China, Sri Lanka, Thailand and South Korea are outliers, with fertility rates much lower at their levels of income than would be predicted by the statistical relationship. So are most nations of sub-Saharan Africa outliers, but they all lie on the other side of the curve. Nevertheless, *cet. par.* there would appear to be a link between income and fertility. A regional breakdown of even the Chinese experience displays the general pattern: fertility is lower in higher-income regions (3). With the notable exception of China and Sri Lanka, poor countries are a long way from the so-called demographic transition, that is, transition to a regime of low fertility and low mortality rates.

Both time series and cross-section data are suggestive of a broad *inverse* (more accurately, declining) relationship between fertility (and mortality) rates and national income per head. That mortality rates would decline with increasing income is to be expected. Rising income usually carries with it

FIGURE 4.4
**Fertility in relation to income in developing countries, 1972 and 1982**

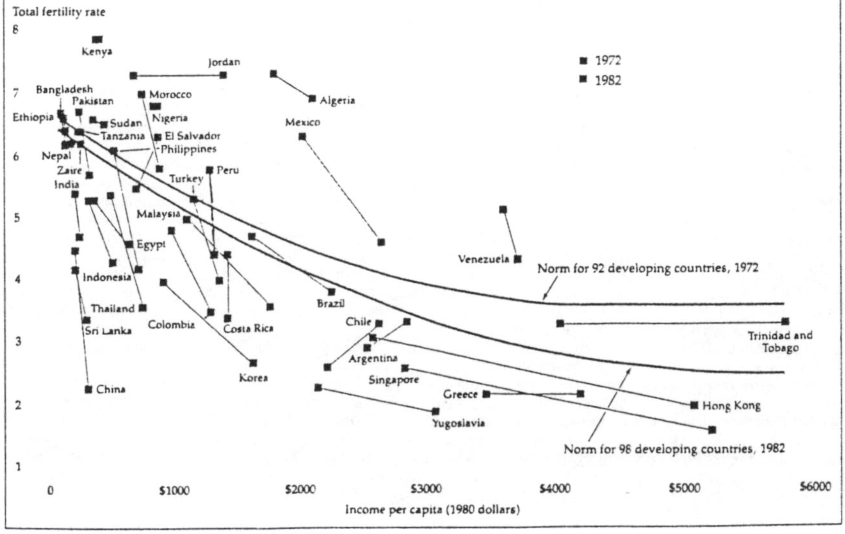


**Fertility in relation to income in developing countries, 1972 and 1982.**

more education, improved diet, better health-care and sanitation (4–7).

While economists, by and large, have neglected these themes, demographers and ecologists have not. Much of this discussion has been conducted at an aggregate plane (8–11). Thus, in the literature on the environment it is a commonplace to read estimates of declining land-man ratios and of dwindling natural-resource bases associated with increases in the size of populations at both the global and regional levels. That rising numbers in the face of a finite environmental resource base will have catastrophic effects has been eloquently argued by Ehrlich and Ehrlich (12). The assertion here is that beyond a point there are no substitution possibilities between environmental resources (e.g. genetic diversity, fresh water, breathable air, and so forth) and manufactured goods. Now, policy-makers often are not sensitive to ecological processes, which in any case are for the most part ill-understood (13). The social value of additional knowledge about ecological processes is therefore large, certainly larger than its private value, and possibly a good deal larger than is officially acknowledged. Moreover, as long as uncertainty about the value of environmental resources is large and environmental damages are at least partially irreversible, there is a case for awarding special weight to keeping our future options open. In the present context this means we ought to pursue what one could call a *conservationist* approach to environmental policy: we should preserve more than what standard cost-benefit analysis of the use of environmental resources will warrant (14, 15). Neither the population growth rate nor the intensity of environmental resource use is exogenously given. They are determined jointly by a complex combination of history, opportunities, human motivation, ecological possibilities, and chance factors. To identify and affect population policy one needs to peer into the locus of decision-making over fertility matters. As human society is currently organized, this locus is in large measure the household. We must then study the household. However, we will see below that for fertility analysis in sub-Saharan Africa and the Caribbean, the household isn't a very useful category.

In this article I shall put resource allocation theory to work on findings in applied demography, so as to identify what we could today call *the population problem* in the poorest regions of the world, namely, the Indian sub-continent and sub-Saharan Africa. Population growth rates in these regions are overly high, and I shall identify the directions in which public policy needs to be put into effect. The population problem in these parts displays itself starkly in the form of unacceptable risks of maternal death for poor, illiterate women, and lives that are doomed to extreme poverty. I have not found anywhere in the literature an exploration of household behavior which yields anything like the population problem we will uncover here. For example, even in the influential and informative report on population and development by the World Bank (1) there are only 3 pages devoted to the question why households may be producing too many childern. The report said that households can get locked in a "Prisoners" dilemma game over fertility matters.

There is a lot more to the population problem than the Prisoners' Dilemma. Among other things, I will suggest that for poor rural households environmental degradation (e.g. vanishing sources of water, receding sources of fodder and household fuel) is likely to be both a cause and an effect of increased family size. To the best of my knowledge, this last has not been given any attention in the applied demographic literature (16–18). In any event, I have not been able to locate any empirical work which tests the thesis. I cannot, therefore, tell how powerful the mutual feedback is in rural communities we know of.

## THE HOUSEHOLD AS A PARTNERSHIP

In economics the household for the most part is treated as a unit of analysis. This obviously makes sense for single-membered households, it does not necessarily make sense otherwise. It is common practice in both theoretical and applied economics to identify household choice with its well-being. However, choice may reflect a ranking which systematically favors some members (for example, males), and it may discriminate against others (for example, higher-birth order girls and elderly relatives). Household choice assumes strong normative significance only when the underlying ranking of options is based upon a defendable aggregate of each member's well-being. But this may not be common; at least not when the family is impoverished, and the stresses and strains of hunger, illness, and physical weakness are felt.

For the State to interfere with household choice and to probe its inner workings systematically can have catastrophic consequences. Nevertheless, there are indirect levers the State can pull which do not amount to direct interference with what happens inside the household, but which protect vulnerable members and enable them to reach a stronger strategic position. Thus, to get a quantitative feel for gender-differences in the costs of reproduction, assume that each successful birth involves a year and a quarter of pregnancy and breast-feeding. Then, on making the obvious corrections, we can conclude that in a society where female life expectancy at birth is 50 years, and where the total fertility rate is 7 (this is approximately the average figure in sub-Saharan Africa today), well over a third of a woman's expected adult life would be spent either carrying a child in her womb, or in breast-feeding it.

In most poor countries maternal mortality is the largest single cause of death among women in their reproductive years, nutritional anaemia playing a central role in this. In parts of sub-Saharan Africa (e.g. Ethiopia), 1 woman dies for every 50 births. By way of contrast, we should note that the maternal mortality rate in Scandinavia today is 1 per 20 000 (1). We may conclude that, at a total fertility rate of 7 and over, the chance the representative woman will not make it through her reproductive years is 1 in 6. The reproductive cycle in a woman's life in these societies involves her playing the Russian Roulette. This is one manifestation of the population problem. It is unacceptable. These statistics tell us that modelling household fertility decisions is not for the faint-hearted: the motivations of the two central parties to a decision may well be quite different. These are early days yet in our understanding of the exact springs of household behaviour, even in poor countries. So it is better to squeeze as much out of a partially unspecified model than to start with a precise model and to work through its implications. Singh, Squire and Strauss (19) pursue this route to good effect. But they weren't concerned with fertility decisions.

At least two parties are involved in a fertility decision. We may begin by thinking of the household as comprising two members who may have concern for each other, but whose motivations aren't the same. As household resources are inevitably scarce, individual well-being interests can never be entirely congruent. Interest lies in those situations where both parties perceive that they add something by acting together (there are gains in forming a household and cooperating), where the pair can break up should either party be placed under undue stress (there is an outside option for each party), and where the parties' motivations aren't the same.

Formal accounts of fertility behavior have not placed the household explicitly in the context of rural poverty, and it is poor rural populations that are growing the fastest. Nor has the household been analyzed in the context of environmental-resource use. We will see that the context matters.

## HOUSEHOLD VERSUS SOCIETAL REASONING

All societies practice some form of birth control. Fertility is below the maximum possible in all societies. Modern techniques are far more humane and much more reliable, but fertility even in poor countries is not unresponsive to the relative resource costs households face. Extended breast-feeding and postpartum female sexual abstinence have been a common practice in Africa. In a noted study on! Kung San foragers in the Kalahari region, Lee (20) observed that among them the nomadic, bush-dwelling women had an inter-birth interval of nearly 4 years, while those settled at cattle-posts gave birth to children at much shorter intervals. From the perspective of the individual nomadic !Kung San woman, it is significant that the social custom is for mothers to nurse their children on demand, and to carry them during their day-long trips in search of wild food through the children's fourth year of life. Anything less than a four-year birth interval would therefore increase mothers' carrying loads enormously, impose a threat on their own capacity to survive, and reduce their children's prospects of survival. In contrast, cattle-post women are sedentary, and are able to wean

Two American Indian children playing among alpaca textiles in their family's market stand. Photo: C. Folke.

their children earlier (21–23).

Excepting under conditions of extreme nutritional stress, nutritional status does not appear to affect fecundity (24, 25). During the 1974 famine in Bangladesh the rural population lost over 1.5 million additional children. The stock was replenished within a year. The central questions in economic demography are then these: what determines fertility, and what grounds are there for our thinking that there is a population problem?

That many parts of the globe are even now experiencing severe resource scarcity is widely recognized. This does not mean individual households are making irrational or abnormal choices. In an otherwise most illuminating essay Bauer (26) goes farther. Arguing that it would be wrong of us to think large families in poor countries necessarily pose a problem, he writes: "The comparatively high fertility and large families in many LDCs (less-developed countries) should not be regarded as irrational, abnormal, incomprehensible or unexpected. They accord with the tradition of most cultures and with the precepts of religious and political leaders... Allegations or apprehensions of adverse or even disastrous results of population growth are unfounded. They rest on seriously defective analysis of the determinants of economic performance; they misconceive the conduct of the peoples of LDCs; and they employ criteria of welfare so inappropriate that they register as deterioration, changes which are in fact improvements in the conditions of people."

This is not convincing. Even when men and women at the household level rationally prefer large numbers of children to small numbers, it does not follow there is no population problem. As in every other field of individual choice we need here to ask as well if a collection of reasoned decisions at the individual level may be sub-optimal at the collective level. Putting it in a slightly different way, we need to ask if there can be a *resource allocation* failure here.

There are two broad reasons for a possible dissonance between household and societal levels of decision-making in the field of procreation. The first is that the relative prices of various goods and services that households face may simply be *wrong*, for whatever reason. The second is provided by the ubiquitous phenomenon of *externalities*.

## POPULATION EXTERNALITIES

Two sources of externalities suggest themselves. The first is simple enough, it has to do with the finiteness of space. Increased population size implies greater crowding, and one would not typically expect households, acting on their own, to take account of the fact that the children they will have will affect others by adding to the crowding. The human epidemiological environment becomes more and more precarious as communication and population densities rise. Crowded centers of population provide a fertile ground for the spread of viruses. That environmental resources are usually common property is also cited as a harbinger of externalities. The point is that because households have access to common property resources, parents do not fully bear the cost of rearing children, and so they produce too many. The second source of externality lies elsewhere, and is more subtle. Procreation is not only a private matter, it is a *social* activity as well. In many societies there are norms encouraging high fertility rates which no household desires unilaterally to break. These norms may well have had a rationale in the past, when mortality rates were high, rural population densities were low, the threat of extermination from outside attack was high, and mobility was restricted. But norms often survive even when their purpose has disappeared.

People differ in the extent of their absorption of social norms, their readiness to digest new information, and to act upon new information. There are inevitably those who, for one reason or another, experiment and take risks. They are the norm-breakers, they often lead the way. In the context of fertility, educated women are among the first to make the move towards smaller families (27). Female education is therefore

A young Peruvian boy assisting his father in a bakery. Photo: C. Folke.

a potent force in creating norm-breakers, as are employment opportunities for women. Special costs are inevitably borne during transitional periods, when established modes of operation are in the process of disintegration without being replaced immediately by new institutions to soften the costs. Demographic transition is potentially a prime example of this.

There is an additional force operating in rural communities of poor countries which further encourages high fertility rates. It has to do with the relative prices of alternative sources of a number of vital household needs. From the household's perspective, the local environmental-resource base offers the relatively cheap sources of such needs. This can also encourage high fertility rates and unsustainable resource use.

## CHILDREN AS CONSUMPTION AND INSURANCE GOODS

The first and most obvious determinant of fertility is the nature of the available technology of fertility control. Traditional methods have consisted of abortion, abstinence or rhythm, prolonged breast-feeding, and coitus interruptus. These options are often inhumane, and usually ineffectual and unsafe. Contraceptives are superior on all three counts. Nevertheless, their use has been uneven within poor countries. The large variations that occur across regions not only reflect a divergence in the public provision of family planning and health-care services, they reflect variations in demand as well. Surveys indicate that women themselves perceive an unmet need for access to methods for reducing their fertility. However, the extent of this felt need varies across regions substantially (1, 28). Successful family-planning programs have proved more difficult to institute than could have been thought possible at first. At one extreme (South-East Asia, Sri Lanka, and the state of Kerala in India), household demand and State commitment to family-planning programs and public-health services have merged in a successful way. At another extreme (sub-Saharan Africa), there has been next to nothing done at the State level in the way of a supply of such services.

At a more foundational level, there is the question of parental demand for children. The *cost* side of the ledger in bearing and rearing children is self-evident. Pregnancy involves foregone work-capacity for women, and as we noted earlier, it can involve a considerable addition to the risk of dying. After birth the offspring have to be fed, clothed, taught and cared for. Each of these tasks involves time and material resources. Reproductive costs differ considerably between men and women. Conflicts of interest between the genders arising from this is a key ingredient of the population problem. Understanding and modelling the cost side of reproduction does not pose any serious intellectual challenge. This is not to say that estimating the cost of having children isn't formidable (29–31).

The *benefit* side is more delicate. Two broad types of reproductive motivations have figured prominently in analyses of population growth in poor countries. The first stems from a regard for children as children. Not only are children desirable in themselves, they carry on the family line or lineage, and they are the clearest avenue open to what one may call *self-transcendence*. We are genetically programmed to want and to value them. In short; children are durable consumption goods. Note that in evolutionary biology phenotypic costs and benefits of reproduction are important only to the extent that they are correlated with reproductive measures. Offspring in this theory are valued in terms of the end of increasing fitness. This isn't the point of view in economic demography, where instead children are valued as means, as durable consumption goods, or as producer and investment goods. This comprises a disparate set, ranging from the desire to have children because they are playful and enjoyable, to the dictates of injunctions emanating from the cult of the ancestor, which sees religion as essentially the reproduction of the lineage. This latter motivation has been emphasized by Caldwell and Caldwell (32, 33) in explaining why sub- Saharan Africa has for the most part proved so resistant to fertility reduction.

The second kind of motivation stems from the old-age security children can provide in an economic environment where capital, or annuity, markets are next to nonexistent. As a numerical example, we may consider the simulation study by May and Heer (34), who estimated that an average Indian couple in the 1960s needed to have 6.3 children in order to be 95% sure of having a surviving son when the father reaches the age of 65 years. This is a high figure, about the same as the total fertility rate in India during the decade of the 1950s. This *safety first* model of fertility decision has recently been much explored in a series of articles by Cain (35–38). In much of sub-Saharan Africa even today, rural women lose something like a third of their offspring by the end of their reproductive years. This provides a strong reason for pro-natalism.

Old-age security as a motivation for having children in poor countries is intuitively appealing. In a significant study Nugent and Gillaspy (39) used Mexican evidence to show that old-age pension and social security do act as a substitute for children. This does not mean fertility rates must inevitably decline when fully-functioning capital markets are introduced. They may well rise if parents display a mixed motivation for having children: viewing them both as investment and durable consumer goods (40, 41).

Old-age security provides a potentially strong motive. In 1980 people aged 65-and-over in South Asia formed about 4% of the total population. In South and Southeast Asia female life expectancy at birth is 59 years, while that of males is about 54 years. In the Indian sub-continent the proportion of the elderly who live with their children (for the most part, sons) is of the order of 80% or more. (In the United States the corresponding figure is about 15%.)

## ENVIRONMENTAL DEGRADATION AND CHILDREN AS PRODUCER GOODS

In poor countries children are also useful as income-earning assets; that is, as *producer goods*. This provides households in these parts with a third kind of motivation for having children. It has important consequences. There are exceptions of course (42), but on the whole this motivation has been neglected in the demographic literature.

Poor countries for the most part are biomass-based subsistence economies. Production through-put is low. Households there do not have access to the sources of domestic energy available to households in advanced industrial countries. Nor do they have water on tap. This means that the relative prices of alternative sources of energy and water faced by rural households in poor countries are quite different from those faced by households elsewhere. In poor countries the indirect sources (e.g. tap water at home) are often prohibitively expensive. This provides a link between high fertility, degradation of the environmental-resource base of a rural community, and an accentuation of hardship among its members.

From about the age of 6 years children in poor households in poor countries mind their siblings and domestic animals, fetch water, and collect fuelwood, dung and fodder. They are needed on a daily basis if the household is to survive. As many as 5 hours a day may be required for obtaining the bare-essential firewood, dung and fodder.

All this may be expected to relate to the high fertility and low literacy rates in rural areas of most poor countries. Poverty, the thinness of markets, and an absence of basic amenities make it essential for households to engage in a number of complementary production activities: cultivation, cattle grazing, fetching water, collecting fodder and fuelwood, cooking food, and producing simple marketable products. Labor productivity is low not only because capital is scarce, but also because environmental resources are scarce too. Cooking in a poor household is a vertically-integrated activity: nothing is processed to be begin with. It is time-intensive. Each household needs many hands, and it can be that the overall usefulness of each additional hand increases with declining resource availability. This can happen especially if households discount the future at a high rate. In their study of work allocation among rural households in the foothills of the Himalayas, C.S.E. 1989, recorded that children in the age range 10–15 years work one-and-a-half times the number of hours adult males do, their tasks consisting of fuelwood, dung, and fodder collection, grazing domestic animals, household chores, and marketing (43). A high rate of fertility and population growth further damages the environmental resource base (to the extent they are unprotected common-property), which in turn in a wide range of circumstances provides further (private) incentives for large families, which in turn further damages the resource base and so on; until some countervailing set of factors (whether public policy, or some form of Malthusian checks) stops the spiralling process. Such an explosive process can be set off by any number of factors. Government or private usurpation of resources to which rural communities have had historical access is a potential source of the problem. The short-period loss in efficiency associated with minor violations is, to be sure, small. Over time the effect can be large.

A study of data from the village Char Gopalpur in Bangladesh showed that male children become net producers at as early an age as 12 years, and work as many hours a day as an adult. Using a zero (caloric) rate of interest, it was also estimated that male children compensate for their own cumulative consumption by the age of 15. The transfer of resources over a life cycle in poor households in poor countries is usually from offspring in the aggregate to their parents. This is in sharp contrast to advanced industrial nations, where resources are transfered on average from the adult to the young. Thus, whether a society has made the demographic transition, that is, the transition from high to low fertility, is related to the direction of the intergenerational flow of resources (44–48). This is also what economic theory would predict.

The motivation for fertility we have been emphasizing in this and the previous section springs from a general absence of certain basic needs in rural parts of poor countries: public health services, old-age security, water, and sources of fuel. Children are born in poverty, and they are raised in poverty. A large proportion suffer from undernourishment, remain illiterate, and are often both stunted and wasted. Labor productivity is dismally low also because of a lack of infrastructure, such as roads. In this background it is hard to make sense of the oft-expressed suggestion that there are potential increasing-returns-to-scale in population size; that human beings are a valuable resource. Historical evidence on the way pressure of population led to new ways of doing things, which is what Boserup (49, 50) studied in her far-reaching work, does not seem to speak to the population problem as it exists in sub-Saharan Africa and the Indian sub-continent today.

## SOME SPECIAL FEATURES OF SUB-SAHARAN AFRICA

Even among poor regions, sub-Saharan Africa is a special case on fertility matters, and it is worth asking why. For our purposes we will lose little by thinking in aggregate terms. There are central tendencies in any broad cultural group, and a number of features within sub-Saharan Africa would seem to be pertinent when we seek to locate them. When we have identified a few, we will contrast them with those prevailing in the Indian sub-continent.

Unlike the Indian sub-continent, the *household* is not a very meaningful organizing unit for production, consumption and fertility decisions in Africa. In the late 1950s, some 35% of all married men in sub-Saharan Africa were polygamists (51). In rural areas matters would not appear to have changed much (27). By *polygamy* we really mean *polygyny* here: it is the men who have more than one spouse. Women in sub-Saharan Africa, just as women among non-caste Hindus in India, often have more than one relationship at any given time. But they are extra-marital relationships, not marriages. In sub-Saharan Africa, it is for the most part men who have to accumulate wealth to obtain a bride. This affords a reason why the median age difference between spouses in Africa is large. The sexual division of labor is powerful, but it assumes a different form from the Indiansub-continent. The primary responsibility for raising subsistence crops for the household usually rests with women who, as a consequence have greater power and control over food distribution than their counterparts in the Indian sub-continent. Sub-Saharan Africa has often been characterized by strong descent lineage and by weak conjugal bonds. For the most part, as in much of the Indian sub-continent, descent is patrilineal and residence is patrilocal.

Even though women do not inherit land, they are active in food cultivation. This allows them considerable independence from their husbands. Nevertheless, women's sexuality and labor power are firmly under control by the husband's lineage. Among other things it is the extent of kinship control of women which differentiates societies in sub-Saharan Africa from those in the Indian sub-continent.

## THE MODELLING OF FERTILITY DECISIONS

Household fertility and savings decisions are inter-related. Indeed, children as old-age security identifies the two. Nevertheless, it will prove useful to consider them separately. It makes for expositional ease.

Should the child mortality rate decline, the fertility rate would be expected to follow suit among households averse to facing risks in the number of children who survive. But even when infant and child mortality rates decline, it takes time for households to recognize this. Demographic transitions in the past have displayed sharp declines in fertility rates following only some time after steep declines in mortality rates.

We may assume that parents are interested in (i) their own consumption, (ii) the *quality* of each child they have, and (iii) the number of children they have. In those circumstances where children are seen at least partially as investment goods the quality of a child would in part reflect future parental consumption. The quality of a child depends on the amount of time and resources devoted to him; it depends as well on the time and effort devoted by the child in acquiring education and skills. The problem is that parents are faced with a tradeoff between current consumption and the quality of each child they raise. They also face a tradeoff between the number of children they have and the quality of each child. As we noted earlier, in poor households there is an additional complication that the average current consumption of household members is itself up to a point an increasing function of the number of children in the household: children are valuable as producer-goods. This accentuates the tradeoff parents face between the quality and quantity of children. Increased life expectancy increases the return on children's education, and so human capital formation could be expected to assume a larger share of total investment.

Improvements in education appear to have a salutary effect on household circumstances. The beneficial effects of parents' education, particularly mothers' education, on the well-being of their children has been much studied in recent years. Studies confirm that education helps mothers process information more effectively, and enables them to use the various social and community services which may be on offer more intensively. Among other things, education appears to impart a degree of self-confidence on one, to avail oneself of whatever new facilities that may be on offer. This is invaluable for rural populations living through changing circumstances. Here is an indication of orders of magnitude. The infant mortality rate in households in Thailand where the mother has no education (resp. has had primary and secondary education) was found to be 122 per 1000 (resp. 39 and 19 per 1000).

It is useful to trace the effect of an increase in parental income on fertility. To begin with, we may trace the increase in parental income to a rise in their labour productivity; as a consequence for example, of rural investment, or more generally, better employment opportunities for men and women in the labour market. Now a rise in women's labor-productivity implies an increase in the opportunity cost of rearing children. At the same time, with increasing parental income children are needed less as producer goods, and possibly less also as investment goods, since rising income will bring in its wake greater access to the capital market. Improvements in labor productivity are often associated with urbanization. Urbanization tends to disintegrate households into *nuclear* units. This raises the cost parents have to bear in rearing their children. Growing urbanization in a growing economy also offers children better employment prospects, which improve their bargaining strength relative to their parents. This in turn lowers the gross return on children as investment goods, since children become less dependable as a source of income to their parents in their old age. Moreover, State legislation on elementary schooling (making it compulsory) and increased private returns to education (arising from general industrialization) make children relatively speaking less useful as producer goods. Compounding all these considerations enables us to have a glimpse of those forces at work which relate fertility to household income.

Both the costs and benefits of having children are experienced in different proportions by the parents. The cost of bearing and nursing a child is inevitably borne by the mother, but the cost of rearing children is culturally conditioned. In some cultures, these costs are diffused across the kinship. When this is so, there is an allocation failure, in that neither parent bears the full cost of their decision. In societies characterized by weak conjugal bonds male parents often bear little of the cost of rearing children. Here, then, we would expect to see another source of asymmetry in parental motivations over reproductive decisions. Men's desire for children would on balance be expected to exceed that of women by far, and this would bring in its wake all the attendant implications we observe in the data. Patriarchy, a weak conjugal bond, and a strong kinship support system of children, taken together, provide a powerful stimulus to fertility.

Matters are different in societies where the conjugal bond is powerful. This is the case in most of Asia. Parents together bear the bulk of the cost of raising their children, even though the sexes typically do so unevenly. The extent of economic dependency of women on men now assumes a central role. This dependency is enormous in the Indian sub-continent, most especially the North. In these types of patriarchal societies women rightly perceive sons as having especially high value as insurance against personal calamities, such as widowhood and abandonment. In East and Southeast Asia, and also southern India and Sri Lanka, women's economic dependency is less. Among those that were the world's poorest countries in the early 1970s, fertility rates have fallen most dramatically in this part of the world. In a wide-ranging essay on the old-age security hypothesis, Cain (38) used the median age difference between spouses as an index of female economic dependence in patriarchal societies to demonstrate a remarkably high correlation between this and the total fertility rate in a cross section study of nations.

There are thus forces at work which move the fertility goals of women relative to men in opposite directions. In poor societies marked by gender-based asymmetry in employment opportunities and power, women's reproductive goals do not differ noticeably from those of men (52). But professed desires are sensitive to the extent to which women are educated: educated women tend to desire smaller families than illiterate ones. A preference for sons is nearly universal in the Indian sub-continent. In sub-Saharan Africa this isn't so (53). Stopping rules based on sex preference provide a different type of information regarding sex preference than sex ratios within a population. The reason is that in a steady state stopping rules have no effect on the sex ratio. To see this, suppose that in a society where sons are preferred, parents continue to have children until a son is born, at which point they stop. Assume for simplicity that at each try there is a 50% chance of a son being conceived. Now imagine a large population of parents, all starting from scratch. In the first round 50% of the parents will have sons and 50% will have daughters. The first group will now stop and the second group will try again. Of this second group, 50% will have sons and 50% will have daughters. The first sub-group will now stop and the second sub-group will have another try. And so on. But at each round the number of boys born equals the number of girls. The sex ratio is 1.

## ALLOCATION FAILURE AND PUBLIC POLICY

A good bit of the motivation underlying analytical work on fertility behavior has been in identifying circumstances where there is no allocation failure; that is, situations in which individual household decisions, unencumbered by any public population policy, yield efficient outcomes. The literature is a picture of economists busily burying any *distortion* they can imagine, and heaving a sigh of relief when they have fashioned a world in which none is visible. In this article I have identified reasons for rejecting this point of view. Public policy does not end when efficiency is in sight.

Earlier, we noted the importance of children as producer and insurance goods in poor households. We observed that the availability of household infrastructure in the form of cheap fuel and potable water makes children less important as income earning assets. Availability of credit and access to the capital market lowers the importance of children as insurance goods. Children as producer goods and as old-age security yield somewhat different implications for public policy.

The provision of such patterns of household infrastructure as we have identified requires resources, and the standard theory of resource allocation has for long shown that it is the State's obligation in poor countries to make attempts at ensuring their supply (54). The aim should not be to force people to change their reproductive behavior. The draconian measures employed in India during the Emergency Period 1975–1977 as regards sterilization are an example of the kinds of activities governments must avoid. The aim should be to identify policies which would so change the options men and women face that their reasoned choices would involve a lowering of their fertility rates to replacement levels. The evidence tells us that poor parents in poor countries *do* calculate when making such decisions as those which bear on household size and assets. It would certainly be unjust of governments to insist on parents sending their children to schools for so many years if this requirement further impoverishes poor households. But it would not be unjust were the complementary household production inputs made available through the provision of family-planning and public-health service, and infrastructural investment, and for governments to then make free school attendance compulsory. The school-year in rural United States until the beginning of this century was shorter than in urban areas, and it took account of seasonal labor requirements.

Taxes required for the provision of such household infrastructure and family-planning and public-health service as we are discussing here can only be obtained from households that are better off. That this is redistributive is of consequence, but isn't nearly of decisive consequence. For reasons we have identified, the bulk of the very poor in poor countries have continually to aim at large household sizes, making it in turn much more difficult for them to lift themselves out of the grip of poverty: household labor productivity remains abysmally low, investment credit is for the most part unavailable to them, and the avenue of savings is consequently that much constrained for them. The matter is different for those with a greater access to resources. They are, as always, in a position to limit their household size and increase the chance of propelling themselves into still-higher income levels. People from the poorest of backgrounds have been known to lift themselves out of the mire. Nevertheless, there are forces at work which pull rich and poor groups away from one another in terms of the quality of life. The Matthew Effect ("For unto everyone that hath shall be given, and he shall have abundance; but from him that hath not shall be taken away even that which he hath") works relentlessly in poor countries (54).

I am putting matters in stark terms so as only to focus on the idea that parents would have a different set of fertility goals were the relative prices of environmental and infrastructure goods different, and were the economic dependency of women on men less. Compulsory schooling, for example, makes children prohibitively expensive as assets for generating current income, and so it reduces their attractiveness as a commodity.

In debating population policy we need to develop a language for considering lives which would have been enjoyed had alternative policies been followed. We need also to develop a way of thinking about those who exist but who wouldn't have existed had alternative policies been followed. These are profoundly difficult matters. What I have tried to argue in this article is that there is much we can establish even were we to leave such conceptual difficulties aside. Population policy involves a good deal more than making family-planning centers available to the rural poor. It also involves more than a recognition that poverty is a root cause of high fertility rates in a number of societies. The problem is deeper, but it is identifiable.

### References and Notes


1. World Bank. 1984. *World Development Report*. Oxford University Press, New York. World Bank. 1988. *World Development Report*. Oxford University Press, New York. World Bank. 1990. *World Development Report*. Oxford University Press, New York.
2. FAO. 1989. *The State of Food and Agriculture*. Food and Agricultural Organization, Rome.
3. Birdsall, N. and Jamison, J. 1983. Income and other factors influencing fertility in China. *Pop. Dev. Rev. 9*.
4. Preston, S.H. 1980. Causes and consequences of mortality declines in less developed countries during the twentieth century. In: *Population and Economic Change in Developing Countries*. Easterlin, R.A. (ed.). Chicago University Press, Chicago..
5. Preston, S.H. 1986. The decline of fertility in non-European industrialized countries. *Pop. Dev. Rev., Suppl. 12*.
6. Simon, J.L. 1981. *The Ultimate Resource*. Princeton University Press, Princeton.
7. Simon, J.L. and Kahn, H. (eds). *The Resourceful Earth: A Response to Global 2000*. Basil Blackwell, New York.
8. Ehrlich, P., Ehrlich, A. and Holdren, J. 1977. *Ecoscience: Population Resources and the Environment*. W.H. Freeman, San Francisco.
9. Birdsall, N. 1988. Economic approaches to population growth. In: *Handbook of Development Economics, Vol. 1*. Chenery, H. and Srinivasan, T.N. (eds). North Holland, Amsterdam.
10. Kelley, A.C. 1988. Economic consequences of population change in the third world. *J. Econ. Lit., 26*.
11. Brown, L.R. et al. 1991. *State of the World*. W.W. Norton, New York.
12. Ehrlich, P. and Ehrlich, A. 1990. *The Population Explosion*. Simon and Schuster, New York.
13. Ehrlich, P. and Ehrlich, A. 1991. The value of biodiversity. In: *The Economics of Transnational Commons*. Dasgupta, P. and Mäler, K.G. (eds). Oxford University Press, Oxford (forthcoming).
14. Arrow, K.J. and Fisher, A. 1974. Preservation, uncertainty and irreversibility. *Quart. J. Econ., 88*.
15. Henry, C. 1974. Investment decisions under uncertainty: the irreversibility effect. *Am. Econ. Rev., 64*.
16. Dasgupta, P. and Mäler, K.G. 1991. The enviornment and emerging development issues. *Proceedings of the World Bank Annual Conference on Development Economics 1990*.
17. Nerlove, M. and Meyer, A. 1991. Endogenous fertility and the environment: a parable of firewood. In: *The Environment and Emerging Development Issues*. Dasgupta, P. and Mäler, K.G. (eds). Oxford University Press (forthcoming).
18. McGuire, J. and Popkin, B.M. 1989. Beating the zero-sum game: women and nutrition in the Third World: part 1. *Food Nut. Bull., 11*.
19. Sing, I., Squire, L. and Strauss, J. (eds). 1986. *Agricultural Household Models: Extensions, Applications and Policy*. Johns Hopkins University Press, Baltimore.
20. Lee, R.D. 1972. Population growth and the beginnings of sedentary life among the !Kung Bushmen. In: *Population Growth: Anthropological Implications*. Spooner, B. (ed.). MIT Press, Cambridge, MA.
21. Blurton Jones, N.G. and Sibly, R.M. 1978 Testing adaptiveness of culturally determined behavior: Do bushmen women maximize their repoductive success by spacing births widely and foraging seldom? In: *Human Behaviour and Adaptions*. Blurton Jones, and Reynolds, V. (eds). Taylor and Francis, London.
22. Lee, R.BI 1980. Lactation, ovolution, infanticide, and women's work: a study of hunter-gatherer population regulation. In: *Biosocial Mechanisms of Population Regulations*. Cohen, M.N., Malpass, R.S. and Klein, H.G. (eds). Yale University Press, New Haven.
23. Page, H.J. and Lesthaeghe, R. (eds). 1981. *Child-spacing in Tropical Africa: Tradition and Change*. Academic Press, London.
24. Bongaarts, J. 1980. Does malnutrition affect fecundity? A summary of the evidence. *Science, 208*.
25. Menken, J., Trussell, J. and Watkings, S. 1981. The nutrition fertility link: An evaluation of the evidence. *J. Interdiscip. Hist., 11*.
26. Bauer, P.T. 1981. *Equality, the Third World and Economic Delusion*. Weidenfeld and Nicolson, London.
27. Farooq, G.M., Ekanem, I.I. and Ojelade, S. 1987. Family size preferences and fertility in south-western Nigeria. In: *Sex Roles, Population and Development in West Africa*. Heinemann, Portsmouth, NH.
28. Chomitz, K.M. and Bridsall, N. 1991. Incentives for small families: concepts and issues. *Proceedings of the World Bank Annual Conference on Development Economics 1990*.
29. Lindert, P. 1980. Child cost and economic development. In: *Population and Economic Change in Developing Countries*. Easterlin, R.A. (ed.). Chicago University Press, Chicago.
30. Lindert, P. 1983. The changing economic costs and benefits of having children. In: *Determinants of Fertility in Developing Countries*, 2 volumes. Bulatao, R.A. and Lee, R.D. (eds). Academic Press, New York.
31. Lee, R.D. 1980. Lactation, ovolution, infanticide, and women's work: a study of hunter-gatherer population regulation. In: Cohen, M.N., Malpass, R.S. and Klein, H.G. (eds). *Biosocial Mechanisms of Population Regulations*. Yale University Press, New Haven.
32. Caldwell, J.C. and Caldwell, P. 1987. The cultural context of high fertility in sub-Saharan Africa. *Pop. Dev. Rev. 13*.
33. Caldwell, J.C. and Caldwell, P. 1990. High fertility in sub-Saharan Africa. *Sci. Am. 262*, (May).
34. May, D.A. and Heer, D.M. 1968. Son survivorship motivation and family size in India: a computer simulation. *Pop. Stud. 22*.
35. Cain, M. 1981. Risk and insurance: perspectives on fertility and agrarian change in India and Bangladesh. *Pop. Dev. Rev. 7*.
36. Cain, M. 1982. Perspectives on family and fertility in developing countries. *Pop. Stud. 36*
37. Cain, M. 1983. Fertility as an adjustment to risk. *Pop. Dev. Rev. 9*.
38. Cain, M. 1984. Women's status and fertility in developing countries: son preference and economic security. *World Bank Staff Working Paper No. 682*.
39. Nugent, J. and Gillaspy, T. 1983. Old age pension and fertility in rural areas of less developed countries: some evidence from Mexico. *Econ. Dev. Cult. Change 31*.
40. Nerlove, M., Razin, A. and Sadka, E. 1987. *Household and Economy. Welfare Economics of Endogenous Fertility*. Academic Press, New York.
41. Nerlove, M., Razin, A. and Sadka, E. 1987. *Population Policy and Individual Choice: A Theoretical Investigation*. Research Report 60. International Food Policy Research Institute, Washington, DC.
42. Mueller, E. 1976. The economic value of children in peasant agriculture. In: *Population and Development: The Search for Selective Interventions*. Ridker, R.G. (ed.). Johns Hopkins University Press, Baltimore.
43. C.S.E. 1990. *Human-Nature Interactions in a Central Himalayan Village: A Case Study of Village Bemru*. Centre for Science and Environment, New Delhi.
44. Caldwell, J.C. 1976. Toward a restatement of demographic theory. *Pop. Dev. Rev. 2*
45. Caldwell, J.C. 1977. The economic rationality of high fertility: an investigation illustrated with Nigerian data. *Pop. Stud. 31*.
46. Caldwell, J.C. 1977. *The Persistence of High Fertility: Population Prospects in the Third World*. Australian National University Press, Canberra.
47. Caldwell, J.C. 1981. The mechanisms of demographic change in historical perspective. *Pop. Stud. 35*.
48. Caldwell, J.C. 1982. *Theory of Fertility Decline*. Academic Press, New York.
49. Boserup, E. 1965. *The Conditions of Agricultural Growth*. George Allen & Unwin, London.
50. Boserup, E. 1981. *Population Growth and Technological Change*. Chicago University Press, Chicago.
51. Goody, J. 1976. *Production and Reproduction: A Comparative Study of the Domestic Terrain*. Cambridge University Press, Cambridge.
52. Mason, K.O. and Taj, A.M. 1987. Differences between women's and men's reproductive goals in developing countries. *Pop. Dev. Rev. 13*.
53. Williamson, N.E. 1976. *Sons or Daughters? A Cross-cultural Survey of Parental Preferences*. Sage Publications, Beverly Hills, CA.
54. Dasgupta, P. 1991. *An Inquiry into Well-Being and Destitution*. Oxford University Press, Oxford. (Forthcoming).

55. This article has been adapted from Chapter 12 of my book: *An Inquiry into Well-Being and Destitution*, forthcoming, Oxford University Press. In preparing it I have gained much from members of the Environmental Studies Forum at the Institute for International Studies, and of the Workshop on Population and Environment at the Morrison Institute for Population and Resources, both at Stanford University, and most especially from discussions with Paul Ehrlich and Marc Feldman. For their comments on an earlier draft, which was presented as a Crafoord Lecture at the University of Lund, I am most grateful to Tommy Bengtsson and Rolf Ohlsson.

**Partha Dasgupta is professor of economics and professor of philosophy at Stanford University; professor of economics at the University of Cambridge; research adviser to the World Institute for Development Economics Research (WIDER), Helsinki; and chairman of the Beijer International Institute of Ecological Economics, Royal Swedish Academy of Science, Stockholm. His current address: Faculty of Economics and Politics, University of Cambridge, Austin Robinson Building, Sidgwick Avenue, Cambridge CB3 9DD, England.**

5 36-55
[96]

O11
Q23
Q32
Q25

# [25]

*Review of International Economics 4(2), 152–171, 1996*

# Sustainable Development and International Distribution: Theory and Application to Rainforests

*Ernst Mohr**


## Abstract

A situation is analyzed in which two countries negotiate the financing of costs that accrue if one of them switches onto a sustainable development path. The other country's incentive to pay arises as it benefits from the developing country's environmental resources, but at an ever declining rate as long as development remains nonsustainable. In an application to the protection of tropical rainforests it is shown that North to South redistribution of welfare would be substantial, yet the North would still gain enormously in efficiency terms. An explanation is given of why the Rio Conference failed in terms of rainforest protection.


> *States shall cooperate in a spirit of global partnership to conserve, protect and restore the health and integrity of the Earth's ecosystem.*
>
> —Rio Declaration, Principle 7

## 1. Introduction

In the face of environmental deterioration in less developed countries (LDCs) a suggestion is that the North should contribute to the financing of the costs which are necessary to bring LDCs onto a sustainable development track. Apart from altruistic motives or ethical responsibilities, this request is justified by a claimed self-interest of the North in environmentally sane development in LDCs. The existence of environmental resources in the South or their services directly benefit the North, so it has a self-interest in protecting them, or so the argument goes. The tropical rainforests and their importance for the global climate and for biodiversity are a case in point. There are interesting distributional implications to the proposal as well as to the self-serving motives behind it.

The argument implicitly suggests that some environmental resources have the property of "producing" nonmarketable transfrontier services: A resource stock is located in an area under exclusive control of an LDC, but it provides a stream of environmental services some or all of which cannot be prevented from seeping abroad. This control problem obstructs trade in environmental services as the foreign beneficiaries prefer to consume these as a free lunch. Welfare is shifted away from the resource owner towards the free riders compared to the case of standard trade in private goods.

Nonsustainable development, however, changes the incentive structure and the international distribution of welfare. If development deteriorates the resource stock and consequently the international transmission of services, then the free riders have

---

*Mohr: University of St. Gallen, CH-9,000 St. Gallen, Switzerland. Tel: +71-302-584, Fax: +71-229-379. Email: ernst.mohr@iwo.unisg.ch. I wish to thank Gernot Klepper, Michael Rauscher, Frank Stähler, and Manfred Wiebelt for their helpful comments and Boris Galonske for his outstanding research assistance.

some incentive to pay if in exchange for their contribution the resource owner invests in sustainability. Assuming that the free riders' benefits from a sustainable path exceed the costs it is suggested that the developed North pays for the South's incremental costs of sustainable development. For example, concerning climate protection, this is envisaged in Art. 11 of the framework convention of the UNCED Conference in Rio, 1992. Welfare in the South would remain unaffected, but welfare in the North, though smaller than under riding a constant resource stock for free, would be greater than under nonsustainable development.

There is an important caveat to this argument. It addresses the normative question of how much the South should obtain. But it does not address the positive question of how much the North *will* pay and the South *will* receive. This article addresses this latter question. Applying noncooperative bargaining theory, the relative bargaining power of two countries negotiating transfer payments to achieve sustainable development and its distributive effects is explored.

It is shown that a resource-owning country, being on a nonsustainable track, can obtain transfer payments systematically above incremental costs of sustainable development. The analysis therefore implies that this type of international environmental cooperation would be more expensive to the North than the normative proposal suggests and that the South would gain in welfare terms.

The bargaining model is then applied to the protection of the tropical rainforests for the purpose of climate policy. Using data on actual deforestation rates, simulations suggest that even for the overall very small actual deforestation rates, equilibrium payments are substantially above incremental costs; and tiny cross-country differences in deforestation rates are associated with huge differences in bargaining power and consequently in the spread between transfers obtained and incremental costs incurred. However, on the basis of numbers for the North's willingness to pay for carbon sequestration as they can be found in the literature and on the basis of land prices (opportunity costs) as approximations for the costs of protecting the forests, the North still can buy into these carbon sinks at a fraction of what domestic carbon dioxide [$CO_2$] abatement (energy conservation) would cost. Hence, despite a hefty surcharge, the tree option is the efficient one. An interesting proposition of the analytical model states that at least for small enough rates of decline of the stream of transfrontier services, the resource owner benefits from an increase in that rate even if it also obtains environmental benefits from the resource. The simulations suggests that on the basis of their actual deforestation rates *alone*, and abstracting from domestic *environmental* benefits from the stock, virtually all examined countries hosting rain forests have an incentive to artificially boost the rate of destruction in a preagreement phase.

The model is reminiscent of the standard transboundary pollution problem. In contrast, however, goods are transferred abroad instead of bads. Also, the problem analyzed here features a dynamic aspect of irreversible environmental degradation, which is essential in triggering international cooperation when nonmarketable environmental goods cross borders. The model is also reminiscent of the common pool extraction problem with one-directional dissipation. It differs, however, in that in the common pool problem the cross-border flows can be influenced by the recipient, while in our model it is exclusively the party in possession of the source which can affect cross-border flows by switching between development tracks. Furthermore, in the common pool problem the stock remains constant if extractors remain inactive, while in our problem the stock declines when parties are passive.

The two-player bargaining game we employ is of the (1, 1) alternating-offer type with complete information. It differs from the standard infinite-horizon constant-size-of-the-pie game (Rubinstein, 1982) in the following respects:

1. During the bargaining process parties receive benefits in money terms from the resource's environmental services.
2. The pie is shrinking while bargaining takes place (Binmore, 1987).
3. The bargaining game is of the finite horizon type (Ståhl, 1972). The terminal bargaining round, $T^*$, however, is endogenous and can be readily interpreted. The finiteness of the bargaining process is due to an ever narrowing and eventually disappearing spread of the North's benefits from environmental services over incremental costs of sustainable development as long as bargaining goes on.
4. The bargaining game features an eventual incentive to remain silent and not make serious offers anymore while the other party continues to negotiate seriously. In Ausubel and Deneckere (1992) a silence motive is derived under conditions of private information, and a silent party remains so during the entire game. In our perfect information game both parties may make serious proposals initially but may become silent later on. Here silence is motivated by the fact that a party making a serious proposal and thus inducing sustainable development one period earlier must fully bear sustainability costs for an additional period. These costs are to be compared with the rent the proposer can appropriate by securing a slightly larger resource stock. As this rent decreases during negotiations it eventually pays to remain silent and let the other party incur the additional costs.

## 2. The Model

We consider two countries, one, the resource owner ($R$), on the territory of which an environmental resource is located, and one, the foreign beneficiary ($B$), which obtains windfall gains from the services the resource provides. In period 0 when negotiations between $R$ and $B$ on the financing of sustainable development begin, $B$ receives in money terms a finite value $V_0$ from the resource's services. As long as $R$ is on a nonsustainable development track, $B$'s service value declines over time. As we are not interested in the reasons behind nonsustainability but only in its consequences for distribution we take it that the resource's services' rate of decline is constant and exogenous. That is,

$$V_t = a^t V_0 \quad \forall\, t = 0, 1, \ldots, \tau, \tag{1}$$

with $a < 1$. The period in which the resource owner switches onto a sustainable track is $\tau$.

Before that track is reached the money value of environmental services which $R$ receives is given by

$$W_t = p^t g V_0 \quad \forall\, t = 0, 1, \ldots, \tau, \tag{2}$$

with $g \geqslant 0$ and $p \leqslant 1$.

Equations (1) and (2) accomodate a number of stylized cases. For example, $g = 0$ represents the case in which $R$ does not cherish a certain species on its territory while its vanishing stock is cherished by $B$. It also accomodates the case in which $B$ benefits from climate services of a rainforest (production of humidity, sequestration of carbon dioxide) while $R$ is not affected by climate change. The situation in which $R$ derives a constant value from a timber stand, say, while $B$ derives a (vanishing) existence value from the remaining biodiversity in it is represented by $g > 0$ and $p = 1$. A purely public service to be consumed by all in equal quantities, such as the utility derived from a global heritage (e.g., the population of the forest elephant), implies $g = 1$ and $a = p$. Different rates of decline ($a \neq p, p < 1, g > 0$) can accomodate cases where both parties derive a vanishing utility from different "services" of the resource. For example, $R$ may value an area of its territory for weekend activities while for $B$ it is valuable solely as the breeding site of a bird. Finally, the rate of decline of $R$'s benefit from the resource may be a function of $B$'s rate of decline, such as when the main recreational activity in $R$ is the hunting of the bird which migrates between $R$ and $B$.

We make the standard "small country" assumption in letting the international price for a unit of services be (and remain) constant. Hence, by assumption, there is a perfect substitute for $R$'s services available to $B$. In the case of rainforests as carbon sinks, for example, this is fulfilled if $B$ levies at home a carbon tax at a constant rate, as carbon sequestration and energy conservation are perfect substitutes in greenhouse policy-making. In case $B$ derives a value from a species located in $R$, the small country assumption implies that $B$ is able to invest at a given price in providing for a home (sanctuary, gene bank) for the species outside $R$.

The literature offers a bounty of definitions for the concept of sustainable development (for a survey see Pezzey, 1989). There is therefore a large degree of freedom in formalizing sustainability. Fortunately, however, competing definitions seem to differ with respect to necessary rather than sufficient conditions for sustainability: there appears to exist agreement that development is sustainable if the value of the environmental resource stock is nondecreasing. We follow this sufficiency condition in defining sustainability (narrowly) as a constant sequence of period gains from the resource's services. If $R$ switches onto a sustainable track in $\tau$,

$$V_t = a^\tau V_0 \tag{3}$$

and

$$W_t = p^\tau g V_0 \quad \forall\, t = \tau,\ \tau + 1, \ldots \tag{4}$$

We assume that sustainability causes costs $S$ per period. For simplicity we take it that $S$ is constant over time. Costs are therefore taken to be independent of the remaining resource stock.[1] This implies increasing costs per unit of environmental services as time goes on. This is given, for example, if costs depend on a given acreage whereas the quantity of the service per acre is declining over time.[2]

Declining environmental services during the bargaining process for $B$ in combination with fixed incremental costs implies a finite time horizon, $T^*$, for negotiations, as for small enough environmental services it does not pay any more to incur the costs of a sustainable track. Given the endogenously determined finite $T^*$, the bargaining solution can be determined recursively.[3]

We take it that $(1 + g)V_0 > S$. We also presume for simplicity that $S > gV_0$, ensuring that $R$ lacks an incentive to switch to sustainable development unilaterally, i.e., without obtaining transfer payments from $B$. Time preferences of players are represented by the constant one-period discount factors $h$, $0 < h < 1$, for $R$, and $k$, $0 < k < 1$, for $B$.

The model is closed by defining the bargaining rules. We make the standard presumption of a (1, 1) alternating-offer game, where the parties ($R$ and $B$) take turns in making offers and where a counteroffer can only be made after one period has elapsed. The game ends when one party accepts the other party's proposal or when $T^* + 1$ is reached, whichever comes sooner. A proposal in period $t$ is a duple $(x_t, S)$ suggesting an eternal transfer payment per period, $x_t$, from $t$ onwards from $B$ to $R$, in exchange for $R$

incurring costs, $S$, in each future period. We take it that an agreement (acceptance of a proposal) is binding.

## 3. Discrete Time Bargaining

Suppose a finite period $T^*$ exists after which $R$ and $B$ cannot or will not bargain seriously anymore. Which party can make the final transfer proposal $x_{T^*}$ in the final bargaining period $T^*$ depends on who can make the first proposal in $t = 0$ and on $T^*$ being odd or even. Suppose $B$ makes the proposal in $t = 0$ and suppose $T^*$ is even. Then, by assumption, $B$ makes the proposal in $T^*$. In infinite-horizon constant-size-of-the-pie games under complete information, rational parties already agree in $t = 0$ to avoid the time costs of waiting. In our shrinking-pie game this incentive is reinforced by the incentive of at least one party ($B$) to stop the resource decline, ceteris paribus the sooner the better. Hence under perfect information $R$ and $B$ will already agree in $t = 0$ on $(x_0, S)$, where $(x_0, S)$ is subgame perfect. Hence $\tau = 0$. Given $T^*$, and $B$ making the final proposal (in $T^*$), $x_0$ can be determined recursively by the following algorithm.

If negotiations are still going on in $T^*$, an agreement on $(x_T, S)$ in $T^*$ will induce a period $T^*$ present value to $B$, $Z^B_{T^*}$, of future net benefits from the resource of

$$Z^B_{T^*} \equiv \left(a^{T^*}V_0 - x_T\right)/\left(1-k\right).$$

Given $Z^B_{T^*}$ $(V_{T^*}, x_{T^*})$, in order to win an agreement from $B$ in $T^* - 1$, $R$ must offer at least $x_{T^*-1}$ such that

$$a^{T^*-1}V_0 + kZ^B_{T^*}\left(V_{T^*}, x_{T^*}\right) = Z^B_{T^*-1} \equiv \left(a^{T^*-1}V_0 - x_{T^*-1}\right)/\left(1-k\right),$$

making $B$ indifferent between accepting $x_{T^*-1}$ in $T^* - 1$ and an agreement in $T^*$. $R$ has no incentive to offer more, so $x_{T^*-1}$ is the optimal offer of $R$ given $x_{T^*}$.

Using the alternating-offer rule, the first offer, $x_0$, $x_0 = x_{T^*-t}$ for $t = T^*$, can thus be recursively derived. If $B$ also makes the proposal in $t = 0$,

$$x_0 = S\left(1-h\right)\sum_{j=0}^{(T^*/2)-1}\left(hk\right)^j + V_0\left[\left(1-a\right)/a\right]\sum_{j=0}^{T^*/2}\left(hk\right)^j a^{2j}$$
$$-gV_0\left[\left(1-p\right)/kp^2\right]\sum_{j=1}^{T^*/2}\left(hk\right)^j p^{2j} + h^{(T^*/2)}kx_{T^*}. \qquad (5)$$

For the bargaining horizon $T^*$, corresponding first-period offers can be similarly derived for each of the three remaining perturbations of who moves first and last. Whichever party's turn it is to make the final proposal in $T^*$, it compares the other party's discounted cumulative gains from the agreement $(x_{T^*}, S)$ with the discounted cumulative gains from the remaining nonsustainable path. If $B$ can make the final offer it is optimal to set

$$x^B_{T^*} = S - gV_0 p^{T^*}\left[h\left(1-p\right)/1-hp\right] \qquad (6)$$

If $R$ can make the offer in $T^*$ it satisfies

$$x^R_{T^*} = a^{T^*}V_0\left[k\left(1-a\right)/1-ka\right] \qquad (7)$$

Given an exogenous $T^*$, $0 < T^* < \infty$, the four possible initial offers, one of which is (5), given (6), represent the relative bargaining power arising from the four possible but arbitrary allocations of the first and last mover advantage. In the next section $T^*$ is endogenously determined for the bargaining game.

## 4. The Bargaining Horizon

The effective bargaining horizon, $T^*$, can be found by considering three periods, $T$, $T_B$, and $T_R$, which are critical for the negotiations. The first period, $T$, relates to the time after which both parties prefer the remaining nonsustainable track over sustainability. After $T$, an agreement is not feasible anymore. The other two periods, $T_B$ and $T_R$, refer to the time after which $B$ (respectively $R$) remains silent to await the other party's offers.

The shrinking size of the pie during negotiations in the face of constant period costs of sustainability, $S$, sets a finite feasible bargaining horizon for the game, beyond which $R$ and $B$ cannot bargain anymore. To determine it, note that it must satisfy

$$Z_T^R \equiv \left(gp^T V_0 - S + x_T\right)/\left(1-h\right) \geqslant gp^T V_0/\left(1-hp\right), \tag{8}$$

$$Z_T^B \equiv \left(a^T V_0 - x_T\right)/\left(1-k\right) \geqslant a^T V_0/\left(1-ka\right). \tag{9}$$

Conditions (8) and (9) imply that each party must be at least as well off when development becomes sustainable in $T$ as under the remaining nonsustainable path.

Replacing $T^*$ by $T$ in (6) and (7) and upon substituting (6) for $x_T$ in (8) and (7) for $x_T$ in (9), it follows immediately that (8) is fulfilled if $B$ makes the final offer and (9) is fulfilled if $R$ offers last. Hence if $R$ offers last $T$ is restricted by (8), and if $B$ offers last the restriction on $T$ is (9).

Both substituting (6) for $x_T$ in (9) and rearranging and substituting (7) for $x_T$ in (8) and rearranging lead to the same condition:

$$\frac{\left(a^T V_0\right)}{S} \geqslant \frac{1-ka}{k\left(1-a\right)} - \frac{gp^T V_0}{S}\frac{1-p}{1-a}\frac{h}{k}\frac{1-ka}{1-hp}. \tag{10}$$

Period $T$ is defined as the largest integer satisfying (10). As the first term on the RHS is positive, the bargaining horizon is necessarily finite as $a < 1$ and $V_0 < \infty$, Condition (10) ensures that the party which can make the final offer prefers the agreement $(x_T, S)$ to the remaining noncooperative and nonsustainable path. Note that (10) holds whichever party moves last. If for $T = 0$ (10) is violated then a bargaining equilibrium does not exist.[4] After $T$, $R$ and $B$ prefer the nonsustainable situation over the sustainable one. Hence, existence of a bargaining equilibrium requires $T \geqslant 0$.

Next consider $T_B$ and $T_R$. These critical periods take account of the incentive to remain silent when the resource stock is small. It is necessary for the algorithm described in Section 3 to lead to a subgame perfect $x_0$ that for $t = 0, 1, 2, \ldots$, each party, whenever it is up to it to make a proposal, does not prefer to remain silent (or make a nonserious offer) in order to accept the serious proposal to be obtained in the subsequent period. Let $T_R$ and $T_B$, respectively, be the period in which $R$ and $B$ make their last (serious) offer.

To determine $T_R$ consider any period $t$ in which $R$ makes an offer. To be serious $R$'s offer must leave $B$ with at least $a^t V_0$ in $t$ and $a^{t+1} V_0 - x_{t+1}$ thereafter. This implies a gain to $R$ of at most $gp^t V_0 - S$ in $t$ and $x_{t+1} - S + a^t V_0(1 - a) + gp^t V_0$ thereafter. Determining the cumulative present value of this offer and comparing it with the cumulative present value of accepting the serious offer obtained in the next period reveals that making a serious offer in $t$ dominates being silent only if

$$\frac{(a^t V_0)}{S} \geqslant \frac{1-h}{h(1-a)} - \frac{gp^t V_0}{S} \frac{(1-p)}{(1-a)}. \tag{11}$$

The largest integer of $t$ fullfilling (11) determines $T_R$. It pays to bargain seriously only if the present value of rents $R$ can appropriate from $B$ in terms of bargaining concessions, by securing a larger eternal flow of environmental services for $B$ through a serious offer in $t$, plus the corresponding gain $R$ receives directly from a larger resource stock are not exceeded by the additional costs of environmental protection, $S$, of achieving sustainability one period earlier, as these costs are borne by the party responsible for this acceleration.

By an isomorphic argument it follows that $B$ bargains seriously in any period $t$ in which it can make an offer if

$$\frac{(a^t V_0)}{S} \geqslant \frac{1-ka}{k(1-a)} - \frac{gp^t V_0}{S} \frac{1-p}{1-a}. \tag{12}$$

Period $T_B$ is given by the largest integer of $t$ satisfying (12).

It follows from (11) and (12) that $R$'s and $B$'s incentives to make serious offers vanishes in finite time.[5] Furthermore, once a party turns silent it remains so forever, and if it makes a serious offer in any period it does so at all earlier times. The silence motive in this complete information game therefore imposes a restriction on the *effective* bargaining horizon $T^*$ (as opposed to the feasible one, $T$). Restrictions (10), (11), and (12) together require the effective bargaining horizon, $T^*$, to satisfy

$$\frac{a^{T^*} V_0}{S} \geqslant \max \begin{bmatrix} \dfrac{1-ka}{k(1-a)} - \dfrac{gp^{T^*} V_0}{S} \dfrac{1-p}{1-a} \dfrac{h}{k} \dfrac{1-ka}{1-hp}, \\ \dfrac{1-h}{h(1-a)} - \dfrac{gp^{T^*} V_0}{S} \dfrac{1-p}{1-a}, \\ \dfrac{1-k}{k(1-a)} - \dfrac{gp^{T^*} V_0}{S} \dfrac{1-p}{1-a} \end{bmatrix} \geqslant \frac{a^{T^*+1} V_0}{S}, \tag{13}$$

provided $T \geqslant 0$, $T_R \geqslant 0$, and $T_B \geqslant 0$. Hence from (10)–(13), $T^* = \min(T, T_R, T_B)$ if neither $T$, $T_R$, or $T_B$ is negative. Condition (13) represents three possible regimes determining the effective bargaining horizon. Note that as all offers in $t = 0, 1, 2, \ldots,$ $T^*$ are serious, the algorithm described in Section 3 implies that $x_0$ is subgame perfect.

Now consider the case $T \geqslant 1$ and either $T_B < 0$ or $T_R < 0$. In this case one party never starts bargaining seriously. It is straightforward that then the other party offers in $t = 0$ or $t = 1$ and thereafter (up to min $(T, T_B)$ respectively min $(T, T_R)$) the minimum offer (6), respectively (7), where $T^*$ is replaced by $t$. Apparently the best a party can do which is silent from the beginning is to accept the minimum offer of the other party instantaneously.

Finally consider the case $T \geqslant 0$, $T_R < 0$, and $T_B < 0$. It can be easily verified that this case is feasible. It implies that when negotiations begin both parties want the agreement ($T \geqslant 0$) but both would also want to remain silent, given the other party speakes out ($T_R$, $T_B < 0$). This case can be treated as a static 2 × 2 noncooperative game.

Obviously, remaining silent cannot be an optimal strategy if the other party remains silent too. The same can be said of an outcome in which both speak out. However, if either speakes out and the other remains silent, neither has an incentive to defect. Hence an equilibrium requires either party to be silent and the other to make proposals. For reasons already given both parties then already agree on the first proposal made.[6]

In conclusion of this section, we have established the existence of a "window of history." Only while this window is open can both parties reach an agreement on the protection of $R$'s resources. If $T < 0$ this window remains closed. If it is open initially ($T \geq 0$) it will, however, remain so only for a while, and close again well before the stock of resources and the services it provides has vanished.

## 5. Continuous-Time Bargaining

In this section the artificial first- and last-mover advantages are eliminated. Let the time delay between successive proposals be $\Delta t$ and let $\Delta t = T^*/n$, where $n$ is the number of proposals which can be made in the interval $[0, T^*]$. The continuous time bargaining equilibrium equivalent to (5) can be derived by letting $\Delta t \to 0$ and $n \to \infty$. It is

$$x_0 = S\frac{1-h}{1-hk}\left[1-e^{-(1-hk)T^*/2)}\right] + V_0\frac{1-a}{1-hka^2}\left[1-e^{-(1-hka^2)T^*/2)}\right]$$
$$-gV_0\frac{1-p}{1-hkp^2}\left[1-e^{-(1-hkp^2)T^*/2)}\right]+e^{-(1-hk)T^*/2)}x_{T^*}. \tag{5'}$$

The condition for the effective bargaining horion (13) is replaced by

$$\frac{e^{-(1-a)T^*}V_0}{S} \geqslant \max\begin{bmatrix} \dfrac{1-ka}{k(1-a)} - \dfrac{ge^{-(1-p)T^*}V_0}{S}\dfrac{1-p}{1-a}\dfrac{h}{k}\dfrac{1-ka}{1-hp}, \\ \dfrac{1-h}{h(1-a)} - \dfrac{ge^{-(1-p)T^*}V_0}{S}\dfrac{1-p}{1-a}, \\ \dfrac{1-k}{k(1-a)} - \dfrac{ge^{-(1-p)T^*}V_0}{S}\dfrac{1-p}{1-a} \end{bmatrix} \tag{13'}$$

provided $T \geqslant 0$, $T_R \geqslant 0$, and $T_B \geqslant 0$. Note that under continuous bargaining, $T$, $T_R$, and $T_B$ respectively, are determined by the equality of the LHS and the first, second, and third term on the RHS of (13′) if $T^*$ is replaced by $T$, $T_R$, and $T_B$. For $T \geqslant 0$ and either $T_B < 0$ or $T_R < 0$ then the effective bargaining horizon is $T^* = 0$. The same holds if both $T_B$ and $T_R$ are negative but $T \geqslant 0$.

Let regimes I, II, and III respectively be those in which $T^*$ is determined by the first, second and third term on the RHS of (13′). The final offers at the effective bargaining horizon $T^*$ are now

$$x^B_{T^*} = S - ge^{-(1-p)T^*}V_0\frac{h(1-p)}{1-hp}, \tag{6'}$$

$$x^R_{T^*} = e^{-(1-a)T^*}V_0\frac{k(1-a)}{1-ka}. \tag{7'}$$

It can be shown that in the bargaining equilibrium defined by (5′), (6′), (7′) and (13′) all first- and last-mover advantages are removed. We summarize Sections 3–5 by:

THEOREM 1. *Under continuous time bargaining a bargaining equilibrium exists only if $T \geqslant 0$. If $T \geqslant 0$, $\tau = 0$ and the equilibrium period transfer payment from B to R, $x_0$, is (a) unique and given by $x_0 = x^B_{T^*}$, where $x^B_{T^*}$ is given by (6′) with $T^* = 0$, if $T_B \geqslant 0$ and $T_R < 0$; (b) unique and given by $x_0 = x^R_{T^*}$, where $x^R_{T^*}$ is given by (7′) with $T^* = 0$, if $T_B < 0$ and $T_R \geqslant 0$; (c) not unique with $x_0$ given as under either (a) or (b) if $T_B < 0$ and $T_R < 0$; (d) unique and given by (5′), where $T^*$, $T \geqslant T^* \geqslant 0$, is given by (13′) and (i) $x_{T^*} = x^R_{T^*} = x^B_{T^*}$ if $T^* \equiv \min(T, T_R, T_B) = T$, (ii) $x_{T^*} = x^B_{T^*}$ if $T^* \equiv \min(T, T_R, T_B) = T_R$, (iii) $x_{T^*} = x^R_{T^*}$, otherwise, in case $T_B \geqslant 0$ and $T_R \geqslant 0$.*

The interesting case is (d). In the next section we explore its properties.

## 6. Properties

We analyze the properties of the transfer payments from $B$ to $R$ induced by the bargaining equilibrium of case (d) in Theorem 1. In most of the analysis we assume $a \in\ ]-1, 1[$, i.e., we take it that the rate of decline of environmental services for $B$ is in this sense moderate. From (13′) it immediately follows that:

LEMMA 1. *The bargaining horizon, $T^*$, is an increasing function of $V_0/S$. Hence the more of the services can be sustained with \$1 the longer can R and B haggle without foresaking the chance for an eventual agreement.*

Let $g = 0 \vee p = 1$. In this case only $B$ suffers from the resource decline. This situation is extreme in shifting onto the side of B the relative loss of letting opportunities to agree fade away. The third term on the RHS of (5′) vanishes and (13′) is given by

$$\frac{e^{-(1-a)T^*}V_0}{S} = \max\left[\frac{1-ka}{k(1-a)}, \frac{1-h}{h(1-a)}\right] \equiv \psi. \qquad (13'')$$

For $g = 0 \vee p = 1$, $B$ will not turn silent as long as cooperation dominates noncooperation. Time $T^*$ is therefore determined either by regime I or II. From (i) or (ii) of Theorem 1 and (6′) it follows therefore $x_{T^*} = S$.

From Lemma 1 there exists $V_0^{min}$ such that $T^* = 0$. Upon using (5′) it immediately follows that:

LEMMA 2. *Given $g = 0 \vee p = 1$, for $V_0 = V_0^{min} \Leftrightarrow T^* = 0$, $x_0 = S$.*

Note that for $g = 0 \vee p = 1$, $R$ cannot gain in terms of environmental benefits from an agreement, so incremental and total period costs are actually the same for $R$. Hence if only $B$ suffers from the resource decline and if the bargaining horizon gives $R$ no opportunity to use the declining resource stock strategically then $B$'s transfer payment is equal to the incremental costs of sustainable development. In this situation bargaining over sustainable development does not affect welfare in the resource-owning country while it increases welfare, compared to the nonsustainable track, in the country benefiting from the resource's existence. The following proposition is important.

PROPOSITION 1. *Given $g = 0 \vee p = 1$, for $V_0 > V_0^{min} \Leftrightarrow T^* > 0$, a sufficient condition for $x_0 > S$ is $a \in ]-1, 1[$.*

Proof of Proposition 1 is given in the Appendix. Compared to the case $T^* = 0$, if $T^* > 0$ bargaining power is shifted towards the resource owner as it is able to use the fading resource strategically to obtain transfer payments in excess of costs. The resource-owning country can secure for itself a net transfer income. Negotiating sustainability is therefore a vehicle to obtain an "export" income for the supply of international services the resource owner cannot obtain from market participation due to the fleeting nature of these services. Bargaining over sustainable development shifts welfare from the beneficiary of environmental services to the resource-owning country. Note that Proposition 1 states that a sufficient condition for this welfare-shifting and income-creating effect is that the rate of decline of the resource is not extremely large.[7]

Now consider the general case $g \geqslant 0$, $p \leqslant 1$. From (5′), (6′), (7′), and (13′) $x_0$ is continuous and differentiable in $g$. From Proposition 1 it therefore follows that:

COROLLARY 1. *If $T^* > 0$ if $g = 0$, then there exists $\varepsilon_l$, $\varepsilon_l > 0$, such that $x_0 > S$ if $0 < g < \varepsilon_l$.*

Hence if $R$ possesses sufficient bargaining power to negotiate a net transfer income if it does not benefit from the resource directly (which is the case if $T^* > 0$), then it also obtains a transfer income above incremental costs if it directly but moderately benefits from the resource's existence. Note that in the case $g > 0$ and $p < 1$, it is not even necessary that $x_0 > S$ for $R$ to gain in welfare terms. With $g > 0$ and $p < 1$, $R$ obtains a benefit from the agreement other than transfer payments and hence can agree to pay for part of the period costs and still be better off than without an agreement.

Let $\gamma \equiv S/V_0$. Hence $\gamma$, $\gamma < 1$, is the cost necessary to sustain one unit of the resource's services for $B$. Let $g \geqslant 0$ and $p \leqslant 1$. Dividing (5′), (6′), and (7′) by $V_0$ it follows that for a given $\gamma$ and $T^*$ the transfer payment per service unit, $x_0/V_0$, is independent of $V_0$. From Lemma 1 it therefore follows that $d(x_0/V_0)/dV_0 = 0$ if $\gamma$ is constant. Consider $n$ strategically independent negotiations between $B$ and $n$ resource owners $R_i$, $i = 1, \ldots, n$. It then follows immediately that:

PROPOSITION 2. *If $a_i = a_j$, $g_i = g_j$, $p_i = p_j$, and $h_i = h_j$, then $x_0^i/V_0^i = x_0^j/V_0^j$ if $\gamma_i = \gamma_j$ $\forall$ $V_0^i \gtreqless V_0^j$, $i, j = 1, \ldots, n$.*

Proposition 2 states that the sheer size of the resource stock (or of its services) has no impact on the bargaining power if $\gamma$ is constant. Other things being equal, a large resource-owning country is therefore unable to negotiate a larger transfer per resource (service) unit compared to a small resource owner if the quantity of resources which can be sustained by \$1 is the same in both. Let $x_0/V_0 \equiv \phi(\gamma)$. It follows that:

COROLLARY 2. *Given $\gamma$, $x_0 - S = [\phi(\gamma) - \gamma]V_0$, with $\phi(\gamma) - \gamma < 1$. If $g = 0 \vee p = 1$ then $0 \leqslant \phi(\gamma) - \gamma < 1$.*

Proof of Corollary 2 is given in the Appendix. Net total period gains for $R$ increase by less than the resource size if the feasible milage per \$, $1/\gamma$, remains constant. If $g > 0$ and $p < 1$, $R$ and $B$ can agree on transfer payment below $S$. If $\phi(\gamma) - \gamma < 0$ this is the case. Then Corollary 2 states that the total contribution of $R$ to the financing of sustainability is linear in $V_0$ with slope $|\phi(\gamma) - \gamma|$.

We have given in Proposition 1 and Corollary 1 conditions under which a resource-owning country can obtain net income and increase its welfare when negotiating sustainability. Critical to this income- and welfare-increasing opportunity is the resource owner being on a nonsustainable track initially. A natural question then is whether transfer payments are larger if $R$ is initially on a track which is "less" sustainable. Put differently, does a resource-owning country have an incentive to shift onto an environmentally more destructive path in order to create a larger bargaining leverage in future negotiations? We can make

PROPOSITION 3. *If* $g = 0 \vee p = 1$, *there exists* $\varepsilon_2$, $\varepsilon_2 < 1$ *such that* $\varepsilon_2 < a < 1$ *is sufficient for* $dx_0/da < 0$.

Proof of Proposition 3 is given in the Appendix. Consider the general case $g \geqslant 0$, $p \leqslant 1$. Suppose $R$'s own rate of decline of environmental services is linked to $B$'s rate by a continuous, differentiable, and finitely sloped function $p = \mu(a)$. By continuity and differentiability of $x_0$ in $g$ it follows immediately from Proposition 3

COROLLARY 3. *Given a continuous, differentiable, and finitely sloped function* $p = \mu(a)$, *for each* $a \in ]\varepsilon_2, 1[$ *there exists* $\varepsilon_3$, $\varepsilon_3 > 0$ *such that* $dx_0/da < 0$ *if* $0 < g < \varepsilon_3$.

Proposition 3 implies that at least for a small enough rate of decline a resource owner not affected by environmental deterioration indeed obtains better terms on $x_0$ if the other bargaining party's rate of decline increases. Corollary 3 implies that whenever this is true it is at least also true if $R$ directly benefits from the resource's services a little bit. Given $R$'s inability to earn regular export income from the sale of environmental services this creates a moral hazard effect on the side of resource-owning countries: If you find yourself being on a sustainable track get off if you can; and if you are off, at least if you are only slightly so, get further off. It should be mentioned, however, that the implicit assumption behind Proposition 3 and Corollary 3 is that switching between different nonsustainable development tracks is sufficiently cheap. From a bargaining theoretic perspective the underlying reason for these results is a simple one. If $R$ is not or is only mildly affected by environmental deterioration it can exert additional pressure on $B$ by allowing faster deterioration. Note that in the bargaining game this haggling on the back of nature is not detrimental to nature as parties already agree in $t = 0$. Contrary to the accelerated destruction incentive, which appears to be rather robust, this latter property is an artefact of the bargaining game not possessing much empirical relevance.

It is interesting to investigate the international distribution in the case in which $g = 1$, $a = p$, and $h = k$. A well-known result of noncooperative bargaining theory states that in a constant-size-of-pie, infinite-horizon game identical parties split the pie evenly; see e.g., Sutton (1986). In our model this would imply $x_0 = S/2$. We can, however, make

PROPOSITION 4. *If* $R$ *and* $B$ *are identical except for the resource ownership, if* $h = k < 1$ *then* $x_0 \geqslant S/2 \Leftrightarrow T^* \geqslant 0$.

Proof of Proposition 4 is given in the Appendix. The following corollary is also proved in the Appendix:

COROLLARY 4. *If R and B are identical except for the resource ownership, then* $lim_{h \to 1} x_0 = S/2 \ \forall \ T^* \geqslant 0$.

Proposition 4 and Corollary 4 imply that the difference in resource ownership alone fails to shift bargaining power and welfare from *B* to *R* only if the parties also fail to be impatient. With impatient parties the difference in resource ownership alone suffices to twist bargaining power and welfare in favor of the resource-owning country compared to an equal sharing of costs. Countries on the territory of which environmental resources are located, which supply the world with services to be consumed in equal quantities by all, do possess an owner advantage in negotiating sustainability. This illustrates the disadvantageous bargaining position in which the beneficiaries of ex-territorial resources are when trying to stop their destruction. In the next section we apply the theory to the protection of tropical rainforests for the purpose of carbon sequestration.

## 7. Application

Huge quantities of carbon are contained in the world's tropical rainforests. In as much as the rainforests disappear carbon is released in the form of $CO_2$ into the atmosphere, thus contributing to the greenhouse effect. Protecting the rainforests, for the purpose of locking carbon in, can be treated in the framework developed. The rainforests are a resource owned by nations on the territory of which they are located. As the resource holds back carbon it produces transboundary environmental services, as the temperature increase which is said to adversely affect the North is thereby slowed down and the total increase is smaller. The resource owners cannot "hold back" these services, so the North would have the luck to get them for free were the rainforest-owning countries on a sustainable development track which preserved the stock. However, the rainforests are on the decline and with them the climate services they provide. This sets the stage for international negotiations on sustaining them. With the model, developed in Sections 2–6, we now explore whether, in the face of the predicted surcharges to be paid, carbon sequestration in the South is still profitable for the North. We also explore the distributive effects of this form of international climate cooperation.

The rainforest countries we study are listed in Table 1. The first column gives the total size of their rainforests and the second column gives the size as a percentage of the world stock. Table 1 contains all tropical rainforest countries with a stock of more than 2% of the world total (including nontropical forests).[8] The third column gives the actual country-specific annual deforestation rates in percent $((1 - a) \cdot 100)$.

The next two pairs of columns give bargaining equilibria of bilaterally negotiating sustainability of the rainforests between the North and each of the countries listed. We know from Proposition 2 that the total size of a country's rainforest stock does not affect the bargaining equilibrium. We can also infer from Corollary 2 that the equilibrium ratio of international transfer payments (from the North to a specific forest-owning country) over necessary costs of preserving the rainforest, $x_0/S$, does depend only on the ratio $V_0/S$.

In Table 1, calculations of the equilibrium surcharge $x_0/S$ are for both bargaining situations based on a fictitious ratio $V_0/S$ of 100:1, common to all countries. As the size of the stock is irrelevant and as $V_0/S$ is taken to be the same for all, countries are therefore taken in Table 1 to be identical except for the rate of decline of their

*Table 1. The Pure Effect of Differing Rates of Decline*

| | Stock of Closed Forests (1000ha) | Stock of Closed Forests (%) | Deforestation Rates in % ((1 – a)·100) | $x_0/S$[d] | T | $x_0/S$[e] | T |
|---|---|---|---|---|---|---|---|
| Bolivia[a] | 44,010 | 3.1 | 0.2 | 5.11 | 1,094 | 1.79 | 405 |
| Brazil[a] | 357,480 | 24.9 | 0.5 | 10.67 | 596 | 3.61 | 338 |
| Columbia[a] | 46,400 | 3.2 | 1.8 | 24.87 | 214 | 10.31 | 157 |
| Mexico[a] | 46,250 | 3.2 | 1.8 | 24.87 | 214 | 10.31 | 157 |
| Peru[a] | 69,680 | 4.9 | 0.4 | 8.97 | 699 | 3.02 | 370 |
| Venezuela[a] | 31,870 | 2.2 | 0.4 | 8.97 | 699 | 3.02 | 370 |
| Zaire[b] | 105,750 | 7.4 | 0.4 | 8.97 | 699 | 3.02 | 370 |
| India[b] | 36,540 | 2.5 | 0.1 | 2.91 | 1,541 | 1.16 | 128 |
| Indonesia[b] | 113,900 | 7.9 | 1.1 | 18.65 | 323 | 6.91 | 219 |
| Total | 851,880 | 59.3 | | | | | |
| World[c] | 1,436,492 | 100.0 | | | | | |

[a] Calculations of a are based on annual deforestation rates for the period 1981–1985 (Amelung and Diehl, 1992); the calculations are the author's.
[b] Rates of decline as reported by the World Resources Institute (1990).
[c] Total forest area in Africa, Asia, Oceania, and Central and South America (World Resources Institute, 1990).
[d] $g = 0$, $h = k = 0.98$, $V_0 = 100$, $S = 1$.
[e] $g = 0$, $h = k = 0.92$, $V_0 = 100$, $S = 1$.

rainforests. Table 1 gives therefore the pure effect of differing actual rates of decline on the bargaining solution.

The first column of bargaining solutions, given by the ratio $x_0/S$ and the equilibrium bargaining horizon $T$ (in years), is based on an annual discount rate $((1 - h)\cdot 100 = (1 - k)\cdot 100)$ of 2%, common to the North and each of the countries listed. This discount rate is advocated by Cline (1992) to be appropriate in evaluating climate policy. The second set of bargaining solutions supposes a larger discount rate of 8% which is more in line with current World Bank evaluation practice (Birdsall and Steer, 1993). All other calculations reported in this section use a common 8% discount rate. All calculations of transfer payments are based on the assumption that countries owning rainforests are themselves not affected by climate change. This assumption in turn implies that they do not benefit from their rainforests' climate services. This corresponds to the case $g = 0$ in the analytical model. From Theorem 1, case (d), and (13′) it then follows that $T < T_B = T_R$ as we presume $h = k$. Hence in the application neither party turns silent before both lose their interest in reaching an agreement. The equilibrium effective bargaining horizon is therefore indeed $T^* = T$.

The assumption that some countries are completely insulated against the greenhouse effect is actually incorrect. However, climate models suggest that this assumption is more innocuous the closer a country is to the equator (as changes in average temperatures would be concentrated at higher latitudes), the more humid a region is (as arid and semi-arid regions are more vulnerable to changes in humidity) and the less vulnerable a country is to sea level rises (Enquete Commission, 1989). This suggests that the earth's tropical rainforest belt is less affected by climate change. For simplicity and lack of data on the costs of climate change in this region we represent this in the calculations by setting $g = 0$ for all rainforest-owning countries.[9] This implies that the values for $S$ are to be taken as the total *and* incremental costs of protecting the forests.

Tables 2 and 3 depart from the assumption of a uniform and fictitious ratio of 100:1 for $V_0/S$. Instead incremental costs are taken to depend on a proxy for the opportunity costs of securing the rainforests for carbon sequestration. We approximate opportunity costs by the relative price of land in these countries, to be converted from forest to agricultural use (Schneider, 1993).[10] In other words, it is presumed that to sustain a hectar of rainforests it must be bought thereby preventing conversion.[11]

The first column in Table 2 gives opportunity costs per hectare of rainforest in present values, $S'$, for the countries listed. Values $S'$ are land prices per hectare of forest. Assuming that land is a consol, the induced annuities are $S$, $S = S'(1 - h)$. The equilibrium transfers from the North to these countries, reported in Table 3, are based on these costs. The land price of $150 for a hectare of Brasilian forest is that which is used in Schneider (1993).[12] For lack of similar data for each of the other countries we induce relative differences between country-specific incremental costs by weighting the price of $150/ha with an index for the relative productivity of agricultural land in the other countries.[13]

Tables 2 and 3 differ with respect to the value used for the North's willingness to pay for carbon sequestration. We represent it by the requested or revealed willingness to pay as it can be inferred from cost-benefit analyses of climate policy, from existing greenhouse-gas taxes, or from otherwise proposed or considered greenhouse policies. In that we again follow Schneider (1993) and examine the values listed there. Willingnesses to pay are calculated presuming that presently 100 tons of carbon are sunk in an average hectare of rainforest throughout the world, which would eventually be released into the atmosphere if countries stayed on a nonsustainable track.[14] On the basis of 100t of carbon released if a hectare of rainforest is completely destroyed, the inclinations to pay represented in Table 2 are $180/ha, $350/ha, $610/ha and $730/ha respectively. They represent the willingness to pay as it is implied by (1) the low cost

*Table 2. Effects of Conservative Climate Policies*

| | $S'$[a] | $V_0/S$[b] | $V_0/S$[c] | $V_0/S$[d] | $V_0/S$[e] |
|---|---|---|---|---|---|
| Bolivia | 63 | 2.87 | 5.58 | 9.73 | 11.65 |
| Brazil | 150 | 1.20 | 2.33 | 4.07 | 4.87 |
| Columbia | 193 | 0.93 | 1.81 | 3.16 | 3.78 |
| Mexico | 239 | 0.75 | 1.46 | 2.55 | 3.05 |
| Peru | 93 | 1.94 | 3.77 | 6.57 | 7.86 |
| Venezuela | 164 | 1.10 | 2.14 | 3.73 | 4.46 |
| Zaire | 236 | 0.76 | 1.48 | 2.59 | 3.09 |
| India | 519 | 0.35 | 0.67 | 1.17 | 1.41 |
| Indonesia | 445 | 0.40 | 0.79 | 1.37 | 1.64 |

[a]The price per ha land, $S'$, is calculated as follows: the Brazilian land price of $150/ha (Schneider, 1993) is weighted by an index based on the ratio of the 1990 national value added in agriculture (World Bank, 1992) and the total national stock of cropland and permanent pastures (World Resources Institute, 1990).

[b]Nordhaus (1991): low estimate, $V_0' =$ US$180/ha.

[c]Penny a gallon of gas, $V_0' =$ US$350/ha.

[d]Enacted tax, Finland $V_0' =$ US$o10/ha (Schneider, 1993).

[e]Nordhaus (1991): medium estimate, $V_0' =$ US$730/ha.

*Table 3. Effects of Dutch and Swedish Enacted Carbon Tax*

| | $V_0/S$ | $x_0/S$ | $x_0/V_0^a$ | T |
|---|---|---|---|---|
| Bolivia | 71.79 | 1.43 | 0.02 | 236 |
| Brazil | 30.00 | 1.45 | 0.05 | 98 |
| Columbia | 23.32 | 2.80 | 0.12 | 76 |
| Mexico | 19.81 | 2.36 | 0.13 | 65 |
| Peru | 48.48 | 1.73 | 0.04 | 189 |
| Venezuela | 27.49 | 1.20 | 0.04 | 47 |
| Zaire | 19.09 | — | — | — |
| India | 8.67 | — | — | — |
| Indonesia | 8.67 | 1.23 | 0.11 | 12 |

[a] Enacted tax, Netherlands and Sweden, $V_0'$ = US$4,500/ha (Schneider, 1993).

estimate of Nordhaus (1991), (2) a tax of a penny per gallon of gas, (3) the enacted Finnish carbon tax, and (4) the Nordhaus (1991) medium estimate. The calculation of equilibrium payments in Table 3 is based on a willingness to pay of $4,500/ha as is implied by the enacted Dutch and Swedish carbon tax. Simulations have furthermore been undertaken for a willingness to pay, as is implied by the Nordhaus (1991) high estimate of $6,600/ha and the US Congressional Budger Office (US-CBO) estimate of $10,000/ha.

These values indicate the value for the North having prevented once and forever the emission of 100t of carbon in the atmosphere, for example by locking it in biomass. They are therefore in present value terms, giving the discounted benefit of having a smaller greenhouse gas concentration in future years. Applying the classic scientific Arrhenius greenhouse model (see for example equations 1 and 2 in Cline [1991]), carbon locked in hectare of trees is therefore in economic terms a consol, the value of which, $V_0'$, relates to its annuity $V_0$ according to $V_0 = V_0'(1 - k)$. As we take a common discount rate ($h = k$), $V_0'/S' = V_0/S$. Hence we can directly use the ratios $V_0'/S'$ in calculating the equilibrium bargaining ratios $x_0/S$ from equation (5′).

The willingnesses to pay which are used are all static. They implicitly imply the presence of a perfect substitute for climate policy (e.g., energy conservation), available at a constant price. They thus conform to the assumptions made in the analytical model. Due to the availability of the policy substitute, in each case $V_0$ ($V_0'$) must be interpreted as the North's willingness to pay.

The construction of the data base suggests the following. First, in approximating costs by weighted land prices per hectare we marginalize negotiations which in the analytical model are formulated in terms of a total stock. Hence, the data set we use in the application presumes a situation as if the North would negotiate with each country the preservation of single (representative) hectares separately. We know from Proposition 2 that this interpretation conforms with the analytical model. The implicit, but important, presumption, however, is that the North bargains with a country's government and cannot operate on the market for land as an ordinary (atomistic) market participant. We shall instantly see that governments owning rainforests have every incentive to prevent this.

Second, using land prices as approximations of costs, in combination with the presumption that a forest is homogeneous, provides a straightforward interpretation of why the costs are invariant to the total stock and of how precisely the resource is supposed to decline: The acreage covered presently by the rainforests will always be so (hence costs are fixed), but as time goes on while development is nonsustainable more and more carbon will have evaporated into the atmosphere. In this interpretation, the forest area does not become smaller but the forest in it becomes thinner.

Third, the construction of the cost data on the basis of Brazilian (Rondonian) land prices suggests that the results are most reliable in the case of this Brazilian province but less so for other provinces and the other countries. Results for other countries may therefore be interpreted as a two-parameter (destruction rate and cost) sensitivity analysis with a suggestion as to which countries might be roughly associable with the parameter constellations. The simulations indicate how the theoretical model can be calibrated in principle to country- or region-specific issues of carbon sequestration. The use of land prices to represent costs must be viewed as an upper bound on the necessary costs to protect carbon sinks. The results of the application of the model to rainforest protection are interpreted in the conclusion.

## 8. Conclusions

The paper analyses a bargaining situation in which two countries negotiate the financing of the costs which accrue if one of them switches from a nonsustainable onto a sustainable development track. The other country's incentive to contribute to the financing of these costs arises from a problem of a fading free-rider position: It benefits free of charge from the other country's environmental resources, but at a declining rate as long as development remains nonsustainable. This bargaining situation catches, so the paper argues, some of the key elements in North-South negotiations on certain international environmental problems such as, for example, the preservation of tropical rainforests or biodiversity.

The paper gives conditions under which such negotiations will induce payments from North to South which are (1) equal to and (2) above incremental costs of sustainability. Such international environmental cooperation generally comes about with a redistribution of welfare from North to South. It is also argued that the South can have an incentive to engage in a more destructive development in a preagreement phase in order to obtain a larger transfer income. Furthermore it is shown that an agreement can be reached only in a "window of history," which, if open at all, will close well before the resource has vanished. The equilibrium transfer payments needed to preserve tropical carbon sinks which are reported in Tables 1–3 suggest:

1. (Table 1.) In order to entice a substantial redistribution from North to South only very small rates of decline of the rainforests are needed. For the hypothetical benefit-cost relation, $V_0/S$, of 100:1 the 0.1% annual rate of decline of the Indian rainforest, for example, suffices to induce a net profit for India from sustaining its forest relative to costs of 191 (16)% in the 2 (8)% discount rate case. For other countries with more quickly disappearing rainforests this net profit is even larger. As the South can win a bounty in bilateral negotiations, the government of a rainforest-hosting country has every incentive to monopolize its domestic supply of carbon sinks to the North.

2. (Table 1.) International redistribution is sensitive to the discount rates applied to climate policy. A smaller discount rate (2% instead of 8%) which is more favorable to a tougher climate policy (Cline, 1992), is also more favorable to transfer from North to South.

3. (Table 1.) International redistribution is highly sensitive to even tiny differences in the rates of decline. For example, in the 8% discount rate case an increase in the rate of decline from 0.1% to 0.2% (India to Bolivia) implies an increase of transfers by 63% of incremental costs, and an increase from 1.1% to 1.8% (Indonesia to Columbia) implies an increase of transfers by almost 3.5 times the necessary costs. As there is considerable uncertainty as to what the correct rates of decline are (Melillo et al., 1985) carbon sink preservation creates a market with a strong willingness to pay for (remote) control and observation services.

4. (Table 1.) Other things being the same and for the range of rates of decline listed in Table 1, virtually every country would benefit from a somewhat larger rate of decline. The North therefore faces a moral hazard problem on the side of rainforest-owning countries. These have an incentive to boost destruction (or at least do nothing against a further acceleration unilaterally) in a pre-agreement phase.

5. (Table 1.) It is particularly expensive to protect forests which are under the threat of quick extinction. Therefore, and counter to popular sentiments, if a carbon sink policy is to be implemented on a limited budget such that not all rainforests can be sustained, it is rational to give up the most perishable ones and concentrate on the protection of those which "need it least."

6. (Table 2.) Up to and including a willingness to pay of $730/ha, which corresponds to Nordhaus' (1991) medium estimate of warming damages, a carbon sink policy is infeasible in the countries listed, unless incremental costs are (substantially) smaller than those assumed. This follows because for the parametric specification listed in Table 2 a bargaining equilibrium does not exist, because the feasible bargaining horizon. $T$, is negative.[15] The interpretation of this is that for these (low) unit valuations, the quantity of carbon caught in the national stocks is already too small. The North is better off riding the remaining nonsustainable track for free. These results also provide an explanation for the failure to reach a substantive agreement on the protection of rainforests at the Rio Conference. In this interpretation the North's revealed low preference for climate protection kept the "window of history" firmly shut. The analysis predicts that an agreement on the protection of rainforests in the ongoing Rio process can only be expected if the North begins to exhibit a willingness to pay for climate protection well above the ones presumed in Table 2.

7. (Table 3.) A carbon sink policy is feasible for a valuation of $4,500/ha such as is induced by the Dutch and Swedish enacted carbon tax. Note that even at this valuation, which is more than 6 times the Nordhaus medium estimate valuation, a sink policy remains infeasible for some rainforests (Zaire, India) because their "window of history" is already closed. The equilibrium transfer payments suggest that even at a benefit-cost ratio substantially below the fictitious 100:1 ratio (Table 1) the surcharges on incremental costs remain hefty (ranging between 20% [Venezuela] and 280% [Columbia]). The results also suggest that despite the redistribution thereby induced the Swedish and Dutch governments pursue on the margin an extremely inefficient climate policy. As the $x_0/V_0$ values show, replacing the Dutch and Swedish carbon tax by buying into carbon sinks (where it is feasible) would permit $CO_2$ emmission abatement at costs which range between only 2% (Bolivia) and 13% (Mexico) of those which are actually borne at home.

8. (Table 3.) The values (in years) for $T$ suggest that even at the relatively high valuation of $4,500/ha time to strike an agreement is quickly running out for some rainforests. In view of 5, this is less troublesome for those rainforests which would be relatively expensive to protect in terms of $x_0/V_0$ (e.g., Indonesian rainforest in the case of Table 3, due to large incremental costs and a large rate of decline). The possibility

of forever forsaking an agreement within a few decades, however, causes concern in the case of rainforests which could be bought into at relatively little cost.

9. (Table 3.) Comparing $x_0/V_0$ values for individual countries across the range between \$4,500/ha and the high CBO estimate of \$10,000/ha (not reported here) suggests that the relative efficiency gains from carbon sequestration are rather insentive to variations in the willingness to pay. For example, the efficiency gain of investing in the Brazilian forest remains almost constant at around the 96% level.

## Appendix

PROOF. Proposition 1: Given Lemma 2 the proof is established if $a \in \,]-1, 1[$ is sufficient for $dx_0/dV_0 > 0$ as from Lemma 1 $dT^*/dV_0 > 0$. For $g = 0 \vee p = 1$ it follows from (5′) that

$$dx_0/dV_0 = \partial x_0/\partial V_0 + (\partial x_0/\partial T^*)(\partial T^*/\partial V_0). \tag{A1}$$

From (5′), $\partial x_0/\partial V_0 > 0$ if $T^* > 0$. Hence it is sufficient for $dx_0/dV_0 > 0$ that $\partial x_0/\partial T^* \geqslant 0$. Using (13″) it follows from (5′) that $\partial x_0/\partial T^* \geqslant 0$ if

$$e^{[(1-a)-hk(1-a^2)/2]T^*} \geqslant h(1-k)/(1-a)\psi. \tag{A2}$$

From (13″) we can replace the denominator on the RHS of (A2) by $\max[(1 - ka)/k, (1 - h)/h]$. From this it follows that the RHS of (A2) is smaller than 1. Therefore sufficient for $\partial x_0/\partial T^* > 0$ is $(1 - a) - hk(1 - a^2)/2 \geqslant 0$, for which it suffices that $(1 - a)/(1 - a^2) \geqslant 1/2$ as $hk \in \,]0, 1[$. This fulfilled if $a \in \,]-1, 1[$.

PROOF. Corollary 2: From the definitions of $\gamma$ and $\phi(\gamma)$, $x_0 - S = [\phi(\gamma) - \gamma]V_0$. We have $\phi(\gamma) - \gamma < 1$ as $\phi(\gamma) < 1$, or else $B$ would lose from the bargaining equilibrium compared to non-cooperation. Also $\phi(\gamma) - \gamma \geqslant 0$ if $g = 0 \vee p = 1$ follows from Lemma 2 and Proposition 1, from which $\phi(\gamma)/\gamma \geqslant 1$.

PROOF. Proposition 3: From Theorem 1, (6′) and (7′),

$$dx_0/da = \partial x_0/\partial a + (\partial x_0/\partial T^*)(\partial T^*/\partial a). \tag{A3}$$

From the proof of Proposition 1, $\partial x_0/\partial T^* > 0$ if $g = 0 \vee p = 1$, Let $\psi = \psi(a)$. From (13″)

$$\partial T^*/\partial a = [T - \psi(a)/\psi(a)]/(1-a), \tag{A4}$$

where

$$\psi'(a)/\psi(a) = (1/1-a)\begin{bmatrix}(1-k)/1-ka \\ 1\end{bmatrix} \quad \text{if} \quad \psi = \begin{bmatrix}(1-h)/h(1-a) \\ (1-ka)/k(1-a)\end{bmatrix}. \tag{A5}$$

From (13″),

$$T^* = -\ln[(S/V_0)\psi]/(1-a). \tag{A6}$$

Substituting (A5) and (A6) in (A4) gives

$$\lim_{a\to 1} \partial T^*/\partial a = -\left(\lim_{a\to 1}(1/1-a)^2\right)\left[\ln\left(\gamma \lim_{a\to 1} \psi(\alpha)\right)+1\right].$$

As from (13″) $\lim_{a\to 1} \psi(a) = \infty$ it follows $\lim_{a\to 1} \partial T^*/\partial a = -\infty$.

Finally from (5′) $\lim_{a\to 1} \partial x_0/\partial a$ is finite (and negative) if $g = 0 \vee p = 1$. Hence from (A3) $\lim_{a\to 1} dx_0/da = -\infty$.

PROOF. Proposition 4: For $g = 1$, $a = p$, $h = k$, (5′) simplifies to

$$x_0 = S(1-h)/(1-h^2)\left[1-e^{-(1-h^2)T^*/2}\right]+e^{-(1-h^2)T^*/2}x_{T^*} \qquad \text{(A7)}$$

and the three regimes in (13′) converge such that $T^*$ is determined by

$$e^{-(1-a)T^*}(V_0/S) = (1-ha)/2h(1-a). \qquad \text{(A8)}$$

As regimes disappear, $x_T^R = x_T^B$. Using this we can replace $x_{T^*}$ in (A7) by (7′), letting $h = k$. Upon using (A8), (A7) simplifies to yield

$$x_0 = S\left[(1-h)/(1-h^2) - e^{-(1-h^2)T^*/2}\left((1-h)/(1-h^2)-1/2\right)\right]. \qquad \text{(A9)}$$

For $h < 1$, $(1 - h)/(1 - h^2) > 1/2$ and hence $dx_0/dT^* > 0$ if $h < 1$. Also from (A9), $x_0 = S/2$ if $T^* = 0$. Hence $x_0 > S/2$ if $T^* > 0$.

PROOF. Corollary 4: $\lim_{a\to 1}(1 - h)/(1 - h^2) = 1/2$. Hence from (A9) $\lim_{a\to 1} x_0 = S/2$.

## References


Amelung, Torsten, and Markus Diehl, *Deforestation of Tropical Rain Forests*, Tübingen: J.C.B. Mohr, 1992.

Ausubel, Lawrence M., and Raymond J. Deneckere, "Bargaining and the Right to Remain Silent," *Econometrica* 60 (1992):597–625.

Binmore, Kenneth, "Perfect Equilibria in Bargaining Models," in Kenneth Binmore and Partha Dasgupta, *The Economics of Bargaining*, Oxford: Blackwell, 1987.

Birdsall, Nancy, and Andrew Steer, "Act Nor on Global Warming—But Don't Cook the Books," *Finance and Development* 30 (1993):6–8.

Cline, William, "Scientific Basis for the Greenhouse Effect," *Economic Journal* 101 (1991):904–19.

Cline, William, *Economics of Global Warming*, Washington D.C.: Institute for International Economics, 1992.

Enquete Commission, *Protecting the Earth's Atmosphere: An International Challenge*, Bonn: Dt. Bundestag, 1989.

Melillo, J.M., C.A. Palm, R.A. Houghton, G.M. Woodwell, and N. Myers, "A Comparison of Two Recent Estimates of Disturbances in Tropical Forests", Environmental Conservation 12 (1985):37–40.

Nordhaus, William, "To Slow or Not to Slow," *Economic Journal* 101 (1991):920–37.

Pezzey, John, "Economic Analysis of Sustainable Growth and Sustainable Development," Environment Department Working Paper no. 15, World Bank, March 1989.

Rubinstein, Ariel, "Perfect Equilibrium in a Bargaining Model," *Econometrica* 50 (1982):97–109.

Schneider, Robert, "The Potential for Trade with the Amazon in Greenhouse Gas Reduction," Latin America Technical Department LATEN Dissemination Note # 2, World Bank, April 1993.

Ståhl, Ingolf, *Bargaining Theory*, Stockholm: EFI, 1972.

Sutton, John, "Non-Cooperative Bargaining Theory: An Introduction", *Review of Economic Studies* 53 (1986):709–24.
Swanson, Timothy, *The International Regulation of Extinction*, London: Macmillan, 1994.
World Bank, *World Development Report 1992*, New York: Oxford University Press, 1992.
World Resources Institute, *World Resources*, New York: Oxford University Press, 1990.

## Notes

1. Empirically one might expect $S$ to depend on the remaining stock, where the functional relationship is not necessarily monotone. To sustain a large stock it may suffice to patrol the area (to prevent trespass) needing the fewer patrolmen the smaller the resource. A small stock may require additional nursing, becoming more intensive the smaller the stock.
2. In the application (Section 7) a precise interpretation of this assumption is given for the case of carbon sequestration.
3. For the solution algorithm described below the assumption of a constant $S$ is innocuous. To see this note that for a finite $T^*$ to exist it is sufficient that the rate of decline of total period services for the free rider eventually exceeds the rate of decline of costs per period. A simple way to represent this is to take $S$ constant.
4. Formally, nonexistence is implied by $T < 0$. Economically $T < 0$ means that in $t = 0$ the value of the resource's service is already too small to warrant its protection at period costs $S$. Note that this can be either due to a small stock of the resource or alternatively due to a small price of the service's perfect substitute.
5. The party which is more impatient (in terms of $h$ and $k$) turns silent earlier.
6. There are two equilibria in this case irrespective of which party can move first. The first equilibrium involves $B$ making a proposal (in $t = 0$ or $t = 1$), given by (6), where $T^*$ is replaced by $t = 0$ or $t = 1$. The second involves $R$ making a proposal, in either $t = 0$ or $t = 1$, given by (7), where $T^*$ is replaced by $t = 0$ or $t = 1$.
7. The intuition for the restriction is that for a rate of decline going to infinity the strategically exploitable "window of history" necessarily vanishes.
8. With the exception of Bangladesh and New Guinea for reasons given below.
9. Because of its vulnerability to a sea level rise we have excluded Bangladesh from the calculations.
10. For a discussion of different approaches see Cline (1992, pp. 220–21).
11. It is sometimes argued that the destruction of forests is to a considerable degree due to free access, suggesting that the purchase of land does not prevent destruction. However, Swanson (1994) has convincingly argued that the property rights regime cannot be considered exogenous from the returns on natural capital and the simulations suggest that these returns will substantially increase in the wake of negotiations, thus creating an enclosure incentive.
12. Schneider lists different land prices for different Brasilian provinces. He bases his own cost-benefit analysis of investing in the Brasilian carbon sink on the relatively high price of \$150/ha of forest in the Rondonia region.
13. The land price for New Guinean forest thus induced is prohibitively high thus making negotiations on its preservation impossible. New Guinea is therefore excluded.
14. This is the net release used by Schneider (1993).
15. See note 4.

[26]

ELSEVIER

Ecological Economics 10 (1994) 221–232

ECOLOGICAL ECONOMICS



# An open economy model of the effects of unilateral environmental policy by a large developing country

Amitrajeet A. Batabyal *

*Department of Agricultural and Resource Economics, 207 Giannini Hall, University of California, Berkeley, CA 94720, USA*

(Received 19 January 1993; accepted 8 July 1993)

**Abstract**

In this paper, we pose the following question. Why is it that despite the universal recognition of the need for global environmental protection, developing countries have been lax in instituting stringent environmental regulations? Addressing this question from an economic standpoint, we show that there are plausible theoretical circumstances in which a large developing country can be worse off if it chooses to implement environmental policy in an uncoordinated fashion. The empirical dimension of this question is stressed and the key parameters – such as elasticities and marginal propensities to consume – which are germane to any policy discussion regarding this issue are identified. Second, we study – once again from the perspective of a large developing country – the possibility of using the domestic tax structure optimally to attain environmental policy objectives in a second-best environment. This scenario involves taxing pollution indirectly, by using product taxes. Finally, keeping the empirical dimension of the question in mind, we show how to compute optimal externality correcting taxes. These taxes are primarily a function of different kinds of elasticities.

*Key words:* Developing country; Environmental policy; Trade

## 1. Introduction

In most developing countries the process of significant policy formation is invariably a long, drawn out, arduous tug-of-war between politicians, businesses and various special interest groups. Given this situation, the fact that the policy response in developing countries to some of the leading issues of the day has been slow – if not absent – is not surprising. What is surprising – given the inherent economic dimension to most of the leading issues of the day – is the dearth of adequate economic explanations as to why this process of policy formation, particularly unilateral policy formation, is lethargic.

The western world's zeal in convincing developing countries to protect the global environment by enacting stringent environmental controls of their own is well known. Some of the larger developing countries such as Brazil, China and India have often been on the receiving end of this developed country zeal regarding environmental protection. For instance, tales of the potential

* Corresponding author. Present address; Department of Economics, College of William and Mary, Williamsburg, VA 23187, USA.

0921-8009/94/$07.00 
*SSDI* 0921-8009(93)E0071-N

catastrophic environmental consequences of rain forest destruction in the Amazon basin are legion. However, despite this great interest in environmental issues, particularly in the developed world, laws in developing countries enacted with the specific intention of controlling environmental degradation have been slow in coming. For example, in India until 1976 "...environment protection as such *did not figure anywhere* in the Constitution" (Danida, 1989, p. 21, emphasis added). It was only after the highly publicized industrial disaster involving Union Carbide at Bhopal that the first serious attempt at controlling environmental pollution was made by way of enacting the Environment (Protection) Act of 1986 (Danida, 1989).

Typically, explanations as to why the unilateral policy response to such issues is slow have focused on political-economic arguments. In this paper, we address this question from an economic standpoint. We study two aspects of this issue that have received scant attention to date. In Section 2, we construct a simple two-factor, two-good, two-country static model of the effects of unilateral environmental controls as embodied in a pollution tax – which takes the form of a production tax – on the polluting good. We find that theoretically plausible circumstances exist in which a large developing country (hereafter LDC) can make itself worse off with the unilateral imposition of environmental controls. Thus if it is indeed true that a LDC such as India can make itself worse off by its own unilateral policies, then it stands to reason that governments in such LDCs are not likely to be very keen on instituting environmental policies unilaterally. Indeed, such countries can be expected to demand that environmental policies be coordinated by *all* countries and be instituted multilaterally. Motivated by these findings, in Section 3 we pose the following question: Suppose that the multilateral institution of environmental policies involving all countries is unlikely, and also suppose that the LDC in question is precluded by institutions such as the GATT from using any direct trade instruments to benefit from its market power in trade. In such a scenario, can a LDC use its *domestic* product tax structure to correct for the externality *and* capture some of the concomitant trade gains arising from the fact that it has market power in the world? Clearly, these are two different objectives. The idea here is to determine whether it is possible for the LDC government to attain two targets with a single instrument. We answer the above question in the affirmative and derive a closed form expression for an optimal pollution tax and show that such a tax is always positive if the polluting good is the export good, but not necessarily positive if the polluting good is the import good. The intuitive reason as to why this is so is that when the polluting good is the export good, the two effects that the tax captures, i.e., the trade effect and the pollution effect, both work in the same direction. However, when the polluting good is the import good, the trade effect and the pollution effect work in opposite directions. Finally, in Section 4 we review our salient findings.

Previous researchers have studied questions tangentially related to ours. On the empirical [1] front, in an early paper d'Arge and Kneese (1972) left the question of the effects of unilateral environmental controls open. Focusing principally on the income effects of environmental policies, they showed that positive income effects resulted for all countries being studied irrespective of whether environmental controls were instituted unilaterally or multilaterally. In another empirical study, Walter (1973, p. 68) came to the tentative conclusion that "...U.S. trade [would] be affected if the world's nations [adopted] different environmental standards and/or ways of implementing such standards." In a rather comprehensive empirical study of the effects of unilateral environmental controls primarily in the USA manufacturing sector, Leonard (1984) found little support for the industrial flight hypothesis. [2] Similarly, Tobey (1990) has shown that the adoption of stringent environmental controls does not per se weaken a nation's comparative advantage in trade. On the

---

[1] Most of the empirical studies known to me appear to have focused on one developed country, namely the USA.

[2] Related issues such as transboundary pollution and the institution of multilateral policy have been studied by McGuire (1982) and Merrifield (1988).

other hand, Whalley (1991, p. 188) has argued that if "...indeed global policy responses to [environmental concerns such as] global warming are enacted, the consequences for ... patterns of trade between regions, are likely to be severe." As this brief review of the empirical literature shows, a consensus on the empirical effects of environmental controls is yet to be achieved. The theoretical literature is more uniform in its findings. Pethig (1976) and Asako (1979) have both demonstrated that under certain conditions, when a nation's pollution-intensive good is exported, increased trade can diminish that country's welfare. In a somewhat different vein, McGuire (1982) has shown that in an open economy with factor mobility across countries, unilateral environmental regulation can drive the regulating country out of producing the regulated good. The issue of the institution of unilateral environmental regulations by developed countries has been studied by Batabyal (1990). He has shown that the question of potential welfare loss is really an empirical question and has identified the relevant policy parameters.

Given the inherent strategic element to the issues that we are analyzing, it should be noted that in recent times there have been a number of game theoretic analyses of these questions. Many of the germane issues have been discussed in Pethig (1992) and Batabyal (1993a). [3]

With regard to the second question we have posed, the problem of optimal open economy, second-best taxation of an externality has been almost entirely neglected in the environmental economics and development economics literature. This despite the increasing awareness that "...the 1990s may see a growing use of trade measures to achieve objectives set for environmental policies" (Whalley, 1991, p. 180). However, there does exist a small literature in international economics which has addressed itself to this issue. Friedlaender and Vandendorpe (1968) and Dornbusch (1971) have considered the second-best taxation problem and derived expressions for the optimal consumption and production tax for an economy with some market power in trade, but with no externality. Vandendorpe (1972) has extended the two-good results of Friedlaender and Vandendorpe (1968) to the $n$-good case, again without externalities. Markusen (1975) has considered the problem of optimal taxation with international externalities. However, Markusen's characterization of the optimal tax expressions is in terms of variables which are difficult to interpret empirically. Further, a number of his results are ambiguously signed. As we shall show later in this paper, when the polluting good is the export good, our pollution tax is unambiguously positive. Since we believe that the question of the effects of unilateral environmental controls is essentially an empirical one, we characterize our tax in terms of elasticities and marginal propensities to consume, to the extent possible. It is hoped that such a characterization will explicitly highlight the variables which are most relevant for policy discussions regarding this issue. The results of Section 3 can be viewed as a natural extension of this research on optimal second-best taxation to the case where the two-country international economy is now characterized by a domestic externality.

## 2. The open economy model

### 2.1. Assumptions

First, the two countries produce two different final goods, $E$ and $I$, both of which are traded and can be substituted. Second, the two factors of production, capital and labor, are supplied inelastically by consumers and not traded. Third, $E$ is the export good of the large developing country (hereafter LDC), and $I$ is the export good of the other country (hereafter OC). The production of $E$ in LDC gives rise to a pure production externality, namely pollution, which is domestic in nature. Fourth, the production externality does not affect production decisions in LDC. However, this externality does enter the utility functions of consumers in LDC in an additively separable manner. Fifth, within LDC and OC, all con-

[3] For more on this, see the references in Pethig (1992) and in Batabyal (1993a).

sumers are identical and all consumers treat $E$ and $I$ as normal goods. Being a large country, LDC possesses some market power in trade. Sixth, the government in LDC distributes the tax proceeds to consumers proportionally in a manner which does not alter the extant income distribution. Finally, OC is assumed not to retaliate in any way against domestic LDC policies which have trade implications. These assumptions are maintained throughout the rest of this paper.

These assumptions are fairly standard in most neoclassical trade models. Since our model is an aggregative model, these assumptions enable us to focus on the variables of interest, i.e., the terms of trade, producer price ratios and national income, without having to worry about less relevant microeconomic variables. Further, as Batabyal (1991) has shown, these kinds of assumptions are important in a practical sense as well since they are often an integral part of computable general equilibrium (CGE) models which are used to quantify the effects of the kinds of policies being analyzed in this paper.

### 2.2. Notation

Superscripts on letters will always refer to the two countries, i.e., LDC and OC. Lower case letters will always refer to demand relationships for the two goods. Uppercase letters will always refer to supply/production relationships. The letter $t$ will refer to the pollution tax, which takes the form of a production tax. The letter $P$ refers to the terms of trade of LDC. $\nabla$ refers to the Balance of Payments condition. $\beta$ refers to the marginal rate of transformation between $E$ and $I$ in LDC. $Z^{LDC}$ refers to the aggregate level of pollution in the economy of LDC. Functions are denoted by lower case or upper case letters depending on whether the function concerned describes a demand or a supply/production relationship. This system of notation is maintained throughout the remainder of this paper.

### 2.3. Method of analysis

Before proceeding to the model, we outline the method by which we propose to conduct the analysis. Whenever possible, we will attempt to characterize our results in terms of elasticities and marginal propensities to consume. The method of analysis itself is well known in trade theory and has been referred to as the "method of comparative statics" by Mundell (1960, 1968) and as the "Samuelsonian two stage derivation" by Bhagwati and Srinivasan (1983). The method actually consists of three distinct steps which can be briefly described as follows. Recognizing that a perturbation of one of the equilibrium values of a variable produces a Balance of Payments disequilibrium for one and hence both countries, in the first step, we compute the excess demand for the export good, holding the terms of trade constant. In the second step, we determine the excess supply for LDC's export good caused by the actual change in the terms of trade. Finally, in the third step, we equate excess demand with excess supply to obtain the condition which characterizes the effect of the parameter change on the variable of interest, which often enough is the terms of trade. [4] In Section 3, we shall use this method to derive a closed form expression for the optimal pollution tax.

### 2.4. Description of the model

Our model is derived from the classical $2 \times 2 \times 2$ model of international trade theory. In what follows, we proceed as in Bhagwati and Srinivasan (1983, appendix C). The two-country economic system is characterized by the following functional relationships:

$$D^{OC} = P \cdot e^{OC} + i^{OC} \equiv P \cdot E^{OC} + I^{OC} \quad \text{and} \qquad (1)$$

$$D^{LDC} = e^{LDC} + (1/P) \cdot i^{LDC} \equiv E^{LDC} + (1/P) \cdot I^{LDC} \qquad (2)$$

[4] Briefly, the method can be illustrated as follows. Suppose that the equilibrium governing a particular system is given by the relationship $g(v,w) = f(w)$ where $v$ is a parameter. Then to determine $dw/dv$, we proceed as follows:
Step 1: Holding $w$ constant, excess $g$ is $(\partial g/\partial v)\,dv$.
Step 2: Excess $f$ due to the change in $w$ is $[(\partial f/\partial w) - (\partial g/\partial w)]\,dw$.
Step 3: Equating excess $g$ to excess $f$, we have $dw/dv = [\partial g/\partial v]/[(\partial f/\partial w) - (\partial g/\partial w)]$.

which tell us that total domestic expenditure in OC and LDC equals national income.

$$e^{OC} = a(D^{OC}, P); \quad (3)$$

$$i^{OC} = b(D^{OC}, 1/P). \quad (4)$$

The demand for $E$ and $I$ in OC depends on national income and the terms of trade.

$$e^{LDC} = c(D^{LDC}, P); \quad (5)$$

$$i^{LDC} = d(D^{LDC}, 1/P). \quad (6)$$

The demand for $E$ and $I$ in LDC depends on national income and the terms of trade.

$$I^{LDC} = M(E^{LDC}). \quad (7)$$

This is the equation of the production possibility frontier in LDC. [5]

$$I^{OC} = F(1/P); \quad (8)$$

$$E^{OC} = G(P). \quad (9)$$

The production of $I$ and $E$ in OC depends on the terms of trade.

$$I^{LDC} = H(1/P); \quad (10)$$

$$E^{LDC} = J(P). \quad (11)$$

The production of $I$ and $E$ in LDC depends on the terms of trade.

$$\nabla = P \cdot (e^{OC} - E^{OC}) = i^{LDC} - I^{LDC}. \quad (12)$$

The Balance of Payments *equilibrium* condition.

$$U^{LDC} = \Omega(i^{LDC}, e^{LDC}) + C(Z^{LDC}). \quad (13)$$

The aggregate utility index of LDC is an additive function of total final good consumption, i.e., $i^{LDC}$, $e^{LDC}$ and the aggregate level of pollution in the economy. $Z^{LDC}$ is itself a function of the total production of $E$, i.e., $Z^{LDC} = S(E^{LDC})$. We assume that $\partial\Omega/\partial i^{LDC} > 0$, $\partial\Omega/\partial e^{LDC} > 0$, $dC/dZ^{LDC} < 0$ and that $dS/dE^{LDC} > 0$. Observe that in writing Eqs. 8–11 we have implicitly assumed that Eq. 7 is satisfied simultaneously.

Since we wish to characterize our results in terms of elasticities, it will be convenient to define five separate trade demand functions. To this end, let

$$\phi^{OC} \equiv e^{OC} - E^{OC} = k(D^{OC}, P) \quad (14)$$

be the import demand function for $E$ in OC. This depends on total domestic expenditure and the terms of trade. Define

$$\phi^{LDC} \equiv i^{LDC} - I^{LDC} = l(D^{LDC}, 1/P) \quad (15)$$

to be the import demand function for $I$ in LDC. Import demand for $I$ in LDC depends on total domestic expenditure and the terms of trade. Let

$$\theta^{OC} \equiv -\phi^{LDC} = y(D^{LDC}, 1/P) \quad (16)$$

be the "offer" function of OC. This function depends on total domestic expenditure in LDC and the terms of trade. Define

$$\psi^{LDC} \equiv e^{LDC} - E^{LDC} = u(D^{LDC}, P) \quad (17)$$

to be the function which tells us that total imports from LDC to OC depend on total domestic expenditure in LDC and the terms of trade. Let

$$\psi^{OC} \equiv -\psi^{LDC} = v(D^{LDC}, P) \quad (18)$$

be the function which tells us that total exports from LDC to OC depend on total domestic expenditure in LDC and the terms of trade. Finally, for subsequent convenience, write Eq. 12 as

$$\nabla = \phi^{LDC} - P \cdot \phi^{OC} = l(D^{LDC}, 1/P) - P \cdot k(D^{OC}, P). \quad (19)$$

### 2.5. Stability

Although stability is not the centerpiece of our analysis, it forms an important part of the analysis in two ways. First, it is nonsensical to apply comparative statics methods to unstable economies. Second, by Samuelson's (1947, p. 258) correspondence principle, much useful information can be gained by a study of the stability condition of the aforementioned two-country system. Stability conditions can be derived in a number of different ways. For our purposes, we differentiate Eq. 19 w.r.t. $P$ and write the stability condition as [6]

$$\frac{d\nabla}{dP} = \phi \cdot [\varepsilon^{LDC} + \varepsilon^{OC} - 1], \quad (20)$$

[5] It is assumed that $dM/dE^{LDC} < 0$ and that $\beta = -dM/dE^{LDC}$.

[6] Mundell (1960, pp. 72–73).

where $\varepsilon^{LDC} > 0$ is the elasticity of demand for imports in LDC and $\varepsilon^{OC} > 0$ is the elasticity of demand for imports in OC.

The stability condition tells us that a change in the Balance of Payments condition due to a small change in the terms of trade can be expressed as a linear combination of the initial equilibrium level of imports ($\phi$) and the elasticities of import demand for LDC and OC, respectively. Intuitively, stability requires that the excess demand for a good decreases when its price increases. In this case, stability requires that a decline in OC's (LDC's) terms of trade improve OC's (LDC's) trade balance. Thus our two-country system is stable if and only if $\mathrm{d}\nabla/\mathrm{d}P = \phi[\varepsilon^{LDC} + \varepsilon^{OC} - 1] > 0$. From this it follows that stability requires

$$\varepsilon^{LDC} + \varepsilon^{OC} > 1. \tag{21}$$

This is the well-known elasticity criterion for stability, sometimes also known as the Marshall–Lerner criterion.

In what follows, we assume that our two-country system is stable. It is important to note that Eq. 20 provides us with the coefficient for a change in the terms of trade. This fact will be used later in determining the economic effects of a pollution tax imposed by LDC.

### 2.6. The effects of a pollution tax

Recall that LDC imposes a pollution tax on the manufacturers of $E$. The tax itself can be levied on a number of variables. It can be levied on gross emissions, in which case we would have to work with a pollution emission function. The tax can be levied on net emissions, an approach which assumes that the $E$ industry in LDC already has pollution abatement facilities available. In this case, we would have to add a pollution abatement and a pollution emission function to our model. Finally, the tax can be levied on the actual production of $E$. This approach gets at the problem indirectly, but has the important advantage of being the simplest to implement practically. Further, this approach is most in keeping with what is likely to be true in most developing countries. That is, while the government would like to regulate pollution by means of the first or second approaches, it typically does not have the information available to do so. Faut de mieux, the government levies a production tax on the manufacturers of $E$. The pollution tax introduces a discrepancy in the prices seen by producers in LDC and all other prices. Thus there is a direct effect and an indirect effect of the pollution tax. The direct effect consists of the *negative price effect* on producers of $E$ in LDC. The indirect effect consists of the *positive income effect* on consumers due to the disbursement of the tax proceeds.

We now distinguish between prices in LDC and OC by denoting them by $P^{LDC}$ and $P^{OC}$, respectively. To obtain the direct effect of the pollution tax on the LDC terms of trade, we first compute the excess demand for $E$ at constant terms of trade. This is given by

$$-\gamma^{LDC}E^{LDC}\,\mathrm{d}t, \tag{22}$$

where $\gamma$ is the elasticity of supply of $E$ in LDC and $\mathrm{d}t$ is the small tax that has been placed on the polluting good. The negative sign follows from the fact that the $E$ production response to the tax is negative.

To Eq. 22 we must now add the positive income effect of the tax. The increased demand for $E$ in LDC is given by

$$r^{LDC}E^{LDC}\,\mathrm{d}t, \tag{23}$$

where $r^{LDC} \in (0,1)$ and $r^{LDC}$ is the marginal propensity to spend income on the home good in LDC.

Thus the total excess demand for $E$ due to the tax is given by adding Eqs. 22 and 23. This yields

$$(r^{LDC} - \gamma^{LDC}) \cdot E^{LDC}\,\mathrm{d}t. \tag{24}$$

We now have to determine the excess supply of $E$ as a result of the actual change in the terms of trade, which has been held constant so far. As has been mentioned earlier, this excess supply is given by the stability condition. It should be noted that $P$ in Eq. 20 is now $P^{LDC}$. Thus the excess supply for $E$ due to the change in $P^{LDC}$ is

$$\phi \cdot (\varepsilon^{LDC} + \varepsilon^{OC} - 1)\,\mathrm{d}P^{LDC}. \tag{25}$$

We equate Eqs. 24 and 25 to obtain

$$\frac{dP^{LDC}}{dt} = \frac{(r^{LDC} - \gamma^{LDC}) \cdot E^{LDC}}{\phi \cdot (\varepsilon^{LDC} + \varepsilon^{OC} - 1)}. \quad (26)$$

Thus we observe that

$$\frac{dP^{LDC}}{dt} > 0 \Leftrightarrow r^{LDC} > \gamma^{LDC}. \quad (27)$$

In other words, the terms of trade of LDC improve as a result of the tax if and only if the positive income effect outweighs the negative price effect.

A pollution tax which takes the form of a production tax on $E$ decreases the production of $E$ and increases the production of $I$. This can be expected to increase the relative price of the taxed good. Thus, intuitively we would expect that $dP^{LDC}/dt > 0$, but as Eq. 27 shows, in a terms of trade sense, LDC can make itself *worse off* by levying a pollution tax unilaterally. Specifically, we can expect this to happen if the supply of $E$ in LDC is highly price elastic and a relatively small marginal proportion of an income increase is spent on it.

To determine the effect of the pollution tax on the domestic LDC producer price ratio, we proceed as follows. Observe that the price seen by $E$ producers in LDC is $[P^{OC}/(1+t)]$. Differentiating this expression w.r.t. $t$ we have

$$\frac{d[P^{OC}/(1+t)]}{dt} = P^{OC} \cdot \left[-1 \cdot (1+t)^{-2} \cdot (1)\right] + \frac{1}{1+t} \cdot \frac{dP^{OC}}{dt}.$$

Letting $P^{OC} = 1$ by appropriate choice of units and letting $t = 0$, assuming initial free trade, the above expression reduces to

$$\frac{d[P^{OC}/(1+t)]}{dt} = -1 + \frac{dP^{OC}}{dt}. \quad (28)$$

Now assuming stability and that $dP^{OC}/dt < 0$, we observe that the LDC $E$ producer price ratio declines, i.e., Eq. 28 is negative. Since $P^{LDC} = 1/P^{OC}$, the $dP^{OC}/dt < 0$ assumption is actually a "no immiserization" assumption. In effect we are assuming that the pollution tax does not make LDC worse off, i.e., Eq. 27 is positive. The negativity of Eq. 28 makes intuitive sense since we would expect that $E$ producers decrease production as a result of the pollution tax owing to a decline in the producer price of their final output. However, if $dP^{OC}/dt > 0$, then it is possible that the pollution tax might actually *increase* the production of $E$ in LDC.

Before concluding this section, we wish to compute the effect of the pollution tax on national income in LDC. To do this, we will use a method known to economists at least since Meade (1955). The method illustrates how the aggregate level of pollution in the LDC economy explicitly affects some of our results. The method consists of differentiating Eq. 13 totally and then denoting the change in national income, i.e., $dD^{LDC}$, by $dU^{LDC}/U_i$ where $U_i$ is the marginal utility of $I$ in LDC. Note that this concept of national income is environmentally adjusted. As such, it is not the usual concept of national income. More informally, in this process, we are decomposing the change in national income due to the tax into its constituent components. Differentiating Eq. 13 totally, we have

$$dU^{LDC} = U_i \cdot di^{LDC} + U_e \cdot de^{LDC} + Z_1 \cdot dZ^{LDC}, \quad (29)$$

where $U_i$, $U_e$ denote the marginal utility of $I$ and $E$ and $Z_1$ denotes the marginal disutility of pollution. Dividing the left-hand side and the right-hand side of Eq. 29 by $U_i$ yields

$$dD^{LDC} \equiv dU^{LDC}/U_i = di^{LDC} + \alpha \cdot de^{LDC} + Z_2 \cdot dZ^{LDC}, \quad (30)$$

where $\alpha$ is the marginal rate of substitution of $E$ for $I$ and $Z_2$ denotes the marginal social rate of substitution between pollution and $I$.

Since $i^{LDC} = I^{LDC} - \theta^{OC}$, $e^{LDC} = E^{LDC} - \psi^{OC}$ and since $\alpha = P^{LDC} = P^{OC} = P$ in the initial equilibrium, we can write Eq. 30 as

$$dD^{LDC} = [dI^{LDC} + P^{LDC} \cdot dE^{LDC}] - [d\theta^{OC} + P^{LDC} \cdot d\psi^{OC}] + Z_2 \cdot dZ^{LDC}. \quad (31)$$

This tells us that a small change in national income from the initial equilibrium can be expressed as the sum of a production effect, a trade effect and a pollution effect.

In order to express Eq. 31 in a more convenient form, we note that Eq. 1 can be expressed as $P \cdot (e^{OC} - E^{OC}) \equiv I^{OC} - i^{OC}$. This in turn can be expressed as $P \cdot \psi^{OC} \equiv -\theta^{OC}$. Totally differentiating this last expression and using Eq. 7, we get

$$\mathrm{d}D^{LDC} = \left[P^{LDC} - \beta\right] \cdot \mathrm{d}E^{LDC} + \psi^{OC} \cdot \mathrm{d}P^{LDC} + Z_2 \cdot \mathrm{d}Z^{LDC}. \qquad (32)$$

Now the change in the production of $E$ due to the imposition of the pollution tax, i.e., $\mathrm{d}E^{LDC}$, is given by $-\gamma^{LDC}E^{LDC}\mathrm{d}t$. Using $Z^{LDC} = S(E^{LDC})$, dividing the left-hand side and right-hand side of Eq. 32 by $\mathrm{d}t$ and substituting for $\mathrm{d}P^{LDC}/\mathrm{d}t$ from Eq. 26 yields

$$\frac{\mathrm{d}D^{LDC}}{\mathrm{d}t} = \frac{[\{(P^{LDC} - \beta) \cdot \gamma^{LDC} \cdot E^{LDC}\} \cdot \{\phi(\varepsilon^{LDC} + \varepsilon^{LDC} - 1)\}]}{\phi \cdot (\varepsilon^{LDC} + \varepsilon^{OC} - 1)} + \frac{\psi^{OC} \cdot (r^{LDC} - \gamma^{LDC}) \cdot E^{LDC}}{\phi \cdot (\varepsilon^{LDC} + \varepsilon^{OC} - 1)} - \frac{\left[Z_2 \cdot \gamma^{LDC} \cdot E^{LDC}\left\{\frac{\mathrm{d}S}{\mathrm{d}E^{LDC}}\right\}\{\phi \cdot (\varepsilon^{LDC} + \varepsilon^{OC} - 1)\}\right]}{\phi \cdot (\varepsilon^{LDC} + \varepsilon^{OC} - 1)}. \qquad (33)$$

This is an important relation. It tells us that the change in national income in LDC due to a small change in the tax rate is given by a combination of three distinct effects. The first term in the right-hand side of Eq. 33 refers to the $E$ production effect and is negative in sign. The second term refers to the terms of trade effect, which is assumed to be positive. Finally, the third term refers to the pollution effect; this is positive.

Thus we observe that LDC will be better off from the imposition of a small pollution tax provided that the sum of the terms of trade effect and the pollution effect outweighs the negative $E$ production effect. In theory, however, once again we note that LDC can make itself *worse off* by instituting a pollution tax unilaterally. The variables which are germane to a resolution of this question of national welfare change are expressed in Eq. 33.

## 3. A characterization of the optimal pollution tax

### 3.1. Motivation

In Section 2 we observed that from a theoretical standpoint, a large developing country could make itself worse off by conducting environmental policy unilaterally. Specifically, when the production of the polluting good is taxed, there are trade effects which cannot reasonably be ignored by the government of LDC.

Suppose that the LDC government is not permitted to capture any trade gains by virtue of its market power in the world by setting a tariff or any other tariff equivalent policy. [7] What steps can the LDC government take to manipulate the terms of trade in its favor by using the domestic tax structure? In this section we address this particular question. We find that the government can use its market power in trade to set an optimal pollution tax on the production of the export good, i.e., $E$. In this context, optimal means that the tax is based on explicitly maximizing the aggregate LDC utility index subject to certain constraints, with the maintained assumption that there is no retaliation from OC. Further, all possible economy wide effects of pollution are taken into account in the determination of the tax.

### 3.2. Derivation of the optimal pollution tax

The model that we shall use to derive the optimal pollution tax is essentially the same as the model used in Section 2. The entire procedure for deriving the pollution tax is based in large part on the Meade method for calculating small changes in national income. [8] In our derivation we will be using Eq. 7 to model the produc-

[7] By tariff equivalent, we mean a policy initiative which in effect has the same result as that of a tariff. An example would be an equal rate tax on the exportable's production and a subsidy on the consumption of the importable.

[8] This method of designating small changes in national income is well known to economists. The method has been used by numerous researchers such as Friedlaender and Vandendorpe (1968), Jones (1969) and Dornbusch (1971).

tion side of the economy. Further, it is important to realize that in the initial equilibrium with no tax, $P = P^{LDC} = P^{OC}$. To derive the optimal pollution tax, we start with Eq. 32. We have

$$dD^{LDC} = (P^{LDC} - \beta) \cdot dE^{LDC} + \psi^{OC} \cdot dP^{LDC} + Z_2 \cdot dZ^{LDC}. \quad (34)$$

The first term on the right-hand side of Eq. 34 reflects the $E$ production effect which arises from the shift in the production of $E$ at constant terms of trade. The second term on the right-hand side of Eq. 34 refers to the change in national income in LDC due to a change in the terms of trade. Finally, the third component on the right-hand side of Eq. 34 refers to the pollution effect. Eq. 34 is identical to an expression obtained by Friedlaender and Vandendorpe (1968, p. 1062) except that the Friedlaender and Vandendorpe expression contains no externality component. Eq. 34 is also similar to Dornbusch's (1971) Eq. 5.

We now follow Friedlaender and Vandendorpe (1968) and Dornbusch (1971) to accomplish our next objective. This involves decomposing the differential of the terms of trade effect on the right-hand side of Eq. 34 in terms of elasticities and marginal propensities to consume. In order to do this, we note that in international equilibrium, it must be true that [9]

$$\phi^{LDC} - P^{LDC} \cdot \psi^{OC} = 0. \quad (35)$$

Writing Eq. 35 as

$$\left[ d\left\{ \left( E^{LDC} + \frac{1}{P^{LDC}} \cdot M(E^{LDC}) \right), \frac{1}{P^{LDC}} \right\} - M(E^{LDC}) \right] - P^{LDC} \cdot k(P^{LDC}) = 0, \quad (36)$$

and recalling that $E^{LDC} + (1/P^{LDC}) \cdot M(E^{LDC}) = D^{LDC}$, we totally differentiate Eq. 36 – holding $D^{OC}$ constant – to obtain the following relation

$$\left[ \frac{\partial d}{\partial D^{LDC}} \cdot \frac{\partial D^{LDC}}{\partial P^{LDC}} + \frac{\partial d}{\partial(1/P^{LDC})} \cdot \frac{d(1/P^{LDC})}{dP^{LDC}} - P^{LDC} \cdot \frac{dk}{dP^{LDC}} - k(P^{LDC}) \right] \cdot dP^{LDC}$$
$$+ \left[ \frac{\partial d}{\partial D^{LDC}} \cdot \frac{\partial D^{LDC}}{\partial E^{LDC}} - \frac{dM}{dE^{LDC}} \right] \cdot dE^{LDC} = 0. \quad (37)$$

Eq. 37 tells us that once the condition for international balance of payments equilibrium has been expressed appropriately, and when all the resulting quantities are allowed to vary simultaneously, the resulting change in international equilibrium can be expressed as the sum of a terms of trade effect and a production effect; both effects arising from the change in the production of $E$.

We will now convert Eq. 37 into another expression which stresses the empirical dimension of the tax by using elasticities and marginal propensities to consume. To this end, let

$$s^{LDC} = (\partial d / \partial D^{LDC}) \cdot (1/P^{LDC}) \quad (38)$$

be the marginal propensity to consume the importable in LDC. Let

$$\partial^{LDC} = [(1/P^{LDC})/\phi^{LDC}] \cdot [\partial d / \partial(1/P^{LDC})] \quad (39)$$

be the incomplete price elasticity of import demand in LDC. Let

$$\xi^{LDC} = I^{LDC}/\phi^{LDC} \quad (40)$$

be the ratio of the aggregate production of the importable to the aggregate quantity of imports demanded by LDC. Finally, let

$$\chi^{OC} = (d\psi^{OC}/dP^{LDC}) \cdot (P^{LDC}/\psi^{OC}) \quad (41)$$

be the price elasticity of imports in OC.

Using Eqs. 35, 38–41 and differentiating the individual terms in Eq. 37, we can rewrite Eq. 37 as follows

$$[s^{LDC} \cdot (P^{LDC} - \beta) + \beta] \cdot dE^{LDC} - \psi^{OC} \cdot [(1 + \chi^{OC}) + (\partial^{LDC} + \xi^{LDC} \cdot s^{LDC})] \cdot dP^{LDC} = 0. \quad (42)$$

[9] Since $e^{OC} - E^{OC} = E^{LDC} - e^{LDC}$ in equilibrium, it is clear that in equilibrium $\psi^{OC} = \phi^{OC}$. Thus we will write $\phi^{OC}$ and $\psi^{OC}$ interchangeably in the remainder of this decomposition procedure. Further, it should be noted that we will supress the $D^{OC}$ argument in the function denoting $\phi^{OC}$, since $D^{OC}$ is held constant in this procedure.

Eq. 42 accomplishes our task of decomposing the differential of the terms of trade effect on the right-hand side of Eq. 42. Eq. 42 says that after a change in the production of $E$, at the new world equilibrium, the excess demand as a result of the change in $E$ production at constant terms of trade must equal the change in the terms of trade when the terms of trade adjusts by $dP^{LDC}$. It should be clear that this is only a minor variation on "the method of comparative statics" that we used in Section 2 to analyze the effects of a small pollution tax.

In our discussion of stability in Section 2, we noted that a decline in LDC's terms of trade must improve LDC's trade balance. Applying the same concept here, we note that stability requires a decrease in the demand for $I$ (the LDC importable) when the price of $I$, $1/P^{LDC}$, increases. Since LDC exports $E$ and imports $I$, in our case stability requires that $[(1+\chi^{OC})+(\partial^{LDC}+\xi^{LDC}\cdot s^{LDC})]<0$.

We can now use our result in Eq. 42 to substitute for $dP^{LDC}$ in Eq. 34 above. Using the fact that

$$dP^{LDC} = \frac{\left[s^{LDC}\cdot(P^{LDC}-\beta)+\beta\right]}{\psi^{OC}\cdot\left[(1+\chi^{OC})+(\partial^{LDC}+\xi^{LDC}\cdot s^{LDC})\right]}\cdot dE^{LDC} \tag{43}$$

and that $Z^{LDC}=S(E^{LDC})$, we can express Eq. 34 as

$$\frac{\left[s^{LDC}\cdot(P^{LDC}-\beta)+\beta\right]}{\left[(1+\chi^{OC})+(\partial^{LDC}+\xi^{LDC}\cdot s^{LDC})\right]} + (P^{LDC}-\beta)+Z_2\cdot\left[\frac{dS}{dE^{LDC}}\right]=0. \tag{44}$$

Letting $[(1+\chi^{OC})+(\partial^{LDC}+\xi^{LDC}\cdot s^{LDC})]\equiv\Gamma<0$ and $dS/dE^{LDC}\equiv\Lambda>0$, we write Eq. 44 as

$$(P^{LDC}-\beta)+\frac{\left[s^{LDC}\cdot(P^{LDC}-\beta)+\beta\right]}{\Gamma} + Z_2\cdot\Lambda=0. \tag{45}$$

To arrive at a closed form expression for the tax, we simplify Eq. 45 and observe that the optimal pollution tax is given by

$$\frac{P^{LDC}-\beta}{\beta}=\frac{-\left[\dfrac{Z_2\cdot\Lambda\cdot\Gamma}{\beta}\right]-1}{s^{LDC}+\Gamma}. \tag{46}$$

We can now state:

**Theorem 1.** *The tax implied by Eq. 46 is positive.*

**Proof.** Since $Z_2<0$, $\Gamma<0$, $\Lambda>0$ and $\beta>0$, the numerator of Eq. 46 is clearly negative. To see that the denominator of Eq. 46 is also negative, let

$$\begin{aligned}\tau &\equiv \partial^{LDC}+\xi^{LDC}\cdot s^{LDC}\\ &= \left[(1/P^{LDC})/\phi^{LDC}\right]\cdot\left[\partial d/\partial(1/P^{LDC})\right]\\ &\quad+\left[I^{LDC}/\phi^{LDC}\right]\cdot\left[\partial d/dD^{LDC}\right]\cdot\left[1/P^{LDC}\right]\end{aligned} \tag{47}$$

from the definitions $\partial^{LDC}$, $\xi^{LDC}$ and $s^{LDC}$, respectively.[10] Now observe that we can express $\tau$ alternately as

$$\begin{aligned}&[(1/P^{LDC})/\phi^{LDC}]\cdot[\{\partial d/\partial(1/P^{LDC})\}\\ &\quad+(\partial d/\partial D^{LDC})\{d(.,.)\}]\\ &\quad-[\{(1/P^{LDC})/\phi^{LDC}\}(\partial d/\partial D^{LDC})\{d(.,.)-I^{LDC}\}],\end{aligned} \tag{48}$$

which is identical to the earlier decomposition. Let the first term of Eq. 48, i.e., the term before the negative sign, equal $\hat{\tau}<0$, the pure substitution effect of $\tau$. The second term of Eq. 48 is, of course, $s^{LDC}$. Thus $\tau=\hat{\tau}-s^{LDC}$ and $\Gamma=(1+\chi^{OC})+(\hat{\tau}-s^{LDC})$.

Since $(P^{LDC}/\beta)=[-\{(Z_2\cdot\Gamma\cdot\Lambda)/\beta\}+\chi^{OC}+\hat{\tau}]/[1+\chi^{OC}+\hat{\tau}]>0$, it follows that $s^{LDC}+\Gamma<0$. *QED.*

---

[10] $\tau$ is the imperfect price elasticity of import demand. The word "imperfect" refers to the fact that in the computation of this elasticity, total production in LDC is held constant. Further, since $\tau$ is a price elasticity, it can always be decomposed into a substitution effect which is negative (strictly speaking nonpositive) and an income effect which is (since $E$ and $I$ have been assumed to be normal goods) positive.

A comparison of Eq. 46 with some previously derived optimal tax expressions in the literature suggests some obvious similarities. Specifically, Eq. 46 is related to eq. 28 of Markusen (1975), to Eq. 9 of Friedlaender and Vandendorpe (1968) and to Eq. 14 of Dornbusch (1971). However, Eq. 46 is most closely related to Markusen's eq. 28, which is his version of the optimal production tax with environmental pollution. Holding $S_2 = 0$ in his Eq. 28 to make our Eq. 46 and his Eq. 28 comparable, we find that both expressions contain a pollution term and a trade effect term. The similarities notwithstanding, we note that as opposed to the motivation underlying this paper, the work of the researchers cited above is motivated by, inter alia, an interest in determining the second-best policy initiatives available to the government of a country with some monopoly power in trade which is precluded from using its first-best policy alternative.

It is of some interest to determine the nature of an optimal tax expression for an externality when the externality is the result of domestic production of the LDC import good. Using a procedure similar to the above, it can be shown that the optimal tax is now not necessarily positive. This result arises from the fact that the $\Lambda$ term in Eq. 46 for the case of an import sector externality is negative. We discuss the policy implications of this fact in the next section.

## 4. Conclusions

In this paper we have drawn upon current research in environmental economics and international trade theory to address two questions of considerable importance to developing countries, particularly large developing countries. First, in Section 2 we showed that theoretically plausible circumstances exist in which a large developing country can make itself worse off by pursuing environmental policy unilaterally. This concept of immiserization holds along three measures. An LDC can be worse off in a terms of trade sense, in a "perverse incentives to polluting producers" sense or in an environmentally adjusted national income sense. In a specific practical setting, any one or more of these measures may be applicable. This analysis lends credence to LDC demands – at international meetings such as the recent Earth Summit at Rio de Janeiro – for monetary transfers to ensure environmental protection. Clearly, if unilateral action is likely to lead to immiserization, the two remaining routes to environmental protection lie in multilateral action or in monetary transfers from the Northern countries to the Southern countries.

Second, this paper has shown that the question of being better off or worse off is really an empirical one. A thorough analysis of the empirical factors impinging on the question of immiserization is beyond the scope of this paper. Such an analysis lies in the realm of research with computable general equilibrium (CGE) models. There are a number of links between our model and many CGE models currently in use. These links and other related empirical issues have been discussed in Batabyal (1991, pp. 461–464).

Third, in Section 3 we demonstrated that the LDC government could use its market power to set an optimal pollution tax to correct for the domestic distortion and capture the trade gains arising from its market power. Since this tax is positive – when the externality is in the export sector – an optimal program always involves taxing the polluting sector. Since the LDC government can attain two targets with one instrument, under certain circumstances it will *not* be necessary for the government to protect environmentally intensive export sectors of the economy. This result lessens the significance of arguments which suggest that because "history matters", LDCs might need to protect environmentally intensive sectors of the economy. This line of reasoning need not hold if the externality happens to be in the import sector of the economy. As mentioned in the previous section, in this case the optimal corrective tax can be positive or negative. As a result, it may make sense to subsidize environmentally intensive import sectors of the economy.

The present line of research can be extended in a number of directions. Three of the most important directions include an analysis of strategy, an analysis of dynamics and an analysis of the effects of uncertainty. The issues of strategy and dynamics have been addressed in Batabyal (1993a,b). Batabyal (1993a) shows how game theoretic concerns can alter the results of the present paper; this paper also analyzes the informational requirements of alternate environmental policies. Batabyal (1993b) discusses how to cast the global environmental protection problem as a mechanism design problem. The impact of uncertainty in environmental policy formation is the subject of our current research and we hope to report the results of this research shortly.

## References


Asako, K., 1979. Environmental pollution in an open economy. Econ. Rec., 55: 359–367.

Batabyal, A.A., 1990. A model of potentially immiserizing unilateral environmental controls. University of Minnesota Department of Agricultural and Applied Economics Staff Paper P90-53 (unpubl.), 23 pp.

Batabyal, A.A., 1991. Environmental pollution and unilateral control in an open economy. Nat. Resour. Model., 5: 445–467.

Batabyal, A.A., 1993a. Game models of environmental policy in an open economy. Draft manuscript (unpubl.), 33 pp.

Batabyal, A.A., 1993b. Development, trade and the environment: which way now? Draft manuscript (unpubl.), 7 pp.

Bhagwati, J.N. and Srinivasan, T.N., 1983. Lectures on International Trade. MIT Press, Cambridge, MA, 414 pp.

Danida, 1989. Environmental Profile: India. Ministry of Foreign Affairs, Copenhagen, Denmark, 109 pp.

d'Arge, R.C. and Kneese, A.V., 1972. Environmental quality and international trade. Int. Organ., 26: 419–465.

Dornbusch, R., 1971. Optimal commodity and trade taxes. J. Polit. Econ., 79: 1360–1368.

Friedlaender, A.F. and Vandendorpe, A.L., 1968. Excise taxes and the gains from trade. J. Polit. Econ., 76: 1058–1068.

Jones, R.W., 1969. Tariffs and trade in general equilibrium: comment. Am. Econ. Rev., 59: 418–424.

Leonard, H.J., 1984. Are Environmental Regulations Driving U.S. Industries Overseas? The Conservation Foundation, Washington, DC, 155 pp.

Markusen, J., 1975. International externalities and optimal tax structures. J. Int. Econ., 5: 15–29.

McGuire, M.C., 1982. Regulation, factor rewards, and international trade. J. Publ. Econ., 17: 335–354.

Meade, J., 1955. Trade and Welfare Mathematical Supplement. Oxford University Press, Oxford, 165 pp.

Merrifield, J., 1988. The impact of selected abatement strategies on transnational pollution, the terms of trade, and factor rewards: a general equilibrium approach. J. Environ. Econ. Manage., 15: 259–284.

Mundell, R., 1960. The pure theory of international trade. Am. Econ. Rev., 50: 67–110.

Mundell, R., 1968. International Economics. Macmillian Press, New York, NY, 332 pp.

Pethig, R., 1976. Pollution, welfare and environmental policy in the theory of comparative advantage. J. Environ. Econ. Manage., 2: 160–169.

Pethig, R. (Editor), 1992. Conflicts and Cooperation in the Management of Environmental Resources. Springer-Verlag, Berlin, 338 pp.

Samuelson, P.A., 1947. Foundations of Economic Analysis. Harvard University Press, Cambridge, MA, 447 pp.

Tobey, J., 1990. The effects of domestic environmental policies on patterns of world trade: an empirical test. Kyklos, 43: 191–209.

Vandendorpe, A.L., 1972. Optimal tax structures in a model with traded and non-traded goods. J. Int. Econ., 2: 235–256.

Walter, I., 1973. The pollution content of american trade. Western Econ. J., 11: 61–70.

Whalley, J., 1991. The interface between environmental and trade policies. Econ. J., 101: 180–189.

# [27]

# Marginal urban environments as havens for low-income housing: Third World regional comparisons

*Hamish Main and Stephen Wyn Williams*



Third World urbanisation has produced a number of unexpected outcomes in recent decades, notably the rapidity of urban growth overall and the mega-populations of the largest cities. This chapter derives from another, related, feature of Third World urbanisation that was unforeseen by social scientists: the spate of disasters that has befallen cities around the Third World, especially since the 1970s. Such urban disasters are clearly a part of the wide range of environment-related calamities suffered by Third World people, but the apparently enhanced vulnerability of Third World cities to natural environmental hazards arises principally from the residential occupation of marginal urban environments by those who are unable to secure residence in less vulnerable sites. It is argued below that this is an outcome of the operation of urban land and housing markets, as these markets develop in Third World societies in ways that increasingly favour those with sufficient wealth and marginalise those without. Unable to afford accommodation in preferred sites, the urban poor become increasingly constrained to accommodation on land not wanted by the better-off.

The most visible result of residential marginalisation has been the concentration of legal and illegal low-income housing towards the urban periphery, especially in Latin America. But when journeys to the city centre become too long, or when land at the periphery becomes scarce, the urban poor begin to look for inner-city sites previously discounted as unavailable not because they are required for the better-off but specifically because they are *not* required due to their awkward or dangerous nature.

Thus, when a Third World city's land and housing markets are sufficiently developed, the chief locational determinant of low-income housing is the attribute of low evaluation by middle- and high-income housing markets and by non-residential land markets. The urban poor obtain shelter on land, left over from other markets, that is marginal either in a spatial sense (locationally peripheral) or in an environmental sense (of intrinsically poor site quality).

But the development of land and housing markets is a lengthy and uneven process in Third World societies, involving squatter demolitions as the stick where land is required for others' legal purposes, as well as the carrot of cheap land and/or housing where competition is less severe and the poor can find safe residential havens. The market guides relegation of the urban poor into marginal residential havens – all too often dominated by negative externalities and peripherality, yet havens from the predations of formal land and housing markets supported by the state. This process is less advanced overall in Africa than in Latin America, with much of Asia being in an intermediate position.

This is not a novel explanation; these issues have been considered *inter alia* by Angel *et al.* (1983); Baross (1983); Gilbert and Ward (1985); Doebele (1987); Hardoy and Satterthwaite (1989); and Baross and van der Linden (1990). It is applied in this chapter to a comparison of Latin American and African cities. Such a broad regional comparison is by no means intended to suggest that differences between cities and urban cultures within each continent are insignificant, but we believe that sufficient regional similarities are discernible to make such an exercise worthwhile. Wealthier and more powerful urban residents tend to reside in a city's more desirable sites in most societies, pre-industrial as well as industrial, but recent urban environmental disasters have been sufficiently frequent and damaging to sufficient numbers of urban residents to warrant close scrutiny of the forces acting upon those who are worse affected in Third World cities towards the end of the twentieth century.

The chapter begins with a brief survey of what constitutes marginal urban environments. It may appear at first glance that Latin American cities have to cope with more difficult topographic and other *in situ* conditions than do African cities, but closer examination reveals site problems of one kind or another in almost every urban area in Africa. Yet it is apparent that the urban poor in Latin American cities today are constrained to reside in these marginal environments to an extent markedly greater than in the case of the African urban poor. It is therefore unsurprising that the list of environmental disasters which have recently befallen the poor in so many Latin American cities is longer than in the African case. The chapter proceeds by offering a model of urban residential development which indicates spatially how the urban poor are constrained to marginal environments and by briefly considering some aspects of the development of land and housing markets and associated processes which bring about this situation. The logic of the model is that as African societies become increasingly urbanised, as African cities grow in population and in area and as their land and housing markets develop, they will in coming decades be increasingly threatened by environmental disasters that wreak widespread damage to homes and to lives.

## Marginal urban environments

Marginal urban environments are sited in and/or around negative externalities. These negative externalities are natural or man-made features of urban environments that make nearby residence unattractive because they entail actual or potential ongoing problems for local residents and/or threats of disaster (see Table 9.1). The most widespread features of the natural environment are probably steep slopes, which make access and construction difficult and may threaten landslides; flood plains, swamps and other water margins, which may cause problems for access and construction and health, and may threaten flood; and zones threatened by tectonic activity. Industrial production sites are probably the most problematic man-made feature of urban environments, with their threat of environmental pollution or even major disaster, but rubbish dumps, burial grounds, borrow pits, airport flight-paths and high-tension electric cables also figure prominently in creating undesirable residential locations in Third World cities.

Where a dominant wind direction is more or less constant throughout the year, residential areas downwind of noxious urban activities are readily identifiable as marginal environments; but it is more usual for variation in wind direction to reduce the role of wind pollution in determining which urban locations are environmentally marginal for desirable residence. Downstream sites, drawing water that has already passed through much of the urban system, are more commonly identifiable as marginal, given the health risks posed by polluted water in Third World cities: a cholera outbreak in Jakarta in August 1977, for example, was traced to spring water polluted by waste infiltrated upstream. Zones of tectonic activity are perhaps the least site-specific of negative externalities in their effects on residential areas. But, as Table 9.1. suggests, the areas of the city that are affected by most negative externalities can be identified fairly closely.

Few cities are located on anything like the featureless isotropic plain of the theoretical models. Buenos Aires is unusual among major Latin American cities in its flat site. Africa appears at first glance to offer more sites for unconstrained urban expansion than other Third World continents: the monotonous plateau of Zambia's Copperbelt towns is interrupted less by natural features than by open-cast mines and their waste dumps, while Casablanca's 'topography is permissibly favorable, rising as it does gently inland from the ocean front' (Hance, 1970, p. 306). But actual urban development may provoke an apparently generous topography into

**Table 9.1** Negative externalities and threats of disaster as determinants of marginal urban residential environments

| | Ongoing problem | | Threat of disaster | |
|---|---|---|---|---|
| *Negative externality* | *Problem* | *Site specificity within city* | *Disaster* | *Site specificity within city* |
| Tectonic zone | construction | low | earthquake/volcano | low |
| Steep slope | construction | very high | landslide | very high |
| | access | very high | | |
| Swampy land | construction | very high | flooding | high |
| | access | very high | | |
| | insects/disease | high | epidemic | high |
| Floodable land | insects/disease | very high | epidemic | very high |
| | construction | very high | flooding | very high |
| | access | very high | | |
| Industrial production zone | airborne pollution | high/low | gas leak/explosion | very high |
| | waterborne pollution | high | epidemic | high |
| | noise | very high | | |
| | crowds of workers | high | | |
| Rubbish dump | airborne pollution | high/low | methane explosion | very high |
| | waterborne pollution | high | epidemic | high |
| | insects/disease | high | | |
| Burial ground | waterborne pollution | high | epidemic | high |
| | superstitious fears | high | | |
| Borrow pit | insects/disease | high | epidemic | high |
| | construction | very high | | |
| Airport flight path | noise | high | crash | high |
| High-tension electricity cables | noise/illness | very high | electrocution | very high |
| Railway line, main road | airborne pollution | very high | crash | very high |
| | noise | very high | | |
| Sewer | waterborne pollution | high | gas leak/explosion | high |
| | insects/disease | high | | |
| | | | epidemic | high |

difficult or disastrous consequences, if development plans are not sufficiently thorough. Suez's superficially easy terrain encouraged imaginative geometrical urban development plans for high-density housing – until geomophologists identified a substructure of very steep slopes, underground wadis constituting flood hazard, a high water table and very saline soils that would attack concrete foundations (Doornkamp, 1985, pp. 76–7). Development constraint maps in the town plans of reliable survey and planning companies may show severely limited directions for the desirable future expansion of even small towns on extensive plains, though all too often less thorough planning surveys do not identify flood threats, poorly drained soils, steep slopes and other potential physical constraints.

Clearly, one person's negative externality may be another's positive externality. It was common in pre-industrial Islamic cities, for example, for noxious activities like dyeing and tanning to be confined to locations outside the city wall, or at least towards the periphery of the built-up area; these were negative externalities for the majority of the urban population, but not so for the dyers and tanners themselves who resided close to their workplaces. Similarly in the industrial city, factory employees without reliable transport have a reason to seek accommodation close to their workplaces despite the pollution suffered there. Lagos is unusual in that some of the low-density residential areas surrounding the city centre are closer to major industrial areas (for example at Apapa) than are poorer neighbourhoods. This is partly a function of the awkward island site, reflecting especially the difficulties of transport between the centre and periphery of Lagos. Transport routes may be considered either positive or negative externalities; but low-income neighbourhoods under airport flight paths (for example Kano, Lima) and alongside railway tracks (for example Delhi, Kuala Lumpur) and precarious residence on street pavements (for example Bombay, Calcutta) are clearly undesirable sites in major respects.

The quality of urban environments is perceived to some extent through the filter of culture, and such perceptions may change through time. In Britain council housing became a major negative externality for private housing markets between the world wars, for example, as did many major football grounds during the 1970s as a result of football hooliganism. The question of whether hillsides are desirable residential locations depends only partly on their topography and geology (accessibility and construction quality), and it is complicated by altitude. Europeans colonising tropical lands often expressed their preference for cooler climates by locating their centres of administration at higher altitudes. This was most evident in Spanish America (for example Bogota, Caracas, San Jose), where in places it followed the ancient precedent of the Maya and Inca cities. In India the colonial summer capital was located for some years in the Himalayas at Shimla, but such sites were more often used by colonials for the establishment of hill stations for recreation (for example Darjeeling, Baguio City, Yogjakarta) (King, 1991). Today, hillside residential sites are dominated by the wealthier members of many North American cities, while flat lowlands are left over for the poor. But this situation is reversed in Latin American cities like Rio de Janeiro and Caracas, Bogota and Lima, where it is predominantly the poor who reside on the hillsides. The altitude of La Paz is sufficient for those born in the city to prefer the lower hill slopes to the flat land of the higher El Alto above 4,000 metres, whereas migrants from the Altiplano, accustomed to harsh climatic conditions there, are now moving to El Alto in large numbers (van Lindert, 1991, p. 455). Those who resided until the mid-twentieth century in inner-city mansions in many Latin American societies moved out in large numbers to new peripheral suburbs as industrial development began close to city centres and when the increasing availability of private motor transport made suburbs more accessible. This automobile-encouraged surbanisation took a unique form in Salvador, where the elite had for centuries resided at the summit of the escarpment, leaving the flood-prone valley floors for gardening while the poor came to occupy the upper and middle hill slopes. In the 1950s, with the construction of motor roads along the coast, the elite descended *en masse* to new high-rise flats along the ocean shore, while the growing volume of *favelas* occupied not only the steeper hill slopes but also flood-prone locations alongside coastal streams and lagoons (Claval, 1991, p. 24) and even islands of garbage in the bay (Dwyer, 1975, p. 32).

The results of a brief survey of recent published literature, on the presence or absence of some major negative externalities and of major environmental disasters, are presented in Table 9.2. Twenty large cities in each of Latin America, Africa and southern Asia are listed in the table, which omits cities for which no such sites or events have been encountered in the literature; but such cities are few, especially in Latin America. The brevity of the survey and the interim nature of these results are stressed, and conclusions drawn from the table must be interpreted in this light. The table suggests that the volume of negative externalities is not dissimilar in each of the three regions surveyed, but that there are clear differences between the three in the predominant type of major negative externality: steep slopes are by far the most apparent in Latin American cities, whereas industrial production zones are most ubiquitous in southern Asian cities, and in African cities both of these appear to be about as widespread as swampy land. But it appears that urban environmental disasters arising out of negative externalities have been far more numerous in Latin America than in Africa, which has experienced far fewer earthquakes and landslides and industrial disasters and slightly fewer urban floods. The Asian cities surveyed appear to have been intermediate in this respect.

We have also sought to identify where low-income neighbourhoods have been markedly more affected by negative externalities than have middle- and high-income neighbourhoods, and preliminary findings appear in Table 9.2. Low-income neighbourhoods do indeed appear to have been much worse affected in a great majority of the cities surveyed in Latin America, but this is much less apparent in the African cases encountered. Steep slopes and swampy land are evidently inhabited by better-off residents in many African cities as well as by those less well off, though industrial production zones which are reported as major negative externalities are clearly associated far more with low-income housing. And, unlike Latin America, rarely has it been reported in African cities that environmental disasters have affected the urban poor markedly more than better-off urbanites.

Each continent has its notorious industrial areas: Sao Paulo's Cubatao ('Pollution Valley'), Rio's Belford Roxo and some of the eastern districts of Mexico City; Jakarta's Cibubur and the east coast of Bombay Island; the industrial districts of southern Tunis and south-western Alexandria. In each of these cases, the factories are surrounded by low-income neighbourhoods. Neither these residents, nor those who can afford to reside on the other side of the city, know what dangers exist in the factories or what disasters they might create. In some cases, air pollution is suffered by all urban residents more-or-less regardless of class or location; but neighbourhoods downstream from industrial zones, with their water pollution problems, are more likely to house low-income people. And when disaster strikes, it is the local neighbourhoods and their residents that almost inevitably suffer most. The escape of gas from Union Carbide's Bhopal plant in December 1984 killed perhaps 2,500 people mostly in neighbouring high-density *bastis*, while middle- and upper-class neighbourhoods on the other side of the city were largely unaffected (Jones, 1988, p. 58). The strong spatial correlation between areas affected by the gas and the city's high-density residential areas is clear; Bhopal's low-density residential areas are located very largely on the other side of the city centre, south of the Lower Lake. It was not only the *bastis'* location, but also the nature of their construction, that brought disaster out of hazard: those fortunate enough to stay on the upper floors of multi-storey buildings, or inside well-sealed buildings, suffered markedly less (Weir, 1986, p. 3). The explosion from a leaking petrol pipeline in Cubatao, Sao Paulo in February 1984 set off fires in a nearby shanty town and killed over 500 people (Weir, 1986, p. 115).

It is striking that only one of the thirteen industrial disasters indicated in Table 9.2 has occurred in any of the African cities listed. Flooding appears to have been the greatest urban environmental threat in Africa: it has become an almost annual hazard for some of the residents of Nigerian cities like Lagos and Port Harcourt (see Peil's Chapter Ten in this volume for example). But urban flood damage here has so far been minor compared with that faced by Khartoum residents in August 1988, when heavy rains combined with the annual Nile flood to wash away entire neighbourhoods, many of them temporary settlements of refugees from the war in southern Sudan (Ahmad, 1989, p. 54). A government source estimated that over 800,000 of Khartoum's population of about 2,500,000 had been 'affected' by the floods, though no number of lives lost was given

**Table 9.2** Major negative externalities and environmental disasters in selected large Third World cities

| | *Major negative externality* | | | *Disaster* | | | |
|---|---|---|---|---|---|---|---|
| City | Steep slope | Swampy or floodable land | Industrial pollution | Earth-quake | Land-slide | Flood | Industrial |
| *Latin America* | | | | | | | |
| Bogota | * | | * | | * | * | |
| Caracas | * | | * | * | * | | x |
| Cartagena | | * | x | | | | |
| Guatemala City | * | | x | * | * | x | |
| Guayaquil | | * | | | | x | |
| La Paz | * | | | | * | | |
| Lima | * | | * | x | | | x |
| Managua | x | | x | x | x | x | |
| Medellin | * | | | | * | | |
| Mexico City | * | * | * | * | | * | * |
| Quito | * | * | | | | | |
| Recife | * | * | | | | x | |
| Rio de Janeiro | * | * | * | | * | * | |
| Salvador | * | * | | | | * | |
| San Jose | * | | | x | * | * | |
| San Juan | | * | | | | * | x |
| San Salvador | * | | | * | x | * | |
| Santiago | x | | x | | | | |
| Sao Paulo | | * | * | | | | * |
| Tijuana | | | | | | * | |
| *Africa* | | | | | | | |
| Abidjan | x | * | * | | | | |
| Accra | * | x | x | x | | x | |
| Addis Ababa | x | | | | x | | |
| Alexandria | | | * | | | | x |
| Cairo | | | * | * | | x | |
| Dar es Salaam | | * | * | | | x | |
| Douala | | * | * | | | | |
| Johannesberg | | * | * | | * | * | |
| Kampala | | * | | | | x | |
| Khartoum | | x | | | | * | |
| Kumasi | x | x | | | | | |
| Lagos | | x | x | | | * | |
| Luanda | x | | | | x | | |
| Maputo | * | * | | | | | |
| Monrovia | | * | * | | | | |
| Nairobi | x | * | * | | | | |
| N'Djamena | | x | | | x | x | |
| Port Harcourt | | * | | | | * | |
| Rabat | * | * | | | | | |
| Yaounde | | * | * | | | | |

**Table 9.2** (*continued*)

| | *Major negative externality* | | | *Disaster* | | | |
|---|---|---|---|---|---|---|---|
| City | Steep slope | Swampy or floodable land | Industrial pollution | Earth-quake | Land-slide | Flood | Industrial |
| *Asia* | | | | | | | |
| Ankara | * | | | | * | | |
| Baguio City | * | * | | x | x | * | |
| Bangkok | | * | * | | | * | x |
| Bhopal | | | * | | | | * |
| Bombay | | * | * | | | * | x |
| Calcutta | | * | x | | | * | |
| Delhi | | * | x | | | * | * |
| Hong Kong | * | * | | | * | x | |
| Jakarta | * | * | * | | | * | x |
| Karachi | | * | * | | | | |
| Kuala Lumpur | * | x | x | | | * | x |
| Madras | | * | * | | | | |
| Manila | | * | x | | | * | |
| Pusan | * | | | | | | |
| Seoul | * | | x | | | | |
| Shanghai | | | x | | | | x |
| Surabaya | | * | | | | * | |
| Taichung | | | * | | | | |
| Tehran | | | x | | | | |
| Tel Aviv | x | | | x | | x | |

x Given externality is present/disaster has occurred, but no evidence found that low-income housing areas affected markedly more than other housing areas.
* Given externality is present/disaster has occurred, and low-income housing areas affected markedly more than other housing areas.
NB The twenty large cities in each of the Third World regions selected for Table 9.2 are the twenty for which the most information on major negative externalities and disasters has been encountered in the brief survey of recent literature undertaken for this chapter.

Sources: various, including Clarke *et al*, 1989; Douglas, 1983; Hance, 1970; Jones, 1988; Susman *et al.*, 1983; *Environment and Urbanization*, 1989a; *Environment and Urbanization*, 1989b; *Regional Development Dialogue*, 1991

(Ministry of Social Affairs, 1989; quoted by Abu Sin and Harbi, 1991, p. 123). Even though the 1988 Nile flood was lower than that of 1946, the devastation caused was estimated to be ten times greater due to housing encroaching on to unsuitable sites. Squatter settlements without drainage or open spaces or building regulations had grown very rapidly in Khartoum during the 1980s, accounting by the end of the decade for over 40 per cent of the built-up area; at the same time, 50 per cent of this area was 'exposed with its occupants to the risk of disaster from any abnormalities in Nile level and rainfall' (Abu Sin and Harbi, 1991, p. 121).

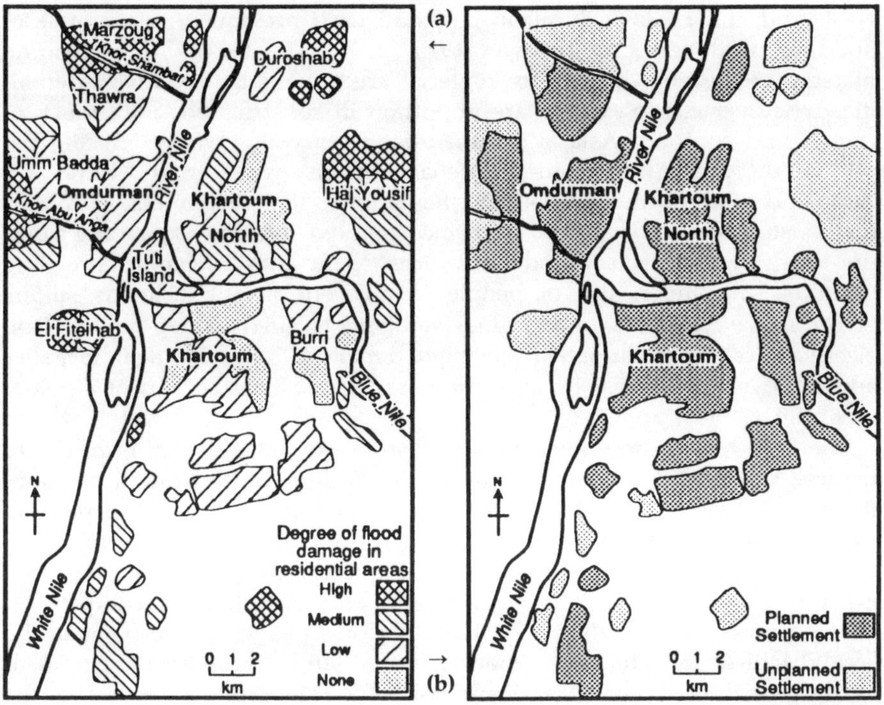


**Figure 9.1** (a) Flood damage in greater Khartoum, August 1988. Source: after Abu Sin and Harbi, 1991; (b) Planned and unplanned settlements in Khartoum. Source: after Ahmad, 1989, p. 51

A comparison of Figure 9.1(a) with Figure 9.1(b) confirms that unplanned settlements around Khartoum's periphery took the brunt of the damage.

One of the squatter settlements most damaged by the 1988 Khartoum flood was Hilat Kusha ('Place of Rubbish'), a dump covering about one square mile sited next to the city's largest industrial estate, where over 5,000 refugees from the south dwelt among some of the factories' worst by-products (Save the Children Fund, 1990, pp. 36–7). Multiple negative externalities are not unusual in Third World cities, but this was a particularly abysmal combination. About 20,000 residents, many of them long established, were reported (Jimenez and Valasquez, 1989, p. 53) around 'Smokey Mountain', a Manila rubbish dump where many earn a living by scavenging garbage. Immigrants to Beirut used to be quarantined in Quarantina, subsequently abandoned and declared by the government as unsuitable for housing because it was adjacent to the municipal rubbish dump; squatters were sufficiently established by the 1970s to be renting accommodation here to Kurds and other newcomers (UNCHS, 1987, p. 140). Almost 40,000 people dwelt during the 1950s in Asima, an area of wasteland and rubbish dump in Baghdad used previously as a source of building mud and clay (Dwyer, 1975, p. 4). The borrow pits yielding material created by digging for material are potentially negative externalities wherever clay and mud are important in construction, as in much of central and southern Asia and the Andes (Agarwal, 1990, p. 35). Borrow pits for the construction and maintenance of city walls around Kano and Zaria and other northern Nigerian cities prior to the colonial era, as well as for housing today, have now been incorporated into the expanding built-up area; rainy-season inundation turns them into mosquito breeding grounds, and the health of people in adjacent neighbourhoods suffers accordingly. Residents of marginal settlements sited under high-tension electricity cables in Surabaya pay high rental costs despite their illegality and the overhead threat because they are located near centres of employment (Silas, 1989, pp. 65–6).

The 1988 Khartoum flood disaster illustrates the maxim that hazards are natural, whereas disasters are man-made. Well-organised urban development would avoid such disasters chiefly by diverting residential expansion to land not threatened by floodwaters, which after all are a recurring element of the Khartoum landscape. The question of why urban development is in fact not well organised here and elsewhere is complex; in keeping with much of the recent literature on the subject, we point in the second half of this chapter to market forces within capitalist development as the principal motor. A starting point for this explanation lies in the assumption that, as Table 9.2 indicates, urban environmental disasters, even of a magnitude much smaller than that of the 1988 Khartoum floods, have been far rarer in Africa than in Latin America.

## Urban spatial development and marginal urban environments

Baross (1983) argues that the supply of land for low-income groups divides into three main categories: non-commercial, commercial and administrative. Within this broad classification marginal urban environments fall predominantly into the first of these, in so far as a monetary transfer price (at least initially) is not involved. According to Baross the settling of marginal land is a by-product of the increasing commercial articulation of land supply, and two basic reasons for its utilisation are posited. First, when no land is available from other non-commercial sources or administrative measures, 'those who cannot pay for land at all (not even for the cheaper rents) have no other option but to seek out parcels where nobody else wants to build' (p. 192). Second, where marginal land is centrally located it provides ready access to city-centre employment opportunities, thus 'if for topographic or land-use planning reasons marginal land exists near the city centre, these become strategic locations for popular development' (p. 192). However, this supply of 'free' land can be eroded over time as the established settlers start selling plots, becoming in effect petty landlords. In some countries, a greater threat to the continued use of marginal land is posed by the state, whose efficiency in administering master plans, and applying stricter zoning by-laws and building regulations prohibits the creation of new settlements and encourages the demolition of existing ones. However, in other countries the state's influence is much less pronounced.

With these basic ideas in mind it is possible to construct a relatively simple dynamic 'model' which illustrates over time how marginal urban environments acquire significance in the housing strategies of low-income groups. The emergence and expansion of marginal urban environments is presented in Figure 9.2, a three-stage model of urban development based on Latin America in the twentieth century. Three types of negative externality are evident in the model: (a) a river and its banks, which are unsuitable for housing construction and liable to flood; (b) steep slopes, difficult to access and to build on, and potentially provoked into landslides by such human intervention; and (c) an industrial zone, developing after the first stage of the model, which emits airborne pollutants especially in the direction of the prevailing winds towards the south and east. The model focuses on the spatial pattern of low-income residential areas *vis-à-vis* other residential areas and these negative externalities.

The first stage of the model is characteristic of Latin American cities prior to 1930, when motor transport was unimportant and most place-to-place movement was on foot. Wealthier urban residents lived close to the city centre, while the urban poor (many of whom worked as domestic servants in the mansions) resided mainly in rented accommodation or on communal land further from the centre. City population was small, and intra-urban distances sufficiently short for housing needs to be met from available land without major problems. Hardly anybody resided on the riverbank or on the steep slopes.

Industrial development, and the expansion of private transport for the better-off along with public transport for the urban masses, are incorporated into the second stage of the model. This typically represents a date after the middle of the twentieth century, perhaps about the 1960s. Wealthier residents have moved out of the urban centre some decades previously into extensive, well-serviced suburbs. Their former mansions have been subdivided and inhabited by lower-income residents, but most low-income neighbourhoods are located beyond the comfortable suburbs in poorly serviced shanty towns. Pressures on land are reflected in the variety of legal and illegal forms of access to land, in the incorporation of former communal land into the commercial sector and in evictions of squatters to make way for legal suburban development. Difficulties of access to the city centre and other major sources of employment, notably

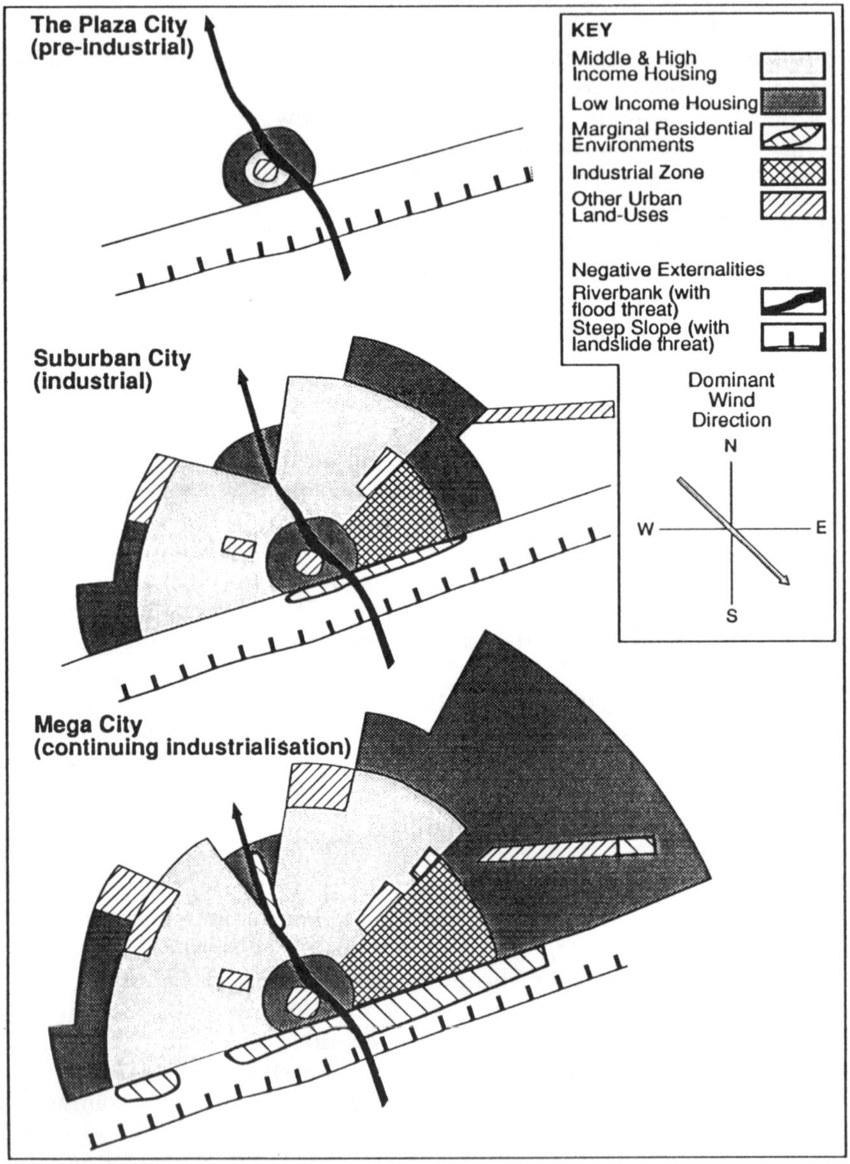


**Figure 9.2** Marginal urban environments and low-income housing: a model

the industrial zone, are resolved by some of the peripheral poor through colonisation of the lower steep slopes.

The third stage of the model corresponds to the situation in some Latin American mega-cities today. Urban population has grown so large, and low-income neighbourhoods have become so constrained to the urban periphery through the expansion of middle-class suburbs and other legal developments, that despite widespread public transport daily commuting has become prohibitive for many in time and/or money costs. Accommodation costs are too high for them also in the central tenements, where very high residential densities yield lucrative profits for landlords and others investing in the land and housing markets. The poor and some of the not-so-poor are now largely squeezed out of existing accommodation possibilities, legal and illegal, other than marginal urban environments on the riverbanks and up the slopes. The problems and dangers of these sites are usually understood; but these are outweighed by their proximity to central and industrial workplaces, by the fact that they are cheap or even free of rent and their unattractiveness to formal land markets. Sites like these are havens for the urban poor, who are unlikely to be evicted from them because those with money and power and contacts have no use for them. Health problems are at their worst among those who inhabit the river banks downstream from the city centre; some of their shacks are washed away almost every year when the river is in spate, and many lives are lost in occasional floods. Those who inhabit the rocky slopes adjacent to the industrial zone suffer particularly badly from airborne pollution, though the shanty towns on the higher slopes towards the western periphery are relatively healthy places to live in; but the elderly find the climb hard where the roads cannot reach, and shacks are sometimes swept away by landslides.

In applying this model to African cities, the logic of our argument is as follows. The urban poor suffer marginal urban environments, disproportionate to urban populations as a whole, to a much greater extent in Latin America than in Africa. But this regional difference is not explained by intrinsically more awkward natural environments in Latin America: as Table 9.2 shows, it seems that major negative externalities are approximately as much of a feature of African cities as of Latin American and also Asian cities. Rather, explanation of the growing association between low-income housing and marginal urban environments lies in the progressive squeezing out of low-income neighbourhoods from land that is valuable for residential or other land-uses through the operation of increasingly developed land and housing markets in cities that are growing beyond a manageable size. Support for this explanation is yielded both by the evident rarity of environmental disasters in African cities compared with Latin American cities and by the apparently much lower bias towards the urban poor in the damage inflicted by African disasters.

If explanation indeed lies predominantly in the development of land and housing markets, and associated processes within overall urbanisation, two outcomes are noteworthy. First, the second stage of the model outlined above is more applicable than the third stage to African cities today; industrialisation, suburbanisation and the development of public transport networks began and expanded some decades later in Africa than in Latin America. Second, continuing urbanisation in Africa entailing development of land and housing markets along lines even approximately similar to those in Latin American cities will in coming years produce a significant increase in the African urban poor's occupation of marginal urban environments; and the probability of major urban environmental disasters will rise accordingly. Khartoum's flood disaster in 1988 might be indicative of an emerging trend of urban environmental calamities in African cities.

## Marginal urban environments and the land issue

Thus far the discussion has focused on the nature, characteristics and spatio-temporal location of marginal urban environments, illustrating how these sites have become havens for low-income dwellers. From the discussion the environmentally marginal nature of these sites is apparent in terms both of their inherent and acquired characteristics (Gilbert and Ward, 1985). The former refers essentially to physical (natural) geographic features, while the latter refers to location in terms of services, transportation and, importantly in this context, exposure to a broad range of environmental problems.

Without significant changes in the attitudes and policies of governments to the housing problems of low-income groups, it would be expected that the future for most low-income dwellers will be one of constant insecurity. It would appear probable that low-income groups will locate increasingly on dangerous sites, either because these are the cheapest sites available or, alternatively, because they minimise the chance of eviction. Consequently, intra-urban segregation will become more marked with 'the poor in the worst-quality, worst-serviced and often worst-located sites with richer groups in the best-located, best-quality and best-serviced locations'. Furthermore, such processes will have a more profound impact in so far as 'cities' physical growth will be defined by where poorer groups can invade or illegally negotiate for land' (Hardoy and Satterthwaite, 1990, p. 235). Although the problem of marginal urban environments is very often discussed in technocratic terms (for example appropriate materials, structure and designs etc.), the canvas on which the problem of such environments is located is quintessentially political and institutional in nature. At the heart of these considerations is the relationship between a land policy and a low-cost housing policy. Specifically, it would seem apparent that the central issue is simply the failure of governments to provide an adequate supply of affordable, legal land sites for housing. As Angel *et al.* noted in 1983, 'land for housing the poor is gradually becoming an insurmountable obstacle in the housing struggle facing the growing cities of the Third World' (p. 3).

However, the 'land crisis' has not always been a characteristic feature of Third World cities. As the UNCHS (1987, p. 131) notes, given the pace of urban growth since 1950, urban land markets have been extraordinarily adaptive and 'what is surprising is not that they now face severe problems but that they function at all'. Thus at the end of the Second World War many cities were still quite 'porous' (Doebele, 1987) with large city-centre buildings encouraging subdivision, while the existence of large land lots allowed additional dwellings to be readily installed. Furthermore, well-located land owned by public and other institutions constituted informal 'land banks'. At greater distances from the city centre, settlements were established on land of low commercial value by invasion, quiet encroachment or by illegal subdivision.

However, for most of the major cities of the Third World the relatively easy availability of land for low-income dwellers has ended. In the central areas, saturation point has been reached, and in many instances expansion is only possible by an enlarged rental sector or by locating in the most marginal of environments. In peripheral areas the markets for both public and private land have tightened considerably. Over the years the attitudes and policies of governments towards squatting and invasion on public land moved from a relatively permissive position to one which viewed land as an irreplaceable asset which must be defended. This was reinforced by a planning environment which according to McAuslan (1985) focused on negative controls involving 'planning, zoning and any other measure which limits the use to which land can be put' (p. 64). At the present time land-use controls remain in place although they may be weak or unevenly applied, and as Mattingley (1993, p. 113) observes 'a number of market forces are working against government efforts to determine the uses of urban land'. In the private sector, with the lack of other secure investment opportunities, peripheral land has been the subject of speculative activity by high- and middle-income families, while construction companies who have prospered from urban growth buy land in the periphery to assure adequate sites for future projects.

As a consequence of the processes noted above the land market has tightened considerably for low-income dwellers. Nevertheless, as Hardoy and Satterthwaite (1989, p. 102) note, there is 'no lack of undeveloped or partially developed land on which low income housing sites could be developed'. In Sao Paulo, for example, it has been estimated that the extent of undeveloped land could accommodate a two-thirds' increase in population without any further expansion. However, as the above authors indicate, 'much of this land . . . is owned by individuals or institutions who keep it vacant because the growth of the city and the development of its economy is rapidly pushing up its value, despite the fact that no investment is made in developing it . . . Such land is rarely invaded; low income groups know that any attempt to do so would be crushed.'

Some, albeit limited, attempt to ease the land-supply problem for low-income housing has been associated with the sites-and-services projects which have been implemented in a number of developing countries. However successful these interventions are at a project level, the sites-and-services approach remains a negligible source of land supply for shelter for low-income groups. Attempts to scale up these pilot projects into continuous housing programmes have encountered major obstacles. Specifically, the process of land acquisition is a slow and expensive process (Zetter, 1984) and to avoid delays governments will tend to opt for less expensive low-value sites on the periphery which are easier to obtain. However, for the recipient of the plot this clearly is far from the ideal site-location, involving not only construction costs but also transport costs to and from work.

What, therefore, is to be done? In essence the solution is simple: what is required is a substantial increase in the supply of land available for low- and moderate-income families. However, as Table 9.3 illustrates, there exists a variety of approaches and instruments which could stimulate an increase in the supply of land of this type. Some writers recommend the use of positive government controls such as land-banking, land-pooling and compulsory acquisition (for example, McAuslan, 1985). However, there is a growing body of opinion which advocates the reduction of state intervention in the land and housing markets. In addition, a number of governments have stressed the importance of 'unblocking' the market as part of the solution to housing problems and lack of services. Certainly a number of important basic 'technical' actions exist which can help to 'unblock' a city's land market. For example, an adequate local cadastral and property registration system would appear to be essential to the lowering of urban land prices by increasing accessibility between buyers and sellers. Similarly, accurate inventories of publicly owned land are necessary for any effective policy concerning land and land supply. It is perhaps true that unblocking the market could increase the proportion of middle-income and lower-income households who can find legal housing solutions. Nevertheless, as Hardoy and Satterthwaite (1989) argue there will still remain a large proportion of individuals and households too poor to enter this market. For many of these households 'market solutions' are clearly not sufficient, and in some situations 'negotiated solutions' involving some concession to the households concerned would be appropriate. An example of this latter type of solution would be the land-sharing schemes as implemented in Bangkok (Angel and Boonyabancha, 1988).

**Table 9.3** Increasing the supply of land for low-income housing: a typology

A. INCREASING SUPPLY THROUGH DIRECT PUBLIC ACTIONS

1. Accelerated construction of service systems and improvement of transportation.
2. Improved methods of cost recovery (that is the unearned increment resulting from public investment).
3. Reducing the attractiveness of urban land as a vehicle for the storage of capital (taxation, land-use controls, credit controls, price freezing).
4. Prevention of unnecessary destruction of existing low-income settlements.
5. The need to modernise cadastral and land-registration systems.
6. Better legislation for compulsory acquisition.
7. Inventories of all publicly owned land.

B. INCREASING SUPPLY THROUGH IMPROVED INTERACTION OF PUBLIC AND PRIVATE (INCLUDING INFORMAL) SECTORS

1. Supporting informal systems.
2. Joint private-public development.

C. MAKING EXISTING SUPPLY MORE EFFICIENT

1. The need to re-examine the question of appropriate standards:
   — lot sizes
   — excessive building codes and standards for infrastructure and services.
2. Community participation: mobilising the energies and ideas of local organisations.

Source: Adapted from Doebele, 1987; pp. 120–30.

The implication of the foregoing discussion is quite clearly that in many countries there is a pressing need for the reform of urban land policies and institutions (see Farvacque and McAuslan, 1992). In this context, the immediate issues requiring attention are readily identifiable and would include *inter alia*, the respective roles of public interventions, market mechanisms and traditional authorities; the balance between social and economic considerations; and the form of appropriate administrative and legal institutions. However, it would be naive to suggest that in such a complex arena as land and its management simple administrative and managerial solutions are sufficient. In addition to the proximate issues just noted, the reform of urban land policies is premised on a wider set of issues of governance, including participation and decentralisation in government, and transparency and accountability in adminstration. The consequences of failing to address this agenda will inevitably reinforce the tendency for many low-income dwellers to locate in the most marginal of environments, and one can only venture the pessimistic prognosis that the types of chronic problems and environmental disasters discussed earlier in this chapter will become increasingly common.

## References


Abu Sin, M.E. and Harbi, M., 1991, 'Greater Khartoum's vulnerability to disaster hazards: the case of the 1988 rains and Nile flood', in M.E. Abu Sin and H.R.J. Davies (eds), *The Future of Sudan's Capital Region Khartoum*, Khartoum University Press.

Agarwal, A., 1990, 'Here's mud in your house', in *Third World Guide 91/92*, Montevideo, Instituto del Tercer Mundo, p. 35.

Ahmad, A.M., 1989, 'Housing submarkets for the urban poor: the case of Greater Khartoum', *Environment and Urbanization*, **1**(2), pp. 50–9.

Angel, S. *et al.* (eds), 1983, *Land for Housing the Poor*, Singapore, Select Books.

Angel, S. and Boonyabancha, S., 1988, 'Land-sharing as an alternative to eviction: the Bangkok experience', *Third World Planning Review*, **10**(2), pp. 107–8.

Baross, P., 1983, 'The articulation of land supply for popular settlements in Third World cities', in S. Angel *et al.* (eds), 1983, *Land for Housing the Poor*, Singapore, Select Books.

Baross, P. and Linden, J. van der, 1990, *The Transformation of Land Supply Systems in Third World Cities*, Aldershot, Avebury.

Clarke, J.I. *et al.* (eds), 1989, *Population and Disaster*, Oxford, Blackwell.

Claval, P., 1991, 'Specificities and problems of hillside cities', *Regional Development Dialogue*, **12**(2), pp. 14–28.

Doebele, W.A., 1987, 'Land policy', in Rowdin, L. (ed.), *Shelter, Settlement and Development*, Boston, Allen & Unwin, pp. 110–32.

Doornkamp, J.C., 1985, *The Earth Sciences and Planning in the Third World*, Liverpool, Liverpool University Press.

Douglas, I., 1983, *The Urban Environment*, London, Edward Arnold.

Dwyer, D.J., 1975, *People and Housing in Third World Cities*, London, Longman.

*Environment and Urbanization*, 1989a, 'Environmental problems in Third World cities', **1**(1).

—, 1989b, 'Beyond the stereotypes of slums; how the poor find accommodation in Third World cities **1** (2).

Farvacque, C. and McAuslan, P., 1992, *Reforming Urban Land Policies and Institutions in Developing Countries*, Urban Management Program, Policy Paper 5, Washington, World Bank.

Gilbert, A. and Ward, P., 1985, *Housing, the State and the Poor: Policy and Practice in Three Latin American cities*, Cambridge, Cambridge University Press.

Goethert, R., 1991, 'Lessons from squatters in Latin America: housing on hillsides for low income groups', *Regional Development Dialogue*, **12**(2), pp. 57–75.

Hance, W.A., 1970, *Population, Migration and Urbanisation in Africa*, New York, Columbia University Press.

Hardoy, J. and Satterthwaite, D., 1989, *Squatter Citizen: Life in the Urban Third World*, London, Earthscan.

Hardoy, J. and Satterthwaite, D., 1990, 'The future city', in S. Cairncross, J. Hardoy and D. Satterthwaite (eds), *The Poor Die Young: Housing and Health in Third World Cities*, London, Earthscan.

Jimenez, R.D. and Valasquez, A., 1989, 'Metropolitan Manila: a framework for its sustained development', *Environment and Urbanization*, **1**(1), pp. 51–8.

Jones, T., 1988, *Corporate Killing: Bhopals Will Happen*, London, Free Association Books.

King, A.D., 1991, 'History and culture in the development of the Himalayan hill station: the case of Shimla', *Regional Development Dialogue*, **12**(2), pp. 114–26.

McAuslan, P., 1985, *Urban Land and Shelter for the Poor*, London, Earthscan.

O'Connor, A., 1983, *The African City*, London, Hutchinson.

Silas, J., 1989, 'Marginal settlements in Surabaya', *Environment and Urbanization*, **1** (2).

Save the Children Fund, 1990, *Prospects for Africa's Children*, London, Hodder & Stoughton.

Susman, P., O'Keefe, P. and Wisner, B., 1983, 'Global disasters, a radical interpretation', in K. Hewitt (ed.), *Interpretations of Calamity: From the Viewpoint of Human Ecology*, London, Allen & Unwin, pp. 263–83.

UNCHS (HABITAT), 1987, *Global Report on Human Settlements 1986*, Oxford, Oxford University Press.

van Lindert, P., 1991, 'Moving up or staying down? Migrant-native differential mobility in La Paz', *Urban Studies*, **28**(3), pp. 433–63.

Ward, P., 1990, *Mexico City: The Production and Reproduction of an Urban Environment*, London, Belhaven.

Weir, D., 1986, *The Bhopal Syndrome – Pesticide Manufacturing and the Third World*, London, Earthscan.

Zetter, R., 1984, 'Land issues in low-income housing', in G.K. Payne (ed.), *Low Income Housing in the Developing World, The Role of Sites and Services and Settlement Upgrading*, Chichester, John Wiley, pp. 221–32.

# [28]

# Urban Environmental Sustainability: Critical Issues and Policy Measures in a Third-World Context

Peter Nijkamp and Hans Opschoor

## INTRODUCTION AND CONTEXT

Economic restructuring, sociopolitical transformation, technological innovation and global networking have all had a profound impact on the position of cities and regions in our world. Cities tend increasingly to become both centrifugal and centripetal nodes in a national – and also increasingly international – society linked by means of networks. This also holds for cities in developing countries. They face the urgent need to solve problems of poverty, housing and unemployment, and at the same time they are also facing the need to generate competitive advantages in order to be sustainable and to survive among fierce national or international competition (Porter (1990)). Against the background of competition and gains or losses of trade (of goods and services), the idea of sustainable development is increasingly coming to the fore.

The notion of 'sustainable development' (SD) has been discussed extensively in recent years (see WCED (1987); Archibugi and Nijkamp (1989); Opschoor (1992)). However, these discussions have often considered sustainability on a global scale, and to a large extent they have focused on conceptual issues. Consequently, it is not surprising that the lack of empirical applicability in a concrete policy context has been a major source of criticism. A more operational treatment of this abstract concept of SD seems the only way for it to survive in the current debate on our common future, as was strongly emphasized at the UNCED conference held in Rio de Janeiro in 1992.

SD has been defined as 'a pattern of development that meets the needs of present generations without jeopardizing the ability of future generations to meet their own needs' (WCED, 1987). In the context of our chapter this can be interpreted to mean that economic development should occur such that it leaves its resource base intact, in order to offer future generations an equal access to possibilities of using the natural environment as an input into the process of welfare generation (James *et al.*, 1989). This resource base refers to two elements: (i) the resources themselves, that is, the total of all relevant environmental stocks (such as fisheries, forests, arable land, water, air quality and so on); and (ii) the 'environmental infrastructure', that is, the environmental processes and life support systems (for example, resource regeneration processes and waste absorption systems).

SD does not only have an inter-generational dimension, but it also contains other aspects, notably spatial allocative aspects. Such spatial dimensions range from global to local. Global examples include sea level rise of the oceans, caused mainly by global warming or climatic changes; depletion of the ozone layer; deforestation; desertification; and extinction of species. Local examples relate to, for example, pollution in areas that face strong urban development; hazards from chemical, nuclear, and radioactive toxic industries; road construction; and local catastrophes. A common attribute of these examples is that they threaten human and environmental survival and hence are 'negative' or 'undesirable' changes that one should try to avoid or cope with. 'Positive' changes (regeneration of natural environmental stocks, advances in environmental technology and so on) are, by definition, 'welcome'. Intensified scientific action is needed to support and enhance such 'positive' changes. An operationally relevant SD analysis should offer concrete and viable guidelines for the contents, and the steps to be taken in order to meet the objective of SD.

Within this general context, tools should be developed to analyze and manage economic processes at the local level; this approach we suggest calling 'local sustainable development' (LSD) analysis or management. As we shall see below, the inherent logic of a LSD analysis stems from the belief that such an analysis may make functional interdependencies at the local level more manageable in view of the ongoing process of development of cities and regions. From a management and policy point of view, the local level is more suitable for control and transformation than the global scale. Hence it is evident that the objective of SD may be achieved more easily if the processes of socioeconomic development and environmental change on a local scale are more clearly understood and properly managed.

In this chapter we aim to develop the notion of LSD (in the second section) and to see how and to what extent it can be used in urban development planning (in the third and fourth sections), especially in developing countries (in the fifth section). We conclude by discussing the feasibility of LSD and its prospects (in the sixth section).

## LOCAL SUSTAINABLE DEVELOPMENT

### Introduction

Within the framework of SD an integrated economic and environmental approach to local-level policy-making is needed in order to: (i) minimize conflicts between resource-using activities; (ii) enhance socio-economic opportunities (for instance, by optimising employment opportunities); and (iii) bequeath an environmental estate for the benefit of future generations (Cloke and Park, 1985). Hence the need for an LSD strategy. Quite often an LSD-orientated strategy is carried out by evaluating the implications of environmental standards or by putting constraints on industry, land use, housing or transport developments.

In view of these observations, it seems meaningful, from a welfare viewpoint, to define LSD as 'a development which ensures that the local population can attain and maintain an acceptable and non-declining level of welfare, without jeopardizing the opportunities of people in adjacent areas'. This entails a need for local development to be compatible with ecological conditions in the long run while, at the same time, it does not interfere with supra-local (and preferably global) sustainable development (Nijkamp *et al.,* 1992). Consequently, LSD has to fulfil two goals: (i) it should ensure for the local population an acceptable level of welfare, which can be sustained in the future; and (ii) it should not be in conflict with SD at the national level. We may have different interpretations of sustainability: weak versus strong sustainability, and internal versus overall sustainability. We proceed with our analysis by addressing these aspects.

### Internal versus overall sustainability

One could say that the biosphere provides humankind with a certain environmental utilization space (defined in terms of sustainable exploitation of renewable resources, land, absorptive capacities for pollution and waste and so on). Within this environmental utilization space, national subspaces could be defined as the level of overall environmental pressure that an economy can sustainably exert (defined in terms of national emission targets, nature conservation objectives and energy consumption reduction targets and so on). From these national environmental utilization spaces, urban economies may be regarded as having a fair share in proportion to, for example their population size or their contribution to the national economy in terms of gross domestic product (GDP).

A local treatment of sustainable development thus falls in between a macro (or global) systems level and a micro (or project) level approach, as analysis of LSD is spatially a meso level analysis. Of course, LSD runs the risk of transferring the 'global rhetoric' (Pezzy, 1989) of sustainability towards a micro or meso level of application. However, practical, efficiency or analytical reasons may necessitate a flexible use of different spatial scales. Also, management reasons may necessitate a differentiated level of treatment of LSD, both for legislative tasks and for control (or executive) tasks. Thus, LSD presupposes a meso level of analysis, though not on an a priori fixed spatial scale of a region or city.

LSD differs from SD in three essential aspects: (i) the *degree of openness* (or interrelatedness) of a city or region; (ii) *socioeconomic imbalances* which are – in contrast to global treatment – not levelled out on a local or regional scale; and (iii) the *local or regional authority over common goods*. These aspects should be considered explicitly to make SD operational on the basis of (supra-)local, regional or supra-regional – but locally or regionally differentiated – policies. These three dimensions justify separate attention for LSD. Here we elaborate on them by considering the scale at which urban development may generate environmental effects and what this may mean in terms of sustainability.

Urban economic activity makes use of environmental resources that are available in the cities considered: land, air, water, amenities and biodiversity. Implicitly it depends on the regenerative and absorptive processes underlying these resources; we refer to these processes as the 'environmental infrastructure'. Urban activities also draw on economic resources (produced capital, labour) and the social and economic infrastructure underlying these. In so far as these activities take place without affecting adversely the level of supply and the productivity of these resources and their infrastructural foundations (social, economic and environmental), one may say that these urban activities are the urban agglomeration itself. However, both in terms of inputs into the urban economic activities and in terms of environmental outputs (pollution and waste), urban economies typically resort to environmental resources and environmental infrastructure beyond the internal urban resource base: elsewhere in the country or even beyond national boundaries. Energy and food resources and acid depositions are examples of this.

In a wider spatial sense, urban economies can only be called sustainable if two conditions are met: (i) they should be internally sustainable as defined above, and (ii) their claim on resource bases elsewhere should not exceed their environmental utilization space. If these two conditions are met, the urban economy is both internally and externally sustainable; that is, it meets the conditions of what may be called 'overall sustainability'.

**Strong versus weak sustainability**

We now come to the other aspect or goal of LSD: the provision of an acceptable and sustainable level of welfare. The question here is: What do we mean by sustainable welfare? Restricting ourselves to LSD as economic and ecological co-evolutionary development at a local scale, we regard local development as non-negative changes of local social welfare over time, with social welfare being made up of two correlated components, namely the consumption of man-made products and services (the socioeconomic system) and the consumption of environmental amenities (the ecological system). In Figure 5.1, a schematic simplified representation is given of the above definition. Both systems (economic and ecological) produce corresponding functions that include quantitative and qualitative components.

As we move towards concrete SD concepts, we observe that the condition that social welfare changes should be positive ($dW/dt \geq 0$) may hold in two different ways, namely, either the change in one welfare constituent is positive, and negative in the other one (provided the net overall change in $W$ is still positive), or the changes in both welfare constituents are non-negative. In the first case we speak of 'weak sustainability', whereas in the second case we have 'strong sustainability' (Daly, 1991). Although these distinctions are conceptually sound, the absence of a 'numéraire' again makes an actual numerical illustration or application very difficult.

It is clear that spatial substitution and substitution between welfare components are closely related phenomena. The above discussion can be summarized in the matrix of Figure 5.2 on the scopes and domains at which sustainability must be defined, even in an LSD context.

*Figure* 5.1 The main components of the social welfare function

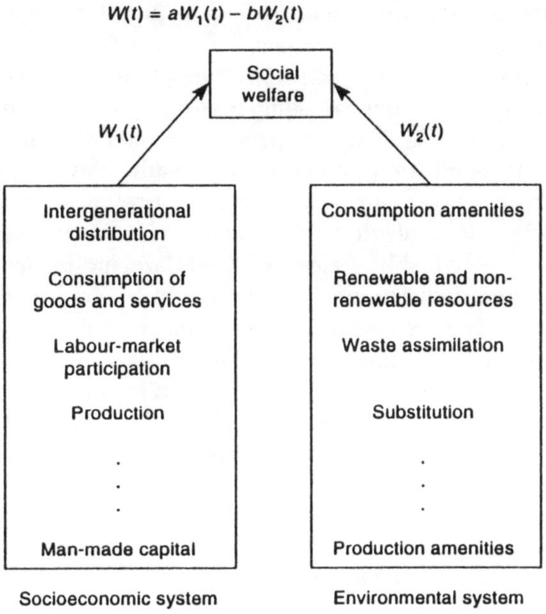


*Figure* 5.2 Criteria for local sustainability

| *Scope\Domain* | *Internal sustainability* | *External sustainability* | *Overall sustainability* |
|---|---|---|---|
| Weak sustainability | ($w,i$) conditions | ($w,e$) conditions | ($w,e$) + ($w,i$) conditions |
| Strong sustainability | ($s,i$) conditions | ($w,s$) conditions | ($s,e$) + ($s,i$) conditions |

The ($w$, $i$) conditions relate to the total local resource base (that is, the sum of environmental and economic resources) and require non-negative changes over time. The ($w$, $e$) conditions ensure that local claims on resources elsewhere remain within limits derived from sustainability standards at a higher (for example, national) level; overall (weak) sustainability is achieved when both sets of criteria are met. Analogously, ($s$, $i$) conditions relate to the economic and environmental resource bases (stocks and infrastructures) *separately* and require non-negative changes over time; ($w$, $s$) conditions ensure that the urban claim on the natural (and economic) resource base remains within the environmental utilization and economic possibilities frontier; overall (strong) sustainability implies that both sets of conditions must be met. Note that an urban centre could in principle meet internal and external sustainability conditions by compensating (in environmental or economic terms) for the loss of specific resources or infrastructure, for example, through environmental, economic and social development projects to be written off against current revenues drawn from the resource base. Thus substitution between welfare components (especially in the weak sustainability approach), welfare and resource endowments over time and between spatial units could be envisaged.

Finally, it is noteworthy that the nature of the spatial substitution phenomena in the context of spatial analysis and modelling may be depicted more adequately and in a visually appealing way by using geographic information systems (GIS) (see Fischer and Nijkamp, 1992); especially since this methodology allows for an incorporation of spatial modelling.

## TOWARDS SUSTAINABLE CITIES

The network character of our societies is clearly reflected in the increasingly important role of cities as nodal centres in a network. Consequently, cities have an important task in a sustainability policy. This opportunity is gaining more importance, as our world is exhibiting a massive transition towards urbanization. The majority of the world's population towards the end of the 1990s is living in urban areas, and this share is still increasing. For the time being, there are no signs of a change in this pattern of worldwide urbanization (UN Population Fund, 1996). By the year 2000 there will be twenty-one cities with populations of over 10 million people (seventeen of these cities are in what are called 'developing countries') (World Bank, 1992). At face value, it seems as though cities are exerting a strong centripetal force, which is so strong that all negative externalities of the city appear to be accepted.

Sustainable development of cities refers to continuity in a changing situation, and these changing situations are clearly reflected in the new role of the city, for example, as an industrial centre, as a service centre, as a high-tech centre and so on. In general, if the self-organization of an urban system fails (for example, because of lack of consensus among different individual institutions), a phase of non-sustainability is likely to start. Environmental decay is one of the first overt signs of non-sustainability. Modern cities are suffering badly from environmental costs (for example, Delhi, Bangkok, Rome, Athens), and it is precisely these externalities which are decisive for the shape the city is going to take in the future.

In order to explain urban dynamics from the viewpoint of urban externalities, it is necessary to recognize that cities throughout world history have played a critical role as nodal points in the spatial–economic network of a country. This role has always attracted urban immigrants, in both the developed and the underdeveloped world. However, the movement towards urban territory as a whole has at the same time caused urban sprawl, leading to city regions or functional urban regions. Land prices and environmental externalities in central areas of the cities were both often impediments to new household and firm locations, so that an outward shift took place. Industries moved to urban fringes or to special industrial parks in the neighbourhood of cities. People moved to suburban – and even more distant – locations, but this massive movement meant essentially only an expansion of the functional urban territory. Despite a broadening of the spatial range, the urban system has still kept its original function and has even reinforced its position over the years. In the wake of this sprawl, urban environmental damage tends to show a wider spatial coverage (see Orishimo, 1982). In most cases, the external costs of diseconomies are not (fully) internalized in the price system, so that a distorted urban locational pattern emerges. In addition, government policies aiming at restoring the balance are often hampered by severe failures so that the ultimate situation may be even less sustainable.

Although it is likely that environmental quality problems may become more severe with urban size, there is no clear evidence that urban size as such causes environmental decay. According to Orishimo (1982), it is not the sheer city size, but rather the implied land use, the transport system and the spatial layout of a city that are critical factors for urban environmental quality. There are clear correlations with urban environmental quality and average income levels (World Bank, 1992); see also below). Moreover, the rising material needs of an urbanizing society and especially the inherent claims on nearby natural resources, must be mentioned. Overall, modern cities tend to show drastic evolutionary changes, in which the human resource potential in a city – composed of creativity, competence and communication – is exerting a dominant role. The attainment of urban sustainability is undoubtedly a complex and dynamic problem. Modern urban systems – with their high density of population and economic activities, their nodal position in interwoven geographical and functional–economic (inter)national networks and their ambition to act as engines in the competitive process of open regions – are faced with increasingly severe environmental problems, ranging from air, soil and water pollution to intangible externalities such as noise nuisance, lack of safety, or visual pollution. Thus an improvement of the current unfavourable situation requires a mobilization of a wide range of forces.

Policies addressing sustainable development of cities should cover multiple urban fields such as rehabilitation, land use, transport, energy management, architecture and conservation policy, and cultural policy. Measurable indicators, including minimum performance levels and critical threshold levels, will then have to be defined, estimated and used in forecasting tools, to improve awareness of sustainable development issues of modern cities. Local authorities will have to share their tasks with all other actors in the urban space (including the private sector) in enforcing and maintaining these critical thresholds. It goes without saying that urban sustainable development is a process rife with conflicts and incompatibilities. Commitment to a strict environmentally sustainable urban development by key actors in a city is necessary for a successful implementation of sustainability policies. In doing so, economic (market-based) incentives may also be desirable in order to cope with the negative externalities of modern city life. Failure to develop an effective balanced urban development policy will reinforce urban sprawl and will externalize inner-city problems to a much larger area.

A necessary condition for implementing an effective planning system for urban environmental management geared towards maintaining sustainability is the development of a system of suitable *urban environmental indicators* (see OECD, 1978). Such indicators, which should represent a balance between the necessary quality of information and the costs involved, would have to be related to economic, social, spatial and cultural dimensions of the city. The OECD has drawn up a long list of elements that are decisive for urban environmental quality and which would have to be included in such an indicator system. Examples are: housing, services and employment, ambient environment and nuisances, social and cultural concerns and so on. However, it appears to be extremely difficult to operationalize such an indicator system. This means that precise empirical evidence on urban environmental quality and on the implications for both household and firm behaviour is not always available.

In light of the previous observations, the conclusion seems warranted that the route towards sustainable cities is not an easy one. Cities often face the most severe environmental problems, such as air and water pollution, noise disturbance, waste, degradation of the quality of urban life, and visual destruction of urban landscapes and architecture. Urban policies aiming to achieve sustainable development need to be more strategic in nature, more integrative, more visionary regarding the role of the private sector, more focused on the provision of market incentives, and more orientated towards the needs of citizens. Examples show that such strategic and integrative approaches do exist; lessons should be drawn from them, and extended.

## ELEMENTS OF URBAN SUSTAINABILITY

The previous section demonstrated the need for sustainable city policy. If modern cities want to maintain and improve their role as the 'home of human beings', intensified efforts are needed to safeguard both the historico-cultural heritage left to the present generation by our predecessors, and the socioeconomic and environmental potential of modern cities needed to host future generations. Local energy and environmental planning is a *sine qua non* for the fulfilment of the latter task. Sustainable cities aim at achieving a balanced (co-evolutionary) development in which economic forces (for example, efficiency), social considerations (for example, equity and access to facilities) and environmental concerns (for example, quality of life) are brought together from the viewpoint of a 'green society' (see also Pearce *et al.*, 1989). Enhancing local energy efficiency is likely to be one of the critical success factors for sustainable cities, as energy management and use provides a substantial support to an improvement of the local economy (that is, a higher degree of competitiveness), to a more affordable – and hence equitable – distribution of scarce resources (that is, a better access to public services), and to a reduction in the environmental burden (that is, reduction in emissions of $CO_2$).

The main problem in building 'sustainable cities' is *not* the lack of arguments supporting the need for 'green-based' cities, but the question of designing proper concrete co-evolutionary urban development strategies that can boast sufficient public support.

It is increasingly recognized that urban environmental quality requires an active urban energy policy reducing the consumption of fossil fuels; for instance, through the introduction of district heating, co-generation or combined heat and power (CHP) technologies. By employing strict energy savings measures, a considerable element of the pollution caused by households, industries and transport can be avoided. An interesting example can be found in a study undertaken for an urban revitalization project of a run-down district (Neukölln) in Berlin, where energy policy was regarded as the key force of urban environmental management (see, for details, Nijkamp and Volwahsen, 1990). A computer model carrying out all steps of a comprehensive energy–environment study was designed for this urban revitalization project in Berlin–Neukölln.

It is also increasingly recognized that a favourable environmental quality in cities is a *conditio sine qua non* for a balanced urban economic development and that urban development is not necessarily at odds with a favourable environmental quality, and certainly not in the long run. In the context of a balanced urban development policy it is strictly necessary that systematic attempts be made to assess, monitor and evaluate the various elements of urban development. In this framework, it seems plausible to design a systematic environmental and community impact analysis (see Lichfield, 1990), which – analogous to environmental impact analysis in many countries – would provide policy-makers with all relevant information for sustainable city planning. A high environmental quality offers a great potential for many activities (for example, recreation, tourism, research), without significant negative externalities. However, overuse of scarce environmental resources will not only cause environmental conditions to deteriorate, but is in the long run also to the detriment of the local or regional economy. A good quality of life is often an important locational motive for new entrepreneurs. Thus it is in the interest of the economy at large when the highest possible environmental quality is striven for.

This scheme is based on a balance between urban development, environmental quality and energy efficiency; these different forces are also schematized in Figure 5.3 opposite.

## SUSTAINABLE CITIES IN DEVELOPING COUNTRIES

### Introduction

The world population is likely to double between 1990 and 2040; virtually all this growth is expected to occur in the Third World (World Bank, 1992). Most of that population growth there is probably going

*Figure* 5.3 The energy–environment–urban development triangle

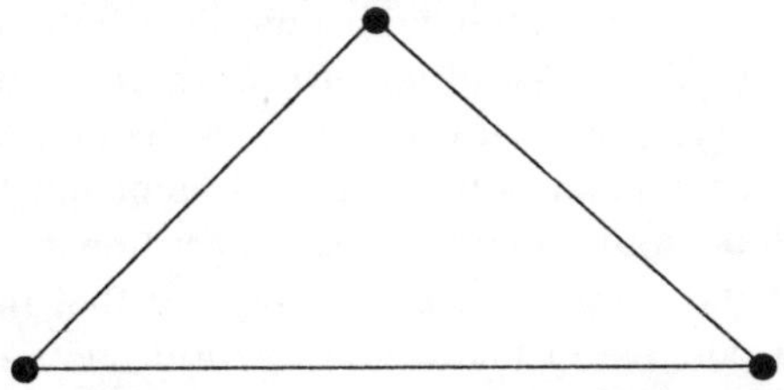


to show up in urban population figures: the urban population in developing countries will rise sixteen times as fast as the rural population. Average urban air quality is dropping in low-income countries; in middle-income countries it is improving, but is still far from adequate. Growing motorized mobility and inadequate heating systems are likely to aggravate this situation substantially over the decades to come. The above figures are just illustrations of a much more widespread environmental deterioration, both in terms of environmental quality levels and in terms of numbers of people exposed.

Urban and regional energy and environmental planning is gaining in importance as an effective strategy for implementing ecologically sustainable economic development, as advocated in the Brundtland Report (WCED, 1987). Does this also apply to urban policies in developing countries? Are there specific elements which make the notion of urban sustainability more problematic in developing countries? Such questions will be dealt with in the present section.

One problem peculiar to developing countries is the formidable density of people in many Third-World cities. This density leads to diseconomies of scale which tend to interface exponentially with negative environmental externalities caused by polluting activities.

Next, environmental interests are usually not fully incorporated in regional and urban development planning, so that normative guidelines (based, for example, on carrying capacity, regenerative capacity and so on) are often missing in the practice of planning. Economic progress is often more focused on quantity than on quality.

A third main factor is formed by urban poverty itself. According to the South Commission (1990), poverty causes environmental decay. Agarwal (1992) wonders, for example, why at international forums the main focus is on conventions on biodiversity and not on poverty abatement. The 'fight for daily bread' leads to short-term decisions which shift environmental and multi-generational interests beyond the horizon.

Another problem is the relatively unequal distribution of income and productive assets in Third-World countries. There is often a bi-modal distribution of income and wealth which is to the detriment of a rigorous and effective abatement policy for environmental decay.

Finally, the administrative competence regarding strict enforcement of environmental measures is often lacking, so that the effectiveness of environmental policies in many Third-World cities is poor. And in the case of public interventions in favour of environmental quality in cities we often observe a situation of government failure (as well as market failures).

In urban planning in developing countries even more than in industrialized countries, the need to consider equity aspects is thus obvious. These equity aspects are additional to the two main sets of policy-relevant aspects implicitly referred to above: efficiency and sustainability. These three elements will now be discussed in succession.

**Efficiency**

Efficiency has been a key criterion in policy frameworks in conventional (economic) project appraisal for developing countries (milestones have been Little and Mirrlees, 1974; UNIDO, 1972; Squire and van der Tak, 1975; Squire, 1989). Efficiency considerations are geared towards maximizing the difference between gross aggregate welfare changes (benefits) and all uses of scarce resources (costs). Assuming a broader interpretation of welfare, the availability of environmental amenities with a direct impact on the well-being of individuals has also been considered a welfare attribute. On the cost side, basic resources comprise man-made capital and natural or environmental capital (see, for example, James *et al.*, 1989). Each of these categories can be further subdivided. Natural capital, for instance, may be subdivided into classes related to its functions: assimilation of waste, provision of renewable and non-renewable resources, or supply of environmental amenities essential to production processes (see also above, p. 000). It has been proposed to differentiate between irreversible *vis-à-vis* reversible changes in environmental capital (Hedman, 1990).

Traditionally, cost–benefit analysis (CBA) techniques have been applied, whereby prices serve as weights. If fully available and to the extent that they provide a true reflection of the value to society (present and future), market prices can indeed be applied. However, if markets are imperfect, or even absent (such as is the case of many futures markets), and if market forces generate external effects, market prices must be considered as being distorted. In such situations (which are quite general, especially in developing countries) shadow prices may – or even *must* – be applied. Problems occur if no shadow price can be determined for one or more efficiency attributes, particularly environmental amenities (benefits) and environmental resource use (costs). In such circumstances there are two possible approaches. The first is to replace the (comprehensive) efficiency criterion by at least two other criteria, namely a partial-efficiency criterion (covering all monetarized efficiency attributes) and other criteria covering the remaining efficiency attributes (such as environment). An alternative approach would be to decompose fully the comprehensive efficiency criterion in its respective attributes: contributions to material welfare, contributions to environmental amenities, use of man-made capital, use of natural capital and so on (see, for example, James *et al.*, 1978). Both approaches require weighting mechanisms other than prices to arrive at conclusions regarding efficiency. The emphasis is then likely to be on weights derived from views of policy-makers, by using multi-criteria methods (see Nijkamp *et al.*, 1991).

## Equity

Equity in the urban setting in developing countries has at least two aspects: intra-generational equity (that is, the urban poverty issue) and inter-generational equity. In many developing countries the political importance of the urban population has frequently overreached its significance in terms of numbers: hence the effective distribution of income and assets (including environmental assets or access to them) between the urban economy and the rural economy surrounding and even supporting it, may be out of balance. Therefore, spatial equity is a major concern indeed in urban development planning. The issue of distribution between groups is quite a different matter. In terms of income distribution this matter is beyond the scope of our chapter; here we draw attention to the substantial inequalities in access to, for example, land, water, energy, and environmental and sanitation facilities. The most basic urban environmental services are clean drinking water, sanitation and solid waste collection; the degree to which these services are available has been reviewed by Coolidge *et al.*, (1993). Generally speaking, there has been progress but far too little; provision of these services has not kept up with the pace of urbanization. This is especially true for the poorer segments of the population. Urban planning will have to address these differences in resource endowment, either by enhancing the level of supply of public facilities (for example, water, electricity, housing, sanitation) or by defining and (more equitably) allocating private property rights to environmental assets. Very often, individual rights of access to common property resources are defined inadequately and this in itself leads to degradation of the resource base. Urban development thus has a number of reasons to engage in activities as outlined here in addition to the equity aspect.

The LSD policy framework should also provide an insight into preferences regarding intertemporal equity, namely the distribution of welfare over time. In view of the long-term focus implied by sustainability concerns, questions arise: How important is the welfare of the present generation compared to welfare of future generations? How much welfare are those who are living now willing to sacrifice in order to safeguard the interests of future generations? Moreover, what are the views on the possibility of compensating future generations for a lower level of environmental amenities with higher material welfare levels?

Sustainability concerns draw particular attention to long-term ecological risks. Such risks may have various specific characteristics (Quiggin and Anderson, 1990). One is that 'surprises' may occur, events that cannot be predicted, and particularly unpleasant surprises at that, with potentially disastrous effects for future generations. Often, probabilities associated with various possible events cannot be estimated. Judgements on the present generation's responsibility to future generations should therefore, on inter-generational equity grounds, contain a risk strategy, describing subjective attitudes towards risks and associated extreme events. In terms of the size of the environmental utilization space, risk aversion implies that 'safe' estimates are made of it, and that its boundaries are protected by 'safe' environmental standards (Ciriacy Wantrup, 1952; Opschoor, 1992). Risk-aversive strategies imply a larger willingness to sacrifice present welfare than optimistic views on future possibilities to respond to eventual harmful events: for example, through technological progress. It may be relevant to observe that such a risk-aversive approach is implied in the so-called Precautionary Principle as discussed (and given partial legitimacy) at the UNCED conference and incorporated in its Declaration of Rio (Principle 15).

One approach is to follow the 'maximin' strategy, whereby the alternative is preferred where the worst possible outcome is better than the worst possible outcomes of other alternatives. An alternative approach consists of assigning weights to risks and their possible consequences. Reijnders (1990), for instance, argues that long-term ecological risks are unacceptable. 'No-regret' strategies aim at avoiding highly uncertain but potentially disastrous events and surprises by embarking on measures that can also be justified on the basis of their impact on related, but more predictable, fields. It goes without saying that we are facing here an enormous research challenge for sustainable city policy.

**Sustainability**

Sustainability, whatever its definition and operationalization (see Figure 5.1 on page 57), always refers to a certain threshold level regarding the use of environmental capital (or the total stock of capital, comprising man-made capital as well). In its basic form (actual resource use is either lower or higher than sustainable levels), this third key criterion is therefore of a different nature from efficiency and equity motives, which are expressed in terms of desired directions of change (maximization of aggregate real income, or enhancement of the part of income accruing to target groups). The sustainability criterion in fact operates as a constraint on environmental utilization analogous to the production possibility frontier in welfare economics (Opschoor, 1992), albeit that the sustainability frontier can be ignored temporarily at the expense of future environmental space. More data demanding forms of sustainability criteria involve measurement of the degree of sustainability on a cardinal or ordinal scale expressing the relative difference between normative threshold levels and actual resource use.

As we saw in our discussion on equity aspects, the choice of threshold levels for sustainable resource use depends to a large extent on how the present generation judges its responsibility to future generations (the so-called 'trustee' principle), including assessment of risks and possibilities for substitution in production functions (inter-generational equity).

Clearly, the question remains which critical success factors are to be fulfilled in order to ensure a viable urban sustainability policy. Here we shall use the notion of the pentagon model. This model takes for granted the existence of five necessary and crucial conditions which have to be met in order to ensure that a policy favouring urban sustainability is feasible in principle (see Figure 5.4). In the context of sustainable city policies these five factors have the following meaning:

*Figure* 5.4 A pentagon prism with necessary conditions for policy success

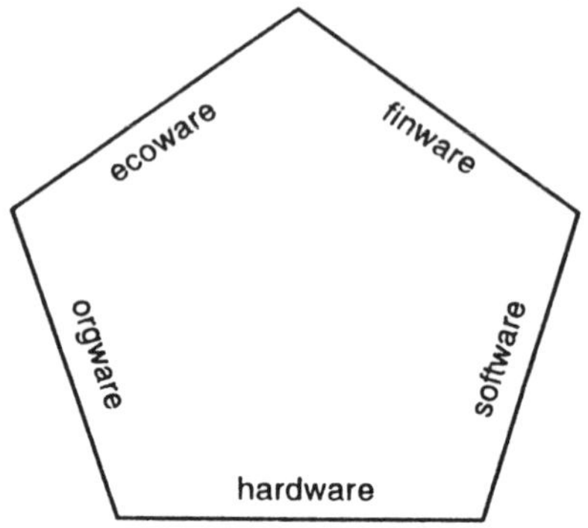


*Hardware* The need to implement sophisticated technologies for pollution and waste treatment, route guidance and so on.

*Software* The existence of and access to up-to-date information and decision support systems for an effective combat against urban environmental degradation.

*Orgware* The presence of an efficient, alert and proactive administrative system with sufficient co-ordination and co-operation among different institutional configurations, aiming at improving the quality of urban life.

*Ecoware* Sufficient recognition of environmental interests and presence of a legislative and institutionalized system ensuring an adequate incorporation of environmental interests in urban development planning.

*Finware* The existence of an economic and financial support system which is able to generate the necessary financial resources for those urban development and environmental projects or programmes which have a net positive social benefit.

It goes without saying that the latter condition is often a weak link in a sustainability chain and hence deserves due attention.

## THE FEASIBILITY OF URBAN ENVIRONMENTAL POLICIES

Are urban LSD programmes feasible? There are at least two sets of concerns here: (i) on physical feasibility; and (ii) on financial feasibility.

To begin with *physical feasibility*: the conditions shown in Figure 5.2 on page 57 are not necessarily compatible with non-negative changes in economic welfare. Maintaining economic and environmental assets and hence making allowance for their depreciation if used, might in principle result in infeasibility in terms of income or consumption demands. If that is the case, unsustainable use of environmental resources is likely to be the result. Unless this is compensated for or mitigated by economic and/or environmental programmes from higher levels, the city has no sustainable future. Increasing pressure on urban policy-makers from higher administrative levels to adhere to external sustainability is therefore to be expected. This situation becomes more likely as one moves from a policy or assessment based on weak internal sustainability towards one geared towards strong overall sustainability. Most urban development is at best concerned with weak internal sustainability.

But even if LSD is physically feasible, this does not imply that it will in fact materialize. As mentioned above, *financing* possibilities are one of the most critical conditions for a substantial improvement of urban quality of life conditions. Does an urban sustainability policy generate sufficient 'value for money' which would justify the mobilization of huge financial resources? Similar questions have also been raised recently in the context of other 'non-productive' assets such as housing, infrastructure and culture (see, for example, Montarari and Petraroia, 1991, and Struyk *et al.*, 1990). Despite the indigenous merits of housing, infrastructure and culture, it was necessary to also show that these assets would create a positive contribution to social welfare to such an extent that it was worth investing in them. In effect, what is required is that a net positive contribution is made to the present value of flows of incremental social welfare over time. But this net present value is determined to a large degree by time preference and hence by discount rates. Especially in the context of developing countries, this means that the net contributions of sustainability-orientated urban programmes may appear to be relatively low, given the relatively high prevailing rates of individual and entrepreneurial time preference.

It is evident that net positive socioeconomic benefits are a *sine qua non* to justify public intervention in the urban environment. Such benefits comprise both primary economic benefits (for example, extra tourist revenues as a result of a strict urban environmental policy) and secondary benefits (for example, new enterprises attracted by an attractive urban climate). Clearly, the distributional effects would have to be considered as well, so that a careful analysis of the beneficiaries (and externalities) of environmental policies favouring a sustainable city is necessary.

The previous remarks can be illustrated by some cases. In *industry*, new technologies and better insulation of buildings may lead to a considerable rise in energy efficiency, although this clearly has a long lead time in normal circumstances. In the *residential* sector, housing insulation programmes may also lead to drastic energy savings for both space heating and air conditioning (for example, by means of better insulation, heat pumps, solar energy installations, wind turbines, and economizers for central heating systems). Also, in the *transport* sector, considerable savings are possible in principle (for example, through more energy-efficient engines, vehicle weight reduction or – in the long run – through more energy -efficient physical planning aimed at a reduction of commuting distance and/or a shift of the model split in favour of public transport) (see Button, 1992). At a more integrated and meso level of urban energy planning, various possibilities are offered by central heat distribution; recycling of energy from heat; by combined heat and power, either in district heating or in co-generation; or by using urban/industrial waste as a fuel for generating plants. Especially at a local level these energy saving options are likely to be more efficient than at a more region-wide level, as in general such options require fairly high densities of energy demand. In addition, land use zoning and physical planning might also provide some of the regulatory regions for environmental policy.

In all cases, environmental programmes are expensive and require much public money. In light of severe public budget constraints and deficits of governments at all levels (national, regional and local), a strong plea seems in order for private financing of public programmes or projects, especially in the wake of the deregulation movement. In most cases, however, fully private financing is not regarded as a desirable option. Hence, in practice, we see the emergence of various types of public private partnership (PPP) configurations. Our analysis earlier in this section demonstrates the need to engage in such partnerships, especially when public and private rates of time preference, or public and private valuation for environmental quality, diverge.

In conclusion, defining and implementing an urban sustainability policy is a formidable task which needs political attention urgently. This is especially true in developing countries. LSD can be defined with various domains and scopes in mind; the more stringest one chooses to be, the lower the physically feasible sustainable level of socioeconomic welfare. The less stringent one is, the more the costs of urban development are shifted on to a city's own future population, or on to other parts of the economy beyond the urban sphere, either now or in the future. LSD is a challenge for creative urban policy and for technological and administrative innovators; prime movers in the direction of LSD may find this to be beneficial, not only in environmental terms but also in socioeconomic terms. At the same time, LSD poses complicated questions regarding private–public co-operation and financial matching. But the concept is likely to offer a new departure for a more balanced approach to development planning of Third-World cities.

## References

Agarwal, A. K. (1992) 'International Trade and Sustainable Development from a Southern Non-governmental Perspective', in J. W. Arntzen, I. Hemmer and O. Kuik (eds), *International Trade and Sustainable Development* (Amsterdam: Free University Press) pp. 121–44.

Archibugi, F. and P. Nijkamp (eds) (1989) *Economy and Ecology: Towards Sustainable Development* (Dordrecht: Kluwer).

Bergh, J. C. J. M. van den (1991) *Dynamic Models for Sustainable Development* (Amsterdam: Thesis).

Berry, R. (1985) 'Islands of Renewal in Seas of Decay', in P. Peterson (ed.), *The New Urban Reality* (Washington DC: The Brookings Institution) pp. 123–40.

Button, K. J. (1992) 'Transport Regulation and the Environment in Low Income Countries', *Utilities Policy*, July, pp. 248–57.

Ciriacy Wantrup, S. V. (1952) 'Resources Conservation', *Economics and Policies* (Berkeley, Calif: University of California Press) pp. 1–15.

Cloke, P. J. and C. C. Park (1985) 'Integrated Management Strategies', in *Rural Resource Management* (Andover: Croom Helm) pp. 408–48.

Coolidge, J. G., R. C. Porter and Z. J. Zhang (1993) *Urban Environmental Services in Developing Countries*, EPAT/Mucia Working Paper No. 9 (Dept of Economics, University of Michigan).

Daly, H. E. (1991) *Steady State Economics* (Washington, DC: Island Press).

Fischer, M. M. and P. Nijkamp (1992) 'Geographic Information System and Spatial Analysis', *Annals of Regional Science* (Special issue), vol. 26.

Giaoutzi, M. and P. Nijkamp (1993) *Decision Support for Regional Sustainable Development* (Aldershot: Avebury).

Hedman, S. (1990) *Reversibility as a Weighting Factor in Integrated Least Cost Planning Methodologies*, revised version of paper presented at the International Congress, 'The Ecological Economics of Sustainability', World

Bank, Washington DC, University of Maryland, College Park.

Heggie, I. G. (1992) 'Can Charging for Negative Externalities Help Finance Improved Urban Transport Facilities; The Case of Developing Countries', *Public/Private Partnerships in Urban Mobility* (Paris: OECD) pp. 207–17.

James, D. E., H. M. A. Jansen and J. B. Opschoor (1978) *Economic Approaches to Environmental Problems* (Amsterdam/New York: Elsevier).

James, D. E., P. Nijkamp and J. B. Opschoor (1989) 'Ecological Sustainability and Economic Development', in F. Archibugi and P. Nijkamp, *Economy and Ecology* (Dordrecht: Kluwer) pp. 21–42.

Kairiukstis, L. (1989) 'Ecological Sustainability of Regional Development: Background to the Problem', in *Ecological Sustainability of Regional Development* (Laxenburg, Austria: International Institute for Applied Systems Analysis) pp. 1–5.

Lichfield, N. (1990) *Economics of Conservation* (Cambridge University Press).

Little, I. N. D. and J. A. Mirrlees (1974) *Project Appraisal and Planning for Developing Countries* (London: Heinemann).

Lovelock, J. (1979) *Gaia: A New Look at Life on Earth* (Oxford University Press).

Marahrens, W., Chr. Ax and G. Buck (1991) *Stadt und Umwelt* (Basel: Birkhaüser).

Montarari, A. and P. Petraroia (1991) *Polluted City* (Rome: Istituto Poligrafico).

Nijkamp, P. (ed.) (1991) *Urban Sustainability* (Aldershot: Gower).

Nijkamp, P., P. Lasschuit and F. Soeteman (1992) 'Sustainable Development in a Regional System', in M. Breheny (ed.), *Sustainable Development Planning* (London: Pion) pp. 112–36.

Nijkamp, P. and A. Volwahsen (1990) 'New Directions in Integrated Regional Energy Planning', *Energy Policy*, October, pp. 764–74.

Nijkamp, P., J. Vleugel, R. Maggi and I. Masser (1991) *Missing Networks in Europe* (Brussels: European Round Table of Industrialists).

OECD (1978) *Urban Environmental Indicators* (Paris: OECD).

Opschoor, J. B. (1992) 'Sustainable Development, the Economic Process and Economic Analysis', in J. B. Opschoor (ed.), *Environment, Economy and Sustainable Development* (Groningen: Wolters Noordhoff) pp. 1–23.

Opschoor, J. B. and L. Reijnders (1991) 'Towards Sustainable Development Indicators', in O. Kuik and H. Verbruggen (eds), *In Search of Sustainable Development Indicators* (Dordrecht: Kluwer) pp. 7–29.

Orishimo, I. (1982) *Urbanisation and Environmental Quality* (Dordrecht: Kluwer).

Pearce, D., A. Markandya and E. B. Barbier (1989) *Blueprint for a Green Economy* (London: Earthscan).

Pelt, M. J. F. van, A. Kuyvenhoven and P. Nijkamp (1990) 'Project Appraisal and Sustainability: Methodological Challenges', *Project Appraisal*, vol. 5, no. 3, pp. 139–58.

Pelt, M. J. F. van, A. Kuyvenhoven and P. Nijkamp (1991) 'Sustainability, Efficiency and Equity: Project Appraisal in Economy', Research Memorandum 1991–96, Dept of Economics, Free University, Amsterdam.

Pezzy, J. (1989) 'Economic Analysis of Sustainable Growth and Sustainable Development', WP15, Environment Department (Washington, DC: The World Bank).

Porter, M. (1990) *The Competitive Advantage of Nations* (New York: Free Press).

Quiggin, J. and J. Anderson (1990) *Risk and Project Appraisal*, Paper presented at the World Bank Annual Conference on Development Economics, Washington, DC, 26–27 April.

Reijnders, L. (1990) 'Normen voor Milieuvervuiling met het Oog op Duurzaamheid', *Milieu*, no. 5, pp. 138–40.

Schuster, J. M. D. (1989) 'Government Leverage of Private Support', in M. Wyszomirski and P. Clubb (eds), *The Cost of Culture* (New York: American Council for the Arts) pp. 63–97.

Simon, H. A. (1967) *Models of Man: Mathematical Essays on Rational Human Behaviour in a Social Setting* (New York: John Wiley).

South Commission (1990) *The Challenge to the South* (Oxford University Press).

Squire, L. and H. G. van der Tak (1975) *Economic Analysis of Projects* (Baltimore, Md: Johns Hopkins University Press).

Squire, L. (1989) 'Project Evaluation in Theory and Practice', in H. Chenery and T. N. Srinivasan (eds), *Handbook of Development Economics*, vol. II (Amsterdam: Elsevier) pp. 311–48.

Struyk, R. J., M. L. Hoffman and H. M. Katsura (1990) *The Market for Shelter in Indonesian Cities* (Washington, DC: The Urban Institute Press).

UNIDO (1972) *Guidelines for Project Evaluation* (New York: United Nations).

UN Population Fund (1996) *World Population Report 1996* (New York: UNFPA).

WCED (1987) *Our Common Future* (Bruntland Report), World Commission on Environment and Development (Oxford University Press).

World Bank (1992) *World Development Report 1992* (Washington, DC).

Young, M. D. (1992) *Sustainable Investment and Resource Use* (Paris: UNESCO).

# Name Index